Modern Mathematics

with Applications to Business and the Social Sciences

FOURTH EDITION

Modern Mathematics

with Applications to Business and the Social Sciences

FOURTH EDITION

Ruric E. Wheeler
W. D. Peeples, Jr.
SAMFORD UNIVERSITY

Brooks/Cole Publishing Company

Monterey, California / A Division of Wadsworth, Inc.

Dedicated to our wives, Joyce and Katie

Contemporary Undergraduate Mathematics Series

Robert J. Wisner, Consulting Editor

Printed in the United States of America

10   9   8   7   6   5   4   3   2   1

Library of Congress Cataloging-in-Publication Data

Wheeler, Ruric E., [date]
    Modern mathematics with applications to business
and the social sciences.

    Includes index.
    1. Business mathematics.   2. Social sciences—
Mathematics.   I. Peeples, W. D., [date]   II. Title.
HF5691.W45   1986   510′.2465   85-19494
ISBN 0-534-05826-4

Acquisition Editor: Jeremy Hayhurst
Production Services Coordinator: Joan Marsh
Manuscript Editor: Betty Berenson
Production: Cece Munson, The Cooper Company
Interior and Cover Design: Albert Burkhardt
Illustrations: Reese Thornton
Typesetting: Syntax International

Preface

What are the advantages of adopting a book that has been used in classrooms across the United States for **17 years?** Probably the most significant advantage is that the authors through experimentation have tried to find the optimum procedures for presenting solid (and sometimes complicated) mathematical concepts at a level that can be understood by students who are not mathematical experts. Little things do make a difference, and here are a few of the many procedures that make the teaching/learning process in this book easier for both the teacher and the student:

1. Review material is presented just prior to the place it is needed in the book.
   a. Material needed for linear algebra (systems of linear equations, matrices, linear programming, and probability applications) is presented in an easy-to-cover first chapter.
   b. The concepts needed for the study of calculus, especially functions, are placed in Chapter 8 immediately preceding calculus.
2. Material is introduced as a natural response to need instead of the usual "theory then application" approach.
   a. Matrix theory is introduced in the process of solving a system of linear equations rather than introduced as an abstract theory with the solving of a system of equations as a later application.
   b. Counting techniques, such as tree diagrams, permutations, and combinations, are introduced in response to solving probability problems rather than presented as an abstract idea and later used in probability applications.
   c. Probability distributions are presented as an outgrowth of sample statistics.
3. Difficult material is presented in small bits.
4. Complicated procedures are presented as goals (or what is to be accomplished), the steps to accomplish these goods, and the end result.

The following are special features of this fourth edition:

1. The most important feature of the book is that it is student-oriented; that is, it can be read easily by the average student. It does not emphasize mathematical developments but instead appeals to intuition.

2. There is a personal note to the student at the beginning of each chapter and at the beginning of each section. Not only is the content of each section described in nonmathematical language but an attempt is made to indicate how the material of the section will be used.

3. A key motivation for the study of each section is the large number of real-world illustrations. Application problems in each exercise set are classified as business, economics, life sciences, and social science.

4. The textual material is illustrated with more than 500 solved examples. Every new idea is illustrated with a solved example.

5. There are more than 4000 problems in the exercise sets. These problems vary from easy to those that challenge superior students. The first problems in an exercise set are marked A and are easy, routine problems; problems marked B are of medium difficulty; those with a C are difficult and possibly tedious.

6. The pivot operations used in the simplex method of linear programming are the same as row operations in Chapter 2. This allows the student to use the simplex method without having to learn an entirely new procedure.

What's new in this edition? Here is a partial list:

1. Enlargement of algebra review topics to cover topics needed in the study of calculus
2. Coverage of calculus enlarged from three chapters to six chapters
3. New material on descriptive statistics
4. New material on probability distributions
5. New material on Markov chains
6. New material on game theory

The material in this book offers instructors maximum flexibility in designing their courses. Chapter 8 can be presented after Chapter 1 for those who want to emphasize algebra at the beginning of the course. Or both Chapters 1 and 8 can be omitted for well-prepared classes. Chapters 3, 4, and 5 can be taught in any order or omitted, but Chapter 5 must be taught before Chapters 6 and 7. Sections that are not essential to the rest of the book are indicated by asterisks. Suggested course outlines are given as part of this preface.

An Instructor's Manual is available from the publisher; it contains suggestions for presenting the material, multiple-choice tests, and answers to all problems not answered in the book.

Acknowledgments

While writing this book we have received assistance from many persons. We are most grateful for this assistance. We would especially like to thank the following persons, who took the time to share their ideas and criticism with us.

Alabama: Fred Blackman, University of Montevallo

California: Mary Kay Beavers, City College of San Francisco; Alfred S. Beebe, University of Southern California; Philip Clarke, Los Angeles Valley College; A. E. Halteman, San Jose State University; V. Haroutunian, City College of San Francisco; A. E. Hurd, University of California, Los Angeles; Don Mazukelli, Los Angeles Valley College; Mary Mehlman, Los Angeles Pierce College; Mark A. Meller, Pepperdine University; Roland Sink, Pasadena City College; Karl J. Smith, Santa Rosa Junior College; James W. Strain, Midwestern State University

Canada: Hendrick J. Boom, University of Manitoba; P. Cuttle, University of Saskatchewan

Colorado: Charles E. Lienert, Metro State College

Florida: Douglas Cenzer, University of Florida; Frank L. Cleaver, University of South Florida

Georgia: Richard Cowan, Shorter College

Illinois: Wilson Banks, Illinois State University

Iowa: Gayle Baylor, Cedar Rapids

Kentucky: Bivi Ritchie, Morehead State University

Maryland: Donald R. Barr, U. S. Naval Postgraduate School

Massachusetts: Paul T. Banks, Boston College; Doris S. Stockton, University of Massachusetts; John Sullivan, North Shore Community College

New Hampshire: Christopher Toy, New Hampshire College

New Jersey: Ruth O'Dell, County College of Morris

New Mexico: Mary Sittel, New Mexico State University

New York: Frederick Byham, State University of New York at Fredonia

Ohio: Leonard Bruening, Cleveland State University; Allen W. Brunson, Cleveland State University

Oregon: Ruhard Byrne, Portland State University

Pennsylvania: Alan Gart, Franklin and Marshall College

Texas: Chaney Anderson, South Texas Junior College; Stewart Angell, Texarkana College; Katherine Bell, Lamar University; Julius Burkett, Stephen Austin State University; Gene Evans, Abilene Christian University; J. R. Hickey, Baylor University; S. E. McReynolds, Jr., Abilene Christian University; Ram Misra, University of Houston; Mike Murphy, University of Houston; Joseph Norstrom, University of Houston; J. N. O'Brien, Sam Houston University; G. Edgar Parker, Pan American University; Marian Paysinger, University of Texas at Arlington; R. C. Pierce, Jr., University of Houston; Paul Pontius, Pan American University; Wesley Sanders, Sam Houston State University; Andrew Thacker, University of Houston; Faye Thomas, Lamar University; Jeffrey Valler, University of Texas at Austin

Virginia: E. A. Newburg, Virginia Commonwealth University

Washington: D. R. Horner, Eastern Washington State University

West Virginia: Franz X. Hiergeist, West Virginia University

Wisconsin: Gene A. Deboth, St. Norbert College

We also wish to express our sincere appreciation to the reviewers who offered valuable suggestions for this revision. They are Kenneth Broun, University of Wisconsin; David Cochener, Angelo State University; Henry Decell, University of Houston; Robert Pruitt, San Jose State University; Bernard Schroeder, University of Wisconsin; and David Zalewski, Northern Michigan University.

Credit is due Craig Barth and the Brooks/Cole staff for excellent workmanship. We are also grateful for the assistance given by Karen Jones, Cathie Mitchell, Teresa Morrison, June Myer, and Stephen Peeples.

To the Student

At the beginning of each chapter and at the beginning of each section of a chapter, we have written notes to you. In these notes we describe in elementary terms the content of the section. Often we indicate where the material of a section is used elsewhere in the book or in everyday problems. Occasionally we share some historical perspective or special application of the material at hand. In general, we place the specifics of what you are learning in the larger context of the goals of the course.

As you begin this study, it is appropriate to consider the question, "What is mathematics?" Some say that mathematics consists of operations with numbers used to answer the questions, "How many?" and "How much?" In this role, mathematics is a tool. It is an indispensable tool in our modern world of business transactions, industrial production, research in both the life sciences and social sciences, and the never-ending flow of statistics.

Mathematics is also a language. It can be a simple language allowing us to communicate effectively in the marketplace, in public affairs, and even at home. It can be a sophisticated language teaching us how to use new and fascinating procedures for decision-making—for finding models and patterns to fit situations, and for determining the risk and uncertainty of optimum solutions.

The one thing that mathematics is not is a spectator sport. To enjoy mathematics, you must become involved. Make sure you solve a large number of the problems. Remember, you are the one who will benefit if you learn to use the language of mathematics to solve the problems in this book and in the real world. Good luck!

Ruric E. Wheeler
William D. Peeples, Jr.

Course Outlines

One-semester courses	Students with average mathematical background (chapters)	Better-prepared students (chapters)
Emphasis on business management, accounting, finance, insurance, production, and marketing	1–6 not starred*	1–6, 7 not starred
Preparation for advanced study of statistics, decision theory, and operations research	1–7 not starred	1–8 not starred
Preparation for marketing, production, and economics	1–4, 8, 9, 10 not starred	1–4, 8, 9, 10
Emphasis on social science	1–3, 5–8 not starred	1–3, 5–8
Two-semester courses		
Emphasis on business management, accounting, finance, insurance, production, and marketing	1–6, 8–12 not starred	1–6, 8–12
Preparation for advanced study of statistics, decision theory, and operations research	1–14 not starred	1–14
Preparation for marketing, production, and economics	1–13 not starred	1–13
Emphasis on social science	1–3, 5–14 not starred	1–3, 5–14

* Throughout the book, sections marked with asterisks (starred) are not needed for subsequent material in the book and may be omitted at the discretion of the instructor.

Background (or Equivalent) Needed for Understanding Each Chapter

Chapter	Prerequisite chapters	Chapter	Prerequisite chapters
2	1		
3	1, 2	8	1, 2
4	1, 2	9	1, 2, 8
5	1, 2	10	1, 2, 8, 9
6	1, 2, 5	11	1, 2, 8, 9
7	1, 2, 5	12	1, 2, 8, 9, 10, 11
		13	1, 2, 8, 9, 10, 11, 12
		14	1, 2, 8, 9, 10, 11, 12, 13

Contents

CHAPTER ***7**

Applications of Probability   332

CHAPTER **8**

Functions and Graphs   382

CHAPTER **9**

Differential Calculus   422

CHAPTER 10

Additional Derivative Topics   473

CHAPTER 11

Integral Calculus   506

CHAPTER 12

The Calculus of Exponential and Logarithmic Functions   543

Modern Mathematics

with Applications to Business and the Social Sciences

FOURTH EDITION

1

Fundamental Concepts of Modern Mathematics

How much stock should a company have on inventory? How many warehouses should be planned by a company and where should they be located in order to provide the cheapest transportation and storage? How many machines should be in operation, and at what capacity, for cheapest production? Which article should have the greatest production in order to assure maximum profit? How can one predict with some degree of accuracy that an operation will be profitable? What strategies should be employed to overcome competition? These are a few questions concerning strategies and calculated decisions that are confronted by businesses. Similar problems arise in decision-making in economics and in the social and life sciences.

In this book, we study the application of mathematics to such problems. We relate mathematical models to real-world problems. Most of the time in this book the mathematical model is an equation. For example, you are familiar with the mathematical model that relates distance, rate, and time

$$d = r \cdot t$$

You know that if you travel 60 miles per hour for 5 hours you have traveled

$$d = 60 \cdot 5 = 300 \text{ miles}$$

Most mathematical models involve *algebra*. In elementary algebra you manipulate not only numbers but symbols that represent numbers. This chapter briefly reviews some facts about real numbers and presents the fundamental ideas of algebra.

Algebra is vital to the application of mathematics to real-world problems. Be sure you fully understand the material of this chapter.

During the latter part of the nineteenth century, a man by the name of Georg Cantor found it helpful to borrow a word from common usage to describe a mathematical idea. The word he borrowed was *set*. Mathematicians of the twentieth century have found the idea of a set very useful, and many areas of modern business mathematics are based on the concept of sets. For example, business analysis involves sets of data, sets of legal documents, sets of orders, and sets of favorable or unfavorable decisions. This chapter begins with a review of the basic concepts and terminology of set theory in order to provide a convenient mathematical language and notation. You will use set terminology at various places in the book, such as sets of feasible solutions in linear programming.

The word *set* is synonymous with collection, class, or aggregate. We describe a set as a **well-defined collection** of objects or symbols having the property that we can determine when a given object or symbol is or is not in the set.

The individual objects of a set are called the **elements** of the set. They are said to **belong to** or to **be members of** or to **be in** the set. The relationship between an object of the set and the set itself is expressed in the form "is an element of" or "is a member of." For example, the counting numbers, 1, 2, 3, . . ., are the elements of the set we call, in the next section, the **set of natural numbers.** (In mathematics three dots indicate the omission of numbers or terms; in this example the numbers continue indefinitely.) The symbol $\in$ is used to denote "is an element of."

Element

$x \in A$ means   x is an element of set A

$x \notin A$ means   x is not an element of set A

Braces are also used to indicate a set in **set-builder notation.** We let x represent the elements of set A and give a description of these elements after a vertical line.

Set-Builder Notation

$A = \{x \mid x \text{ is an element such that (the description) is true}\}$. The vertical line is read "such that" or "satisfying the condition that."

EXAMPLE 1 Use set-builder notation to describe the set of counting numbers less than 140.

Solution $\{x \mid x$ is a counting number less than $140\}$

This set is read, "The set of all x such that x is a counting number less than 140," and can be tabulated as $\{1, 2, 3, \ldots, 139\}$.

The set of all people over 20 feet tall is an example of an **empty set.**

Null Set | A set that contains no elements is called the empty or null set and is denoted by $\emptyset$.

The relationship between two sets such as $A = \{1, 3, 5, 7\}$ and $B = \{1, 2, 3, 4, 5, 6, 7, 8, 9, 10\}$ where each element of A is also an element of B is described by the term **subset.** A is said to be a subset of B.

Subset | Set A is said to be a subset of set B, denoted by $A \subseteq B$, if and only if each element of A is an element of B.

EXAMPLE 2 **a.** The set of all vice presidents of the XYZ Corporation is a subset of the set of all administrative personnel.
b. The set $\{$Kaye, Aster, Brenda$\}$ is a subset of $\{$Brenda, Aster, Kaye$\}$. (Why?) Note that $\emptyset$ is a subset of every set. (Why?)

Proper Subset | Set A is said to be a proper subset of set B, denoted by $A \subset B$, if and only if each element of A is an element of B and there is at least one element of B that is not an element of A.

Since all dogs are animals, the set of all dogs is a subset of the set of animals. Moreover, the set of all dogs is a proper subset of the set of animals because there are animals that are not dogs.

EXAMPLE 3 List all the subsets of $\{3, 5, 7\}$. First list the different subsets with two elements. Then list the subsets with one element. Then list all other subsets.

Solution The subsets of $\{3, 5, 7\}$ are $\{3, 5\}$, $\{3, 7\}$, $\{5, 7\}$, $\{3\}$, $\{5\}$, $\{7\}$, $\emptyset$, and $\{3, 5, 7\}$. Notice there are eight subsets.

Let $A = \{m, n, o, p\}$ and $B = \{n, m, p, o\}$. By the definition of a subset, A is a subset of B and B is a subset of A. This fact suggests a definition for equality of sets.

Equal Sets

Two sets A and B are said to be equal, denoted by $A = B$, if and only if $A \subseteq B$ and $B \subseteq A$. That is, A and B have exactly the same elements.

If there is a fixed set of objects to which a discussion will be limited, and if all of the sets to be discussed are subsets of this set, then this "over-all" set is often called the **universal set,** or simply the **universe.**

A useful device for visualizing sets under discussion is the **Venn** (or **Euler**) **diagram.** An English logician named John Venn used closed figures, usually circular, in a plane to portray relationships between sets. In this book a set of points under discussion can be represented by those points within a region bounded by a closed curve. For example, if a circular region represents set A, then the statement $x \in A$ means that x is represented by a point within the circle, as illustrated in Figure 1.1. In Figure 1.2 the complete region within the rectangle represents the universe.

Figure 1.1

Figure 1.2

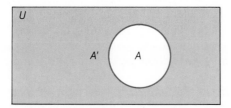

Complement

The complement of set A (denoted by A') is the set of all elements in the universe U that are not in A.

If the universe consists of all bonds, and if A consists of all bonds that have interest rates exceeding 8%, then the set of all bonds bearing interest of 8% or less is the complement of A. In Figure 1.2 the shaded region outside the circle but inside the rectangle represents A'. If the universe is all college students, and if *A* is the set of college students who have made all *A*'s, then all college students who have one or more grades lower than *A* make up the complement of *A*.

EXAMPLE 4   If $U = \{x \mid x \text{ is a counting number less than } 10\}$ and if $A = \{x \mid x \text{ is a counting number less than } 8\}$, then $A' = \{8, 9\}$.

In the preceding example, if $A = \{1, 2, 3, \ldots, 9\}$, then $A' = \varnothing$. In general,

$$U' = \varnothing \qquad \text{and} \qquad \varnothing' = U$$

Special notations are used for discussing the relationship among members of two or more sets. First consider elements that sets have in common.

Intersection

If *A* and *B* are any two sets, the intersection of *A* and *B*, denoted by $A \cap B$, is the set consisting of all the elements that belong to both *A* and *B*. Symbolically,

$$A \cap B = \{x \mid x \in A \text{ and } x \in B\}$$

The five diagrams in Figure 1.3 represent $A \cap B$ under different conditions. In (a), *A* and *B* overlap (have elements in common), and the intersection is the shaded area. If *A* and *B* are **disjoint** (have no elements in common), as shown in (b), then the intersection, $A \cap B$, is the null set. If $A \subset B$ (*A* is a proper subset of *B*), then the elements in set *A* are all in set *B*, so $A \cap B = A$, as depicted in (c). In a similar manner, if $B \subset A$, then $A \cap B = B$, as shown in (d). If *A* and *B* are equal, then $A \cap B = A = B$, as depicted in (e).

Figure 1.3

(a)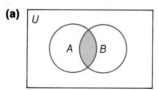

(b)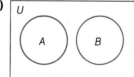

(c)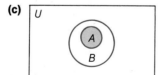

(d)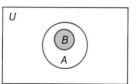

(e)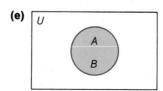

Notice the relationship between the word **and** and the definition of intersection: $x \in A \cap B$ if and only if $x \in A$ **and** $x \in B$. We now relate the word **or** to an operation on sets called **union**.

<table>
<tr><td>**Union**</td><td>The union of two sets A and B, denoted by $A \cup B$, is the set of all elements that belong to A or to B. Symbolically,

$$A \cup B = \{x \mid x \in A \quad \text{or} \quad x \in B\}$$</td></tr>
</table>

The three Venn diagrams in Figure 1.4 illustrate the basic relationships for union that might exist between two sets A and B. In Figure 1.4(a), A and B overlap, and the union of A and B is the shaded area. Notice that $A \cup B$ is the set of all elements that belong to A or B or to both A and B. If some elements are common to both sets, they are listed only once when tabulating the union of the sets. For example, given

$$A = \{a, b, c, d, e\} \qquad \text{and} \qquad B = \{c, d, e, f, g\}$$

then

$$A \cup B = \{a, b, c, d, e, f, g\}$$

Figure 1.4 **(a)**   **(b)**   **(c)**

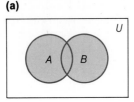   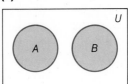   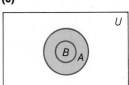

The elements c, d, and e, which are common to A and B, are listed only once. In Figure 1.4(b), A and B are disjoint, and the union of A and B is represented by the shaded area, which consists of the interiors of both circles. In Figure 1.4(c), $B \subset A$. Here the union of A and B is the interior of the circle representing set A.

EXAMPLE 5   If $U = \{x \mid x \text{ is a counting number less than } 10\}$, $A = \{2, 4, 6\}$, $B = \{1, 2, 3, 4, 5\}$, and $C = \{3, 5, 7\}$, find $A \cap B$, $A \cap C$, $A \cup C$, and B'.

Solution

$A \cap B = \{2, 4\}$ elements in common

$A \cap C = \varnothing$ no elements in common

$A \cup C = \{2, 3, 4, 5, 6, 7\}$ elements in either A or C or both

$B' = \{6, 7, 8, 9\}$ elements in the universe, not in B

Now let's consider the number of elements in a set A, sometimes denoted by $n(A)$.

EXAMPLE 6 An investigator found in a poll of 100 people that 40 used brand *A* and 25 used both brand *A* and brand *B*. Everyone contacted used either brand *A* or brand *B*. But, alas, the poor investigator lost the tabulation of those who used brand *B*. Can you help find the answer?

Solution Let *A* be the set of people who used brand *A*, and let *B* be the set of people who used brand *B*. Note that $n(A) = 40$, $n(A \cap B) = 25$, and $n(A \cup B) = 100$. [See Figure 1.5(a).]

Figure 1.5 **(a)**   **(b)**

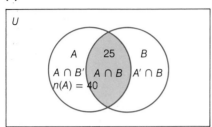   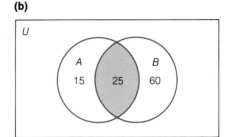

In Figure 1.5(b), 25 has been placed in the region containing the elements of $A \cap B$. Since $n(A) = 40$, there are 15 elements in *A* that are not in $A \cap B$, as noted in the figure. Since $n(A \cup B) = 100$, and $100 - 15 - 25 = 60$, then 60 elements are in *B* but not in $A \cap B$. Thus,

$$n(B) = 25 + 60 = 85$$

Therefore, because of a knowledge of sets, the investigator now knows that 85 people used brand *B*.

Exercise Set **1.1**

A   **1.** If *A* is the set of all counting numbers less than or equal to 16, which of the following statements are true and which are false?
   a. $11 \in A$ **b.** $16 \subset A$ **c.** $5 \in A$ **d.** $\frac{1}{3} \in A$ **e.** $-4 \in A$
   f. $0 \subset A$ **g.** $81 \in A$ **h.** $\varnothing \in A$ **i.** $\varnothing \subseteq A$ **j.** $A \in A$

   2. Use set-builder notation to express the following:
   a. The counting numbers less than or equal to 16
   b. The set of even counting numbers
   c. The set of counting numbers between 8 and 15, inclusive
   d. The set of female presidents of the United States
   e. The counting numbers greater than 10
   f. The set of all odd counting numbers

   3. Compute the number of elements in each of the following sets.
   a. $A = \{201, 1, 2, 3\}$
   b. $B = \{x, y, z\}$

    c. $C = \{x \mid x$ is a counting number less than 8$\}$

    d. $D = \{x \mid x$ is a counting number greater than 5 and less than 6$\}$

    e. $E = \{x \mid x$ is a counting number less than 3$\}$

    f. $F = \{x \mid x$ is a counting number less than 10 and greater than 4$\}$

4. Form the union and the intersection of the following pairs of sets.

    a. $R = \{5, 10, 15\}$ $T = \{15, 20\}$

    b. $M = \{1, 2, 3\}$ $N = \{101, 102, 103, 104\}$

    c. $A = \{0, 10, 100, 1000\}$ $B = \{10, 100\}$

    d. $G = \{$odd counting numbers less than 100$\}$

       $H = \{$even counting numbers between 1 and 31$\}$

    e. $A = \{x, y, z, t\}$ $B = \{x, y, r, s\}$

5. Shade the portion of the diagram that illustrates each of the following sets.

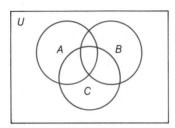

    a. $A \cap B$ **b.** $A' \cap C$ **c.** $A \cup B$

    d. $A' \cup B$ **e.** $A \cap (B \cap C)$ **f.** $A \cup (B \cup C)$

B   **6.** Describe the differences among sets $\varnothing$, $\{\varnothing\}$, and $\{0\}$.

7. Let $A = \{1, 2, 3, 4\}$, $B = \{1, 2\}$, $C = \{3, 4\}$, and $D = \{3, 4, 5\}$. Classify the following relationships as either true or false.

    a. $B \subset A$ **b.** $C \subset D$ **c.** $D \subset \varnothing$ **d.** $D \subset C$ **e.** $\varnothing \subset A$

    f. $\{3\} \subset C$ **g.** $3 \in D$ **h.** $\{3\} \in D$ **i.** $\varnothing \subset C$ **j.** $A \subset A$

8. Let

$$U = \{x \mid x \text{ is a student at Hard College}\}$$

$$B = \{y \mid y \text{ is a student majoring in business}\}$$

$$W = \{z \mid z \text{ reads } The\ Wall\ Street\ Journal\}$$

Describe each of the following in words, given that $B \subseteq U$ and $W \subseteq U$.

    a. B' **b.** W' **c.** U' **d.** $(B')'$

9. Given $U = \{a, b, c, d, e, f, g\}$, $X = \{a, b, c, d\}$, and $Y = \{c, d, e, f\}$, tabulate the elements of the following sets.

    a. $X \cup Y$ **b.** X' **c.** $X \cap Y$ **d.** $X \cup Y'$

    e. $Y \cap X'$ **f.** $X' \cap Y'$ **g.** $(X \cup Y)'$ **h.** $(X' \cap Y')'$

10. List all the subsets of the following sets.

    a. $\{a, b\}$ **b.** $\{a, b, c, d\}$ **c.** $\{a\}$

11. a. Explain in words the difference between $A \subseteq B$ and $A \subset C$.

    b. If $A \subseteq B$ and $B \subseteq C$, is $A \subseteq C$? Explain.

    c. If $\{a, b\} = \{b, c\}$, does $a = c$? Explain.

    d. Is $\varnothing \in \{0\}$?   **e.** Is $\varnothing \subseteq \{0\}$?   **f.** Is $0 \in \varnothing$?

C **12.** How many subsets are there for a set
  a. with zero elements?   **b.** with one element?   **c.** with two elements?
  d. with three elements?   **e.** with four elements?   **f.** with five elements?

13. Can you see a pattern in exercise 12? A set with *n* elements has how many subsets?

14. Out of 1000 first-year students in a certain university, 300 failed mathematics, 200 failed English, and 150 failed both mathematics and English.
  a. How many failed English or failed mathematics?
  b. How many failed English and did not fail mathematics? (*Hint:* Use ∩.)
  c. How many failed mathematics and did not fail English?
  d. How many failed mathematics or did not fail English?
  e. How many failed English or did not fail mathematics?
  f. How many did not fail English or did not fail mathematics?
  g. How many did not fail English and did not fail mathematics?

Business **15.** **Market Analysis.** A market analysis was made on the first 100 purchases of a new model car at Lassiter Motors: 65% had automatic transmissions, 55% had air conditioning, and 70% had power steering; 35% had automatic transmission and power steering, 30% had both automatic transmission and air conditioning, and 28% had both air conditioning and power steering. How many had all three extras if all of them had at least one extra? (*Hint:* Use the formula below.)

$$n(A \cup B \cup C) = n(A) + n(B) + n(C) - n(A \cap B) - n(A \cap C)$$
$$- n(B \cap C) + n(A \cap B \cap C)$$

Economics **16.** **Dow Average.** Of the 120 economists who gave advice to banks at the beginning of the year, 84 advised that the interest rates on government securities would decrease in the first 3 months of the year, and 70 advised that the Dow average would increase. How many recommended that both would occur?

Life Sciences **17.** **Blood Classification.** Blood can be classified as A (having type A antigen), B (having type B antigen), AB (having both), and O (having neither). Additionally, blood may contain the Rh antigen (called Rh positive and indicated by +). If the blood does not contain the Rh antigen, it is Rh negative (indicated by −).
  a. Draw a Venn diagram to show the eight types of blood: A−, A+, B−, B+, AB−, AB+, O+, O−.
  b. Out of a random sample of 1000 people, the following data were obtained: 204 had A antigen, 256 had B antigen, 801 had Rh antigen, 52 had both A and B antigens, 104 had both A and Rh antigens, 206 had both B and Rh antigens, and 42 had all three antigens. How many had blood type O−?

Social Sciences **18.** **Voting Coalitions.** Set theory can be used to analyze the power of voting coalitions. A **winning coalition** consists of any set of voters who can carry a proposal. A committee has five members, A, B, C, D, and E. In order for a proposal to be passed, it must have at least three votes. List all the possible winning coalitions.

19. A town council consists of five members whose votes are weighted according to the number of citizens in their districts. Councilperson A has six votes; B, five votes; C, four votes; and D and E, one vote each. Nine or more votes are required to carry an issue.
  a. List all winning coalitions.
  b. From the winning coalitions, pick the ones having the property that if one councilperson were removed, thus removing all of that person's votes, the coalition would fail to win.

In our everyday use of numbers we seldom think about the numbers we use. The main reason for reviewing these numbers is to call attention to their characteristics. In addition, *less than, greater than,* and *absolute value* are defined to assist in performing operations involving negative numbers. The representation of numbers on the number line aids understanding. As you have probably realized, the material of this section is used not only throughout this book but also in most application problems in everyday life.

We shall frequently refer to the following five sets of numbers.

Table 1.1 Sets of Numbers

Name	Number Set	Description	Examples
Natural numbers	$N = \{1, 2, 3, \ldots\}$	The counting numbers	5, 8, 100, 101
Integers	$I = \{\ldots -2, -1, 0, 1, 2 \ldots\}$	The counting numbers, their negatives, and zero	$-7, 0, 2002$
Rational numbers	$Q = \left\{x \mid x = \dfrac{a}{b}, a \text{ and } b \in I, b \neq 0\right\}$	Quotient of two integers (also written as a/b or $a \div b$ or as decimals)	$-\frac{2}{3}, \frac{15}{2}, 2.01$
Irrational numbers	$H = \{x \mid x \text{ is not rational}\}$	When written as decimals, the decimals are nonterminating and nonrepeating	$\sqrt{3}, \pi, -3\sqrt{5}$ 3.131131113 $\ldots$
Real numbers	$R = Q \cup H$	Contains all the elements of the rational *and* the irrational numbers	$\frac{2}{3}, 3\sqrt{7}, -6.01$

Figure 1.6 shows how these sets are related.

Figure 1.6

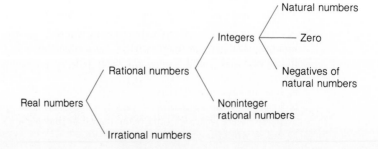

There is a one-to-one correspondence between the real numbers and the points on a line (to each real number there corresponds one and only one point on the line, and vice versa). To illustrate this concept, we draw a line with a uniform scale of a convenient size having the positive direction toward the right. This line is called the **real number line** or real line; the real number corresponding to a point on the line is called the **coordinate** of the point, and the point is called the **graph** of the number. The point corresponding to 0 is called the **origin.** Points or graphs representing the irrational number $-\sqrt{10}$ and the rational numbers 2 and 6.5 are shown in Figure 1.7.

Figure 1.7

The operations of addition and multiplication on the set of negative numbers are performed by using the following definition.

Addition and Multiplication of Negative Numbers

a. The symbol $|x|$ represents the **absolute value** of x.

$$|x| = \begin{cases} x & \text{if x is positive or zero} \\ -x & \text{if x is negative} \end{cases}$$

b. $-(-x) = x$

c. $x + (-y) = x - y$ if $|x|$ is greater than $|y|$
$= -(y - x)$ if $|x|$ is less than $|y|$
$= 0$ if $|x| = |y|$

d. $-x + (-y) = -(x + y)$

e. $-x(y) = -xy$ (unlike signs)

f. $(-x)(-y) = xy$ (like signs)

EXAMPLE 7

a. $|-3| = 3$ and $|17| = 17$

b. $-(-6) = 6$

c. $5 + (-9) = -(9 - 5) = -4$ since $|-9|$ is larger than $|5|$
$-3 + 5 = (5 - 3) = 2$ since $|5|$ is larger than $|-3|$

d. $-5 + (-6) = -(5 + 6) = -11$

e. $(-3) \cdot (5) = -15$ (unlike signs)

f. $(-4) \cdot (-8) = 32$ (like signs)

Properties of rational numbers expressed as fractions are summarized as follows.

a. $\dfrac{cp}{cq} = \dfrac{p}{q}$ and $\dfrac{pc}{qc} = \dfrac{p}{q}$ $c \neq 0, \quad q \neq 0$

b. $\dfrac{p}{q} + \dfrac{r}{q} = \dfrac{p+r}{q}$ $q \neq 0$

c. $\dfrac{p}{q} + \dfrac{r}{s} = \dfrac{ps}{qs} + \dfrac{qr}{qs} = \dfrac{ps+qr}{qs}$ $q \neq 0, \quad s \neq 0$

d. $\dfrac{p}{q} \cdot \dfrac{r}{s} = \dfrac{pr}{qs}$ $q \neq 0, \quad s \neq 0$

Observe that $\dfrac{p}{q}$ requires that $q \neq 0$; that is, division by 0 is not defined.

EXAMPLE 8

a. $\dfrac{-10}{15} = \dfrac{-2 \cdot 5}{3 \cdot 5} = \dfrac{-2}{3}$ and $\dfrac{-10}{15} = \dfrac{5 \cdot -2}{5 \cdot 3} = \dfrac{-2}{3}$

b. $\dfrac{2}{7} + \dfrac{3}{7} = \dfrac{5}{7}$

c. $\dfrac{2}{5} + \dfrac{3}{7} = \dfrac{2 \cdot 7}{5 \cdot 7} + \dfrac{5 \cdot 3}{5 \cdot 7} = \dfrac{14 + 15}{35} = \dfrac{29}{35}$

d. $\dfrac{-2}{7} \cdot \dfrac{-5}{6} = \dfrac{-2 \cdot (-5)}{7 \cdot 6} = \dfrac{10}{42} = \dfrac{5}{21}$

For mixed fractions, recall that $2\frac{1}{3}$ means $2 + \frac{1}{3}$; thus, $3\frac{1}{2}$ equals

$$3 + \dfrac{1}{2} = \dfrac{6}{2} + \dfrac{1}{2} = \dfrac{7}{2}$$

By using the operations of addition and multiplication, we can define two *inverse operations* on real numbers: subtraction (finding a difference) and division (finding a quotient).

a. *Subtraction:* $p - q = p + (-q)$

b. *Division:* $p \div q = p \cdot \dfrac{1}{q} = \dfrac{p}{q}$ $q \neq 0$

c. $\dfrac{p}{q} \div \dfrac{r}{s} = \dfrac{p}{q} \cdot \dfrac{s}{r}$ $q, s, r \neq 0$

EXAMPLE 9

a. $3 - (-5) = 3 + [-(-5)] = 3 + 5 = 8$ and
$-17 - 4 = (-17) - (4) = -17 + (-4) = -21$

b. $-3 \div 6 = \dfrac{-3}{6} = -3 \cdot \dfrac{1}{6} = -\dfrac{1}{2}$

c. $\dfrac{-2}{3} \div \dfrac{5}{7} = \dfrac{-2}{3} \cdot \dfrac{7}{5} = \dfrac{-14}{15}$

In all the work that follows, we adopt the usual custom of writing $2 \cdot x$ as $2x$. The 2 is called the **coefficient** of x. Recall that $2x + 3x = (2 + 3)x = 5x$ and $6x - 4x = (6 - 4)x = 2x$ (classified later as the *distributive property of multiplication over addition or subtraction*).

Algebraic expressions often involve symbols of grouping such as **parentheses, brackets,** and **braces.** Note that these symbols always come in pairs. Two properties of grouping state that

$$-(a + b) = -a - b \qquad \text{and} \qquad -(a - b) = -a + b$$

That is, if a negative sign precedes a symbol of grouping, the signs of all terms within the grouping are changed when the symbols of grouping are removed. When a numeral is written adjacent to a symbol of grouping, each term within the grouping is multiplied by the number represented by the numeral.

EXAMPLE 10

$$\begin{aligned}
7x - [4x - (2x - 1)] &= 7x - [4x - 2x + 1] \\
&= 7x - [2x + 1] \\
&= 7x - 2x - 1 \\
&= 5x - 1
\end{aligned}$$

EXAMPLE 11

$$\begin{aligned}
x - \{y - 2[3y - (2 + y)]\} &= x - \{y - 2[3y - 2 - y]\} \\
&= x - \{y - 2[2y - 2]\} \\
&= x - \{y - 4y + 4\} \\
&= x - \{-3y + 4\} \\
&= x + 3y - 4
\end{aligned}$$

It is generally agreed that the following order of operations is used when working with real numbers or algebraic expressions representing real numbers.

Order of Operations

> **a.** Do any work inside parentheses or brackets.
> **b.** Do multiplications or divisions, in order, from left to right.
> **c.** Do additions or subtractions, in order, from left to right.
> **d.** If the problem involves a fraction bar, simplify the numerator and the denominator separately and then divide.

EXAMPLE 12   Simplify the following.

a. $8 \div 4 + 3 \cdot 5 = 2 + 3 \cdot 5 = 2 + 15 = 17$

b. $\dfrac{-7(-3) + (-5)}{4(-3) - (-4)} = \dfrac{21 + (-5)}{-12 - (-4)} = \dfrac{16}{-8} = -2$

We conclude this section by comparing the size of two real numbers. If a is to the left of b on a number line, then a is said to be less than b. If a is to the right of b on a number line, then a is greater than b. If a is to the left of b, then a positive number must be added to a to equal b.

<table>
<tr><td>Less Than and
Greater Than</td><td>If a and b are any real numbers, then a is said to be less than b, denoted by $a < b$, and b is said to be greater than a, denoted by $b > a$, if and only if there exists a positive number c such that $a + c = b$.</td></tr>
</table>

EXAMPLE 13
    a. $-7 < -5$ because $-7 + 2 = -5$. (2 is a positive number.)
    b. $\frac{3}{5} < \frac{7}{8}$ because $\frac{3}{5} + \frac{11}{40} = \frac{7}{8}$. ($\frac{11}{40}$ is a positive number.)

Sometimes the equality symbol is combined with inequalities to state a "less than or equal to" relationship. The statement "$a \leq b$" means "$a < b$ or $a = b$" or "a is not greater than b."

EXAMPLE 14
    a. $-4 \leq -4$ is true because -4 is equal to -4.
    b. $-3 \leq -2$ because $-3 < -2$.

Remember that algebraic statements involving less than and greater than have distinct meanings on the real number line. Some of the more common correspondences are summarized in Table 1.2 where in each case $a, b, c \in R$ (are real numbers).

Table 1.2

Algebraic Statement	Number Line Interpretation
a. x is positive ($x > 0$)	**a.** The graph of x lies to the right of the origin.
b. x is negative ($x < 0$)	**b.** The graph of x lies to the left of the origin.
c. $x > y$	**c.** The graph of x lies to the right of the graph of y.
d. $x < y$	**d.** The graph of x lies to the left of the graph of y.
e. $x < y < z$	**e.** The graph of y is to the right of the graph of x and to the left of the graph of z.
f. $\lvert x \rvert < c$	**f.** The graph of x is less than c units from the origin.
g. $\lvert x \rvert < \lvert y \rvert$	**g.** The graph of x is closer to the origin than the graph of y.

Exercise Set 1.2

A
    1. Classify the following numbers as natural numbers (N), integers (I), rational numbers (Q), irrational numbers (H), and/or real numbers (R). (For example, -5 is I, Q, and R.)
    a. $\sqrt{3}$ **b.** $\frac{1}{2}$ **c.** 0.125 **d.** 0
    e. 0.17 **f.** π **g.** $\sqrt[3]{3}$ **h.** $-1/\pi$

2. State whether each statement is true (T) or false (F).
   a. Every integer is a rational number.
   b. Every integer is a natural number.
   c. Every rational number is a natural number.
   d. No natural numbers are rational.
   e. No irrational numbers are natural numbers.
   f. $Q \cap H = \varnothing$ g. $I \subset H$ h. $I \cap Q = N$

3. Express each statement by means of the symbols $<$, $\leq$, $>$, or $\geq$.
   a. x is at least 7
   b. x is not greater than 3
   c. x is at most 5
   d. x is between 1 and 3, inclusive
   e. x is at least 1 and less than 3
   f. x is greater than 5 and not greater than 7

4. Remove the symbols of grouping and combine terms.
   a. $3x^2 + (x^2 - 4z) - (4z - 3x) - 2x$
   b. $x + 4 - 2\{2 - 3(x - y)\}$
   c. $4x^2 - \{3x^2 - 2[x - 3(x^2 - x)] + 4\}$
   d. $3(x - 2y) - (-x + 2y)$
   e. $3\{3x - [3x - (3x + 1) + 3] - x\}$
   f. $x - [x + 2(y + z) - \{x - 2(y - z)\}]$

5. Rewrite the expressions below without absolute value notation.
   a. $|-11|$ b. $|x|$ c. $|-(-11)|$
   d. $|-x|$ e. $|3 - 5 \cdot 2|$ f. $-|-5| - |-2 - (-14)|$

6. Simplify the following expressions by using the correct order of operations.
   a. $12 \div 4 - 8 \div 2$ b. $-75 \div 3 \cdot 5$
   c. $\dfrac{-9 + (-4)(-3) \div 6}{2 \cdot 2 - (-3)}$ d. $(-9 + 2 \cdot 2 \cdot 3)(-3)$

7. In each of the following lists of numbers, arrange from smallest to largest.
   a. $-1, |-3|, 0$ b. $\left|\dfrac{-3}{4}\right|, \left|\dfrac{-5}{6}\right|, \dfrac{2}{3}$
   c. $-1, -|2|, |-2|$ d. $\dfrac{1}{2} - \left|\dfrac{-1}{2}\right|, \dfrac{-1}{2}, \dfrac{1}{2}$

B   8. Perform the following operations:

   a. $-\frac{4}{3}(\frac{1}{4} - \frac{2}{5})$ b. $\dfrac{3}{ab} + \dfrac{5}{a}$

   c. $-8(\frac{2}{3} - 4)$ d. $-11\frac{8}{9} - 3\frac{5}{9}$

   e. $\dfrac{6 - 5}{4 - 4}$ f. $\dfrac{17}{-3 - (2 - 5)}$

   g. $-(\frac{3}{8} - \frac{7}{8})$ h. $\dfrac{4}{3} + \dfrac{7}{9} \cdot \dfrac{-3}{5}$

   i. $(\frac{2}{3} \cdot \frac{9}{1})\frac{13}{2}$ j. $-\frac{4}{3}(\frac{1}{3})(-\frac{1}{2})$
   k. $(-\frac{3}{2} + \frac{17}{2}) \div (-\frac{2}{5} + \frac{3}{8})$ l. $(\frac{4}{3} \div -\frac{7}{8}) \cdot (-\frac{1}{2} - \frac{3}{4})$
   m. $6xy + (-4xy)$ n. $3\frac{1}{2} + (-7\frac{1}{4})$
   o. $-(-3 + 4)$ p. $-(7 - 10)$

9. Place the correct symbol $<$, $>$, or $=$ between the two expressions.

  a. $-|-6| - |-12 - 4|$ $|4 - 1| - |-5| - |1|$

  b. $-|-3| - |-1 - 5|$ $|-3 - 2| - |3| \cdot |-2|$

C 10. Perform the indicated operations.

  a. $3\frac{5}{9} + 2\frac{2}{3}$ **b.** $-17\frac{7}{12} + 7\frac{2}{5}$ **c.** $-11\frac{8}{21} - 3\frac{5}{9}$

  d. $7\frac{1}{8} \cdot 6\frac{1}{4}$ **e.** $-8\frac{1}{7} \cdot 3\frac{1}{2}$ **f.** $16\frac{2}{3} \cdot -4\frac{1}{4}$

  g. $0.312(-5.4)$ **h.** $4\frac{7}{8} \cdot 1\frac{3}{4}$ **i.** $-7\frac{1}{2} \cdot 4\frac{1}{3}$

  j. $(0.132 - 5.6)(-7.1)$ **k.** $\left(-\frac{7}{10} + \frac{3}{25}\right) \cdot \left(\frac{24}{5} \div \frac{22}{15}\right)$ **l.** $\left(\frac{3}{8} + \frac{1}{3}\right) \div \left(\frac{17}{2} - 4\right)$

11. Use a calculator to simplify. (Watch out for the order of computation.)

  a. $\dfrac{16 \div 2 \cdot 4 - 5 \div (-3)}{16 - 2 - 4 \div 5}$ **b.** $\dfrac{13.1 \div 0.12 \cdot (-4.7) - 3.621}{13.1 - 7.6(-0.17) - 16.3}$

  c. $\dfrac{-7.2(-4.3) - 0.01 \div -2.5}{4.61 - 2.73 \div 0.1}$ **d.** $\dfrac{-9.76 - 4.67(0.017)}{13.1(-6.4) - 0.471}$

12. Let a and b be any real numbers. Is it always true that

  a. $|a - b| = |b - a|$?   **b.** $|a| + |b| = |a - b|$?

  c. $|a - b| \geq |a| - |b|$?   **d.** $|a - b| \leq |a|$?

Business   13. **Sum of Digits Depreciation.** Suppose that an asset has a life of 6 years and a value of $1,000. To find the sum of digits depreciation, we add the natural numbers representing each of the 6 years:

$$1 + 2 + 3 + 4 + 5 + 6 = 21$$

We then use 21 as the denominator and each year in reverse order as the numerator (that is, year 1 would be $\frac{6}{21}$) to find the depreciation by multiplying the resulting fraction by the initial value of the asset.

Year	Fraction	Allowable Depreciation
1	$\left(\frac{6}{21}\right)$ 1,000	285.71
2	$\left(\frac{5}{21}\right)$ 1,000	238.09
3	$\left(\frac{4}{21}\right)$ 1,000	190.48
4	$\left(\frac{3}{21}\right)$ 1,000	142.86
5	$\left(\frac{2}{21}\right)$ 1,000	95.24
6	$\left(\frac{1}{21}\right)$ 1,000	47.62
		1,000.00

    Use the sum of digits method to find the yearly depreciation of an office computer valued at $5,000 with a life of 8 years.

Economics   14. **Total Revenue.** A firm determines that its total revenue in dollars from the sale of x items of a product is $4x + 500$. Show this fact as an inequality if the total revenue must be at least $25,000. If it must be more than $30,000.

Life Sciences   15. **Mathematical Models.** Sometimes algebraic expressions are used to describe reactions as they occur in time. For example,

$$E = \frac{1 - 0.2t}{2 + t}$$

has been used to describe muscle efficiency E during maximum contraction during the time t that the muscle is contracted. Find a value for E when $t = 0$, 0.5, $4\frac{1}{2}$, and 5.

16. Psychology. Intelligence quotient (IQ) is equal to 100 multiplied by the mental age divided by the chronological age. An 8-year-old girl has a mental age of 12. What is her IQ?

17. Using exercise 16, what is the mental age of a 12-year-old boy with an IQ of 150?

3 Solution Sets for Equations and Inequalities

Equations and inequalities involving only numbers (or constants) can be classified as true or false. For example,

$$4 + 2 = 6 \quad \text{true} \qquad 7 < 9 - 1 \quad \text{true} \qquad \left| -3 \right| < 0 \quad \text{false}$$

Equations and inequalities involving unknowns (such as x, y, z) are called **open sentences** since they cannot in general be classified as true or false without a value being substituted for the unknown. For example,

$$x + 3 = 7 \qquad \text{and} \qquad 3x - 1 < 5$$

are open sentences. In this section, we seek values for the unknowns that will make open sentences true statements. In other words, we solve linear equations and inequalities.

The equation $2x - 1 = 13$ is of the first degree in x (that is, the power of x is 1) and is called a **linear equation.** If the number 7 is substituted for x in this linear equation,

$$2(7) - 1 = 13$$
$$13 = 13$$

the result is true. Thus, 7 is said to *satisfy* (or to be a *solution* of) the equation $2x - 1 = 13$. The set $\{7\}$ is called the *solution set* of $2x - 1 = 13$. In general, we have the following definition.

Solution Set

If an equation (or inequality) involves only one variable and there is a number that, if substituted for that variable, makes the equation (or inequality) a true statement, then that number is called a **solution** of the equation (or inequality); the set of all the solutions is called the *solution set*. (A solution of an equation is also sometimes called a *root* of the equation.)

Equations (or inequalities) that have the same solution sets are said to be **equivalent.** The following properties of equations are very important because they yield equivalent equations and thus can be used in the equation-solving process.

<table>
<tr><td>**Properties of
Equality**</td><td>Let a, b, and c be real numbers.
a. If $a = b$, then $a + c = b + c$.   Addition property
b. If $a = b$, then $a - c = b - c$.   Subtraction property
c. If $a = b$, then $ca = cb$.   Multiplication property

d. If $a = b$ and $c \neq 0$, then $\dfrac{a}{c} = \dfrac{b}{c}$.   Division property</td></tr>
</table>

These four properties may be used to isolate the unknown (or variable) with a coefficient of 1 on one side of an equation and thus obtain a value for the variable (or a solution).

EXAMPLE 15   Solve $3x + 5 = 11$.

Solution   To isolate the term involving x on a side by itself, we first subtract 5 from both sides (or members) of the equation.

$$3x + 5 - 5 = 11 - 5 \quad \text{Subtraction property}$$
$$3x = 6$$

Then, to isolate x on the left side by itself, we divide both sides by 3.

$$\frac{3x}{3} = \frac{6}{3} \quad \text{Division property}$$
$$x = 2$$

The solution can be checked by substituting it into the original equation:

$$3(2) + 5 = 11$$
$$11 = 11$$

EXAMPLE 16   Solve $\dfrac{x}{2} - 3 = 1$.

Solution

$$\frac{x}{2} - 3 + 3 = 1 + 3 \quad \text{Addition property}$$
$$\frac{x}{2} = 4$$
$$2\left(\frac{x}{2}\right) = 2 \cdot 4 \quad \text{Multiplication property}$$
$$x = 8$$

$$\text{Check:} \quad \frac{8}{2} - 3 = 1$$
$$1 = 1$$

EXAMPLE 17   Solve $3x - 2(2x - 5) = 3(x - 2)$.

Solution This time we need to get all terms involving x on one side of the equation. First we simplify,

$$3x - 2(2x - 5) = 3(x - 2)$$
$$3x - 4x + 10 = 3x - 6$$
$$-x + 10 = 3x - 6$$
$$-x + 10 - 3x = 3x - 6 - 3x \quad \text{Subtraction property}$$
$$-4x + 10 = -6$$
$$-4x + 10 - 10 = -6 - 10 \quad \text{Subtraction property}$$
$$-4x = -16$$
$$x = 4 \quad \text{Division property}$$

Check: $3 \cdot 4 - 2(2 \cdot 4 - 5) = 3(4 - 2)$
$$12 - 6 = 3 \cdot 2$$
$$6 = 6$$

EXAMPLE 18 Solve $|x + 2| = 3$.

Solution The equation is equivalent to $x + 2 = -3$ or $x + 2 = 3$, with solutions $x = -5$ or $x = 1$.

The procedures for solving equations in the preceding examples may also be used for solving equations involving letters.

EXAMPLE 19 Solve $I = Prt$ for t.

Solution To solve for t, we divide both members by Pr, where $Pr \neq 0$.

$$\frac{I}{Pr} = \frac{Prt}{Pr} \quad \text{Division property}$$

$$\frac{I}{Pr} = 1 \cdot t$$

or $\qquad t = \dfrac{I}{Pr}$

Check: $I = Pr\left(\dfrac{I}{Pr}\right)$

$$I = I$$

EXAMPLE 20 Solve $y = mx + b$ for $x \qquad (m \neq 0)$.

Solution $\qquad y + (-b) = mx + b + (-b) \quad \text{Addition property}$

$$y - b = mx$$

$$\frac{(y - b)}{m} = \frac{mx}{m} \quad \text{Division property}$$

$$\frac{y - b}{m} = x \qquad \text{or} \qquad x = \frac{y - b}{m}$$

$$\text{Check:} \quad y = m\left(\frac{y-b}{m}\right) + b$$

$$y = y - b + b$$

$$y = y$$

The procedures used for solving inequalities are almost the same as those used for solving equations. See if you can discover the differences.

Properties of Inequalities

For real numbers a, b, and c,

a. If $a < b$, then $a + c < b + c$.

b. If $a < b$ and $c > 0$, then $ca < cb$.

c. If $a < b$ and $c < 0$, then $ca > cb$.

d. If $a < b$ and $c > 0$, then $\dfrac{a}{c} < \dfrac{b}{c}$.

e. If $a < b$ and $c < 0$, then $\dfrac{a}{c} > \dfrac{b}{c}$.

Property **a** states that if the same quantity is added to both sides of an inequality, the inequality is still true. Property **b** is sometimes stated as follows: If both members of an inequality are multiplied by the same positive number, the inequality is still true. Property **c** can be stated as: If both members of an inequality are multiplied by the same negative number, the inequality is reversed; that is, "less than" changes to "greater than" when the inequality is multiplied by a negative number. Difficulty arises in multiplying both sides of an inequality by an expression involving a variable in that the sign of the expression is generally unknown.

EXAMPLE 21 Each of the properties of inequalities is illustrated with numbers as follows.

a. $-1 < 5$, so $-1 + 6 < 5 + 6$ or $5 < 11$

b. $-1 < 5$, so $3(-1) < 3(5)$ or $-3 < 15$

c. $-1 < 5$, so $-2(-1) > -2(5)$ or $2 > -10$

d. $6 < 8$, so $\dfrac{6}{2} < \dfrac{8}{2}$ or $3 < 4$

e. $6 < 8$, so $\dfrac{6}{-2} > \dfrac{8}{-2}$ or $-3 > -4$

EXAMPLE 22 Find the solution set of $\dfrac{x}{3} - 2 < 4$.

Solution

$$\frac{x}{3} - 2 + 2 < 4 + 2 \qquad \text{Property } \mathbf{a} \text{ for inequalities}$$

$$\frac{x}{3} < 6$$

$$3\left(\frac{x}{3}\right) < 3 \cdot 6 \qquad \text{Property } \mathbf{b} \text{ for inequalities}$$

$$x < 18$$

The solution set consists of all real numbers less than 18.

A visual representation of the solution set of an inequality is often more useful than the algebraic answer. The following examples illustrate the graphs of the solution sets of some simple inequalities.

EXAMPLE 23 On a real number line, draw the graphs of the following inequalities.

a. $x < 3$ **b.** $x \leq 3$ **c.** $x > -1$

d. $x \geq -1$ **e.** $-1 < x < 3$ **f.** $-1 \leq x < 3$

g. $-1 < x \leq 3$ **h.** $-1 \leq x \leq 3$ **i.** $|x| > 1$

Figure 1.8

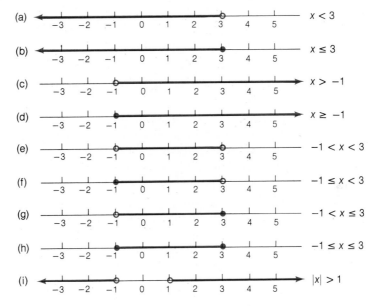

Solution Note in Figure 1.8(a) that an open dot shows that 3 is not an element in the solution set. The arrow indicates that the graph extends indefinitely to the left since all negative numbers are part of the solution set. In (b), a solid dot shows that 3 is an element of the solution set. What does the open dot indicate in (c)? What does the solid dot indicate in (d)? Why do the graphs in (c) and (d) extend indefinitely to the right?

EXAMPLE 24 Find and graph the solution set of $-3x + 2 < 7$.

Solution

$$-3x + 2 + (-2) < 7 + (-2) \quad \text{Property } \mathbf{a} \text{ for inequalities}$$

$$-3x < 5$$

Divide both members by -3.

$$\frac{-3x}{-3} > \frac{5}{-3} \quad \text{Property } \mathbf{e} \text{ for inequalities}$$

$$x > -\frac{5}{3}$$

The solution set consists of all real numbers greater than $\frac{-5}{3}$, or $\{x \mid x \text{ is a real number} > \frac{-5}{3}\}$. The graph of the solution set is given in Figure 1.9.

Figure 1.9

Many students have difficulty reading, analyzing, and setting up an equation (or inequality) for real-world situations. The following three steps are helpful.

1. List facts to understand the problem; determine the quantities asked for and represent them by symbols called unknowns or variables.
2. Determine a pattern and form an equation. Solve the equation.
3. Look back and check to see if your answer makes sense.

EXAMPLE 25   John's coin collection contains nickels and dimes, and he has 3 times as many nickels as he has dimes. The value of his collection is $4.50. How many coins of each kind does he have?

Solution
1. *Understand the problem.*
   a. There are 3 times as many nickels as dimes.
   b. A nickel is worth $0.05 and a dime $0.10.
   c. The value of all coins is $4.50.
   d. We are to find the number of nickels and the number of dimes in the collection.
   e. Let d be the number of dimes in the collection.
2. *Form and solve the equation.*   By **a**, there are $3 \cdot d = 3d$ nickels. By **b**, the value of the nickels is $0.05(3d)$ and the value of the dimes is $0.10(d)$. Then, by **c**,

$$0.05(3d) + 0.10(d) = 4.50$$

$$0.15d + 0.10d = 4.50$$

$$0.25d = 4.50$$

$$d = 18$$

So there are 18 dimes and $3 \cdot 18 = 54$ nickels.
3. *Check.*   The value of 18 dimes is $18(\$0.10) = \$1.80$ and the value of 54 nickels is $54(\$0.05) = \$2.70$ and $\$1.80 + \$2.70 = \$4.50$.

EXAMPLE 26   A will provides that an estate is to be divided among a wife and two children, with each child receiving the same amount. The wife is to receive $10,000; the remainder is to be divided so that the wife receives in addition twice as much of the remainder as each child. If the estate is valued at $50,000, how much does each receive?

Solution

1. *Understand the problem.* List the given facts and identify what is to be found.
   a. There is an estate to be divided among a wife and two children.
   b. The wife receives a lump sum of $10,000 before the children receive anything.
   c. In addition to the lump sum, the wife receives twice as much of the remainder as each child.
   d. The value of the estate is $50,000.
   e. We are to find the part of the estate that the wife receives and the part that each child receives.
   f. Let x be the amount that each child receives.

2. *Form and solve the equation.* The wife receives $10,000 + 2x. The total that the wife and both children receive is

$$\begin{array}{ccc} \text{wife} & \text{child 1} & \text{child 2} \\ \$10{,}000 + 2x + & x & + & x \end{array}$$

Therefore, the equation is

$$2x + (2x + \$10{,}000) = \$50{,}000$$
$$4x + \$10{,}000 = \$50{,}000$$
$$4x = \$40{,}000$$
$$x = \$10{,}000 \text{ (each child's share)}$$
$$2x + \$10{,}000 = 2(\$10{,}000) + \$10{,}000$$
$$= \$30{,}000 \text{ (wife's share)}$$

3. *Check.* Now verify that the answer satisfies the facts. Each child receives $10,000 and the wife, $30,000. Does the wife receive $10,000 plus double what a child receives? The answer is yes. Does the sum of the allotments equal $50,000? The answer is again yes because

$$\$10{,}000 + \$10{,}000 + \$30{,}000 = \$50{,}000$$

Exercise Set **1.3**

A In exercises 1–12, solve for the variable and check.

1. $2x - 7 = 3$

2. $1 - 2x = -5$

3. $4x - 7 = 5$

4. $17 - 5x = -3$

5. $4 - 2x = (8 + 3x) + 1$

6. $-5 - x = (3 + 2x) + 1$

7. $2x - (-5) = 6 - (-x)$

8. $4x + (-7) = 3x - (-1)$

9. $\dfrac{x}{5} - 3 = -2$

10. $-\dfrac{x}{7} - 2 = -3$

11. $\dfrac{x}{5} - \dfrac{1}{3} = \dfrac{x}{3} + \dfrac{1}{5}$

12. $\dfrac{x}{2} - \dfrac{1}{4} = \dfrac{3x}{4} + 1$

Solve and graph each of the following inequalities.

13. $-x + (-4) < -7$

14. $-2x - 3 < 5$

15. $\dfrac{x}{3} + 2 < -5$

16. $-3x - 4 < -5$

17. $\dfrac{x}{3} + \dfrac{4}{6} < \dfrac{x}{2} - \dfrac{4}{15}$

18. $\dfrac{x}{7} + 3 \le 4 - \dfrac{x}{3}$

B   *Solve for the variable indicated.*

19. $A = P + Prt$; r

20. $I = A(1 - dt)$; t

21. $y = mx + b$; b

22. $y = mx + b$; m

23. $S = \dfrac{a}{1 - r}$; r

24. $l = a + (n - 1)d$; d

Solve and check the following equations.

25. $-[2x - (3 - x)] = 4x - 11$

26. $x^2 - 3 = 1 + (x + 1)(x - 2)$

27. $2 - x - x^2 = 1 - (x - 1)^2$

28. $\dfrac{3x + 4}{5} = \dfrac{7x + 6}{10}$

29. $\dfrac{x - 5}{4} = 1 + \dfrac{x - 9}{12}$

30. $\dfrac{x}{3} - 1 = \dfrac{2x - 3}{3}$

31. $|4 - x| = 1$

32. $|3 - x| = 4$

33. $|2x + 1| = 3$

34. $|3x - 2| = 4$

Solve and check the following inequalities.

35. $-1 \le x + 5 < 6$

36. $-4 \le \dfrac{3x + 2}{5} < -2$

37. $5 \le \dfrac{2x + 1}{-3} < 8$

38. $-2 \le \dfrac{2x + 5}{2} \le 0$

Use the three-step suggestion of this section to solve exercises 39–42.

39. Carol is twice as old as Ed. Ed is 10 years younger than Carol. How old is Ed?

40. The sum of two integers is 62. The second integer is 11 more than twice the first. What are the integers?

41. Tom has twice as many books as Joe. Together they have 75 books. How many does each boy have?

42. Twenty pounds added to 4 times Tom's weight is 500 pounds. How much does Tom weigh?

C   *Solve for the variable indicated.*

43. $A = P + Prt$; P

44. $\dfrac{x}{a} + \dfrac{4}{b} = 1$; x

45. $x^2y^2 - 3x - 2z^3y^2 = 1$; y^2

46. $3x_1x_3 + x_1x_2 = x_4$; x_1

Solve exercises 47 and 48 by using a calculator.

47. $6.310x - 8 < 1.60x - 0.011$

48. $-3.41(1 - 0.62x) > 4.071x - 6.3$

Business   49. **Statements.** Mr. Smith's electric bill was 6 times Mr. Jones' bill. The two bills totaled $84. What was the cost of each man's bill?

50. **Investments.** A woman has an annual income of $6,500 from two investments. She has $15,000 more invested at 10% than she has invested at 12%. How much does she have invested at each rate?

51. **Investments.** A sum of $2,000 is invested, part at 8% and the remainder at 10%. Find the amount invested at each rate if the yearly income from the two investments is $180.

52. At weekend performances, a theater sells 400 adult tickets and 520 children's tickets, each of which is 75¢ cheaper than an adult ticket. If total ticket receipts are $1,680, what is the cost of an adult ticket? A child's ticket?

53. **Mixture Problem.** A grocer mixes 40 pounds of 80¢-a-pound nuts with 60 pounds of 60¢-a-pound nuts. If he wants to receive at least the same amount of money as when he sold the nuts separately, how much should he charge for the mixture?

54. **Mixture Problem.** Carl is pricing different brands of coffee. Brand A sells for 25¢ a pound more than brand B, and brand C sells for 37¢ less than twice the price of brand B. Carl decides to taste the coffee before making a decision on which coffee is the best buy; so he buys 1 pound of each brand and spends $5.08. How much does a pound of each brand cost?

Economics   55. **Supply and Demand Equations.** Let the supply (S) and demand (D) equations for a certain commodity be given in terms of price (x) by

$$D = \frac{400 - 5x}{2} \quad \text{and} \quad S = \frac{5x}{2}$$

For what price are supply and demand equal? (Set the expression S equal to the expression for D and solve for x.)

Life Sciences   56. **Temperature.** $F = \frac{9}{5}C + 32$ relates temperature in degrees Celsius to temperature in degrees Fahrenheit. Solve for C in terms of F.

Social Sciences   57. **SAT Scores.** The average SAT verbal scores at a high school have been increasing since new graduation requirements were inaugurated in 1980. If y represents the average verbal score and t the number of years since 1980, then

$$y = 1.5t + 430$$

Solve for t in terms of y and then find when the school can expect a 450 verbal score.

Expressing Ideas with Graphs

In this section, we introduce the rectangular (or Cartesian) coordinate system and learn to draw the graphs of both linear equations and linear inequalities.

Managers and economists use equations and graphs to study costs, sales, supply, and demand. Social scientists are interested in demographic data showing voting behavior or population growth. The number of ways that linear equations can be used is endless.

We form a **rectangular** (or Cartesian) **coordinate system** with two perpendicular real number lines that intersect at the origin O, such as in Figure 1.10. The two lines are called **coordinate axes**. Traditionally, the horizontal line is called the **x-axis**, and the vertical line is called the **y-axis**. The point of intersection of the two lines is called the **origin**. The plane in which the two axes lie is called the **coordinate plane**. The four parts into which the two axes divide the plane are called **quadrants**. The four quadrants are labeled I, II, III, and IV, as in Figure 1.10.

Figure 1.10

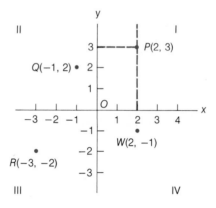

To each **ordered pair** of numbers, such as (2, 3), there corresponds a point, such as P in Figure 1.10; conversely, an ordered pair of real numbers (called **coordinates**) exists for each point in the coordinate plane. In Figure 1.10, W is identified by the coordinates $(2, -1)$, Q by $(-1, 2)$, and R by $(-3, -2)$.

Now consider the equation $x + y = 4$. Let a and b be two real numbers. We say that the ordered pair (a, b) **satisfies** $x + y = 4$, or is a **solution** of $x + y = 4$, if the equation $x + y = 4$ becomes a true statement when a is substituted for x and b is substituted for y. To find a solution to this equation, we select a value for

Figure 1.11

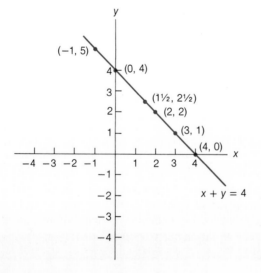

x and then solve the equation for y. For example, (2, 2) is a solution, and so are (3, 1), $(1\frac{1}{2}, 2\frac{1}{2})$, (−1, 5), (4, 0), and (0, 4). In fact, there are infinitely many solutions for this equation in the real number system. Now that we have defined the coordinate axes, we can give a geometric description of the set of all solutions of x + y = 4. Each ordered pair (a, b) of the solution set corresponds to a unique point in the coordinate plane. If we plot all the points of the solution set, the resulting figure is called the **graph** of the solution set or the graph of the equation. Since the solution set is infinite, we cannot possibly plot every ordered pair that satisfies the equation. We can, however, get an idea of what the graph looks like by plotting several representative points. For example, we use six solutions of x + y = 4 to obtain the graph in Figure 1.11.

All six points seem to lie on the same straight line. In fact, it can be shown that this straight line contains all points represented by ordered pairs satisfying x + y = 4, and that each point on the line is represented by such a pair. A more complete explanation will be given in the next section.

EXAMPLE 27   Sketch the graph of w = u + 1, where w and u are real numbers.

Solution   For this example, we choose to plot w along the vertical axis and u along the horizontal axis. Now {(1, 2), (0, 1), (−1, 0)} is a subset of the ordered pairs in the solution set of w = u + 1. If we represent these ordered pairs on a rectangular coordinate system, we note (Figure 1.12) that a straight line contains all three points. We might say that two of the points determine the line and the third point serves as a check.

Figure 1.12

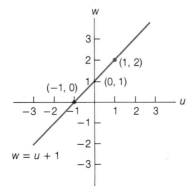

The y-coordinate of the point where the line crosses the y-axis is called the **y-intercept.** The x-coordinate of the point where the line crosses the x-axis is called the **x-intercept.** To find the y-intercept, set x = 0 in the equation of a line and solve for y. To find the x-intercept, set y = 0 and solve for x. In Figure 1.11 the x-intercept is 4 and the y-intercept is 4. In Figure 1.12 the u-intercept is −1 and the w-intercept is 1.

EXAMPLE 28   Find the x-intercept and the y-intercept of the graph of 2x − 3y = 6, and use these to sketch the graph of the equation.

Solution To find the x-intercept, set $y = 0$. Then

$$2x - 3 \cdot 0 = 6$$

$$x = 3 \quad \text{x-intercept}$$

To get the y-intercept, set $x = 0$. Then

$$2 \cdot 0 - 3y = 6$$

$$y = -2 \quad \text{y-intercept}$$

The graph of $2x - 3y = 6$ is shown in Figure 1.13.

Figure 1.13

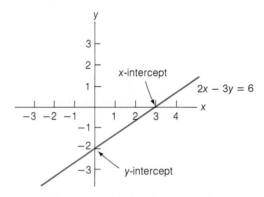

If the graph is parallel to an axis, only one intercept is needed to determine the graph of a linear equation.

EXAMPLE 29 Graph $x = 4$.

Solution The x-intercept is 4. Since $x = 4$ for each point on the graph, the graph is parallel to the y-axis, as seen in Figure 1.14.

Figure 1.14

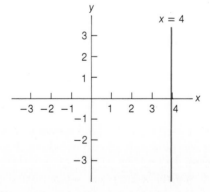

Now let's look at one of many applications of the graphing of linear equations. The intersection of the graph of an equation involving demand D and price x and an equation involving supply S and price x is called the **equilibrium point** for supply and demand.

EXAMPLE 30 Suppose the equation

$$D = \frac{320 - 4x}{3}$$

approximates a relationship between demand D and price x, where D and x are measured in appropriate units. Furthermore, suppose the relationship between supply and price is approximated by $S = 20x$. Find the point of equilibrium (intersection point) for these by graphing the equations on the same coordinate system with both D and S on the vertical axis.

Solution Note that when $x = 2$, $D = 104$; when $x = 5$, $D = 100$. Use these two points to graph

$$D = \frac{320 - 4x}{3}$$

Use $x = 4$, $S = 80$ and $x = 6$, $S = 120$ to graph $S = 20x$, as shown in Figure 1.15. The intersection of the two graphs seems to be at $x = 5$, $S = D = 100$. Thus, the **equilibrium price** is $x = 5$, and the **equilibrium supply and demand** are both 100. If the price of the item is more than 5, the supply will exceed the demand. If the price is less than 5, the demand will exceed the supply.

Figure 1.15

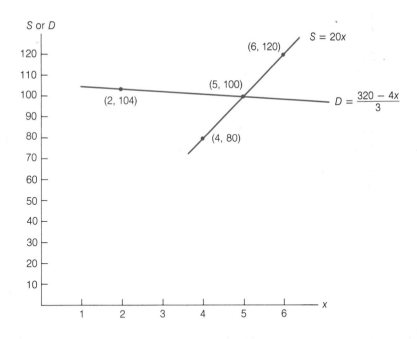

As seen in the preceding example, the graphing of equations is useful in solving application problems. Just as important is the graphing of inequalities. (The ideas we develop here are also applied in the chapters on linear programming.)

As shown in Figure 1.16, a line divides the coordinate plane into two parts called **half-planes.** Just as the points on a line are described by the equation of the line, the points in a half-plane are described by means of an inequality. To

Figure 1.16

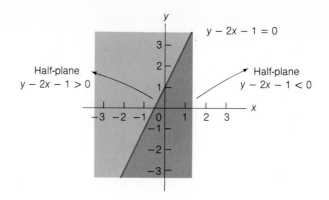

illustrate, consider the line

$$y - 2x - 1 = 0$$

shown in Figure 1.16. If (x, y) is any point on the line, it will satisfy the equation $y - 2x - 1 = 0$. If (x, y) is any point above the line, then it satisfies

$$y - 2x - 1 > 0$$

For example, $(-1, 2)$ is above the line, and $(-1, 2)$ satisfies the inequality

$$2 - 2(-1) = 4 > 0$$

In a similar manner $(0, 0)$ is in the solution set of

$$y - 2x - 1 < 0$$

since $0 - 0 - 1 < 0$. This agrees with the fact that the half-plane below the line consists of all points that satisfy

$$y - 2x - 1 < 0$$

In general, we state the following relationship.

Half-Planes

One half-plane determined by the line

$$ax + by + c = 0$$

is the set of points satisfying

$$ax + by + c > 0$$

and the other half-plane is the set of points satisfying

$$ax + by + c < 0$$

EXAMPLE 31 Represent on a graph the number pairs of the set $\{(x, y) | y \geq x + 1\}$.

Solution The set of ordered pairs that satisfy $y = x + 1$ is represented by points on a straight line. The ordered pairs that satisfy $y > x + 1$ are represented by points that lie in a half-plane.

We may locate the half-plane of points that satisfy $y > x + 1$ by finding one point whose coordinates satisfy $y > x + 1$. For example, $(-1, 1)$ is one such point since $1 > -1 + 1$. All other ordered pairs that satisfy $y > x + 1$ are on the same side of $y = x + 1$ as $(-1, 1)$. The solution set is indicated by the shaded portion of Figure 1.17. Verify this solution by finding additional ordered pairs in the solution set.

Figure 1.17

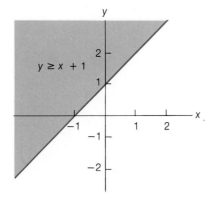

EXAMPLE 32 Graph $3x + y > 6$.

Solution First we graph the straight line $3x + y = 6$. It is represented in Figure 1.18 by a dashed line since the points on the line do not satisfy the given inequality. However, this line does divide the rectangular coordinate plane into two half-planes, and one of these half-planes contains all of the points in the solution set of $3x + y > 6$. The ordered pair $(0, 0)$ will be tested to see if it satisfies the inequality. Since $3 \cdot 0 + 0$ is not greater than 6, $(0, 0)$ is not in the solution set of $3x + y > 6$. The graph of $3x + y > 6$ (indicated by shaded region) is the half-plane that does not contain $(0, 0)$.

Figure 1.18

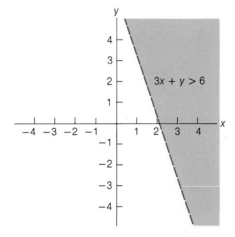

Exercise Set 1.4

A 1. Graph the following points and name their quadrants.
   a. (2, 4) **b.** (−5, 6) **c.** (−3, −2) **d.** (4, −1)

2. Find one or two points that satisfy the following equations and inequalities. Graph them. Do you see any patterns?
   a. $x = 7$ **b.** $x = -2$ **c.** $y = -4$ **d.** $y = 3$
   e. $x \leq 3$ **f.** $x > -1$ **g.** $y < 4$ **h.** $y \geq -2$

3. Plot five points (x, y) satisfying the expression $y = 3x + 1$. Draw a straight line connecting any two of these points and observe the results.

4. Construct a graph for the set of points satisfying each equation or inequality.
   a. $\{(x, y) \mid y = 2x - 3\}$ **b.** $\{(x, y) \mid y > x + 2\}$
   c. $\{(x, y) \mid 2x + 3y < 6\}$ **d.** $\{(x, y) \mid 5x + 3y = 7\}$
   e. $\{(x, y) \mid 2x + y = 1\}$ **f.** $\{(x, y) \mid x + 1 = 0\}$
   g. $\{(x, y) \mid y + 1 = 0\}$ **h.** $\{(x, y) \mid y < x - 1\}$
   i. $\{(x, y) \mid y > x\}$ **j.** $\{(x, y) \mid y = 2x\}$
   k. $\{(s, t) \mid 2s + t = 7\}$ **l.** $\{(x, y) \mid x + y < 9\}$

B 5. Graph $y = 2x - 3$ for $-1 \leq x \leq 4$. (*Hint:* The line extends from $x = -1$ to $x = 4$.)

6. Graph $y = 0.1x + 1.3$ for $-10 \leq x \leq 5$.

7. Graph $y = -2x + 4$ for $-2 \leq x \leq 4$.

8. Graph $w < 2x - 4$ for $-1 \leq x \leq 3$.

9. Graph $w > 3x - 2$ for $-2 \leq x \leq 2$.

10. Find the x- and y-intercepts and graph each of the following equations.
   a. $2x - 3y = -6$ **b.** $\frac{1}{2}y = 2x + 4$
   c. $x - 3y = 6$ **d.** $5x - 3y = 15$

C 11. Graph on the same coordinate system $y = mx + 2$ for various values of m. (Note the pattern since we use it in the next section.)

12. Graph $\dfrac{x}{2} + \dfrac{y}{2} \leq 5$ for $x \geq 0$ and $y \geq 0$.

13. Draw a graph of the line that passes through the points $\{(1, -1), (0, -3), (2, 1), (3, 3), (\frac{3}{2}, 0), (-1, -5)\}$. Can you guess the equation of the line?

Business 14. **Simple Interest.** Draw a graph of the amount of money owed if $200 is borrowed at 8% simple interest for different periods of time. Use the equation

$$A = \$200(1 + 0.08t)$$

15. **Depreciation.** Let x in the equation $y = -60x + 10,000$ represent months and y represent the average undepreciated dollar value of a machine.
   a. Prepare a table of values for $x = 0, 5, 10, 15, 20, 25, 30, 35, 40$.
   b. Sketch the graph of the equation, letting x assume all real values greater than or equal to zero.

Economics 16. **Supply and Demand.** Suppose the demand D for a certain item is affected by price x so that

$$D = \frac{50 - 5x}{4}$$

   a. What is the demand when $x = 0$?
   b. What is the demand when $x = 4$?

c. What happens to the demand when $x = 10$?

d. Graph the equation.

17. **Supply and Demand.** Suppose the supply for the item in exercise 16 is given by

$$S = \frac{5x}{6}$$

where S represents supply expressed in terms of price x.

a. What is the supply when $x = 3$; when $x = 9$?

b. Graph this equation on the same coordinate axes you used in exercise 16.

c. Find the equilibrium price.

d. Find D at the equilibrium price to obtain the equilibrium demand. What is the equilibrium supply?

e. When is the supply greater than the demand?

18. **Supply and Demand.** The supply S and demand D for a certain commodity are affected by price x so that

$$D = \frac{400 - 5x}{2} \quad \text{and} \quad S = \frac{5x}{2}$$

a. Graph the equation involving D and the equation involving S on the same axes.

b. Find the equilibrium price.

c. Find the equilibrium demand; the equilibrium supply.

d. When is the supply less than the demand?

Life Sciences

19. **Height, Weight Chart.** The Slim-Up Health Club considers the following weights to be desirable for women who are either 60 or 72 inches tall.

Height x (in inches)	60	72
Weight y (in pounds)	110	150

Draw a graph of a straight line through these two points and then estimate from the line the desirable weight for a woman who is 63, 66, or 69 inches tall.

Social Sciences

20. **Population.** The population of a small town seems to be increasing linearly. In 1980 the population was 15,000. In 1986 it was 20,000. Graph the linear equation that represents population in terms of time. Estimate the population in 1990 and 1994.

Slopes and Linear Equations

In Section 3 of this chapter we considered the solution of linear equations, and in Section 4 we studied the drawing of graphs of such equations. These are important mathematical skills. Just as important is the ability to develop an equation that accurately describes a situation. So, in this section we develop equations of lines from data representing real-life situations. We define the slope of a line and use this concept to find the graph of the line and also to find the equation of the line. In addition, we learn to find the equation of a line through two points.

You will find this section relatively easy—and very important in your accumulation of strategies to solve everyday problems.

Any two points in a plane can be considered the endpoints of some line segment. Let $P_1(x_1, y_1)$ and $P_2(x_2, y_2)$ be endpoints of a line segment as in Figure 1.19. If we now construct through P_2 a line parallel to the y-axis and through P_1 a line parallel to the x-axis, the lines will meet at P_3. Note that the x-coordinate of P_3 is the same as the x-coordinate of P_2 and that the y-coordinate of P_3 is the same as the y-coordinate of P_1. The distance from P_3 to P_2 is $y_2 - y_1$, and the distance from P_1 to P_3 is $x_2 - x_1$.

Figure 1.19

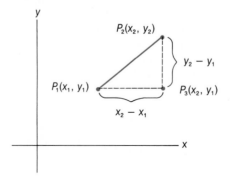

These concepts are important in discussing the *inclination* of a line, which is measured by comparing the **rise** $(y_2 - y_1)$ to the **run** $(x_2 - x_1)$ as shown in Figure 1.20.

Figure 1.20

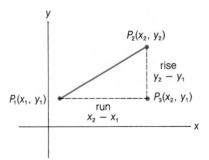

Slope of a Line Segment

The ratio of the rise to the run of a line segment is called the **slope** and is designated by the letter m. Thus, the slope of the line segment from $P_1(x_1, y_1)$ to $P_2(x_2, y_2)$ is

$$m = \frac{y_2 - y_1}{x_2 - x_1}$$

If P_2 is to the right of P_1, $x_2 - x_1$ will necessarily be positive, and the slope will be positive or negative as $y_2 - y_1$ is positive or negative. Thus, positive slope indicates that a line rises to the right; negative slope indicates that it falls to the right. Since

$$\frac{y_2 - y_1}{x_2 - x_1} = \frac{-(y_1 - y_2)}{-(x_1 - x_2)} = \frac{y_1 - y_2}{x_1 - x_2}$$

the restriction that P_2 be to the right of P_1 is not necessary, and the order in which the points are considered is immaterial in determining the slope.

If a line segment is parallel to the x-axis, then $y_2 - y_1 = 0$, and the line has slope 0; but if it is parallel to the y-axis, then $x_2 - x_1 = 0$, and its slope is not defined. These two special cases are shown in Figure 1.21.

Figure 1.21

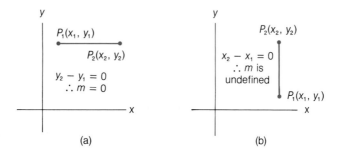

(a)   (b)

EXAMPLE 33 The slope of the line in Figure 1.22 is given by

$$m = \frac{y_2 - y_1}{x_2 - x_1} = \frac{5 - 2}{2 - 1} = \frac{3}{1} = 3$$

Figure 1.22

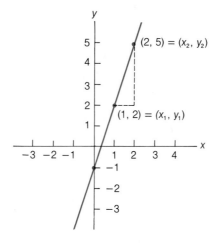

Let's now look at slopes in relation to linear equations of the form $ax + dy + c = 0$, where a and d are not both zero.

In the preceding section, we noted that graphs of $y = x + 1$, $x + y = 4$, and $w = u + 1$ were straight lines. In fact, the graph of any linear equation with no more than two unknowns is a straight line. In fact, any line may be described by an equation of the form $ax + dy + c = 0$. So, a given graph is a line if and only if it has an equation of the form $ax + dy + c = 0$, where a and d are not both zero.

A linear equation may be solved for y, if $d \neq 0$, to obtain

$$y = \frac{-a}{d} x + \frac{-c}{d}$$

By letting $m = -a/d$ and $b = -c/d$, the expression becomes

$$y = mx + b$$

Now consider the graph of $y = mx$ ($b = 0$ for this example) when m has values $\frac{1}{2}$, 1, 2, and 4 (see Figure 1.23). Since $(0, 0)$ and $(1, \frac{1}{2})$ are two points on the line $y = \frac{1}{2}x$, we note that the y value increases by $\frac{1}{2}$ as x increases by 1. Thus, the slope is $\frac{1}{2}$.

Figure 1.23

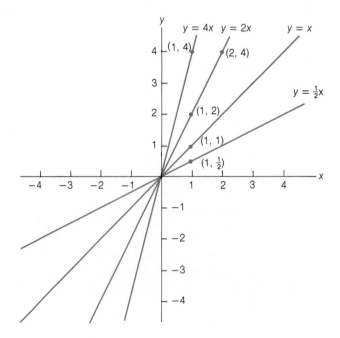

Note also that $m = \frac{1}{2}$. Since $(0, 0)$ and $(1, 2)$ are points on $y = 2x$, the slope is $(2 - 0)/(1 - 0) = 2$, and the coefficient of x in $y = 2x$ is likewise 2. Intuitively you may have already decided that in $y = mx + b$, m is the slope of the line.

Slope of a Line

For the line $ax + dy + c = 0$, when expressed as

$$y = \frac{-a}{d} x + \frac{-c}{d} \qquad \text{where } d \neq 0$$

the slope is

$$m = \frac{-a}{d}$$

The y-intercept is given by $b = -c/d$.

If (x_1, y_1) is a fixed point on a given straight line, and (x, y) is any point on the line, then the slope from (x_1, y_1) to (x, y) is

$$m = \frac{y - y_1}{x - x_1} \qquad \text{or} \qquad y - y_1 = m(x - x_1)$$

Since the coordinates x and y are variables denoting any point on the line, the equation $y - y_1 = m(x - x_1)$ represents the relationship between x and y. Thus, the equation of the line with slope m passing through the fixed point (x_1, y_1) is $y - y_1 = m(x - x_1)$. A linear equation written in this form is said to be in **point-slope form.** If the slope and one point of the line are known, then the equation of the line can be easily obtained.

Point-Slope Form

If a line has slope m and passes through the point (x_1, y_1), then the equation of the line is given by

$$y - y_1 = m(x - x_1)$$

EXAMPLE 34 Find the equation of the line through $(2, 1)$ with a slope of 3.

Solution
$$y - 1 = 3(x - 2)$$
$$y = 1 + 3x - 6$$
$$y = 3x - 5$$

As a special case, the fixed point may be chosen to be the point where the line crosses the y-axis. The coordinates of this point are usually written as $(0, b)$. Then the equation of the line becomes $y = mx + b$, the equation discussed earlier. The b in this equation is the value of y when $x = 0$, or the **y-intercept.**

Slope-Intercept Form

If a line has a slope of m and a y-intercept of b, then the equation of the line is given by

$$y = mx + b$$

EXAMPLE 35 If the slope of a line is 3 and the y-intercept is 2, what is the equation of the line?

Solution Since $m = 3$ and $b = 2$, the equation is $y = mx + b$ or $y = 3x + 2$.

EXAMPLE 36 Find the equation of the line that crosses the y-axis at $(0, -5)$ and has a slope of 2.

Solution
$$y = 2x - 5$$

Sometimes, instead of being given a point and the slope, you are given only two points along the line. The *two-point method* of finding the equation of a line consists of using these two points to determine the slope of the line and then using the point-slope formula to establish the equation.

EXAMPLE 37 Find the equation of the line containing the points (2, 3) and (−1, 4).

Solution The two points can be used in either order to find the slope of the line; one way is

$$m = \frac{4 - 3}{-1 - 2} = -\frac{1}{3}$$

The slope along with either of the fixed points can now be used to determine the equation of the line; that is,

$$y - 3 = \left(-\frac{1}{3}\right)(x - 2) \qquad \text{or} \qquad y - 4 = \left(-\frac{1}{3}\right)(x + 1)$$

Both of these may be simplified to give $y = -\frac{1}{3}x + \frac{11}{3}$ as the equation of the line in slope-intercept form.

As a special case, the graph of a linear equation may be a horizontal line or a vertical line. The equation of a **horizontal line** is of the form $y = b$ and has a slope of 0. The equation $y = 1$ is the equation of a horizontal line as seen in Figure 1.24. By choosing two points, say, (2, 1) and (4, 1), the slope is seen to be 0. That is,

$$m = \frac{1 - 1}{4 - 2} = \frac{0}{2} = 0$$

Figure 1.24

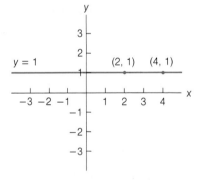

The equation of a **vertical line** is of the form $x = h$, and the slope is undefined. The equation of the line shown in Figure 1.25 is $x = 3$. By choosing two points on the line, say, (3, 5) and (3, 2), we can see that the slope is undefined. That is,

$$m = \frac{5 - 2}{3 - 3} = \frac{3}{0}$$

which does not exist.

Figure 1.25

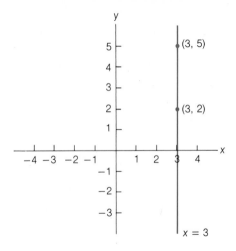

The box below contains a summary of the types of equations introduced in this section.

$y - y_1 = m(x - x_1)$	**Point-slope form:** slope is m; line passes through (x_1, y_1)
$y = mx + b$	**Slope-intercept form:** slope is m; y-intercept is b
$y = b$	**Horizontal line:** y-intercept is b; line has slope of 0
$x = h$	**Vertical line:** x-intercept is h; slope of the line is undefined

Exercise Set **1.5**

A **1.** Compute the slope or indicate that the slope is not defined for the line through each pair of points.

   a. (3, 6), (4, 1)   **b.** (0, 1), (2, 3)

   c. $(-3, -5)$, (4, 2)   **d.** $(7, -1)$, $(-3, 1)$

   e. (0, 4), (4, 0)   **f.** $(-1, -7)$, $(-6, -5)$

   g. (4, 3), $(4, -1)$ **h.** $(7, -1)$, (7, 4)

   i. (3, 1), (7, 1)   **j.** $(-1, 2)$, (7, 2)

2. Find an equation for and graph the line that has:

   a. a slope of 4 and goes through the point (2, 3)

   b. a slope of -2 and goes through the point $(4, -1)$

   c. a slope of $\frac{1}{2}$ and goes through the point $(-1, 1)$

   d. a slope of $\frac{7}{-2}$ and goes through the point (3, 4)

3. In each of the following linear equations, what is the slope? What is the y-intercept of each? Graph each equation.

a. $y = 3x + 2$ **b.** $y + 2x - 1 = 0$

c. $y = 3x - 1$ **d.** $2y = 1 - x$

e. $y = \dfrac{x - 4}{2}$ **f.** $x = \dfrac{y - 1}{3}$

g. $4x + 3y - 7 = 0$ **h.** $3x - 2y = 5$

4. Classify the following statements as either true or false.
   a. The slope of the y-axis is 0.
   b. The line segment joining (a, b) and (c, b) is horizontal.
   c. The line with a negative slope rises to the right.
   d. The line that is almost vertical has a slope close to 0.

5. Find an equation of the line ℓ with slope m containing point Z.
   a. $m = \frac{1}{2}$, $Z = (1, 3)$ **b.** $m = 1$, $Z = (0, 2)$
   c. $m = \frac{-1}{3}$, $Z = (-1, -2)$ **d.** $m = 0$, $Z = (-3, 1)$

B   6. Find an equation of the line through each of the following pairs of points.
   a. $(1, 1), (2, 5)$ **b.** $(-1, 1), (2, 5)$ **c.** $(1, 3), (1, -2)$ **d.** $(2, 4), (4, 2)$

7. Find an equation of each line with the following characteristics:
   a. The line contains the two points $(1, -3)$ and $(4, 5)$.
   b. The line has a slope of -3 and goes through the point $(7, 1)$.
   c. The line has a slope of 1 and goes through the point $(-7, 1)$.
   d. The line contains the two points $(0, 1)$ and $(4, 3)$.
   e. The line has a y-intercept of 4 and a slope of 5.
   f. The line has a y-intercept of 6 and a slope of -3.

8. **a.** Find an equation of the horizontal line through $(-4, -6)$.
   b. Find an equation of the vertical line through $(-5, 4)$.
   c. Write the equation of the x-axis.
   d. Write the equation of the y-axis.

9. Suppose the equation of a line is written in the form

$$\frac{x}{a} + \frac{y}{b} = 1$$

What is the x-intercept? The y-intercept?

10. Use the intercept form of the equation of a line (exercise 9) to find equations for lines with the following intercepts:
   a. $x = 2$, and $y = -3$ **b.** $x = 3$, and $y = 5$

C   11. Find the y-intercept of the line that passes through the point $(3, -2)$ with a slope of 2.

12. What is the slope of a line with a y-intercept of -3 that passes through the point $(-4, 1)$?

If two lines are parallel, they have the same slope. Lines that are perpendicular to a given line whose slope is m have slopes of $\dfrac{-1}{m}$, $m \neq 0$. *Use this information in the next two problems.*

13. For each part of exercise 5, find the equation of the line parallel to ℓ through the point $(2, 3)$.

14. For each part of exercise 5, find the equation of the line perpendicular to ℓ through the point $(2, 3)$.

Business **15. Depreciation.** The decrease in value of property over a period of time is called **depreciation** of the property. One accounting procedure for determining depreciation is the **straight-line method** or **linear depreciation.** In this procedure the loss in value over a specified time is a given percentage of the original value. For example, if an item depreciates linearly at a rate of 5% per year, then its loss in value at the end of 1 year is $0.05C$, where C is the cost. At the end of 4 years its loss in value is

$$4(0.05)C = 0.20C$$

Let r be the annual rate of linear depreciation, t the length of time in years, and C the original cost of an item. At the end of 1 year, the item depreciates in value by Cr. At the end of t years, the item has depreciated by Crt. Therefore, its current value (original cost minus depreciation) is

$$V = C - Crt \quad \text{or} \quad V = C(1 - rt)$$

a. If a machine costing $10,000 depreciates at a rate of 5% per year, find its value at the end of t years.
b. What is the value of the machine at the end of 3 years?
c. When is the value zero?

16. Depreciation. A truck costing $12,000 has a useful life of 10 years with a scrap value of $3,000 at the end of this time. Find an equation representing value (V) in terms of time (t).

17. Sales. Assume the amount of sales for the XYZ Corporation is given by a linear equation. Suppose the amount of sales was $150,000 in 1980 and $110,000 in 1984.
a. Let $t = 0$ in 1980; find an expression for the amount of sales (S) in terms of time (t).
b. What was the amount of sales in 1983?
c. Estimate the amount of sales in 1986.

Economics **18. Marginal Cost, Revenue, and Profit.** In a linear equation representing cost, such as $C = mx + b$, the slope m is called **marginal cost.** In revenue equations, such as $R = m_1x + c$, the slope m_1 is called the **marginal revenue.** In profit equations, such as $P = m_2x + d$, the slope m_2 is called the **marginal profit.** Given that $C = 400 + 3x$ and $R = 7x + 100$, find the marginal cost, the marginal revenue, and the marginal profit. $P = R - C$.

Life Sciences **19. Pollution.** In a certain industrial city, it is believed that the pollution count increases linearly from 7:00 A.M. to 2:00 P.M. At 8:00 A.M., the pollution count is 140. At 10:00 A.M., the count is 200. Use 7:00 A.M. as the origin and t as the time in hours after 7:00 A.M. to find the linear equation representing the pollution count in terms of time. Predict the pollution count at 11:00 A.M. and at 1:00 P.M.

Applications of Percentage in Business

In this section we review working with percents and decimals, concepts used continuously in all areas of everyday business activities. We will also introduce some concepts with which you may not be familiar: cost, selling price, markup, and profit.

When the denominator of a fraction is 100, the fraction may be written as a percent using the symbol %. Thus, 37/100 may be written as 37%. That is, a *percent* is a ratio with a denominator of 100 when expressed as a fraction.

EXAMPLE 38 Convert to decimals: 1.6%, 247%, and $16\frac{2}{3}$%.

Solution

$$1.6\% = \frac{1.6}{100} = \frac{16}{1000} = 0.016$$

$$247\% = \frac{247}{100} = 2.47$$

$$16\frac{2}{3}\% = \frac{16\frac{2}{3}}{100} \approx 0.167$$

In the next example, note that the writing of a decimal fraction as a percent is merely a process of moving the decimal point two places to the right and adding the symbol %.

EXAMPLE 39 Convert to percents: 0.047, 0.769, 3.56, and 0.00071.

Solution

$$0.047 = 4.7\% \qquad 0.769 = 76.9\%$$
$$3.56 = 356\% \qquad 0.00071 = 0.071\%$$

To convert a fraction to a percent, follow two steps. Change the fraction to a decimal, and then change the decimal to a percent.

EXAMPLE 40 Change $\frac{15}{40}$ and $\frac{1}{3}$ to percents.

Solution

$$\frac{15}{40} = 0.375 = 37.5\% \qquad \frac{1}{3} = 0.33\frac{1}{3} = 33\frac{1}{3}\%$$

Problems involving percent can be classified into three categories. The first type of problem is to find a given percent of a number.

EXAMPLE 41
a. Find 25% of 12,000.
b. In a class of 48 people, 25% made As. How many made As?

Solution
a. 0.25(12,000) = 3000.
b. 0.25(48) = 12, so 12 people made As.

The second type of problem involves finding what percent one number is of another number.

EXAMPLE 42
a. 92 is what percent of 400?
b. A solution contains 100 grams of substance A and 20 grams of substance B. What percent of the solution is substance B?

Solution
a. Let x be the percent expressed as a decimal. Then

$$x(400) = 92$$

$$x = \frac{92}{400} = 0.23 \qquad \text{or } 23\%$$

b. Let x be the percent of the solution that is B. Then

$$x(100 + 20) = 20$$

$$x = \frac{20}{120} = 0.16\tfrac{2}{3} \quad \text{or } 16\tfrac{2}{3}\%$$

The third type of problem involves finding a number when a certain percent of it is known.

EXAMPLE 43   Eighteen percent of the first-year students at Swan University failed first-year English. If 396 first-year students failed English, how many first-year students are enrolled at Swan University?

Solution   Let n represent the number of first-year students at Swan University. Then

$$0.18n = 396$$

$$n = \frac{396}{0.18} = 2200$$

so 2200 first-year students are enrolled.

Merchants purchase goods with the expectation of selling them at a profit. The difference in the cost of the goods and the selling price is called the **markup** or **profit.** The rate of markup is usually expressed as a percentage of either cost or selling price. The most common approach is to consider the rate of markup based on the cost. If r is the rate of markup based on the cost C, and if S is the selling price, then

$$S = C + rC = C \cdot 1 + C \cdot r = C(1 + r)$$

EXAMPLE 44   Find the selling price of a suit that costs $72 if the markup (based on cost) is 40%. What is the profit?

Solution   Let S, C, and r be as indicated above, and let P denote the number of dollars of profit.

$$S = C(1 + r) = 72(1 + 0.40) = 100.80$$
$$P = S - C = 100.80 - 72.00 = 28.80$$

The selling price is $100.80, and the profit is $28.80.

EXAMPLE 45   What is the rate of markup on an article that cost $180 if the selling price is $223.20?

Solution   Since $S = C(1 + r)$,

$$223.20 = 180(1 + r)$$
$$223.20 = 180 + 180r$$
$$43.20 = 180r$$
$$0.24 = r$$

Thus, the rate is 24%.

EXAMPLE 46 What is the cost of an automobile that sells for $5,265.00 if the markup is 30% of the cost?

Solution

$$5265 = C(1 + 0.30)$$
$$5265 = C(1.30)$$
$$4050 = C$$

Thus, the cost is $4,050.

Let's consider now several applications of rates based on the selling price. For example, as mentioned earlier, the rate of markup can be based on selling price. Also, as a promotion scheme, retailers may advertise marking down the price of a given article by a stated rate. This **markdown** rate is based on the selling price. Also, when trade discounts are given, these are based on selling price.

If d represents a markdown rate based on selling price, then dS is the decrease in selling price. So

$$S - dS = S \cdot 1 - S \cdot d = S(1 - d)$$

gives the discounted value (sometimes cost, and sometimes a new selling price).

EXAMPLE 47 An article sells for $45. The store requires a markup of 30% based on selling price. What is the cost of the article?

Solution

$$C = S(1 - d)$$
$$C = 45(1 - 0.30)$$
$$= 45(0.70)$$
$$= 31.50$$

Thus, the cost is $31.50.

EXAMPLE 48 A store manager plans to reduce the selling price of an item by 10%. If the item costs $8.95 and presently sells for $10.50, will the sale of the item after the markdown be profitable?

Solution

$$S_2 = 10.50(1 - 0.10)$$
$$= 10.50(0.90)$$
$$= 9.45$$
$$P = S_2 - C$$
$$P = 9.45 - 8.95$$
$$= 0.50$$

Thus, the profit is $0.50 after the markdown of 10%.

EXAMPLE 49 An article that costs $100 has a 20% markup based on cost. The operating expenses of the store are 10% of the selling price. If the markdown of the article is 8%, does the store enjoy a profit or sustain a loss?

Solution
$$\text{Selling price} = \$100(1 + 0.20) = \$120$$
$$\text{Operating expenses} = 0.10(\$120) = \$12$$
$$\text{Markdown} = 0.08(\$120) = \$9.60$$
$$\text{Total cost} = \text{cost} + \text{operating expenses} = \$100 + \$12$$
$$= \$112$$
$$\text{Final selling price} = \text{selling price} - \text{markdown} = \$120 - \$9.60$$
$$= \$110.40$$

The store sustains a loss of $\$112 - \$110.40 = \$1.60$.

EXAMPLE 50   Find the cost of a dozen shirts quoted at $60 per dozen less 40%. The "less 40%" means that the company will allow a merchant a trade discount of 40%.

Solution

List price	$60.00	List price	$60.00
Rate of discount	0.40	Discount	$24.00
Amount of discount	$24.00	Billing price	$36.00

EXAMPLE 51   The list price of an article is quoted as $560. However, the current price is quoted with discounts of 10% and 2%. What are the current price and the **effective discount rate** (the one discount rate that will yield the same price as both the two discount rates of 10% and 2%)?

Solution
$$560(0.10) = 56$$
$$560 - 56 = 504$$
$$504(0.02) = 10.08$$
$$504 - 10.08 = 493.92$$

The current price is $493.92.

$$560 - 493.92 = 66.08$$
$$\frac{66.08}{560} = 0.118$$

The effective discount rate is 11.8%.

Exercise Set **1.6**

A   **1.** Convert to decimals.
    a. 5.5%   **b.** 0.012%   **c.** 0.31%
    d. 426%   **e.** 43.6%   **f.** 18.4%

    2. Convert to percents.
    a. $\frac{18}{15}$ **b.** $\frac{33}{150}$ **c.** $\frac{6}{15}$ **d.** $\frac{18}{4}$ **e.** $\frac{11}{40}$ **f.** $\frac{143}{80}$

    3. a. What percent of 48 is 12?   **b.** 24 is what percent of 96?
    c. Find 16% of 200.   **d.** Find 0.01% of 1.632.

e. What is 78% of 16?   **f.** What percent of 150 is 6?

g. What percent of 18 is 54?   **h.** What number is 130% of 96?

B   **4.** There are 23 girls and 19 boys in a first-year history class at Simmons College. Seven people failed the first test. What percent of the class failed the first test?

5. If your automobile payments are $50 a month, what percent of your $750-per-month salary must be set aside to pay for your automobile?

6. In exercise 5 you receive a 4% raise. What is your new monthly salary? What percent of your salary now must be set aside to pay for your automobile?

7. Of the 80,000 football seats in the stadium, 48,640 were filled. What percent of the stadium was filled?

8. If you spend 65% of your leisure time reading, how much leisure time do you have if you spend 13 hours a week reading?

C   **9.** Ms. Taylor is considering buying a dress that costs $76.00, but she would rather have the dress made if she can save at least 25% of the cost. The materials for the dress cost $37.00. She finds out the dressmaker's fee and decides to purchase the ready-made dress. What is the minimum amount of the fee?

Business   **10. Profit.** A merchant sells a suit for $87, thereby gaining a profit of 30% of cost. What was the cost of the suit?

11. Markup. Fill in the missing entries.

	Cost	% Markup based on cost	Selling price
a.	$1,400	24	—
b.	$50	—	$62.50
c.	—	20	$84

12. In exercise 11 compute the percent markup based on selling price for each article.

13. Compute the current selling price for an article with a list price of $50.00 with trade discounts of 40% and $33\frac{1}{3}$%.

14. Discount Rate.
   a. Find the effective discount rate for a list price of $1,000 with discounts of 50%, 10%, and 5%.
   b. Do part **a** for a $400 list price.
   c. Which answer is the larger?
   d. Can you make a general statement about this situation?

15. Find the effective discount rate equivalent to a series of discount rates of 20%, 10%, and 5%.

16. Markup. Fill in the missing entries.

	Cost	% Markup based on cost	Regular selling price	Rate (%) of markdown	Reduced selling price	% Operating expenses based on cost	Profit or loss
a.	$1,000	40	—	20	—	20	—
b.	—	20	$1,000	8	—	10	—
c.	—	20	—	8	$1,000	10	—
d.	—	14	—	10	$400	20	—

17. What can you conclude about a business in which the percent profit based on cost is the same as the percent profit based on selling price?

Economics	**18. Inflation.** If the rate of inflation is 8% per year, what will be the cost of a $100 item 1 year from now? What will be the cost at the end of the second year?
Life Sciences	**19. Rate of Growth.** Suppose the rate of growth of the fish population in a lake is 10% per year. If a lake contains 100,000 fish now, determine the number of fish in the lake at the end of 1 year; then at the end of 2 years.
Social Sciences	**20. Population.** If the population of a city of 60,000 is increasing at a rate of 4% per year, what will be the population in 1 year? In 2 years?

7 Summary and Review

Review to ensure that you understand and can use the following concepts: set-builder notation, proper subset, equal sets, complement of a set, universe, intersection of two sets, union of two sets, null set, number of a set, addition of integers, multiplication of integers, absolute value, inverse operations, order of operations, parentheses, braces, brackets, solutions of equations, solutions of inequalities, solution sets, rectangular Cartesian coordinate system, coordinate axes, graphs of equations, graphs of inequalities, equilibrium point for supply and demand, depreciation, slopes of lines (formula for, slope of a horizontal line, slope of a vertical line, slopes of parallel and perpendicular lines), equations of lines (point-slope form, slope-intercept form, horizontal line, vertical line), markup, markdown, and effective discount rate.

Can you use the following formulas presented in this chapter? Do you understand each one?

$$\frac{pc}{qc} = \frac{p}{q} \qquad c \neq 0$$

$$\frac{p}{q} + \frac{r}{q} = \frac{p+r}{q} \qquad q \neq 0$$

$$\frac{p}{q} + \frac{r}{s} = \frac{ps+qr}{qs} \qquad q, s \neq 0$$

$$p - q = p + (-q)$$

$$p \div q = p \cdot \frac{1}{q} \qquad q \neq 0$$

$$\frac{p}{q} \div \frac{r}{s} = \frac{p}{q} \cdot \frac{s}{r} \qquad q, s, r \neq 0$$

$$m = \frac{y_2 - y_1}{x_2 - x_1}$$

$$y - y_1 = m(x - x_1)$$

$$y = mx + b$$

$$x = h$$

$$S = C(1 + r)$$

$$y = b$$

$$C = S(1 - d)$$

Review Exercise Set **1.7**

A **1.** Let $A = \{1, 2, 3, 5, 7\}$, $B = \{3, 6, 9\}$, and $U = \{x \mid x$ is a natural number less than 10$\}$. List the elements of the following.

a. A' **b.** $A \cap B$ **c.** $A \cup B$
d. $A \cap (B \cap \varnothing)$ **e.** $A \cap B'$ **f.** $B \cup (A \cap \varnothing)$

2. Let $A = \{-2, -\frac{1}{2}, -\sqrt{2}, 0, \frac{1}{\sqrt{2}}, \sqrt{2}, 2\}$. List the elements of A in the following sets.

    a. Set of natural numbers   **b.** Set of integers
    c. Set of rational numbers   **d.** Set of irrational numbers
    e. Set of negative numbers   **f.** Set of real numbers

3. First put the following equations into the $y = mx + b$ form. Find the slope of each line. Then graph the lines.

    a. $3x + 4y + 7 = 0$ **b.** $6x + 6y + 6 = 0$
    c. $4x - 5y - 3 = 0$ **d.** $-4x - y + 0 = 0$

4. Find the equation of the line through $(-1, 4)$ and $(-1, 6)$.

5. Find the equation of the line through the point $(-1, 7)$ parallel to the line $3y + 2x = 7$.

6. Find the equation of the line through the points $(1, -2)$ and $(6, 4)$, and predict the value of y when $x = 5$.

7. Construct a graph for each of the following.

    a. $\{(x, y) \mid y < 3x + 2\}$ **b.** $\{(x, y) \mid x = 2y - 7\}$
    c. $\{(x, y) \mid 3x + 2y = 1\}$ **d.** $\{(x, y) \mid 3y + 2x > 1\}$
    e. $\{(x, y) \mid x + y < 5\}$ **f.** $\{(x, y) \mid 2x + y < 6\}$

8. Solve each equation.

    a. $5 + \dfrac{x}{5} = \dfrac{7}{10}$ **b.** $\dfrac{3x}{4} - \dfrac{5x - 1}{8} = \dfrac{1}{4}$

9. Solve and graph each inequality on a number line.

    a. $\dfrac{y}{2} + 5 \geq 4y - 7$ **b.** $\dfrac{x}{5} + 7 \leq \dfrac{x}{3} - 2$

    c. $\dfrac{x - 2}{-5} \leq 2$ **d.** $-2(x + 1) > \dfrac{x}{4}$

B   **10.** If the $180 you spend each month on room and board represents 60% of your monthly income, what is your monthly income?

11. An article sells for $1.45. If the store uses a 40% markup on selling price, how much did the article cost? What is the selling price of an article that costs $2.00?

12. What is the selling price of an article that costs $8.00 if the markup is 20% based on cost? What would be the cost of an article that sells for $2.40?

13. Find a discount rate equivalent to a series of 10%, 8%, and 4% discounts.

14. According to the National Safety Council, about 60% of all automobile-accident fatalities for a year occurred during daylight hours. If, during the year, 23,000 automobile-accident fatalities occurred during daylight hours, how many automobile-accident fatalities occurred that year?

15. If an article costs $76.98 and sells for $132.98, what is the percentage of markup based on the cost? On the selling price?

16. A brand of paint costs $4.50 a liter and is sold for $6.50 a liter. What is the markup on 100 liters of paint? What is the percentage of markup based on cost?

17. Two men are waiting for trains. David waits 10 minutes, then impatiently gets on a local averaging 30 miles per hour. Lin waits 30 minutes and gets on the express which averages 50 miles per hour. Both arrive at their destination at the same time. How long did it take the express to make the trip? How far did they travel?

18. An artist displays her paintings at a county fair. One of her landscapes is priced at $950. No one buys the picture, so on the last day of the fair, the artist reduces the price to $875. What percent of the original price, correct to the nearest 1%, is the markdown?

19. Stanley Secretarial Service furnishes part-time help for salespeople staying at the local hotel. They charge $5.70 per hour for a typist. If the markup of the company is $33\frac{1}{3}\%$ of the total bill, what is the hourly rate of the typists who work for the service?

20. A can contains 454 grams of corn. A recipe for a salad serving 50 people calls for $2\frac{1}{2}$ kilograms (1000 grams = 1 kilogram) of corn. How many cans of corn are needed to make the salad?

C **21.** Solve $x + [3.4 - (5 + 4.9x)] = [6 - (3 - 2.1x) - 4]$.

22. Solve for x using your calculator.

    a. $1.233x - 4.007 = 32.1 - 0.0043x$ **b.** $\dfrac{x}{7.114} - 14.745 = 0.001x + 2.1141$

23. A school year lasts 9 months. Two-thirds of the time already passed in this school year is equal to $\frac{1}{3}$ of the entire school year. How many months of this school year have passed?

24. Bank robbers smash through a road block and proceed at 90 miles per hour. Fifteen minutes later, the police follow at 100 miles per hour. How long after the road block was smashed will it take the cops to catch the robbers?

25. A candy maker wishes to make a mixture of nuts to sell for $2.42 a pound. How many pounds of the $1.92-per-pound nuts should be mixed with 100 pounds of $2.88-per-pound nuts?

26. Solve and graph the following inequality: $|3x + 1| < 5$.

27. Lynn took her 100-point history final yesterday. She missed twice as many questions on the multiple-choice section as on the true-false section. She missed a total of nine questions. Each true-false question was worth 1 point; each multiple-choice question was worth 5 points. She earned 2 points on the bonus question. What was her grade on the test?

28. John J. Johnson, Jr., earned $13,750 annually 3 years ago. At the end of the first year, he received a 13% increase. The second year his salary was cut by 7.75%, and last year he received an increase of 19.5%. What is his annual salary at present?

29. Solve for t in $at + b = 2t$.

30. Show with an example that when finding an equation of a line, given two fixed points on that line, it does not matter which of the two points you use to obtain the equation.

31. **a.** Why is the slope of a vertical line undefined?
    b. Explain why, if two lines have the same slopes and one point in common, *all* points on the lines have to be in common.

2

Systems of Linear Equations and Matrices

n the preceding chapter we observed that the solution set of linear equations such as

$$ax + by + c = 0$$

contains an infinite number of ordered pairs of real numbers. In fact, we graphed such linear equations in two unknowns and observed that the graphs were straight lines.

It is often useful to determine if equations have common solutions. The equations are then referred to as a **system of equations** and the ordered pairs that satisfy all equations are the **solutions to the system.**

A linear system is particularly applicable to the economic laws of *supply* and *demand*, to the study of *break-even analysis*, and to the study of linear trends in various fields of the life sciences and social science.

We begin our study of solving systems of equations by looking for graphical solutions; then we review the algebraic procedures of substitution and elimination. These techniques are suitable for systems involving two or three variables, but they are not suitable for systems involving larger numbers of variables. The new techniques introduced form a basis for computer solutions of large systems. These techniques lead naturally to a study of mathematical entities called **matrices.** We conclude this chapter with a study of matrices and their many applications. The mathematics studied in this chapter is sometimes called **linear algebra.**

1 Finding Solutions for Linear Systems

We begin our discussion with a pair of linear equations called a **system of two linear equations.** Recall that the solution set of any equation involving two unknowns is the set of ordered pairs that satisfy the equation. The **solution set of a system of two equations** is defined to be the intersection of the solution sets of the individual equations. Such solutions are called **simultaneous solutions** since each ordered pair satisfies both equations simultaneously.

We first find simultaneous solutions by graphing the equations in a system of linear equations and noting the points of intersection or common ordered pairs that are in the solution set of each equation in the system. We then use algebraic procedures called *substitution* and *addition* to find solutions for the system of equations.

We complete the section by considering systems involving three equations and three unknowns. This discussion leads to a procedure for solving systems involving n equations and n unknowns.

Linear systems involving two unknowns may be solved graphically. The graph of the solution set of each linear equation in two unknowns is a straight line. Suppose now that two such equations are graphed on the same coordinate system. The **solution set** of the system of two linear equations in two unknowns is then given by the intersection of the two lines.

EXAMPLE 1   Solve the following system graphically.

$$3x + y = 3$$
$$x + 2y = -4$$

Solution   The first equation is satisfied by infinitely many ordered pairs, three of which are $(0, 3)$, $(1, 0)$, and $(3, -6)$. Likewise, some ordered pairs that satisfy $x + 2y = -4$ are $(-4, 0)$, $(0, -2)$, and $(2, -3)$. The graphs of these two equations are given in Figure 2.1. The intersection of the two lines in Figure 2.1 seems to be the point $(2, -3)$. We can check to see whether or not this ordered pair is a solution of the system of equations by checking it in each equation. Substituting $x = 2$ and $y = -3$ in the first equation gives

$$3(2) + (-3) = 3$$
$$6 - 3 = 3$$

Figure 2.1

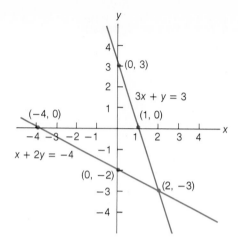

Substituting $x = 2$ and $y = -3$ in the second equation gives

$$(2) + 2(-3) = -4$$
$$2 - 6 = -4$$

Hence, $\{(2, -3)\}$ is the solution set of the system.

Geometrically, we are confronted with three possibilities for the straight line graphs of equations in a system of two linear equations in two unknowns:

One of these possibilities must occur for the graph of two lines in a plane:
1. The two lines intersect at exactly one point.
2. The two lines coincide.
3. The two lines are parallel.

These possibilities lead, correspondingly, to the conclusion that one and only one of the following is true for two linear equations in two unknowns, x and y:

1. The intersection of the two solution sets contains exactly one ordered pair.
2. The intersection of the two solution sets contains all those ordered pairs found in either one of the given solution sets; that is, the solution sets are equal.
3. The intersection of the two solution sets is the null set.

Each of these possibilities is illustrated in the following example.

EXAMPLE 2   Find the solution set of each of the following systems of equations.

a. $6x + 2y = 8$ **b.** $3x + y = 3$ **c.** $3x + y = 3$

$3x - 2y = 1$ $6x + 2y = 6$ $6x + 2y = 12$

Solution

Figure 2.2

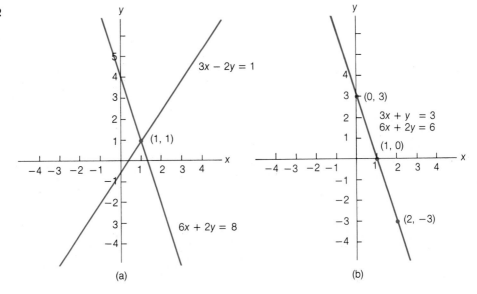

(a)

(b)

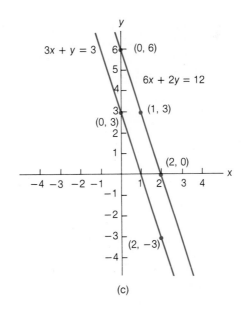

(c)

In **a**, the solution is (1, 1). There is an infinite number of solutions in **b** as all the solutions of one equation are solutions of the other. One equation can be obtained from the other by multiplying both sides of the equation by a constant. There are no common ordered pairs in **c** since the lines are parallel.

Although the graphic solution of a system of two linear equations with two variables gives an excellent picture of the relationship between the two variables, the method is time consuming and may not be accurate if the numbers that compose the ordered pairs in the solution set are not integers. Consequently, algebraic methods for solving the system are often more practical. Algebraically, we obtain a second system of equations that is **equivalent** to the given system (that is, it has the same solution set). One such method involves the elimination of one of the variables by **substitution.** We use this procedure to solve the following system of equations.

$$3x + y = 3 \quad (1)$$
$$x + 2y = -4 \quad (2)$$

Procedure	Illustration
1. In one of the equations solve for one of the variables in terms of the other.	1. In (1) solve for y in terms of x: $$y = 3 - 3x$$
2. Substitute this expression for the variable in the other equation.	2. Substituting for y in (2) gives $$x + 2(3 - 3x) = -4$$
3. Solve this linear equation for the unknown.	3. $x + 6 - 6x = -4$ $$-5x = -10$$ $$x = 2$$
4. Substitute this solution in one of the original equations and solve.	4. $3(2) + y = 3$ $$y = -3$$
5. Write down the solution.	5. The solution is $(2, -3)$.
6. Check the solution by substituting for x and y in both original equations.	6. $3(2) + (-3) = 3 \quad (1)$ $$6 - 3 = 3$$ $$3 = 3$$ $2 + 2(-3) = -4 \quad (2)$ $$2 - 6 = -4$$ $$-4 = -4$$

Another method for solving a system of equations is called the **method of addition.** We use this procedure now to solve the following system of equations:

$$6x + 2y = 10 \quad (1)$$
$$3x - y = 1 \quad (2)$$

Procedure	Illustration
1. Multiply one or both of the equations by a nonzero number that will make the coefficients of one variable numerically alike but with opposite signs. The system obtained is **equivalent** to the original system (has the same solutions).	1. In this illustration we multiply both sides of the second equation by -2 so that the coefficients of x will satisfy our requirement. $$6x + 2y = 10 \quad (1)$$ $$-6x + 2y = -2 \quad (2)$$
2. Add the equations to eliminate one variable.	2. We add term by term to obtain $$0 + 4y = 8$$
3. Solve for the variable in the equation obtained.	3. $y = 2$
4. Substitute the value for one variable in one of the original equations to obtain the other variable.	4. $6x + 2(2) = 10$ $$6x = 6$$ $$x = 1$$
5. Write down the solution.	5. The solution is (1, 2).
6. Check in both original equations. We make this check by substituting the coordinates of the solution into the original equations to see if the equations are satisfied.	6. $6(1) + 2(2) = 10 \quad (1)$ $$6 + 4 = 10$$ $$10 = 10$$ $$3(1) - (2) = 1 \quad (2)$$ $$3 - 2 = 1$$ $$1 = 1$$

EXAMPLE 3   Find the solution set of

$$3x + y = 3$$
$$x + 2y = -4$$

Solution   In order to make the coefficients of y additive inverses in the two equations, multiply each term of the first equation by -2 to obtain

$$-6x - 2y = -6$$

Add to this equation the like terms of the second equation

$$\begin{aligned} -6x - 2y &= -6 \\ x + 2y &= -4 \\ \hline -5x &= -10 \end{aligned}$$

Divide both sides by -5 to obtain

$$x = 2$$

Substituting $x = 2$ into the first equation gives

$$3(2) + y = 3$$

Hence,

$$y = 3 - 6 = -3$$

The solution set is $\{(2, -3)\}$, and we can check that this point lies on both lines by substituting its coordinates into both equations. Note that this is the same solution as was obtained by graphical procedures.

EXAMPLE 4 Find the solution set of

$$3x + \ y = 3$$
$$6x + 2y = 6$$

Solution Multiply both sides of the first equation by -2 to obtain

$$-6x - 2y = -6$$

Add this equation to the second equation to obtain

$$0 = 0$$

This result means that any point satisfying the first equation will also satisfy the second equation, and vice versa. If (x, y) satisfies

$$3x + y = 3$$

then multiplying by 2 gives

$$2(3x + y) = 2 \cdot 3$$

or

$$6x + 2y = 6$$

Hence, any point that satisfies the first equation will satisfy the second equation. That is, the graphs of the two equations coincide [see Figure 2.2(b)].

EXAMPLE 5 Find the solution set of

$$3x + \ y = \ 3$$
$$6x + 2y = 12$$

Solution Multiplying the first equation by -2 gives

$$-6x - 2y = -6$$

Adding the second equation to this equation yields 0 on the left side of the equation and 6 on the right side of the equation. Since $0 \neq 6$, no numbers x and y satisfy both equations.

Solving for y in the two equations gives

$$y = -3x + 3$$
$$y = -\tfrac{6}{2}x + \tfrac{12}{2}$$

The slopes of the two lines are equal, and since the lines don't intersect, the lines are parallel.

These examples have illustrated all the possibilities that can occur when solving a general system of two linear equations in two unknowns.

The following illustrations are examples of the use of systems of two linear equations in two unknowns in solving practical problems.

EXAMPLE 6 The total number of Democrats and Republicans in a community is 40,000. In a recent election 60% of the Democrats and 40% of the Republicans voted. If only Democrats and Republicans voted and the total vote was 21,400, find the number of Democrats and the number of Republicans in the community.

Solution Let

$$x = \text{number of Democrats}$$
$$y = \text{number of Republicans}$$

Then

$$0.60x = \text{number of Democrats who voted}$$

and

$$0.40y = \text{number of Republicans who voted}$$

The equations that form a mathematical model for this problem are

$$x + \quad y = 40{,}000$$
$$0.60x + 0.40y = 21{,}400$$

Solving this system gives

$$x = 27{,}000 \quad \text{and} \quad y = 13{,}000$$

A word problem should always be checked by seeing if the conditions of the stated problem are satisfied and not by substituting the values into the equations because the system of equations may not be a true mathematical representation for the problem. To check this problem, note that the sum of 27,000 Democrats and 13,000 Republicans gives a total of 40,000. If 60% of the Democrats voted, the number of Democrats who voted was $(0.60)(27{,}000) = 16{,}200$. Similarly, if 40% of the Republicans voted, the number of Republicans who voted was $(0.40)(13{,}000) = 5200$. The total vote cast was $16{,}200 + 5200 = 21{,}400$. Hence, the statements given in the problem are satisfied.

When an equation expressing total cost C in terms of x (the number of items produced) and an equation expressing revenue R in terms of x are graphed on the same coordinate system, then the **break-even point** is the intersection of the two lines. Of course, the break-even point can be found by solving the system of linear equations by setting $C = R$.

EXAMPLE 7 A university is offering a special course in crafts for which tuition is $60 per student. The university has found that the cost of the course is $600 plus $20 for each student who registers for the course. How many students must take the course for the university to break even?

Solution Let $x = $ the number of students taking the course. Then the revenue equation becomes $R = 60x$, and the cost equation becomes $C = 20x + 600$. Setting these two equations equal to each other gives

$$R = C$$
$$60x = 20x + 600$$
$$40x = 600$$
$$x = 15$$

Check to see that 15 students are required in order to obtain the break-even point. The graph of these two functions is given in Figure 2.3. The solution (15, $900) means that the university receives $900 if 15 students take the course. Likewise, $900 is the cost for 15 students.

Figure 2.3

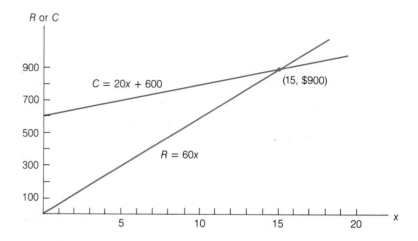

R or C

$C = 20x + 600$

(15, $900)

$R = 60x$

Exercise Set 2.1

A   **1.** Solve the following systems graphically.

a. $x + y = 5$	**b.** $x + y = 1$	**c.** $2x + y = 4$
$x - y = -1$	$x - y = 5$	$4x + 2y = 8$
d. $2x + y = 4$	**e.** $3x - y = 0$	**f.** $3x - y = 0$
$x - y = -1$	$x + y = 4$	$6x - 2y = 2$
g. $3x - 2y = 1$	**h.** $2x - y = 3$	**i.** $x - 2y = -3$
$6x - 4y = 1$	$4x - 2y = 6$	$2x + y = 4$

2. Solve algebraically each system of equations in exercise 1 and explain why the solution set is empty in some cases.

3. Solve the following systems by the addition method.

a. $3x + 2y = 1$	**b.** $4x - 3y = 5$	**c.** $2x + 3y = 9$
$5x + 3y = 4$	$8x - 6y = 7$	$3x + 5y = 11$
d. $4x - 3y = 5$	**e.** $5x - 2y = -4$	**f.** $4x - 3y = 5$
$8x - 6y = 10$	$3x + 5y = 10$	$3x + 2y = 8$

4. Solve the following systems by the substitution method.

a. $x + y = 5$	**b.** $x + 2y = 1$	**c.** $5x - 2y = -4$
$2x - 3y = -5$	$3x + 4y = 5$	$3x - y = -1$

d. $2x + y = -1$
$3x - 2y = -12$

e. $x - 2y = -1$
$2x + 3y = 19$

f. $2x + y = 1$
$-3x - y = -5$

B

5. Solve the following systems of equations.

a. $\frac{5}{2}x - \frac{2}{3}y = \frac{-4}{3}$
$\frac{3}{5}x + \frac{5}{2}y = 2$

b. $0.4x - 0.3y = 0.05$
$0.3x + 0.2y = 0.08$

c. $0.01x - 0.2y = -0.1$
$0.02x + 0.3y = 1.9$

d. $\frac{2}{3}x + \frac{1}{4}y = \frac{1}{6}$
$-\frac{3}{4}x = \frac{y}{3} + \frac{5}{2}$

6. The sum of two test scores is 175. The difference between the two scores is 11. Find the scores.

7. The average of two test scores is 78. The difference between the two scores is 12. Find the scores.

8. Fifty coins totaling $7.40 are removed from a soft-drink machine. If the coins are all dimes and quarters, determine the number of each.

C

9. Solve the following systems by using a calculator.

a. $17.05x - 3.24y = 22.63$
$3.21x - 4.56y = 3.96$

b. $35.7x + 103y = 104.759$
$-23.4x + 37y = 118.412$

c. $123x - 37y = 6890$
$47x - 31y = 896$

d. $137x - 41y = -10,688$
$105x + 13y = -2994$

Business

10. Mixture Problem. Small Dairy has 5 gallons of milk that is 4% butterfat. How much low-fat milk (1% butterfat) should Small Dairy mix with the 5 gallons to make a mixture that is 2% butterfat?

11. Mixture Problem. A candy-store proprietor wishes to mix candy that sells for $3 per pound with candy selling for $4 per pound to make a mixture to sell for $3.60 per pound. How many pounds of each kind of candy should be used to make 80 pounds of the mixture?

12. Commission. Jim is trying to decide between two positions. The first pays $225 per week plus 5% commission on gross sales. The second pays 9% on gross sales. Graph the two pay equations on the same axes and find the amount of gross sales for which the pay from the two positions would be the same. What would you advise Jim to do?

Economics

13. Revenue Equation, Cost Equation. A local club has membership dues of $25 per month for each member. (The revenue function is written as $R = 25x$.) Management has been studying the cost of operation and has found the monthly cost to be $C_1 = \$6000 + \$15x$, where x represents the number of members. A service company states that by remodeling, it will provide similar services for the monthly cost $C_2 = \$10,500 + \$10x$. Draw the graphs of the revenue equation and the two cost equations. Should management allow the service company to operate the club?

14. Break-even Point. A producer knows that she can sell as many items at $0.25 each as she can produce in a day. If her cost is $C = \$0.20x + \$70$, find her break-even point.

15. Break-even Point. If the producer in exercise 14 can change her cost equation to $C(x) = \$0.15x + \$150$ by hiring an assistant, should she make the change? Explain your answer.

16. Break-even Point. A firm knows that it can sell as many items at $1.25 each as it can produce in a day. If the cost is $C = \$0.90x + \$105$, find the break-even point.

17. Break-even Point. If the firm in exercise 16 can change the cost equation to $C(x) = \$0.80x + \$120$, should the change be made? Explain.

18. Nutrition. A special diet requires 4 milligrams of iron and 52 grams of protein each day. A person decides to attain these requirements by drinking skim milk and eating fish. A glass of skim milk provides 0.2 milligram of iron and 1 gram of protein. One-fourth pound of fish provides 8 milligrams of iron and 10 grams of protein. How many glasses of milk and how many pieces of fish ($\frac{1}{4}$ pound) are need to attain the diet's requirements?

19. Population. A town has a population of 1000. The number of men is 80 less than twice the number of women. Find the number of men and the number of women.

20. Psychological Attraction and Repulsion. A psychologist has been studying reactions of attraction and repulsion by first feeding mice and then later giving them mild electric shocks from the same box. With this procedure the psychologist established the following functions where a represents attraction, r represents repulsion, and x represents the distance in centimeters of the mouse from the box.

$$a = -\tfrac{1}{4}x + 70$$
$$r = -\tfrac{4}{3}x + 200$$

Graph the attraction function and the repulsion function on the same coordinate axes and find the distance where attraction equals repulsion. (*Hint:* Find the intersection point of the two lines.) Check your graphical result by setting $a = r$ and solving for x.

2 Systems of Linear Equations and Matrices

In practical applications most systems of linear equations involve a large number of equations and unknowns. Usually these systems are solved using computers. In this section we introduce a procedure for solving systems of equations that can be extended to any number of equations and unknowns. Our discussion of this procedure leads naturally into the study of mathematical concepts called **matrices.** A study of the theory of matrices will be postponed until the next section; however, the application of matrices in this section should suggest the importance of this subject.

The step-by-step procedure that we use to solve equations in this section is called the **Gauss-Jordan elimination method.**

Let us use a step-by-step procedure to solve the system of equations

$$2x + 3y = -5$$
$$x - 2y = 8$$

There are many ways of solving this system, and some are easier than others; but we shall follow a procedure that can be applied to any system and is suitable for machine computation. This procedure consists of replacing the original system by an equivalent one from which the solution is apparent. The following are operations that may be performed on a system of equations to give an equivalent system.

---

1. Interchange any two equations.
2. Multiply each term of any equation by a nonzero constant.
3. Replace any equation by the sum of that equation and a constant times any other equation.

Changing the order or arrangement of the equations certainly will not change the solution of the system. Likewise, if $(2, -3)$ satisfies $2x + 3y = -5$, then it should satisfy the result of multiplying this equation by a constant such as 4 $(8x + 12y = -20)$. Check to be certain. Note that $(2, -3)$ also satisfies $x - 2y = 8$. Let's multiply this equation by 2 and add it to the first equation

$$
\begin{array}{rcrr}
2x + 3y &=& -5 & \\
+\,2(x - 2y &=& & 8) \\
\hline
4x - y &=& 11 &
\end{array}
$$

Does $(2, -3)$ satisfy $4x - y = 11$? Thus, we see that each of the three operations listed transforms a system of linear equations into one with the same solution set (an equivalent system).

Now we will use these operations to replace our system of equations with an equivalent system in which the solution is apparent. In general, when the process is possible, it may be summarized as follows:

---

1. Make the coefficient of the first unknown equal to 1 in the first equation and 0 in all other equations.
2. Make the coefficient of the second unknown equal to 1 in the second equation and 0 in all other equations.
3. Make the coefficient of the third unknown equal to 1 in the third equation and 0 in all other equations.
4. Continue this process for all equations (if possible).

To understand how this procedure is performed, let's apply it to the following system:

$$
\begin{array}{rcr}
2x + 3y &=& -5 \\
x - 2y &=& 8
\end{array}
$$

Goal	Operation	Equivalent System
1. To make the coefficient of x in the first equation 1.	Multiply the first equation by $\frac{1}{2}$.	$x + (\frac{3}{2})y = -\frac{5}{2}$ $x \quad -2y = \quad 8$
2. To get the coefficient of x in the second equation to be 0.	Multiply the first equation by -1 and add to the second equation.	$x + (\frac{3}{2})y = -\frac{5}{2}$ $-(\frac{7}{2})y = \quad \frac{21}{2}$
3. To get the coefficient of y in the second equation to be 1.	Multiply the second equation by $-\frac{2}{7}$.	$x + (\frac{3}{2})y = -\frac{5}{2}$ $y = -3$
4. To make the coefficient of y in the first equation 0.	Multiply the second equation by $-\frac{3}{2}$ and add to the first equation.	$x = \quad 2$ $y = -3$

The answer is apparent: $x = 2$, $y = -3$.

For a system with several equations and several unknowns it is obvious that the unknowns could be omitted since all operations are performed on coefficients. Let's write the coefficients of our original system as

$$\begin{bmatrix} 2 & 3 & | & -5 \\ 1 & -2 & | & 8 \end{bmatrix}$$

where the vertical line replaces the equals signs. Such a rectangular array of numbers is called an **augmented matrix.** It is a special case of the general definition of a **matrix** to be discussed in the next section. In general, matrices (plural of matrix) are rectangular arrays (usually numbers) within brackets such as:

$$\begin{bmatrix} 5 & 1 \\ 3 & 7 \end{bmatrix} \quad \begin{bmatrix} 2 & 1 & 4 \\ 5 & 6 & 8 \end{bmatrix} \quad \text{and} \quad \begin{bmatrix} 8 & -1 & 3 \\ 2 & 1 & -1 \\ 3 & 2 & 7 \end{bmatrix}$$

For our purposes at this time let's replace the operations used to obtain equivalent systems of equations by operations on the rows of numbers (*elements*) of the augmented matrices. These row operations in matrices produce equivalent matrices (called *row equivalent matrices*) just as we obtained equivalent systems of equations previously.

Row equivalent matrices are obtained by the following operations:

Row Operations on Matrices

1. Interchange any two rows.
2. Multiply each element of any row by a nonzero constant.
3. Replace any row by the sum of that row and a constant times any other row.

We now use these matrix operations to solve the system of equations represented by the augmented matrix

$$\begin{bmatrix} 2 & 3 & | & -5 \\ 1 & -2 & | & 8 \end{bmatrix}$$

Goal	Row Operation	Row Equivalent Matrix
1. To get a 1 in row 1, column 1.	Multiply the first row by $\frac{1}{2}$	$\begin{bmatrix} 1 & \frac{3}{2} & \mid & -\frac{5}{2} \\ 1 & -2 & \mid & 8 \end{bmatrix}$
2. To get the other entry in column 1 to be 0.	Multiply the first row by -1 and add it to the second row	$\begin{bmatrix} 1 & \frac{3}{2} & \mid & -\frac{5}{2} \\ 0 & -\frac{7}{2} & \mid & \frac{21}{2} \end{bmatrix}$
3. To get a 1 in row 2, column 2.	Multiply the second row by $-\frac{2}{7}$	$\begin{bmatrix} 1 & \frac{3}{2} & \mid & -\frac{5}{2} \\ 0 & 1 & \mid & -3 \end{bmatrix}$
4. To get the other entry in column 2 to be 0.	Multiply the second row by $-\frac{3}{2}$ and add it to the first row	$\begin{bmatrix} 1 & 0 & \mid & 2 \\ 0 & 1 & \mid & -3 \end{bmatrix}$

The last matrix is the augmented matrix of the system

$$1 \cdot x + 0 \cdot y = 2$$
$$0 \cdot x + 1 \cdot y = -3$$

or $x = 2$, $y = -3$.

EXAMPLE 8 Solve the system

$$2x + 5y = 9$$
$$3x - 2y = 4$$

using augmented matrices.

Solution To form the augmented matrix, write down as the first column the coefficients of x, as the second column the coefficients of y, and as the last column the constant terms (appearing on the right side of the equation):

$$\begin{bmatrix} 2 & 5 & \mid & 9 \\ 3 & -2 & \mid & 4 \end{bmatrix}$$

To put the augmented matrix in a form where the solution to the system is evident, perform the following row operations. Multiply the first row by $\frac{1}{2}$.

$$\begin{bmatrix} 1 & \frac{5}{2} & \mid & \frac{9}{2} \\ 3 & -2 & \mid & 4 \end{bmatrix}$$

Multiply the first row by -3 and add to the second row.

$$\begin{bmatrix} 1 & \frac{5}{2} & \mid & \frac{9}{2} \\ 0 & -\frac{19}{2} & \mid & -\frac{19}{2} \end{bmatrix}$$

Multiply the second row by $-\frac{2}{19}$.

$$\begin{bmatrix} 1 & \frac{5}{2} & \mid & \frac{9}{2} \\ 0 & 1 & \mid & 1 \end{bmatrix}$$

Multiply the second row by $-\frac{5}{2}$ and add to the first row.

$$\begin{bmatrix} 1 & 0 & \mid & 2 \\ 0 & 1 & \mid & 1 \end{bmatrix}$$

This matrix is the augmented matrix of the system

$$1 \cdot x + 0 \cdot y = 2 \qquad \text{or} \qquad x = 2$$
$$0 \cdot x + 1 \cdot y = 1 \qquad\qquad\qquad y = 1$$

EXAMPLE 9 Show that the following system has no solution by using permissible row operations on the augmented matrix of the system.

$$2x + y = 5$$
$$2x + y = 7$$

Solution The augmented matrix is

$$\left[\begin{array}{cc|c} 2 & 1 & 5 \\ 2 & 1 & 7 \end{array}\right]$$

Multiply the first row by $\frac{1}{2}$ to get

$$\left[\begin{array}{cc|c} 1 & \frac{1}{2} & \frac{5}{2} \\ 2 & 1 & 7 \end{array}\right]$$

Multiply the first row by -2 and add the result to the second row to obtain

$$\left[\begin{array}{cc|c} 1 & \frac{1}{2} & \frac{5}{2} \\ 0 & 0 & 2 \end{array}\right]$$

This is the augmented matrix for the system

$$x + \tfrac{1}{2}y = \tfrac{5}{2}$$
$$0 \cdot x + 0 \cdot y = 2$$

and because the second equation has no solution, the system has no solution.

EXAMPLE 10 Solve the system of equations

$$3x - 2y = 1$$
$$6x - 4y = 2$$

by using augmented matrices.

Solution The augmented matrix of the system can be written as

$$\left[\begin{array}{cc|c} 3 & -2 & 1 \\ 6 & -4 & 2 \end{array}\right]$$

Multiply the first row by $\frac{1}{3}$ to get

$$\left[\begin{array}{cc|c} 1 & -\frac{2}{3} & \frac{1}{3} \\ 6 & -4 & 2 \end{array}\right]$$

Add -6 times the first row to the second row

$$\left[\begin{array}{cc|c} 1 & -\frac{2}{3} & \frac{1}{3} \\ 0 & 0 & 0 \end{array}\right]$$

The system of equations can be written as

$$x - \tfrac{2}{3}y = \tfrac{1}{3}$$
$$0 \cdot x + 0 \cdot y = 0$$

Since any pair of values that satisfies the first equation will obviously satisfy the second equation, there are infinitely many solutions.

Summary of Solutions

$$\begin{bmatrix} 1 & 0 & | & a \\ 0 & 1 & | & b \end{bmatrix} \qquad \begin{bmatrix} 1 & a & | & b \\ 0 & 0 & | & 0 \end{bmatrix} \qquad \begin{bmatrix} 1 & a & | & b \\ 0 & 0 & | & c \end{bmatrix}$$

Unique solution: $\qquad$ Infinitely many $\qquad\qquad$ $c \neq 0$
$x = a, y = b$ $\qquad\quad$ solutions $\qquad\qquad\quad$ No solutions

Exercise Set **2.2**

A Write the system of equations for each of the following augmented matrices.

1. $\begin{bmatrix} 3 & 1 & | & 13 \\ 2 & -1 & | & 2 \end{bmatrix}$ $\qquad\qquad$ **2.** $\begin{bmatrix} 16 & -4 & | & 0 \\ 8 & 1 & | & 12 \end{bmatrix}$

3. $\begin{bmatrix} 1 & 0 & | & 4 \\ 0 & 1 & | & 6 \end{bmatrix}$ $\qquad\qquad$ **4.** $\begin{bmatrix} 1 & 0 & | & 2 \\ 0 & 1 & | & -1 \end{bmatrix}$

Write the augmented matrix for each of the following systems.

5. $2x + 3y = 5$
$\quad\ 4x - \ y = 3$

6. $7u - 4w = 6$
$\quad\ 3u + \ w = 8$

7. $5x + 2y = \ \ 3$
$\quad\ 3y + \ x = -2$

8. $6x + 4 = 5y$
$\quad\ 2y + 3 = 7x$

9. $6 + 2y = 2x$
$\quad\ x + 5 \ \ = 2y$

10. $2s - 1 = 7t$
$\quad\ \ 5 - t = s$

Solve each of the following systems of equations by using augmented matrices.

11. Exercise 1. $\qquad\qquad$ **12.** Exercise 2. $\qquad\qquad$ **13.** Exercise 5.

14. Exercise 6. $\qquad\qquad$ **15.** Exercise 7. $\qquad\qquad$ **16.** Exercise 8.

17. Exercise 9. $\qquad\qquad$ **18.** Exercise 10.

B Discuss the solutions for the following systems of equations.

19. $4x + 3y = 7$
$\quad\ 8x + 6y = 14$

20. $2x + 4y = 6$
$\quad\ 3x + 6y = 9$

21. $2x - \ y = 3$
$\quad\ 4x - 2y = 9$

22. $2x + 4y = 7$
$\quad\ 3x + 6y = 11$

C   *Use a calculator to solve the following systems of equations.*

23. $1.1x + 2.5y = 7$
$2.1x - 3.5y = 6$

24. $0.1x + 0.6y = 7$
$1.1x + 1.6y = 4$

Business   **25.** **Mixture Problem.** The Fresh Roasted Nut store wishes to mix nuts that sell for $1.40 per pound with nuts that sell for $2 per pound in order to make a mixture that will sell for $1.60 per pound. How many pounds of the $1.40-per-pound nuts should be mixed with 50 pounds of the $2-per-pound nuts?

26. **Mixture Problem.** At a recent concert, tickets were $5 for adults and $3 for students. There were 2000 more adult tickets sold than student tickets. How many tickets of each kind were sold if the total receipts were $42,000?

27. **Mixture Problem.** The Reused Paper Company uses both scrap paper and scrap cloth to make their paper. Their Best Paper requires 3 tons of cloth and 15 tons of paper for each run while Good Paper requires 1 ton of cloth and 12 tons of paper for each run. How many runs of Best Paper and how many runs of Good Paper should be made if Reused Paper has 34 tons of scrap cloth and 261 tons of scrap paper on hand? Assume Reused Paper wishes to use all its scrap paper and scrap cloth.

28. **Investments.** The Easy Investment Club has $100,000 invested in bonds. Type A bonds pay 8% interest while Type B bonds pay 10%. How much money is invested in each type if the club receives $9,360 in interest?

Economics   **29.** **Break-even Point.** A production equation is given by $R = 1.40x + 60$, where x is the number of items produced. The cost equation is $C = 0.95x + 105$. Find the break-even point.

Getting Acquainted with Matrices

In this section you will be given the definition of a matrix and will be introduced to **matrix algebra:**   that is, you will learn the rules by which matrices are combined. You will learn that matrices of the same order can be added and subtracted, that all matrices can be multiplied by a constant, and that some matrices can be multiplied together. Note carefully which matrices can or cannot be multiplied.

Matrix algebra has many important applications. It is most valuable in dealing with large systems with many variables. Not only will applications of matrices be considered in this chapter, but you will also discover that matrices are very useful in the *simplex method* of solving linear programming problems in the next chapter.

After this section on the theory and applications of matrices, we return to solving systems of equations by using matrices. A thorough knowledge of matrices will be most valuable as we consider systems with more than two equations and two unknowns.

As introduced in the preceding section, **matrices** are rectangular arrays of elements (usually numbers) written within brackets.

EXAMPLE 11   The following rectangular arrays are matrices:

$$\begin{bmatrix} 2 & 1 \\ 3 & 2 \end{bmatrix} \qquad \begin{bmatrix} 2 & 1 \\ 3 & 2 \\ 4 & 5 \end{bmatrix} \qquad \begin{bmatrix} 2 & 3 & 2 \\ 1 & 5 & 7 \end{bmatrix}$$

In the above example the first matrix has two **rows** (horizontal entries) and two **columns** (vertical entries). The second matrix has three rows and two columns. The third matrix has two rows and three columns. The **dimension** or **size** of a matrix gives the number of rows and columns it has, with the number of rows being given first. The first matrix is 2×2 (read "2 by 2"). The second is 3×2, and the third is 2×3.

A matrix may in general have m rows and n columns and be written as

$$\begin{bmatrix} a_{11} & a_{12} & a_{13} & \cdots & a_{1n} \\ a_{21} & a_{22} & a_{23} & \cdots & a_{2n} \\ \vdots & \vdots & \vdots & & \vdots \\ a_{m1} & a_{m2} & a_{m3} & \cdots & a_{mn} \end{bmatrix}$$

and sometimes it may be denoted as $\mathbf{A} = [a_{ij}]$. The dimension of this matrix is $m \times n$, where m represents the number of rows and n the number of columns. The objects in the matrix are called **elements** of the matrix. Usually, the elements are numbers. Notice that in the subscript notation the first subscript gives the row in which the element lies and the second subscript gives the column. For example, a_{35} is the element in the third row and fifth column. The given $m \times n$ matrix is sometimes written as $[a_{ij}]$, where a_{ij} represents each element with the appropriate subscript.

EXAMPLE 12 $[a_{ij}] = \begin{bmatrix} 2 & 3 & 4 \\ 1 & 5 & 7 \end{bmatrix}$ is a 2×3 matrix. Its elements are $a_{11} = 2$, $a_{12} = 3$, $a_{13} = 4$, $a_{21} = 1$, $a_{22} = 5$, $a_{23} = 7$.

A matrix consisting of a single row of elements is called a **row matrix** (or a **row vector**). Similarly, a matrix consisting of a single column is called a **column matrix** (or a **column vector**).

EXAMPLE 13 $[a_{ij}] = \begin{bmatrix} 1 & 3 & 7 \end{bmatrix}$ is called a row matrix (or row vector), with $a_{11} = 1$, $a_{12} = 3$, and $a_{13} = 7$. $[b_{ij}] = \begin{bmatrix} 7 \\ -1 \\ 4 \end{bmatrix}$ is called a column matrix (or column vector), with $b_{11} = 7$, $b_{21} = -1$, and $b_{31} = 4$.

When new mathematical objects are introduced, one of the first questions that must be answered is, "When are two of these objects equal?" In our case the question would be "When are two matrices equal?" The answer comes fairly easily:

| Equal Matrices | Two matrices are **equal** if and only if they have the same **dimensions** (same number of rows and columns) and if all corresponding elements are equal. |

EXAMPLE 14

$$\begin{bmatrix} 3 & 2 & 1 \\ 5 & 0 & 2 \end{bmatrix} = \begin{bmatrix} \frac{-6}{-2} & \frac{14}{7} & \frac{1}{1} \\ \frac{10}{2} & \frac{0}{3} & 2 \end{bmatrix}$$

These two matrices are equal because they have the same dimensions (that is, they are both 2 × 3), and all corresponding elements are equal:

$$3 = \frac{-6}{-2} \qquad 2 = \frac{14}{7} \qquad 1 = \frac{1}{1} \qquad 5 = \frac{10}{2} \qquad 0 = \frac{0}{3} \qquad 2 = 2$$

EXAMPLE 15

$$\begin{bmatrix} 3 & 2 & 1 \\ 5 & 0 & 2 \end{bmatrix} \neq \begin{bmatrix} 3 & 2 & 1 & 0 \\ 5 & 0 & 2 & 0 \end{bmatrix}$$

These two matrices are not equal because they are not the same size; that is, the first matrix is 2 × 3, while the second is 2 × 4.

How should matrices such as $\begin{bmatrix} 1 & 0 \\ 2 & 3 \end{bmatrix}$ and $\begin{bmatrix} -2 & 1 \\ 1 & 2 \end{bmatrix}$ be added? It seems obvious that corresponding elements should be added:

$$\begin{bmatrix} 1 & 0 \\ 2 & 3 \end{bmatrix} + \begin{bmatrix} -2 & 1 \\ 1 & 2 \end{bmatrix} = \begin{bmatrix} 1 + (-2) & 0 + 1 \\ 2 + 1 & 3 + 2 \end{bmatrix} = \begin{bmatrix} -1 & 1 \\ 3 & 5 \end{bmatrix}$$

| Sum of Two Matrices | The sum of two matrices **A** and **B** of the same dimension is the matrix **A** + **B**, in which the entry in the ith row and jth column is $a_{ij} + b_{ij}$. |

EXAMPLE 16   Find the sum of $\begin{bmatrix} 1 & 2 & -3 \\ 0 & -3 & 4 \end{bmatrix} + \begin{bmatrix} 2 & -1 & 3 \\ 1 & -1 & 2 \end{bmatrix}$

Solution

$$\begin{bmatrix} 1+2 & 2+-1 & -3+3 \\ 0+1 & -3+-1 & 4+2 \end{bmatrix} = \begin{bmatrix} 3 & 1 & 0 \\ 1 & -4 & 6 \end{bmatrix}$$

Note that according to the preceding definition, matrices cannot be added unless they have the same dimension. Then, the sum of two matrices of the same dimension is obtained by adding the corresponding entries.

A matrix with each element equal to 0 is a *zero matrix*, usually denoted by 0. For example,

$$\begin{bmatrix} 0 & 0 & 0 \\ 0 & 0 & 0 \end{bmatrix}$$

is a 2 × 3 zero matrix.

We shall be interested in two kinds of products involving matrices: (1) the product of a real number and a matrix and (2) the product of two matrices. For the product of a real number and a matrix, the real number is multiplied by each element of the matrix. For example,

$$2\begin{bmatrix} 3 & 1 \\ 0 & 2 \end{bmatrix} = \begin{bmatrix} 2 \cdot 3 & 2 \cdot 1 \\ 2 \cdot 0 & 2 \cdot 2 \end{bmatrix} = \begin{bmatrix} 6 & 2 \\ 0 & 4 \end{bmatrix}$$

Product of a Real Number and a Matrix

The product of a real number c and a matrix $\mathbf{A} = [a_{ij}]$ is the matrix $[ca_{ij}]$.

EXAMPLE 17

$$5\begin{bmatrix} 1 & -1 & 2 \\ 3 & 0 & 4 \end{bmatrix} = \begin{bmatrix} 5 \cdot 1 & 5 \cdot (-1) & 5 \cdot 2 \\ 5 \cdot 3 & 5 \cdot 0 & 5 \cdot 4 \end{bmatrix} = \begin{bmatrix} 5 & -5 & 10 \\ 15 & 0 & 20 \end{bmatrix}$$

The following properties can be easily developed:

If c and d are any real numbers:
1. $c(d\mathbf{A}) = (cd)\mathbf{A}$
2. $c\mathbf{A} + d\mathbf{A} = (c + d)\mathbf{A}$
3. $c(\mathbf{A} + \mathbf{B}) = c\mathbf{A} + c\mathbf{B}$

The preceding definition can be used to find the additive inverse of a matrix. Two matrices are **additive inverses** if their sum is the zero matrix.

Additive Inverse of a Matrix

The additive inverse of a matrix $\mathbf{A} = [a_{ij}]$, denoted by $-\mathbf{A}$, is the product of -1 and $\mathbf{A}$. That is, $-\mathbf{A} = [-a_{ij}]$.

EXAMPLE 18 If $\mathbf{A} = \begin{bmatrix} 2 & -1 \\ 4 & -2 \\ -3 & 3 \end{bmatrix}$, then $-\mathbf{A} = \begin{bmatrix} -2 & 1 \\ -4 & 2 \\ 3 & -3 \end{bmatrix}$

EXAMPLE 19 Find the additive inverse of

$$\begin{bmatrix} 2 & 3 & 1 \\ -1 & 0 & 2 \end{bmatrix}$$

Solution The additive inverse of a matrix is found by multiplying each element by -1. Hence, the additive inverse is

$$\begin{bmatrix} -2 & -3 & -1 \\ 1 & 0 & -2 \end{bmatrix}$$

To prove that these matrices are additive inverses, note that

$$\begin{bmatrix} 2 & 3 & 1 \\ -1 & 0 & 2 \end{bmatrix} + \begin{bmatrix} -2 & -3 & -1 \\ 1 & 0 & -2 \end{bmatrix} = \begin{bmatrix} 0 & 0 & 0 \\ 0 & 0 & 0 \end{bmatrix}$$

$A - B$, called the difference of A and B, can be defined to be the sum of A and the additive inverse of B, or $A + (-B)$.

EXAMPLE 20

$$\begin{bmatrix} 1 & -1 & 2 \\ 3 & 1 & 4 \end{bmatrix} - \begin{bmatrix} -1 & 2 & 2 \\ 2 & -4 & 3 \end{bmatrix} = \begin{bmatrix} 1 & -1 & 2 \\ 3 & 1 & 4 \end{bmatrix} + \begin{bmatrix} 1 & -2 & -2 \\ -2 & 4 & -3 \end{bmatrix}$$

$$= \begin{bmatrix} 1+1 & -1-2 & 2-2 \\ 3-2 & 1+4 & 4-3 \end{bmatrix}$$

$$= \begin{bmatrix} 2 & -3 & 0 \\ 1 & 5 & 1 \end{bmatrix}$$

To define the product of two matrices, we first introduce what is called the **dot product.**

Dot Product

The dot product of the row matrix A (also called a row vector) with elements $a_1, a_2, \ldots, a_p$ and the column matrix B (also called a column vector) with entries $b_1, b_2, \ldots, b_p$ is a real number,

$$A \cdot B = a_1 b_1 + a_2 b_2 + \cdots + a_p b_p$$

EXAMPLE 21   Find the dot product of $[3 \quad 1 \quad 2]$ and $\begin{bmatrix} 1 \\ 4 \\ -2 \end{bmatrix}$

Solution $3(1) + 1(4) + 2(-2) = 3$

EXAMPLE 22   Find the dot product of $[3 \quad 2 \quad 1]$ and $\begin{bmatrix} 1 \\ 2 \end{bmatrix}$.

Solution   The dot product of these two matrices cannot be found because the number of elements in the row is different from the number of elements in the column.

Product of Matrices

The product of the $m \times p$ matrix A and the $p \times n$ matrix B is the $m \times n$ matrix AB whose i, j element is the dot product of the ith row of A and the jth column of B.

Consider the multiplication of two matrices such as

$$\begin{bmatrix} 3 & 1 & 2 \\ -1 & 0 & 5 \end{bmatrix} \quad \text{and} \quad \begin{bmatrix} 1 & 0 \\ 4 & 6 \\ -2 & 3 \end{bmatrix}$$

Since we are multiplying matrices, we would expect our answer to be a matrix. To obtain our product matrix, we proceed as follows. To find the element in the first row and first column of the product matrix, we find the dot product of the first row

$$[3 \quad 1 \quad 2]$$

of the first matrix (matrix on the left) with the first column

$$\begin{bmatrix} 1 \\ 4 \\ -2 \end{bmatrix}$$

of the second matrix (matrix on the right). In this example

$$[3 \quad 1 \quad 2] \cdot \begin{bmatrix} 1 \\ 4 \\ -2 \end{bmatrix} = (3)(1) + (1)(4) + (2)(-2) = 3 + 4 - 4 = 3$$

This element goes in the first row, first column of the product matrix. If the product matrix is denoted by c_{ij}, then $c_{11} = 3$. Now we take the dot product of the first row of the left-hand matrix with the second column of the right-hand matrix.

$$[3 \quad 1 \quad 2] \cdot \begin{bmatrix} 0 \\ 6 \\ 3 \end{bmatrix} = 3(0) + 1(6) + 2(3) = 0 + 6 + 6 = 12$$

This element goes in the first row, second column of the product matrix: $c_{12} = 12$. Now we take the dot product of the second row of the matrix on the left and the first column of the matrix on the right.

$$[-1 \quad 0 \quad 5] \cdot \begin{bmatrix} 1 \\ 4 \\ -2 \end{bmatrix} = (-1)(1) + 0(4) + 5(-2) = -1 + 0 - 10 = -11$$

This element goes in the second row, first column of the product matrix: $c_{21} = -11$. Then we take the dot product of the second row of the left-hand matrix with the second column of the right-hand matrix.

$$[-1 \quad 0 \quad 5] \cdot \begin{bmatrix} 0 \\ 6 \\ 3 \end{bmatrix} = (-1)(0) + 0(6) + 5(3) = 0 + 0 + 15 = 15$$

This element goes in the second row, second column of the product matrix: $c_{22} = 15$. Thus,

$$\begin{bmatrix} 3 & 1 & 2 \\ -1 & 0 & 5 \end{bmatrix} \begin{bmatrix} 1 & 0 \\ 4 & 6 \\ -2 & 3 \end{bmatrix} = \begin{bmatrix} 3 & 12 \\ -11 & 15 \end{bmatrix}$$

Notice that *the product of two matrices is not defined unless the number of columns of the first matrix is the same as the number of rows of the second matrix.* Another important item to note in the definition is the dimension of the matrices involved. A 3×2 matrix multiplied by a 2×3 matrix gives a 3×3 matrix, whereas, if the order is reversed, the product of a 2×3 matrix with a 3×2 matrix gives a 2×2 matrix. Thus, the order of multiplication is important when multiplying matrices.

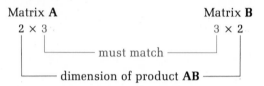

The following example indicates that the commutative property of multiplication does not hold for all pairs of matrices. Many times, the product will not be defined if the order of multiplication is reversed. For example, a 2×3 matrix times a 3×5 matrix equals a 2×5 matrix. However, multiplication is not defined for a 2×5 matrix times a 3×5 matrix. Even when both products are defined, **AB** may not be the same as **BA**.

In the example given earlier,

$$\begin{bmatrix} 3 & 1 & 2 \\ -1 & 0 & 5 \end{bmatrix} \begin{bmatrix} 1 & 0 \\ 4 & 6 \\ -2 & 3 \end{bmatrix} = \begin{bmatrix} 3 & 12 \\ -11 & 15 \end{bmatrix}$$

If the order is reversed, the product becomes

$$\begin{bmatrix} 1 & 0 \\ 4 & 6 \\ -2 & 3 \end{bmatrix} \begin{bmatrix} 3 & 1 & 2 \\ -1 & 0 & 5 \end{bmatrix} = \begin{bmatrix} 3 & 1 & 2 \\ 6 & 4 & 38 \\ -9 & -2 & 11 \end{bmatrix}$$

Hence, the commutative property does not hold for the product of these two matrices.

In much of the work with matrices in this book, we will use only *square matrices*, that is, matrices where the number of rows and the number of columns are the same. The product of square matrices of the same dimension always exists. In particular, we denote the products

$$(\mathbf{A})(\mathbf{A}) \qquad \text{as} \quad \mathbf{A}^2$$

$$(\mathbf{A})(\mathbf{A})(\mathbf{A}) \qquad \text{as} \quad \mathbf{A}^3$$

$$\vdots \qquad\qquad \vdots$$

$$\underbrace{(\mathbf{A})(\mathbf{A}) \cdots (\mathbf{A})}_{n \text{ factors}} \quad \text{as} \quad \mathbf{A}^n$$

For example, if $\mathbf{A} = \begin{bmatrix} 2 & 3 \\ -4 & 1 \end{bmatrix}$, then $\mathbf{A}^2 = \begin{bmatrix} 2 & 3 \\ -4 & 1 \end{bmatrix}\begin{bmatrix} 2 & 3 \\ -4 & 1 \end{bmatrix} = \begin{bmatrix} -8 & 9 \\ -12 & -11 \end{bmatrix}$.

The **identity matrix** for multiplication is very important in the sections that follow. Just as 1 is the identity for multiplication of real numbers (that is, $1 \cdot 6 =$

$6 \cdot 1 = 6$ or $1 \cdot x = x \cdot 1 = x$), we define

$$I = \begin{bmatrix} 1 & 0 \\ 0 & 1 \end{bmatrix}$$

as the identity matrix for 2×2 matrices. For example,

$$\begin{bmatrix} 1 & 0 \\ 0 & 1 \end{bmatrix} \begin{bmatrix} 3 & -4 \\ 2 & 7 \end{bmatrix} = \begin{bmatrix} 3 & -4 \\ 2 & 7 \end{bmatrix}$$

and

$$\begin{bmatrix} x & y \\ z & w \end{bmatrix} \begin{bmatrix} 1 & 0 \\ 0 & 1 \end{bmatrix} = \begin{bmatrix} x & y \\ z & w \end{bmatrix}$$

In general,

$$I = \begin{bmatrix} 1 & 0 & 0 & \cdots & 0 \\ 0 & 1 & 0 & \cdots & 0 \\ 0 & 0 & 1 & \cdots & 0 \\ \vdots & \vdots & \vdots & & \vdots \\ 0 & 0 & 0 & \cdots & 1 \end{bmatrix} \quad n \times n$$

is the identity matrix for $n \times n$ matrices.

Although the commutative property of multiplication does not hold for all matrices (remember that some multiplications of matrices are not defined), many properties do follow from similar properties of real numbers. Let $M =$ the set of all $m \times n$ matrices with real elements; then the following properties hold for M:

Properties of Matrices

1. M is closed under addition.
2. Addition is associative in M.
3. Addition is commutative in M.
4. There exists an $m \times n$ matrix,

$$\begin{bmatrix} 0 & 0 & \cdots & 0 \\ \vdots & \vdots & & \vdots \\ 0 & 0 & \cdots & 0 \end{bmatrix}$$

   denoted by [0] and called the **zero matrix,** whose elements are all zero such that $[a_{ij}] + [0] = [a_{ij}]$ for all $[a_{ij}]$ in M.
5. For each $[a_{ij}]$ in M, there exists an **additive inverse,** $[-a_{ij}]$ in M such that $[a_{ij}] + [-a_{ij}] = [0]$.
6. There exists an $m \times m$ identity matrix I such that

$$I[a_{ij}] = [a_{ij}]$$

   and such that

$$[a_{ij}]I = [a_{ij}]$$

Matrix theory can be used on most problems that can be defined using an array of numbers. Let's investigate three of many possibilities.

EXAMPLE 23   A bakery makes three types of bread using the ingredients listed in Table 2.1 in convenient units per loaf of bread.

Table 2.1

Type of Bread	Ingredients Required				
	A	B	C	D	E
I	3	2	1	1	0
II	1	1	1	1	1
III	2	1	2	1	1

If an order is placed for 60 loaves of type I, 75 loaves of type II, and 50 loaves of type III, find the number of units of each ingredient required by the bakery to fill the order. The order can be represented as the matrix [60   75   50], and the required ingredients can be written as the matrix

$$\begin{bmatrix} 3 & 2 & 1 & 1 & 0 \\ 1 & 1 & 1 & 1 & 1 \\ 2 & 1 & 2 & 1 & 1 \end{bmatrix}$$

The ingredients required to fill the order are given by the product of the two matrices.

$$[60 \quad 75 \quad 50] \cdot \begin{bmatrix} 3 & 2 & 1 & 1 & 0 \\ 1 & 1 & 1 & 1 & 1 \\ 2 & 1 & 2 & 1 & 1 \end{bmatrix} = [355 \quad 245 \quad 235 \quad 185 \quad 125]$$

If the per-unit costs to the bakery of the ingredients A, B, C, D, and E are given by

$$\begin{bmatrix} \$0.10 \\ \$0.08 \\ \$0.06 \\ \$0.05 \\ \$0.07 \end{bmatrix}$$

then the cost for each type of bread can be found by multiplying

$$\begin{bmatrix} 3 & 2 & 1 & 1 & 0 \\ 1 & 1 & 1 & 1 & 1 \\ 2 & 1 & 2 & 1 & 1 \end{bmatrix} \quad \text{and} \quad \begin{bmatrix} \$0.10 \\ \$0.08 \\ \$0.06 \\ \$0.05 \\ \$0.07 \end{bmatrix}$$

to obtain

$$\begin{bmatrix} \$0.57 \\ \$0.36 \\ \$0.52 \end{bmatrix}$$

The cost for the ingredients required to fill the order is then obtained by multiplying the order matrix by this cost matrix.

$$[60 \quad 75 \quad 50] \cdot \begin{bmatrix} \$0.57 \\ \$0.36 \\ \$0.52 \end{bmatrix} = (60)(\$0.57) + 75(\$0.36) + 50(\$0.52)$$

$$= \$34.20 + \$27.00 + \$26.00$$

$$= \$87.20$$

It could also be obtained by multiplying the number of unit ingredients required by the cost per unit:

$$[355 \quad 245 \quad 235 \quad 185 \quad 125] \cdot \begin{bmatrix} \$0.10 \\ \$0.08 \\ \$0.06 \\ \$0.05 \\ \$0.07 \end{bmatrix} = \$35.50 + \$19.60 + \$14.10 \\ + \$9.25 + \$8.75$$

$$= \$87.20$$

If the bakery sells the bread for $0.76 a loaf for type I, $0.62 a loaf for type II, and $0.72 a loaf for type III, the amount received by the bakery for the order would be

$$[60 \quad 75 \quad 50] \cdot \begin{bmatrix} \$0.76 \\ \$0.62 \\ \$0.72 \end{bmatrix} = \$45.60 + \$46.50 + \$36.00$$

$$= \$128.10$$

The profit received by the bakery is then $128.10 - $87.20 = $40.90 for the order. This amount could have been obtained by noticing that the bakery makes the following profit on each loaf of bread:

$$\begin{matrix} \text{Type I} \\ \text{Type II} \\ \text{Type III} \end{matrix} \begin{bmatrix} \$0.19 \\ \$0.26 \\ \$0.20 \end{bmatrix}$$

Multiplying the order matrix by this profit matrix gives the same result for profit:

$$[60 \quad 75 \quad 50] \cdot \begin{bmatrix} \$0.19 \\ \$0.26 \\ \$0.20 \end{bmatrix} = \$11.40 + \$19.50 + \$10.00 = \$40.90$$

Matrices can also be used to replace a system of equations by a single matrix equation.

EXAMPLE 24   Write the following system of equations in matrix form.

$$\begin{aligned} 3x_1 + 4x_2 - 2x_3 + x_4 &= 5 \\ -x_1 + 3x_2 \qquad\quad - 2x_4 &= 7 \\ 2x_1 + 3x_2 + x_3 - x_4 &= 0 \\ x_1 - x_2 - x_3 + 3x_4 &= -2 \end{aligned}$$

This set of four equations in four unknowns can be replaced by the single matrix equation

$$\begin{bmatrix} 3 & 4 & -2 & 1 \\ -1 & 3 & 0 & -2 \\ 2 & 3 & 1 & -1 \\ 1 & -1 & -1 & 3 \end{bmatrix} \begin{bmatrix} x_1 \\ x_2 \\ x_3 \\ x_4 \end{bmatrix} = \begin{bmatrix} 5 \\ 7 \\ 0 \\ -2 \end{bmatrix}$$

as can be seen by multiplying the two matrices on the left to obtain

$$\begin{bmatrix} 3x_1 + 4x_2 - 2x_3 + x_4 \\ -x_1 + 3x_2 \qquad - 2x_4 \\ 2x_1 + 3x_2 + x_3 - x_4 \\ x_1 - x_2 - x_3 + 3x_4 \end{bmatrix} = \begin{bmatrix} 5 \\ 7 \\ 0 \\ -2 \end{bmatrix}$$

Since the two matrices are equal, the definition of equality demands that their corresponding elements be equal. Hence, we obtain the given system of equations. If

$$\mathbf{A} = \begin{bmatrix} 3 & 4 & -2 & 1 \\ -1 & 3 & 0 & -2 \\ 2 & 3 & 1 & -1 \\ 1 & -1 & -1 & 3 \end{bmatrix}, \quad \mathbf{X} = \begin{bmatrix} x_1 \\ x_2 \\ x_3 \\ x_4 \end{bmatrix}, \quad \text{and} \quad \mathbf{B} = \begin{bmatrix} 5 \\ 7 \\ 0 \\ -2 \end{bmatrix}$$

then the given system becomes the simple matrix equation $\mathbf{AX} = \mathbf{B}$.

Mathematical models use matrices extensively. The following example illustrates how a mathematical model using matrices can aid college administrators in their plans and decisions.

EXAMPLE 25 The National Center for Higher Education Management Systems uses matrices as models to study college management. The elements of an important matrix in this model, the induced course-load matrix, are the average numbers of units taken in each field by students classified according to majors.

Majors

Fields		History	English	Biology	Chemistry	Business	Undecided
	History	3.5	3.8	1.5	1.0	1.5	2.8
	English	3.8	4.5	1.5	1.5	2.5	3.2
	Mathematics	2.5	1.8	1.6	2.6	2.0	2.5
	Biology	1.6	1.8	6.0	1.9	1.0	2.0
	Chemistry	0.2	0.1	1.4	5.0	0.0	1.2
	Accounting	0.4	0.0	0.0	0.0	3.5	0.3
	Economics	1.5	1.5	1.5	1.5	3.0	1.5
	Physical Ed.	1.5	1.5	1.5	1.5	1.5	1.5
	Total	15	15	15	15	15	15

For example, English majors on the average take 3.8 units per year of history, and business majors take 3.5 units of accounting.

Suppose a hypothetical college, Micro U, decides to limit enrollment to 100 majors each in history, English, and business; 40 majors each in biology and chemistry; and 200 students classified as undecided. How many units of each field will need to be taught?

We first write the enrollment by majors as a column matrix:

$$
\begin{bmatrix} 100 \\ 100 \\ 40 \\ 40 \\ 100 \\ 200 \end{bmatrix}
\begin{array}{l} \text{history} \\ \text{English} \\ \text{biology} \\ \text{chemistry} \\ \text{business} \\ \text{undecided} \end{array}
$$

Multiplying the induced course-load matrix by the enrollment matrix gives a matrix answer in which the components are the units to be taught in each field.

$$
\begin{bmatrix}
3.5 & 3.8 & 1.5 & 1.0 & 1.5 & 2.8 \\
3.8 & 4.5 & 1.5 & 1.5 & 2.5 & 3.2 \\
2.5 & 1.8 & 1.6 & 2.6 & 2.0 & 2.5 \\
1.6 & 1.8 & 6.0 & 1.9 & 1.0 & 2.0 \\
0.2 & 0.1 & 1.4 & 5.0 & 0.0 & 1.2 \\
0.4 & 0.0 & 0.0 & 0.0 & 3.5 & 0.3 \\
1.5 & 1.5 & 1.5 & 1.5 & 3.0 & 1.5 \\
1.5 & 1.5 & 1.5 & 1.5 & 1.5 & 1.5
\end{bmatrix}
\begin{bmatrix} 100 \\ 100 \\ 40 \\ 40 \\ 100 \\ 200 \end{bmatrix}
=
\begin{bmatrix} 1540 \\ 1840 \\ 1298 \\ 1156 \\ 526 \\ 450 \\ 1020 \\ 870 \end{bmatrix}
$$

Exercise Set **2.3**

A **1.** Perform the following indicated operations when possible. If impossible, explain why.

a. $[1 \quad 3] \begin{bmatrix} 4 & 2 & 3 \\ -1 & 0 & 2 \end{bmatrix}$

b. $\begin{bmatrix} 4 & 2 & 3 \\ -1 & 0 & 2 \end{bmatrix} + [1 \quad 3]$

c. $5 \begin{bmatrix} 4 & 2 & 3 \\ -1 & 0 & 2 \end{bmatrix} + \begin{bmatrix} 3 \\ -1 \end{bmatrix} [1 \quad 7 \quad 5]$

d. $\begin{bmatrix} 3 & 2 \\ 4 & 1 \end{bmatrix} \begin{bmatrix} 3 \\ 1 \end{bmatrix}$

e. $\begin{bmatrix} 3 & 2 & 5 \\ 1 & 6 & 7 \\ 0 & 5 & -2 \end{bmatrix} + \begin{bmatrix} -2 & 5 & 1 \\ 1 & 2 & 3 \\ 3 & 2 & 1 \end{bmatrix}$

f. $\begin{bmatrix} 2 & 1 \\ 3 & 5 \end{bmatrix} + \begin{bmatrix} 3 & 0 & 5 \\ 2 & 1 & 3 \\ 5 & 2 & 1 \end{bmatrix}$

2. Combine each into a single matrix.

a. $3 \begin{bmatrix} 2 & 1 \\ 0 & 5 \end{bmatrix}$

b. $2 \begin{bmatrix} 2 & 1 & -1 & 3 \\ 4 & 2 & 0 & -1 \\ 0 & 0 & 2 & -1 \end{bmatrix}$

c. $5 \begin{bmatrix} 7 & 3 & 1 \\ 2 & 4 & -1 \end{bmatrix} - 4 \begin{bmatrix} 0 & 5 & -1 \\ 3 & -2 & 4 \end{bmatrix}$

3. Find the dot product of the following matrices (or vectors) if defined.

a. $\begin{bmatrix} 3 & -2 & 5 \end{bmatrix} \cdot \begin{bmatrix} 3 \\ 4 \end{bmatrix}$ **b.** $\begin{bmatrix} 3 & -2 & 5 \end{bmatrix} \cdot \begin{bmatrix} 1 \\ 0 \\ 4 \\ 1 \end{bmatrix}$

c. $\begin{bmatrix} 3 & -2 & 5 \end{bmatrix} \cdot \begin{bmatrix} 1 \\ 0 \\ 4 \end{bmatrix}$ **d.** $\begin{bmatrix} 1 & 2 \end{bmatrix} \cdot \begin{bmatrix} 1 \\ 2 \\ 3 \end{bmatrix}$

4. Find the additive inverses of the following matrices.

a. $\begin{bmatrix} 1 & -2 \\ 3 & 4 \end{bmatrix}$ **b.** $\begin{bmatrix} 2 & 3 & 4 & 5 \\ 1 & 0 & 5 & 2 \end{bmatrix}$ **c.** $\begin{bmatrix} 0 & 0 & 0 \\ 0 & 0 & 0 \end{bmatrix}$ **d.** $\begin{bmatrix} -1 & 2 & 3 \\ 1 & -2 & -3 \end{bmatrix}$

5. Find x if $\begin{bmatrix} 3 & -2 & 0 & 5 \end{bmatrix} \cdot \begin{bmatrix} 4 \\ 5 \\ 3 \\ x \end{bmatrix} = -13.$

6. Find x, y, and z (where given) in the following matrices.

a. $\begin{bmatrix} x \\ y \\ z \end{bmatrix} = 4 \begin{bmatrix} -1 \\ 2 \\ 5 \end{bmatrix}$ **b.** $\begin{bmatrix} 3 \\ 4 \end{bmatrix} + \begin{bmatrix} x \\ y \end{bmatrix} = \begin{bmatrix} 7 \\ 10 \end{bmatrix}$

c. $\begin{bmatrix} 0 \\ 0 \\ 0 \end{bmatrix} = 3 \begin{bmatrix} x \\ y \\ z \end{bmatrix}$ **d.** $\begin{bmatrix} 6 \\ x \end{bmatrix} = \begin{bmatrix} x + y \\ -3 \end{bmatrix}$

B 7. Find the product of the following matrices if possible.

a. $\begin{bmatrix} 3 & 5 & 1 & 2 \\ 2 & 4 & 0 & -1 \end{bmatrix} \begin{bmatrix} 1 & 1 & 3 \\ 2 & -1 & 5 \\ 3 & 0 & 2 \\ 4 & 2 & 1 \end{bmatrix}$ **b.** $\begin{bmatrix} 1 & 1 & 3 \\ 2 & 1 & 5 \\ 3 & 0 & 2 \\ 4 & 2 & 1 \end{bmatrix} \begin{bmatrix} 3 & 5 & 1 & 2 \\ 2 & 4 & 0 & -1 \end{bmatrix}$

c. $\begin{bmatrix} 3 & 2 & 1 \\ 1 & 0 & -1 \\ 2 & 1 & 1 \end{bmatrix} \begin{bmatrix} 1 & 5 & 2 \\ 0 & 2 & 1 \\ 0 & 0 & 5 \end{bmatrix}$ **d.** $\begin{bmatrix} 1 & 5 & 2 \\ 0 & 2 & 1 \\ 0 & 0 & 5 \end{bmatrix} \begin{bmatrix} 3 & 2 & 1 \\ 1 & 0 & -1 \\ 2 & 1 & 1 \end{bmatrix}$

e. $\begin{bmatrix} 2 & 0 & 0 \\ 0 & 1 & -1 \\ 7 & 0 & 0 \end{bmatrix} \begin{bmatrix} 0 & 0 & 0 \\ 3 & 3 & 3 \\ 3 & 3 & 3 \end{bmatrix}$ **f.** $\begin{bmatrix} 0 & 0 & 0 \\ 3 & 3 & 3 \\ 3 & 3 & 3 \end{bmatrix} \begin{bmatrix} 2 & 0 & 0 \\ 0 & 1 & -1 \\ 7 & 0 & 0 \end{bmatrix}$

g. $\begin{bmatrix} 1 & 4 \\ 2 & 5 \\ 3 & 6 \end{bmatrix} \begin{bmatrix} 3 & 1 & 5 \\ 2 & 0 & 3 \end{bmatrix}$ **h.** $\begin{bmatrix} 3 & -1 & 5 \\ 2 & 0 & 3 \end{bmatrix} \begin{bmatrix} 1 & 4 \\ 2 & 5 \\ 3 & 6 \end{bmatrix}$

i. $\begin{bmatrix} 3 \\ 7 \\ 2 \end{bmatrix} \cdot \begin{bmatrix} 1 & 5 & 4 \end{bmatrix}$ **j.** $\begin{bmatrix} 2 & 1 \\ 3 & 4 \end{bmatrix} \begin{bmatrix} 1 & 2 & 3 \\ 0 & 1 & 5 \\ -1 & 1 & 1 \end{bmatrix}$

8. Perform the indicated operations when possible. When impossible, explain why.

a. $\begin{bmatrix} 3 & 5 & 1 & 2 \\ 2 & 4 & 0 & -1 \end{bmatrix} \begin{bmatrix} 1 & 1 \\ 2 & -1 \\ 3 & 0 \\ 4 & 2 \end{bmatrix}$

b. $\begin{bmatrix} 1 & 1 & 3 \\ 2 & 1 & 4 \\ 3 & 1 & 5 \end{bmatrix} \begin{bmatrix} 3 & 5 & 2 \\ 6 & 1 & 4 \end{bmatrix}$

c. $\begin{bmatrix} 2 & 0 & 0 \\ 0 & 1 & -1 \\ 7 & 0 & 0 \end{bmatrix} \begin{bmatrix} 0 & 0 & 0 \\ 3 & 3 & 3 \\ -1 & -1 & -1 \end{bmatrix}$

d. $\begin{bmatrix} 3 & -1 & 5 \\ 2 & 0 & 3 \end{bmatrix} \begin{bmatrix} 2 & 3 \\ 1 & -1 \end{bmatrix}$

9. If $\begin{bmatrix} 3 & 5 \\ 2 & 1 \end{bmatrix} \mathbf{X} = \begin{bmatrix} -9 \\ 1 \end{bmatrix}$, find $\mathbf{X}$. $\left(\textit{Hint:} \quad \text{Let } \mathbf{X} = \begin{bmatrix} x_1 \\ x_2 \end{bmatrix}. \right)$

10. If $\begin{bmatrix} 3 & 7 & 2 & 5 \\ 4 & -1 & 2 & 0 \end{bmatrix} + \mathbf{X} = \begin{bmatrix} -1 & 3 & 2 & 1 \\ 0 & 2 & 3 & 1 \end{bmatrix}$, find $\mathbf{X}$.

11. Show that

$$\begin{bmatrix} 1 & 0 & 0 \\ 0 & 5 & 0 \\ 0 & 0 & 9 \end{bmatrix} \begin{bmatrix} 3 & 0 & 0 \\ 0 & -1 & 0 \\ 0 & 0 & 2 \end{bmatrix} = \begin{bmatrix} 3 & 0 & 0 \\ 0 & -1 & 0 \\ 0 & 0 & 2 \end{bmatrix} \begin{bmatrix} 1 & 0 & 0 \\ 0 & 5 & 0 \\ 0 & 0 & 9 \end{bmatrix}$$

12. Show that

$$\begin{bmatrix} 3 & 4 \\ 2 & 1 \end{bmatrix} \begin{bmatrix} 5 & 2 \\ 3 & 4 \end{bmatrix} \neq \begin{bmatrix} 5 & 2 \\ 3 & 4 \end{bmatrix} \begin{bmatrix} 3 & 4 \\ 2 & 1 \end{bmatrix}$$

C **13.** Let $\mathbf{A} = \begin{bmatrix} 1 & -2 \\ 2 & 0 \end{bmatrix}$, $\mathbf{B} = \begin{bmatrix} -1 & 2 \\ 1 & 1 \end{bmatrix}$, and $\mathbf{C} = \begin{bmatrix} -1 & 2 \\ 2 & 1 \end{bmatrix}$.

Compute the following products.

a. $\mathbf{AB}$ **b.** $\mathbf{BA}$ **c.** $(\mathbf{AB})\mathbf{C}$
d. $\mathbf{BC}$ **e.** $\mathbf{A}(\mathbf{BC})$ **f.** $\mathbf{A}^2$
g. $\mathbf{B}^2$ **h.** $\mathbf{A}^3$ **i.** $(\mathbf{A} + \mathbf{B})(\mathbf{A} + \mathbf{B})$

14. **a.** From exercise 13, verify that the multiplication of matrices is not commutative.
b. With an example show that the multiplication of matrices is associative if all multiplications are defined.
c. Verify that $\mathbf{A}^2 - \mathbf{B}^2 \neq (\mathbf{A} + \mathbf{B})(\mathbf{A} - \mathbf{B})$.
d. Verify that $(\mathbf{A} + \mathbf{B})^2 \neq \mathbf{A}^2 + 2\mathbf{AB} + \mathbf{B}^2$.

Business **15.** **Investments.** An investment club purchases the following stocks.

Number of Shares	Company	Price per Share
150	IBM	$120
200	Pfizer	54
300	American Home Products	62
100	Delta Airlines	54

a. Form a row matrix showing the number of shares purchased.
b. Form a column matrix showing the price of each stock.
c. Find the dot product to give the total cost of the stocks.

16. **Profit.** If the bakery referred to in this section receives an order for 70 loaves of type I, 60 loaves of type II, and 80 loaves of type III bread, find the ingredients required to fill the order and the profit that the bakery makes.

Life Sciences   **17. Pollution.** Lownes Chemical is accused of polluting Bacon Creek by dumping industrial wastes from four manufacturing processes. Three pollutants are found in the creek. The following milliliters of pollutants are found per 1000 liters of water.

$$
\begin{array}{c}
 \\
\begin{array}{cccc}
 & \text{Pollutant 1} & \text{Pollutant 2} & \text{Pollutant 3}
\end{array} \\
\begin{array}{c}
\text{Process A} \\
\text{Process B} \\
\text{Process C} \\
\text{Process D}
\end{array}
\begin{bmatrix}
6 & 1 & 4 \\
3 & 2 & 2 \\
7 & 4 & 1 \\
8 & 10 & 3
\end{bmatrix}
\end{array}
$$

Equipment is purchased to reduce the three pollutants as follows:

$$
\begin{array}{c}
\text{Pollutant 1} \\
\text{Pollutant 2} \\
\text{Pollutant 3}
\end{array}
\begin{bmatrix}
0.80 \\
0.40 \\
0.60
\end{bmatrix}
$$

How many milliliters of pollutants still remain for each process?

Social Sciences   **18. Education.** If Micro U, the hypothetical college referred to in this section, decides to limit enrollment to 150 majors each in history and English, 100 majors in business, 50 majors each in biology and chemistry, and 200 undecided, how many units of each field will need to be taught?

19. Incidence Matrix. Incidence matrices are used in communication network studies and in sociological relationships.

$$
\begin{array}{c}
\phantom{\text{Sender}} \\
\begin{array}{ccccc}
 & & \text{Possible Receivers} & & \\
\text{Sender} & 1 & 2 & 3 & 4
\end{array} \\
\mathbf{A} =
\begin{array}{c}
1 \\
2 \\
3 \\
4
\end{array}
\begin{bmatrix}
0 & 1 & 0 & 1 \\
1 & 0 & 0 & 1 \\
1 & 1 & 0 & 0 \\
1 & 1 & 1 & 0
\end{bmatrix}
\end{array}
$$

A 1 under possible receiver 2 in row 1 indicates that station 2 does receive a transmission from sender 1. A 0 under possible receiver 3 in row 1 indicates that station 3 does not receive the transmission from sender 1.

$\mathbf{A}^2$ is used to summarize two-stage transmissions. That is, a 1 indicates that there is a transmission from one station to another through a third station. A 2 indicates that there are two ways to go through an intermediate station. Find $\mathbf{A}^2$ and $\mathbf{A}^3$ and explain the elements of each.

20. Transportation. The following figure shows the routes of direct air flights among five cities.

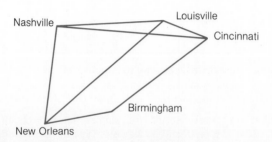

The same information can be represented by the following matrix:

	New Orleans	Birmingham	Nashville	Louisville	Cincinnati
New Orleans	0	1	1	1	0
Birmingham	1	0	0	0	1
A = Nashville	1	0	0	1	1
Louisville	1	0	1	0	1
Cincinnati	0	1	1	1	0

Verify that $\mathbf{A}^2$ is the number of one-stop flights among these five cities.

4 Systems with Three or More Variables

> Now that we know how to solve a system of two equations in two variables by using augmented matrices and have a better understanding of the theory of matrices, there is no reason why we should not extend this theory to three variables. In fact, we could study the solution of n equations in n unknowns. Systems with a large number of equations and variables are very common today because of the accessibility of high-speed computers.

The solution of an equation in three variables, such as

$$x + 2y - 3z + 6 = 0$$

is an ordered triplet (x, y, z). For example, $(-3, 0, 1)$ is a solution since

$$1(-3) + 2(0) - 3(1) + 6 = 0$$
$$-3 - 3 + 6 = 0$$

The solution set for a system of three equations in three unknowns is the intersection of the three sets of ordered triplets that satisfy the three equations.

EXAMPLE 26　Solve the system of equations

$$x + 2y - 3z + 6 = 0$$
$$2x - y + z + 1 = 0$$
$$3x + 2y + z - 4 = 0$$

Solution　The augmented matrix for this system is

$$\begin{bmatrix} 1 & 2 & -3 & | & -6 \\ 2 & -1 & 1 & | & -1 \\ 3 & 2 & 1 & | & 4 \end{bmatrix}$$

Goal	Row Operation	Row Equivalent Matrix
1. Make the coefficient of x in the first equation 1.	1. No operation is necessary.	1. Same as given
2. Make the coefficient of x in the second and third equation 0.	2. Multiply the first row by -2 and add to the second row. Then multiply the first row by -3 and add to the third row.	2. $\begin{bmatrix} 1 & 2 & -3 & \vert & -6 \\ 0 & -5 & 7 & \vert & 11 \\ 0 & -4 & 10 & \vert & 22 \end{bmatrix}$
3. Make the coefficient of y in the second equation 1.	3. Multiply the second row by $-\frac{1}{5}$.	3. $\begin{bmatrix} 1 & 2 & -3 & \vert & -6 \\ 0 & 1 & -\frac{7}{5} & \vert & -\frac{11}{5} \\ 0 & -4 & 10 & \vert & 22 \end{bmatrix}$
4. Make the coefficients of y in the first and third equations 0.	4. Multiply the second row by -2 and add to the first row. Then multiply the second row by 4 and add to the third row.	4. $\begin{bmatrix} 1 & 0 & -\frac{1}{5} & \vert & -\frac{8}{5} \\ 0 & 1 & -\frac{7}{5} & \vert & -\frac{11}{5} \\ 0 & 0 & \frac{22}{5} & \vert & \frac{66}{5} \end{bmatrix}$
5. Make the coefficient of z in the third equation 1.	5. Multiply the third row by $\frac{5}{22}$.	5. $\begin{bmatrix} 1 & 0 & -\frac{1}{5} & \vert & -\frac{8}{5} \\ 0 & 1 & -\frac{7}{5} & \vert & -\frac{11}{5} \\ 0 & 0 & 1 & \vert & 3 \end{bmatrix}$
6. Make the coefficients of z in the first and second equations 0.	6. Multiply the third row by $\frac{1}{5}$ and add to the first row. Then multiply the third row by $\frac{7}{5}$ and add to the second row.	6. $\begin{bmatrix} 1 & 0 & 0 & \vert & -1 \\ 0 & 1 & 0 & \vert & 2 \\ 0 & 0 & 1 & \vert & 3 \end{bmatrix}$

The system becomes

$$1 \cdot x + 0 \cdot y + 0 \cdot z = -1 \qquad\qquad x \qquad\quad = -1$$
$$0 \cdot x + 1 \cdot y + 0 \cdot z = 2 \quad \text{or} \qquad\quad y \quad = 2$$
$$0 \cdot x + 0 \cdot y + 1 \cdot z = 3 \qquad\qquad\qquad z = 3$$

Sometimes it is not possible to reduce a matrix of coefficients to an identity matrix. Then we need to define what we mean by a matrix in reduced form.

Reduced Matrix

A matrix is in reduced form if:
1. The leftmost nonzero element in each row is 1.
2. The leftmost nonzero element in a row has all 0s above it and all 0s below it in its column.
3. The first nonzero element in each row is to the right of the first nonzero element in each row above it.
4. Rows containing all 0s are below the rows containing nonzero elements.

EXAMPLE 27 Solve

$$x + 2y - 3z = -7$$
$$2x - y + z = -1$$
$$3x + 2y + z = 7$$

The augmented matrix for this system is

$$\left[\begin{array}{ccc|c} 1 & 2 & -3 & -7 \\ 2 & -1 & 1 & -1 \\ 3 & 2 & 1 & 7 \end{array}\right]$$

Goal	Row Operation	Row Equivalent Matrix
1. To change the 2 and then the 3 to 0s in column 1	-2(row 1) + (row 2) and -3(row 1) + (row 3)	$\left[\begin{array}{ccc\|c} 1 & 2 & -3 & -7 \\ 0 & -5 & 7 & 13 \\ 0 & -4 & 10 & 28 \end{array}\right]$
2. To change -5 to a 1 in row 2	$-\frac{1}{5}$(row 2)	$\left[\begin{array}{ccc\|c} 1 & 2 & -3 & -7 \\ 0 & 1 & -\frac{7}{5} & -\frac{13}{5} \\ 0 & -4 & 10 & 28 \end{array}\right]$
3. To change the 2 and the -4 in column 2 to 0s	-2(row 2) + (row 1) and 4(row 2) + (row 3)	$\left[\begin{array}{ccc\|c} 1 & 0 & -\frac{1}{5} & -\frac{9}{5} \\ 0 & 1 & -\frac{7}{5} & -\frac{13}{5} \\ 0 & 0 & \frac{22}{5} & \frac{88}{5} \end{array}\right]$
4. To change $\frac{22}{5}$ to a 1 in row 3	$\frac{5}{22}$(row 3)	$\left[\begin{array}{ccc\|c} 1 & 0 & -\frac{1}{5} & -\frac{9}{5} \\ 0 & 0 & -\frac{7}{5} & -\frac{13}{5} \\ 0 & 0 & 1 & 4 \end{array}\right]$
5. To change $-\frac{1}{5}$ and $-\frac{7}{5}$ to 0s in column 3	$\frac{1}{5}$(row 3) + (row 1) and $\frac{7}{5}$(row 3) + (row 2)	$\left[\begin{array}{ccc\|c} 1 & 0 & 0 & -1 \\ 0 & 1 & 0 & 3 \\ 0 & 0 & 1 & 4 \end{array}\right]$

Note that the last equivalent matrix satisfies the requirements of a reduced matrix. Thus,

$$\begin{array}{lll} 1(x) + 0(y) + 0(z) = -1 & & x = -1 \\ 0(x) + 1(y) + 0(z) = 3 & \text{or} & y = 3 \\ 0(x) + 0(y) + 1(z) = 4 & & z = 4 \end{array}$$

Suppose the last equivalent matrix of a system is of the form

$$\left[\begin{array}{ccc|c} 1 & 0 & 2 & -3 \\ 0 & 1 & -1 & 4 \\ 0 & 0 & 0 & 0 \end{array}\right]$$

This matrix is in reduced form but does not give a unique solution:

$$\begin{array}{l} 1 \cdot x + 0 \cdot y + 2 \cdot z = -3 \\ 0 \cdot x + 1 \cdot y - 1 \cdot z = 4 \\ 0 \cdot x + 0 \cdot y + 0 \cdot z = 0 \end{array}$$

The value of z is arbitrary or can be anything to satisfy the last equation. We can assign $z = c$. Then x, y, and z are all given in terms of the parameter c: $x = -3 - 2c$, $y = 4 + c$, and $z = c$.

When there are more variables than equations, the reduced matrix generally gives answers that must be expressed in terms of a parameter, say, c. For example, the reduced matrix for the system

$$2x - y + z = 4$$
$$x + y + 2z = 5$$

is

$$\begin{bmatrix} 1 & 0 & 1 & | & 3 \\ 0 & 1 & 1 & | & 2 \end{bmatrix}$$

So $x = 3 - z$ and $y = 2 - z$. Now let z be any parameter c. Then $x = 3 - c$ and $y = 2 - c$.

EXAMPLE 28 Solve the following system by operations on the augmented matrix.

$$2y + 3z - 7t = 3$$
$$2x + z - 2t = -5$$
$$4x + y + z - 5t = -6$$
$$y + 2z - 4t = 1$$

Solution The augmented matrix is

$$\begin{bmatrix} 0 & 2 & 3 & -7 & | & 3 \\ 2 & 0 & 1 & -2 & | & -5 \\ 4 & 1 & 1 & -5 & | & -6 \\ 0 & 1 & 2 & -4 & | & 1 \end{bmatrix}$$

Interchange the first and second rows to give a matrix that has a nonzero element in the first row and first column:

$$\begin{bmatrix} 2 & 0 & 1 & -2 & | & -5 \\ 0 & 2 & 3 & -7 & | & 3 \\ 4 & 1 & 1 & -5 & | & -6 \\ 0 & 1 & 2 & -4 & | & 1 \end{bmatrix}$$

Multiply the first row by $\frac{1}{2}$ to obtain

$$\begin{bmatrix} 1 & 0 & \frac{1}{2} & -1 & | & -\frac{5}{2} \\ 0 & 2 & 3 & -7 & | & 3 \\ 4 & 1 & 1 & -5 & | & -6 \\ 0 & 1 & 2 & -4 & | & 1 \end{bmatrix}$$

Multiply the first row by -4 and add the result to the third row:

$$\begin{bmatrix} 1 & 0 & \frac{1}{2} & -1 & | & -\frac{5}{2} \\ 0 & 2 & 3 & -7 & | & 3 \\ 0 & 1 & -1 & -1 & | & 4 \\ 0 & 1 & 2 & -4 & | & 1 \end{bmatrix}$$

Multiply the second row by $\frac{1}{2}$ to obtain

$$\left[\begin{array}{cccc|c} 1 & 0 & \frac{1}{2} & -1 & -\frac{5}{2} \\ 0 & 1 & \frac{3}{2} & -\frac{7}{2} & \frac{3}{2} \\ 0 & 1 & -1 & -1 & 4 \\ 0 & 1 & 2 & -4 & 1 \end{array}\right]$$

Multiply the second row by -1 and add the result to the third row and to the fourth row to obtain

$$\left[\begin{array}{cccc|c} 1 & 0 & \frac{1}{2} & -1 & -\frac{5}{2} \\ 0 & 1 & \frac{3}{2} & -\frac{7}{2} & \frac{3}{2} \\ 0 & 0 & -\frac{5}{2} & \frac{5}{2} & \frac{5}{2} \\ 0 & 0 & \frac{1}{2} & -\frac{1}{2} & -\frac{1}{2} \end{array}\right]$$

Multiply the third row by $-\frac{2}{5}$ to get

$$\left[\begin{array}{cccc|c} 1 & 0 & \frac{1}{2} & -1 & -\frac{5}{2} \\ 0 & 1 & \frac{3}{2} & -\frac{7}{2} & \frac{3}{2} \\ 0 & 0 & 1 & -1 & -1 \\ 0 & 0 & \frac{1}{2} & -\frac{1}{2} & -\frac{1}{2} \end{array}\right]$$

Multiply the third row by $-\frac{1}{2}$ and add the result to the fourth row; multiply the third row by $-\frac{1}{2}$ and add the result to the first row; and multiply the third row by $-\frac{3}{2}$ and add the result to the second row to obtain

$$\left[\begin{array}{cccc|c} 1 & 0 & 0 & -\frac{1}{2} & -2 \\ 0 & 1 & 0 & -2 & 3 \\ 0 & 0 & 1 & -1 & -1 \\ 0 & 0 & 0 & 0 & 0 \end{array}\right]$$

Note that the augmented matrix is now in reduced form. It is the augmented matrix for the system

$$\begin{aligned} x + 0 \cdot y + 0 \cdot z - \quad \tfrac{1}{2}t &= -2 \\ 0 \cdot x + \quad y + 0 \cdot z - \quad 2t &= \quad 3 \\ 0 \cdot x + 0 \cdot y + \quad z - \quad t &= -1 \\ 0 \cdot x + 0 \cdot y + 0 \cdot z + 0 \cdot t &= \quad 0 \end{aligned}$$

Since the bottom row of the matrix consists entirely of 0s, the value of t is arbitrary. Let c be a number chosen in any fashion but left fixed for a moment; then let

$$t = c$$

Then from the third equation,

$$z = c - 1$$

and from the second equation,

$$y = 2c + 3$$

and finally from the first equation,

$$x = \tfrac{1}{2}c - 2$$

For each value of c, a solution is obtained, so there is an infinite number of solutions. Assigning values to c gives some of the solutions. For example, $c = 0$ gives by substitution $x = -2$, $y = 3$, $z = -1$, and $t = 0$, which can be expressed as $(-2, 3, -1, 0)$. Similarly, $c = 2$ gives $(-1, 7, 1, 2)$. All of these solutions are contained in the solution set, which is written

$$\{(x, y, z, t) \,|\, x = \tfrac{1}{2}c - 2, \, y = 2c + 3, \, z = c - 1, \, t = c\}$$

Exercise Set 2.4

A The augmented matrices below are given in reduced form. Determine whether each system has a solution and find the solution or solutions if they exist. Use variables x, y, z, and possibly w.

1. $\begin{bmatrix} 1 & 0 & 0 & | & 3 \\ 0 & 1 & 0 & | & -1 \\ 0 & 0 & 1 & | & 4 \end{bmatrix}$

2. $\begin{bmatrix} 1 & 0 & 0 & | & 0 \\ 0 & 1 & 0 & | & 0 \\ 0 & 0 & 1 & | & 2 \end{bmatrix}$

3. $\begin{bmatrix} 1 & 0 & 2 & | & 3 \\ 0 & 1 & 1 & | & 1 \\ 0 & 0 & 0 & | & 0 \end{bmatrix}$

4. $\begin{bmatrix} 1 & 0 & 0 & | & 2 \\ 0 & 1 & 0 & | & -4 \\ 0 & 0 & 1 & | & 0 \end{bmatrix}$

5. $\begin{bmatrix} 1 & 0 & 0 & | & 6 \\ 0 & 1 & 0 & | & 1 \\ 0 & 0 & 0 & | & 4 \end{bmatrix}$

6. $\begin{bmatrix} 1 & 0 & 0 & | & 7 \\ 0 & 1 & 0 & | & 3 \\ 0 & 0 & 0 & | & 2 \end{bmatrix}$

7. $\begin{bmatrix} 1 & 0 & 0 & 0 & | & -2 \\ 0 & 1 & 0 & 0 & | & 4 \\ 0 & 0 & 1 & 0 & | & 6 \\ 0 & 0 & 0 & 1 & | & 1 \end{bmatrix}$

8. $\begin{bmatrix} 1 & 0 & 0 & 0 & | & 2 \\ 0 & 1 & 0 & 0 & | & 0 \\ 0 & 0 & 1 & 0 & | & 0 \\ 0 & 0 & 0 & 1 & | & 0 \end{bmatrix}$

9. $\begin{bmatrix} 1 & 0 & 0 & 0 & | & 3 \\ 0 & 1 & 0 & 0 & | & 4 \\ 0 & 0 & 1 & 0 & | & 5 \\ 0 & 0 & 0 & 0 & | & 2 \end{bmatrix}$

10. $\begin{bmatrix} 1 & 0 & 0 & 0 & | & 3 \\ 0 & 1 & 0 & 0 & | & 4 \\ 0 & 0 & 1 & 0 & | & 5 \\ 0 & 0 & 0 & 0 & | & 0 \end{bmatrix}$

Use augmented matrices to solve the following systems of three equations in three unknowns.

11. $\begin{aligned} x \quad\;\; + z &= 1 \\ y - 2z &= 3 \\ 3x + y + z &= 6 \end{aligned}$

12. $\begin{aligned} x + 2y + z &= 8 \\ 2x - y + 3z &= 9 \\ x - 2y - z &= -6 \end{aligned}$

13. $\begin{aligned} z - 4y &= 3 \\ 2x - z &= 5 \\ x - 3y &= 1 \end{aligned}$

14. $\begin{aligned} x + 2y &= 3 \\ x - 2z &= 7 \\ 3y + z &= 9 \end{aligned}$

15. $\begin{aligned} 3x + y + z &= 3 \\ 5x + 2y - 3z &= 0 \\ x + 2y + 2z &= 1 \end{aligned}$

16. $\begin{aligned} 2x - y + z &= 3 \\ x + 2y - z &= 2 \\ 3x - y + z &= 4 \end{aligned}$

17. $\begin{aligned} x \quad\;\; - z &= 1 \\ y + 2z &= 3 \\ 3x + y + z &= 6 \end{aligned}$

18. $\begin{aligned} x + 3y &= 10 \\ x - y - 4z &= -6 \\ 2x + 4y - 2z &= 12 \end{aligned}$

19.
$$x + 3y \qquad\quad = 10$$
$$2x + 6y \qquad\quad = 20$$
$$2x + 4y - 2z = 12$$

20.
$$x + 3y \qquad\quad = 10$$
$$2x + 6y \qquad\quad = 5$$
$$2x + 4y - 2z = 12$$

Solve the following systems in terms of an arbitrary parameter c. Let z = c.

21.
$$x - y + z = 4$$
$$2x + y - 2z = 6$$

22.
$$2x - y + 3z = 5$$
$$x + 2y - z = 2$$

B   **23.** Determine whether or not the following systems have solutions and solve those that have solutions.

a.
$$x + y + z = 5$$
$$2x - 3y + 2z = 4$$
$$4x - y + 4z = 10$$

b.
$$x - y - z = -3$$
$$3x - 4y - 2z = -11$$
$$5x - 6y - 4z = -17$$

c.
$$x - 2y - 3z = -3$$
$$7x - 14y - 21z = -21$$
$$11x - 22y - 33z = -33$$

d.
$$x + y + z = 5$$
$$2x + 3y - 2z = -19$$
$$3x + 2y + 3z = 20$$

C   **24.** Determine whether or not the following systems have solutions and solve those that have solutions.

a.
$$x + y + z - 2t = 2$$
$$2x + y + 6z + t = 18$$
$$3x + 2y + 4z - 4t = 11$$
$$4x + 3y + 8z - 3t = 22$$

b.
$$x + y + z + t = 2$$
$$x - y + z - t = 10$$
$$2x + y + z + t = 6$$
$$x + 2y + z - 2t = 2$$

c.
$$x + y + 3z + t = 2$$
$$x - y + 2z - t = 0$$
$$2x + y + z + t = 3$$
$$x + 2y - z - t = -3$$

d.
$$x + y - z - 3t = 0$$
$$2x - y - 5z = 3$$
$$5x + 2y - 8z - 9t = 3$$
$$9x - 18z - 9t = 9$$

e.
$$2x - y + z - t = 8$$
$$x + y - 3z = -4$$
$$3x + y - 5t = 3$$
$$x + y - z - 2t = -2$$

f.
$$x + y - 5z - t = -1$$
$$x - y + z - 5t = -9$$
$$2x + y - 7z - 4t = -6$$
$$x + 2y - 8z + t = 3$$

Business   **25. Bonds.** Sarah has a total of $12,400 invested in three types of bonds that pay 9%, 10%, and 11%, respectively. She receives $100 more interest from the 10% bonds than from the 11% bonds. If the total income from the bonds during a year is $1,250, how much has she invested in each type?

26. Bonds. Jeannette has $9,000 invested in bonds paying 14%, 16%, and 18% interest per year. She has $1,000 more invested at 16% than at 18%. If she receives $1,430 interest each year, how much money does she have invested in each type of bond?

27. Payroll. Large Company has 2000 laborers and 3000 office workers with a payroll of $46,000 per hour. The union has negotiated a contract that calls for an average pay raise of 7% per hour for laborers and 6% per hour for office workers for next year. Large Company officials have decided that only an additional $2,980 per hour will be available for pay raises next year. Help Large Company determine what the average pay per hour for laborers and office workers must be this year in order for Large Company to be able to satisfy the union's contract next year.

Economics   **28. Demand Curve.** The economist at Acme Corporation has noted that the demand curve for a given product is in the form of a parabola, $D = ap^2 + bp + c$. The demand was for two (actually two units of 100,000 each) when the price was $1, that is, $D = 2$ when $p = \$1$; $D = 1$ when $p = \$2$; and $D = \frac{1}{2}$ when $p = \$3$. Substitute these values for p and D and solve the three equations for a, b, and c. Predict the demand when the price is $4.

Life Sciences   **29. Pollution.** The pollution count for Big City on a particular day is 600. Assume that this pollution is produced by three industries—A, B, and C. Industry A contributes twice as much to the pollution count as industry B. It is known that the pollution count would be 500 if the pollution count from industry A were reduced by 50%. Find the pollution count of industries A, B, and C, respectively.

Social Sciences   **30. Traffic Flow.** The number of cars entering and leaving four intersections of one-way streets has been tabulated as shown in the diagram.

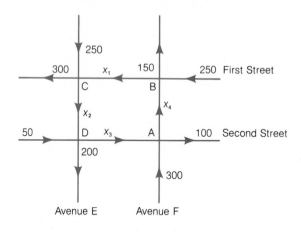

$$\text{At B:} \quad x_4 + 250 = x_1 + 150$$
$$\text{At C:} \quad x_2 + 300 = x_1 + 250$$

Find the equations at D and A. Set up and find a reduced augmented matrix. Note that you can solve for the three variables in terms of x_4. What is the smallest value x_4 can attain to have meaning? What are the other variables when x_4 takes on this value?

31. Student Enrollment. A well-known university has an enrollment of 2900 students composed of lower-division, upper-division, and graduate or professional students. A proud spokesperson for the graduate or professional students announces that 3 times their number of students is 100 students more than the number in the upper and lower divisions combined. Not to be outdone, the dean of lower-division students states that her enrollment is 150 more than the upper-division enrollment. Find the number of lower-division students, the number of upper-division students, and the number of graduate or professional students enrolled in the university.

 Geometric Interpretation of Linear Equations in Three-Space

> In order to discuss geometrically why unique solutions do not always exist, we now investigate geometric solutions in **three-space.** First we learn to locate points in three-space. Then we discuss the graph of a linear equation in three-space. Finally, we discuss the intersection of graphs of linear equations to determine why a system does not have a unique solution.

A coordinate system consisting of two perpendicular lines describes the set of all points in a plane, and these points make up what we call **two-space.** Now consider the lines formed by the intersection of the sides of a room; that is, consider a corner as the origin of a coordinate system. These lines and all the points in space located by this coordinate system constitute what is called **three-space.**

Figure 2.4 illustrates three mutually perpendicular lines that may be considered coordinate axes in three-space. Note that the axes are called x-, y-, and z-axes. The y- and z-axes are usually drawn in the plane of the paper, and the x-axis is drawn to look as if it were perpendicular to the plane of the paper. The dashed extensions of the axes in Figure 2.4 represent the negative portions of the axes.

Figure 2.4

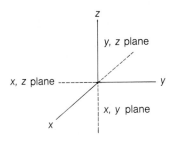

The plane formed by the x-axis and the y-axis is called the x, y-coordinate plane; the plane formed by the x-axis and the z-axis is called the x, z-coordinate plane; and the plane formed by the y-axis and the z-axis is called the y, z-coordinate plane.

Figure 2.5 illustrates the plotting of (5, 2, 4) or x = 5, y = 2, and z = 4 in three-space. The point (5, 2, 4) is located by moving 5 units in the direction of the positive x-axis, 2 units in the direction of the positive y-axis, and 4 units in the direction of the positive z-axis.

Figure 2.5

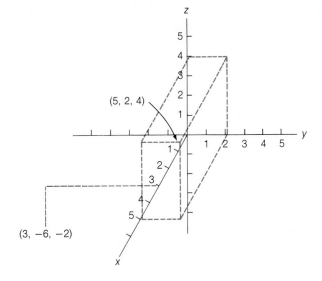

EXAMPLE 29   Plot the point $(3, -6, -2)$ on the coordinate system in Figure 2.5.

Solution   First measure 3 units in a positive direction on the x-axis. Then measure 6 units in a negative direction parallel to the y-axis, and finally measure 2 units in a negative direction parallel to the z-axis and mark the point $(3, -6, -2)$.

Any linear equation in three-space may be written as

$$ax + by + cz = d$$

where not all of a, b, and c are equal to 0. The graph of a linear equation in three-space consists of the set of points that constitute a plane. The easy way to draw a representation of a plane in three-space involves sketching *traces* of the plane. A **trace** of a plane on a coordinate plane is the line formed by the intersection of the coordinate plane and the given plane. For example, the trace of $3y + 4z + 2x = 16$ on the x, y-plane is $3y + 2x = 16$ because $z = 0$ on the x, y-plane. Since $y = 0$ on the x, z-plane, $4z + 2x = 16$ is the trace on the x, z-plane. The trace on the y, z-plane $(x = 0)$ is $3y + 4z = 16$. To represent the graph of the plane $3y + 4z + 2x = 16$ in three dimensions, we draw the three traces as shown in Figure 2.6 and shade the region bounded by the traces.

Figure 2.6

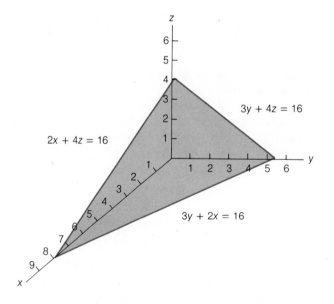

The traces can be obtained by determining the points (or intercepts) in which the coordinate axes intersect a given plane, as illustrated by the following example.

EXAMPLE 30   Sketch the traces of $2x + 5y + 4z = 10$ by finding the intercepts, and then shade the plane.

Solution   By letting $y = 0$ and $z = 0$, $2x = 10$ or $x = 5$ (the x-intercept). From $z = 0$ and $x = 0$, $5y = 10$ or $y = 2$ (the y-intercept). The z-intercept is obtained by setting

$y = 0$ and $x = 0$; that is, $4z = 10$, so $z = 2\frac{1}{2}$. The three intercepts are plotted in Figure 2.7; the lines connecting these points are the traces of the plane, which is shaded.

Figure 2.7

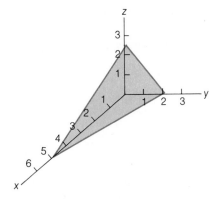

Special planes are obtained when some of the variables are missing in the three-dimensional linear equation.

EXAMPLE 31   Sketch the plane $y = -3$ in three-space.

Solution   This plane is parallel to the x, z-plane and 3 units in a negative direction from the x, z-plane (see Figure 2.8).

Figure 2.8

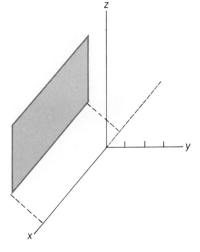

EXAMPLE 32   Sketch the plane $3y + 2z = 6$ in three-space.

Solution   The traces of the plane are $3y + 2z = 6$ on the y, z-plane, $y = 2$ on the x, y-plane, and $z = 3$ on the x, z-plane, as shown in Figure 2.9. This plane is perpendicular to the y, z-plane.

Figure 2.9

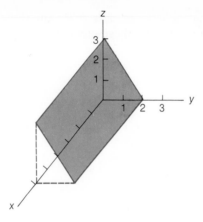

From this discussion of graphs in three-space, it should be evident now that the solution of three linear equations in three variables consists of the coordinates of the common intersection of three planes. The chart in Figure 2.10 summarizes the possibilities and gives the graphical interpretations.

Figure 2.10

Description	Graph
1. The common intersection consists of a single point	
2. The intersection is a line, and the system has infinitely many solutions	
3. The three planes coincide, and the system has infinitely many solutions	

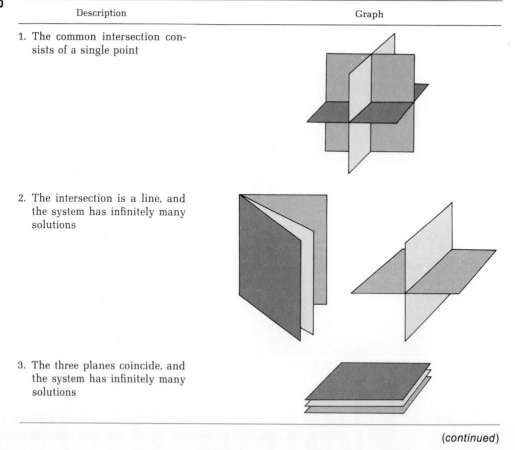

(*continued*)

Figure 2.10
(*continued*)

Description	Graph
4. The three planes are parallel and have no common intersection, and the solution set is the null set.	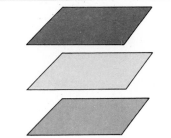
5. Two planes are parallel, and thus the solution set is the null set	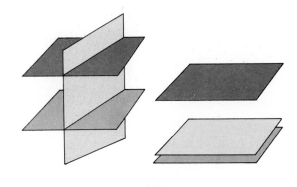
6. The planes intersect only in pairs of parallel lines, and the solution is the null set	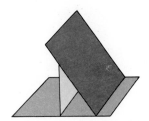

EXAMPLE 33   Find the graphical solution of

$$y + z + 2x = 4$$
$$y = 1$$
$$z = 2$$

and then verify your work by solving the system algebraically for the solution.

Solution   The traces of the plane of $y + z + 2x = 4$ are drawn in Figure 2.11. Both planes $y = 1$ and $z = 2$ are shaded. The intersection of the three planes is $(\frac{1}{2}, 1, 2)$.

Figure 2.11

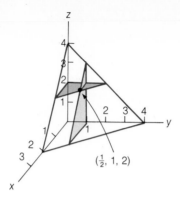

$(\frac{1}{2}, 1, 2)$

To find the algebraic solution, substitute $y = 1$ and $z = 2$ in $y + z + 2x = 4$

$$1 + 2 + 2x = 4$$
$$x = \tfrac{1}{2}$$

so the solution is $(\tfrac{1}{2}, 1, 2)$.

Exercise Set **2.5**

A **1.** Plot the following points in a three-space coordinate system.
  a. $(2, 4, 3)$ **b.** $(3, -1, -2)$ **c.** $(-2, 0, 1)$
  d. $(-1, 0, -2)$ **e.** $(-1, 2, -3)$ **f.** $(0, 0, -1)$

2. Obtain the equations of the traces, find the coordinate intercepts, and then shade the parts of the following planes.
  a. $3x + 7y + 2z = 14$ **b.** $x + y + z = 3$
  c. $5x + 2y + 3z = 15$ **d.** $x - y + z = 4$
  e. $2x - 3y - 4z = 12$ **f.** $-x + y - z = 3$

3. Classify the following statements as true or false.
  a. $3x + y = 7$ is a line in three-space.
  b. In three-space, $y = 0$ is the equation of the x-axis.
  c. One trace of $x - 3y + 4z = 6$ is $3y - 4z = -6$.
  d. In three-space, $z = 0$ represents the x, z-plane.
  e. In three-space, every linear equation represents a plane.
  f. The trace of $6z + 4x = 12$ in the y, z-plane is $z = 2$.
  g. The x-intercept of $y + 6z + 4x = 12$ is 3.
  h. The point $(1, 3, -2)$ is a point on the plane $x - y + 2z = -6$.
  i. $y = 4$ in three-space is a plane perpendicular to the y-axis.
  j. The plane $2z + 3y = 6$ never intersects the z-axis.

4. Shade the following planes in three-space.
  a. $z = 5$ **b.** $x = -2$ **c.** $y = -4$
  d. $x + 3y = 6$ **e.** $2x - y = 4$ **f.** $3y - 4x = 8$

B *Find a graphical solution of the following systems of equations and then verify your work by solving algebraically for the solution.*

5.
$$z = 2$$
$$2x + 2y + z = 4$$
$$x = 1$$

6.
$$y = 3$$
$$x + y + z = 4$$
$$x = 1$$

C *Geometrically explain why the following systems do or do not have solutions.*

7.
$$x = 5$$
$$x = 7$$
$$x + y + 2z = 8$$

8.
$$x + 2y = 4$$
$$2x + 4y = 3$$
$$x + y + z = 2$$

9.
$$x + y - 4z = 6$$
$$2x + 2y - 8z = 3$$
$$x + y + z = 2$$

10. Find the trace of the plane $3x + y - 2z = 6$ on
    a. $x = 2$ **b.** $y = -2$ **c.** $z = 1$

Business   **11. Investments.** Juan has a total of $35,000 invested in 10%, 12%, and 15% bonds. He receives the same amount of interest on the 10% bonds as on the 15% bonds. Interest on the 12% bonds is $1,200. Use geometrical methods to find how much Juan has invested in each type of bond.

Economics   **12. Supply and Demand.** The supply and demand equations for a one-commodity market are given by

$$D = S + 5$$
$$D = -2p + 30$$
$$S = 3p + 20$$

Locate the equilibrium solution geometrically.

Life Sciences   **13. Bacteria Culture.** In a bacteria culture, species A requires 4 units per day of phosphate source; species B, 6 units per day; and species C, 8 units per day. There are 1000 more bacteria of type A than type C. It is desired to have exactly 1000 of species B. If there are 60,000 units of phosphate source, find the number of each type of species geometrically.

Social Sciences   **14. Traffic Flow.** The number of cars entering and leaving four intersections of one-way streets is given in the following diagram.

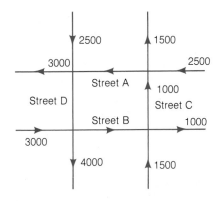

Set up the equations for traffic flow and solve the system geometrically.

In this section, we present a matrix algebra concept that is not only useful as we discuss another method for solving simultaneous systems of linear equations but is also essential in constructing and finding solutions of models of various application problems. For example, in the next section as we consider an economics model called the Leontief model, we need the **inverse** of a matrix.

When the product of two square matrices is equal to the identity matrix, then each matrix is said to be the **inverse** of the other. In this section we study a procedure for finding the inverse of a square matrix if the inverse exists.

Two second-order square matrices **A** and **B** are inverse matrices if

$$\mathbf{AB} = \mathbf{I}$$

EXAMPLE 34

$$\mathbf{A} = \begin{bmatrix} 1 & -\frac{1}{2} \\ 0 & \frac{3}{2} \end{bmatrix} \quad \text{and} \quad \mathbf{B} = \begin{bmatrix} 1 & \frac{1}{3} \\ 0 & \frac{2}{3} \end{bmatrix}$$

are inverse matrices since

$$\begin{bmatrix} 1 & -\frac{1}{2} \\ 0 & \frac{3}{2} \end{bmatrix} \begin{bmatrix} 1 & \frac{1}{3} \\ 0 & \frac{2}{3} \end{bmatrix} = \begin{bmatrix} 1 & 0 \\ 0 & 1 \end{bmatrix}$$

Inverse of a Matrix

If there exists a matrix $\mathbf{A}^{-1}$, such that $\mathbf{AA}^{-1} = \mathbf{A}^{-1}\mathbf{A} = \mathbf{I}$, then $\mathbf{A}^{-1}$ is called the **inverse** of the matrix **A**.

This definition states that for the inverse $\mathbf{A}^{-1}$ to exist, both $\mathbf{A}^{-1}\mathbf{A} = \mathbf{I}$ and $\mathbf{AA}^{-1} = \mathbf{I}$. However, for square matrices it can be proved that if $\mathbf{AA}^{-1} = \mathbf{I}$, then $\mathbf{A}^{-1}\mathbf{A} = \mathbf{I}$ and conversely. Hence, to prove that a square matrix is the inverse of another square matrix, it is necessary to check only one of these conditions, not both.

It can be shown easily that not every matrix has an inverse. First of all, a matrix must be square in order to have an inverse. Then not all square matrices have inverses. See if you can find the inverse of

$$\begin{bmatrix} -1 & 2 \\ -2 & 4 \end{bmatrix}$$

Let $\begin{bmatrix} x & y \\ z & w \end{bmatrix}$ be such an inverse. Then

$$\begin{bmatrix} -1 & 2 \\ -2 & 4 \end{bmatrix}\begin{bmatrix} x & y \\ z & w \end{bmatrix} = \begin{bmatrix} 1 & 0 \\ 0 & 1 \end{bmatrix}$$

$$\begin{bmatrix} -x + 2z & -y + 2w \\ -2x + 4z & -2y + 4w \end{bmatrix} = \begin{bmatrix} 1 & 0 \\ 0 & 1 \end{bmatrix}$$

This is obviously impossible. There are no numbers x and z such that

$$-x + 2z = 1$$

$$2(-x + 2z) = 0 \quad \text{Why?}$$

Likewise, no numbers y and w exist to satisfy the matrix equation. Thus, $\begin{bmatrix} -1 & 2 \\ -2 & 4 \end{bmatrix}$ has no inverse.

EXAMPLE 35 The inverse of the matrix $\begin{bmatrix} 2 & 3 \\ 1 & 2 \end{bmatrix}$ is $\begin{bmatrix} 2 & -3 \\ -1 & 2 \end{bmatrix}$ because

$$\begin{bmatrix} 2 & 3 \\ 1 & 2 \end{bmatrix}\begin{bmatrix} 2 & -3 \\ -1 & 2 \end{bmatrix} = \begin{bmatrix} 1 & 0 \\ 0 & 1 \end{bmatrix}$$

EXAMPLE 36 The inverse of the matrix $\begin{bmatrix} 1 & 3 & 0 \\ 0 & 1 & 2 \\ 0 & 0 & 1 \end{bmatrix}$ is $\begin{bmatrix} 1 & -3 & 6 \\ 0 & 1 & -2 \\ 0 & 0 & 1 \end{bmatrix}$ because

$$\begin{bmatrix} 1 & 3 & 0 \\ 0 & 1 & 2 \\ 0 & 0 & 1 \end{bmatrix}\begin{bmatrix} 1 & -3 & 6 \\ 0 & 1 & -2 \\ 0 & 0 & 1 \end{bmatrix} = \begin{bmatrix} 1 & 0 & 0 \\ 0 & 1 & 0 \\ 0 & 0 & 1 \end{bmatrix}$$

Not all square matrices have inverses, but, for those that do, the inverse may be found by writing the nth-order identity adjacent to the matrix **A** to form an augmented matrix. The permissible row operations are then performed on this new matrix until the matrix that was **A** is reduced to the nth-order identity matrix and the nth-order matrix, which was adjacent to it, becomes the inverse of the matrix **A**. This procedure is illustrated by the following examples.

EXAMPLE 37 Find the inverse of $\begin{bmatrix} 5 & -3 \\ 2 & -1 \end{bmatrix}$.

Solution   Place the 2 × 2 identity matrix next to this original matrix to form the new 2 × 4 matrix

$$\begin{bmatrix} 5 & -3 & 1 & 0 \\ 2 & -1 & 0 & 1 \end{bmatrix}$$

Now operate on this new matrix so that the original matrix is reduced to the identity matrix by permissible row operations. Multiply the first row by $\frac{1}{5}$ to obtain

$$\begin{bmatrix} 1 & -\frac{3}{5} & \frac{1}{5} & 0 \\ 2 & -1 & 0 & 1 \end{bmatrix}$$

Multiply the first row by -2 and add the result to the second row to get

$$\begin{bmatrix} 1 & -\frac{3}{5} & \frac{1}{5} & 0 \\ 0 & \frac{1}{5} & -\frac{2}{5} & 1 \end{bmatrix}$$

Multiply the second row by 5 to get

$$\begin{bmatrix} 1 & -\frac{3}{5} & \frac{1}{5} & 0 \\ 0 & 1 & -2 & 5 \end{bmatrix}$$

Multiply the second row by $\frac{3}{5}$ and add the result to the first row to obtain

$$\begin{bmatrix} 1 & 0 & -1 & 3 \\ 0 & 1 & -2 & 5 \end{bmatrix}$$

Thus, the inverse of $\begin{bmatrix} 5 & -3 \\ 2 & -1 \end{bmatrix}$ is $\begin{bmatrix} -1 & 3 \\ -2 & 5 \end{bmatrix}$, which can be proved by noting that

$$\begin{bmatrix} 5 & -3 \\ 2 & -1 \end{bmatrix} \begin{bmatrix} -1 & 3 \\ -2 & 5 \end{bmatrix} = \begin{bmatrix} 1 & 0 \\ 0 & 1 \end{bmatrix}$$

EXAMPLE 38   Find the inverse of

$$\begin{bmatrix} 1 & 2 & 1 \\ -1 & 1 & 1 \\ 2 & 3 & 1 \end{bmatrix}$$

Solution   Write the third-order identity adjacent to the given matrix to give the new 3×6 matrix

$$\begin{bmatrix} 1 & 2 & 1 & 1 & 0 & 0 \\ -1 & 1 & 1 & 0 & 1 & 0 \\ 2 & 3 & 1 & 0 & 0 & 1 \end{bmatrix}$$

Multiply the first row by 1 and add the result to the second row; then multiply the first row by -2 and add the result to the third row to obtain

$$\begin{bmatrix} 1 & 2 & 1 & 1 & 0 & 0 \\ 0 & 3 & 2 & 1 & 1 & 0 \\ 0 & -1 & -1 & -2 & 0 & 1 \end{bmatrix}$$

Multiply the third row by 2 and add the result to the second row to obtain

$$\begin{bmatrix} 1 & 2 & 1 & 1 & 0 & 0 \\ 0 & 1 & 0 & -3 & 1 & 2 \\ 0 & -1 & -1 & -2 & 0 & 1 \end{bmatrix}$$

Multiply the second row by -2 and add the result to the first row; add the second row to the third row to obtain

$$\begin{bmatrix} 1 & 0 & 1 & 7 & -2 & -4 \\ 0 & 1 & 0 & -3 & 1 & 2 \\ 0 & 0 & -1 & -5 & 1 & 3 \end{bmatrix}$$

Multiply the third row by -1:

$$\begin{bmatrix} 1 & 0 & 1 & 7 & -2 & -4 \\ 0 & 1 & 0 & -3 & 1 & 2 \\ 0 & 0 & 1 & 5 & -1 & -3 \end{bmatrix}$$

Now multiply the third row by -1 and add the result to the first row:

$$\begin{bmatrix} 1 & 0 & 0 & 2 & -1 & -1 \\ 0 & 1 & 0 & -3 & 1 & 2 \\ 0 & 0 & 1 & 5 & -1 & -3 \end{bmatrix}$$

Hence, the inverse of

$$\begin{bmatrix} 1 & 2 & 1 \\ -1 & 1 & 1 \\ 2 & 3 & 1 \end{bmatrix} \quad \text{is} \quad \begin{bmatrix} 2 & -1 & -1 \\ -3 & 1 & 2 \\ 5 & -1 & -3 \end{bmatrix}$$

This fact can be proved by multiplying:

$$\begin{bmatrix} 1 & 2 & 1 \\ -1 & 1 & 1 \\ 2 & 3 & 1 \end{bmatrix} \begin{bmatrix} 2 & -1 & -1 \\ -3 & 1 & 2 \\ 5 & -1 & -3 \end{bmatrix} = \begin{bmatrix} 1 & 0 & 0 \\ 0 & 1 & 0 \\ 0 & 0 & 1 \end{bmatrix}$$

If the inverse of the coefficient matrix of a system of equations exists, it can be used to solve the system. For example, the system

$$5x - 3y = 29$$
$$2x - y = 11$$

can be written as

$$\begin{bmatrix} 5 & -3 \\ 2 & -1 \end{bmatrix} \begin{bmatrix} x \\ y \end{bmatrix} = \begin{bmatrix} 29 \\ 11 \end{bmatrix}$$

or

$$\mathbf{AX} = \mathbf{B}$$

where $\mathbf{A}$ is the coefficient matrix

$$\begin{bmatrix} 5 & -3 \\ 2 & -1 \end{bmatrix}$$

and

$$\mathbf{X} = \begin{bmatrix} x \\ y \end{bmatrix} \quad \text{and} \quad \mathbf{B} = \begin{bmatrix} 29 \\ 11 \end{bmatrix}$$

The inverse of $\mathbf{A} = \begin{bmatrix} 5 & -3 \\ 2 & -1 \end{bmatrix}$ has been found to be $\mathbf{A}^{-1} = \begin{bmatrix} -1 & 3 \\ -2 & 5 \end{bmatrix}$. Multiplying on the left by $\mathbf{A}^{-1}$ both sides of the equation $\mathbf{AX} = \mathbf{B}$ yields

$$\mathbf{A}^{-1}\mathbf{AX} = \mathbf{A}^{-1}\mathbf{B} \quad \text{or} \quad \mathbf{X} = \mathbf{A}^{-1}\mathbf{B}$$

that is,

$$\begin{bmatrix} -1 & 3 \\ -2 & 5 \end{bmatrix}\begin{bmatrix} 5 & -3 \\ 2 & -1 \end{bmatrix}\begin{bmatrix} x \\ y \end{bmatrix} = \begin{bmatrix} -1 & 3 \\ -2 & 5 \end{bmatrix}\begin{bmatrix} 29 \\ 11 \end{bmatrix}$$

$$\begin{bmatrix} 1 & 0 \\ 0 & 1 \end{bmatrix}\begin{bmatrix} x \\ y \end{bmatrix} = \begin{bmatrix} 4 \\ -3 \end{bmatrix}$$

$$\begin{bmatrix} x \\ y \end{bmatrix} = \begin{bmatrix} 4 \\ -3 \end{bmatrix}$$

Hence, $x = 4$ and $y = -3$. This example suggests the following theorem.

> If the coefficient matrix $\mathbf{A}$ of the system has an inverse $\mathbf{A}^{-1}$, the solution $\mathbf{X}$ of the matrix equation $\mathbf{AX} = \mathbf{B}$ may be found as $\mathbf{X} = \mathbf{A}^{-1}\mathbf{B}$.

EXAMPLE 39   Find the solution of the system

$$\begin{aligned} x + 2y + z &= 0 \\ -x + y + z &= -4 \\ 2x + 3y + z &= 1 \end{aligned}$$

Solution   In matrix notation this system becomes

$$\begin{bmatrix} 1 & 2 & 1 \\ -1 & 1 & 1 \\ 2 & 3 & 1 \end{bmatrix}\begin{bmatrix} x \\ y \\ z \end{bmatrix} = \begin{bmatrix} 0 \\ -4 \\ 1 \end{bmatrix}$$

The inverse of

$$\begin{bmatrix} 1 & 2 & 1 \\ -1 & 1 & 1 \\ 2 & 3 & 1 \end{bmatrix}$$

was shown to be

$$\begin{bmatrix} 2 & -1 & -1 \\ -3 & 1 & 2 \\ 5 & -1 & -3 \end{bmatrix}$$

Hence, by the theorem,

$$\begin{bmatrix} x \\ y \\ z \end{bmatrix} = \begin{bmatrix} 2 & -1 & -1 \\ -3 & 1 & 2 \\ 5 & -1 & -3 \end{bmatrix} \begin{bmatrix} 0 \\ -4 \\ 1 \end{bmatrix} \quad \text{or} \quad \begin{bmatrix} x \\ y \\ z \end{bmatrix} = \begin{bmatrix} 3 \\ -2 \\ 1 \end{bmatrix}$$

Thus, $x = 3$, $y = -2$, and $z = 1$.

As indicated earlier, many square matrices do not have inverses. The procedure for finding the inverse indicates this fact; that is, sometimes it is impossible to reduce the nth-order matrix **A** to the identity matrix by permissible row operations.

EXAMPLE 40 Show that the matrix $\begin{bmatrix} 1 & 2 \\ 3 & 6 \end{bmatrix}$ does not have an inverse.

Solution If the procedure as outlined for determining the inverse is applied to this matrix, we have

$$\begin{bmatrix} 1 & 2 & 1 & 0 \\ 3 & 6 & 0 & 1 \end{bmatrix}$$

Multiply the first row by -3 and add the result to the second row to obtain

$$\begin{bmatrix} 1 & 2 & 1 & 0 \\ 0 & 0 & -3 & 1 \end{bmatrix}$$

Since it is impossible to reduce the matrix $\begin{bmatrix} 1 & 2 \\ 0 & 0 \end{bmatrix}$ to $\begin{bmatrix} 1 & 0 \\ 0 & 1 \end{bmatrix}$ by permissible row operations, the procedure fails and the inverse does not exist.

EXAMPLE 41 Suppose an airline has three types of cargo planes, labeled I, II, and III. They can carry the following numbers of pieces of equipment of types A, B, and C, respectively.

Planes

		I	II	III
	A	8	6	10
Equipment	B	5	4	2
	C	3	6	4

Determine the planes required to deliver 46 pieces of type A equipment, 25 pieces of type B, and 25 pieces of type C.

Solution Let

$$x = \text{number of planes of type I used}$$
$$y = \text{number of planes of type II used}$$
$$z = \text{number of planes of type III used}$$

The equations to be solved are:

$$8x + 6y + 10z = 46$$
$$5x + 4y + 2z = 25$$
$$3x + 6y + 4z = 25$$

In matrix notation these equations become

$$\begin{bmatrix} 8 & 6 & 10 \\ 5 & 4 & 2 \\ 3 & 6 & 4 \end{bmatrix} \begin{bmatrix} x \\ y \\ z \end{bmatrix} = \begin{bmatrix} 46 \\ 25 \\ 25 \end{bmatrix}$$

The inverse of

$$\begin{bmatrix} 8 & 6 & 10 \\ 5 & 4 & 2 \\ 3 & 6 & 4 \end{bmatrix} \quad \text{is} \quad \begin{bmatrix} \frac{2}{64} & \frac{18}{64} & -\frac{14}{64} \\ -\frac{7}{64} & \frac{1}{64} & \frac{17}{64} \\ \frac{9}{64} & -\frac{15}{64} & \frac{1}{64} \end{bmatrix}$$

Prove this. Now, by multiplying the matrix equation on the left by this inverse, we obtain the following result:

$$\begin{bmatrix} \frac{2}{64} & \frac{18}{64} & -\frac{14}{64} \\ -\frac{7}{64} & \frac{1}{64} & \frac{17}{64} \\ \frac{9}{64} & -\frac{15}{64} & \frac{1}{64} \end{bmatrix} \begin{bmatrix} 8 & 6 & 10 \\ 5 & 4 & 2 \\ 3 & 6 & 4 \end{bmatrix} \begin{bmatrix} x \\ y \\ z \end{bmatrix} = \begin{bmatrix} \frac{2}{64} & \frac{18}{64} & -\frac{14}{64} \\ -\frac{7}{64} & \frac{1}{64} & \frac{17}{64} \\ \frac{9}{64} & -\frac{15}{64} & \frac{1}{64} \end{bmatrix} \begin{bmatrix} 46 \\ 25 \\ 25 \end{bmatrix}$$

$$\begin{bmatrix} 1 & 0 & 0 \\ 0 & 1 & 0 \\ 0 & 0 & 1 \end{bmatrix} \begin{bmatrix} x \\ y \\ z \end{bmatrix} = \begin{bmatrix} 3 \\ 2 \\ 1 \end{bmatrix}$$

$$\begin{bmatrix} x \\ y \\ z \end{bmatrix} = \begin{bmatrix} 3 \\ 2 \\ 1 \end{bmatrix}$$

This result shows that the airline should use three planes of type I, two planes of type II, and one plane of type III to deliver the equipment.

In the preceding discussion, the matrix solution does not appear to have any advantage over the elimination method of solving the system. Notice, however, that, once the inverse matrix has been obtained, it can be used over and over again to fill future deliveries without the necessity of recomputing it. Thus, if another delivery is required for 132 pieces of type A, 54 pieces of type B, and 70 pieces of type C, it is easy to determine the planes required by using the inverse matrix previously obtained:

$$\begin{bmatrix} x \\ y \\ z \end{bmatrix} = \begin{bmatrix} \frac{2}{64} & \frac{18}{64} & -\frac{14}{64} \\ -\frac{7}{64} & \frac{1}{64} & \frac{17}{64} \\ \frac{9}{64} & -\frac{15}{64} & \frac{1}{64} \end{bmatrix} \cdot \begin{bmatrix} 132 \\ 54 \\ 70 \end{bmatrix} = \begin{bmatrix} 4 \\ 5 \\ 7 \end{bmatrix}$$

Hence, to make the new delivery, the airline would use four planes of type I, five planes of type II, and seven planes of type III.

It is important to remember that, *once the inverse matrix has been found, it can be used for all future deliveries.* This is a very important advantage of the matrix solution over the elimination method, which would require that the entire method be repeated for each new delivery. Other uses of the inverse of a matrix are given and interpreted in later sections.

Exercise Set **2.6**

A
1. Show that the following matrices are inverses of each other.

a. $\begin{bmatrix} 1 & 2 \\ 1 & 3 \end{bmatrix}$ and $\begin{bmatrix} 3 & -2 \\ -1 & 1 \end{bmatrix}$ b. $\begin{bmatrix} 4 & -6 \\ 2 & 2 \end{bmatrix}$ and $\begin{bmatrix} \frac{1}{10} & \frac{3}{10} \\ -\frac{1}{10} & \frac{2}{10} \end{bmatrix}$

c. $\begin{bmatrix} 5 & 7 \\ 3 & 4 \end{bmatrix}$ and $\begin{bmatrix} -4 & 7 \\ 3 & -5 \end{bmatrix}$ d. $\begin{bmatrix} 2 & 0 & 2 \\ 4 & 2 & 0 \\ 2 & -2 & 2 \end{bmatrix}$ and $\begin{bmatrix} -\frac{1}{4} & \frac{1}{4} & \frac{1}{4} \\ \frac{1}{2} & 0 & -\frac{1}{2} \\ \frac{3}{4} & -\frac{1}{4} & -\frac{1}{4} \end{bmatrix}$

2. Find the inverses of the following matrices if they exist.

a. $\begin{bmatrix} 5 & -3 \\ 2 & 3 \end{bmatrix}$ b. $\begin{bmatrix} 3 & 0 \\ 2 & 0 \end{bmatrix}$ c. $\begin{bmatrix} 5 & 19 \\ 1 & 4 \end{bmatrix}$ d. $\begin{bmatrix} 3 & 3 \\ 3 & 3 \end{bmatrix}$

3. Solve the following systems by finding the inverse of the coefficient matrix and then using the theory of this section.

a. $x + y = 2$ b. $x + y = 1$ c. $x - y = 1$ d. $2x + y = 3$
   $2x + 3y = 2$ $3x + y = 7$ $x + y = 5$ $x + 3y = 4$

4. Find the inverses of the following matrices if they exist.

a. $\begin{bmatrix} 0 & 0 & 1 \\ 0 & 1 & 0 \\ 1 & 0 & 0 \end{bmatrix}$ b. $\begin{bmatrix} 1 & 0 & 1 \\ 0 & 1 & 0 \\ 1 & 0 & 0 \end{bmatrix}$ c. $\begin{bmatrix} 0 & 4 & 0 \\ 1 & 0 & 0 \\ 0 & -1 & 1 \end{bmatrix}$

d. $\begin{bmatrix} 1 & -1 & 1 \\ 1 & 1 & 1 \\ 1 & 1 & 1 \end{bmatrix}$ e. $\begin{bmatrix} 1 & -1 & 2 \\ 3 & 1 & 0 \\ 2 & 3 & 1 \end{bmatrix}$ f. $\begin{bmatrix} 1 & 0 & 2 \\ 1 & 3 & 1 \\ 0 & -2 & 1 \end{bmatrix}$

B
5. Solve the following systems by finding the inverse of the coefficient matrix and then using the theory of this section.

a. $x - y + 3z = 8$ b. $x + y + z = 5$
     $2x + y + 2z = 6$ $x - y + z = 7$
     $x + 2y + z = 0$ $2x + y + z = 9$
c. $-2x - 3y + z = 3$ d. $x + y + z = 2$
     $x + 2y + z = 1$ $x - y + z = 6$
     $-x - y + 3z = 6$ $-x + y + z = -4$

6. Show that the inverse of

$$\begin{bmatrix} a_{11} & a_{12} \\ a_{21} & a_{22} \end{bmatrix} \text{ is } \begin{bmatrix} \dfrac{a_{22}}{\Delta} & \dfrac{-a_{12}}{\Delta} \\ \dfrac{-a_{21}}{\Delta} & \dfrac{a_{11}}{\Delta} \end{bmatrix}$$

If $\Delta = a_{11}a_{22} - a_{12}a_{21} \neq 0$.

7. Use exercise 6 to find the inverse of the following matrices.

a. $\begin{bmatrix} 3 & 5 \\ 2 & 7 \end{bmatrix}$ **b.** $\begin{bmatrix} 3 & 5 \\ 2 & 4 \end{bmatrix}$ **c.** $\begin{bmatrix} 6 & 1 \\ 5 & 1 \end{bmatrix}$ **d.** $\begin{bmatrix} 3 & -2 \\ 1 & -1 \end{bmatrix}$

8. Let $A = \begin{bmatrix} 2 & 1 \\ -3 & -1 \end{bmatrix}$.

 a. Find A^{-1}.
 b. Find $[A^{-1}]^{-1}$.
 c. In general, conjecture an answer for $[A^{-1}]^{-1}$.

9. Show that the following matrices do not have inverses.

a. $\begin{bmatrix} 2 & 1 \\ 6 & 3 \end{bmatrix}$ **b.** $\begin{bmatrix} 6 & -3 \\ 4 & -2 \end{bmatrix}$ **c.** $\begin{bmatrix} 2 & 4 & -2 \\ 3 & -1 & 0 \\ 5 & 3 & -2 \end{bmatrix}$

C   **10.** Find the inverses of the following matrices if they exist.

a. $\begin{bmatrix} 1 & 0 & 1 & 1 \\ 0 & 1 & 0 & 0 \\ 1 & 0 & 1 & 0 \\ 1 & 1 & 1 & 1 \end{bmatrix}$ **b.** $\begin{bmatrix} 1 & 0 & 0 & 1 \\ 1 & 1 & 0 & 0 \\ 0 & 0 & 1 & 1 \\ 1 & 1 & 0 & 1 \end{bmatrix}$ **c.** $\begin{bmatrix} 1 & 1 & 0 & 5 \\ 1 & 1 & 1 & 2 \\ 1 & -1 & 2 & 3 \\ 1 & 0 & 2 & 4 \end{bmatrix}$

11. Let $A = \begin{bmatrix} 3 & 1 \\ 5 & 2 \end{bmatrix}$ and $B = \begin{bmatrix} 5 & 2 \\ 7 & 3 \end{bmatrix}$. Show that $(AB)^{-1} = B^{-1}A^{-1}$.

12. Use A and B from exercise 11 along with $C = \begin{bmatrix} 1 & 0 \\ 1 & 1 \end{bmatrix}$ to show that

$$(ABC)^{-1} = C^{-1} \cdot B^{-1} \cdot A^{-1}$$

Business

13. Investments. The Easy Investment Club has $100,000 invested in bonds. Type A bonds pay 8% interest while type B bonds pay 10%. How much money is invested in each type if the club receives $9,360 in interest?

14. Investments. Jane has money invested through Merrill Lynch at 12% annual interest, a bank investment certificate that pays 10% interest, and a personal loan to a friend at 5% interest. She remembers that she has $16,000 invested and that the amount with Merrill Lynch is $4,000 more than that invested at the bank and loaned to the friend. Her annual interest is $1,750. Use the inverse of a matrix to help Jane determine how much she has invested in each account.

Economics

15. Break-Even Analysis. A country club has been studying its cost of operation and has found the monthly cost to be $C = \$6,000 + \$15x$, where x represents the number of members. A service company states that by remodeling it can provide a similar service for a monthly cost of $C = \$10,500 + \$10x$. Use the inverse of a matrix to find the break-even point, or find the number of members necessary to undertake the remodeling.

Life Sciences

16. Herbicides. Three herbicides are available to kill weeds, grass, and vines. One gallon of one herbicide contains 1 unit of chemical A, which kills weeds, and 2 units of chemical B, which kills grass. One gallon of the second herbicide contains 2 units of chemical B and 3 units of chemical C, which kills vines. One gallon of the third herbicide contains 3 units of chemical A and 4 units of chemical C. It is desired to spread 10 units of chemical A, 16 units of chemical B, and 20 units of chemical C. How many gallons of each herbicide should be purchased?

Social Sciences

17. Polling. A company has been engaged to make 4850 phone polls and 2650 home polls. The company has two teams of pollsters. Team I can make 60 phone polls and 40 home polls a day while team II can make 70 phone polls and 30 home polls each day. How many days should each team be scheduled in order to complete the engagement?

In recent years, matrix arithmetic has played a significant role in economic theories, especially in the branch of economics called **input-output analysis.** The first significant work in this field of economics was done by the famous economist Wassily Leontief, who was awarded a Nobel Prize in Economics in 1973 for his use of input-output analysis to study how much output must be produced by each segment of an economy in order to meet consumption and export demands. His study of the American economy involved 500 sections of the American economy interacting together. As you would expect, such analysis needed matrix calculations and, in particular, inverses of matrices.

    We will attempt to illustrate input-output analysis in this section with a very small model in view of the fact that many of you do not have available large-scale computer facilities. Luckily, even small models illustrate the potential of the theory.

Suppose we divide an economy into a number of industries—aluminum, steel, transportation, and so on. Each industry produces a certain output using raw materials (*input*). Of course, the input of some industries is the *output* of others (automobile manufacturers, for example, use steel as input). This interdependence among the industries is recorded in a matrix, called the **input-output matrix.** Given the internal demands for each other's outputs, the theory of input-output analysis attempts to establish conditions in an economy where the output will satisfy exactly each sector's demands as well as outside demands.

    To illustrate input-output analysis, suppose there are n industries, each of which produces a single item. Each item may be used as an input to any industry. Let a_{ij} be the fractional amount of the jth item required as input by industry i to produce a unit quantity of the ith item as output. Written as a matrix, this becomes

$$
\begin{array}{cc}
 & \textbf{Output item} \\
 & \begin{array}{cccc} 1 & 2 & \cdots & n \end{array}
\end{array}
$$

$$
\textbf{Input item} \quad
\begin{array}{c} 1 \\ 2 \\ \vdots \\ n \end{array}
\begin{bmatrix}
a_{11} & a_{12} & \cdots & a_{1n} \\
a_{21} & a_{22} & \cdots & a_{2n} \\
\vdots & \vdots & & \vdots \\
a_{n1} & a_{n2} & \cdots & a_{nn}
\end{bmatrix}
$$

This matrix is called a **technology** or a *Leontief input-output matrix.*

    The simplest Leontief model is called a **closed** Leontief system and occurs when the output of each industry is used only as input to the industries and no other inputs are required. For simplification, assume that each industry produces only one of the items. Let x_1 represent the number of units of item 1 of output of industry 1, x_2 the number of units of item 2 of output of industry 2, ..., and x_n the number of units of item n of output of industry n.

The expression $a_{i1}x_1 + a_{i2}x_2 + \cdots + a_{in}x_n$ represents the total input requirements of industry i of all the items. For a closed Leontief system, the number x_i of output units of item i by industry i must equal the total input requirements by industry i of all the items. Hence,

$$x_1 = a_{11}x_1 + a_{12}x_2 + \cdots + a_{1n}x_n$$
$$x_2 = a_{21}x_1 + a_{22}x_2 + \cdots + a_{2n}x_n$$
$$\vdots \qquad \vdots \qquad \vdots$$
$$x_n = a_{n1}x_1 + a_{n2}x_2 + \cdots + a_{nn}x_n$$

In matrix notation this becomes $\mathbf{X} = \mathbf{AX}$, where

$$\mathbf{A} = \begin{bmatrix} a_{11} & a_{12} & \cdots & a_{1n} \\ a_{21} & a_{22} & \cdots & a_{2n} \\ \vdots & \vdots & & \vdots \\ a_{n1} & a_{n2} & \cdots & a_{nn} \end{bmatrix} \quad \text{and} \quad \mathbf{X} = \begin{bmatrix} x_1 \\ x_2 \\ \vdots \\ x_n \end{bmatrix}$$

For a closed Leontief system the sum of each column of the Leontief input-output matrix must equal 1 (unity) because all of the output is consumed as input.

EXAMPLE 42 Consider Rural City, which has only a farmer (to provide food) and a tailor (to provide clothes). Suppose the farmer uses one-half of the food he grows, and the tailor requires the other one-half. Assume the tailor uses two-thirds of the clothes he produces, and the farmer requires one-third. Write these requirements as a Leontief input-output matrix.

Solution The Leontief input-output matrix for this closed system is

$$\begin{array}{cc} & \begin{array}{cc} \text{Food} & \text{Clothes} \\ \text{produced} & \text{produced} \end{array} \\ \textbf{Input requirements} \begin{array}{c} \text{Farmer} \\ \text{Tailor} \end{array} & \begin{bmatrix} \frac{1}{2} & \frac{1}{3} \\ \frac{1}{2} & \frac{2}{3} \end{bmatrix} \end{array}$$

This matrix indicates that in order for the farmer to produce food, he requires one-half of the food produced and one-third of the clothes produced. Similarly, in order for the tailor to produce clothes, he requires one-half of the food produced and two-thirds of the clothes produced. Let x_1 represent the number of units of food produced and x_2 represent the number of units of clothes produced. The requirements can be represented by the equations

$$x_1 = \tfrac{1}{2}x_1 + \tfrac{1}{3}x_2$$
$$x_2 = \tfrac{1}{2}x_1 + \tfrac{2}{3}x_2$$

In matrix notation this system can be written

$$\begin{bmatrix} x_1 \\ x_2 \end{bmatrix} = \begin{bmatrix} \frac{1}{2} & \frac{1}{3} \\ \frac{1}{2} & \frac{2}{3} \end{bmatrix} \begin{bmatrix} x_1 \\ x_2 \end{bmatrix}$$

An **open** Leontief system consists of n production industries as before and a consumer section that demands items in addition to their use as inputs for production. Suppose **X** and **A** are defined as before and d_i represents the number of units of item i demanded by the consumer. Let **D** $= [d_i]$ represent the column matrix of the consumer demands. Then, in matrix notation,

$$\mathbf{X} = \mathbf{AX} + \mathbf{D}$$

Thus, **D** $=$ **X** $-$ **AX** represents the output available to the consumer section of the economy. A very fundamental problem is whether or not the economy can satisfy the consumer demand. Another way of stating this problem is: Given a demand matrix **D** of the consumer section, does there exist a matrix **X** with nonnegative components such that **X** $-$ **AX** $=$ **D**? This question will be answered after the next example.

EXAMPLE 43   To illustrate an **open** Leontief system, let us return to Rural City and assume that the farmer and the tailor decide to sell some of the items they produce to a consumer. Suppose the farmer requires one-third of the food and the tailor requires one-third of the food and the other one-third is sold to a consumer. Suppose the tailor requires one-half of the clothes and the farmer requires one-fourth of the clothes and the other one-fourth is sold to a consumer. Write these requirements as an open Leontief input-output matrix.

Solution

		Food produced	Clothes produced
Input requirements	Farmer	$\frac{1}{3}$	$\frac{1}{4}$
	Tailor	$\frac{1}{3}$	$\frac{1}{2}$

This matrix indicates that in order for the farmer to produce food he requires one-third of the food produced and one-fourth of the clothes produced. Similarly, in order for the tailor to produce clothes he requires one-third of the food produced and one-half of the clothes produced. Let x_1 represent the number of units of food produced and x_2 represent the number of units of clothes produced. Suppose d_1 represents the units of food required by the consumer and d_2 represents the units of clothes required by the consumer. The requirements can be written

$$\begin{bmatrix} \frac{1}{3} & \frac{1}{4} \\ \frac{1}{3} & \frac{1}{2} \end{bmatrix} \begin{bmatrix} x_1 \\ x_2 \end{bmatrix} + \begin{bmatrix} d_1 \\ d_2 \end{bmatrix} = \begin{bmatrix} x_1 \\ x_2 \end{bmatrix}$$

We are now ready to return to the fundamental question raised concerning the open Leontief system. Remember that the question was: Given a demand vector **D** of the consumer section, does there exist a vector **X** such that

$$\mathbf{X} - \mathbf{AX} = \mathbf{D}$$

If **I** is the identity matrix, this equation becomes

$$\mathbf{I} \cdot \mathbf{X} - \mathbf{A} \cdot \mathbf{X} = \mathbf{D} \qquad \text{or} \qquad (\mathbf{I} - \mathbf{A}) \cdot \mathbf{X} = \mathbf{D}$$

If $(\mathbf{I} - \mathbf{A})^{-1}$ exists, then

$$\mathbf{X} = (\mathbf{I} - \mathbf{A})^{-1} \cdot \mathbf{D}$$

Hence, if $(\mathbf{I} - \mathbf{A})^{-1}\mathbf{D}$ exists and has nonnegative components, it provides a yes answer to the fundamental question.

EXAMPLE 44 In Example 43 $\mathbf{AX} + \mathbf{D} = \mathbf{X}$ was

$$\begin{bmatrix} \frac{1}{3} & \frac{1}{4} \\ \frac{1}{3} & \frac{1}{2} \end{bmatrix}\begin{bmatrix} x_1 \\ x_2 \end{bmatrix} + \begin{bmatrix} d_1 \\ d_2 \end{bmatrix} = \begin{bmatrix} x_1 \\ x_2 \end{bmatrix}$$

or $(\mathbf{I} - \mathbf{A})\mathbf{X} = \mathbf{D}$ can be written as

$$\left(\begin{bmatrix} 1 & 0 \\ 0 & 1 \end{bmatrix} - \begin{bmatrix} \frac{1}{3} & \frac{1}{4} \\ \frac{1}{3} & \frac{1}{2} \end{bmatrix} \right)\begin{bmatrix} x_1 \\ x_2 \end{bmatrix} = \begin{bmatrix} d_1 \\ d_2 \end{bmatrix}$$

$$\begin{bmatrix} \frac{2}{3} & -\frac{1}{4} \\ -\frac{1}{3} & \frac{1}{2} \end{bmatrix}\begin{bmatrix} x_1 \\ x_2 \end{bmatrix} = \begin{bmatrix} d_1 \\ d_2 \end{bmatrix}$$

$$\begin{bmatrix} x_1 \\ x_2 \end{bmatrix} = \begin{bmatrix} 2 & 1 \\ \frac{4}{3} & \frac{8}{3} \end{bmatrix}\begin{bmatrix} d_1 \\ d_2 \end{bmatrix}$$

where $\begin{bmatrix} 2 & 1 \\ \frac{4}{3} & \frac{8}{3} \end{bmatrix}$ is the inverse of $\begin{bmatrix} \frac{2}{3} & -\frac{1}{4} \\ -\frac{1}{3} & \frac{1}{2} \end{bmatrix}$. If the consumer requires 300 units of food and 500 units of clothes, then the number of units that must be produced is

$$\begin{bmatrix} x_1 \\ x_2 \end{bmatrix} = \begin{bmatrix} 2 & 1 \\ \frac{4}{3} & \frac{8}{3} \end{bmatrix}\begin{bmatrix} 300 \\ 500 \end{bmatrix} = \begin{bmatrix} 1100 \\ 1733.3 \end{bmatrix}$$

Therefore, 1100 units of food and 1733.3 units of clothes must be produced.

EXAMPLE 45 A three-industry open Leontief system has the following input coefficient matrix:

$$\begin{array}{l} \text{Services} \\ \text{Manufacturing} \\ \text{Farming} \end{array} \begin{bmatrix} 0.3 & 0.2 & 0.3 \\ 0.5 & 0.2 & 0.1 \\ 0.1 & 0.3 & 0.1 \end{bmatrix}$$

If the demands from the consumer section are for 21, 5, and 1 units, respectively, find the output needed to satisfy these demands.

Solution

$$\mathbf{I} - \mathbf{A} = \begin{bmatrix} 1 & 0 & 0 \\ 0 & 1 & 0 \\ 0 & 0 & 1 \end{bmatrix} - \begin{bmatrix} 0.3 & 0.2 & 0.3 \\ 0.5 & 0.2 & 0.1 \\ 0.1 & 0.3 & 0.1 \end{bmatrix}$$

$$\mathbf{I} - \mathbf{A} = \begin{bmatrix} 0.7 & -0.2 & -0.3 \\ -0.5 & 0.8 & -0.1 \\ -0.1 & -0.3 & 0.9 \end{bmatrix}$$

$$(\mathbf{I} - \mathbf{A})^{-1} = \begin{bmatrix} 2.14 & 0.84 & 0.81 \\ 1.43 & 1.86 & 0.68 \\ 0.71 & 0.71 & 1.43 \end{bmatrix}$$

(correct to two decimal places). Then

$$(\mathbf{I} - \mathbf{A})^{-1}\mathbf{D} = \begin{bmatrix} 2.14 & 0.84 & 0.81 \\ 1.43 & 1.86 & 0.68 \\ 0.71 & 0.71 & 1.43 \end{bmatrix}\begin{bmatrix} 21 \\ 5 \\ 1 \end{bmatrix} = \begin{bmatrix} 49.95 \\ 40.01 \\ 19.89 \end{bmatrix}$$

Rounding the components off to the nearest whole number gives

$$\mathbf{X} = (\mathbf{I} - \mathbf{A})^{-1}\mathbf{D} = \begin{bmatrix} 50 \\ 40 \\ 20 \end{bmatrix}$$

Hence, the outputs needed to satisfy the demands are 50 units of services, 40 units of manufacturing, and 20 units of farming.

Exercise Set **2.7**

A In exercises 1–6, matrix **A** is an input-output matrix associated with an economy, and matrix **D** (in millions of dollars) is the demand matrix (or vector). In each exercise, find the final inputs of each industry so that the demands of both industry and the open sector are met.

1. $\mathbf{A} = \begin{bmatrix} 0.20 & 0.15 \\ 0.25 & 0.10 \end{bmatrix}$ and $\mathbf{D} = \begin{bmatrix} 12 \\ 20 \end{bmatrix}$ **2.** $\mathbf{A} = \begin{bmatrix} 0.30 & 0.50 \\ 0.20 & 0.40 \end{bmatrix}$ and $\mathbf{D} = \begin{bmatrix} 8 \\ 10 \end{bmatrix}$

3. $\mathbf{A} = \begin{bmatrix} \frac{3}{5} & \frac{2}{5} \\ \frac{1}{5} & \frac{3}{5} \end{bmatrix}$ and $\mathbf{D} = \begin{bmatrix} 10 \\ 6 \end{bmatrix}$ **4.** $\mathbf{A} = \begin{bmatrix} \frac{4}{10} & \frac{1}{10} \\ \frac{5}{10} & \frac{2}{10} \end{bmatrix}$ and $\mathbf{D} = \begin{bmatrix} 12 \\ 7 \end{bmatrix}$

5. $\mathbf{A} = \begin{bmatrix} 0.1 & 0.4 & 0.3 \\ 0.3 & 0.2 & 0.2 \\ 0.1 & 0.1 & 0.2 \end{bmatrix}$ and $\mathbf{D} = \begin{bmatrix} 12 \\ 10 \\ 8 \end{bmatrix}$ **6.** $\mathbf{A} = \begin{bmatrix} \frac{1}{5} & \frac{2}{5} & \frac{3}{5} \\ \frac{2}{5} & \frac{4}{5} & \frac{1}{5} \\ \frac{3}{5} & \frac{2}{5} & \frac{3}{5} \end{bmatrix}$ and $\mathbf{D} = \begin{bmatrix} 100 \\ 90 \\ 80 \end{bmatrix}$

B **7.** For the given input-output matrix, determine the following

$$\begin{array}{c} \\ A \\ B \\ C \end{array} \begin{array}{ccc} A & B & C \\ \begin{bmatrix} 0.3 & 0.2 & 0.1 \\ 0.1 & 0.4 & 0.2 \\ 0.2 & 0.3 & 0.1 \end{bmatrix} \end{array}$$

a. The production of 1 unit of B requires how much from A?
b. The production of 1 unit of C requires how much from B?
c. If units are in millions of dollars, what is the value of C to produce $100,000,000 of B?
d. Which sector, A, B, or C, consumes the greatest proportion of C?
e. Which sector, A, B, or C, is least dependent on B?

Economics **8.** The input-output matrix of a closed Leontief system is

$$\mathbf{A} = \begin{array}{c} \\ I \\ II \\ III \end{array} \begin{array}{ccc} I & II & III \\ \begin{bmatrix} \frac{1}{3} & \frac{1}{4} & 0 \\ \frac{1}{3} & \frac{1}{2} & \frac{1}{2} \\ \frac{1}{3} & \frac{1}{4} & \frac{1}{2} \end{bmatrix} \end{array}$$

Suppose that

$$\mathbf{X} = \begin{bmatrix} 3 \\ 8 \\ 6 \end{bmatrix}$$

Show that $\mathbf{X} = \mathbf{AX}$.

9. Suppose that, in a three-industry open system, the Leontief input coefficient matrix is

$$\mathbf{A} = \begin{bmatrix} 0.3 & 0.2 & 0.3 \\ 0.5 & 0.2 & 0.1 \\ 0.1 & 0.3 & 0.2 \end{bmatrix}$$

If the output matrix is

$$\mathbf{X} = \begin{bmatrix} 7 \\ 5 \\ 3 \end{bmatrix}$$

compute $\mathbf{X} - \mathbf{AX}$ to determine the output available for the consumer section.

10. A closed Leontief system consists of three factories—I, II, and III—that produce item I, item II, and item III, respectively. Industry I requires one-third of item I and one-fourth of item II. Industry II requires one-third of item I, one-half of item II, and one-half of item III. Industry III requires one-third of item I, one-fourth of item II, and one-half of item III. Write these requirements as a Leontief input-output matrix, $\mathbf{A}$. If

$$\mathbf{X} = \begin{bmatrix} 15 \\ 40 \\ 30 \end{bmatrix}$$

show that $\mathbf{X} = \mathbf{AX}$.

11. In a three-industry open Leontief system, industry I requires 0.3 of item I, 0.2 of item II, and 0.3 of item III. Industry II requires 0.5 of item I, 0.2 of item II, and 0.1 of item III. Industry III requires 0.1 of item I, 0.3 of item II, and 0.2 of item III. Write these requirements as a Leontief input-output matrix, $\mathbf{A}$. If the output is

$$\mathbf{X} = \begin{bmatrix} 10 \\ 7 \\ 5 \end{bmatrix}$$

compute $\mathbf{X} - \mathbf{AX} = \mathbf{D}$ to determine how much of the output is available for the consumer.

12. A two-industry open Leontief system consisting of a farmer and a tailor has the following input-output matrix:

		Food produced	Clothes produced
Input requirements	Farmer	0.5	0.5
	Tailor	0.2	0.3

Can this system satisfy a consumer demand for 16 units of food and 26 units of clothes?

13. A two-industry open Leontief system has the following input coefficient matrix:

Services	0.5	0.5
Manufacturing	0.2	0.3

If the demands from the consumer section are for 14 units of service and 16 units of manufacturing, find the output needed to satisfy these demands.

14. The energy sector of an economy consists of electricity, oil, and coal. The production of 1 unit of electricity demands 0.05 unit of electricity, 0.2 unit of oil, and 0.6 unit of coal. The production of 1 unit of oil requires 0.1 unit of electricity, 0.4 unit of oil, and 0.001 unit of coal. The production of 1 unit of coal requires 0.2 unit of electricity, 0.6 unit of oil, and 0.002 unit of coal. What gross production is required to meet an external demand for 50 units of electricity, 60 units of oil, and 30 units of coal?

8 Summary and Review

Review to ensure you understand and can use the following concepts:

System of two linear equations: graphical solutions, parallel lines, coincident lines, equivalent system, solution by substitution, solution by the method of addition.

System of three linear equations: solution, three-space coordinate system, planes, trace of a plane.

Matrices: definition, row matrix, column matrix, equal matrices, zero matrix, identity matrix, additive inverse of a matrix.

Augmented matrices: solving systems of equations, row operations to give equivalent systems, reduced matrix, Gauss-Jordan elimination.

Matrix operations: sum, product of a real number and a matrix, negative of a matrix, dot product, product.

Inverse of a matrix: coefficient matrix, input-output matrix: Leontief matrix, closed Leontief system, open Leontief system.

Review Exercise Set 2.8

A 1. Determine whether or not the following systems have common solutions, and solve by two different methods those that do.

a. $3x + 2y = 1$
$5x - 3y = 27$

b. $3x - 7y = 2$
$12x - 28y = 6$

c. $11x - 3y = 7$
$55x - 15y = 35$

d. $2x + 3y = 3$
$3x - y = 10$

2. Solve the following systems of equations by first using augmented matrices and then using inverses of matrices.

a. $2x + y = 4$
$3x - 2y = -1$

b. $5x + 3y = -2$
$4x - 3y = -7$

c. $5x - 3y = 1$
$4x + y = 11$

d. $5x - 7y = -1$
$2x - 3y = 0$

B 3. Determine whether or not the following systems have common solutions, and solve those that have solutions.

a. $x + y + z = 5$
$2x - 3y + 2z = 4$
$4x - y + 4z = 10$

b. $x - y - z = -3$
$3x - 4y - 2z = -11$
$5x - 6y - 4z = -17$

c. $x - 2y - 3z = -3$
$7x - 14y - 21z = -21$
$11x - 22y - 33z = -33$

d. $x + y + z = 5$
$2x + 3y - 2z = -19$
$3x + 2y + 3z = 20$

4. Solve the following systems of equations by using augmented matrices.

a. $x + y + 2z = 4$
$3x - y + z = 3$
$5x + 3y - 4z = 4$

b. $3x - y - z = 2$
$x + 4y - 3z = 11$
$x - y + 2z = 1$

5. Solve the systems of equations in exercise 4 by using inverses of matrices.

C **6.** Determine whether or not the following systems have solutions, and solve those that have solutions.

a. $x + y + z - 2t = 2$
$2x + y + 6z + t = 18$
$3x + 2y + 4z - 4t = 11$
$4x + 3y + 8z - 3t = 22$

b. $x + y + z + t = 2$
$x - y + z - t = 10$
$2x + y + z + t = 6$
$x + 2y + z - 2t = 2$

c. $x + y + 3z + t = 2$
$x - y + 2z - t = 0$
$2x + y + z + t = 3$
$x + 2y - z - t = -3$

d. $x + y - z - 3t = 0$
$2x - y - 5z = 3$
$5x + 2y - 8z - 9t = 3$
$9x - 18z - 9t = 9$

Business **7. Investments.** Kim has a total of $13,700 invested in three types of bonds that pay 9%, 10%, and 11%, respectively. She receives $100 more interest from the 9% bonds than from the 11% bonds. If the total income from the bonds during a year is $1,350, how much does she have invested in each type?

8. Retailing. A clothing store buys 110 suits. For one type it pays $90 per suit and for the other type $75 per suit. The owner wishes to sell the $75 suits for $100. What price must he receive for the other suits if he wishes to make a 50% profit over his cost of $9,000?

9. Investments. Roberto has $9,000 invested in bonds paying 7%, 8%, and 9% interest per year. He has $1,000 more invested at 8% than he has invested at 9%. If he receives $715 interest each year, how much money does he have invested in each type of bond?

Economics **10. Transportation.** An airline has three types of cargo planes, labeled I, II, and III. They can carry the following pieces of equipment:

Planes

	I	II	III
A	8	6	5
Equipment B	4	5	8
C	4	5	3

Suppose a request is received for 76 pieces of type A equipment, 55 pieces of type B, and 45 pieces of type C. How many planes of each type will the company need to make the delivery?

Life Sciences **11. Pollution.** The pollution count for Big City on a particular day is 575. Assume this pollution is produced by three industries, A, B, and C. Industry C contributes twice as much to the pollution count as industry B. It is known that the pollution count would be 450 if the pollution from industry C were reduced by 50%. Find the pollution count of industries A, B, and C, respectively.

Social Sciences **12. Population.** The number of men, women, and children in a city is 850,000. The number of children is equal to the sum of the number of men and women. There are 25,000 more women than men. Find the number of men, women, and children in this city.

13. **Education.** A university has 300 employees classified as faculty, administration, or staff. The number of faculty members is equal to the sum of the number of administration members and staff members. The number of staff members is 50 more than the number of administration members. Find the number of employees in each classification.

14. **Politics.** An organization has its members classified as liberal, conservative, or middle-of-the-roaders. There are five more conservatives than liberals. The number of middle-of-the-roaders is five more than 3 times the number of conservatives. Find the number in each classification if there are 150 members.

3

Introduction to Linear Programming

We all like to get as much as possible in exchange for the least amount of effort or expenditure. Do you remember the last time you went shopping? Of course, you wanted to get the most for your money. And have you ever tried to satisfy your appetite with only the 1000 calories a day a severe diet will allow? All of us have struggled with our daily schedule, trying to find enough time for classes, for study, for a part-time job, and still have the maximum amount of leisure time for club activities, movies, dates, and other activities.

During World War II, the military forces faced similar questions involving purchasing, transportation, job assignments, scheduling, and mixing. To help answer some of these questions, a mathematical process called **linear programming** was formulated.

Linear programming is one of the important developments in applied mathematics in the last half-century. To solve a problem using linear programming, a **mathematical model** (consisting of a set of equations or inequalities) is constructed representing the problem. The model is used to solve the problem by geometric procedures or by a technique originated by George Dantzig called the **simplex method**. Both of these methods of solution will be presented in this chapter.

> Mathematical models often contain inequalities that express limitations. For example, the size of a school building limits the number of students who may attend the school; the amount of money a person has limits the amount he or she can invest; the quality of steel a company wishes to produce places conditions on the ingredients; and so on. **Linear programming** is a procedure that helps optimize a function subject to limitations.

In Chapter 1 we studied the graphs of linear equations and linear inequalities. Then, in Chapter 2, we studied the graphs of a system of linear equations. In this section we study the graph of a set of linear inequalities called **a system of inequalities.** The **solution set for a system of inequalities in two unknowns** is the set of ordered pairs that satisfies all of the inequalities. To solve the system we draw the graph of each inequality and then take the intersection of all the solution sets of all the inequalities in the system. The ordered pairs in the solution set that are also intersection points of the lines that bound the solution set are called **corner points.** (We will see in the next section why corner points are important.) A method for solving a system of inequalities and finding the corner points is illustrated by the following examples.

EXAMPLE 1 Graph the solution set and find the corner points of the system

$$2x + y - 1 \geq 0$$
$$x - y + 1 \leq 0$$

Solution Solutions of linear inequalities were graphed in Section 1.4. In Figure 3.1 the lightest shading represents the solution set for $2x + y - 1 \geq 0$, and the medium shading represents the solution set for $x - y + 1 \leq 0$. The coordinates of any point in the darkest shaded region form a solution of this system. The bounding

Figure 3.1

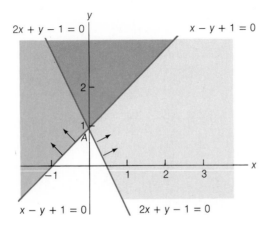

lines of the solution set are $2x + y - 1 = 0$ and $x - y + 1 = 0$. The intersection of these two lines can be found by any of the methods of Chapter 2 to be $(0, 1)$. This point is the only corner point and is represented by $A = (0, 1)$ in Figure 3.1.

EXAMPLE 2 Graph the solution set and find the corner points of the system

$$2x + y \leq 3$$
$$-x + y \leq 0$$
$$y \geq 0$$

Solution   The solution sets for the inequalities $2x + y \leq 3$, $-x + y \leq 0$, and $y \geq 0$ are graphed in Figure 3.2, and the solution set of the points satisfying all the inequalities is shaded. The corner points for this system are $A = (1, 1)$, $B = (0, 0)$, and $C = (\frac{3}{2}, 0)$, as illustrated in Figure 3.2.

Figure 3.2

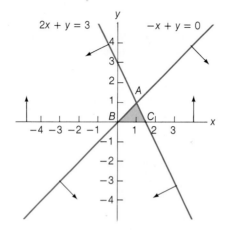

EXAMPLE 3 Find the corner points and graph the solution set of the system

$$2x + y \leq 3$$
$$-x + y \leq 0$$
$$x \leq 0$$

Figure 3.3

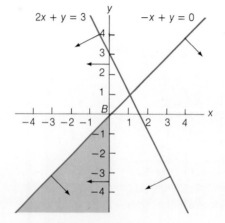

Solution The lines $2x + y = 3$, $-x + y = 0$, and $x = 0$ are graphed, and then the solution set of the points satisfying all of the inequalities is shaded in Figure 3.3. The only corner point is $B = (0, 0)$. The points $(0, 3)$ and $(1, 1)$ are intersections of boundary lines but are not corner points because they are not part of the solution set of the system.

The following examples are simple illustrations of how mathematical models may be constructed to aid in problem solving. The solution set and corner points are found for Example 4, but they are assigned as exercises for Examples 5 and 6. (In the next section we illustrate how corner points are used to maximize or minimize a linear function.)

EXAMPLE 4 A supermarket mixes its regular ground beef as 60% beef and 40% fat. For extra lean ground beef, the market uses 75% beef and 25% fat. The store has 225 pounds of beef and 125 pounds of fat available to make ground beef. Write the system of inequalities that expresses these conditions, graph the solution set, and find the corner points.

Solution Let x represent the number of pounds of regular ground beef made and y represent the number of pounds of extra lean ground beef. Since x and y are both number of pounds, we have $x \geq 0$ and $y \geq 0$. The other conditions are

$$0.60x + 0.75y \leq 225 \quad \text{condition on beef}$$

$$0.40x + 0.25y \leq 125 \quad \text{condition on fat}$$

The graph of the solution set is given in Figure 3.4.

Figure 3.4

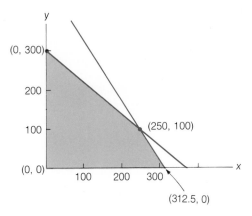

The corner points are $(0, 0)$, $(312.5, 0)$, $(250, 100)$, and $(0, 300)$.

EXAMPLE 5 A doctor has prescribed a diet in which the total number of calories cannot exceed 1200. She insists that twice the number of protein calories added to the number of carbohydrate calories must equal or exceed 1600. Write these conditions as a system of inequalities.

Solution Let x represent the number of protein calories and y represent the number of carbohydrate calories. The conditions are

$$x + y \leq 1200$$
$$2x + y \geq 1600$$
$$x \geq 0$$
$$y \geq 0$$

EXAMPLE 6 A school system has only enough money to hire 300 teachers. Each teacher has either a class A or a class B certificate. The school board desires that at least one-third of its teachers have the class A certificate. Express these conditions as a system of inequalities.

Solution Let x represent the number of teachers with class B certificates and y represent the number of teachers with class A certificates. The mathematical model is

$$x + y \leq 300$$
$$y \geq \tfrac{1}{3}(x + y)$$
$$x \geq 0$$
$$y \geq 0$$

Note that only integral solutions have meaning.

Exercise Set **3.1**

Graph the solution sets and find the corner points in exercises 1–20.

A   **1.** $x \geq 0$
       $y \geq 0$

2. $x \geq 3$
    $y \geq 2$

3. $x \geq 0$
    $y \geq 3$

4. $x \geq 2$
    $y \geq 0$

5. $y \geq x$
    $x \geq 0$

6. $y \geq x$
    $y \geq 0$

B   **7.** $y \geq x$
       $x \geq 0$
       $y \leq 3$

8. $y \geq x$
    $y \geq 0$
    $y \leq 3$

9. $y \leq x$
    $x \geq 0$
    $y \leq 3$

10. $y \leq x$
      $y \geq 0$
      $y \leq 3$

11. $-x + y \geq 0$
     $x + y \geq 0$

12. $-x + y \geq 0$
     $2x + y \geq 3$

13. $y \geq x - 1$
      $y \geq -x + 1$
      $y \leq 1$

14. $y \geq x - 1$
     $y \geq -x + 1$
     $y \geq 1$

C   **15.** $y \geq x - 1$
       $y \leq -x + 1$
       $y \leq 1$
       $x \geq 0$
       $y \geq 0$

16. $y \geq x - 1$
     $y \leq -x + 1$
     $y \geq 1$
     $x \geq 0$
     $y \geq 0$

17. $2y \leq x + 6$
            $y + x \geq 2$
            $y - x \geq -4$
            $y \geq 0$

18. $2y \leq x + 6$
$y \geq -x + 2$
$y - x \geq -4$
$y \geq 0$
$x \geq 0$

19. $2y \leq x + 6$
$y + x \geq 2$
$y - x \geq -4$
$-y \geq 0$

20. $x + y \geq 1$
$x + y \leq 2$
$x \geq 0$
$y \geq 0$

21. Graph the solution set for Example 5, and locate the corner points.

22. Graph the solution set for Example 6, and locate the corner points.

Business

23. Manufacturing. A manufacturer makes two products, valves and reducers. A valve requires 1 hour on machine A and 2 hours on machine B, while a reducer requires 2 hours on A and 2 hours on B. Let x be the number of valves produced in a day and y be the number of reducers produced in a day. If the machines operate 8 hours a day, write the mathematical model for this manufacturer, graph the solution set, and find the corner points.

24. Rework exercise 23 if the manufacturer decides to operate the machines 16 hours a day.

25. Investment. An investor has up to $30,000 to invest in AA bonds or B bonds. The AA bonds yield 8%, and the B bonds yield 12%. If the investor wishes to invest at least 2 times as much in AA as B bonds, write the mathematical model, graph the solution set, and find the corner points for the investor.

26. Assignment. The Sanitation Department of Clean City has 100 garbage trucks and 250 employees. A full-strength collection team consists of one truck and three employees. while a partial-strength team consists of one truck and two employees. A full-strength team collects 12 tons of garbage per day, while a partial-strength team collects only 6 tons. The city manager wishes to collect the maximum amount of garbage each day, but the numbers of operating trucks and available employees vary. How many full-strength teams and how many partial-strength teams should be formed in order to maximize the amount of garbage collected on a day when all trucks are operating and a maximum of 240 employees is available for assignment? Write the mathematical model and graph the solution for Clean City's assignment problem. Then find the corner points.

Life Sciences

27. Agriculture. George has a 50-acre farm on which he plans to plant two crops, wheat and corn. Wheat requires 2 days of labor per acre, and corn requires 3 days of labor per acre. The other costs for wheat amount to $40 per acre, and for corn the other costs amount to $30 per acre. George has evaluated his assets and found that he has 150 days of labor available and $1800 capital. Let x represent the number of acres of wheat planted and y represent the number of acres of corn planted. Graph the solution set and find the corner points for George.

Social Sciences

28. Education. A classroom has space for 50 students. Let x represent the number of girls and y represent the number of boys. Graph the set that represents the possible number of boys and girls, and find the corner points.

29. There are 210 students in the school referred to in exercise 28. The principal requests that the number y of boys and the number x of girls in the classroom satisfy the additional requirement $7x + 3y \leq 210$. Graph the set of possibilities that would satisfy this condition and the space condition of exercise 28. Find the corner points of this set.

30. The teacher in the classroom of exercise 28 insists that the number of boys in the classroom be at least 7. Use this additional restriction to graph the set of possibilities and find the corner points.

Many practical problems in business, economics, life sciences, and social science involve complex relationships among variables. These relationships are often stated in terms of inequalities. In addition, we may wish to find the maximum or minimum value of a linear function subject to the conditions imposed by the inequalities. For example, a set of linear inequalities may represent the relationship between available raw material and labor. If we can express production linearly in terms of available raw material and labor, we can find the conditions for maximum production.

Problems of this type are typical of the problems faced by many individuals and many companies each day. Linear programming was developed to help solve some of these problems. In this section we give a geometric explanation of how a linear programming problem may be solved.

Let us first describe in general terms a linear programming problem.

Linear Programming

1. A **linear programming problem** is one that is concerned with maximizing or minimizing a linear function defined on a solution set of a system of linear equations or inequalities.
2. The solution set of a system of equations or inequalities in a linear programming problem is called the **set of feasible solutions.**
3. The equations or inequalities expressing the restrictions or conditions of the problem are called **constraints.**
4. The linear function to be maximized or minimized is called the **objective function.**
5. A **convex set** in a plane is a set in which for any two points P and Q of the set, all of the points on the line segment PQ are in the set.
6. If the boundaries of a plane convex set consist of lines, the set is called a **polyhedral convex set.**
7. If a polyhedral convex set is bounded by a polygon, it is called a **bounded polygonal convex set.**

The shaded regions of Figures 3.2 and 3.5(a) illustrate bounded polygonal convex sets. Sets that are polyhedral convex but not bounded are illustrated in Figures 3.1 and 3.3. A set that is not convex is illustrated in Figure 3.5(b).

The following example is a simple geometric explanation of how the maximum and minimum values of an objective function defined on a bounded polygonal convex set may be found.

Figure 3.5

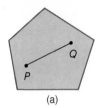

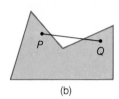

(a)   (b)

EXAMPLE 7 Find the maximum and the minimum values of the cost objective function $C = 10x + 5y$ subject to the constraints

$$x + y \leq 12$$
$$2 \leq x \leq 6$$
$$3 \leq y \leq 8$$

Solution The set of feasible solutions is shown in Figure 3.6. Note that this set is bounded by a five-sided polygon with corner points $(2, 3)$, $(2, 8)$, $(4, 8)$, $(6, 6)$, and $(6, 3)$. The corner points are very important in finding the maximum or minimum value of the objective function. To find the maximum and minimum values of $C = 10x + 5y$ subject to the constraints let us assign values to C and plot the lines obtained. When C is assigned a particular value and the graph drawn, any point (x, y) in the set of feasible solutions that lies on this line would produce this same cost.

Figure 3.6

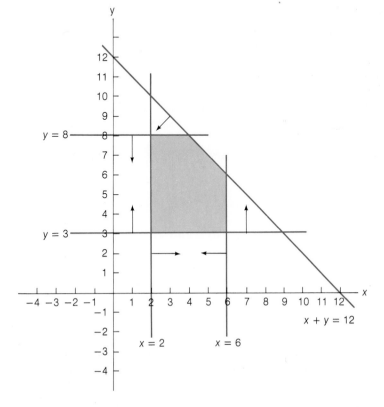

Suppose, for example, we let the cost C take on a number of different values and plot a number of constant cost lines. Note that these lines are parallel to each other since they have the same slope (only the constant term varies). Let's plot these lines when $C = 35, 60, 75, 80, 90$, and 100. Note that all except the last are values of C at corner points.

$$C_1: \quad 10x + 5y = 35$$
$$C_2: \quad 10x + 5y = 60$$
$$C_3: \quad 10x + 5y = 75$$
$$C_4: \quad 10x + 5y = 80$$
$$C_5: \quad 10x + 5y = 90$$
$$C_6: \quad 10x + 5y = 100$$

In Figure 3.7 we observe that as C increases, the y-intercept increases. (This relationship holds for functions of the form $C = ax + by$ where $b > 0$.) Thus, the maximum C occurs at a point where the y-intercept is the largest and the line contains at least one point of the solution set. This occurs on C_5, which goes through the corner point $(6, 6)$. Note also that the minimum value of the y-intercept occurs for the line C_1 through the corner point $(2, 3)$. The line when the cost is 100 contains no points in the solution set. Hence, the cost can never be 100 for a point in the solution set. (If $b < 0$, the minimum value of C occurs when the

Figure 3.7

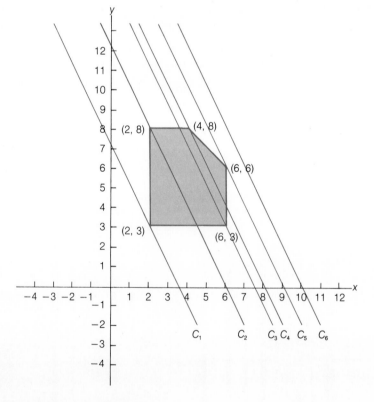

line has the largest y-intercept and the maximum occurs for the line with the smallest y-intercept.)

A study of Figure 3.7 suggests that maximum and minimum values of a linear function occur at corner points. This is indeed true, as indicated by the following important theorem:

Maximum Value, Minimum Value

> An **objective function** defined on a bounded polygonal convex set has both a **maximum value** and a **minimum value** on the set, and these **values occur at corner points** of the set. If the set is not bounded, the objective function may not have a maximum value or a minimum value, but if it does have one or both, they will occur at corner points of the set.

Consequently, to find maximum or minimum values of an objective function we find all corner points and evaluate the objective function at each of the corner points. The corner points for the problem are (2, 3), (2, 8), (6, 3), (4, 8), and (6, 6), and these are the points for which C was found. The minimum value for C was 35 at (2, 3), and the maximum value was 90 at (6, 6).

The procedure for finding the maximum and minimum values of an objective function is outlined below:

> **Steps for Finding the Maximum and Minimum Values of an Objective Function Defined on a Bounded Polygonal Convex Set**
>
> **1.** Graph the solution set of the constraints to form a bounded polygonal convex set. This set is called the **feasible region.**
> **2.** Find the corner points of the solution set.
> **3.** Evaluate the objective function at each corner point.
> **4.** The smallest value obtained from step 3 is the minimum value of the function and the largest value obtained is the maximum value of the function on the bounded polygonal convex set.

EXAMPLE 8 Find the maximum and minimum values of the function

$$P = 4x + 3y$$

subject to the constraints

$$x \geq 0$$
$$y \geq 0$$
$$5x + 3y \leq 30$$
$$2x + 3y \leq 21$$

Solution Step 1.

Figure 3.8

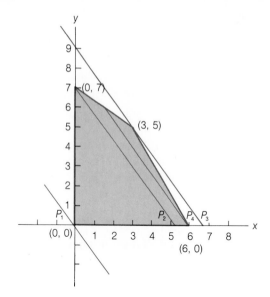

Step 2. The corner points of the set of constraints are found to be $(0, 0)$, $(0, 7)$, $(3, 5)$, and $(6, 0)$.

Step 3. Evaluating P at each of these corner points gives

$$P_1 = 4(0) + 3(0) = 0$$
$$P_2 = 4(0) + 3(7) = 21$$
$$P_3 = 4(3) + 3(5) = 27$$
$$P_4 = 4(6) + 3(0) = 24$$

and the lines corresponding to these P values are drawn in Figure 3.8.

Step 4. The maximum value of P is 27 and the minimum value is 0.

   If the objective function is defined on a convex set that is not a bounded polygonal set, it might not have a maximum or a minimum value on the solution set. A study of the objective function for different values of the constant can help you decide when maximum and minimum values do not exist.

EXAMPLE 9 Find the maximum and minimum values of

$$f = 2x + 3y$$

subject to the constraints

$$x + y \geq 0$$
$$-2x + y \geq -4$$
$$y \geq 0$$

Solution Let's look at the objective function for different values of f. At $(0, 0)$, f is 0, and at $(2, 0)$, f is 4. Let f also have values 6, 12, and 18. Then plot the following lines in Figure 3.9:

Figure 3.9

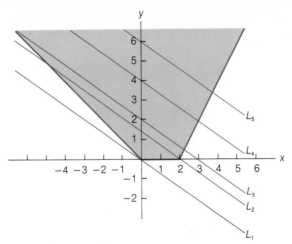

L_1: $0 = 2x + 3y$

L_2: $4 = 2x + 3y$

L_3: $6 = 2x + 3y$

L_4: $12 = 2x + 3y$

L_5: $18 = 2x + 3y$

The solution set is shown in Figure 3.9. Notice that this set is not bounded. The corner points are $(0, 0)$ and $(2, 0)$.

It is obvious that the minimum value occurs at $(0, 0)$ and is 0. Since the y-intercept can get larger and larger for larger values of f, the function does not have a maximum value on the solution set.

Now take a look at a new function over this solution set, $f = 3x + 2y$. Let f take on several values and plot the lines. Are you surprised that f has neither a maximum nor a minimum?

There are many different types of problems that can be solved by constructing a linear programming model. This variety contributes to the difficulty of the construction. We cannot possibly demonstrate a procedure that will always work, but there are certain steps that are helpful in constructing and solving a linear programming problem:

Linear Programming Model

1. Locate and identify the variables.
2. Express the objective function (that is, the linear function to be maximized or minimized) in terms of the variables.
3. Express the constraints as equations or inequalities in terms of the variables.
4. Consider the constraints as a system of equations or inequalities and graph the system of constraints.
5. Find the corner points.
6. Evaluate the objective function at each corner point to locate any maximum or minimum that exists.

We shall now see how each step of the procedure is applied to a problem. Study the example to ensure your understanding of the steps in the construction.

EXAMPLE 10   Suppose a sociologist wishes to maximize the time he can spend on his favorite research project. He plans 14 morning sessions and 12 afternoon sessions for a week. The project is such that he does not want more than 3 morning sessions and 2 afternoon sessions during 8 hours, nor more than 2 morning sessions and 4 afternoon sessions during 8 hours. How long should each session be in order for him to maximize the time spent on his project for the week?

Solution   The first step in the construction of the linear programming model is to locate and identify the variables. The sociologist wants to know how long each session should be, so we let

$$x = \text{time in hours of each morning session}$$
$$y = \text{time in hours of each afternoon session}$$

The quantity he wishes to maximize is time, P, spent on the project for the week. Since he plans 14 morning sessions and 12 afternoon sessions,

$$P = 14x + 12y$$

is the linear function to be maximized. This expression for P is the objective function and completes the second step of the construction. The third step consists of expressing the constraints as equations or inequalities in terms of the variables. Since x and y represent time in hours and we know that time is nonnegative, we must have $x \geq 0$ and $y \geq 0$. The statements in the problem require that

$$3x + 2y \leq 8$$
$$2x + 4y \leq 8$$

Step 4 involves graphing the system of constraints, as shown in Figure 3.10. Step 5 requires the corner points, which are found to be (0, 0), (0, 2), (2, 1), and $(\frac{8}{3}, 0)$. When the objective function is evaluated at each of these corner points as required by step 6, we obtain

$$P_1 = 14(0) + 12(0) = 0$$
$$P_2 = 14(0) + 12(2) = 24$$

Figure 3.10

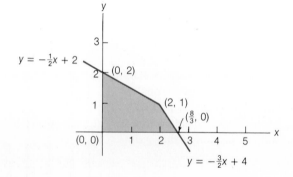

$$P_3 = 14(2) + 12(1) = 40$$
$$P_4 = 14(\tfrac{8}{3}) + 12(0) = 37.33$$

Hence, the sessions should be 2 hours long in the morning and 1 hour long in the afternoon to maximize the time spent on the project subject to the constraints.

Exercise Set **3.2**

Exercises 1–3 involve the following sets.

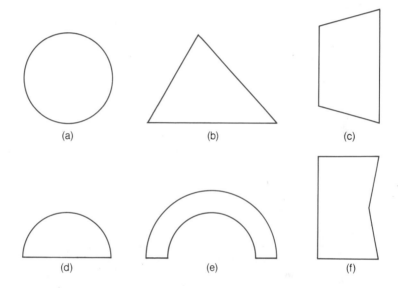

(a)   (b)   (c)

(d)   (e)   (f)

A **1.** Which sets are convex?

2. Which sets are polyhedral convex?

3. Which sets are bounded polygonal convex?

4. Graph the solution set of the following systems of linear inequalities. Locate corner points. Is each solution set convex? Polyhedral convex? Bounded polygonal convex?

a.
$x \geq 0$
$y \geq 0$

b.
$x + y \leq 2$
$x \geq 0$
$y \geq 0$

c.
$x + 3y \leq 4$
$x \geq 0$
$y \geq 0$

d.
$x + y \geq 2$
$x + 3y \geq 4$

e.
$x + y \leq 2$
$x + 3y \leq 4$
$x \geq 0$
$y \geq 0$

f.
$x + y \geq 2$
$x + 3y \geq 4$
$x + y \leq 4$

g.
$x + y \geq 2$
$x + 3y \geq 4$
$x + y \leq 4$
$x \geq 0$

5. Find the maximum and minimum values (if they exist) of $P = x + 2y$ over each of the solution sets given in exercise 4. Do both maximum and minimum values exist for all problems? Explain.

6. Answer the questions of exercise 5 for the function $P = x - 2y$.

7. Find the maximum and minimum values of the function $P = 25x + 35y$ subject to the following sets of constraints.

<table>
<tr><td>a.</td><td>$x \geq 0$</td><td>b.</td><td>$x \geq 0$</td><td>c.</td><td>$x \geq 0$</td></tr>
<tr><td></td><td>$y \geq 0$</td><td></td><td>$y \geq 0$</td><td></td><td>$y \geq 0$</td></tr>
<tr><td></td><td>$2x + 3y \leq 15$</td><td></td><td>$2x + y \leq 7$</td><td></td><td>$x + y \leq 7$</td></tr>
<tr><td></td><td>$3x + y \leq 12$</td><td></td><td>$3x + y \leq 8$</td><td></td><td>$2x + y \leq 9$</td></tr>
<tr><td></td><td></td><td></td><td></td><td></td><td>$3x + y \leq 12$</td></tr>
<tr><td>d.</td><td>$x \geq 0$</td><td>e.</td><td>$x \geq 0$</td><td></td><td></td></tr>
<tr><td></td><td>$y \geq 0$</td><td></td><td>$y \geq 0$</td><td></td><td></td></tr>
<tr><td></td><td>$x + y \geq 2$</td><td></td><td>$x + y \geq 2$</td><td></td><td></td></tr>
<tr><td></td><td>$2x + 3y \leq 15$</td><td></td><td>$2x + y \leq 7$</td><td></td><td></td></tr>
<tr><td></td><td>$3x + y \leq 12$</td><td></td><td>$3x + y \leq 8$</td><td></td><td></td></tr>
</table>

8. Find the maximum and minimum values of the function $P = 35x + 25y$ subject to the sets of constraints given in exercise 7.

9. Find the maximum and minimum values of the function $P = 25x - 35y$ subject to the sets of constraints given in exercise 7.

10. Find the maximum and minimum values of the function $P = 25x + 35y$ subject to the following sets of constraints.

<table>
<tr><td>a.</td><td>$x \geq 0$</td><td>b.</td><td>$x \geq 0$</td><td>c.</td><td>$x \geq 0$</td></tr>
<tr><td></td><td>$y \geq 0$</td><td></td><td>$y \geq 0$</td><td></td><td>$y \geq 0$</td></tr>
<tr><td></td><td>$2 \leq x + y \leq 7$</td><td></td><td>$x + 3y \leq 21$</td><td></td><td>$2x + 3y \geq 6$</td></tr>
<tr><td></td><td>$2x + y \leq 9$</td><td></td><td>$2x + 3y \leq 24$</td><td></td><td>$x + 3y \leq 21$</td></tr>
<tr><td></td><td>$3x + y \leq 12$</td><td></td><td>$2x + y \leq 16$</td><td></td><td>$2x + 3y \leq 24$</td></tr>
<tr><td></td><td></td><td></td><td></td><td></td><td>$2x + y \leq 16$</td></tr>
</table>

11. Find the maximum and minimum values of the function $P = 25x - 35y$ subject to the sets of constraints given in exercise 10.

12. Find the maximum and minimum values of the function $P = 50x + 20y$ subject to the sets of constraints in exercise 10.

13. **Manufacturing.** A manufacturer makes two products, item 1 and item 2. Item 1 requires 1 hour on machine A and 1.5 hours on machine B, while item 2 requires 2 hours on A and 1 hour on B. If the machines operate 8 hours a day and the manufacturer makes a profit of $600 each for item 1 and $700 each for item 2, find the number of each product that should be produced for maximum profit.

14. Redo exercise 13 for profits of $800 each for item 1 and $700 each for item 2.

15. **Investment.** An investor has up to $50,000 to invest in AA bonds or B bonds. The AA bonds yield 10%, and the B bonds yield 15%. If the investor wishes to invest at least 3 times as much in AA bonds as in B bonds, find the amount the investor should invest in each type of bond to maximize income.

16. **Assignment.** Redo exercise 26 in Section 3.1 to help the city manager decide how many full-strength teams and how many partial-strength teams should be formed to maximize the amount of garbage collected.

17. **Agriculture.** George has found that he can make $250 per acre profit for each acre of wheat he plants on his 50-acre farm (see exercise 27 in Section 3.1). He can make $225 per acre profit for each acre of corn he plants. Write his total profit as a linear function of the acres planted, and use the corner points found in exercise 27 to help George decide how many acres of each crop he should plant in order to maximize his profit.

18. Redo exercise 17 with a profit of $200 per acre for wheat and $300 per acre for corn.

Social Sciences

19. **Education.** A university plans to use instructors and graduate assistants in a research project. The university needs at least 400 hours of labor spent in gathering data, with each instructor spending 8 hours and each graduate student spending 20 hours gathering data. After the data are gathered, at least 304 hours are required for processing. Each instructor can process data for 8 hours and each graduate assistant for 4 hours. If instructors cost $10 per hour and graduate assistants cost $7 per hour, find the number of each the university should use for minimum cost. Assume that the university uses the same instructors and graduate assistants to gather and process the data.

20. Redo exercise 19 for an instructor cost of $15 per hour while the graduate assistant's cost remains at $7 per hour.

3 The Simplex Method

The first two sections of this chapter have presented a geometric solution to simple linear programming problems. They have provided the intuitive foundation to help you understand the theory involved in the **simplex method** of solution. Many people, including the Russian Leonid Kantorovich and the economist Tjalling Loopmans, who received the Nobel Prize in 1975, have contributed to the development of linear programming. George Dantzig, who received the National Medal of Service, originated the technique for solving linear programs by the simplex method presented in this section.

A linear programming problem becomes more difficult as the number of restrictions or the number of variables increases. Finding all the corner points and evaluating the linear function at each corner point may become very time consuming and tedious as the number of variables increases. Consequently, a method called the **simplex method** has been developed for solving linear programming problems. Briefly, the simplex method is a procedure for evaluating the objective function at certain selected corner points instead of evaluating the objective function at all corner points.

To illustrate how the simplex method works, we consider Example 8 again. We are to find the maximum value of the objective function

$$P = 4x + 3y$$

subject to the constraints

$$x \geq 0$$
$$y \geq 0$$
$$5x + 3y \leq 30$$
$$2x + 3y \leq 21$$

Mathematically, the constraints are changed into equations by the introduction of additional variables, called **slack variables.** Recall that $5x + 3y \leq 30$ means that there exists a real number $r \geq 0$ such that $5x + 3y + r = 30$. Also, $2x + 3y \leq 21$ means that there exists a real number $s \geq 0$ such that $2x + 3y + s = 21$. The variables r and s are examples of slack variables. The system of equations may now be written

$$
\begin{aligned}
5x + 3y + r &= 30 \\
2x + 3y \quad + s &= 21 \\
-4x - 3y \qquad\quad + P &= 0
\end{aligned}
$$

with the constraints $x \geq 0$, $y \geq 0$, $r \geq 0$, and $s \geq 0$.

Notice that we now have three equations containing five unknowns subject to the constraints. Since the coefficients of r, s, and P are all 1, we see that setting $x = 0$ and $y = 0$ gives the obvious solution $r = 30$, $s = 21$, $P = 0$. The solution $x = 0$, $y = 0$, $r = 30$, $s = 21$, $P = 0$ is called an **obvious basic feasible solution.** Note that this solution is a 5-tuple $(x, y, r, s, P) = (0, 0, 30, 21, 0)$, but for simplification we shall state that $P = 0$ is the value of the linear function at the basic feasible solution $(0, 0)$. Because the coefficients of x and y are negative in the third equation of the system, the value $P = 0$ is a minimum for $x = 0$ and $y = 0$. Any positive value for x or y would make P larger. We emphasize that $P = 0$ is the value of the linear function at the basic feasible solution $(0, 0)$. To make P larger, we operate on the system in a manner that will give the value of P at another basic feasible solution. Suppose we operate on the system so that the coefficient of x will be 1 in the first equation and 0 in the other equations. Such operations are called **pivot operations,** and x is called a **pivot element.** In this illustration, the coefficient of x is 5, and the multiplicative inverse of 5 is $\frac{1}{5}$. Hence, each term of the first equation is multiplied by $\frac{1}{5}$ to give

$$x + \tfrac{3}{5}y + \tfrac{1}{5}r = 6 \tag{1}$$

To eliminate x in the second equation, we multiply each term of equation (1) by -2 and add the resulting equation to the second equation of the system, giving

$$\tfrac{9}{5}y - \tfrac{2}{5}r + s = 9$$

Finally, to eliminate x in the third equation, we multiply each term of equation (1) by 4 and add the resulting equation to the third equation of the system, giving

$$-\tfrac{3}{5}y + \tfrac{4}{5}r + P = 24$$

The system may now be written

$$
\begin{aligned}
x + \tfrac{3}{5}y + \tfrac{1}{5}r &= 6 \\
\tfrac{9}{5}y - \tfrac{2}{5}r + s &= 9 \\
-\tfrac{3}{5}y + \tfrac{4}{5}r \quad + P &= 24
\end{aligned}
$$

If we set $y = 0$ and $r = 0$, we obtain $P = 24$, $x = 6$, and $s = 9$.

We note that $P = 24$ is the value of P at the basic feasible solution $(6, 0)$. Since the coefficient of y in the third equation for P is still negative, P can be made larger by increasing y. Hence, we pivot on y. We multiply the second equation by $\frac{5}{9}$ to give

$$y - \tfrac{2}{9}r + \tfrac{5}{9}s = 5 \tag{2}$$

To eliminate y in the first equation, we multiply each term of equation (2) by $-\frac{3}{5}$ and add the resulting equation to the first equation to yield

$$x + \tfrac{1}{3}r - \tfrac{1}{3}s = 3$$

To eliminate y in the third equation, we multiply each term of equation (2) by $\frac{3}{5}$ and add the resulting equation to the third equation to obtain

$$\tfrac{2}{3}r + \tfrac{1}{3}s + P = 27$$

The new system is

$$
\begin{aligned}
x \qquad + \tfrac{1}{3}r - \tfrac{1}{3}s \qquad &= 3 \\
y - \tfrac{2}{9}r + \tfrac{5}{9}s \qquad &= 5 \\
\tfrac{2}{3}r + \tfrac{1}{3}s + P &= 27
\end{aligned}
$$

Setting $r = 0$ and $s = 0$ gives $P = 27$ in the third equation, $x = 3$ in the first equation, and $y = 5$ in the second equation. Notice that in the equation containing P, the coefficients of r and s are both positive. Since $r \geq 0$ and $s \geq 0$, the maximum value of P is obtained by setting $r = 0$ and $s = 0$. Any positive value for r or s would make P have a smaller value. Hence, the maximum value of P subject to the constraints has been found to be $P = 27$ at the extreme point (3, 5).

This example introduces the simplex method of linear programming. Instead of writing the systems of equations, the simplex method uses matrices to simplify notation. We illustrate this use of matrix notation by solving the same problem again.

Maximize

$$P = 4x + 3y$$

subject to

$$
\begin{aligned}
x &\geq 0 \\
y &\geq 0 \\
5x + 3y &\leq 30 \\
2x + 3y &\leq 21
\end{aligned}
$$

Introducing the slack variables $r \geq 0$ and $s \geq 0$ allows us to change the form of the problem to a system of equations:

$$
\begin{aligned}
5x + 3y + r \qquad\qquad &= 30 \\
2x + 3y \qquad + s \qquad &= 21 \\
-4x - 3y \qquad\qquad + P &= 0
\end{aligned}
$$

where $x \geq 0$, $y \geq 0$, $r \geq 0$, and $s \geq 0$. This system is written in the following matrix form, called the **simplex tableau:**

$$
\begin{array}{ccccc}
x & y & r & s & P \\
\end{array}
$$
$$
\left[
\begin{array}{ccccc|c}
\boxed{5} & 3 & 1 & 0 & 0 & 30 \\
2 & 3 & 0 & 1 & 0 & 21 \\
\hline
-4 & -3 & 0 & 0 & 1 & 0
\end{array}
\right]
$$

The columns of the matrix are the coefficients of the variables, which are written above the first row, with the exception of the last column. The last column gives the constants in the equations and is separated from the other columns by a vertical line. Note that the last row represents the linear function to be maximized. It is separated from the other rows by a dashed line.

The element 5 in the first row and first column is circled to indicate that it is the **pivot element.** The row containing the pivot element is called the **pivot row,** and the column containing the pivot element is called the **pivot column.** (The manner of selecting the pivot element will be explained later.) The second matrix is

$$
\begin{array}{ccccc}
x & y & r & s & P \\
\end{array}
$$

$$
\left[
\begin{array}{ccccc|c}
1 & \frac{3}{5} & \frac{1}{5} & 0 & 0 & 6 \\
0 & \textcircled{$\frac{9}{5}$} & -\frac{2}{5} & 1 & 0 & 9 \\
\hline
0 & -\frac{3}{5} & \frac{4}{5} & 0 & 1 & 24 \\
\end{array}
\right]
\begin{array}{l}
\frac{1}{5}\text{row } 1_1 \\
\text{Row } 2_1 - 2\text{row } 1_2 \\
\text{Row } 3_1 + 4\text{row } 1_2 \\
\end{array}
$$

The instructions for obtaining this second matrix are written to the right of each row with the subscripts denoting the matrix from which the row is obtained. The instruction "$\frac{1}{5}$row 1_1" to the right of the first row means that the first row of the second matrix was obtained by multiplying the first row of the first matrix by $\frac{1}{5}$. The instruction "Row $2_1 - 2$row 1_2" means that the second row of the second matrix was obtained by adding to the second row of the first matrix -2 multiplied by the first row of the second matrix. The instruction "Row $3_1 + 4$row 1_2" means that the third row of the second matrix was obtained by adding to the third row of the first matrix 4 multiplied by the first row of the second matrix. The element $\frac{9}{5}$ is circled to indicate that it is the pivot element from which the third matrix will be obtained. Note that the last column now gives the values $x = 6$, $s = 9$, and $P = 24$ when $y = 0$ and $r = 0$. $P = 24$ is the value of the linear function at the extreme point $(6, 0)$. The third matrix is

$$
\begin{array}{ccccc}
x & y & r & s & P \\
\end{array}
$$

$$
\left[
\begin{array}{ccccc|c}
1 & 0 & \frac{1}{3} & -\frac{1}{3} & 0 & 3 \\
0 & 1 & -\frac{2}{9} & \frac{5}{9} & 0 & 5 \\
\hline
0 & 0 & \frac{2}{3} & \frac{1}{3} & 1 & 27 \\
\end{array}
\right]
\begin{array}{l}
\text{Row } 1_2 - \frac{3}{5}\text{row } 2_3 \\
\frac{5}{9}\text{row } 2_2 \\
\text{Row } 3_2 + \frac{3}{5}\text{row } 2_3 \\
\end{array}
$$

When obtaining the new matrix from the previous matrix, the pivoting operation of multiplying the pivot row of the previous matrix by the multiplicative inverse of the pivot element is the first operation performed. Notice that since the pivot element was $\frac{9}{5}$, the second row was multiplied by $\frac{5}{9}$ and given as the second row of the new matrix. Since this makes 1 the coefficient of y, the constant 5 in this row is now the value of y when $r = 0$ and $s = 0$.

To obtain the other rows of the new matrix, we multiply this new row by the additive inverse of the value in the pivot column of each of the other rows and add the result to each of those rows. These operations should result in a column that has a 1 where the pivot element had been and 0s for all other elements in the column. Since the coefficients of the last row of this third matrix are now all positive, this matrix is the final matrix and gives the maximum value $P = 27$ when $x = 3$, $y = 5$, $r = 0$, and $s = 0$. The operations performed on the simplex tableau in the preceding discussion are called **pivot operations.**

| | Pivot Operations | Pivot operations are row operations except interchanges performed on a matrix to make the pivot element 1 and to make 0 all other entries in the pivot column. |

EXAMPLE 11 Perform a pivot operation on the following simplex tableau to obtain a second matrix. Write the system of equations represented by the second matrix.

Solution

$$\begin{array}{cccccc}
x & y & r & s & P & \\
\left[\begin{array}{ccccc|c}
③ & 2 & 1 & 0 & 0 & 8 \\
2 & 4 & 0 & 1 & 0 & 8 \\
\hline
-14 & -12 & 0 & 0 & 1 & 0
\end{array}\right]
\end{array}$$

The pivot operation gives the following second matrix:

$$\begin{array}{ccccc}
x & y & r & s & P \\
\left[\begin{array}{ccccc|c}
1 & \frac{2}{3} & \frac{1}{3} & 0 & 0 & \frac{8}{3} \\
0 & \frac{8}{3} & -\frac{2}{3} & 1 & 0 & \frac{8}{3} \\
\hline
0 & -\frac{8}{3} & \frac{14}{3} & 0 & 1 & \frac{112}{3}
\end{array}\right]
\end{array}
\begin{array}{l}
\frac{1}{3}\text{row }1_1 \\
-2\text{row }1_2 + \text{row }2_1 \\
14\text{row }1_2 + \text{row }3_1
\end{array}$$

This second matrix represents the system

$$x + \tfrac{2}{3}y + \tfrac{1}{3}r \qquad\qquad = \tfrac{8}{3}$$
$$\tfrac{8}{3}y - \tfrac{2}{3}r + s \qquad = \tfrac{8}{3}$$
$$-\tfrac{8}{3}y + \tfrac{14}{3}r \qquad + P = \tfrac{112}{3}$$

The constants in the last column of the second matrix give $x = \frac{8}{3}$, $s = \frac{8}{3}$, and $P = \frac{112}{3}$ when $y = 0$ and $r = 0$.

Exercise Set **3.3**

Indicate whether the following statements are true or false.

A   1. Slack variables are always positive.

2. Slack variables are nonnegative.

3. Slack variables are used to change the constraints to equations.

4. The simplex method evaluates the objective function at certain corner points instead of evaluating the objective function at all corner points.

5. Row interchanges are not permitted in the simplex method.

6. Pivot operations are column operations with the exception of an interchange performed on a matrix to make the pivot element 1 and all other entries in the pivot column 0.

7. Pivot operations are row operations with the exception of an interchange performed on a matrix to make the pivot element 1 and all other entries in the pivot column 0.

8. To get 0 below the pivot element multiply each element of that row by 0.

9. A fraction larger than 1 cannot be used as a multiplier to make the pivot element 1.

10. A fraction less than 1 cannot be used as a multiplier to make the pivot element 1.

11. Complete the blanks for the following simplex tableau.

$$
\begin{array}{ccccc}
x & y & r & s & P \\
\end{array}
$$

$$
\left[
\begin{array}{ccccc|c}
2 & ③ & 1 & 0 & 0 & 2 \\
4 & 1 & 0 & 1 & 0 & 3 \\
\hline
-5 & -7 & 0 & 0 & 1 & 4
\end{array}
\right]
$$

a. The pivot element is _____.
b. The first equation is _____.
c. The second equation is _____.
d. The linear function is _____.
e. The variables set equal to zero are _____.

B 12. Perform the pivot operation indicated for the simplex tableau given in exercise 11 in order to obtain the second matrix.

Find the second matrices for the following simplex tableaus. Write the systems of equations represented by the second matrices.

13.
$$
\begin{array}{ccccc}
x & y & r & s & P \\
\end{array}
$$
$$
\left[
\begin{array}{ccccc|c}
5 & 2 & 1 & 0 & 0 & 10 \\
④ & 3 & 0 & 1 & 0 & 6 \\
\hline
-10 & -5 & 0 & 0 & 1 & 0
\end{array}
\right]
$$

14.
$$
\begin{array}{ccccc}
x & y & r & s & P \\
\end{array}
$$
$$
\left[
\begin{array}{ccccc|c}
5 & 2 & 1 & 0 & 0 & 10 \\
4 & ③ & 0 & 1 & 0 & 6 \\
\hline
-5 & -10 & 0 & 0 & 1 & 0
\end{array}
\right]
$$

15.
$$
\begin{array}{ccccc}
x & y & r & s & P \\
\end{array}
$$
$$
\left[
\begin{array}{ccccc|c}
1 & \frac{2}{3} & \frac{1}{3} & 0 & 0 & \frac{8}{3} \\
0 & ⑧/③ & -\frac{2}{3} & 1 & 0 & \frac{8}{3} \\
\hline
0 & -\frac{8}{3} & \frac{14}{3} & 0 & 1 & \frac{112}{3}
\end{array}
\right]
$$

16.
$$
\begin{array}{ccccc}
x & y & r & s & P \\
\end{array}
$$
$$
\left[
\begin{array}{ccccc|c}
2 & 0 & ④ & 1 & 0 & 7 \\
3 & 1 & 2 & 0 & 0 & 5 \\
\hline
4 & 0 & -3 & 0 & 1 & 12
\end{array}
\right]
$$

C *Given the following simplex tableaus, find the second matrices and the systems of equations represented by the second matrices.*

17.
$$
\begin{array}{cccccc}
x & y & r & s & t & P \\
\end{array}
$$
$$
\left[
\begin{array}{cccccc|c}
3 & 2 & 1 & 0 & 0 & 0 & 3 \\
2 & 3 & 0 & 1 & 0 & 0 & 4 \\
1 & ④ & 0 & 0 & 1 & 0 & 5 \\
\hline
-4 & -6 & 0 & 0 & 0 & 1 & 0
\end{array}
\right]
$$

18.
$$
\begin{array}{cccccc}
x & y & r & s & t & P \\
\end{array}
$$
$$
\left[
\begin{array}{cccccc|c}
1 & 2 & 3 & 0 & 0 & 0 & 5 \\
0 & 5 & ⑥ & 1 & 0 & 0 & 7 \\
0 & 4 & 2 & 0 & 1 & 0 & 9 \\
\hline
0 & -5 & -7 & 0 & 0 & 1 & 4
\end{array}
\right]
$$

19.
$$
\begin{array}{cccccc}
x & y & r & s & t & P \\
\end{array}
$$
$$
\left[
\begin{array}{cccccc|c}
2 & 0 & 1 & 0 & 4 & 0 & 5 \\
3 & 1 & 0 & 0 & ① & 0 & 1 \\
4 & 0 & 0 & 1 & 2 & 0 & 6 \\
\hline
2 & 0 & 0 & 0 & -3 & 1 & 8
\end{array}
\right]
$$

20.
$$
\begin{array}{cccccc}
x & y & r & s & t & P \\
\end{array}
$$
$$
\left[
\begin{array}{cccccc|c}
1 & ⑤ & 1 & 0 & 0 & 0 & 3 \\
2 & 6 & 0 & 1 & 0 & 0 & 4 \\
3 & 7 & 0 & 0 & 1 & 0 & 5 \\
\hline
4 & -2 & 0 & 0 & 0 & 1 & 6
\end{array}
\right]
$$

Find the second matrices for the following simplex tableaus by using a calculator or micro-computer. If you use a microcomputer, test your program by using your program to verify the second matrices for exercises 19 and 20 also.

21.

$$
\begin{array}{ccccc}
x & y & r & s & P \\
\end{array}
$$

$$
\left[
\begin{array}{ccccc|c}
1.35 & \boxed{2.46} & 1 & 0 & 0 & 1.78 \\
2.58 & 1.48 & 0 & 1 & 0 & 2.54 \\
\hline
-1.36 & -2.58 & 0 & 0 & 1 & 1.34 \\
\end{array}
\right]
$$

22.

$$
\begin{array}{ccccc}
x & y & r & s & P \\
\end{array}
$$

$$
\left[
\begin{array}{ccccc|c}
3.48 & 1 & 2.98 & 0 & 0 & 5.34 \\
5.64 & 0 & \boxed{1.46} & 1 & 0 & 2.18 \\
\hline
2.44 & 0 & -4.98 & 0 & 1 & 9.38 \\
\end{array}
\right]
$$

Application problems for this section are given in Exercise Set 3.5.

4 Forming the Simplex Tableau

> We have seen that the simplex method is a technique for moving from one basic feasible solution to another basic feasible solution until the maximum of the linear function is obtained. This section explains how the simplex tableau is formed and how the very important pivot element is obtained.

Suppose we return to the sociologist's linear programming problem (Example 10), which was solved in Section 3.2 by finding the corner points and then evaluating the linear function at each of the corner points. Let us now see how a simplex tableau can be formed to enable us to solve this problem by using the simplex method. The mathematical model for this problem was: Maximize

$$P = 14x + 12y$$

subject to the constraints

$$x \geq 0$$
$$y \geq 0$$
$$3x + 2y \leq 8$$
$$2x + 4y \leq 8$$

By the definition of less than or equal to, $3x + 2y \leq 8$ means that there exists a real number $r \geq 0$ such that

$$3x + 2y + r = 8$$

Similarly, $2x + 4y \leq 8$ means that there exists a real number $s \geq 0$ such that

$$2x + 4y + s = 8$$

These equations can be written as the system

$$3x + 2y + r \qquad = 8$$
$$2x + 4y \qquad + s \qquad = 8$$
$$-14x - 12y \qquad + P = 0$$

subject to the constraints $x \geq 0$, $y \geq 0$, $r \geq 0$, and $s \geq 0$. This system is expressed in the simplex tableau as follows:

$$
\begin{array}{ccccc}
x & y & r & s & P
\end{array}
$$

$$
\left[
\begin{array}{ccccc|c}
3 & 2 & 1 & 0 & 0 & 8 \\
2 & 4 & 0 & 1 & 0 & 8 \\
\hline
-14 & -12 & 0 & 0 & 1 & 0
\end{array}
\right]
$$

Now let us see how the pivot element is selected. Notice that the last column of the initial matrix gives the values of r, s, and P when $x = 0$ and $y = 0$. For example, P at $x = 0$, $y = 0$ is

$$P = 14x + 12y = 14(0) + 12(0) = 0$$

This is clearly not the maximum value of P that we seek. Since the coefficient of x in the function to be maximized is larger than the coefficient of y, we shall try to increase P by increasing x while keeping $y = 0$. When $y = 0$,

$$P = 14x$$
$$r = 8 - 3x$$
$$s = 8 - 2x$$

Hence, P becomes larger as x becomes larger, but we cannot make x too large without making r or s negative. We cannot let r or s be negative since our constraints state that $r \geq 0$ and $s \geq 0$. To find the value of x that will make $r = 0$, we set $r = 0$ and solve the equation $0 = 8 - 3x$. This gives $x = \frac{8}{3}$. Any larger value of x will make r negative, which is a violation of the constraint $r \geq 0$.

Similarly, to find the value of x that will make $s = 0$, we set $s = 0$ and solve the equation $0 = 8 - 2x$. This gives $x = 4$. Any larger value of x will make s negative and thus violate the constraint $s \geq 0$. Since we do not want either r or s to be negative, the largest value of x we can use is $\frac{8}{3}$. This value for x was obtained from the equation $3x + 2y + r = 8$; hence, the pivot element is chosen to be in the first row and x column, which in our illustration is 3. Therefore, the simplex tableau with the pivot element indicated is

$$
\begin{array}{ccccc}
x & y & r & s & P
\end{array}
$$

$$
\left[
\begin{array}{ccccc|c}
③ & 2 & 1 & 0 & 0 & 8 \\
2 & 4 & 0 & 1 & 0 & 8 \\
\hline
-14 & -12 & 0 & 0 & 1 & 0
\end{array}
\right]
$$

To avoid going through this procedure each time to find the pivot element, let us analyze what was done and summarize the steps as a procedure for finding the pivot element.

1. Choose as the **pivot column** the variable column that has a negative number in the last row that is the largest number in absolute value. If the negative number in the last row with the largest absolute value occurs in two or more variable columns, choose any one of these columns as the pivot column and proceed to the next step.
2. Divide each **positive** element of the pivot column into the constant in the same row as the positive element.
3. Choose as the **pivot row** the row for which the quotient obtained in step 2 is smallest. If two or more quotients are the same, choose any one of these rows as the pivot row.
4. The **pivot element** is the element in both the pivot row and the pivot column and is indicated by a circle.

When these steps are applied to our initial matrix, the x column is chosen as the pivot column because it is the variable column that has the negative number with the largest absolute value in the last row. Dividing 2 into 8 gives $\frac{8}{2} = 4$, while dividing 3 into 8 gives $\frac{8}{3}$. Since $\frac{8}{3}$ is smaller, the first row is chosen as the pivot row. The element in the pivot row and the pivot column is the pivot element, written ③.

Exercise Set 3.4

A 1. Mark the following statements as either true or false.
   a. A slack variable is a positive real number.
   b. A slack variable is a nonnegative integer.
   c. The pivot element is the element in both the pivot row and the pivot column.
   d. The pivot column is the variable column that has the negative number with the largest absolute value in the row obtained from the linear function to be maximized.
   e. Each element of the pivot column is divided into the constants, and the smallest value for the quotient indicates the pivot row.

Form the simplex tableau and indicate the pivot elements for the following linear programming problems, where $x \geq 0$ and $y \geq 0$.

2. Maximize $P = 25x + 35y$
   subject to $2x + 3y \leq 15$
                 $3x + y \leq 12$

3. Maximize $P = 35x + 25y$
   subject to $2x + y \leq 7$
                 $3x + y \leq 8$

4. Maximize $P = 35x - 25y$
   subject to $2x + 3y \leq 15$
                 $3x + y \leq 12$

5. Maximize $P = 25x - 35y$
   subject to $2x + 3y \leq 15$
                 $3x + y \leq 12$

6. Maximize $P = 35x + 25y$
subject to $2x + 3y \leq 15$
$3x + y \leq 12$

7. Maximize $P = 25x + 35y$
subject to $2x + y \leq 7$
$3x + y \leq 8$

B **8.** Maximize $P = 25x + 35y$
subject to $x + y \leq 7$
$2x + y \leq 9$
$3x + y \leq 12$

9. Maximize $P = 35x + 25y$
subject to $x + y \leq 7$
$2x + y \leq 9$
$3x + y \leq 12$

10. Maximize $P = 25x + 35y$
subject to $x + 3y \leq 21$
$2x + 3y \leq 24$
$2x + y \leq 16$

11. Maximize $P = 35x - 25y$
subject to $x + y \leq 7$
$2x + y \leq 9$
$3x + y \leq 12$

C **12.** Maximize $P = 25x + 35y$
subject to $x + y \leq 2$
$x + y \leq 7$
$2x + y \leq 9$
$3x + y \leq 12$

13. Maximize $P = 25x + 35y$
subject to $2x + 3y \leq 6$
$x + 3y \leq 21$
$2x + 3y \leq 24$
$2x + y \leq 16$

14. Maximize $P = 40x + 25y$
subject to $x + 2y \leq 3$
$x + 3y \leq 5$
$2x + 3y \leq 7$
$4x + 2y \leq 9$

15. Maximize $P = 30x + 18y$
subject to $x + y \leq 5$
$3x + 2y \leq 7$
$x + 4y \leq 9$
$3x + 5y \leq 12$

Application problems are given in Exercise Set 3.5.

5 The Simplex Method of Maximization

> The previous section showed how the initial simplex tableau can be formed and how the pivot element is selected. This section explains how the simplex technique is performed to lead to the final solution.

Given a simplex tableau with the pivot element indicated for a linear programming problem, how does the simplex method enable us to find the solution to the problem?

We shall answer this question by returning to the sociologist's problem described in Section 3.4. Recall that the simplex tableau with pivot element indicated is

$$
\begin{array}{ccccc}
x & y & r & s & P \\
\end{array}
$$

$$
\left[
\begin{array}{ccccc|c}
③ & 2 & 1 & 0 & 0 & 8 \\
2 & 4 & 0 & 1 & 0 & 8 \\
\hline
-14 & -12 & 0 & 0 & 1 & 0 \\
\end{array}
\right]
$$

The second matrix is

$$
\begin{array}{ccccc}
x & y & r & s & P
\end{array}
$$

$$
\left[
\begin{array}{ccccc|c}
1 & \frac{2}{3} & \frac{1}{3} & 0 & 0 & \frac{8}{3} \\
0 & \frac{8}{3} & -\frac{2}{3} & 1 & 0 & \frac{8}{3} \\
\hline
0 & -\frac{8}{3} & \frac{14}{3} & 0 & 1 & \frac{112}{3}
\end{array}
\right]
\quad
\begin{array}{l}
\frac{1}{3}\text{row } 1_1 \\[4pt]
-2\text{row } 1_2 + \text{row } 2_1 \\[4pt]
14\text{row } 1_2 + \text{row } 3_1
\end{array}
$$

When $r = y = 0$, the last column of the second matrix gives the values $x = \frac{8}{3}$, $s = \frac{8}{3}$, and $P = \frac{112}{3}$. Recall that $(\frac{8}{3}, 0)$ is one of the corner points and gives the value $P = \frac{112}{3}$. In this example the simplex tableau gives the value $P = 0$ at the corner point $(0, 0)$, and the second matrix gives the value $P = \frac{112}{3}$ at the corner point $(\frac{8}{3}, 0)$.

The entire process is repeated by taking the second matrix as a new simplex tableau and obtaining a third matrix from it by pivot operations. As we go through the procedure again for review, you should work it out on paper yourself, using this development only as a check. The y column is chosen as the pivot column since it is the variable column containing the negative number with the largest absolute value in the last row. Dividing $\frac{8}{3}$ by $\frac{8}{3}$ gives 1, while dividing $\frac{8}{3}$ by $\frac{2}{3}$ gives 4. Since 1 is the smaller value, the s row is chosen as the pivot row. Hence, the pivot element is $\frac{8}{3}$.

The second matrix with pivot element indicated is

$$
\begin{array}{ccccc}
x & y & r & s & P
\end{array}
$$

$$
\left[
\begin{array}{ccccc|c}
1 & \frac{2}{3} & \frac{1}{3} & 0 & 0 & \frac{8}{3} \\
0 & \boxed{\frac{8}{3}} & -\frac{2}{3} & 1 & 0 & \frac{8}{3} \\
\hline
0 & -\frac{8}{3} & \frac{14}{3} & 0 & 1 & \frac{112}{3}
\end{array}
\right]
$$

The third matrix is

$$
\begin{array}{ccccc}
x & y & r & s & P
\end{array}
$$

$$
\left[
\begin{array}{ccccc|c}
1 & 0 & \frac{1}{2} & -\frac{1}{4} & 0 & 2 \\
0 & 1 & -\frac{1}{4} & \frac{3}{8} & 0 & 1 \\
\hline
0 & 0 & 4 & 1 & 1 & 40
\end{array}
\right]
\quad
\begin{array}{l}
\text{Row } 1_2 - \frac{2}{3}\text{row } 2_3 \\[4pt]
\frac{3}{8}\text{row } 2_2 \\[4pt]
\text{Row } 3_2 + \frac{8}{3}\text{row } 2_3
\end{array}
$$

This matrix represents the system

$$
\begin{aligned}
x + \tfrac{1}{2}r - \tfrac{1}{4}s &= 2 \\
y - \tfrac{1}{4}r + \tfrac{3}{8}s &= 1 \\
4r + s + P &= 40
\end{aligned}
$$

When $r = s = 0$, this system gives the value $P = 40$ at the corner point $(2, 1)$. Notice that since r and s both must be nonnegative, the positive coefficients of r and s in the equation for P imply that the maximum value of P occurs when $r = s = 0$ since any positive choice for r or s would make P smaller. Hence, we have solved the linear programming problem. The values $x = 2$ and $y = 1$ make P a maximum of 40. This also indicates that we should stop forming new matrices as soon as the linear function to be maximized has all positive or zero elements in each position of its row except in the constant position (last position).

The simplex method for maximizing a linear function can be summarized as follows:

Simplex Method

1. Form the simplex tableau with pivot element indicated.
2. Develop the second matrix from the simplex tableau as explained in Section 3.3.
3. If the elements of the row corresponding to the linear function are all positive or zero, except for the element in the constant position, the second matrix gives the solution.
4. If the elements of the row corresponding to the linear function other than the element in the constant position are not all positive or zero, take the second matrix as a new initial matrix and develop a third matrix. If the third matrix satisfies the condition stated in step 3, it gives the optimal solution. If it does not satisfy the condition stated in step 3, take it as a new simplex tableau and develop a fourth matrix.
5. Continue the process of developing new matrices until a matrix is obtained that has positive or zero elements in the linear function row for all positions except the constant position. The element in the constant position of the linear function row may be positive, negative, or zero. This matrix, when obtained, gives the solution.

EXAMPLE 12 Use the simplex method to solve the following problem.

Maximize

$$P = \$0.68x + \$0.70y$$

subject to

$$x \geq 0$$
$$y \geq 0$$
$$6x + 5y \leq 960$$
$$10x + 11y \leq 1760$$

The simplex tableau with the pivot element indicated is

$$
\begin{array}{ccccc}
x & y & r & s & P \\
\end{array}
$$
$$
\left[
\begin{array}{ccccc|c}
6 & 5 & 1 & 0 & 0 & 960 \\
10 & \boxed{11} & 0 & 1 & 0 & 1760 \\
\hline
-\frac{68}{100} & -\frac{70}{100} & 0 & 0 & 1 & 0
\end{array}
\right]
$$

The second matrix is

$$
\begin{array}{ccccc}
x & y & r & s & P \\
\end{array}
$$
$$
\left[
\begin{array}{ccccc|c}
\frac{16}{11} & 0 & 1 & -\frac{5}{11} & 0 & 160 \\
\frac{10}{11} & 1 & 0 & \frac{1}{11} & 0 & 160 \\
\hline
-\frac{12}{275} & 0 & 0 & \frac{7}{110} & 1 & 112
\end{array}
\right]
\quad
\begin{array}{l}
\text{Row } 1_1 - 5\text{row } 2_2 \\
\frac{1}{11}\text{row } 2_1 \\
\text{Row } 3_1 + \frac{7}{10}\text{row } 2_2
\end{array}
$$

Since there is still a negative element in the first column of the last row, repeat the process using the first column as the pivot column.

$$160 \div \frac{10}{11} = 176$$
$$160 \div \frac{16}{11} = 110$$

Thus, $\frac{16}{11}$ is chosen to be the pivot element.

The new simplex tableau with the pivot element indicated is

$$
\begin{array}{ccccc}
x & y & r & s & P \\
\end{array}
$$

$$
\left[
\begin{array}{ccccc|c}
\boxed{\frac{16}{11}} & 0 & 1 & -\frac{5}{11} & 0 & 160 \\
\frac{10}{11} & 1 & 0 & \frac{1}{11} & 0 & 160 \\
\hline
-\frac{12}{275} & 0 & 0 & \frac{7}{110} & 1 & 112 \\
\end{array}
\right]
$$

The third matrix is

$$
\begin{array}{ccccc}
x & y & r & s & P \\
\end{array}
$$

$$
\left[
\begin{array}{ccccc|c}
1 & 0 & \frac{11}{16} & -\frac{5}{16} & 0 & 110 \\
0 & 1 & -\frac{5}{8} & \frac{3}{8} & 0 & 60 \\
\hline
0 & 0 & \frac{3}{100} & \frac{1}{20} & 1 & 116.80 \\
\end{array}
\right]
\quad
\begin{array}{l}
\frac{11}{16}\text{row } 1_2 \\
\text{Row } 2_2 - \frac{10}{11}\text{row } 1_3 \\
\text{Row } 3_2 + \frac{12}{275}\text{row } 1_3 \\
\end{array}
$$

Since all the elements of the P row are now positive or zero, this matrix gives the maximum solution:

$$P = \$116.80 \text{ at } x = 110 \text{ and } y = 60$$

EXAMPLE 13   A company is considering two products, type I and type II. Type I requires $\frac{1}{4}$ hour on a drill and $\frac{1}{8}$ hour on a lathe. Type II requires $\frac{1}{2}$ hour on a drill and $\frac{3}{4}$ hour on a lathe. The profit from type I is \$50 per product, and the profit from type II is \$102 per product. If the machines are limited to 8 hours per day, how many of each product should be produced to maximize profit? What is the maximum daily profit?

Solution   To develop a mathematical model for this problem, let x_1 = number of type I products produced and x_2 = number of type II products produced. The model is:

Maximize

$$P = \$50x_1 + \$102x_2$$

subject to

$$\frac{1}{4}x_1 + \frac{1}{2}x_2 \leq 8$$
$$\frac{1}{8}x_1 + \frac{3}{4}x_2 \leq 8$$
$$x_1 \geq 0$$
$$x_2 \geq 0$$

The simplex tableau for this problem is

$$
\begin{array}{ccccc}
x_1 & x_2 & r & s & P \\
\end{array}
$$

$$
\left[
\begin{array}{ccccc|c}
\frac{1}{4} & \frac{1}{2} & 1 & 0 & 0 & 8 \\
\frac{1}{8} & \boxed{\frac{3}{4}} & 0 & 1 & 0 & 8 \\
\hline
-50 & -102 & 0 & 0 & 1 & 0 \\
\end{array}
\right]
$$

The final matrix is

$$
\begin{array}{ccccc}
x_1 & x_2 & r & s & P
\end{array}
$$

$$
\left[
\begin{array}{ccccc|c}
1 & 0 & 6 & -4 & 0 & 16 \\
0 & 1 & 1 & 2 & 0 & 8 \\
\hline
0 & 0 & 198 & 4 & 1 & 1616
\end{array}
\right]
$$

Since all the elements of the last row are nonnegative, this matrix gives the maximum daily profit as $P = \$1,616$, which occurs when 16 type I products and 8 type II products are produced.

Exercise Set 3.5

Indicate whether the following statements are true or false.

A 1. In the simplex method, the initial matrix is never the final matrix.

2. In the simplex method, the second matrix is never the final matrix.

3. In the simplex method, the third matrix is never the final matrix.

4. In the simplex method, if the elements of the row corresponding to the objective function are all positive or zero, with the possible exception of the element in the constant position, the matrix is the final matrix.

5. The solution for the linear programming problem can be obtained from the final matrix.

Form a simplex tableau with the pivot element indicated for the following linear programming problems, and then solve the problems by using the simplex method.

6. Maximize $P = 2x + 3y$
   subject to
   $$x \geq 0$$
   $$y \geq 0$$
   $$x + y \leq 4$$
   $$3x + 2y \leq 9$$

7. Maximize $P = 3x + 2y$
   subject to
   $$x \geq 0$$
   $$y \geq 0$$
   $$x + y \leq 4$$
   $$3x + 2y \leq 9$$

8. Maximize $P = 4x + 3y$
   subject to
   $$x \geq 0$$
   $$y \geq 0$$
   $$x + y \leq 4$$
   $$3x + 2y \leq 9$$

9. Maximize $P = 5x + 4y$
   subject to
   $$x \geq 0$$
   $$y \geq 0$$
   $$x + y \leq 4$$
   $$3x + 2y \leq 9$$

B 10. Maximize $P = 25x + 35y$
   subject to
   $$x \geq 0$$
   $$y \geq 0$$
   $$2x + 3y \leq 15$$
   $$3x + y \leq 12$$

11. Maximize $P = 25x + 35y$
   subject to
   $$x \geq 0$$
   $$y \geq 0$$
   $$2x + y \leq 7$$
   $$2x + y \leq 8$$

12. Maximize $P = 35x + 25y$
   subject to
   $$x \geq 0$$
   $$y \geq 0$$
   $$2x + 3y \leq 15$$
   $$3x + y \leq 12$$

13. Maximize $P = 35x + 25y$
   subject to
   $$x \geq 0$$
   $$y \geq 0$$
   $$2x + y \leq 7$$
   $$3x + y \leq 8$$

C 14. Maximize $P = 25x + 35y$
subject to
$$x \geq 0$$
$$y \geq 0$$
$$x + 3y \leq 21$$
$$2x + 3y \leq 24$$
$$2x + y \leq 16$$

15. Maximize $P = x + 8y + 9z$
subject to
$$x \geq 0$$
$$y \geq 0$$
$$z \geq 0$$
$$5x - 2y - 3z \leq 0$$
$$-3x + y + z \leq 0$$
$$-5x + 3y + 4z \leq 200$$

16. Maximize $P = x - 3y + 2z$
subject to
$$x \geq 0$$
$$y \geq 0$$
$$z \geq 0$$
$$x + 6y + 3z \leq 6$$
$$x + 2y + 4z \leq 4$$
$$x - y + z \leq 3$$

17. Maximize $P = 2x + 9y + 5z$
subject to
$$x \geq 0$$
$$y \geq 0$$
$$z \geq 0$$
$$3x + 2y - 5z \leq 12$$
$$-x + 2y + 3z \leq 3$$
$$x + 3y - 2z \leq 2$$

18. Maximize $P = 7.3x + 5.2y$
subject to
$$x \geq 0$$
$$y \geq 0$$
$$1.3x + 2.4y \leq 25$$
$$3.5x + 4.6y \leq 30$$

19. Maximize $P = 1.25x + 2.35y$
subject to
$$x \geq 0$$
$$y \geq 0$$
$$0.17x + 0.38y \leq 33$$
$$0.35x + 0.23y \leq 13$$

20. Maximize $P = 2.36x + 4.23y$
subject to
$$x \geq 0$$
$$y \geq 0$$
$$0.23x + 0.37y \leq 1.5$$
$$0.33x + 0.42y \leq 3.5$$

21. Maximize $P = 1.3x + 2.4y$
subject to
$$x \geq 0$$
$$y \geq 0$$
$$0.9x + 0.6y \leq 7$$
$$0.8x + 0.8y \leq 5$$

Business 22. **Manufacturing.** A manufacturer makes two types of products, type I and type II. Type I requires 4 hours on machine A and 3 hours on machine B, while type II requires 2 hours on machine A and 3 hours on machine B. If the profit for type I is $14 per product and the profit for type II is $13 per product, how many of each type should be produced to maximize the profit? Assume the machines can operate 12 hours per day.

23. Redo exercise 22 for a profit of $14 per product for both products.

24. **Mixture Problem.** A nut company has at most 64 pounds of pecans and at most 132 pounds of peanuts that it wishes to mix. A package of mixture I contains 2 ounces of pecans and 11 ounces of peanuts, while mixture II contains 8 ounces of pecans and 12 ounces of peanuts per package. If a profit of $0.64 per package is obtained from mixture I and a profit of $0.70 per package is obtained from mixture II, how many packages of each mixture should be made to obtain the maximum profit?

25. Redo exercise 24 for a profit of $0.68 per package from mixture I and a profit of $0.70 per package from mixture II.

Economics 26. **Investments.** An investment club has at most $27,000 to invest in bonds of two types, good quality and high risk. Good quality bonds average a yield of 7% while high risk yield 10%. The policy of the club requires that the amount invested in high risk be not more than twice the amount invested in good quality. How should the club invest its money to receive the maximum return subject to its investment policy?

27. Redo exercise 26 assuming that a conservative member of the club gets the club policy changed so that the club must invest at least twice as much money in good quality as it invests in high risk.

28. Pollution. Government regulations for pollution control have forced Chemical Needs to install a new process to help reduce pollution caused by production of a certain chemical. The old process releases 12 grams of pollutant A and 30 grams of pollutant B into the air for each liter of chemical produced. The new process releases 5 grams of pollutant A and 15 grams of pollutant B for each liter produced. Chemical Needs makes a profit of $0.40 for each liter produced by the old process and only $0.18 for each liter produced by the new process. If the regulations do not allow more than 10,000 grams of pollutant A and no more than 27,000 grams of pollutant B each day, how many liters of the chemical should be produced by the old process and how many liters should be produced by the new process to maximize Chemical Needs' profit?

29. Redo exercise 28 for a profit of $0.35 for each liter produced by the old process and $0.25 for each liter produced by the new process.

30. Education. Eddy is given a set of test questions from which he is to select 20 questions. The test is in two parts; the first part contains true/false questions, and the second part requires short answers. The true/false questions score 4 points each, and the short-answer questions score 6 points each. Determine the number of questions of each type that Eddy should select to maximize his grade if the teacher imposes the restriction that the number of short-answer questions plus one-half the number of true/false questions cannot exceed 16. Assume that Eddy can answer all questions correctly.

31. Redo exercise 30 if the teacher imposes the additional restriction that not more than six questions may be true/false.

Minimization Using the Dual Problem

We have now seen how the simplex method can be used to solve a linear programming problem involving maximization. Associated with each maximum problem is a minimum problem called its **dual.** Similarly, each minimum linear programming problem has a corresponding maximum problem, called its **dual,** associated with it. To solve a minimum problem, we simply use the simplex method to solve the dual maximum problem.

As stated in the section introduction, there is associated with each linear programming problem a dual problem. Study the following dual problems to see how they are related.

Maximize	Minimize
$8x_1 + 6x_2 = P$	$2y_1 + 5y_2 = C$
subject to	subject to
$3x_1 + x_2 \leq 2$	$3y_1 + 2y_2 \geq 8$
$2x_1 + 4x_2 \leq 5$	$y_1 + 4y_2 \geq 6$
$x_1 \geq 0$	$y_1 \geq 0$
$x_2 \geq 0$	$y_2 \geq 0$

We note the following relations:

1. **a.** The dual of a maximum problem is a minimum problem.
   b. The dual of a minimum problem is a maximum problem.
2. **a.** The constraints in a maximum problem are given as $\leq$.
   b. The constraints in a minimum problem are given as $\geq$.
3. **a.** The coefficients of the variables in the objective function to be maximized are the constants in the $\geq$ constraints of the dual minimum problem.
   b. The coefficients of the variables in the objective function to be minimized are the constants in the $\leq$ constraints of the dual maximum problem.
4. **a.** The coefficients of x_1 and x_2 in the first maximum constraint are the coefficients of y_1 in the first two minimum constraints. The coefficients of x_1 and x_2 in the second maximum constraint are the coefficients of y_2 in the first two minimum constraints.
   b. The coefficients of y_1 and y_2 in the first minimum constraint are the coefficients of x_1 in the first two maximum constraints. The coefficients of y_1 and y_2 in the second minimum constraint are the coefficients of x_2 in the first two maximum constraints.

The relationship between the dual problems is easy to see from a simplex tableau. The simplex tableau for this problem is

$$
\begin{array}{ccccc}
x_1 & x_2 & y_1 & y_2 & P \\
\end{array}
$$
$$
\left[
\begin{array}{ccccc|c}
③ & 1 & 1 & 0 & 0 & 2 \\
2 & 4 & 0 & 1 & 0 & 5 \\
\hline
-8 & -6 & 0 & 0 & 1 & 0 \\
\end{array}
\right]
$$

Note that we have replaced the slack variable headings of the columns by the variables in the dual problem. This replacement will enable us to give the solution to the dual problem when the final matrix is obtained. The coefficients of the dual problem appear in the first columns rather than rows.

The second matrix for this problem is

$$
\begin{array}{ccccc}
x_1 & x_2 & y_1 & y_2 & P \\
\end{array}
$$
$$
\left[
\begin{array}{ccccc|c}
1 & \frac{1}{3} & \frac{1}{3} & 0 & 0 & \frac{2}{3} \\
0 & \frac{10}{3} & -\frac{2}{3} & 1 & 0 & \frac{11}{3} \\
\hline
0 & -\frac{10}{3} & \frac{8}{3} & 0 & 1 & \frac{16}{3} \\
\end{array}
\right]
\begin{array}{l}
\frac{1}{3}\text{row } 1_1 \\
\text{Row } 2_1 - 2\text{row } 1_2 \\
\text{Row } 3_1 + 8\text{row } 1_2 \\
\end{array}
$$

The third matrix is

$$
\begin{array}{ccccc}
x_1 & x_2 & y_1 & y_2 & P \\
\end{array}
$$
$$
\left[
\begin{array}{ccccc|c}
1 & 0 & \frac{2}{5} & -\frac{1}{10} & 0 & \frac{3}{10} \\
0 & 1 & -\frac{1}{5} & \frac{3}{10} & 0 & \frac{11}{10} \\
\hline
0 & 0 & 2 & 1 & 1 & 9 \\
\end{array}
\right]
\begin{array}{l}
\text{Row } 1_2 - \frac{1}{3}\text{row } 2_3 \\
\frac{3}{10}\text{row } 2_2 \\
\text{Row } 3_2 + \frac{10}{3}\text{row } 2_3 \\
\end{array}
$$

Since all the elements of the last row are positive or zero, the third matrix is the final matrix and gives the solution $P = 9$ when $x_1 = \frac{3}{10}$ and $x_2 = \frac{11}{10}$. The bottom row gives the solution to the dual problem $C = 9$ when $y_1 = 2$ and $y_2 = 1$. The bottom row always gives the solution to the dual problem and is the reason why the headings of the slack variable columns were changed to the variables in the dual problem.

In order to be very clear about what is meant by dual problems, we define the following problems to be *dual* to each other. For purposes of simplification we shall assume that $c_i \geq 0$ for $i = 1, 2, \ldots, m$.

If you become lost in the general notation, proceed to the examples and then return to the general problem.

Maximize

$$b_1 x_1 + b_2 x_2 + \cdots + b_n x_n = P$$

subject to

$$a_{11} x_1 + a_{12} x_2 + \cdots + a_{1n} x_n \leq c_1$$
$$a_{21} x_1 + a_{22} x_2 + \cdots + a_{2n} x_n \leq c_2$$
$$\vdots \qquad\qquad\qquad \vdots$$
$$a_{m1} x_1 + a_{m2} x_2 + \cdots + a_{mn} x_n \leq c_m$$
$$x_1 \geq 0, x_2 \geq 0, \ldots, x_n \geq 0$$

Minimize

$$c_1 y_1 + c_2 y_2 + \cdots + c_m y_m = C$$

subject to

$$a_{11} y_1 + a_{21} y_2 + \cdots + a_{m1} y_m \geq b_1$$
$$a_{12} y_1 + a_{22} y_2 + \cdots + a_{m2} y_m \geq b_2$$
$$\vdots \qquad\qquad\qquad \vdots$$
$$a_{1n} y_1 + a_{2n} y_2 + \cdots + a_{mn} y_m \geq b_n$$
$$y_1 \geq 0, y_2 \geq 0, \ldots, y_m \geq 0$$

A simplex tableau for the maximum and the dual minimum is

$$
\begin{array}{c}
\begin{array}{ccccccccc}
x_1 & x_2 & \cdots & x_n & y_1 & y_2 & \cdots & y_m & P
\end{array} \\
\left[
\begin{array}{ccccccccc|c}
a_{11} & a_{12} & \cdots & a_{1n} & 1 & 0 & \cdots & 0 & 0 & c_1 \\
a_{21} & a_{22} & \cdots & a_{2n} & 0 & 1 & \cdots & 0 & 0 & c_2 \\
a_{31} & a_{32} & \cdots & a_{3n} & 0 & 0 & \cdots & 0 & 0 & c_3 \\
\vdots & \vdots & & \vdots & \vdots & \vdots & & \vdots & \vdots & \vdots \\
a_{m1} & a_{m2} & \cdots & a_{mn} & 0 & 0 & \cdots & 1 & 0 & c_m \\
\hline
-b_1 & -b_2 & \cdots & -b_n & 0 & 0 & \cdots & 0 & 1 & 0
\end{array}
\right]
\end{array}
$$

Note that the headings of the slack variable columns have been changed to the minimum variables.

EXAMPLE 14 Minimize

$$2y_1 + 5y_2 = C$$

subject to

$$3y_1 + 2y_2 \geq 8$$
$$y_1 + 4y_2 \geq 6$$
$$y_1 \geq 0$$
$$y_2 \geq 0$$

Solution The dual problem is to maximize

$$8x_1 + 6x_2 = P$$

subject to

$$3x_1 + x_2 \leq 2$$
$$2x_1 + 4x_2 \leq 5$$
$$x_1 \geq 0$$
$$x_2 \geq 0$$

The simplex tableau for this problem is

$$
\begin{array}{ccccc|c}
x_1 & x_2 & y_1 & y_2 & P & \\
\hline
③ & 1 & 1 & 0 & 0 & 2 \\
2 & 4 & 0 & 1 & 0 & 5 \\
\hline
-8 & -6 & 0 & 0 & 1 & 0
\end{array}
$$

The second matrix is

$$
\begin{array}{ccccc|c}
x_1 & x_2 & y_1 & y_2 & P & \\
\hline
1 & \frac{1}{3} & \frac{1}{3} & 0 & 0 & \frac{2}{3} \\
0 & \frac{10}{3} & -\frac{2}{3} & 1 & 0 & \frac{11}{3} \\
\hline
0 & -\frac{10}{3} & \frac{8}{3} & 0 & 1 & \frac{16}{3}
\end{array}
$$

$\frac{1}{3}\text{row } 1_1$

Row $2_1 - 2\text{row } 1_2$

Row $3_1 + 8\text{row } 1_2$

The third matrix is

$$
\begin{array}{ccccc|c}
x_1 & x_2 & y_1 & y_2 & P & \\
\hline
1 & 0 & \frac{2}{5} & -\frac{1}{10} & 0 & \frac{3}{10} \\
0 & 1 & -\frac{1}{5} & \frac{3}{10} & 0 & \frac{11}{10} \\
\hline
0 & 0 & 2 & 1 & 1 & 9
\end{array}
$$

Row $1_2 - \frac{1}{3}\text{row } 2_3$

$\frac{3}{10}\text{row } 2_2$

Row $3_2 + \frac{10}{3}\text{row } 2_3$

Since all the elements of the last row are positive or zero, the third matrix gives the solution $C = 9$ when $y_1 = 2$, $y_2 = 1$. Of course, this also gives the solution $P = 9$ when $x_1 = \frac{3}{10}$ and $x_2 = \frac{11}{10}$ for the dual maximum problem.

EXAMPLE 15 Find the dual problem that corresponds to the maximization problem in Example 12 in Section 3.5. Solve the dual problem.

Solution Recall that the maximization problem was to maximize

$$0.68x_1 + 0.70x_2 = P$$

subject to

$$6x_1 + 5x_2 \le 960$$
$$10x_1 + 11x_2 \le 1760$$
$$x_1 \ge 0$$
$$x_2 \ge 0$$

The dual minimum problem is to minimize

$$960y_1 + 1760y_2 = C$$

subject to

$$6y_1 + 10y_2 \ge 0.68$$
$$5y_1 + 11y_2 \ge 0.70$$
$$y_1 \ge 0$$
$$y_2 \ge 0$$

The final matrix of the solution of the maximization problem was found to be

$$
\begin{array}{ccccc}
x_1 & x_2 & y_1 & y_2 & P \\
\end{array}
$$

$$
\begin{bmatrix}
1 & 0 & \frac{11}{16} & -\frac{5}{16} & 0 & | & 110 \\
0 & 1 & -\frac{5}{8} & \frac{3}{8} & 0 & | & 60 \\
\hline
0 & 0 & \frac{3}{100} & \frac{1}{20} & 1 & | & 116.80
\end{bmatrix}
$$

This matrix gives the maximum solution

$$P = 116.80 \quad \text{at} \quad x_1 = 110 \quad \text{and} \quad x_2 = 60$$

It also gives the solution to the dual minimum problem

$$C = 116.80 \quad \text{at} \quad y_1 = \tfrac{3}{100} \quad \text{and} \quad y_2 = \tfrac{1}{20}$$

EXAMPLE 16 Minimize

$$2y_1 + 5y_2 + 6y_3 + 1 = C$$

subject to

$$-3y_1 + 2y_2 - 4y_3 \le 1$$
$$y_1 + 2y_2 + 2y_3 \ge 2$$
$$2y_1 + 3y_2 + y_3 \ge 5$$
$$y_1 \ge 0$$
$$y_2 \ge 0$$
$$y_3 \ge 0$$

Solution Notice that the first inequality constraint is stated as less than or equal to instead of greater than or equal to as required in order to set up an initial matrix. To change the sense of the first inequality, multiply each term by -1. The problem then becomes:

Minimize

$$2y_1 + 5y_2 + 6y_3 + 1 = C$$

subject to

$$3y_1 - 2y_2 + 4y_3 \geq -1$$
$$y_1 + 2y_2 + 2y_3 \geq 2$$
$$2y_1 + 3y_2 + y_3 \geq 5$$
$$y_1 \geq 0$$
$$y_2 \geq 0$$
$$y_3 \geq 0$$

The simplex tableau for this problem is

$$
\begin{array}{ccccccc|c}
x_1 & x_2 & x_3 & y_1 & y_2 & y_3 & P & \\
3 & 1 & ② & 1 & 0 & 0 & 0 & 2 \\
-2 & 2 & 3 & 0 & 1 & 0 & 0 & 5 \\
4 & 2 & 1 & 0 & 0 & 1 & 0 & 6 \\
\hline
1 & -2 & -5 & 0 & 0 & 0 & 1 & 1 \\
\end{array}
$$

The second matrix is

$$
\begin{array}{ccccccc|cl}
x_1 & x_2 & x_3 & y_1 & y_2 & y_3 & P & & \\
\frac{3}{2} & \frac{1}{2} & 1 & \frac{1}{2} & 0 & 0 & 0 & 1 & \frac{1}{2}\text{row } 1_1 \\
-\frac{13}{2} & \frac{1}{2} & 0 & -\frac{3}{2} & 1 & 0 & 0 & 2 & \text{Row } 2_1 - 3\text{row } 1_2 \\
\frac{5}{2} & \frac{3}{2} & 0 & -\frac{1}{2} & 0 & 1 & 0 & 5 & \text{Row } 3_1 - \text{row } 1_2 \\
\hline
\frac{17}{2} & \frac{1}{2} & 0 & \frac{5}{2} & 0 & 0 & 1 & 6 & \text{Row } 4_1 + 5\text{row } 1_2 \\
\end{array}
$$

Since all the elements of the last row are nonnegative, the second matrix is the final matrix and gives the solution

$$C = 6 \text{ when } y_1 = \tfrac{5}{2}, \; y_2 = 0, \text{ and } y_3 = 0$$

Caution! Do not use this method of multiplying an inequality by -1 in a maximum problem if this will result in negative values in the last column of the simplex tableau. Remember that we assumed that all of the elements of the last column were nonnegative with the possible exception of the element in the last row and last column. A special starting procedure is required for problems in which some of the constants in the last column other than the constant in the last row and last column are negative.

EXAMPLE 17 A mining company owns two mines: mine I, which produces 2 tons of high-grade ore, 3 tons of medium-grade ore, and 3 tons of low-grade ore each hour; and mine II, which produces 1 ton of high-grade ore, 2 tons of medium-grade ore, and 6 tons of low-grade ore each hour. The company needs 100 tons of high-grade ore, 180 tons of medium-grade ore, and 240 tons of low-grade ore. If it costs the company $250 each hour to work mine I and $275 each hour to work mine II, how many hours should each mine be worked in order to satisfy the requirements but keep the company's cost at a minimum?

Solution Let $y_1 =$ number of hours mine I is worked and $y_2 =$ number of hours mine II is worked. The cost function is then

$$C = \$250y_1 + \$275y_2$$

It is subject to the following constraints:

$$y_1 \geq 0$$
$$y_2 \geq 0$$
$$2y_1 + y_2 \geq 100$$
$$3y_1 + 2y_2 \geq 180$$
$$3y_1 + 6y_2 \geq 240$$

The simplex tableau with pivot element indicated is

$$
\begin{array}{cccccc|c}
x_1 & x_2 & x_3 & y_1 & y_2 & P & \\
2 & 3 & 3 & 1 & 0 & 0 & 250 \\
1 & 2 & ⑥ & 0 & 1 & 0 & 275 \\
\hline
-100 & -180 & -240 & 0 & 0 & 1 & 0
\end{array}
$$

The second matrix is

$$
\begin{array}{cccccc|c}
x_1 & x_2 & x_3 & y_1 & y_2 & P & \\
\frac{3}{2} & ② & 0 & 1 & -\frac{1}{2} & 0 & \frac{225}{2} \\
\frac{1}{6} & \frac{1}{3} & 1 & 0 & \frac{1}{6} & 0 & \frac{275}{6} \\
\hline
-60 & -100 & 0 & 0 & 40 & 1 & 11{,}000
\end{array}
$$

The third matrix is

$$
\begin{array}{cccccc|c}
x_1 & x_2 & x_3 & y_1 & y_2 & P & \\
\frac{3}{4} & 1 & 0 & \frac{1}{2} & -\frac{1}{4} & 0 & \frac{225}{4} \\
-\frac{1}{12} & 0 & 1 & -\frac{1}{6} & \frac{1}{4} & 0 & \frac{325}{12} \\
\hline
15 & 0 & 0 & 50 & 15 & 1 & 16{,}625
\end{array}
$$

Since all the elements of the last row are nonnegative, this matrix gives the solution $C = \$16{,}625$ at $y_1 = 50$, $y_2 = 15$, $x_1 = 15$, and $x_2 = x_3 = 0$. Hence, the minimum cost is \$16,625, and it is obtained by working mine I for 50 hours and mine II for 15 hours.

Exercise Set 3.6

Find the dual problem that corresponds to each of the following linear programming problems.

A   1. Maximize $P = 25x_1 + 35x_2$
     subject to $2x_1 + 3x_2 \leq 15$
               $3x_1 + x_2 \leq 12$
               $x_1 \geq 0$
               $x_2 \geq 0$

2. Maximize $P = 3x_1 + 2x_2$
   subject to $x_1 + x_2 \leq 4$
             $3x_1 + 2x_2 \leq 9$
             $x_1 \geq 0$
             $x_2 \geq 0$

3. Minimize $4y_1 + 7y_2 = C$
    subject to $y_1 + y_2 \geq 5$
              $3y_1 + y_2 \geq 21$
              $y_1 \geq 0$
              $y_2 \geq 0$

4. Minimize $4y_1 + 5y_2 = C$
   subject to $y_1 + y_2 \geq 5$
             $3y_1 + y_2 \geq 21$
             $y_1 \geq 0$
             $y_2 \geq 0$

Set up a simplex tableau for each of the indicated linear programming problems and its dual.

5. Exercise 1   **6.** Exercise 2
7. Exercise 3   **8.** Exercise 4

Write the linear programming problems and duals that are represented by the following simplex tableaus.

9.

x_1	x_2	y_1	y_2	P	
3	2	1	0	0	5
1	3	0	1	0	8
−7	−4	0	0	1	0

10.

x_1	x_2	y_1	y_2	P	
4	3	1	0	0	7
2	4	0	1	0	9
−5	−8	0	0	1	0

11.

x_1	x_2	y_1	y_2	y_3	P	
2	3	1	0	0	0	4
1	2	0	1	0	0	7
3	1	0	0	1	0	6
−6	−8	0	0	0	1	0

12.

x_1	x_2	y_1	y_2	y_3	P	
1	2	1	0	0	0	5
2	3	0	1	0	0	6
3	5	0	0	1	0	8
−7	−4	0	0	0	1	0

B Solve the following linear programming problems by using the simplex method.

13. Minimize $4y_1 + 5y_2 = C$
subject to $y_1 + y_2 \geq 5$
$3y_1 + 5y_2 \geq 21$
$y_1 \geq 0$
$y_2 \geq 0$

14. Minimize $5y_1 + 4y_2 = C$
subject to $y_1 + y_2 \geq 5$
$3y_1 + 5y_2 \geq 21$
$y_1 \geq 0$
$y_2 \geq 0$

15. Minimize $4y_1 + 7y_2 = C$
subject to $y_1 + y_2 \geq 5$
$3y_1 + y_2 \geq 21$
$y_1 \geq 0$
$y_2 \geq 0$

16. Minimize $7y_1 + 4y_2 = C$
subject to $y_1 + y_2 \geq 5$
$3y_1 + 5y_2 \geq 21$
$y_1 \geq 0$
$y_2 \geq 0$

17. Minimize $25y_1 + 35y_2 = C$
subject to $2y_1 + 3y_2 \leq 15$
$3y_1 + y_2 \leq 12$
$y_1 \geq 0$
$y_2 \geq 0$

18. Minimize $35y_1 + 25y_2 = C$
subject to $2y_1 + 3y_2 \leq 15$
$3y_1 + y_2 \leq 12$
$y_1 \geq 0$
$y_2 \geq 0$

C 19. Minimize $25y_1 + 35y_2 = C$
subject to $y_1 + y_2 \geq 2$
$2y_1 + 3y_2 \leq 15$
$3y_1 + y_2 \leq 12$
$y_1 \geq 0$
$y_2 \geq 0$

20. Minimize $25y_1 + 35y_2 = C$
subject to $2y_1 + 3y_2 \geq 6$
$2y_1 + 3y_2 \leq 15$
$3y_1 + y_2 \leq 12$
$y_1 \geq 0$
$y_2 \geq 0$

21. Minimize $y_1 + 5y_2 + 4y_3 = C$
subject to $y_1 - 2y_2 - 2y_3 \leq -2$
$y_1 + y_2 + y_3 \geq 3$
$2y_2 + y_3 \geq 4$
$y_1 \geq 0$
$y_2 \geq 0$
$y_3 \geq 0$

22. Minimize $25y_1 + 35y_2 = C$
subject to $y_1 + y_2 \geq 2$
$2y_1 + y_2 \leq 7$
$3y_1 + y_2 \leq 8$
$y_1 \geq 0$
$y_2 \geq 0$

Business   **23. Transportation.** A company has two warehouses, A and B, and two stores, I and II. Warehouse A contains 40 tons of a product and warehouse B contains 100 tons of the same product. Store I needs 50 tons of the product and store II needs 75 tons. The shipping costs are:

A to I, $5/ton   B to I, $6/ton

A to II, $8/ton   B to II, $10/ton

Find the shipping instructions that will satisfy each store's need at a minimum shipping cost.

24. Redo exercise 23 for shipping costs of:

A to I, $8/ton   B to I, $6/ton

A to II, $5/ton   B to II, $10/ton

Economics

25. Minimum Cost. An oil company requires 800, 1400, and 500 barrels of low-, medium-, and high-grade oil, respectively. Refinery I produces per day 200, 300, and 100 barrels of low-, medium-, and high-grade oil, respectively, while refinery II produces per day 100, 200, and 100 barrels of low-, medium-, and high-grade oil, respectively. If it costs $150 per day to operate refinery I and $200 per day to operate refinery II, how many days should each be operated to satisfy the requirements at minimum cost?

26. Redo exercise 25 for a cost at refinery I of $250 per day and at refinery II of $200 per day.

Life Sciences

27. Diet. The Get-Slim Company is planning to can a diet product composed of two foods. Food I contains 40 calories per unit, and each unit has 20 grams of protein, 20 grams of carbohydrate, and $\frac{1}{2}$ gram of fat. Food II contains 30 calories per unit, and each unit contains 10 grams of protein, 40 grams of carbohydrate, and $\frac{1}{2}$ gram of fat. How many units of each food should each can contain if the company wishes to minimize the number of calories yet have the mixture satisfy requirements of 60 grams of protein, 4 grams of fat, and 100 grams of carbohydrate?

28. Redo exercise 27 if food I now contains 65 calories per unit and food II now contains 30 calories per unit.

29. Abdul is on a low-carbohydrate diet. He is planning a meal composed of two foods: food I with 7 grams of carbohydrate per unit and food II with 4 grams of carbohydrate per unit. In order to keep him from becoming discouraged with his diet, Abdul's doctor has insisted that he consume at least 500 calories at each meal, of which at least 210 calories must be protein. Both foods contain 100 calories per unit, but food I contains only 30 protein calories per unit, whereas food II contains 50 protein calories per unit. Help Abdul decide how many units of each food he should eat to minimize the amount of carbohydrate.

30. Redo exercise 29 if food I now has 4 grams of carbohydrate per unit and food II now has 7 grams of carbohydrate per unit.

31. Medicine. Dr. Jones has decided her patient needs at least 14 milligrams of drug I and at least 16 milligrams of drug II each day. These drugs are to be obtained by taking medicine I and medicine II. Both medicine I and medicine II contain the undesirable drug X. One gram of medicine I contains 3 milligrams of drug I, 1 milligram of drug II, and 3 milligrams of drug X. One gram of medicine II contains 2 milligrams of drug I, 2 milligrams of drug II, and 2 milligrams of drug X. How many grams of medicine I and medicine II should Dr. Jones prescribe each day if she wishes to minimize the amount of drug X?

32. Redo exercise 31 if medicine II now contains 1 milligram of drug I, 2 milligrams of drug II, and 2 milligrams of drug X. The other conditions remain the same.

Social Sciences   **33. Scheduling.** A sociologist is having trouble arranging his daily activities. He decides to construct a linear program to assist him. In order to maintain good health, he decides that he will spend 10 hours each day sleeping and eating. The 14 remaining hours are to be used in study, play, and work. He wishes to maximize his amount of study time, but he feels that he must spend at least 3 hours each day in play (which includes physical exercise and family recreation). In addition, the requirements of his job are such that the time spent in play plus one and one-fourth of the time on the job must be at least 13 hours. Help the sociologist by constructing a linear program for him and solve the linear program to determine his maximum amount of study time.

Summary and Review

Review to ensure you are familiar with the following terms:

System of inequalities	Solution set for a system
Corner points	Objective function
Constraints	Graphical solution
Convex set	Polygonal convex set
Bounded polygonal convex set	Feasible region
Slack variables	Basic feasible solution
Simplex tableau	Pivot element
Pivot operations	Dual problems

Review Exercise Set **3.7**

Sketch the solution set of the following systems of linear inequalities. Locate the corner points. Is the solution set convex? Polyhedral convex? Bounded polygonal convex?

A   **1.** $x \geq 0$ **2.** $x \geq 0$
            $y \geq 0$ $y \geq 0$
       $3x + 5y \leq 30$ $x + y \geq 5$
       $3x + 5y \leq 21$ $3x + 5y \geq 21$

3. Find the maximum and minimum values, if they exist, of $P = 3x + 4y$ subject to the constraints of exercise 1.

4. Find the maximum and minimum values, if they exist, of $C = 8x + 4y$ subject to the constraints of exercise 2.

5. Set up the simplex tableau with pivot element indicated to maximize the function given in exercise 3.

6. Set up the simplex tableau with pivot element indicated to minimize the function given in exercise 4.

7. Write the dual minimum problem given by the tableau in exercise 5.

8. Write the dual maximum problem given by the tableau in exercise 6.

B   **9.** Solve the maximum problem set up in exercise 3 by using the simplex method. Give also the solution to the dual problem.

10. Solve the minimum problem set up in exercise 4 by using the simplex method. Give also the solution to the dual problem.

11. A company has two warehouses, A and B, and two stores, I and II. Warehouse A contains 100 tons of a product, and warehouse B contains 150 tons of the same product. Store I needs 50 tons of the product, and store II needs 75 tons. The shipping costs are:

A to I, $5/ton	B to I, $6/ton
A to II, $8/ton	B to II, $10/ton

Find shipping instructions that will satisfy the stores' needs at minimum shipping cost.

12. Work exercise 11 if the shipping costs are:

A to I, $8/ton	B to I, $6/ton
A to II, $5/ton	B to II, $10/ton

13. An oil company requires 800, 1400, and 500 barrels of low-, medium-, and high-grade oil, respectively. Refinery I produces per day 200, 300, and 100 barrels of low-, medium-, and high-grade oil, respectively; refinery II produces per day 100, 200, and 100 barrels of low-, medium-, and high-grade oil, respectively. If it costs $350 per day to operate refinery I and $200 per day to operate refinery II, how many days should each be operated to satisfy the requirements at minimum cost?

14. A person on a low-carbohydrate diet plans to eat two foods. A unit of food I contains 5 grams of carbohydrate and 100 calories, of which 10 calories are protein. A unit of food II contains 6 grams of carbohydrate and 100 calories, of which 30 calories are protein. He wishes to minimize the number of grams of carbohydrate while eating at least 400 calories, of which at least 60 are protein calories. Find the number of units that he should eat of each type of food.

15. A diet company is planning to can a diet product composed of two foods. Food I contains 30 calories per unit, and each unit has 20 grams of protein, 20 grams of carbohydrate, and $\frac{7}{6}$ grams of fat. Food II contains 40 calories per unit, and each unit contains 10 grams of protein, 40 grams of carbohydrate, and $\frac{1}{2}$ gram of fat. How many units of each food should each can contain if the company wishes to minimize the number of calories, yet have the mixture satisfy the requirements of 60 grams of protein, 4 grams of fat, and 100 grams of carbohydrate?

Use a calculator or microcomputer to solve the following by the simplex method.

16. Minimize $C = 3x + 2y$
subject to
$$1.5x + y \geq 7$$
$$0.25x + 0.5y \geq 4$$
$$x \geq 0$$
$$y \geq 0$$

17. Minimize $C = 0.3x + 0.2y$
subject to
$$1.5x + 0.5y \geq 7$$
$$0.5x + y \geq 8$$
$$x \geq 0$$
$$y \geq 0$$

18. Maximize the function $P = \$37.25x + \$43.75y$ subject to the following constraints.

$$21.56x + 32.56y \leq 2122.12$$
$$30.52x + 31.54y \leq 2392.88$$
$$x \geq 0$$
$$y \geq 0$$

CHAPTER 4

Mathematics of Finance

his chapter is included primarily for those interested in business problems. However, nearly everyone uses the concepts of this chapter in everyday activities. Few people pay cash for all of their purchases. Financing a car or a home has become common practice. When items are financed, the total amount paid exceeds the price of the purchase. The difference is called *interest.* We search for the lowest possible interest rate. By making equal payments we *amortize* a debt, and we learn in this chapter how to find the size of these equal payments.

Tables have been provided for this chapter in the Appendix. However, we encourage the use of an inexpensive scientific or financial calculator instead of these tables. By solving problems with a calculator you can work problems for interest rates not in the tables. A calculator will also reduce the drudgery of the computations in this chapter.

This chapter discusses simple interest, bank discount, compound interest, annuities, and other topics of a subject area called the mathematics of finance.

1 Simple Interest and Discount

The calculations of **simple interest** and **simple discount** are elementary, but it is still helpful to review these concepts. In everyday practice the use of simple interest and simple discount is usually restricted to short-term loans. However, simple interest is also used for interest periods in both **compound interest** and **annuities,** so a good foundation in simple interest is important.

Simple interest is interest charged or interest earned on the original amount loaned and not on the amount paid back or on interest accrued subsequently. It is the "rent" paid for using someone else's money. Simple interest is computed at a constant percent of the money borrowed for a specified time, usually a single year or less, and is paid at the end of the specified time.

The sum borrowed is called the **principal, P,** or sometimes the **present value;** r denotes the **rate** of interest, usually expressed in percent per year; and t is the **time** expressed in years or fractions of years. By definition, simple interest, I, equals the principal multiplied by the rate multiplied by the time in years.

<table>
<tr><td>**Simple Interest**</td><td>

$I = Prt$

where

$I =$ Simple interest

$P =$ Principal

$r =$ Interest rate per year

$t =$ Time in years

</td></tr>
</table>

The **simple interest amount,** A, owed at the end of t years at $r\%$ per year is given by the following formula.

<table>
<tr><td>**Amount Owed on a Simple Interest Loan**</td><td>

$A = P + I$

$A = P + Prt$

$A = P(1 + rt)$

where

$A =$ Amount (future value)

$P =$ Principal (present value)

$r =$ Annual simple interest rate

$t =$ Time in years

</td></tr>
</table>

EXAMPLE 1 A loan of $1,000 is made for 6 months at a simple interest rate of 12%. How much does the borrower owe at the end of 6 months?

Solution
$$A = P(1 + rt) = \$1,000[1 + (0.12)(\tfrac{1}{2})]$$
$$= \$1,000(1 + 0.06)$$
$$= \$1,060$$

Thus, the borrower owes $1,060.

The relationship between principal or present value and amount or future value for Example 1 is shown in the time diagram of Figure 4.1.

Figure 4.1

$1,000
Principal or
present value

$1,060
Amount or
future value

0

$\frac{1}{2}$ year

To find the present value of an amount at a simple interest rate, r, solve the equation $A = P(1 + rt)$ for P to obtain the following result:

**Present Value
of an Amount**

$$P = \frac{A}{1 + rt}$$

where

P = Present value of an amount

A = Amount

r = Annual simple interest rate

t = Time in years

Note that in this formula the amount includes the interest.

EXAMPLE 2 Compute the present value of $1,000 due in 3 months with interest at 12% annually.

Solution

$$P = \frac{\$1,000}{1 + (0.12)(\frac{3}{12})} = \frac{\$1,000}{1.03} = \$970.87$$

Hence, the present value is $970.87.

The time diagram for Example 2 is shown in Figure 4.2.

Figure 4.2

$970.87
Principal or
present value

$1,000
Amount or
future value

0

3 months

When computing the time, t, many lending agencies use a 360-day year, which is called an **ordinary interest year.** Thus, a loan for 30 days is $\frac{1}{12}$ of an ordinary interest year, and 180 days is $\frac{1}{2}$ of an ordinary year. In contrast, for an interest year of 365 days (except for leap year, 366), we obtain what is called **exact interest.** In the same manner, we may compute the number of days for the loan by using a 30-day month (called **ordinary** or approximate time), or we can compute the **exact time** (exact number of days) for the loan.

In practice, **exact time** and an **ordinary interest year** are employed most commonly and, unless otherwise stated, will be used in this book. The exact number of days is found by subtracting the dates and adding 1; that is, from July 1 to July 2 is $2 - 1 + 1 = 2$ days.

EXAMPLE 3 Find the ordinary interest on a $100 loan at 10% simple interest from July 4 to August 8.

Solution From July 4 to July 31 is 27 days. From July 31 to August 1 is 1 day. From August 1 to August 8 is 7 days. The time of the loan is, consequently, $27 + 1 + 7 + 1 = 36$ days.

$$I = Prt = \$100(0.10)(\tfrac{36}{360}) = \$1.00$$

The interest is $1.00.

EXAMPLE 4 Find the exact interest on a $100 loan at 10% simple interest from July 4 to August 8.

Solution $$I = Prt = \$100(0.10)(\tfrac{36}{365}) = \tfrac{360}{365} = \$0.99$$

Discount or **bank discount,** D, is money charged for money borrowed, and it is based on the amount to be repaid; it is usually deducted at the time the loan agreement is executed. If A is the amount of money to be repaid at the end of time t (expressed in years), and d is the bank discount rate per year, then D is computed as follows:

Bank Discount

$$D = Adt$$

where

D = Bank discount

A = Amount to be repaid

d = Discount rate per year

t = Time in years

The sum received, called the **principal** or **proceeds,** is equal to the amount to be repaid less the discount.

$$P = A - D$$

$$P = A - Adt$$

$$P = A(1 - dt)$$

where

P = Principal received or present value

A = Amount to be repaid or future value

d = Discount rate per year

t = Time in years

EXAMPLE 5 A $1,000 loan for $\frac{1}{2}$ year is consummated at a bank that charges a 10% bank discount rate. What is the principal received by the borrower?

Solution

$$I = Adt$$

$$= \$1,000(0.10)(\tfrac{1}{2})$$

$$= \$50$$

$$P = A - I$$

$$= \$1,000 - \$50$$

$$= \$950$$

Thus, the borrower receives $950. Figure 4.3 contains the time diagram for this example.

Figure 4.3

$950
Principal or
present value

$1,000
Amount or
future value

0 $\frac{1}{2}$ year

EXAMPLE 6 Find the simple interest rate the bank charged the borrower in Example 5.

Solution The principal was $950 and the interest was $50. Substituting in the formula gives

$$I = Prt$$

$$50 = 950r(\tfrac{1}{2})$$

$$50 = 475r$$

$$r = \tfrac{50}{475} = \tfrac{2}{19} = 0.105 = 10.5\%$$

EXAMPLE 7 If the present value of a 2-year loan at a 12% bank discount rate is $897.60, what amount must be repaid at the end of the 2 years?

To understand the problem we construct a time diagram (Figure 4.4).

$$P = A(1 - dt)$$
$$\$897.60 = A(1 - 0.12 \cdot 2)$$
$$\$897.60 = A(0.76)$$
$$A = \$1,181.05$$

Thus, the amount to be repaid is $1,181.05.

Figure 4.4

$897.60
Principal or
present value   Amount

0   2 years

The bank discount rate is especially useful in discounting promissory notes, as indicated by the following example.

EXAMPLE 8 A 2-year 12% simple-interest-bearing note of $1,200 was discounted by a bank at 10% 6 months before it was due. How much did the bank pay for the note? (*Note:* For such a simple-interest-bearing note, the maturity value is $1,200 plus the interest on $1,200 for 2 years.)

Figure 4.5

$1,200   Discounted   Amount
                      value

0                   $1\frac{1}{2}$ 2 years

Solution The amount of the note at maturity (the end of 2 years) will be

$$A = \$1,200[1 + (0.12)2]$$
$$= \$1,200(1.24)$$
$$= \$1,488$$

The value 6 months before the maturity of the note discounted at a 10% discount rate would be

$$P = \$1,488[1 - 0.10(\tfrac{1}{2})] = \$1,488(0.95) = \$1,413.60$$

Exercise Set **4.1**

A **1.** Find the simple interest and the total amount of each of the following loans.
    a. $10,000 for 2 years at 16%
    b. $8,000 for 3 months at 12%
    c. $16,000 for 4 months at 12%
    d. $80,000 for $1\frac{1}{2}$ years at 14%

2. Find the money received if the following bank loans are consummated.
   a. $10,000 for 2 years at 16% discount rate
   b. $8,000 for 3 months at 12% discount rate
   c. $16,000 for 4 months at 12% discount rate
   d. $80,000 for $1\frac{1}{2}$ years at 14% discount rate

3. Find the equivalent simple interest rate for each part of exercise 2.

B 4. What amount of money invested at 12% simple interest will yield an amount of $10,000 2 years from now?

5. You want to have $1,000 in 5 years. How much must you invest now if money earns 10% simple interest?

6. Daniel signed a note to repay $1,120 in 2 years to a friend who is charging him a 6% discount rate. How much did Daniel receive?

7. How much should one borrow from a bank that has a 10% discount rate in order to receive $2,400 if the loan must be repaid in 2 years?

8. Suppose your bank agrees to lend you $1,000 for 2 years at a discount rate of 10%. How much do you receive?

9. Find the amount of a 90-day loan at 12% ordinary interest if you receive $1,500 now.

10. How much can you borrow for 6 months from a credit union which charges 12% simple interest if you wish to pay only $30 interest?

C 11. How much interest will you owe on a $1,000 loan from March 3 to August 7 at 12% simple interest?

12. What is the interest on a $1,500 loan from June 15 to September 11 at a simple interest rate of 8%?

Solve each formula for the indicated variable.

13. $I = Prt$ (r)   14. $A = P + Prt$ (P)

15. $P = A - Adt$ (d)   16. $P = A - Adt$ (A)

Business 17. **Discount Rate.** A discount rate of 8% is equivalent to what simple interest rate for 1 year? (*Hint:* Assume a $1 present value.)

18. **Promissory Note.** A 60-day, $1,000, 6% ordinary-interest-bearing note dated April 1 is discounted on May 15 at a discount rate of 8%. What is the discounted value of the note?

19. **Promissory Note.** A 90-day, $2,000, 7% ordinary-interest-bearing note dated September 2 was discounted on October 15 at a discount rate of 8%. What was the discounted value of the note?

20. **Promissory Note.** Rati signs a note at a bank in which she agrees to pay the bank a certain amount at the end of 2 years. How much must Rati pay if she receives $1,800 today and the bank charges a discount rate of 8%?

21. **Bonus.** Suppose you have a choice to make between a bonus of $500 now or $550 6 months from now. Which would be the best choice, assuming that 10% simple interest is the best interest you can safely receive from an investment of the $500?

22. **Simple Interest.** Find the interest and the amount of a loan of $3,523.42 at 12% simple interest for 3 years.

23. **Discount Rate.** The price of a new roof is $4,327. If this money is to be obtained from a bank that has a 12% discount rate, what should be the amount of a 3-month note?

In this section we discuss a method of computing interest in which, at the end of a given interest period, the interest is reinvested at the same rate. Thus, during the second interest period, both the original principal and the interest for the first period earn interest. Such a procedure for computing interest is called **compounding,** and in this section we study **compound interest.**

You are encouraged to use your calculator in this section. In addition, compound interest tables are provided in the Appendix.

In the preceding section we saw that simple interest I is found by using the formula $I = Prt$, where P represents the principal, r the rate, and t the time. When interest is computed by this formula, the principal always remains the same. If the interest is added to the principal at the end of each interest period so that the principal is increased, the interest is said to be **compounded.** The sum of the original principal and all of the interest is called the **compound amount,** and the difference between the compound amount and the original principal is the **compound interest.** Simple interest and compound interest are compared in the following example.

EXAMPLE 9 Find the simple interest on $1,000 for 3 years at 10%. Then find the compound interest on $1,000 for 3 years at 10% compounded annually.

Solution First we summarize the problem on a time diagram.

Figure 4.6

P	First interest period	Second interest period	A(at end of third period)
0	1	2	3 years

To emphasize the difference between simple and compound interest, both will be computed year by year.

	Simple Interest	Compound Interest
For the first year	$I = \$1{,}000(0.10) = \$100$	$I = \$1{,}000.00(0.10) = \$100$
For the second year	$I = \$1{,}000(0.10) = \$100$	$I = \$1{,}100.00(0.10) = \$110$
For the third year	$I = \$1{,}000(0.10) = \$100$	$I = \$1{,}210.00(0.10) = \$121.00$

Thus, simple interest for 3 years totals $300, while compound interest totals $331.00. The compound amount is $1,331.00. Notice that the principal changes each year when interest is compounded, but it always remains the same when simple interest is used.

Using the preceding example, let's compute in another way the compound amount at the end of each year. At the end of the first year, the compound amount is

$$\$1{,}000 + \$1{,}000(0.10) = \$1{,}000(1 + 0.10) = \$1{,}000(1.10)$$

During the second year, the principal is $\$1{,}000(1.10)$. Thus, at the end of the second year the compound amount is

$$\$1{,}000(1.10) + \$1{,}000(1.10)(0.10) = \$1{,}000(1.10)(1 + 0.10)$$
$$= \$1{,}000(1.10)(1.10)$$
$$= \$1{,}000(1.10)^2$$

At the end of the third year, the compound amount is

$$\$1{,}000(1.10)^2 + \$1{,}000(1.10)^2(0.10) = \$1{,}000(1.10)^2(1 + 0.10)$$
$$= \$1{,}000(1.10)^2(1.10)$$
$$= \$1{,}000(1.10)^3$$

This pattern extends easily to the general case. Suppose that P dollars are deposited at an interest rate of i per period for n periods. Then Table 4.1 can be used to compute the amount that has accrued at the end of that time.

Table 4.1

Period	Principal	+	Interest	=	Amount (at end of period)
1	P	+	Pi	=	$P(1 + i)$
2	$P(1 + i)$	+	$P(1 + i)i$	=	$P(1 + i)^2$
3	$P(1 + i)^2$	+	$P(1 + i)^2 i$	=	$P(1 + i)^3$
$\vdots$	$\vdots$	$\vdots$	$\vdots$	$\vdots$	$\vdots$
n	$P(1 + i)^{n-1}$	+	$P(1 + i)^{n-1} i$	=	$P(1 + i)^n$

This table suggests that the compound amount can be found by multiplying the principal by $(1 + i)^n$ where i is the interest rate per period and n is the number of periods.

Compound Amount

$$A = P(1 + i)^n$$

where

$A = $ Compound amount after n periods

$P = $ Principal invested

$i = $ Interest rate per period

$n = $ Number of periods

EXAMPLE 10 Find the compound amount that would result from investing $500 at 8% interest compounded annually for 4 years.

Solution We first examine a time diagram, Figure 4.7.

Figure 4.7

Substituting $P = \$500$, $i = 0.08$, and $n = 4$ in the formula given in the theorem, $A = P(1 + i)^n$, gives

$$A = \$500(1 + 0.08)^4 = 500(1.08)^4$$

To complete the problem use a hand calculator to obtain

$$A = \$680.24$$

If you do not wish to use a calculator, we have computed $(1 + i)^n$ for different values of i and n and listed the results in Table I of the Appendix. A similar procedure is followed throughout this chapter.

$$(1.08)^4 = 1.360489$$

Hence,

$$A = \$500(1.08)^4 = 500(1.360489) = \$680.24$$

Interest may be compounded for any period of time—annually, semiannually, quarterly, monthly, daily, and so on. When the rate of compound interest is given, it is usually specified as an annual rate called the **nominal rate.** Hence, if the interest is to be compounded semiannually, this rate must be divided by 2; if the interest is to be compounded quarterly, the nominal rate must be divided by 4, and so forth.

EXAMPLE 11 Find the compound amount that would be obtained from an investment of $2,000 at 12% compounded quarterly for 5 years. What is the compound interest?

Figure 4.8

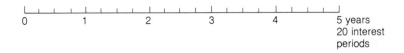

Solution Twelve percent compounded quarterly is $\frac{0.12}{4} = 0.03$ each quarter. Since there are four quarters in a year, the number of interest periods is $n = 4 \cdot 5 = 20$. Thus,

$$A = P(1 + i)^n$$
$$= \$2,000(1 + 0.03)^{20}$$
$$= \$3,612.22$$

Or, from the table, $(1.03)^{20} = 1.806111$. Thus,

$$A = \$2{,}000(1.806111)$$
$$= \$3{,}612.22$$

The compound interest is

$$I = \$3{,}612.22 - \$2{,}000 = \$1{,}612.22$$

Once we have established the relationship $A = P(1 + i)^n$, it is rather easy to change the direction of our thinking. Consider the question "How much principal must we invest now at 8% interest per year compounded semiannually in order to have $6,000 in 4 years to buy a car?" The principal for which we are searching (or the present value) is the value of P in our formula.

Figure 4.9

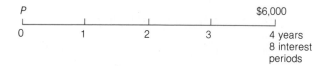

$$A = P(1 + i)^n$$
$$P = \frac{A}{(1 + i)^n} = A(1 + i)^{-n}$$
$$= \$6{,}000(1 + 0.04)^{-8}$$
$$= \$6{,}000(0.730690) \quad \text{Found in Table I}$$
$$= \$4{,}384.14$$

Thus, the present value of $6,000 due in 4 years at 8% interest compounded semiannually is $4,384.14.

EXAMPLE 12 Find the present value of $3,000 due in 5 years at 12% interest compounded quarterly.

Figure 4.10

Solution
$$P = A(1 + i)^{-n}$$
$$= \$3{,}000(1 + 0.03)^{-20}$$
$$= \$3{,}000(0.553676)$$
$$= \$1{,}661.03$$

We have not yet established how to compare the interest rates promised by two institutions. For example, if the bank down the street offers an interest rate of 10% compounded 5 times a year and the bank 12 miles across town offers a rate of 12% compounded 3 times a year, should we undertake the long drive? To compare the two nominal rates we need to introduce the notion of an **effective**

rate of interest. The effective rate of interest is defined to be the rate that, when compounded annually, gives the same amount of interest as the rate i compounded several times a year. That is, $(1 + e)^1 = (1 + i)^k$ where e is compounded 1 time a year and i is compounded k times a year. From this relationship the effective rate can be obtained or the following formula can be used:

Effective Annual Rate

> A rate i per period compounded k times a year produces an effective annual rate of
>
> $$e = (1 + i)^k - 1$$

EXAMPLE 13   Find the effective rate equivalent to the nominal rate of 6% compounded quarterly.

Solution
$$e = (1 + 0.015)^4 - 1$$
$$= 1.0614 - 1$$
$$= 0.0614$$

Thus, a nominal rate of 6% compounded quarterly is equivalent to an effective rate of 6.14%.

EXAMPLE 14   For a savings account, which is the better rate: 12.5% compounded annually, or 12% compounded monthly?

Solution   To compare the two rates, we first find and compare the effective rates:

$$e = (1 + 0.125)^1 - 1 \qquad e = (1 + 0.01)^{12} - 1$$
$$= 1.125 - 1 \qquad\qquad = 1.126825 - 1$$
$$= 12.5\% \qquad\qquad\quad = 12.6825\%$$

The effective rate for 12% compounded 12 times a year is greater than 12.5% compounded 1 time a year.

EXAMPLE 15   How long will it take a dollar to double at 8% compounded semiannually?

Solution   Eight percent compounded semiannually is 4% each period. Substituting $A = 2$, $P = 1$, and $i = 0.04$ gives

$$A = P(1 + i)^n$$
$$2 = 1(1 + 0.04)^n$$
$$2 = (1.04)^n$$

From Table I, n is between 17 and 18 periods.

We have seen that the interest per period is the nominal rate divided by the number of interest periods. Thus, if the nominal rate is denoted by r, the number of interest periods per year by n, and the principal by P, then the compound amount A for 1 year is given by

$$A = P\left(1 + \frac{r}{n}\right)^n$$

For 2 periods (semiannually):

$$A = P\left(1 + \frac{r}{2}\right)^2$$

For 4 periods (quarterly):

$$A = P\left(1 + \frac{r}{4}\right)^4$$

For 365 periods (daily):

$$A = P\left(1 + \frac{r}{365}\right)^{365}$$

Many savings and loan associations compound interest daily, so the formula

$$A = P\left(1 + \frac{r}{365}\right)^n$$

gives the amount for a deposit of P for n days.

Some savings and loan associations advertise that savings are compounded continuously. In this case

$$A = Pe^{tr}$$

where r is the nominal rate and t is the number of years. (The e function, studied in Chapter 12, is evaluated for our use in Table III of the Appendix.)

EXAMPLE 16   Find the compound amount that would be obtained from an investment of $2,000 compounded continuously for 5 years at 6%.

Solution $A = Pe^{tr} = 2000e^{5(0.06)} = 2000e^{0.3} = 2000(1.349859) = \$2{,}699.72$

Exercise Set **4.2**

A   **1.** Make a table to show the difference in interest for $100 invested at 8% simple interest and at 8% compounded annually for 4 years.

Find the effective rates equivalent to the nominal rates for exercises 2–5.

2. 6% compounded semiannually   **3.** 8% compounded semiannually

4. 12% compounded monthly   **5.** 24% compounded monthly

Find the compound interest and compound amount for the investments in exercises 6–11.

6. **a.** $5,000 at 8% compounded annually for 10 years
   b. $5,000 at 8% compounded semiannually for 10 years
   c. $5,000 at 8% compounded quarterly for 10 years

7. **a.** $2,000 at 12% compounded 3 times a year for 8 years
   b. $2,000 at 12% compounded semiannually for 8 years
   c. $2,000 at 12% compounded quarterly for 8 years

8. Find the present value of $5,000 due in 5 years at 8% interest compounded annually.

9. What is the present value of a note for $6,000 due in 5 years at 8% interest compounded semiannually?

10. Find the present value of
    a. $7,000 due in 10 years at 8% interest compounded semiannually
    b. $8,000 due in 6 years at 8% interest compounded quarterly

B 11. Find the compound amount for
    a. $3,000 at 12% compounded continuously for 5 years
    b. $6,000 at 15% compounded continuously for 6 years

C 12. How many years will it take to double $1,000 at 16% interest compounded semiannually?

13. How long will it take for $125 to amount to $375 at 12% interest compounded quarterly?

14. Find the effective annual rate corresponding to 10% interest compounded continuously. (*Note:* You must adjust the formula given.)

15. Approximately how long will it take money to double at 10% interest compounded continuously?

The following exercises require the use of a calculator.

16. Find the compound amount of $10,000 invested for 10 years at 12% interest compounded daily.

17. How long will it take money to double if 8% interest is compounded daily?

Business 18. **Loans.** Paul borrowed $700 and agreed to repay the principal with interest at 8% compounded semiannually. What will he owe at the end of 5 years?

19. **Loans.** On April 1, 1986, Rana borrowed $3,000 at 8% compounded quarterly. What will she owe on October 1, 1998?

20. **Savings.** The sum of $1,000 was deposited in a bank at an interest rate of 6% compounded semiannually. Five years later the rate increased to 8% compounded semiannually. If the money was not withdrawn, how much was in the account at the end of 6 years?

21. **Savings.** How much should parents invest for their daughter at 12% interest compounded semiannually in order to have $5,000 at the end of 20 years?

22. **Cash Value.** A lot is sold for $750 cash and $600 a year for the next 3 years. Find the cash value of the lot if money is worth 6% compounded semiannually.

23. **Debt.** Peter owes $2,000 due in 3 years. If he pays $400 now, what payment after 2 years should satisfy his debt if money is worth 6% compounded semiannually?

24. **Debt.** Assuming that money is worth 6% compounded semiannually, would you discharge a debt by paying $7,500 now or $10,000 in 4 years?

25. Fish Population. Suppose the rate of growth of fish population in a lake is 10% per year. If you stock the lake with 100 fish today, how many fish should the lake contain 6 years from today? (*Hint:* $N = 100e^{6(0.10)}$. Find N and round to the nearest whole number.)

26. Inflation. If inflation continues to increase the cost of an article by 8% per year, how long will it take the cost of the article to double? What will be the cost of the article 5 years from now if the present cost is $300?

Geometric Progressions and Annuities

> The next two sections involve a sequence of payments or deposits that draw interest. In the preceding section we learned that to accumulate a payment with compound interest we multiply by the factor $(1 + i)^n$. To find the sum of such terms we introduce what is known as a **geometric progression.** This work involves a bit of algebraic manipulation and can be omitted since tables are provided in the Appendix and similiar problems are solved in the next section by using these tables.
>
> There are, however, two primary reasons you may wish to study this section: From this study you will obtain an understanding of the formulas used in the next section and an understanding of how the tables are compiled. This understanding will allow you to solve annuity problems with a hand calculator.

A **geometric progression** is characterized by the fact that each term is obtained from the previous term by multiplying by the constant r, called the **common ratio.** Thus, the sum S of the first n terms is

$$S = \underset{\substack{\uparrow \\ \text{1st} \\ \text{term}}}{a} + \underset{\substack{\uparrow \\ \text{2nd} \\ \text{term}}}{ar} + \underset{\substack{\uparrow \\ \text{3rd} \\ \text{term}}}{ar^2} + \cdots + \underset{\substack{\uparrow \\ \text{nth} \\ \text{term}}}{ar^{n-1}}$$

Multiplying by r gives

$$rS = ar + ar^2 + \cdots + ar^{n-1} + ar^n$$

Subtracting the equation for rS from the equation for S gives

$$(1 - r)S = a - ar^n$$

If $r \neq 1$, dividing by $1 - r$ gives

$$S = \frac{a - ar^n}{1 - r}$$

Thus, we have proved the following theorem:

> The sum S of the first n terms of a geometric progression with first term a and common ratio $r \neq 1$ is
>
> $$S = \frac{a - ar^n}{1 - r}$$

EXAMPLE 17   Find the sum of six terms of the following geometric progression:

$$6 + 12 + 24 + \cdots$$

Solution   Since this is a geometric progression, each term is obtained from the preceding term by multiplying by a constant, r. The constant r may be found by dividing the second term by the first term:

$$r = \tfrac{12}{6} = 2$$

After r is found, other terms of the progression may be obtained by multiplying the preceding term by r. The sum of n terms is found by using the formula

$$S = \frac{a - ar^n}{1 - r}$$

$$= \frac{6 - 6(2)^6}{1 - 2}$$

$$= 378$$

An **annuity** is a sequence of equal payments made at equal intervals of time. Paying off a mortgage on a home is an example of an annuity since equal payments are made periodically. We usually denote these payments as R. In an **ordinary annuity,** the payments are made at the end of **payment periods** (the time between successive payments). In an **annuity due,** payments are made at the beginning of a period. The sum of all payments R, plus their interest, is called the **amount of an annuity.** The amount of an ordinary annuity is illustrated in Example 18.

EXAMPLE 18   Suppose at the end of each year you receive $100 and invest it at 6% compounded annually. How much would you have at the end of 5 years?

Figure 4.11

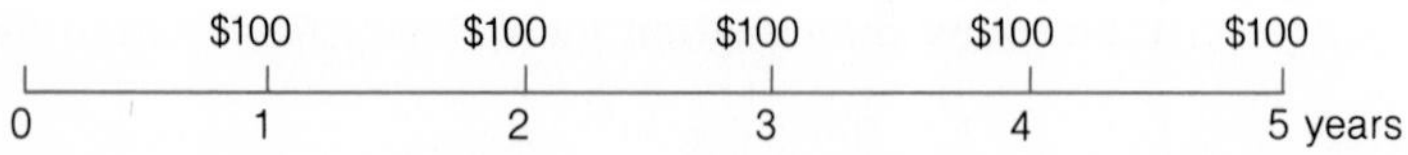

Solution   Let A represent the amount of the annuity. Since the first payment of $100 is not received until the end of the year, it will accumulate interest for 4 years as seen in Figure 4.12. Likewise, the second payment will accumulate interest for 3 years,

Figure 4.12

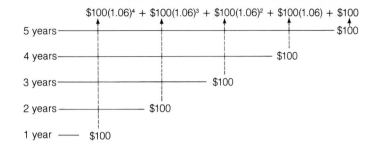

and so on. Hence,

$$A = \$100(1.06)^4 + \$100(1.06)^3 + \$100(1.06)^2 + \$100(1.06) + \$100$$
$$= \$563.71$$

Now let's compute the answer by using geometric progressions. We begin by arranging the terms from last to first.

$$A = \$100 + \$100(1.06) + \$100(1.06)^2 + \$100(1.06)^3 + \$100(1.06)^4$$

Notice that A is now the sum of five terms of a geometric progression whose first term is $100 and whose common ratio is 1.06; hence,

$$A = \frac{a - ar^n}{1 - r} = \frac{\$100 - \$100(1.06)^5}{1 - 1.06} = \frac{\$100[1 - (1.06)^5]}{-0.06}$$

$$= \frac{\$100[(1.06)^5 - 1]}{0.06}$$

$$= \frac{\$100(1.338226 - 1)}{0.06}$$

$$= \$563.71$$

The **present value** of an annuity is the sum of the present values of the payments, each discounted to the time of the present value.

EXAMPLE 19 Compute the present value of an ordinary annuity of $100 per year for 5 years at 6% compounded annually.

Figure 4.13

P	$100	$100	$100	$100	$100
0	1	2	3	4	5 years

Solution Let P represent the present value of the annuity. Actually, P is the sum of the present values of each of the five payments. Thus,

$$P = \$100(1.06)^{-1} + \$100(1.06)^{-2} + \$100(1.06)^{-3} + \$100(1.06)^{-4}$$
$$+ \$100(1.06)^{-5}$$
$$= \$94.34 + \$89.00 + \$83.96 + \$79.21 + \$74.73$$
$$= \$421.24$$

Note that in the preceding example (third equation from the end) the present value can be considered as a geometric progression whose first term is $100(1.06)^{-1}$ and whose common ratio is $(1.06)^{-1}$. Thus,

$$P = \frac{a(1 - r^n)}{1 - r}$$

$$= \frac{\dfrac{\$100}{1.06}\left[1 - \dfrac{1}{(1.06)^5}\right]}{1 - \dfrac{1}{1.06}}$$

$$= \$100\left[\frac{(1.06)^5 - 1}{0.06(1.06)^5}\right]$$

$$= \$100\left[\frac{1.338226 - 1}{0.06(1.338226)}\right]$$

$$= \$421.24$$

The same procedures can be used for finding the amount and present value of an annuity due as illustrated in Example 20. Be sure to remember that in an annuity due the payment is made at the beginning of each payment period.

EXAMPLE 20 Leon deposits $50 at the beginning of each quarter in the Opp Savings and Loan Association. If the account draws 12% interest compounded quarterly, find the amount in the fund at the end of 10 years.

Figure 4.14

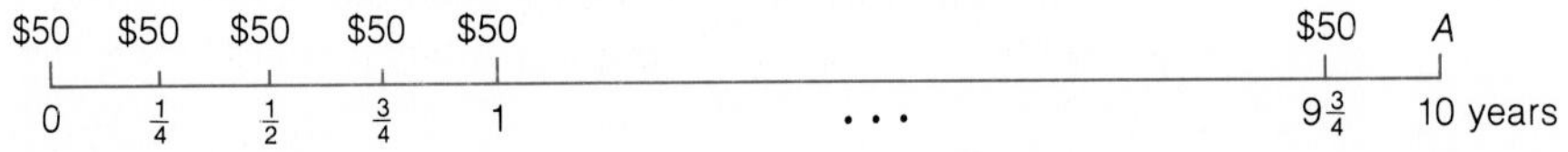

Solution

$$A = \$50(1.03)^{40} + \$50(1.03)^{39} + \cdots + \$50(1.03)$$

or

$$A = \$50(1.03) + \$50(1.03)^2 + \cdots + \$50(1.03)^{40}$$

$$= \frac{a - ar^n}{1 - r}$$

$$= \frac{\$50(1.03)[1 - (1.03)^{40}]}{1 - 1.03}$$

$$= \$50\left[\frac{(1.03)^{41} - 1.03}{0.03}\right]$$

$$= \$3,883.17$$

At the end of 10 years Leon has $3,883.17 in the Opp Savings and Loan Association.

Geometric progressions are also most useful in finding the amounts of annuities that do not fit the regular pattern (see Section 4).

EXAMPLE 21   Lon deposits $1,000 in the First Savings and Loan at the end of each year for 10 years. How much money does he have at the end of 10 years if the savings and loan pays 12% interest compounded quarterly?

Figure 4.15

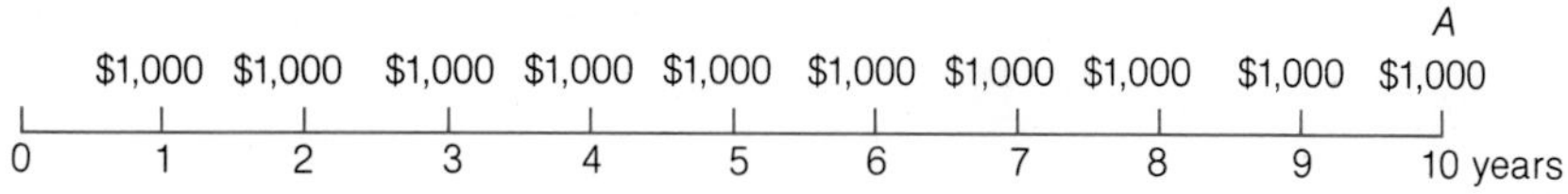

$1,000 $1,000 $1,000 $1,000 $1,000 $1,000 $1,000 $1,000 $1,000 $1,000 A

| 0 | 1 | 2 | 3 | 4 | 5 | 6 | 7 | 8 | 9 | 10 years |

Solution

$$A = \$1,000(1 + 0.03)^{36} + \$1,000(1 + 0.03)^{32} + \cdots +$$
$$\$1,000(1 + 0.03)^{4} + \$1,000$$

or

$$A = \$1,000 + \$1,000(1 + 0.03)^{4} + \cdots + \$1,000(1 + 0.03)^{36}$$

$$= \frac{a(1 - r^{n})}{1 - r}$$

$$= \frac{\$1,000[1 - (1.03)^{4 \cdot 10}]}{1 - (1.03)^{4}}$$

$$= \frac{\$1,000[1 - 3.262038]}{1 - 1.125509}$$

$$= \$18,022.91$$

At the end of 10 years Lon has $18,022.91 in his savings account.

EXAMPLE 22   The Doss family decides to purchase a deferred annuity to finance the graduate school education of newborn Teresa. To provide four annual payments of $5,000 each with the first payment being made 20 years from now, how much should be deposited in a bank paying 8% interest compounded annually?

Figure 4.16

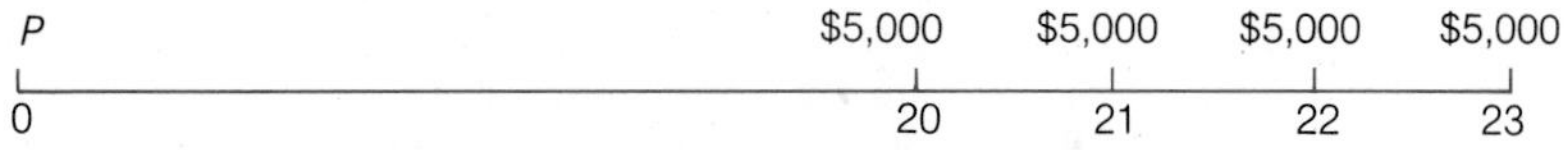

P $5,000 $5,000 $5,000 $5,000

| 0 | | 20 | 21 | 22 | 23 |

Solution

$$P = \frac{\$5,000}{(1.08)^{20}} + \frac{\$5,000}{(1.08)^{21}} + \frac{\$5,000}{(1.08)^{22}} + \frac{\$5,000}{(1.08)^{23}}$$

$$= \frac{a(1 - r^{n})}{1 - r}$$

$$= \frac{\$5,000}{(1.08)^{20}} \frac{\left[1 - \left(\dfrac{1}{1.08}\right)^{4}\right]}{\left[1 - \dfrac{1}{1.08}\right]}$$

$$= \$5,000 \frac{[(1.08)^{4} - 1]}{0.08(1.08)^{23}}$$

$$= \$5,000 \left[\frac{1.36049 - 1}{0.08(5.87146)}\right]$$

$$= \$3,837.30$$

Thus, $3,837.30 must be deposited now in order for Teresa to have $5,000 a year for 4 years starting at age 20.

Exercise Set **4.3**

A
1. Given the following geometric progressions, find the common ratio and the next three terms.
   a. $\frac{1}{3}, 1, 3, \ldots$ **b.** $\frac{1}{2}, -1, 2, \ldots$
   c. $9, -3, 1, \ldots$ **d.** $12, 9, \frac{27}{4}, \ldots$

2. Find the sums of the following geometric progressions.
   a. $4 + 2 + 1 + \cdots + \frac{1}{32}$ **b.** $9 + 3 + 1 + \cdots + \frac{1}{27}$
   c. $4 - 2 + 1 - \cdots - \frac{1}{8}$ **d.** $9 - 3 + 1 - \cdots + \frac{1}{9}$

3. Find the sums of the indicated number of terms of the following geometric progressions.
   a. Six terms of $8 + 4 + 2 + \cdots$
   b. Five terms of $9 + 3 + 1 + \cdots$
   c. Seven terms of $18 + 12 + 8 + \cdots$
   d. Eight terms of $27 - 9 + 3 - \cdots$

B
4. Find the sum of the geometric progression

$$\$6,000 + \$6,000(1.04) + \$6,000(1.04)^2 + \$6,000(1.04)^3$$

5. Find the present value of the following ordinary annuities:
   a. $700 a year for 10 years at 8% compounded annually.
   b. $800 a quarter for 5 years at 12% compounded quarterly.

6. Find the amount of the following ordinary annuities:
   a. $500 a year for 10 years at 8% compounded annually.
   b. $600 a year for 8 years at 6% compounded annually.

C
7. Find the amount of money you would receive from a job that pays 1 cent for the first day, 2 cents for the second day, 4 cents for the third day, 8 cents for the fourth day, and so forth, assuming you work for 30 days.

8. Find the amount at the end of 5 years of $1,000 deposited at the end of each year at 8% interest compounded semiannually.

9. What is the present value of five yearly payments of $3,000 each starting at the end of 10 years at 8% interest compounded yearly?

Business
10. **Investments.** Suppose you deposit $500 each 6 months in a credit union that pays 8% interest compounded semiannually. How much would you have after 5 years?

11. **Investments.** Juan is to receive $1,000 at the end of each year for 5 years. If he invests each year's payment at 8% compounded annually, how much will he have at the end of his 5 years?

12. **Investments.** Ingrid invests $300 at the end of each 6 months in a fund that pays 8% interest compounded semiannually. How much does she have just after the tenth deposit? How much does she have just before the tenth deposit?

13. **Present Value of a Contract.** A contract pays $100 each quarter for 5 years and $1,500 additional at the end of the last quarter. What is the present value of the contract if money is worth 8% interest compounded quarterly?

14. **Annuity.** What is the present value of an annuity of $100 per year for 4 years followed by $300 per year for 5 more years at 8% interest compounded annually?

15. **Insurance.** Find the equivalent cash premium if money is worth 8% interest compounded annually for a 20-year-pay insurance policy which has an annual premium of $100 payable at the beginning of each year for 20 years.

16. **Rent.** Dora pays $300 rent each month, payable in advance. What would be her equivalent yearly rent at 12% interest compounded monthly if she paid her rent for the year in advance?

17. **Installment Purchase.** A car was bought on March 1 with the agreement that there would be 24 monthly payments of $150, the first of which is due on July 1. Find the equivalent cash price if interest is 12% compounded monthly.

18. **Annuity.** Find the amount and the present value of an annuity of $135 a year for 9 years at 8.5% interest compounded annually. (*Note:* This interest rate is not in the tables. A calculator must be used to compute the table entry for both the amount and the present value.)

19. **Contract.** A contract pays $75 each quarter for 6 years and $1,275 additional at the end of the last quarter. What is the present value of the contract if money is worth 8% interest compounded quarterly?

20. **Investments.** Katie deposited $100 when Jeannie was 2 years old and continued to deposit $100 each 6 months thereafter until Jeannie was 16 years old, when the last deposit was made. The savings and loan association paid 8% interest compounded semiannually. If the money was allowed to accumulate until Jeannie was 18 years old, how much did she receive?

21. **Investments.** How much money would Jeannie receive in exercise 20 if the money was allowed to accumulate until she was 21 years old?

Annuities, Amortization, and Sinking Funds

In the preceding section we found the present value and the amount of an annuity by using the formula for the sum of a geometric progression. The numerical values were obtained either by using a calculator or by obtaining values for compound interest factors from Table I of the Appendix.

In this section our work is reduced by evaluating expressions for the amount and the present value of an ordinary annuity in Table II of the Appendix.

In addition, by means of **amortization tables,** we will see how debts are paid through periodic payments. Also, we will see how money is accumulated in **sinking funds.**

Let us now derive an expression for the amount of an ordinary annuity of $R deposits for n periods as shown in Figure 4.17.

Figure 4.17

Let i be the interest rate per period. Note that the value of the $\$R$ at n is simply $\$R$. The $\$R$ at $n - 1$ must involve compound interest for one period, or have a value of $\$R(1 + i)$ at the end of n periods. The $\$R$ at $n - 2$ must accumulate interest for two periods, or have a value at n of $\$R(1 + i)^2$. The $\$R$ at 2 accumulates interest for $n - 2$ periods, or has a value of $\$R(1 + i)^{n-2}$ at n. Finally, the $\$R$ at 1 accumulates interest for $n - 1$ periods and has a value of $\$R(1 + i)^{n-1}$. Thus, the value of A is

$$A = R + R(1 + i) + R(1 + i)^2 + \cdots + R(1 + i)^{n-2} + R(1 + i)^{n-1}$$

Note that this equation is the sum of a geometric progression with the common ratio $1 + i$. Thus,

$$A = \frac{a(1 - r^n)}{1 - r}$$

$$= \frac{R[1 - (1 + i)^n]}{1 - (1 + i)}$$

$$= R\left[\frac{(1 + i)^n - 1}{i}\right]$$

Table II of the Appendix lists a tabulation of this expression for various values of i and n. For brevity this quantity is usually denoted by the symbol $s_{\overline{n}|i}$, read as "s angle n at i." The preceding formula for the amount of an ordinary annuity is usually written as follows:

Amount of an Ordinary Annuity

$$A = R \cdot s_{\overline{n}|i}$$

where

$A = $ Amount of an ordinary annuity

$R = $ Periodic payment of an annuity

$$s_{\overline{n}|i} = \frac{(1 + i)^n - 1}{i}$$

Let's consider now the present value of an ordinary annuity of $\$R$ per period for n periods at $i\%$ per period, as shown in Figure 4.18.

Figure 4.18

The value at $t = 0$ of the first \$R is $R/(1 + i)$. The second \$R has a value at $t = 0$ of $R/(1 + i)^2$. Finally, the last \$R payment has a value of $R/(1 + i)^n$ at $t = 0$. Thus, the present value is given by

$$P = \frac{R}{1 + i} + \frac{R}{(1 + i)^2} + \cdots + \frac{R}{(1 + i)^n}$$

Using the formula for the sum of a geometric progression gives

$$P = \frac{R}{1 + i} \frac{\left[1 - \left(\dfrac{1}{1 + i}\right)^n\right]}{\left[1 - \dfrac{1}{1 + i}\right]}$$

$$= R\left[\frac{(1 + i)^n - 1}{i(1 + i)^n}\right]$$

$$= Ra_{\overline{n}|i} \qquad \text{where} \qquad a_{\overline{n}|i} = \frac{(1 + i)^n - 1}{i(1 + i)^n}$$

Present Value
of an Annuity

$$P = Ra_{\overline{n}|i}$$

where

$P =$ Present value of an annuity

$R =$ Periodic payment

$$a_{\overline{n}|i} = \frac{(1 + i)^n - 1}{i(1 + i)^n}$$

Many types of problems can be solved by using the formulas for A and P. A few of these are illustrated by the following examples.

EXAMPLE 23 Jane deposits \$300 at the end of each year in a savings account that pays 8% interest compounded annually. How much money does she have just after the fifth deposit?

Solution Remember that $A = Rs_{\overline{n}|i}$ gives the amount just after a payment is made. Hence, it can be used to solve the problem.

$$A = \$300s_{\overline{5}|0.08}$$

$$= \$300(5.866601)$$

$$= \$1,759.98$$

EXAMPLE 24 Compute the present value of an ordinary annuity of \$100 each month for 4 years at 12% interest compounded monthly.

Solution	$P = \$100a_{\overline{n}|i}$
	$= \$100a_{\overline{48}|0.01}$
	$= \$100(37.973958)$
	$= \$3{,}797.40$

EXAMPLE 25 Kamilla purchased a refrigerator for $150 down and $30 a month for 12 months. If the interest charge is 12% compounded monthly, find the cash price.

Solution	$C = \$150 + P$
	$= \$150 + 30a_{\overline{12}|0.01}$
	$= \$150 + \$30(11.255077)$
	$= \$150 + \$337.65231$
	$= \$487.65$

EXAMPLE 26 Maria deposited $50 when her son was 1 year old and continued to deposit $50 each 6 months thereafter until her son was 18 years old, when the last deposit was made. The bank paid 8% interest compounded semiannually. If the money was allowed to accumulate until it was presented to her son on his twenty-first birthday, how much did he receive?

Solution The amount of money after the last deposit is

$$A = \$50s_{\overline{35}|0.04}$$
$$= \$50(73.652221)$$
$$= \$3{,}682.61$$

The amount should earn interest for an additional 3 years.

$$A = \$3{,}682.61(1.04)^6 = \$3{,}682.61(1.265319)$$
$$= \$4{,}659.68$$

The computation would be easier if this problem were solved as follows: Find the amount that would result from deposits until age 21 and then subtract the amount that would result from the deposits at the end of each 6 months from ages 18 to 21.

$$A = \$50s_{\overline{41}|0.04} - \$50s_{\overline{6}|0.04}$$
$$= \$50(99.826530) - \$50(6.632975)$$
$$= \$4{,}991.33 - \$331.65$$
$$= \$4{,}659.68$$

EXAMPLE 27 Find the payment needed each month for a year to pay off a debt of $1,000 at 12% interest compounded monthly.

Solution Recall that

$$P = Ra_{\overline{n}|i}$$

Substituting gives

$$\$1{,}000 = Ra_{\overline{12}|0.01}$$

$$\$1{,}000 = R(11.255077)$$

$$R = \frac{\$1{,}000}{11.255077}$$

$$= \$88.85$$

An interest-bearing debt is defined to be **amortized** if both the principal and the interest are paid by a sequence of equal payments made at equal periods of time. The amortization schedule for the $1,000 debt of the preceding example is given in Table 4.2.

Table 4.2

Months	Outstanding Principal	Interest Due	Payment	Principal Repaid Each Period
1	$1,000.00	$10.00	$88.85	$78.85
2	921.15	9.21	88.85	79.64
3	841.51	8.42	88.85	80.43
4	761.08	7.61	88.85	81.24
5	679.84	6.80	88.85	82.05
6	597.79	5.98	88.85	82.87
7	514.92	5.15	88.85	83.70
8	431.22	4.31	88.85	84.54
9	346.68	3.47	88.85	85.38
10	261.30	2.61	88.85	86.24
11	175.06	1.75	88.85	87.10
12	87.96	0.88	88.84	87.96

EXAMPLE 28 The Greens bought a house for $128,500. They paid $23,500 down and amortized the balance at 12% interest compounded monthly for 8 years. What is their equity after the fortieth payment? (**Equity** is the difference obtained by subtracting the present value of any remaining payments from the purchase price.)

Solution The periodic payment must be found first by using the formula $P = Ra_{\overline{n}|i}$. Since $23,500 cash was paid, the balance to be amortized was $128,500 - \$23,500 = \$105,000$. Hence, $\$105,000 = Ra_{\overline{96}|0.01}$ or

$$R = \frac{\$105{,}000}{61.527701}$$

$$= \$1{,}706.55$$

After the fortieth payment the value of the remaining payments is

$$P = \$1{,}706.55a_{\overline{56}|0.01}$$

$$= \$1{,}706.55(42.719991) = \$72{,}903.80$$

Hence, the Greens' equity is $128,500 - \$72{,}903.80 = \$55{,}596.20$.

Sometimes a debtor may make equal deposits into a fund until the deposits plus interest equal the debt plus interest. Such a fund is called a **sinking fund.** The interest a debtor receives from a sinking fund may or may not be the same as the creditor is charging.

EXAMPLE 29 Mr. I. O. You wishes to create a sinking fund to pay off his loan of $1,000 at 8% interest compounded annually in 3 years. If his sinking fund pays 12% interest compounded semiannually, what is his semiannual deposit into the sinking fund?

Solution The amount, A, to pay off the loan is

$$A = \$1,000(1.08)^3$$

$$= \$1,000(1.259712)$$

$$= \$1,259.71$$

The semiannual deposit, R, is found by

$$A = Rs_{\overline{n}|i}$$

$$\$1,259.71 = Rs_{\overline{6}|0.06}$$

$$R = \frac{\$1,259.71}{6.975318}$$

$$= \$180.60$$

A schedule for this fund is given in Table 4.3.

Table 4.3

Period	Interest	Deposit	Increase in Fund	Amount in Fund
1	0	$180.60	$180.60	$180.60
2	$10.84	180.60	191.44	372.04
3	22.32	180.60	202.92	574.96
4	34.50	180.60	215.10	790.06
5	47.40	180.60	228.00	1,018.06
6	61.08	180.57	241.65	1,259.71

EXAMPLE 30 The ABC Company is considering either buying a computer for $90,000 or leasing it for $3,000 per month. Assume that money is worth 12% compounded monthly and that the life of a computer is 5 years, after which time the salvage value will be $20,000. Should the company buy or lease?

Solution To solve this problem, we find the present value of $20,000, which is to be received at the end of 5 years.

$$A = P(1 + i)^{-n}$$

$$P = \$20,000(1.01)^{-60}$$

$$= \$11,009$$

The difference, $\$90,000 - \$11,009 = \$78,991$, represents the present value of the cost of owning the computer. Next we find the present value of the rent for 5 years. Since the formula for $a_{\overline{n}|i}$ does not include a payment at the beginning of the term, the rental, R_P, would be

$$R_P = \$3,000 + \$3,000 a_{\overline{59}|0.01}$$
$$= \$3,000 + \$3,000(44.404587)$$
$$= \$3,000 + \$133,213.76$$
$$= \$136,213.76$$

This certainly seems to indicate that the company should buy the computer. This does not, however, consider other factors, such as maintenance, which would be included in the rental price. Suppose the ABC Company could purchase a maintenance contract for $1,000 per month. The present value, M, of the maintenance contract would be

$$M = \$1,000 + \$1,000 a_{\overline{59}|0.01}$$
$$= \$1,000 + \$1,000(44.404587)$$
$$= \$1,000 + \$44,404.59$$
$$= \$45,404.59$$

The present value of the maintenance contract, $45,404.59, plus the present value of the computer, $78,991, is $124,395.59, which is still much less than the rental cost of $136,213.76.

Exercise Set 4.4

A **1.** Find the amount of the following ordinary annuities:
   a. $1,000 per year for 20 years at 8% interest compounded annually
   b. $500 per quarter for 6 years at 8% interest compounded quarterly
   c. $600 per half year for 5 years at 8% interest compounded semiannually

2. Find the present values of the ordinary annuities in exercise 1.

3. Find the amount and present value of the following ordinary annuities:
   a. $100 per month for 8 years at 12% interest compounded monthly
   b. $500 per month for 3 years at 12% interest compounded monthly

B **4.** Compute the monthly payment necessary to finance a used car for $3,500 at 12% interest compounded monthly for 3 years.

5. Find the payment necessary each quarter for 2 years to amortize a debt of $2,000 at 12% interest compounded quarterly.

C **6.** Make an amortization schedule for exercise 4.

7. Make an amortization schedule for exercise 5.

8. Pai Ling bought a house for $60,000. She paid $10,000 down and amortized the balance at 12% interest compounded monthly for 8 years.
   a. What is her equity after 30 payments?
   b. What is her equity after 60 payments?

Business **9. Amortization.** Steven bought a house for $32,000. He paid $5,000 down and amortized the balance at 12% interest compounded monthly for 7 years.
   a. What is his equity after his fiftieth payment?
   b. What is his equity after his eightieth payment?

10. **Sinking Fund.** Compute the quarterly deposit Mr. I. O. You must make to a sinking fund that pays 12% interest compounded quarterly to pay off a loan in 4 years of $2,000 at 8% interest compounded annually.

11. **Sinking Fund.** What deposit must be made to a sinking fund that pays 12% interest compounded quarterly to pay off in 4 years a loan of $1,500 at 8% interest compounded annually?

12. **Investments.** Margaret wishes to know the amount she can pay for a mine that is expected to yield an annual return of $300,000 for the next 30 years, after which it becomes worthless. Find the amount she can pay to yield her a 10% return if a sinking fund earns 8% interest compounded annually.

13. **Investments.** A mine is expected to yield a return of $300,000 a year for the next 30 years and have a salvage value of $200,000 at that time. How much can be paid for the mine in order to yield an 8% annual return?

14. **Sinking Fund.** What deposit must be made to a sinking fund that pays 8% compounded quarterly to pay off in 5 years a loan of $3,200 at 12% interest compounded semi-annually?

Equations of Value, Additional Annuities, and Perpetuities

In this section we pay particular attention to where payments are located on a time scale. Then by either accumulating or discounting values to a selected time we can form an equation relating the values. At the same time, we look at annuities that are not ordinary annuities. However, we use ordinary annuity formulas to find the amounts and present values of such annuities. We conclude with a discussion of **perpetuities.**

We begin by summarizing previous material so we will fully understand the new material. To accumulate a single payment R for n periods at an interest rate of i per period, we multiply by $(1 + i)^n$. To find the value of a payment R n periods before it is due at interest rate i, we multiply by $1/(1 + i)^n$. To accumulate an ordinary annuity of n payments to the date of the last payment, we multiply by $s_{\overline{n}|i}$. To find the value of an ordinary annuity of R one period before the first payment is made, we multiply by $a_{\overline{n}|i}$. See Figure 4.19.

Figure 4.19

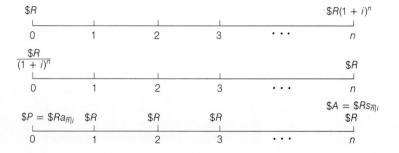

These ideas are now used to find what will be called **equations of values** in the following examples.

EXAMPLE 31 Ari has a $10,000 debt due in 5 years. He wants to pay this debt by making payments of $1,000 each at the end of each year for 6 years. Then, at the end of 6 years, he will make a second payment of $x to retire the debt. If money is worth 8% interest compounded annually, what is the size of the second payment Ari will make at the end of 6 years?

Figure 4.20

	$1,000	$1,000	$1,000	$1,000	$10,000 $1,000	$x $1,000
0	1	2	3	4	5	6 years

Solution We choose the 6-year mark as the time to compare the debt and the payments. At the end of 6 years the debt has a value of $10,000(1 + 0.08)^1$. The annuity has a value of $1,000s_{\overline{6}|0.08}$ and x has a value of x. At the end of 6 years we have the equation

$$10,000(1 + 0.08) = 1,000s_{\overline{6}|0.08} + x$$
$$10,800 = 7,335.93 + x$$
$$x = \$3,464.07$$

Thus, the one additional payment at the end of 6 years that will retire the debt is $3,464.07.

The equation used in Example 31 is called an **equation of value.** In this case it is an equation of value at 6 years.

EXAMPLE 32 Use an equation of value at time 0 to find x for Example 31.

Solution

$$\frac{10,000}{(1 + 0.08)^5} = \$1,000a_{\overline{6}|0.08} + \frac{x}{(1 + 0.08)^6}$$

$$6,805.83 = 4,622.88 + \frac{x}{1.586874}$$

$$x = \$3,464.07$$

As expected, the value of x is the same regardless of the time selected for the equation of value.

As discussed earlier, an annuity whose first payment is made some time after the end of the first period is called a **deferred annuity.**

EXAMPLE 33 A car was bought on January 1 with the agreement that there would be 36 monthly payments of $100, the first of which would be due on April 1. Find the equivalent cash price if interest is 12% compounded monthly.

Figure 4.21

P			$100	$100		$100
Jan. 1	Mar. 1		Apr. 1	May 1		36 monthly payments

Solution   Let's select March 1 as the comparison date for an equation of value.

$$P(1 + 0.01)^2 = 100a_{\overline{36}|0.01}$$

$$1.0201P = 3,010.75$$

$$P = \$2,951.43$$

The equivalent cash price is $2,951.43.

Equations of value are also useful when working with annuities due.

EXAMPLE 34   Amanda pays $400 rent each month, payable in advance. What would be her equivalent yearly rent at 12% interest compounded monthly if she paid it in advance?

Solution   As seen in Figure 4.22, we can use the ideas of equations of value to write this annuity due as an ordinary annuity.

Figure 4.22

At time 0, the equation of value can be written as

$$P = 400 + 400a_{\overline{11}|0.01}$$

$$= \$4,547.05$$

We conclude this chapter with a discussion of perpetuities. An annuity whose payments begin on a certain date and continue indefinitely is called a **perpetuity.** Since the payments continue indefinitely, it would be impossible to compute the amount of a perpetuity; however, the present value can be found. The present value P of a perpetuity that is payable at the end of each interest period at $i\%$ per period is the principal that would in one interest period earn the payment R. Thus,

$$Pi = R \qquad \text{or} \qquad P = \frac{R}{i}$$

EXAMPLE 35   The Go Far Company is expected to pay $3.00 every 6 months on a share of its stock. What is the present value of this stock if money is worth 6% interest compounded semiannually?

Solution $$P = \frac{R}{i} = \frac{\$3.00}{0.03} = \$100$$

Many times, the payment periods and the interest periods for a perpetuity may not be the same. When this happens, the present value may be found by the following theorem.

The present value of a perpetuity that yields the payment R at the end of n interest periods with money worth $i\%$ per interest period is

$$P = \frac{R}{i}\left[\frac{1}{s_{\overline{n}|i}}\right]$$

EXAMPLE 36 Find the present value of the Go Far Company's stock, which is expected to pay $3.00 every 6 months, if money is worth 8% interest compounded quarterly.

Solution Since money is worth 8% interest compounded quarterly, the interest is 2% each quarter. The payment of $3.00 is made after two interest periods; therefore, $n = 2$. Substituting in the theorem gives

$$P = \frac{R}{i}\left[\frac{1}{s_{\overline{n}|i}}\right]$$

$$= \frac{\$3.00}{0.02}\left[\frac{1}{s_{\overline{2}|0.02}}\right]$$

$$= \$150\left[\frac{1}{2.02}\right]$$

$$= \$74.26$$

Exercise Set **4.5**

A 1. Find the present value of a perpetuity of $1,200 per year at 8% interest compounded annually.

2. The annual premium for a 20-year-pay insurance policy is $100 payable at the beginning of each year for 20 years. What is the equivalent cash premium if money is worth 6% interest compounded annually?

3. The Go Far Company is expected to pay $6.00 every 6 months on a share of its stock. What is the present value of this stock if money is worth 8% interest compounded semiannually?

4. A stock pays $22\frac{1}{2}$ cents each quarter. What is the present value of the stock if money is worth 12% interest compounded quarterly?

5. Find the equivalent cash premium if money is worth 8% interest compounded annually for a 20-year-pay insurance policy that has an annual premium of $100 payable at the beginning of each year for 20 years.

B 6. Dora pays $300 rent each month, payable in advance. What would be her equivalent yearly rent at 12% interest compounded monthly if she paid it in advance?

C   **7.** Paul has a debt of $8,000 due in 5 years. He wants to cancel this debt by paying $3,000 1 year from now, $1,000 3 years from now, and a last payment 7 years from now. If money is worth 12% interest compounded semiannually, what will be the amount of the last payment?

8. To cancel three loans of $2,000 due now, $5,000 due in 4 years, and $10,000 due in 6 years, I agree to pay $R at the end of each year for 10 years. If the interest rate is 8% compounded annually, what is my annual payment?

9. Find the present value of an annuity of $1,000 per year with the first payment due 3 years from now and the last occurring 12 years from now if the interest rate is 8% compounded annually.

Business   **10. Installment Purchase.** A car was bought on March 1 with the agreement that there would be 24 monthly payments of $150, the first of which is due on July 1. Find the equivalent cash price if interest is 12% compounded monthly.

11. Installment Purchase. A stereo set sells for $20 down and $30 a month for 12 months. What is the cash price of the set if interest is 24% compounded monthly?

12. Installment Purchase. A TV set that has a cash price of $337.26 is sold for $20 down and $30 a month for 12 months. What is the compound interest rate monthly?

13. Stock Dividend. A stock pays $4.00 every 6 months. What is the present value of the stock if money is worth 8% interest compounded quarterly?

Summary and Review

This chapter contains mathematics commonly referred to as the "mathematics of finance." It consists of simple interest and discount, compound interest and compound amount, present value, annuities, amortization and sinking funds, and perpetuities. Formulas for these are:

Simple interest	$I = Prt$
Bank discount	$D = Adt$
Compound amount	$A = P(1 + i)^n$
Present value	$P = \dfrac{A}{(1 + i)^n}$
Amount of an annuity	$A = Rs_{\overline{n}|i}$
Present value of an annuity	$P = Ra_{\overline{n}|i}$
Present value of a perpetuity	$P = \dfrac{R}{i}\left[\dfrac{1}{s_{\overline{n}|i}}\right]$
Compound amount if a principal is compounded continuously	$A = Pe^{tr}$

The **sum**, S, **of a geometric progression** of n terms is

$$S = \frac{a - ar^n}{1 - r}$$

where the first term is a and each term is obtained from the preceding term by multiplying by the constant $r \neq 1$.

Review Exercise Set 4.6

A   **1.** Find the simple interest due on a loan of $5,000 at 12% interest for 3 months.

2. Find the compound interest and compound amount for an investment of $4,000 at 6% interest compounded semiannually for 10 years.

3. Find the bank discount on $3,000 at 12% interest for 6 months.

4. Compute the compound interest and compound amount for an investment of $4,000 at 8% compounded quarterly for 10 years.

5. Find the effective rate equivalent to 12% interest compounded semiannually.

6. Find the present value of $4,000 due in 5 years at 6% interest compounded semiannually.

7. Compute the present value and the amount of an ordinary annuity of $400 a year for 10 years at 8% interest compounded annually.

B   **8.** Kalid obtained $190 from the bank and signed a 3-month non-interest-bearing note for $200. Compute the simple bank discount rate and the simple interest rate he was charged.

9. Dr. Jones is planning to endow a chair at the university for $15,000 per year. Compute the amount of the endowment if the fund is to be invested at 6% interest compounded semiannually.

10. A contract pays $200 at the end of each quarter for 4 years and $2,000 additional at the end of the last quarter. What is the present value of the contract at 8% interest compounded quarterly?

11. What should be the semiannual deposit to a sinking fund established to pay off a loan of $300 at 6% interest compounded annually in 3 years if the fund pays 6% interest compounded semiannually?

12. You wish to borrow $10,000 today and $5,000 5 years from now. You plan to repay these loans with equal payments at the end of each year for 10 years. If interest is 8% compounded annually, what is your annual payment?

C   **13.** Use geometric progression to find the sum of the annuity

$$\$100 + \$100(1.06) + \$100(1.06)^2 + \cdots + \$100(1.06)^8$$

14. Use a geometric progression to find the present value of the annuity

$$\frac{\$500}{1.08} + \frac{\$500}{(1.08)^2} + \frac{\$500}{(1.08)^3} + \cdots + \frac{\$500}{(1.08)^{12}}$$

15. A $10,000 debt is to be repaid by equal payments at the end of each six months for 3 years. If money is worth 8% interest compounded semiannually, make an amortization table for this debt.

16. A deposit of $500 is made to a bank at the end of each 6 months for $2\frac{1}{2}$ years. If money is worth 8% interest compounded semiannually, make a table showing how much money accumulates in the sinking fund.

17. Find the compound amount the native Americans would have if they had invested $24 for 300 years at 8% interest compounded annually. Use a calculator to work this problem.

18. **Service Charge.** A department store charges 2% interest per month service charge on unpaid balances. Assume that no payments are made for a year and compute the approximate effective rate of interest.

19. **Equity.** A house trailer was bought for $27,500, with $2,500 paid down and the balance amortized at 12% interest compounded monthly for 8 years. What is the equity after the fiftieth payment?

20. **Investments.** An orchard will produce its first crop at the end of 6 years. If after 6 years it is expected to produce an annual income of $6,000 for 15 years, what is the cash value of the orchard? Assume that money is worth 6% interest compounded annually.

21. **Loans.** Mark borrows $6,000 today with interest at 6% compounded annually. He agrees to pay $1,000 in 1 year, $2,000 in 2 years, and the balance 4 years from today. Compute the final payment.

CHAPTER

Counting Techniques and Probability

rchaeological artifacts indicate that many of the early peoples played some version of dice either for recreation or to determine the will of the tribal deity. As more elaborate games were developed, the players began to observe certain patterns in the results, but they did not have the language of **probability** with which to describe and analyze them.

Over time, outstanding mathematicians established probability as a legitimate field of inquiry, but the main application seemed to be games of chance for gamblers.

As more time passed, it became clear that probability was much more than just a technique for gamblers. Physicists now use probability theory when studying various gas and heat laws as well as in the theory of atomic physics. Biologists apply the techniques of probability in genetics, the theory of natural selection, and learning theory. Managers in government and industry use probabilistic techniques in decision-making processes. Furthermore, probability is the theoretical basis of statistics, a discipline that permeates modern thinking. With a knowledge of probability you can solve many problems, as you shall see in this chapter.

 The Language of Probability

One of the significant characteristics of our increasingly complex society is that we must deal with questions for which there is no known answer but instead one or more probable (or improbable) answers. Statements like,

"I am 90% confident that the mean weight is between 76.2 and 78.6 grams"; "This cancer treatment has a .6 chance of leading to complete remission"; and "The candidate has a 20.4% chance of carrying the state of Ohio" are common in conversations. A necessary skill for our times is the ability to measure the degree of uncertainty in an undetermined situation. In this section we discuss **probability**—the language of uncertainty. As the language of the undetermined and the uncertain, probability is an important tool in many phases of our modern uncertain life.

In the study of **probability,** a number between 0 and 1 is assigned to an uncertain outcome. The number indicates how likely or unlikely the outcome may be.

One or Zero Probability

1. If an outcome is impossible, it has a probability of 0.
2. If an outcome will surely happen, it has a probability of 1.

Since probability is a language of uncertainty, any discussion of probability presupposes a process of *observation* or *measurement* in which the outcomes are not certain. Such a process is called an **experiment.** Any possible result of an experiment is called an **outcome.**

EXAMPLE 1   Experiment: A coin is tossed.
Possible outcomes: Head (*H*) or tail (*T*).

EXAMPLE 2   Experiment: A die (one member of a pair of dice) is tossed.
Possible outcomes: The top side of the die shows 1, 2, 3, 4, 5, or 6.

EXAMPLE 3   Suppose we have a spinner that is as likely to stop at one place as another. First consider a spinner divided into four equal sections colored red, black, white, and green (Figure 5.1).

Figure 5.1

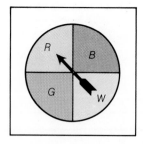

Let an experiment consist of spinning and then observing the color of the region where the needle stops. (If the needle stops on a line separating two regions, we agree to record the color of the region the needle would move into if rotated clockwise.) The set of possible outcomes of this experiment is not numbers but colors: {red, black, white, green}.

EXAMPLE 4 In another possible experiment with a die, we might observe whether the number appearing on the upper face is even or odd. Thus, this experiment would have only two possible outcomes: {even, odd}.

In Examples 2 and 4 the same action was performed; however, the outcomes tabulated were different. In fact, associated with the experiment of tossing a die are several sets that classify the outcomes, as shown in Table 5.1.

Table 5.1

Question	Set of Possible Classifications of Outcomes
Is the number on the die even or odd?	{even, odd}
What is the number on the die?	{1, 2, 3, 4, 5, 6}
Is the number on the die greater than 3?	{less than or equal to 3, greater than 3}

Although the sets of outcomes listed in Table 5.1 are different, you may have noticed that they share certain properties. First, in each example, the set of outcomes **exhausts the possibilities** of what can happen if the experiment is performed. The number of dots on the die is either even or odd; one of the numbers 1, 2, 3, 4, 5, or 6 must appear on the upper face of the die; and the number of dots is either less than or equal to 3 or it is greater than 3. Second, the members of the set of outcomes for an experiment are **distinct**; that is, they do not overlap. In the tossing of a die, the set {even numbers, odd numbers, and numbers divisible by 3} is not a set of possible outcomes because both even numbers and odd numbers overlap with numbers divisible by 3. This discussion suggests the following definition:

Sample Space

> A *sample space* (denoted by S) is a list of the outcomes of an experiment constructed in such a way that:
>
> **1.** The categories do not overlap.
> **2.** No result is classified more than once.
> **3.** The list is complete (exhausts all the possibilities).

EXAMPLE 5 A coin is flipped two times in succession.

Sample space A: One complete listing of the outcomes is $S = \{(H, H), (H, T), (T, H), (T, T)\}$. The letter listed first in each pair indicates the result of the first flip, and the letter listed second gives the result of the second flip.

Sample space B: An alternate way to list the outcomes is to ignore the order in which the heads and tails occur and to record only how many of each appear.

$$S = \{(2H), (1H \text{ and } 1T), (2T)\}$$

EXAMPLE 6   A sack contains five chocolate candies, three butterscotch candies, and one peppermint candy. One piece of candy is drawn from the sack and eaten. Then a second piece of candy is drawn and eaten. What is a sample space for this experiment?

Solution   Notice that the peppermint cannot be chosen on the second draw if the only peppermint was eaten on the first draw.

Sample space $= \{(C, C), (C, B), (C, P), (B, C), (B, B), (B, P), (P, C), (P, B)\}$

Once we have tabulated the sample space of an experiment, we must turn to the task of determining the probabilities of the various outcomes. The techniques of assigning probabilities to outcomes are heavily dependent on the following interpretation of probability.

Relative Frequency Interpretation of Probability	Suppose an experiment is performed N times where N is a very large number. The probability of an outcome A should be approximately equal to the following ratio: $$P(A) = \frac{\text{Number of times } A \text{ occurs}}{N}$$

In other words, the probability of an outcome should represent the **long-range relative frequency** of the outcome.

EXAMPLE 7   A fair die is rolled 10,000 times. Table 5.2 itemizes the number of times a 3 has occurred at various stages of the process. Notice that as N becomes larger, the relative frequency stabilizes in the neighborhood of $.166 \approx \frac{1}{6}$.

Table 5.2

Number of Rolls (N)	Number of 3s Occurring (m)	Relative Frequency (m/N)
10	4	.4
100	20	.2
1000	175	.175
3000	499	.1663
5000	840	.168
7000	1150	.1643
10,000	1657	.1657

The probability describes the fraction of times we could expect the outcome E to occur if the experiment were performed a large number of times.

Suppose a thumbtack lands with "point up" 1000 times out of 10,000 trials. The relative frequency is $1000/10{,}000 = \frac{1}{10}$. If we continue the experiment 10,000 more times and find the ratio is still approximately $\frac{1}{10}$, we would be willing to assign this number as a measure of our degree of belief that the tack would land point up on the next toss. The ratio $\frac{1}{10}$ is the assigned probability that a thumbtack will fall "point up" if dropped.

EXAMPLE 8 A *loaded* die (one in which outcomes are not equally likely) is thrown 7000 times with the results shown in Table 5.3. Determine a rule for assigning a probability to each outcome.

Table 5.3

Outcome	Frequency	Relative Frequency
1	967	$\dfrac{967}{7000} \approx .14$
2	843	$\dfrac{843}{7000} \approx .12$
3	931	$\dfrac{931}{7000} \approx .13$
4	1504	$\dfrac{1504}{7000} \approx .21$
5	1576	$\dfrac{1576}{7000} \approx .23$
6	1179	$\dfrac{1179}{7000} \approx .17$

Solution Use $S = \{1, 2, 3, 4, 5, 6\}$ as a sample space to assign the following probabilities:

$$P(1) = .14 \qquad P(2) = .12 \qquad P(3) = .13$$
$$P(4) = .21 \qquad P(5) = .23 \qquad P(6) = .17$$

EXAMPLE 9 On the basis of observations made over a period of years, we have noted that 99.6% of all young men of age 18 live to be 19, so we conclude that the probability of an 18-year-old young man living to be 19 is about .996. This conclusion is obtained on the basis of the relative frequency, or empirical, approach to probability.

EXAMPLE 10 Seven out of 200 customers did not pay their bills. Assign a number for the probability that a customer is in debt.

Solution The relative frequency $\frac{7}{200} = .035$ is the probability that a customer is in debt.

EXAMPLE 11   Of the last 12,000 carriage bolts produced by the Nuts and Bolts Corporation, 66 were defective (D), and the remaining bolts were good (G). Determine a probability rule for assigning a probability of a good and of a defective bolt when choosing a bolt at random from the production line.

Solution   An appropriate sample space is given by $S = \{D, G\}$. From the experimental frequencies, it seems that a good assignment of probabilities is

$$P(D) = \frac{66}{12,000} \quad \text{and} \quad P(G) = \frac{11,934}{12,000}$$

EXAMPLE 12   A poll was taken of a sample of 500 employees of a company to determine whether they wanted to go on strike. Table 5.4 indicates the results of this poll; the employees are divided into three groups according to salary.

Table 5.4

	In Favor of a Strike	Not in Favor of a Strike	No Opinion
Group A	150	50	10
Group B	100	80	8
Group C	30	70	2

a. What is the probability that an employee, selected at random from group A, is in favor of a strike? (To say that the employee is **selected at random** means that each employee has the same chance of being selected.)

b. What is the probability that an employee, selected at random from group B, has no opinion?

c. What is the probability that an employee selected at random is in group C?

d. What is the probability that an employee selected at random is in group B and in favor of a strike?

e. What is the probability that an employee selected at random has no opinion?

f. What is the probability that an employee selected at random favors a strike?

Solution   The answers are as follows:

a. P (employee selected at random from group A is in favor of a strike) $= \frac{150}{210}$

b. P (employee selected at random from group B has no opinion) $= \frac{8}{188}$

c. P (employee is in group C) $= \frac{102}{500}$

d. P (employee is in group B and in favor of a strike) $= \frac{100}{500}$

e. P (employee has no opinion) $= \frac{20}{500}$

f. P (employee is in favor of a strike) $= \frac{280}{500}$

An inspection of the relative frequencies or the probabilities assigned to getting a 1, a 2, a 3, a 4, a 5, or a 6 as shown in Table 5.3 suggests the following characteristics of a probability rule:

> A **probability rule on a sample space** must satisfy two properties:
>
> **1.** If A is an outcome, then the probability of A, $P(A)$, is between 0 and 1 $[0 \leq P(A) \leq 1]$.
> **2.** The sum of the probabilities of all outcomes in the sample space equals 1.

EXAMPLE 13   In the repeated tossing of a fair coin, it is noted that $P(T) = \frac{1}{2}$ and $P(H) = \frac{1}{2}$. Notice that these probabilities satisfy the properties:

    1. $0 \leq P(T) \leq 1$ and $0 \leq P(H) \leq 1$
    2. $P(H) + P(T) = \frac{1}{2} + \frac{1}{2} = 1$

There is one whole class of sample spaces whose probability assignments are particularly easy to determine.

Uniform Sample Space

> If each outcome of the sample space is equally likely to occur, the sample space is called a *uniform sample space.*

Suppose a uniform sample space consists of n outcomes. Since each of the outcomes is equally likely, it seems reasonable to assign to each outcome the same probability, denoted by $P(A)$.

Since the sum of the probabilities of the n individual outcomes must be 1, we note that

$$n \cdot P(A) = 1 \quad \text{or} \quad P(A) = \frac{1}{n}$$

Thus, each of the n outcomes has a probability of $1/n$.

Equal Probabilities

> In a **uniform sample space** with n outcomes, each outcome has a probability of $1/n$.

EXAMPLE 14   Eight identical balls numbered 1 to 8 are placed in an urn. Find a sample space and a probability rule describing the experiment of randomly drawing one of them from the urn.

Solution   A suitable sample space is $\{1, 2, 3, 4, 5, 6, 7, 8\}$, with each number representing one of the eight balls. Since each ball is equally likely to be drawn, we assign a probability of $\frac{1}{8}$ to each outcome. Then

$$P(1) = \tfrac{1}{8}, \qquad P(2) = \tfrac{1}{8}, \qquad \cdots, \qquad P(8) = \tfrac{1}{8}$$

Notice in Figure 5.2(a) that the sample space consisting of $\{A, B, C, D\}$ is a uniform sample space. In Figure 5.2(b) the sample space is not a uniform sample space since $P(A) = P(B) = P(C) = \frac{1}{6}$ and $P(D) = \frac{1}{2}$.

Figure 5.2

(a) 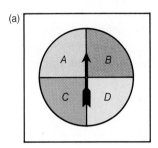   (b)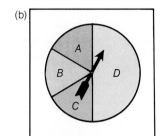

In Section 5.2 we introduce what is called a *compound event*; and in Section 5.3 we describe a *multiplication principle for counting*. As we list the elements of the sample space generated by activating the spinner in Figure 5.2(a) and then in (b), we are illustrating both of these concepts. The sample space of spinning both spinners is

$$\{AA, AB, AC, AD, BA, BB, BC, BD, CA, CB, CC, CD, DA, DB, DC, DD\}$$

where the first letter represents a possible outcome of the spinner in (a), and the second letter represents a possible outcome of (b).

Exercise Set **5.1**

A   **1.** Give the sample space for each of the four spinners.

(a) 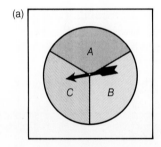   (b)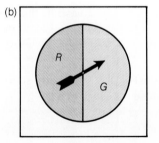

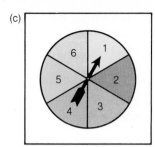

(c)

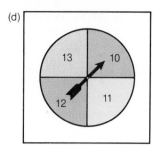

(d)

2. Assign a probability to each outcome in the sample spaces of exercise 1.

3. A fair die is to be rolled. Find a sample space for this experiment and assign a probability to each outcome.

4. Chen, Toshio, Ben, Fred, and Louis place their names in a hat. One name is to be drawn to determine who will confess to breaking a window. Tabulate a sample space and a probability rule.

5. Give a sample space and assign a probability to each outcome of the two spinners.

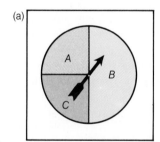

(a)

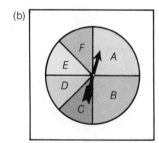

(b)

6. What is the probability of getting heads when a two-headed coin is tossed?

7. In exercise 6, what is the probability of getting tails?

8. Which of the following could not be a probability? Why?

   a. $\frac{-1}{2}$ **b.** $\frac{17}{16}$ **c.** .001   **d.** 0

   e. 1.03   **f.** −.01   **g.** $\frac{5}{4}$ **h.** 1

B   **9.** List the outcomes in the sample space for the simultaneous toss of a coin and a die. (*Hint:* There are 12 outcomes in the space.)

10. An experiment consists of spinning two of the spinners in exercise 1. Tabulate the outcomes in the sample space for each of the following pairs of spinners.

   a. (a) and (b)   **b.** (c) and (a)   **c.** (a) and (d)

   d. (b) and (c)   **e.** (d) and (b)   **f.** (c) and (d)

11. Three coins are tossed, and the number of heads is recorded. Which of the following sets are sample spaces for this experiment? If a set fails to qualify as a sample space, give the reason.

   a. $\{1, 2, 3\}$ **b.** $\{0, 1, 2\}$

   c. $\{0, 1, 2, 3, 4\}$ **d.** $\{0, 2, \text{an odd number}\}$

   e. $\{x \mid x \text{ is a whole number less than 2 and greater than 1}\}$

   f. $\{0, 1, 2, 3\}$

   g. $\{x \mid x \text{ is a whole number and } x < 4\}$

12. An experiment consists of tossing an ordinary coin three times. Tabulate a sample space of possible combinations of heads, H, and tails, T.

13. A box contains three red balls and four black balls. Let R represent a red ball and B a black ball. Tabulate a sample space if
a. one ball is drawn at a time.   **b.** two balls are drawn at a time.
c. three balls are drawn at a time.   **d.** Are these sample spaces uniform?

14. A jar contains four balls numbered 1–4. Record a sample space for the following experiments.
a. A ball is drawn, and the number is recorded. The ball is returned, and a second ball is drawn and recorded.
b. A ball is drawn and recorded. Without replacing the first ball, a second is drawn and recorded.

C   **15.** A bag contains four red marbles, three blue marbles, and three green marbles. A single marble is drawn.
a. Tabulate a sample space with 3 outcomes.
b. Tabulate a sample space with 10 outcomes.

16. Give the sample space for throwing a pair of dice and noting the sum of the numbers that land "up."

Business   **17. Executive Boards.** An executive board of a corporation is made up of five members whom we shall call A, B, C, D, and E. A committee of three is chosen to select a president for the corporation. Find outcomes of the sample space that represent all the possible committees.

18. Commissions. A poll is taken among 100 salespeople of the ABC Corporation concerning how each wishes to be paid. The results of the poll are tabulated by categories—those in the top 25% in sales last year, the next 25%, and the lowest 50%.

	Number of Salespeople		
Method of Payment	Top 25% in Sales	Second 25% in Sales	Lowest 50% in Sales
Flat salary	1	8	23
All commission	20	15	5
$\frac{1}{2}$ salary—$\frac{1}{2}$ commission	4	2	22

If one of the 100 salespeople is chosen at random, what is the probability that this person
a. favors receiving all the salary by commission?
b. wants a flat salary?
c. favors half flat salary and half commission?
d. is in the top 25% of sales?
e. is in the second 25% of sales?
f. is in the lowest 50% of sales and favors being paid by commission?
g. is in the top 25% of sales and favors being paid by a flat salary?

Economics   **19. Unemployment.** A sample of the employment status of the residents in a certain town is given in the following table.

	Employed	Unemployed
Male	1000	40
Female	800	160

Assign a probability that each of the following is true.
a. An unemployed person is female.
b. An unemployed person is male.
c. A male is unemployed.
d. A female is employed.

Life Sciences **20. Causes of Death.** A medical survey of the cause of death among a group of 110 males was categorized according to the cause of death and the age of the subject at the time of death.

Cause of Death	Age at Time of Death Below 40	40–60	Over 60
Heart disease	4	9	14
Cancer	2	4	8
Stroke	1	2	5
Flu or pneumonia	0	1	2
Diabetes	1	0	1
Tuberculosis	0	1	0
Other	17	14	24

If one of these subjects is chosen at random, what is the probability that he
a. died of cancer?
b. died of heart disease while in the 40–60 age group?
c. was over 60 years old when he died?
d. died of diabetes?
e. died of a stroke or of heart disease?
f. died at an age below 40 or died of cancer?

21. Medicine. Dr. Wong believes he has found a cure for a certain blood disease. Out of 80,000 patients, 74,000 recovered after using his medication. Assign a probability that a person suffering from the blood disease will recover using Dr. Wong's medicine.

Social Sciences **22. On-the-Job Accidents.** A sociology class made a study of the relationship between a worker's age and the number of on-the-job accidents. The following table summarizes the findings.

Age Group	Number of Accidents 0	1	2	3 or More
Under 20	18	22	8	12
20–39	26	18	8	10
40–59	34	14	8	6
60 and over	42	10	12	2

a. What is the probability that an employee who had one accident is in the 20–39 age group?
b. What is the probability that an employee under 20 years of age will have two accidents?
c. What is the probability that an employee 60 years old or older will have more than one accident?
d. What is the probability that an employee under 20 years of age will have no accidents?

e. What is the probability that an employee 40 years of age or older will have more than two accidents?

f. What is the probability of an employee having an accident?

2 The Probability of Events

We were introduced to the assigning of probabilities in Section 5.1. A poor means of assigning probabilities to outcomes in a sample space is subjective judgment; yet subjective judgment is often the only tool accessible when very limited data are available. Thus, a sales manager might project that "We have a probability of $\frac{2}{3}$ of getting the XYZ contract" and the ubiquitous man on the street might prophesy that "The probability of Mickey Mouse being elected mayor is $\frac{60}{100}$." Generally, such assignments are merely measures of the strength of the person's belief. However, if the person making the projection has much experience in the area and a keen sense of intuition, the probability model might still be of use. This fact is demonstrated daily in the decision-making centers of government, education, and industry.

In this section, we study rules for assigning probabilities to events. The rules are correct, but decisions made using them can be disastrous if the experiment in question does not meet the assumptions under which the rule was devised. For example, if we assume a coin is fair and assign $P(H) = \frac{1}{2}$ and $P(T) = \frac{1}{2}$, and the coin has been modified to be unbalanced, the probability rule is not useful. And if we base a decision about production in the Nuts and Bolts Factory on the evidence from last month's output, and this month a new machine is installed, the decision might be very inappropriate. Certainly any probability rule built on subjective judgment is suspect. One of the greatest sources of error in the practical application of probability (and its sister science, statistics) is the use of an inappropriate probability rule to make decisions.

In general, we are interested not in the probability of a single outcome in a sample space but in the probability of an *event*. For instance, in drawing a card from a set numbered 1 through 6, we may be interested in the outcomes that are even numbers: 2, 4, 6. We note that these numbers are elements of a subset of the sample space $\{1, 2, 3, 4, 5, 6\}$. This observation leads to the definition of an event.

Event

An *event* is a subset of a sample space.

The occurrence of any collection of outcomes of an experiment can be considered as an event.

EXAMPLE 15   Consider an experiment that consists of tossing an ordinary die and observing the number of dots that appear on the upper face.

Some Possible Events	Corresponding Subsets
a. Observing a 1	$\{1\}$
b. Observing a 3	$\{3\}$
c. Observing a 6	$\{6\}$
d. Observing an even number	$\{2, 4, 6\}$
e. Observing an odd number	$\{1, 3, 5\}$
f. Observing a number divisible by 3	$\{3, 6\}$
g. Observing a number less than 4	$\{1, 2, 3\}$
h. Observing a number greater than 2	$\{3, 4, 5, 6\}$
i. Observing a number greater than 17	$\varnothing$

Of course, these are not all the events that could be listed relative to the experiment. But the events listed have certain apparent characteristics. Events **a**, **b**, and **c** differ from the remaining events listed in that each contains only one point of the whole sample space, whereas events **d** through **h** all involve more than one point, and **i** is empty.

When an event comprises only one outcome of the sample space, it is called a **simple event**; a **compound event** involves more than one sample outcome. There are only six simple events associated with the preceding experiment of tossing a die. Can you name them? In like manner, there are many compound events associated with this experiment. Can you name some of those not already listed?

EXAMPLE 16   Tabulate the sample space and the event of getting at least one head when two coins are tossed.

Solution   The sample space is tabulated as

$$\{HH, HT, TH, TT\}$$

The event of getting at least one head is $\{HH, HT, TH\}$.

EXAMPLE 17   A nickel, a dime, and a penny are tossed. List the sample space of possible outcomes and the event of getting at least two heads.

Solution   The outcomes of this experiment are tabulated in Figure 5.3. The event of getting at least two heads is contained in the shaded area.

Figure 5.3

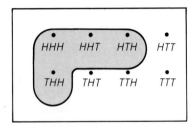

Now let's summarize, for event A, the properties of probability we discussed in Section 5.1.

1. If *A* is the empty set, then $P(A) = 0$.
2. If *A* is the universe (consists of all outcomes), then $P(A) = 1$.
3. If *A* is an event with one outcome from a uniform sample space with $n(S)$ outcomes, then $P(A) = \dfrac{1}{n(S)}$.
4. If *A* is an event that consists of two outcomes from a uniform sample space, then

$$P(A) = \frac{1}{n(S)} + \frac{1}{n(S)} = \frac{2}{n(S)}$$

EXAMPLE 18 What is the probability of getting a 1 or a 3 in the roll of a die?

Solution The sample space for rolling a fair die is

$$S = \{1, 2, 3, 4, 5, 6\}$$

and is a uniform sample space. Therefore, the probability of getting a 1 or a 3 is the sum of separate (but equal) probabilities, or

$$P(1 \text{ or } 3) = P(1) + P(3)$$
$$= \tfrac{1}{6} + \tfrac{1}{6} = \tfrac{2}{6}$$

Notice that if *A* is the event of getting a 1 or a 3, then in the preceding example,

$$P(A) = \frac{2}{6} = \frac{\text{number of elements in } A}{\text{number of elements in } S}$$

This example leads to the following discussion.

In a uniform sample space consisting of $n(S)$ outcomes, it is easy to determine the probability of an event since the probability of each simple event in the sample space is the same. More precisely, if the event *A* consists of $n(A)$ outcomes, then the probability of *A* (called **a priori probability**) is

$$P(A) = \frac{n(A)}{n(S)}$$

Let *S* be a uniform sample space (each outcome in *S* is equally likely). Suppose further that event *A* is a subset of *S*. Then $P(A)$, the probability of event *A*, is given by

$$P(A) = \frac{\text{number of equally likely outcomes in event } A}{\text{number of possible equally likely outcomes}} = \frac{n(A)}{n(S)}$$

This rule is the classical definition of probability. Suppose that there are N possible equally likely outcomes of an experiment. If r of these outcomes have a particular characteristic, so that they can be classified as a success, then the probability of a success is defined to be r/N.

EXAMPLE 19   Consider the experiment of tossing a die. Let the occurrence of a multiple of 3 be denoted as event E. There are six equally likely possible outcomes of the experiment of tossing a die, and two of these, namely, a 3 and a 6, give event E. Thus,

$$P(E) = \frac{n(E)}{n(S)} = \frac{2}{6} = \frac{1}{3}$$

EXAMPLE 20   A card is dealt from a shuffled deck (52 cards with four suits: clubs, diamonds, hearts, and spades). What is the probability that the card is an ace?

Solution   There are 52 cards in the deck; so $n(S) = 52$. Only 4 cards are aces; therefore, $n(A) = 4$. So

$$P(\text{ace}) = P(A) = \frac{n(A)}{n(S)} = \frac{4}{52} = \frac{1}{13}$$

EXAMPLE 21   Consider the experiment of tossing two coins. What is the probability of tossing two heads? At this juncture, we must be careful. We have discussed two sample spaces for this experiment: $\{HH, HT, TT\}$, in which we do not observe which coin has a head and which coin has a tail, and $\{HH, HT, TH, TT\}$, in which we classify each toss with an ordered pair that takes into consideration which coin has a head and which has a tail. Note that we cannot apply the previous definition in the first case because it is not a uniform sample space; however, the definition is applicable to the second sample space. Now let A be the event of tossing two heads. By using the second sample space,

$$P(A) = \frac{n(A)}{n(S)} = \frac{1}{4}$$

EXAMPLE 22   Consider the two spinners in Figure 5.4. If both spinners are activated, find the probability of spinning a total of five points.

Figure 5.4

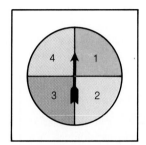 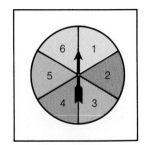

Solution   Spinning both spinners results in 24 equally likely outcomes. Four of them,

$$\{(1, 4), (2, 3), (3, 2), (4, 1)\}$$

give a total of five points. Thus,

$$P(5 \text{ points}) = \frac{4}{24} = \frac{1}{6}$$

Exercise Set **5.2**

A   **1.** A card is drawn from an ordinary deck of cards.
   a. What is the probability of drawing a heart?
   b. What is the probability of drawing an ace?
   c. What is the probability of drawing the jack of spades?
   d. What is the probability of drawing a red card?

2. Suppose there is an equally likely probability that the spinner below will stop at any one of the six numbered sections.

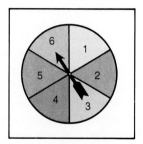

   a. What is the probability that the spinner will stop at an odd-numbered section?
   b. What is the probability that it will stop at an even-numbered section?
   c. What is the probability that it will stop at a section whose number is divisible by 3?
   d. What is the probability that it will stop at a section numbered less than 6?
   e. What is the probability that it will stop at a section numbered 6 or less?
   f. What is the probability that it will stop at a section whose number is a multiple of 7?

3. A die is thrown.
   a. What is the probability of getting an odd number?
   b. What is the probability of getting a number less than 4?
   c. What is the probability of getting a number greater than 6?
   d. What is the probability of getting a number less than or equal to 6?

4. A multiple-choice question has five possible answers. You haven't studied and hence have no idea which answer is correct, so you randomly choose one of the five answers. What is the probability that you have selected the correct answer? An incorrect answer?

5. A survey course in history contains 20 first-year students, 8 second-year students, 6 third-year students, and 1 fourth-year student. A student is chosen at random from the class roll.

a. Describe in words a uniform sample space for this experiment.
b. What is the probability that the student is a first-year student?
c. What is the probability that the student is a fourth-year student?
d. What is the probability that the student is a third- or fourth-year student?
e. What is the probability that the student is a first-year student or a second-year student or a third-year student or a fourth-year student?

6. A professor has decided to award the following grades in her class:

5   As
8   Bs
16   Cs
7   Ds
4   Fs

The 40 grades are placed on cards and put in a box. You randomly select a card. What is the probability that you select

a. a C?   **b.** an F?   **c.** a B or a C?
d. a grade higher than C?   **e.** a grade lower than C?

7. You have forgotten the last digit of a telephone number. You randomly try a digit. What is the probability that you have selected the correct number?

B   **8.** Two spinners with three and six equally likely sections are spun simultaneously. What is the probability that the sum of the numbers is
a. greater than 7?
b. equal to 8?
c. equal to 3?
d. less than 5?

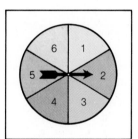 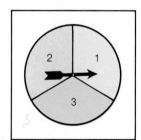

9. Two coins are tossed. What is the probability of getting
a. two heads?   **b.** exactly one head?
c. at least one head?   **d.** at most one head?

10. A box contains four black balls, seven white balls, and three red balls. If a ball is drawn, what is the probability of getting the following colors?
a. black   **b.** red   **c.** white
d. red or white   **e.** black or white   **f.** red or white or black

11. Discuss the following statements.
a. Since there are 50 states, the probability that a person selected at random in the United States was born in Rhode Island is $\frac{1}{50}$.
b. A's chances of winning an election are $\frac{6}{10}$, B's chances are $\frac{3}{10}$, and C's chances are $\frac{1}{10}$. If C withdraws from the race, A believes her chances of winning will decrease.
c. Twenty tosses of a coin yield 18 heads and 2 tails.
d. A candidate is running for two offices, A and B. He assigns a probability of .4 of being elected to A, a probability of .3 of being elected to B, and a probability of .6 of being elected to both A and B.

12. If you flipped a fair coin 15 times and got 15 heads, what would be the probability of getting a head on the sixteenth toss?

13. In drawing a card from a standard deck of cards, you reason that you can get a spade (S) or cannot get a spade. Therefore, there are two outcomes. Hence, $P(S) = \frac{1}{2}$. Is this reasoning correct? Explain.

C **14.** An experiment consists of tossing a die. List the outcomes in the following events:
  a. observing an odd number.
  b. observing a number greater than 4.
  c. observing events **a** and **b**.
  d. observing either **a** or **b** or both.

15. Two dice are tossed. (Note that the two dice can fall in 36 different ways.) What is the probability that the sum of the numbers is
  a. greater than 10?   **b.** 9?   **c.** 7?
  d. greater than 1?   **e.** greater than 12?

16. A pair of fair tetrahedral (four-faced) dice with the numbers 1 through 4 on the faces is rolled. Let

   A represent the sum is 4

   and

   B represent the sum exceeds 4

  a. Tabulate a uniform sample space for this experiment.
  b. Compute $P(A)$.
  c. Compute $P(B)$.

17. A sample space is $\{HH, HT, TH, TT\}$. List all possible events and describe each in words.

Business **18.** **Sales.** Consider the following sales record indicating the number of days on which a certain number of sales were made.

Units Sold	Days
0	20
1	80
2	120
3	250
4	260
5	190
6	80

  a. Assign a probability to the event of selling three units per day.
  b. Assign a probability of selling four or five units per day.
  c. Assign a probability of selling no units per day.
  d. Assign a probability of selling fewer than three units per day.

Economics **19.** **Quality Control.** A shipment is believed to contain 100 good articles, 5 articles with minor defects, and 3 articles with major defects. If 1 article is drawn from the shipment, what is the probability that it will
  a. not have a defect?   **b.** have a defect?   **c.** have a major defect?

Life Sciences **20.** **Drug Analysis.** A medical research institute is experimenting with possible cures for cancer. Dr. Stewart, the scientist in charge of the experiment, initially selects three of five possible drugs, V, W, X, Y, and Z, for concentrated research.
  a. List the sample outcomes where Z is one of the chosen drugs.

b. List the sample outcomes where X and Y are both among the chosen drugs.

c. Another scientist suddenly announces that drug V is definitely not a cure for cancer. If drug V is dropped, list the sample space from which Dr. Stewart can choose three of four possible drugs.

d. Dr. Stewart decides that a new drug, drug A, will definitely be one of the three drugs used for experimentation. She now needs to choose two of the four possible drugs. List the sample outcomes where W is one of these chosen drugs.

Social Sciences   **21. Polls.** In an opinion poll to determine whether people favored a proposition aimed at increasing state income taxes, the following information was obtained.

Group by Income	For	Against
Low income	80,000	60,000
Middle income	60,000	80,000
High income	10,000	50,000

a. What is the probability that a respondent favors the proposition?

b. What is the probability that a respondent favors the proposition and belongs to the low-income group?

c. What is the probability that a respondent favors the proposition and belongs to the high-income group?

d. What is the probability that a middle-income respondent is against the proposition?

3   Tree Diagrams and the Fundamental Principle of Counting

> If we can count the number of outcomes in a uniform sample space and in an event, we can always assign a probability to an event. However, many times counting outcomes becomes tedious.
>
> In this section, we introduce two tools that may be of help—**tree diagrams** and the **Fundamental Principle of Counting.**

The college chorale is planning a concert tour with performances in three cities—Dallas, St. Louis, and New Orleans. In how many ways can they arrange their itinerary?

If there is no restriction on the order of the performances, any one of the three cities can be chosen as the first stop. After the first city is selected, either of the other cities can be second, and the remaining city is then the last stop. A **tree diagram** can aid the chorale in determining their possible tour schedule. Starting at the campus, we draw lines to each of the three cities. We then draw lines from these cities to each of the remaining choices. The result is a diagram resembling the branches of a tree (Figure 5.5). A quick glance at the tree diagram in Figure 5.5 reveals that there are six ways the chorale can arrange its tour.

The following procedure is used in constructing a tree diagram. Draw at the position called **start** a number of **branches** corresponding to the number of ways

Figure 5.5

the *first step* can be performed. At the end of each branch in this first step, draw branches corresponding to the ways the second step can be performed. Any sequence of branches that moves from *start* to the *end of the last branch* is called a **path.** Count the number of paths to obtain the number of ways the experiment can be performed.

Whenever a task can be done in two or more stages and each stage can be done in a number of ways, tree diagrams provide good illustrations of the choices involved and serve as an aid in determining the number of ways the whole task can be accomplished.

EXAMPLE 23 In how many ways can a two-toned car be painted with red, white, and black paint?

Solution As shown in Figure 5.6 there are six paths; so with three paints, six two-toned color combinations are possible.

Figure 5.6

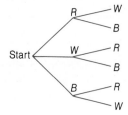

EXAMPLE 24 A coin is tossed twice. Draw a tree diagram to illustrate the possible outcomes.

Solution The four branches of the diagram in Figure 5.7 correspond to the outcomes *HH*, *HT*, *TH*, and *TT*.

Figure 5.7

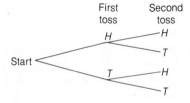

EXAMPLE 25 Albert and Chu play in a Ping-Pong tournament. The first player to win three games wins the tournament. Make a tree diagram showing all the possible ways in which the tournament can turn out.

Solution   In Figure 5.8 the letter A represents a win by Albert, and the letter C represents a win by Chu.

Figure 5.8

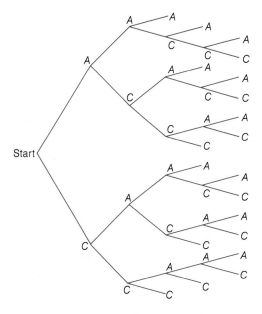

Now let's return to the first example of this section.

E X A M P L E   26   The members of the chorale decide to sing first in New Orleans, next in Dallas, and then to close in St. Louis. Now, they must decide on their modes of transportation. They can travel from the campus to New Orleans by bus or plane and from New Orleans to Dallas by bus, plane, or train, and from Dallas to St. Louis by bus or train. The tree diagram in Figure 5.9 indicates the choices of the chorale. The first part of the trip can be made in two ways, the second part in three ways, and the last part in two ways. Notice that the number of ways the transportation can be chosen is $2 \cdot 3 \cdot 2 = 12$ ways.

Figure 5.9

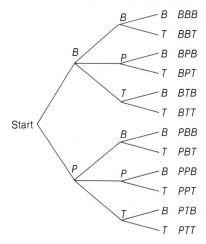

This example introduces the following principle:

<table>
<tr><td>

The Fundamental Principle of Counting

</td><td>

1. If two experiments are performed in order with n_1 possible outcomes of the first experiment and n_2 possible outcomes from the second experiment, then there are

$$n_1 \cdot n_2$$

combined outcomes of the first experiment followed by the second.
2. In general, if k experiments are performed in order with possible number of outcomes $n_1, n_2, n_3, \ldots, n_k$, respectively, then there are

$$n_1 \cdot n_2 \cdot n_3 \cdot \cdots \cdot n_k$$

possible outcomes of the experiments performed in order.

</td></tr>
</table>

For example, if the first stage of a task can be accomplished in m ways, the second stage in n ways, and so forth, and the last stage can be done in z ways, then the whole task can be performed in $m \cdot n \cdot \cdots \cdot z$ ways. The Fundamental Principle of Counting is helpful in solving problems such as the following.

EXAMPLE 27   A coin is tossed and a die is rolled. In how many ways can the two fall?

Solution   The coin can fall in two ways: $\{H, T\}$. The die can fall in six ways: $\{1, 2, 3, 4, 5, 6\}$. Therefore, the two can fall in

$$2 \cdot 6 = 12 \text{ ways}$$

EXAMPLE 28   In many states, automobile license plates have on them a combination of three letters and three numbers. If all letters and numbers may be used repeatedly, how many combinations are available to each of these states?

Solution   There are 26 letters to choose from for each of the three letter places, and there are 10 digits to choose from for the digit places. By the Fundamental Principle of Counting, the number of combinations is

$$26 \cdot 26 \cdot 26 \cdot 10 \cdot 10 \cdot 10 = 17,576,000$$

EXAMPLE 29   An urn contains five red balls and seven white balls. A ball is drawn, its color noted, and a second ball is drawn. What is the probability of drawing a red ball followed by a white ball?

Solution   By the counting principle, there are 12 ways of drawing the first ball and 11 ways of drawing the second. Therefore, there are

$$12 \cdot 11 = 132$$

ways of drawing the two balls. At the same time, there are 5 ways of drawing the red ball on the first draw and 7 ways of drawing the white ball on the second draw. Therefore, the number of ways of drawing a red ball and then a white ball is

$$5 \cdot 7 = 35$$

Thus,

$$P(R \text{ followed by } W) = \tfrac{35}{132}$$

EXAMPLE 30   If a couple plans to have three children, what is the probability that exactly two will be boys? (Assume that it is equally likely for a child to be a boy or a girl.)

Solution   The tree diagram in Figure 5.10 indicates eight paths or ways that the couple can have three children. By counting, we note that three of these have exactly two boys. Therefore,

$$P(\text{exactly 2 boys}) = \tfrac{3}{8}$$

Figure 5.10

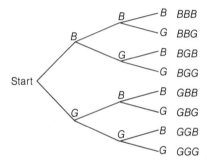

EXAMPLE 31   A card is drawn from a deck of cards. Then the card is replaced, the deck is reshuffled, and a second card is drawn. What is the probability of an ace on the first draw and a king on the second?

Solution   Since the first card is returned, there are $52 \cdot 52$ ways of drawing the 2 cards. There are four ways of drawing an ace on the first draw and four ways of drawing a king on the second draw, or $4 \cdot 4$ ways of drawing both. Thus,

$$P(\text{ace followed by a king}) = \frac{4 \cdot 4}{52 \cdot 52} = \frac{1}{169} \approx .0059$$

EXAMPLE 32   A red die and a blue die are rolled, and the outcome of each is recorded. Find a uniform sample space, and determine the probability of the following events:

    a. $E = \{\text{the sum of the two numbers is 7}\}$
    b. $R = \{\text{the red die shows a 4}\}$
    c. $A = \{\text{the sum of the two numbers is greater than 10}\}$

Solution   The tree diagram in Figure 5.11 is helpful in determining all possible outcomes. Note that for each possible result showing on the red die, there are six possibilities for the blue die.

Figure 5.11

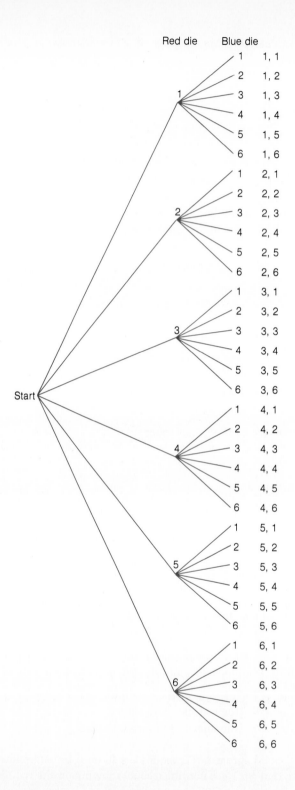

A suitable sample space is

$$S = \left\{ \begin{array}{l} (1, 1), (1, 2), (1, 3), (1, 4), (1, 5), (1, 6), \\ (2, 1), (2, 2), (2, 3), (2, 4), (2, 5), (2, 6), \\ (3, 1), (3, 2), (3, 3), (3, 4), (3, 5), (3, 6), \\ (4, 1), (4, 2), (4, 3), (4, 4), (4, 5), (4, 6), \\ (5, 1), (5, 2), (5, 3), (5, 4), (5, 5), (5, 6), \\ (6, 1), (6, 2), (6, 3), (6, 4), (6, 5), (6, 6) \end{array} \right\}$$

where the first number of each ordered pair represents the number on the red die and the second number of each pair represents the number on the blue die. Furthermore, since each die is fair, we conclude that each of these outcomes is equally likely. There are 36 ordered pairs in the sample space, so we assign to each outcome the probability $\frac{1}{36}$.

a. $E = \{(1, 6), (2, 5), (3, 4), (4, 3), (5, 2), (6, 1)\}$ and has six elements. Hence, $P(E) = \frac{6}{36} = \frac{1}{6}$.

b. $R = \{(4, 1), (4, 2), (4, 3), (4, 4), (4, 5), (4, 6)\}$ and has six elements. Hence, $P(R) = \frac{6}{36} = \frac{1}{6}$.

c. $A = \{(5, 6), (6, 5), (6, 6)\}$ and has three elements. Hence, $P(A) = \frac{3}{36} = \frac{1}{12}$.

Exercise Set **5.3**

A   **1.** A student plans a trip from Atlanta to Boston to London. From Atlanta to Boston, he can travel by bus, train, or airplane. However, from Boston to London, he can travel only by ship or airplane.
  a. In how many ways can the trip be made?
  b. Verify your answer by drawing an appropriate tree diagram and counting the routes.

2. There are six roads from A to B and four roads between B and C.
  a. In how many ways can Joy drive from A to C by way of B?
  b. In how many ways can she drive round-trip from A to B to C and return to A through B?

3. A die is tossed and a chip is drawn from a box containing three chips numbered 1, 2, and 3. How many possible outcomes can be obtained from this experiment? Verify your answer with a tree diagram.

4. By means of a tree diagram, analyze the number of possibilities in tossing a coin four times.

5. In how many ways can two speakers be arranged on a program?

B   **6.** In how many ways can three speakers be arranged on a program?

7. In how many ways can four speakers be arranged on a program?

8. A box contains six different-colored balls: red, white, blue, black, green, and yellow. If two balls are drawn at random, one at a time, and replaced, what is the probability of getting
  a. a yellow ball followed by a red ball?
  b. a red ball followed by a blue ball?
  c. a yellow ball and a red ball? (*Hint:* This event can happen in more than one way.)

9. Four coins are tossed. What is the probability of getting
  a. four tails? **b.** exactly two tails?
  c. at least three heads? **d.** exactly one head?

C **10.** An ice chest contains five cans of cola, seven cans of ginger ale, and three cans of root beer. Al randomly selects a can, and then Sheila takes one. What is the probability that
  a. Al gets a cola and Sheila a root beer? **b.** Al gets a ginger ale and Sheila a cola?
  c. both get root beers? **d.** neither gets a cola?

11. A restaurant offers the following menu:

Main Courses	Vegetables	Beverages
Beef	Potatoes	Milk
Ham	Green beans	Coffee
Fried chicken	Green peas	Tea
Shrimp	Asparagus	

If you choose one main course, two vegetables, and one beverage, in how many ways could you order a meal?

12. Hue and May play in a Ping-Pong tournament. The first player to win four games wins the tournament. Make a tree diagram showing the possible ways in which the tournament can turn out.

13. How many four-letter words are possible out of the alphabet if
  a. no letter can be used more than once?
  b. adjacent letters cannot be alike?
  c. letters can be repeated?

14. Two cards are drawn from a standard deck of playing cards. What is the probability that a king is drawn followed by an ace
  a. if the first card is replaced before the second is drawn?
  b. if the first card is not replaced before the second is drawn?

Business **15.** **Stocks.** Suppose you are considering the purchase of three stocks. Each stock may go up (*U*), stay the same (*S*), or go down (*D*). Draw a tree diagram showing what could happen to your three purchases.

Economics **16.** **Quality Control.** Suppose that, in a shipment of 100 items, 4 are defective. Items from the shipment are drawn one at a time and tested. The testing terminates when 2 defective items are found or after five tests. Show the testing process with a tree diagram.

Life Sciences **17.** **Medicine.** A doctor classifies the results from a new drug according to five levels of dosage (1, 2, 3, 4, 5), male or female, smoker or nonsmoker, and the results (excellent, average, poor). How many combined classifications are possible?

18. **Family Planning.** In a family of exactly two children, what is the probability that
  a. both are girls? **b.** the first is a boy and the second a girl?
  c. at least one is a boy? **d.** neither is a girl?

19. **Family Planning.** Find the probability that a couple having three children will have
  a. all girls. **b.** at least one boy.
  c. at least two girls.

20. **Family Planning.** Assume that a family wishes to have four children and that they are as likely to have a boy as a girl. What is the probability that

    a. exactly four will be girls?   **b.** all the children will be the same sex?

    c. at least three will be boys?   **d.** at most three will be boys?

21. Redo exercise 20 for a family with five children.

Social Sciences   **22. Politics.** Suppose that in a local election only two parties are represented, D and R. Draw a tree diagram illustrating four consecutive elections and determine how many possibilities result in

    a. at least one party change.   **b.** no party changes.

    c. exactly one party change.   **d.** more than two party changes.

23. Interviewing. In an interview, people are classified according to sex (M or F), political affiliation (D, I, R), and age (Y, M, O). Construct a tree diagram showing all possible classifications. Does the number of paths agree with the Fundamental Principle of Counting?

Counting Techniques Using Permutations and Combinations

> The Fundamental Principle of Counting can be used to develop two extremely important concepts for counting: **permutations** and **combinations.** Both of these concepts are useful not only in solving complicated probability problems but also in other types of application problems. The main thing to remember is that permutations involve order or arrangement and that combinations do not.

Suppose we have four letters,

$$\{A, B, C, D\}$$

and list them two at a time:

$$\{AB, AC, AD, BA, BC, BD, CA, CB, CD, DA, DB, DC\}$$

Note that *AB* is listed and so is *BA*. Likewise, *BD* and *DB*. In this listing the order is important. When order is important, arrangements of objects are called **permutations.**

Permutations   The *ordered arrangements* of *r* objects selected from a set of *n* different objects ($r \leq n$) are called **permutations.**

That is, in permutations the order of arrangement is important. *ABCD* is different from *BACD*, where the letters (or objects) are *A*, *B*, *C*, and *D*.

    Now let's list the same four letters

$$\{A, B, C, D\}$$

two at a time without regard to order:

$$\{AB,\ AC,\ AD,\ BC,\ BD,\ CD\}$$

These arrangements of four letters taken two at a time are called **combinations.** We begin our discussion with permutations.

EXAMPLE 33　Tabulate the permutations of $\{A, B, C\}$.

Solution　There are six different permutations:

$$
\begin{array}{ccc}
ABC & BAC & CBA \\
ACB & BCA & CAB
\end{array}
$$

EXAMPLE 34　How many permutations are there of the set $\{A, B, C, D\}$?

Solution　First we draw a tree diagram (Figure 5.12).

Figure 5.12

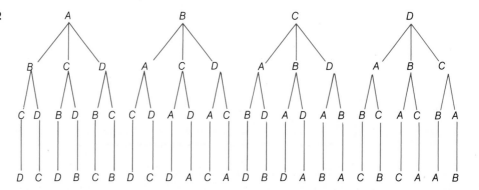

The first row of the diagram represents the first choice of one of the four letters. There are, of course, four choices. The second row represents the choice of a second letter after the first letter has been selected. Note that there are three choices after each first choice and a total number of

$$4 \cdot 3 \text{ ways}$$

the first letter and the second letter can be selected. (Count and verify that there are 12 branches ending on the second row.)

The third row indicates the third choice after the first and second choices have been selected. Note from this row there are two choices for the third letter after each selection of a first and second letter. In this third row verify that there are

$$4 \cdot 3 \cdot 2 \text{ ways}$$

of selecting a first, second, and third letter.

Finally, the fourth letter can be selected in only one way, so there are

$$4 \cdot 3 \cdot 2 \cdot 1$$

permutations of four letters.

In general:

**Number of
Permutations of
n Objects**

> The number of permutations of *n* distinct objects is
>
> $$n \cdot (n - 1) \cdot (n - 2) \cdot \, \cdots \, \cdot 3 \cdot 2 \cdot 1$$
>
> which can be written as *n*! (read *n*-factorial).

The preceding definition defines *n*! to be the product of positive integers 1 to *n*, inclusive. The product $6 \cdot 5 \cdot 4 \cdot 3 \cdot 2 \cdot 1$ may be denoted by 6!, called *6-factorial*. For example,

$$10! = 10 \cdot 9 \cdot 8 \cdot 7 \cdot 6 \cdot 5 \cdot 4 \cdot 3 \cdot 2 \cdot 1 = 3,628,800$$

$$8! = 8 \cdot 7 \cdot 6 \cdot 5 \cdot 4 \cdot 3 \cdot 2 \cdot 1 = 40,320$$

$$6! = 6 \cdot 5 \cdot 4 \cdot 3 \cdot 2 \cdot 1 = 720$$

$$5! = 5 \cdot 4 \cdot 3 \cdot 2 \cdot 1 = 120$$

$$4! = 4 \cdot 3 \cdot 2 \cdot 1 = 24$$

$$3! = 3 \cdot 2 \cdot 1 = 6$$

$$2! = 2 \cdot 1 = 2$$

To complete this list, we define both 1! and 0! to be 1. The statement that 0! = 1 may seem unusual, but you will learn later in your work with factorials that this definition is reasonable and consistent with the factorial idea for positive integers.

EXAMPLE 35 Six workers are assigned six different jobs. In how many ways can the assignments be made?

Solution $6! = 720$ ways

Our objective now is to develop a formula for the number of permutations of *n* objects taken *r* at a time, denoted by *P*(*n*, *r*). Consider the following example.

EXAMPLE 36 A first-year class is to elect a president, a vice president, a secretary, and a treasurer from six class members who qualify. How many ways may the class officers be selected?

Solution If we consider the order as president, vice president, secretary, and treasurer, then {Maria, Tom, Jim, Tomoko} is certainly different from {Tomoko, Tom, Maria, Jim}. Thus, the answer to the problem is *P*(6, 4), the number of permutations of six things taken four at a time. Use the Fundamental Principle of Counting and note that the position of president can be filled in six ways. After this occurs, the position of vice president can be filled in five ways, or the two positions can be filled in $6 \cdot 5$ ways. Then the secretary can be selected in four ways, or the three positions in $6 \cdot 5 \cdot 4$ ways. Finally, there are only three people left to be selected for treasurer. Hence, the number of ways that all four positions can be filled is $6 \cdot 5 \cdot 4 \cdot 3$ or

$$P(6, 4) = 6 \cdot 5 \cdot 4 \cdot 3$$

To express $P(6, 4)$ in terms of factorials, multiply and divide by $2 \cdot 1$:

$$P(6, 4) = \frac{6 \cdot 5 \cdot 4 \cdot 3 \cdot 2 \cdot 1}{2 \cdot 1}$$

Now we can write

$$P(6, 4) \text{ as } \frac{6!}{2!} = \frac{6!}{(6 - 4)!}$$

in order to express everything in terms of the only numbers (six and four) given in the example.

By reasoning in the same way, the number of permutations of n things taken r at a time is

$$P(n, r) = n(n - 1)(n - 2) \cdot \cdots \cdot [n - (r - 1)]$$
$$= n(n - 1)(n - 2) \cdot \cdots \cdot (n - r + 1)$$

In order for the expression for $P(n, r)$ to be in terms of factorials, we multiply and divide by $(n - r)(n - r - 1) \cdot \cdots \cdot 2 \cdot 1$ to get

$$P(n, r) = \frac{n(n - 1) \cdot \cdots \cdot (n - r + 1)}{1} \cdot \frac{(n - r)(n - r - 1) \cdot \cdots \cdot 2 \cdot 1}{(n - r)(n - r - 1) \cdot \cdots \cdot 2 \cdot 1}$$

$$= \frac{n!}{(n - r)!}$$

The **number of permutations** of n things taken r at a time is given by

$$P(n, r) = \frac{n!}{(n - r)!} \qquad 1 \leq r \leq n$$

E X A M P L E 37 In how many ways can a president, a vice president, and a secretary be selected from 10 people?

Solution The answer is

$$P(10, 3) = \frac{10!}{(10 - 3)!} = \frac{10 \cdot 9 \cdot 8 \cdot 7 \cdot 6 \cdot 5 \cdot 4 \cdot 3 \cdot 2 \cdot 1}{7 \cdot 6 \cdot 5 \cdot 4 \cdot 3 \cdot 2 \cdot 1}$$

$$= 10 \cdot 9 \cdot 8 = 720$$

Suppose we wish to find the number of arrangements of n objects where not all objects are distinguishable. For example, suppose we permute the letters in *seem*. If the letters were all different, 4! would be the answer. However, the two *e*'s are indistinguishable. Now suppose the two *e*'s are marked e_1 and e_2; 2! would be the number of ways of arranging these two letters. The number, P, of ways of arranging the letters in *seem* when the *e*'s are indistinguishable times the number of arrangements of the *e*'s (when considered as different) equals the number of ways of arranging the four letters if all were distinguishable; that is,

$$P \cdot 2! = 4! \qquad \text{or} \qquad P = \frac{4!}{2!}$$

EXAMPLE 38 The number of permutations of the letters $AAABCD$ is $\frac{6!}{3!}$ because the letter A occurs three times.

If we have a set of n objects to be arranged when there are n_1 of one indistinguishable type, n_2 of a second indistinguishable type, continuing until there are n_k of the kth indistinguishable type, then the **number of possible permutations** of the n objects is

$$\frac{n!}{n_1! \cdot n_2! \cdot \,\cdots\, \cdot n_k!}$$

where $n_1 + n_2 + \cdots + n_k = n$.

EXAMPLE 39 The number of arrangements of the letters in *toot* is

$$\frac{4!}{2! \cdot 2!} = 6$$

This number can be verified by listing the possible arrangements: {*ttoo, toto, toot, otto, otot, oott*}, as seen in the tree diagram of Figure 5.13.

Figure 5.13

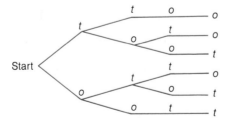

We now turn to combinations. Consider the following example:

EXAMPLE 40 The first-year class is to elect four class officers from six class members who qualify. How many sets of class officers are possible?

Solution   The answer is of course $C(6, 4)$—the number of combinations of six things taken four at a time. The order does not matter. In this case {Mai, Toshio, Ron, Jill} is the same as {Jill, Toshio, Mai, Ron}. By writing down the different sets of four officers from six prospects, let's say, {M, T, J, R, B, C}, we get the following possibilities:

$$\{M, T, J, R\}, \{M, T, J, B\}, \{M, T, J, C\}, \{M, T, R, B\}, \{M, T, R, C\},$$
$$\{M, T, B, C\}, \{M, J, R, B\}, \{M, J, R, C\}, \{M, J, B, C\}, \{M, R, B, C\},$$
$$\{T, J, R, B\}, \{T, J, R, C\}, \{T, J, B, C\}, \{T, R, B, C\}, \{J, R, B, C\}$$

We see that

$$C(6, 4) = 15$$

Now let's obtain the answer another way. Take each combination of officers and arrange the four officers as president, vice president, secretary, and treasurer. There would be $P(4, 4)$. Now if we multiply this result by the number of selections of four officers, $C(6, 4)$, the answer should be the number of arrangements of six things taken four at a time or

$$P(6, 4) = C(6, 4) \cdot P(4, 4)$$

Thus,

$$C(6, 4) = \frac{P(6, 4)}{P(4, 4)} = \frac{6!/2!}{4!}$$

$$= \frac{6!}{2!4!}$$

$$= \frac{6 \cdot 5 \cdot 4 \cdot 3 \cdot 2 \cdot 1}{2 \cdot 1 \cdot 4 \cdot 3 \cdot 2 \cdot 1} = 15$$

In general, by reasoning as we did in Example 40, the number of combinations of n objects taken r at a time, $C(n, r)$, relates to permutations as

$$P(n, r) = C(n, r) \cdot P(r, r)$$

$$C(n, r) = \frac{P(n, r)}{P(r, r)}$$

$$C(n, r) = \frac{n!}{(n - r)!r!}$$

Combination of _n_ Things Taken _r_ at a Time	The number of ways of selecting r objects from n objects without regard to order (the number of combinations of n things taken r at a time) is $$C(n, r) = \frac{n!}{r!(n - r)!} \qquad 1 \leq r \leq n$$

Counting techniques using combinations and permutations are especially useful in applying the definitions of probability to certain types of problems, as demonstrated by the following examples.

EXAMPLE 41 A box contains four red balls and six other balls. Two balls are drawn. What is the probability that they are red?

Solution Two red balls are to be selected from four red balls. This selection can happen in $C(4, 2)$ ways. The number of ways that two balls can be drawn from ten balls is $C(10, 2)$. Thus,

$$P(2 \text{ red}) = \frac{C(4, 2)}{C(10, 2)} = \frac{\dfrac{4!}{2!2!}}{\dfrac{10!}{2!8!}} = \frac{2}{15}$$

EXAMPLE 42 A fair die is rolled four times.

    a. How many outcomes are in the sample space of this experiment that records the number showing for each roll?

    b. Consider the event $E = \{$all 4 rolls show different numbers$\}$. How many outcomes are in this event?

    c. What is the probability of E?

Solution **a.** There are four steps (rolls) to the process, each with six possible results. The sample space contains

$$6 \cdot 6 \cdot 6 \cdot 6 = 6^4 \text{ outcomes}$$

    b. In effect, each roll chooses one of the numbers 1, 2, 3, 4, 5, or 6. For an outcome to be in this event, no number is chosen more than once. After four rolls, four distinct numbers have been chosen and ordered (according to the roll on which they occurred). Thus, there are $P(6, 4)$ different outcomes in E.

$$\textbf{c. } P(E) = \frac{n(E)}{n(S)} = \frac{P(6, 4)}{6^4} = \frac{6 \cdot 5 \cdot 4 \cdot 3}{6 \cdot 6 \cdot 6 \cdot 6} = \frac{5}{18}$$

EXAMPLE 43 A quality control inspector at the Glo-Worm Factory randomly selects 5 bulbs from each lot of 100 bulbs that is produced and inspects them for defects. If a lot has 96 good bulbs and 4 defective bulbs, what is the probability that the inspector will find 3 good bulbs and 2 defective bulbs in her sample?

Solution The sample space consists of all possible combinations of 5 bulbs that can be chosen from 100. Hence, the number of outcomes in the sample space is $C(100, 5)$. An outcome is in the event if exactly 3 of the bulbs are good and 2 are defective. The 3 bulbs are selected without regard for order from 96 good bulbs in $C(96, 3)$ ways. In a like manner, the 2 defective bulbs are selected from 4 in $C(4, 2)$ ways. By the Fundamental Principle of Counting, there are $C(96, 3) \cdot C(4, 2)$ outcomes in the event. Thus,

$$P(F) = \frac{C(96, 3)C(4, 2)}{C(100, 5)} \approx .01$$

EXAMPLE 44 A history professor requires each student to write research papers on 2 of 15 topics. Of the 15 topics, 5 are easy to research, 7 are difficult to research, and 3 are practically impossible to research. One student chooses his 2 topics at random. What is the probability of his getting

- **a.** 2 easy topics?
- **b.** 1 difficult topic and 1 practically impossible topic?
- **c.** 2 practically impossible topics?

Solution The answers are as follows:

a. $P(2 \text{ easy topics}) = \dfrac{C(5, 2) \cdot C(7, 0) \cdot C(3, 0)}{C(15, 2)}$

$$= \frac{10 \cdot 1 \cdot 1}{105} = \frac{2}{21}$$

b. $P(1 \text{ difficult topic and 1 impossible topic}) = \dfrac{C(7, 1) \cdot C(3, 1) \cdot C(5, 0)}{C(15, 2)}$

$$= \frac{7 \cdot 3 \cdot 1}{105} = \frac{1}{5}$$

c. $P(2 \text{ impossible topics}) = \dfrac{C(7, 0) \cdot C(5, 0) \cdot C(3, 2)}{C(15, 2)}$

$$= \frac{1 \cdot 1 \cdot 3}{105} = \frac{1}{35}$$

Exercise Set 5.4

A
1. Consider the four objects $\{W, X, Y, Z\}$.
   a. How many combinations of two objects can be chosen from this set? List them.
   b. How many combinations of three objects can be chosen from this set? List them.
   c. List all combinations of one object chosen from this set.

2. Write in factorial notation.
   a. $P(5, 3)$ **b.** $C(4, 2)$ **c.** $C(44, 22)$
   d. $C(8, 8)$ **e.** $P(6, 6)$ **f.** $P(7, 5)$
   g. $C(7, 5)$ **h.** $C(100, 89)$ **i.** $C(100, 11)$

3. Evaluate each of the following.
   a. $C(10, 6)$ **b.** $C(10, 0)$ **c.** $C(15, 1)$
   d. $C(4, 2)$ **e.** $C(r, 2)$ **f.** $C(r, r - 1)$

4. Evaluate each of the following.
   a. $P(5, 3)$ **b.** $P(6, 5)$ **c.** $P(8, 1)$
   d. $P(9, 2)$ **e.** $P(7, 2)$ **f.** $P(8, 7)$

5. In how many ways can five speakers be arranged on a program?

6. A coach of a football team must choose a first-string quarterback and a second-string quarterback from eight aspiring superstars. In how many ways can the choice be made?

7. In how many ways can seven students line up outside Professor Smith's door to complain about grades?

8. A student-body president is asked to appoint a committee consisting of 5 boys and 3 girls. A list of 12 boys and 10 girls is provided from which to make the appointments. How many different committees can be selected?

9. How many different hands consisting of five cards can be drawn from an ordinary deck of cards?

10. A special committee of 3 persons must be selected from a 12-person board of directors. In how many ways can the committee be selected?

B **11.** Write a simple expression for each of the following.

    a. $P(r, 1)$ **b.** $P(k, 2)$ **c.** $P(r, r-1)$

    d. $P(k, k-2)$ **e.** $P(k, 3)$ **f.** $P(k, k-3)$

12. The license plates for a certain state display three letters followed by three numbers. (Examples: MFT–986 or APT–098.) How many different license plates can be manufactured if no repetitions are allowed?

13. Employee I.D. numbers at a large factory consist of four-digit numbers such as 0133, 4499, and 0000.

    a. How many possible I.D. numbers are there?

    b. How many possible I.D. numbers are there in which all four digits are different?

14. A typical Social Security number is 416-64-8664. How many possible Social Security numbers are there?

15. The Gamma Gamma Alpha fraternity sells lottery tickets for a free spring trip to Florida. They sell 400 tickets in all, of which 4 are drawn as winners. Frank buys 6 tickets.

    a. In how many ways can 4 tickets be selected from 400?

    b. In how many ways can the 4 tickets be drawn so Frank does not hold a winning ticket?

    c. What is the probability that Frank does not win a free trip to Florida?

    d. What is the probability that exactly 1 of the winning tickets belongs to Frank?

C **16.** A bowl contains 8 red marbles and 14 black marbles. Three marbles are selected at random from the bowl without replacement.

    a. What is the probability that all 3 are black?

    b. What is the probability that 1 is red and 2 are black?

17. A hat contains 20 slips of paper numbered 1 to 20. If 3 are drawn without replacement, what is the probability that all are numbered less than 10?

18. The license plates of a certain state display three letters followed by three numbers.

    a. What is the probability that the letters of a randomly selected tag read HOT?

    b. What is the probability that none of the digits on the tag exceeds 4?

19. Employee I.D. numbers at a large factory consist of four-digit numbers. What is the probability that if a number is chosen at random from the list of I.D. numbers, all four of its digits would be different?

20. A typical Social Security number is 413-22-9802. If a Social Security number is chosen at random, what is the probability that all the digits would be the same?

21. From a standard deck of cards how many different hands consisting of seven cards can be drawn consisting of
    a. seven spades? b. five clubs, two hearts?
    c. four clubs, one spade, two hearts? d. three clubs, two hearts, two diamonds?

22. If $n > 1$, then $n \cdot (n - 1)!$ can be simplified to what expression?

23. Find all the positive integers n such that $(2n)! = 2 \cdot n!$.

24. If $(n + 1)! = 80 \cdot n!$, what is n?

25. Demonstrate by using numbers, and then verify the following assertions.
    a. If $n \geq 2$, then $(n^2 - n) \cdot (n - 2)! = n!$.
    b. If $n \geq k$, then $(n - k + 1) \cdot n! + k \cdot n! = (n + 1)!$.
    c. If $n \geq 2$, then $n! - (n - 1)! = (n - 1)^2 \cdot (n - 2)!$.

26. a. Compute $C(n, 0)$ for $n = 4, 6$, and 8.
    b. What is the value of $C(n, 0)$ for all n?

27. a. Compute $C(n, 1)$ for $n = 3, 7$, and 9.
    b. What is the value of $C(n, 1)$ for all n?

28. a. Compute $C(n, n)$ for $n = 2, 5, 9$.
    b. What is the value of $C(n, n)$ for all n?

29. Compute $C(n, r)$ for
    a. $n = 8, \quad r = 6$ b. $n = 10, \quad r = 4$

30. Compute $C(n, n - r)$ for
    a. $n = 8, \quad r = 6$ b. $n = 10, \quad r = 4$

31. Use exercises 29 and 30 to conjecture a relationship between $C(n, r)$ and $C(n, n - r)$. Verify the conjecture.

Business 32. **Sales.** A sales force is made up of four people. There are 10 prospects on file, but each prospect needs a great deal of individual attention. In how many ways can the 10 prospects be considered by the four salespeople without regard to order?

33. **Sales.** A file contains 20 good sales contracts and 5 canceled contracts. In how many ways can 4 good contracts and 2 canceled contracts be selected?

34. **Purchasing.** A firm buys material from three local companies and five out-of-state companies. Four orders are submitted at one time. In how many ways can two orders be submitted to a local firm and two to an out-of-state firm?

35. **Purchasing.** A firm buys material from three local companies and five out-of-state companies. Four orders are randomly submitted at one time. What is the probability that two are submitted to a local firm and two to an out-of-state firm?

36. **Organization.** A company has two divisions. Division A has four supervisors and division B has six supervisors. In how many ways can two supervisors be selected
    a. without regard to their division?
    b. from division B?
    c. if one is selected from division A and one from division B?

37. **Organization.** Among the 30 employees in the Lappup Poll Corporation, there are 20 women and 10 men; there are 18 pollsters, 6 sales employees, and 6 management employees. Three employees are chosen to form a committee. In how many ways can a committee be selected to have
    a. 2 women and 1 man?
    b. 2 pollsters and 1 salesperson?
    c. 1 salesperson, 1 pollster, and 1 management employee?

d. no women?

e. no pollsters?

38. Organization. A company has two divisions. Divison A has four supervisors, and division B has six supervisors. Two supervisors are to be laid off by a random drawing.

a. What is the probability that they will both be from division B?

b. What is the probability that one will be from B and one from A?

Economics **39. Quality Control.** In a quality control check at the Acme Tire Company, 3 tires are randomly selected and inspected from each lot of 20 tires produced. Suppose a lot contains 4 defective tires and 16 good tires.

a. How many ways can 3 tires be selected from 20?

b. How many different selections of 3 tires from 20 will contain exactly 1 defective tire?

c. What is the probability that exactly 1 of the 3 tires selected will be defective?

d. What is the probability that no defective tires will be among the 3 selected?

Life Sciences **40. Dispensing Drugs.** The order of administering five different drugs is important.

a. In how many ways can all five drugs be administered?

b. In how many ways can three of the five drugs be administered?

41. Experiment Design. Ten rats are selected for an experiment. Each trial run is to involve three rats at a time. How many trials can be performed using each group only once?

42. Experiment Design. On a day's rounds at a hospital, an intern is to examine 12 patients. Of the 12 patients, 4 have heart disease. During the course of the morning, the intern randomly selects and examines 6 patients. What is the probability that she will examine exactly 2 patients with heart disease?

Social Sciences **43. Politics.** Five men seek the governorship. Candidates A and B have equal probabilities of winning, and candidates C, D, and E also have equal probabilities of winning. However, A has a probability that is twice that of C.

a. Find the probability that A will win.

b. Find the probability that C will win.

c. Find the probability that C, D, or E will win.

d. Find the probability that A or C will win.

5 Properties of Probability

> Consider the following problems. A card is drawn from a standard deck of cards. What is the probability that it is either an ace or a spade? Of the first-year students who entered Samson University last year, 12% failed first-year English, 16% failed mathematics, and 6% failed both English and mathematics. An admissions counselor would like to know what percent failed English or mathematics. The new notations introduced in this section will help us find solutions to problems like these.

We are now ready to consider some additional combinations of events. Three of these relationships are of such importance that we list them as special events. These events are defined by using the operators of set theory: **union, intersection,** and **complementation.**

And, Or, and Complement

> 1. The event $A \cup B$ is the collection of all outcomes that are **in A or in B or in both A and B.**
> 2. The event $A \cap B$ is the set of all outcomes that are in **both A and B.**
> 3. The **complement** of an event A, denoted A', is the collection of all outcomes that are in the sample space and are not in A.

We illustrate these concepts with examples involving the roll of a die.

EXAMPLE 45 In the rolling of a fair die, what is the probability of an odd number or a 4?

Solution We let O represent an odd number and F represent a 4 and seek $P(O \cup F)$. In Figure 5.14(b) we see that

$$P(O \cup F) = \tfrac{4}{6} = \tfrac{2}{3}$$

Figure 5.14

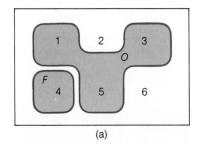

(a)

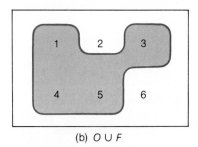

(b) $O \cup F$

Note in Figure 5.14(a) that

$$P(O) = \tfrac{3}{6} \quad \text{and} \quad P(F) = \tfrac{1}{6}$$

Thus,

$$P(O \cup F) = P(O) + P(F)$$

as

$$\tfrac{4}{6} = \tfrac{3}{6} + \tfrac{1}{6}$$

EXAMPLE 46 In the rolling of the same fair die, what is the probability of an even number or a 4?

Solution Let E represent an even number and F represent a 4. We seek $P(E \cup F)$. In Figure 5.15(b) we see that

$$P(E \cup F) = \tfrac{3}{6}$$

Note in Figure 5.15(a) that

$$P(E) = \tfrac{3}{6} \quad \text{and} \quad P(F) = \tfrac{1}{6}$$
$$P(E \cup F) \neq P(E) + P(F)$$
$$\tfrac{3}{6} \neq \tfrac{3}{6} + \tfrac{1}{6}$$

Figure 5.15

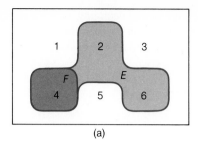

(a)

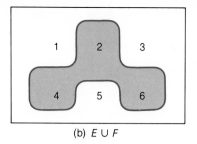

(b) $E \cup F$

What is the difference in the problems in Examples 45 and 46? For $P(O \cup F)$ in Example 45, F and O had no points in common. For $P(E \cup F)$, E and F overlapped. This discussion suggests the following definition and property of probability:

Mutually Exclusive Events	**1.** Events A and B are **mutually exclusive** if they have no outcomes in common. **2.** If events A and B are mutually exclusive, $$P(A \cup B) = P(A) + P(B)$$

EXAMPLE 47   If we toss two dice, what is the probability of getting a sum of 7 or 8?

Solution   Since getting a 7 and getting an 8 are mutually exclusive events,

$$P(7 \text{ or } 8) = P(7) + P(8) = \tfrac{6}{36} + \tfrac{5}{36} = \tfrac{11}{36}$$

EXAMPLE 48   From a standard deck of cards, we draw one card. What is the probability of our getting a spade or a red card?

Solution   Verify that

$$P(S) = \tfrac{13}{52} \quad \text{and} \quad P(R) = \tfrac{26}{52}$$

Since getting a spade and getting a red card are mutually exclusive,

$$P(S \cup R) = P(S) + P(R)$$
$$= \tfrac{13}{52} + \tfrac{26}{52} = \tfrac{39}{52} = \tfrac{3}{4}$$

Now let's return to Example 46 where we noted that $P(E \cup F) = \tfrac{3}{6}$, $P(E) = \tfrac{3}{6}$, and $P(F) = \tfrac{1}{6}$. Why is $P(E \cup F) \neq P(E) + P(F)$? The outcome 4 is in both E and F and is thus counted twice in $P(E) + P(F)$ (see Figure 5.15(a)). The probability that 4 is in both E and F is

$$P(E \cap F) = \tfrac{1}{6}$$

Since $E \cap F$ is included twice in $P(E) + P(F)$ we subtract one of these and note that

$$P(E \cup F) = P(E) + P(F) - P(E \cap F)$$
$$\tfrac{3}{6} = \tfrac{3}{6} + \tfrac{1}{6} - \tfrac{1}{6}$$

We can generalize this concept by realizing that in set theory the number of outcomes in event A or in event B is the number in A plus the number in B less the number in $A \cap B$, which has been counted in both A and B. (See Figure 5.16.)

Figure 5.16

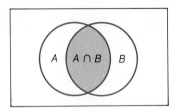

Thus,

$$n(A \cup B) = n(A) + n(B) - n(A \cap B)$$

Divide both sides of the equation by N, the number of elements in a sample space, to obtain

$$\frac{n(A \cup B)}{N} = \frac{n(A)}{N} + \frac{n(B)}{N} - \frac{n(A \cap B)}{N}$$

or

$$P(A \cup B) = P(A) + P(B) - P(A \cap B)$$

Probability of
A or B

For any two events A and B, the probability of A **or** B is given by

$$P(A \cup B) = P(A) + P(B) - P(A \cap B)$$

EXAMPLE 49   Of the first-year students at Hard College last year, 12% failed English, 8% failed history, and 4% failed both English and history. What percent failed English or history?

$$P(E) = .12$$
$$P(H) = .08$$
$$P(E \cap H) = .04$$
$$P(E \cup H) = P(E) + P(H) - P(E \cap H)$$
$$= .12 + .08 - .04$$
$$= .16$$

Thus, 16% failed English or history.

EXAMPLE 50   In drawing a card from eight cards numbered 1 through 8, what is the probability of getting an even number or a number less than 5?

Solution Let A represent the event of getting a number less than 5 and B the event of getting an even number. Now

$$S = \{1, 2, 3, 4, 5, 6, 7, 8\}$$
$$A = \{1, 2, 3, 4\}$$
$$B = \{2, 4, 6, 8\}$$
$$A \cap B = \{2, 4\}$$

and

$$P(A) = \tfrac{4}{8} = \tfrac{1}{2} \quad \text{and} \quad P(B) = \tfrac{4}{8} = \tfrac{1}{2}$$

But 2 and 4 are both even and less than 5; consequently,

$$P(A \cap B) = \tfrac{2}{8} = \tfrac{1}{4}$$

Thus,

$$P(A \cup B) = P(A) + P(B) - P(A \cap B)$$
$$= \tfrac{1}{2} + \tfrac{1}{2} - \tfrac{1}{4} = \tfrac{3}{4}$$

The preceding discussion can be extended to three events A, B, and C:

Probability of A or B or C

$$P(A \cup B \cup C) = P(A) + P(B) + P(C) - P(A \cap B) - P(A \cap C)$$
$$- P(B \cap C) + P(A \cap B \cap C)$$

EXAMPLE 51 A survey of 100 first-year students taking social science courses at Lamor University gave the following information as diagramed in Figure 5.17: 55 were taking history (H), 45 were taking psychology (P), 25 were taking sociology (S), 12 were taking history and psychology, 10 were taking history and sociology, 8 were taking psychology and sociology, and 5 were taking all three social sciences.

Figure 5.17

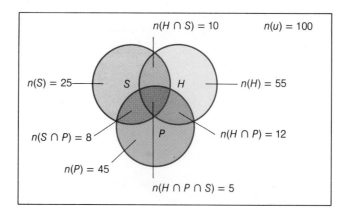

$n(H \cap S) = 10$ $n(u) = 100$
$n(S) = 25$ S H $n(H) = 55$
$n(S \cap P) = 8$ P $n(H \cap P) = 12$
$n(P) = 45$
$n(H \cap P \cap S) = 5$

$$n(H \cup P \cup S) = 100 \qquad \text{so} \qquad P(H \cup P \cup S) = 1$$

$$n(H) = 55 \qquad \text{so} \qquad P(H) = \tfrac{55}{100}$$

$$n(P) = 45 \qquad \text{so} \qquad P(P) = \tfrac{45}{100}$$

$$n(S) = 25 \qquad \text{so} \qquad P(S) = \tfrac{25}{100}$$

$$n(H \cap P) = 12 \qquad \text{so} \qquad P(H \cap P) = \tfrac{12}{100}$$

$$n(H \cap S) = 10 \qquad \text{so} \qquad P(H \cap S) = \tfrac{10}{100}$$

$$n(P \cap S) = 8 \qquad \text{so} \qquad P(P \cap S) = \tfrac{8}{100}$$

$$n(H \cap P \cap S) = 5 \qquad \text{so} \qquad P(H \cap P \cap S) = \tfrac{5}{100}$$

We use this example to verify the formula for $P(H \cup P \cup S)$:

$$P(H \cup P \cup S) = P(H) + P(P) + P(S) - P(H \cap P) - P(H \cap S)$$
$$- P(P \cap S) + P(H \cap P \cap S)$$
$$1 = \tfrac{55}{100} + \tfrac{45}{100} + \tfrac{25}{100} - \tfrac{12}{100} - \tfrac{10}{100} - \tfrac{8}{100} + \tfrac{5}{100} = \tfrac{100}{100}$$

EXAMPLE 52　Consider a group of 200 sales prospects with the following characteristics: last year 80 of them purchased material from the ABC Corporation, 60 of them purchased electronic equipment, and 25 bought more than $100,000 worth of lumber. Now, of those who purchased from the ABC Corporation last year, suppose 40 bought electronic equipment and 10 bought more than $100,000 worth of lumber. Also 6 of those who purchased electronic equipment bought more than $100,000 worth of lumber last year. Likewise, 4 of those who purchased from the ABC Corporation also purchased electronic equipment last year and purchased more than $100,000 worth of lumber. If a sales prospect is chosen at random, what is the probability that he either purchased from the ABC Corporation last year, or purchased electronic equipment, or purchased more than $100,000 worth of lumber last year?

Solution　Let A represent those who purchased from the ABC Corporation last year, B those who purchased electronic equipment last year, and C those who purchased more than $100,000 worth of lumber. The relationship among A, B, and C can be demonstrated by the Venn diagrams in Figure 5.18(a). A contains 80 prospects; $A \cap B$ contains 40 prospects; $A \cap C$ contains 10 prospects; and $A \cap B \cap C$ contains 4 prospects. Since $A \cap B \cap C$ contains 4 prospects, there are 6 for the remainder of $A \cap C$, 36 for the remainder of $A \cap B$, and 34 for the remainder of

Figure 5.18

(a)

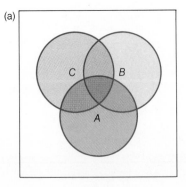

(b)

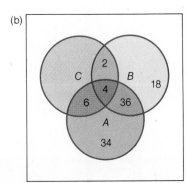

A. Since $B \cap C$ contains 6 prospects, 2 are contained in the part of $B \cap C$ not in $A \cap B \cap C$. From the Venn diagrams in Figure 5.18(b) we see that $A \cup B \cup C$ contains 113 prospects. Therefore, $P(A \cup B \cup C) = \frac{113}{200}$. By the formula.

$$P(A \cup B \cup C) = P(A) + P(B) + P(C) - P(A \cap B) - P(A \cap C)$$
$$- P(B \cap C) + P(A \cap B \cap C)$$
$$= \frac{80}{200} + \frac{60}{200} + \frac{25}{200} - \frac{40}{200} - \frac{10}{200} - \frac{6}{200} + \frac{4}{200} = \frac{113}{200}$$

Let us now make an observation concerning the probability that an event does **not** occur. The probability of getting a 6 on the toss of a die is $\frac{1}{6}$. What is the probability of *not* getting a 6? There are five equally likely ways of not getting a 6—namely, getting a 1, 2, 3, 4, or 5. Thus, the probability of *not getting* a 6 is $\frac{5}{6}$. Note that $\frac{5}{6} = 1 - \frac{1}{6}$.

In general, let's divide all the events in the sample space into two mutually exclusive sets A and A' as shown in Figure 5.19. The set A' is called the **complement** of A in relation to the sample space S.

Figure 5.19

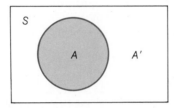

Note that

$$A \cap A' = \emptyset \quad \text{and} \quad A \cup A' = S$$

Thus

$$P(A \cup A') = P(A) + P(A') - P(A \cap A')$$
$$1 = P(A) + P(A') - 0$$
$$P(A') = 1 - P(A)$$

Probability of a Complement

If A is any event in the sample space S, and if set A' denotes the complement of A, then

$$P(A') = 1 - P(A)$$

EXAMPLE 53 What is the probability of not getting an ace when drawing a card from a standard deck of cards?

Solution
$$P(\text{no ace}) = 1 - P(\text{ace})$$
$$= 1 - \frac{4}{52} = \frac{12}{13}$$

Exercise Set 5.5

A 1. A number x is selected at random from the set of numbers $\{1, 2, 3, \ldots, 8\}$. What is the probability that
   a. x is less than 5?   **b.** x is even?
   c. x is less than 5 and even?   **d.** x is less than 5 or a 7?

2. If A and B are events in a sample space such that $P(A) = .6$, $P(B) = .2$, and $P(A \cap B) = .1$, compute each of the following.
   a. $P(A')$ **b.** $P(B')$ **c.** $P(A \cup B)$ **d.** $P(A' \cup B')$

3. An experiment consists of tossing a coin seven times. Describe the complement of each of the following.
   a. Getting at least two heads   **b.** Getting three, four, or five tails
   c. Getting one tail   **d.** Getting no heads

4. In Brooks College, 30% of the first-year students failed mathematics, 20% failed English, and 15% failed both mathematics and English. What is the probability that a first-year student failed mathematics or English?

5. A single card is drawn from a 52-card deck. What is the probability that it is
   a. either a heart or a club?   **b.** either a heart or a king?
   c. not a jack?   **d.** either red or black?

B 6. If A and B are events with $P(A \cup B) = \frac{5}{8}$, $P(A \cap B) = \frac{1}{3}$, and $P(A') = \frac{1}{2}$, compute the following.
   a. $P(A)$ **b.** $P(B)$ **c.** $P(B')$ **d.** $P(A' \cup B)$

7. A card is drawn from a deck of cards. Find the probability of drawing
   a. an ace or a king.
   b. a heart or a diamond.
   c. an ace or a heart.
   d. a diamond or a number less than 3.
   e. a card other than a spade, a heart, or a diamond.

8. From a bag containing six red balls, four black balls, and three green balls, one ball is drawn. What is the probability that it is
   a. red or black?   **b.** red or black or green?
   c. not black?   **d.** not red or not black?
   e. not red, or not black, or not green?
   f. red, or not green, or not black?

C 9. Suppose you roll a pair of tetrahedral (four-faced) dice with one blue die and one red die. Consider the events, $E = \{$the sum is $6\}$ and $F = \{$the blue die shows a $3\}$.
   a. Tabulate E.   **b.** Tabulate F.
   c. Tabulate $\{E$ and $F\}$.   **d.** Tabulate $\{E$ or $F\}$.
   e. Tabulate F'.

10. Assume that the dice in exercise 9 are fair. Compute $P(E)$, $P(F)$, $P(E$ or $F)$, and $P(E$ and $F)$, and verify that $P(E$ or $F) = P(E) + P(F) - P(E$ and $F)$.

11. A fair coin is flipped four times.
   a. Tabulate the uniform sample space of the set of all possible outcomes involving H and T.
   b. Tabulate the event $A = \{$exactly one head appears$\}$.
   c. Tabulate the event $B = \{$at least one tail occurs$\}$.

d. Tabulate $\{A \text{ or } B\}$.

e. Tabulate $\{A \text{ and } B\}$.

f. Tabulate A'.

12. For the event A from exercise 11, compute $P(A)$ and $P(A')$, and verify that $P(A) = 1 - P(A')$.

13. Three-digit numbers range all the way from 100 to 999. A three-digit number is selected at random. Give the probability that it

a. is even.

b. is composed of only even digits.

c. is not composed of only even digits.

d. is a square.

e. has all prime digits.

f. has all composite digits.

Business

14. Marketing Survey. A recent survey found that 60% of the people in a given community drink Lola Cola and 40% drink other soft drinks; 15% of the people interviewed indicated that they drink both Lola Cola and other soft drinks. What percent of the people drink either Lola Cola or other soft drinks?

Economics

15. Forecasting. In a survey of the presidents of leading banks by an economics consulting group, the following information was obtained relative to their forecast for next year:

65%	expect higher inflation
15%	expect a recession
5%	expect both higher inflation and a recession
75%	expect higher interest rates
50%	expect higher interest rates and higher inflation
10%	expect higher interest rates and a recession
3%	expect higher interest rates, higher inflation, and a recession

What is the probability that a bank president selected at random

a. would forecast no recession and lower interest rates?

b. would forecast no increase in inflation and no increase in interest rates?

c. would forecast no recession, no increase in interest rates, and no increase in inflation?

Life Sciences

16. Prediction Relative to Children and Divorce. In a survey, families were classified as C, children, and C', no children. At the same time, families were classified according to D, husband and wife divorced, and D', not divorced. Out of 200 families surveyed, the following results were obtained.

	C	C'	Total
D	60	20	80
D'	90	30	120
Total	150	50	200

a. What is the probability that a family selected at random has children?

b. What is the probability that in a family selected at random the parents are not divorced?

c. What is the probability that for a family selected at random there are children or the parents are divorced?

d. What is the probability that in a family selected at random the parents are not divorced or there are no children?

Social Sciences

17. Survey of Family Characteristics. In a survey of 100 families of a school district in 1970, each family was asked the following questions: (1) Do you have children in public school? (2) Do you object to the modern approach of teaching mathematics? (3) Do you object to placing students in classes according to IQ tests? The yes answers to these questions were tabulated as follows, where A, B, and C represent questions (1), (2), and (3), respectively:

$$n(A) = 70 \qquad\qquad n(A \cap B) = 15$$
$$n(B) = 30 \qquad\qquad n(A \cap C) = \ \ 6$$
$$n(C) = 10 \qquad\qquad n(B \cap C) = \ \ 8$$
$$n(A \cap B \cap C) = \ \ 5$$

a. If a family is selected at random, what is the probability that the answer from this family was yes on either (1) or (2)?

b. If a family is selected at random, what is the probability that it answered yes to one of the three questions?

c. If a family is selected at random, what is the probability that it did not object to modern mathematics or did not object to placing students in classes by IQ tests?

18. Politics. In a sample of 50 people, it was found that 28 planned to vote for the Democratic candidates for mayor and assistant to the mayor, 10 planned to vote for the Republican candidates for mayor and assistant to the mayor, and 5 planned to vote for a Republican mayor and a Democratic assistant to the mayor.

a. What is the probability that a person plans to vote for a Republican mayor?

b. What is the probability that a person plans to vote for at least one Republican?

c. What is the probability of a person voting for a Republican mayor and a Democratic assistant mayor?

d. What is the probability of a person voting for a Republican mayor or a Democratic assistant mayor?

Conditional Probability

> When dealing with an uncertain situation, we might expect that as more information is obtained, the probabilities would change. Alternatively, we might say that as more information is available, the sample space is modified. Suppose, for instance, that the top executives for the P. G. and Y. Corporation are evaluating their chances of obtaining a large fabrication contract. They feel that P. G. and Y., the Go-Slo Corporation, and Leary Enterprises are equally likely to win the bidding. Hence, in their minds, the probability is $\frac{1}{3}$ that they will win the contract. Then comes information that Go-Slo has withdrawn from the bidding. Excitement reigns at P. G. and Y. because in this modified sample space, the probability of success for P. G. and Y. is reevaluated at $\frac{1}{2}$. Is this true?

Conditional probability is the mathematical term used to describe probability with additional information. The symbol $P(A|B)$ denotes the conditional probability that event A will occur, given the information or condition that event B

has occurred; $P(A|B)$ is read "the probability of A, given B." We consider in this section two procedures for computing conditional probability. In the first procedure, information is used to obtain a new sample space reflecting the fact that event B has occurred. This procedure is demonstrated by the next four examples.

EXAMPLE 54 Find the probability of obtaining an even sum when tossing two dice, given that a 4 appears on at least one die.

Solution Of all the possible outcomes for tossing two dice, we use only those outcomes that contain a 4 on one of the dice: $\{(1, 4), (2, 4), (3, 4), (4, 4), (5, 4), (6, 4), (4, 1),$ $(4, 2), (4, 3), (4, 5), (4, 6)\}$. Thus, knowing that a 4 appears on one die reduces the sample space from 36 possible outcomes to 11, five of which are favorable to obtaining an even sum.

$$P(\text{even sum}|\text{a 4 is showing}) = \tfrac{5}{11}$$

Also, knowing that a 4 is showing *decreases* the probability of an even sum since the probability of an even sum is $\tfrac{1}{2}$.

EXAMPLE 55 Find the probability of obtaining a sum of 7 when tossing two dice, given that a 4 appears on at least one die.

Solution We know from Example 54 that there are 11 possible outcomes, of which two have a sum of 7. Thus,

$$P(7|\text{a 4 is showing}) = \tfrac{2}{11}$$

Note that knowing a 4 is showing *increases* the probability of getting a sum of 7, since $P(7) = \tfrac{6}{36} = \tfrac{1}{6}$.

EXAMPLE 56 Suppose in a sample of 120 students, 80 are enrolled in English, 60 in mathematics, and 20 in both English and mathematics (see Figure 5.20). What is the probability that a student selected at random is enrolled in English? What is the probability that a student selected at random is enrolled in English, given that the same student is enrolled in mathematics?

Figure 5.20

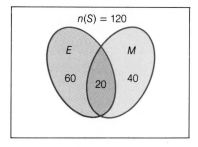

Solution The probability that a student is enrolled in English is

$$P(E) = \tfrac{80}{120} = \tfrac{2}{3}$$

The given condition of being enrolled in mathematics reduces the number of possibilities to 60, of which 20 are enrolled in English; thus,

$$P(E|M) = \tfrac{20}{60} = \tfrac{1}{3}$$

EXAMPLE 57 A poll is taken to determine whether 700 hourly employees of a company favor a strike. The 700 employees are divided into three groups, X, Y, and Z, according to salary (see Table 5.5). Suppose an hourly employee is selected at random. The probability that he is in favor of a strike is $\tfrac{380}{700}$. Now suppose an hourly employee is selected at random from group X. What is the probability that she is in favor of a strike?

Table 5.5

	In Favor of a Strike	Not in Favor of a Strike	No Opinion	Total
Group X	150	50	10	210
Group Y	100	80	8	188
Group Z	130	170	2	302
Total	380	300	20	700

Solution This conditional probability is denoted by

$$P(\text{in favor of a strike}|\text{group X}) = \tfrac{150}{210}$$

Other conditional probabilities are

$$P(\text{not in favor of a strike}|\text{group Z}) = \tfrac{170}{302}$$

and

$$P(\text{group Y}|\text{in favor of a strike}) = \tfrac{100}{380}$$

From our assignment of probabilities in this example, we note an interesting relationship among $P(A|B)$, $P(A \cap B)$, $P(A)$, and $P(B)$. Let A represent the fact that an employee favors a strike and B represent the fact that an employee is in group Y. Then $P(A|B) = \tfrac{100}{188}$. The probability that an employee selected at random is in group Y and simultaneously favors a strike is $P(A \cap B) = \tfrac{100}{700}$. Also, note that $P(B) = \tfrac{188}{700}$. We now observe that, for this example,

$$P(A|B) = \frac{P(A \cap B)}{P(B)}$$

since

$$\frac{100}{188} = \frac{\tfrac{100}{700}}{\tfrac{188}{700}}$$

It is interesting to consider the case in which A and B are interchanged. We investigate to determine whether it is true that

$$P(B|A) = \frac{P(B \cap A)}{P(A)}$$

Of course, it is true from the definition that $P(A \cap B) = P(B \cap A)$. Now $P(B|A)$, the probability that an employee is in group Y, given that he favors a strike, is equal to $\frac{100}{380}$, and $P(A) = \frac{380}{700}$. Therefore,

$$P(B|A) = \frac{P(A \cap B)}{P(A)}$$

since

$$\frac{100}{380} = \frac{\frac{100}{700}}{\frac{380}{700}}$$

Consider now the conditional probability relative to a sample space composed of N simple events. For example, consider two events A and B in the sample space depicted in Figure 5.21. Suppose there are n_1 sample points in $A \cap B$, n_2 sample points in A and not in B, n_3 in B and not in A, and n_4 sample points in neither A nor B, where $N = n_1 + n_2 + n_3 + n_4$. Obviously,

$$P(A) = \frac{n_1 + n_2}{N} \qquad P(B) = \frac{n_1 + n_3}{N} \qquad \text{and} \qquad P(A \cap B) = \frac{n_1}{N}$$

Figure 5.21

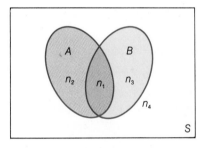

If it is given that the sample points are in B, then

$$P(A|B) = \frac{n_1}{n_1 + n_3}$$

Therefore,

$$P(A|B) = \frac{P(A \cap B)}{P(B)}$$

because

$$\frac{P(A \cap B)}{P(B)} = \frac{n_1/N}{(n_1 + n_3)/N} = \frac{n_1}{n_1 + n_3} = P(A|B)$$

Probability of A and B

If A and B are **any events** and $P(B) \neq 0$, then

$$P(A|B) = \frac{P(A \cap B)}{P(B)}$$

The formula above provides a second procedure for finding conditional probability. Note that $P(A|B) \neq P(B|A)$ unless $P(A) = P(B)$.

EXAMPLE 58   Let A and B be events with $P(A) = \frac{1}{3}$, $P(B) = \frac{1}{4}$, and $P(A \cap B) = \frac{1}{6}$. Find $P(A|B)$, $P(B|A)$, $P(A'|B')$, and $P(B'|A')$.

Solution   Table 5.6 is constructed so that the sum of the probabilities in the first column is $P(A)$, and the sum in the second column is $1 - P(A) = P(A')$. Likewise, the sum of the probabilities listed in the first row is $P(B)$, and the sum in the second row is $1 - P(B) = P(B')$.

Now $P(A \cap B)$ is given as $\frac{1}{6}$. This entry occurs in the table in the first row and first column. The element in the first row and second column is found as

Table 5.6

	A	A'	Total
B	$\frac{1}{6}$	$(\frac{1}{12})$	$\frac{1}{4}$
B'	$(\frac{1}{6})$	$(\frac{7}{12})$	$(\frac{3}{4})$
Total	$\frac{1}{3}$	$(\frac{2}{3})$	1

follows: $(B \cap A) \cup (B \cap A') = B$ since A and A' are mutually exclusive and exhaustive. Thus,

$$P(B \cap A) + P(B \cap A') = P(B)$$
$$\tfrac{1}{6} + P(B \cap A') = \tfrac{1}{4}$$
$$P(B \cap A') = \tfrac{1}{12}$$

This answer is circled in the B row and A' column in Table 5.6. Likewise, since $P(A \cap B) + P(A \cap B') = P(A)$,

$$\tfrac{1}{6} + P(A \cap B') = \tfrac{1}{3}$$
$$P(A \cap B') = \tfrac{1}{6} \quad \text{circled}$$

Now

$$P(A') = 1 - P(A) = 1 - \tfrac{1}{3} = \tfrac{2}{3} \quad \text{and} \quad P(B') = 1 - P(B) = 1 - \tfrac{1}{4} = \tfrac{3}{4}$$
$$P(A' \cap B') = P(B') - P(A \cap B') = \tfrac{3}{4} - \tfrac{1}{6} = \tfrac{7}{12}$$

To check,

$$P(A') = P(B \cap A') + P(B' \cap A') = \tfrac{1}{12} + \tfrac{7}{12} = \tfrac{8}{12} = \tfrac{2}{3}$$

Thus,

$$P(A|B) = \frac{P(A \cap B)}{P(B)} = \frac{\frac{1}{6}}{\frac{1}{4}} = \frac{2}{3}$$

$$P(B|A) = \frac{P(A \cap B)}{P(A)} = \frac{\frac{1}{6}}{\frac{1}{3}} = \frac{1}{2}$$

$$P(A'|B') = \frac{P(A' \cap B')}{P(B')} = \frac{\frac{7}{12}}{\frac{3}{4}} = \frac{7}{9}$$

$$P(B'|A') = \frac{P(A' \cap B')}{P(A')} = \frac{\frac{7}{12}}{\frac{2}{3}} = \frac{7}{8}$$

Sometimes it is easier to visualize the preceding probabilities by using Venn diagrams (see Figure 5.22). Since $P(A \cap B) = \frac{1}{6}$ and $P(A) = \frac{1}{3}$, the probability of that part of A not in $A \cap B$ is

$$\tfrac{1}{3} - \tfrac{1}{6} = \tfrac{2}{12} = P(A \cap B')$$

Figure 5.22

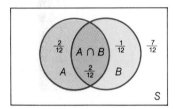

The probability of that part of B not in $A \cap B$ is

$$\tfrac{1}{4} - \tfrac{1}{6} = \tfrac{1}{12} = P(B \cap A')$$

The probability of $A \cup B$ is

$$\tfrac{2}{12} + \tfrac{2}{12} + \tfrac{1}{12} = \tfrac{5}{12}$$

The probability of the complement of $A \cup B$ is

$$1 - \tfrac{5}{12} = \tfrac{7}{12}$$
$$P(A') = 1 - \tfrac{1}{3} = \tfrac{2}{3}$$
$$P(B') = 1 - \tfrac{1}{4} = \tfrac{3}{4}$$

EXAMPLE 59   Thirty mathematics professors out of one hundred examined were found to be overweight (W). Ten of these had high blood pressure (H). Only four of the professors who were not overweight had high blood pressure. Show this information in a table similar to Table 5.6, and then find the probability that a mathematics professor will not have high blood pressure if he is not overweight.

Solution   Now $P(W) = \frac{30}{100}$, $P(W \cap H) = \frac{10}{100}$, and $P(W' \cap H) = \frac{4}{100}$. These give us a start in constructing our table (Table 5.7).

$$P(H'|W') = \frac{P(H' \cap W')}{P(W')}$$

$$= \frac{\frac{66}{100}}{\frac{70}{100}} = \frac{66}{70} = \frac{33}{35}$$

Table 5.7

	W	W'	Total
H	$\frac{10}{100}$	$\frac{4}{100}$	$\frac{14}{100}$
H'	$\frac{20}{100}$	$\frac{66}{100}$	$\frac{86}{100}$
Total	$\frac{30}{100}$	$\frac{70}{100}$	1

Conditional Probability

We have demonstrated two ways to compute conditional probability, $P(A|B)$.

1. Consider a new sample space reflecting the fact that event B has occurred.
2. Use the relationship

$$P(A|B) = \frac{P(A \cap B)}{P(B)}$$

where $P(A \cap B)$ and $P(B)$ are computed in the original sample space.

In cases in which the actual sample spaces are easily accessible, the first technique is the most straightforward way to compute conditional probability.

EXAMPLE 60 As Rod draws a card from a deck of 52 cards, Larry peeks over his shoulder and signals to Lois that the card is red. What is the probability that Lois will correctly guess the card?

Solution Prior to receiving Larry's help, Lois knew that the sample space consisted of the 52 cards in the deck. Upon receiving Larry's signal, Lois realizes that she is now concerned with only the 26 red cards, her new sample space. Since only 1 of the 26 cards was drawn,

$$P(\text{Lois is correct}|\text{card is red}) = \tfrac{1}{26}$$

Sometimes it is best to use the second technique.

EXAMPLE 61 Of the visitors at the recent Olympic games, 45% were from the United States. The visitors were polled on the question, "Should future Olympic games be subdivided into smaller units?" Twenty percent of those polled were from the United States and answered yes. What is the probability that a randomly selected visitor from the United States would answer the question yes?

Solution Let W represent the event {person from the U.S.} and Y represent the event {answered yes}. Converting the percentages into probabilities, we have $P(W) = .45$ and $P(Y \cap W) = .20$. Hence,

$$P(Y|W) = \tfrac{.20}{.45} = \tfrac{4}{9}$$

Exercise Set **5.6**

A

1. A single card is drawn at random from a standard deck. Let $B = \{\text{the card is black}\}$, $H = \{\text{the card is a heart}\}$, and $C = \{\text{the card is a club}\}$.

  a. Describe in words a sample space for the experiment.

  b. How is the sample space changed if we have the additional information that a black card is drawn?

  c. Compute $P(H|B)$.

  d. Compute $P(C|B)$.

  e. Compute $P(B|C)$.

2. Roll a single fair die. Let $A = \{\text{the die shows less than 4}\}$ and $B = \{\text{the die shows an odd number}\}$. Compute

  a. $P(A|B)$ **b.** $P(B|A)$

3. If $P(A) = .6$, $P(B|A) = .7$, and $P(B) = .6$, compute

  a. $P(A \cap B)$ **b.** $P(A|B)$ **c.** $P(B')$ **d.** $P(A \cup B)$

B

4. Given the following table, compute the probabilities requested.

	C	D	E	Total
A	.20	.10	.05	.35
B	.30	.20	.15	.65
Total	.50	.30	.20	1

  a. $P(A)$ **b.** $P(E)$ **c.** $P(B \cap C)$ **d.** $P(A \cap E)$ **e.** $P(E')$

  f. $P(B')$ **g.** $P(C|A)$ **h.** $P(A|C)$ **i.** $P(B|D)$

5. If $P(A) = .70$, $P(B) = .30$, and $P(A \cap B) = .20$, compute

  a. $P(A|B)$ **b.** $P(B|A)$ **c.** $P(A \cup B)$ **d.** $P(A|B')$

  e. $P(A \cup B)'$ **f.** $P(A' \cap B')$ **g.** $P(A'|B)$ **h.** $P(A \cup B')$

6. If $P(A) = \frac{1}{3}$, $P(B) = \frac{1}{4}$, and $P(A \cup B) = \frac{1}{2}$, compute

  a. $P(A|B)$ **b.** $P(B|A)$ **c.** $P(A \cap B')$ **d.** $P(A' \cap B')$

  e. $P(A|B')$ **f.** $P(A'|B)$ **g.** $P(A'|B')$ **h.** $P(A \cup B')$

7. In a certain college, 30% of the students failed mathematics, 20% failed English, and 15% failed both mathematics and English.

  a. If a student failed English, what is the probability that she failed mathematics?

  b. If a student failed mathematics, what is the probability that he failed English?

  c. What is the probability that a student failed mathematics or English?

  d. If a student did not fail mathematics, what is the probability that he failed English?

  e. If a student did not fail English, what is the probability that she did not fail mathematics?

C

8. A pair of dice is rolled on a table. What is the probability that a 2 or a 5 appears on either or both of the dice, given that the sum of the dots on the two dice is more than 6?

9. An urn contains the following balls: five colored red and white, three black and white, four green and white, six red and black, four red and green, and five black and green.

  a. Given that you have drawn a ball that is partly green, what is the probability that it is partly white?

b. Given that the ball you have drawn is partly white, what is the probability that it is partly red?

10. Investments. Of 100 businesspeople polled, 50 have investments in common stocks, 35 have investments in bonds, and 25 have investments in both stocks and bonds. What is the probability that a person chosen at random from the businesspeople polled

a. invests in common stocks and not in bonds?

b. invests in bonds and not in common stocks?

c. does not invest in stocks or does not invest in bonds?

d. invests in stocks or bonds?

e. invests in stocks, if you know she invests in bonds?

f. invests in bonds, if you know he invests in stocks?

g. invests in stocks, if you know he does not invest in bonds?

h. invests in bonds, if you know she does not invest in stocks?

11. Contracting. Five companies have submitted bids on a contract, and it is known that a portion of this contract will be awarded to three of the companies. The representative of one of the companies tries to figure her probability of being selected if the choices are made at random. She persuades the manager who will award the contracts to designate one of the companies (other than her own company) that will be selected for a portion of the contract. She then reevaluates her probability of being randomly selected for a contract. Does the new information give her more (or less) confidence that her company will be selected?

12. Quality Control. You know that 4% of all light bulbs produced by a given company weigh less than specifications, and 2% of all bulbs are both defective and weigh less than specifications. What is the probability that a light bulb selected at random is defective, if you know it weighs less than specifications?

13. Genetics. In a study of genetics, a class used a sample of 100 people to obtain the following information.

	Male (M)	Female (F)	Total
Color blind (C)	4	1	5
Not color blind (C')	40	55	95
Total	44	56	100

What is the probability that a person is

a. color blind, given that the person is a female?

b. color blind, given that the person is a male?

c. not color blind, given that the person is a male?

d. not color blind, given that the person is a female?

14. Politics. The Democratic Party is planning a special campaign in city A, where 40% of the voters are Democrats and 60% are Republicans. If a Democrat is personally contacted, the probability that he will vote is .80; if a Republican is personally contacted, the probability that he will vote is .70. If the Democrat votes after the personal contact, the probability that he will vote for the Democratic candidate is .90. If the Republican votes after the personal contact, the probability that he will vote Democratic is .30. What percent of the voters contacted will vote for the Democratic candidate?

In this section we are interested in experiments in which the probabilities for each outcome need not be fixed. Instead, they take on different values based on what events take place before the trial under consideration. Such problems are a part of the broad area of probability problems called **finite stochastic processes.** The term *stochastic* is derived from the Greek word meaning "guess."

As you probably have already guessed, applications of finite stochastic processes extend all the way from the genetic theories of Mendel to quality control techniques of manufacturing.

We also consider compound events in which the probability of the second event in no way depends on the occurrence or nonoccurrence of the first event.

We have observed that

$$P(A|B) = \frac{P(A \cap B)}{P(B)} \quad \text{and} \quad P(B|A) = \frac{P(A \cap B)}{P(A)}$$

If we multiply by the denominators, we get

$$P(A \cap B) = P(B) \cdot P(A|B) \quad \text{and} \quad P(A \cap B) = P(A) \cdot P(B|A)$$

Multiplication Rule

The probability that both of two events will occur is equal to the probability that the first event will occur multiplied by the conditional probability that the second event will occur when it is known that the first event has occurred:

$$P(A \cap B) = P(A) \cdot P(B|A)$$
$$P(A \cap B) = P(B) \cdot P(A|B)$$

We quickly observe that this rule gives a procedure for computing the probability of A and B, something that has been missing from our repertoire of skills. However, it should be noted that this relationship is helpful only if one of the relevant conditional probabilities is known or can be computed.

EXAMPLE 62 If $P(A) = .72$ and $P(B|A) = .35$, what is $P(B \cap A)$?

Solution $P(B \cap A) = P(A) \cdot P(B|A) = (.72)(.35) = .252$

EXAMPLE 63 A basket contains two red balls and two white balls. A ball is drawn and its color is noted. Then a second ball is drawn. What is the probability that both balls are red?

Solution Let R_1 be the event of drawing a red ball on the first draw. Then

$$P(R_1) = \tfrac{2}{4}$$

To find $P(R_2|R_1)$, where R_2 represents a red ball on the second draw, we consider only the outcomes after R_1 has occurred. Since the red ball has not been replaced, there are three balls in the basket and one of these is red. Thus,

$$P(R_2|R_1) = \tfrac{1}{3}$$

Substituting these values in the appropriate multiplication rule gives

$$P(R_1 \cap R_2) = P(R_1) \cdot P(R_2|R_1) = \tfrac{2}{4} \cdot \tfrac{1}{3} = \tfrac{1}{6}$$

The tree diagram in Figure 5.23 should help you understand the preceding example. From this diagram,

$$P(R_1 \cap R_2) = P(R_1) \cdot P(R_2|R_1)$$
$$= \tfrac{1}{2} \cdot \tfrac{1}{3} = \tfrac{1}{6}$$

Figure 5.23

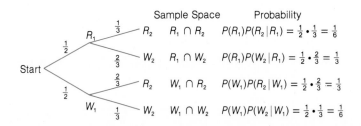

EXAMPLE 64 We are given three urns with red and white balls as follows: urn A has six red balls and four white balls; urn B has five red balls and one white ball; urn C has five red balls and three white balls. We select an urn at random and then draw a ball. What is the probability that the ball is red?

Solution Note here the sequence of two experiments. First an urn is selected; then a ball is drawn. The tree diagram in Figure 5.24 lists the mutually exclusive possibilities

Figure 5.24

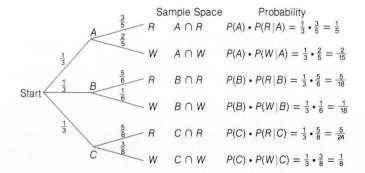

along with their probabilities. The probability that any particular path leads to a red ball is the product of the probabilities along the path. The probability of a red ball along the first path is $\frac{1}{3} \cdot \frac{3}{5} = \frac{1}{5}$. Since there are three mutually exclusive paths that lead to a red ball,

$$P(R) = \tfrac{1}{3} \cdot \tfrac{3}{5} + \tfrac{1}{3} \cdot \tfrac{5}{6} + \tfrac{1}{3} \cdot \tfrac{5}{8} = \tfrac{247}{360} = .686$$

EXAMPLE 65   Urn I contains three red and four black balls; urn II contains 4 red and 5 black balls. A ball is drawn from urn I and placed in urn II; then a ball is drawn from urn II. What is the probability that the second ball is red?

Solution   The first experiment involves drawing a ball from urn I with two possible outcomes, a red or a black ball, denoted by R_1 and B_1, and with probabilities as indicated in Figure 5.25. The second experiment involves drawing a ball from urn II after a ball has been drawn from urn I and placed in urn II. Four possibilities exist, as Figure 5.25 shows. A red ball, R_2, or a black ball, B_2, may be drawn after a red ball has been placed in urn II; or a red ball, R_2, or a black ball, B_2, may be drawn from urn II after a black ball has been placed in urn II. There are two mutually exclusive paths for getting a red ball on the second draw; a red ball on the first draw and a red ball on the second draw, or a black ball on the first draw and a red ball on the second draw. The probability of a particular path is the product of the dependent probabilities along the path. Therefore,

$$P(\text{red ball on the second draw}) = P(R_1) \cdot P(R_2|R_1) + P(B_1) \cdot P(R_2|B_1)$$
$$= \tfrac{3}{7} \cdot \tfrac{5}{10} + \tfrac{4}{7} \cdot \tfrac{4}{10} = \tfrac{31}{70}$$

Figure 5.25

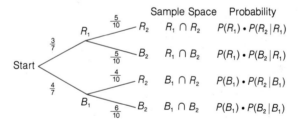

EXAMPLE 66   Two cards are drawn from a standard deck of cards. What is the probability of getting an ace and a king?

Solution 1   There are two mutually exclusive ways this event can occur. We can get an ace on the first draw and a king on the second or a king on the first draw and an ace on the second. We denote this as

$$P(A \cap K) = P[(A_1 \cap K_2) \cup (K_1 \cap A_2)] = P(A_1 \cap K_2) + P(K_1 \cap A_2)$$
$$= P(A_1)P(K_2|A_1) + P(K_1)P(A_2|K_1)$$
$$= \tfrac{4}{52} \cdot \tfrac{4}{51} + \tfrac{4}{52} \cdot \tfrac{4}{51}$$
$$= \frac{8}{13 \cdot 51} = .012$$

Solution 2 By using the theory of combinations, we note that we are choosing 1 ace from 4 and 1 king from 4. At the same time, we are taking 2 cards from 52.

$$P(A \cap K) = \frac{C(4,\,1) \cdot C(4,\,1)}{C(52,\,2)}$$

$$= \frac{\dfrac{4!}{3!1!} \cdot \dfrac{4!}{3!1!}}{\dfrac{52!}{50!2!}}$$

$$= \frac{4 \cdot 4}{26 \cdot 51} = \frac{8}{13 \cdot 51} = .012$$

EXAMPLE 67 In a certain community 60% of those registered to vote are registered as Democrats, 30% are registered as Republicans, and 10% are registered as Independents. A proposed new tax for schools is to be voted on by the community. It is known that 70% of the registered Democrats, 50% of the registered Republicans, and 20% of the registered Independents favor the tax. If a registered resident is selected at random, what is the probability that she will favor the tax?

Solution The tree diagram in Figure 5.26 lists the respective probabilities on each branch. The event of favoring the tax consists of three mutually exclusive outcomes: (1) being a Democrat and favoring the tax, (2) being a Republican and favoring the tax, and (3) being an Independent and favoring the tax. Thus, the probability of a registered resident favoring the tax is

$$P(\text{favor tax}) = .60(.70) + .30(.50) + .10(.20)$$

$$= .59$$

Figure 5.26

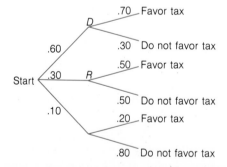

EXAMPLE 68 The probability that a chest X ray will be positive for a person with lung cancer or tuberculosis is .90, while the probability that the X ray will be positive for a person who does not have either disease is .05. Four percent of the people in a city have lung cancer or tuberculosis. If a person is selected at random, what is the probability that the X ray will be positive?

Solution As indicated in Figure 5.27, the X ray can be positive in two ways: (1) when the person has cancer or TB and (2) when the person does not have either disease.

Figure 5.27

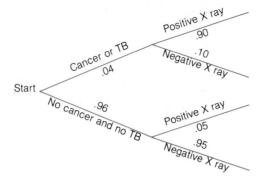

Thus,

P(positive X ray)

$\quad = [P(\text{cancer or TB}) \cdot P(\text{positive X ray}|\text{cancer or TB})]$

$\qquad + [P(\text{no cancer and no TB}) \cdot P(\text{positive X ray}|\text{no cancer and no TB})]$

$\quad = .04(.90) + .96(.05)$

$\quad = .084$

The product formula may be extended to the occurrence of three events in the following manner:

$$P(A \cap B \cap C) = P(A) \cdot P(B|A) \cdot P(C|A \cap B)$$

We can extend this argument to any number k of events, as indicated in the following formula:

$$P(A_1 \cap A_2 \cap \cdots \cap A_k)$$
$$= P(A_1) \cdot P(A_2|A_1) \cdot P(A_3|A_1 \cap A_2) \cdot \; \cdots \; \cdot P(A_k|A_1 \cap A_2 \cap \cdots \cap A_{k-1})$$

EXAMPLE 69   A class has 10 boys and 2 girls. If 3 students are selected at random, what is the probability that all will be boys?

Solution   The probability that the first student selected is a boy is $\frac{10}{12}$ since there are 10 boys in the class of students. If the first student selected is a boy, the probability that the second student selected is a boy is $\frac{9}{11}$ since there are 9 boys left out of 11 students. Likewise, the probability that the third student selected is a boy is $\frac{8}{10}$ since there are 8 boys left out of 10 students. Thus, by the preceding multiplication theorem,

$$P(\text{all boys}) = \tfrac{10}{12} \cdot \tfrac{9}{11} \cdot \tfrac{8}{10} = \tfrac{6}{11}$$

EXAMPLE 70   Suppose that, in a shipment of 100 items, 4 are defective. Items from the shipment are drawn one at a time and tested. The testing will continue until 2 defective items are discovered. What is the probability that 2 defective items will be discovered on or before the third draw?

Solution Figure 5.28, which demonstrates the paths leading to exactly 2 defective items, stops with the third draw. Note that the paths also stop when 2 defective items are discovered. The probability that 2 defective items may be found on or before the third draw is

$$P(G) \cdot P(D|G) \cdot P(D|G \cap D) + P(D) \cdot P(D|D) + P(D) \cdot P(G|D) \cdot P(D|D \cap G)$$

$$= \tfrac{96}{100} \cdot \tfrac{4}{99} \cdot \tfrac{3}{98} + \tfrac{4}{100} \cdot \tfrac{3}{99} + \tfrac{4}{100} \cdot \tfrac{96}{99} \cdot \tfrac{3}{98} = \tfrac{29}{8085}$$

Figure 5.28

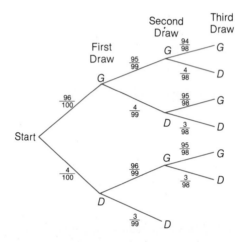

EXAMPLE 71 Three machines, A, B, and C, produce 50%, 25%, and 25%, respectively, of all the items produced in a given area of a factory. It has been found that defective items make up about 5% of the items produced from machine A, 3% of those from machine B, and 1% from machine C. If an item is selected out of a day's production from the three machines, what is the probability that it is defective?

Solution A defective item can be produced in three mutually exclusive, exhaustive paths: through machine A, B, or C. The probability that an item is produced by machine A and is defective is .50(.05) = .0250. In like manner, for machine B this probability is .25(.03) = .0075, and for machine C it is .25(.01) = .0025. Therefore,

$$P(\text{article is defective}) = .025 + .0075 + .0025 = .035$$

EXAMPLE 72 According to the genetic theories of Mendel, a parent with genes of type AA can transmit only an A gene to offspring. A parent with type aa can transmit only an a gene. However, a parent of type Aa can transmit either an A or an a gene, each with probability $\tfrac{1}{2}$. For each of the following mates, find the probability of the offspring being

    a. type AA
    b. type aa
    c. type Aa

(1) AA mates with AA; (2) aa mates with aa; and (3) Aa mates with Aa.

(1) *AA* mates with *AA*:

      a. $P(AA) = 1$
      b. $P(aa) = 0$
      c. $P(Aa) = 0$

(2) *aa* mates with *aa*:

      a. $P(AA) = 0$
      b. $P(aa) = 1$
      c. $P(Aa) = 0$

(3) *Aa* mates with *Aa*:

      a. To be of type *AA*, the offspring must inherit an *A* gene from each parent. It is assumed that the genes are inherited independently.

$$P(AA) = \tfrac{1}{2} \cdot \tfrac{1}{2} = \tfrac{1}{4}$$

      b. Similarly,

$$P(aa) = \tfrac{1}{2} \cdot \tfrac{1}{2} = \tfrac{1}{4}$$

      c. To be of type *Aa*, the offspring can inherit an *A* gene from one parent and an *a* gene from the other, and vice versa. Thus,

$$
\begin{aligned}
P(Aa) &= P(A) \cdot P(a) + P(a) \cdot P(A) \\
&= \tfrac{1}{2} \cdot \tfrac{1}{2} + \tfrac{1}{2} \cdot \tfrac{1}{2} \\
&= \tfrac{1}{2}
\end{aligned}
$$

If $P(A|B) = P(A)$, it indicates that knowing that B has occurred does not yield any additional information about the occurrence or nonoccurrence of A. If $P(A|B) = P(A)$, we say event A is **independent** of event B. In this instance $P(A \cap B) = P(B) \cdot P(A|B) = P(B) \cdot P(A)$. Thus, in this very special case the probability of the intersection of the events is equal to the product of the probabilities of the events. We can use the relationship $P(A \cap B) = P(A) \cdot P(B)$ in situations in which two events are performed and it is clear that what happens on the first trial has no influence on what occurs on the second trial.

Independent Events

> If two events, A and B, are **independent,** then
>
> $$P(A \cap B) = P(A) \cdot P(B)$$

EXAMPLE 73 A card is drawn from a deck of cards. Then the card is replaced, the deck is reshuffled, and a second card is drawn. What is the probability of an ace on the first draw and a king on the second?

Solution $P(A_1 \cap K_2) = P(A_1) \cdot P(K_2|A_1)$. However, knowing that an ace is drawn on the first draw yields no information about what occurs on the second draw since the first card is replaced and the deck is reshuffled. Hence, $P(K_2|A_1) = P(K_2)$.

$$P(A_1 \cap K_2) = P(A_1) \cdot P(K_2)$$
$$= \left(\tfrac{4}{52}\right) \cdot \left(\tfrac{4}{52}\right)$$
$$\approx .0059$$

EXAMPLE 74   A basket contains two red balls and two white balls. A ball is drawn, inspected, and returned to the box. Then a second ball is randomly drawn. What is the probability of drawing two red balls?

Solution   Let R_1 represent getting a red ball on the first draw and R_2 represent getting a red ball on the second draw. Since the ball was returned after the first draw, R_1 and R_2 are independent events.

$$P(R_1 \cap R_2) = P(R_1) \cdot P(R_2) = \tfrac{2}{4} \cdot \tfrac{2}{4} = \tfrac{1}{4}$$

The theorem on the probability of the occurrence of two independent events can be extended as follows:

$$P(A_1 \cap A_2 \cap A_3 \cap \cdots \cap A_k) = P(A_1) \cdot P(A_2) \cdot P(A_3) \cdots \cdot P(A_k)$$

where $A_1, A_2, A_3, \ldots, A_k$ are independent.

EXAMPLE 75   A box contains eight red balls and two black balls. If we randomly draw one ball at a time and return the ball before the next draw, what is the probability of drawing four red balls?

Solution   Since the event of drawing a red ball in each of the four draws is independent of the other draws,

$$P(R_1 \cap R_2 \cap R_3 \cap R_4) = P(R_1) \cdot P(R_2) \cdot P(R_3) \cdot P(R_4)$$
$$= \tfrac{4}{5} \cdot \tfrac{4}{5} \cdot \tfrac{4}{5} \cdot \tfrac{4}{5} = \tfrac{256}{625}$$

Exercise Set 5.7

A   **1.** A new low-flying missile has a probability of .9 of penetrating the enemy defenses and a probability of .7 of hitting the target if it penetrates the defenses. What is the probability that the missile will penetrate the defenses and hit the target?

2. A card is drawn from a standard deck of cards. What is the probability that it is a jack, given that it is a face card (that is, a king, queen, or jack)?

3. From an urn containing five red balls and three white balls, two balls are drawn successively at random without replacement. What is the probability that the first is white and the second is red?

4. Two dice are tossed. What is the probability that the first die shows a 3 and the second die an even number? What is the probability that one die shows a 3 and the other die shows an even number?

5. Two dice are rolled one after the other. What is the probability that the first die shows an even number and the second die shows an odd number?

6. Assume that two cards are drawn from a standard deck of playing cards. What is the probability that a king is drawn, followed by an ace

a. if the first card is replaced before the second is drawn?

b. if the first card is not replaced before the second is drawn?

7. A box contains three red balls and four white balls. What is the probability of drawing two white balls

a. if the first is replaced before the second one is drawn?

b. if the first ball is not replaced?

8. Box A contains three red chips and four black chips. Box B contains five red chips and two black chips. A chip is drawn from box A and placed in box B, and then a chip is drawn from box B. What is the probability that the chip is black?

9. Box A contains six cards numbered 1 through 6, and box B contains four cards numbered 1 through 4. A card is drawn from box A. If it is even, a card is then drawn from box B; if it is odd, a second card is drawn from box A. What is the probability that

a. both cards are odd?

b. both cards are even?

c. one card is odd and the other is even?

10. A box contains two coins, one of which has two tails. A coin is selected at random and tossed. What is the probability of getting a tail?

11. In exercise 10 if a head occurs on the first toss, the second coin is tossed. If a tail occurs on the first toss, the same coin is tossed. What is the probability of getting a tail on the second throw?

B **12.** Two coins are tossed. Find the probability of the following events by using a tree diagram.

a. Both coins show a head.

b. The first coin shows a head, and the second coin shows a tail.

c. The first coin shows a tail, or both coins show tails.

d. One coin shows a head, or both coins show tails.

e. One coin shows a tail, or the coins fall alike.

f. At least one coin shows a head, or the coins fall differently.

13. If it rains within one week of planting, there is a .95 chance that a certain kind of lettuce seed will germinate. If there is a .70 chance of rain in the next week, what is the probability of both rain and germination?

14. A candy jar contains 6 pieces of peppermint, 4 pieces of chocolate, and 12 pieces of butterscotch candy. A small boy reaches into the jar, snatches a piece, and eats it rapidly. He repeats this act quickly.

a. What is the probability that he eats a peppermint and then a chocolate?

b. What is the probability that he eats 2 chocolates?

c. What is the probability that he eats a chocolate and then a butterscotch?

d. What is the probability that he eats a chocolate and a butterscotch?

15. Suppose that the small boy of exercise 14 is caught by his mother immediately after he snatches his first piece. She makes him return the candy to the jar. He waits an appropriate length of time and then again snatches a piece.

a. What is the probability that the frustrated thief snatches a peppermint, then a chocolate?

b. What is the probability that he gets chocolate on both tries?

16. Slips of paper marked with digits 1, 2, 3, 4, and 5 are placed in a box, and two slips are drawn without replacement. Set up two different procedures for finding the probability that one is odd and the other is a 4.

17. Complete one of the procedures in exercise 16 to get an answer.

18. Four executives of a company decide independently whether or not to diversify the company. It is known that two are definitely in favor of diversification, but three votes are required for a decision. What is the probability that the company will be diversified if $P = \frac{1}{2}$ for each executive not definitely in favor?

19. Two cards are drawn from a standard deck of cards. What is the probability of getting an 8 and 9 in any order?

C **20.** Urn A contains five red and three white marbles; urn B contains three red and two white marbles; and urn C contains two red and one white marble. Two coins are tossed. If two heads appear, a marble is drawn from urn A; if one head appears, a marble is drawn from urn B; and if no heads appear, a marble is drawn from urn C. One marble is drawn by this process. What is the probability that it is red?

21. Professor Ab Stract gives hard tests but allows students to take them as many times as they wish. On the average the probability of passing one of his tests on the first try is .40, on the second try .60, and on the third try .80. What is the probability that a student will
   a. fail all three?
   b. pass if Professor Ab Stract gives the test only three times?
   c. require at least two times to pass the test if it is given three times?

Business **22.** **Employment Risks.** At CBF Enterprises, 60% of the workers are men. From a personnel study it is found that 11% of the men and 8% of the women are "employment risks" because of health problems or excessive use of alcohol and drugs. What percent of the employees of this company are employment risks?

23. **Unions.** An election to accept or reject a union is held for all the employees of the Harrison Corporation. Of the employees, 30% are salaried, 35% are clerical workers, and 35% are laborers paid on an hourly basis. In the election 80% of the salaried employees, 20% of the clerical workers, and 5% of the laborers vote to reject the union. What is the probability that the union is rejected?

24. **Sales.** A salesman is known to make a sale in 60% of his calls. What is the probability that he will not make a sale in the next three calls? (Assume that each call is independent of the other calls.)

Economics **25.** **Quality Control.** A machine is assembled using components A and B. The two components are each built in separate fabricating plants. Experience indicates that the probability that A is defective is .01, and the probability that B is defective is .05. (*Hint:* Since A and B are fabricated in different plants, whether A is good or defective is independent of the quality of B.)
   a. What is the probability that both components are defective?
   b. What is the probability that both components are good?

26. **Quality Control.** A manufacturer receives a shipment of 20 articles. Unknown to him, 6 are defective. He selects 2 articles at random and inspects them. What is the probability that the first is defective and the second is satisfactory?

27. **Quality Control.** In exercise 26, what is the probability that one is defective and the other satisfactory?

28. **Quality Control.** Three machines, A, B, and C, produce 60%, 30%, and 10%, respectively, of all the items produced in a section of a factory. It has been determined that 6% of the items produced by machine A are defective, 4% from machine B are defective, and 2% from machine C are defective. If an item is selected out of a day's production from the three machines, what is the probability that it is defective?

29. Quality Control. Out of 10 radio tubes, 3 are defective. The tubes are tested until 2 defective tubes are discovered. What is the probability that the process stops on
a. the second test?   **b.** the third test?   **c.** the fourth test?

Life Sciences **30. Medicine.** The probability that a blood test will show a disease if it exists is .96. The probability that the blood test will indicate the disease if it does not exist is .02. It is believed that 5% of the adults in a small city have this disease. If blood tests are made on a random selection of adults in this city, what is the expected percentage of adults with this disease?

31. Medicine. The probability that a healthy person has a temperature .5 degree above normal is .10. The probability that a sick person has a temperature .5 degree above normal is .80. Of any randomly selected sample of people, 90% are healthy. What is the probability that a randomly selected individual has a temperature .5 degree above normal?

32. Genes. An animal with BB genes is crossed with one with Bb genes. Suppose there is a litter of four. What is the probability that
a. all will be Bb?
b. two will be BB and two Bb?
c. all will be BB?

33. Genes. Do exercise 32 for both animals having Bb genes.

34. Family Composition. Consider a family with three children. Assume for each child that the probability that the child is a boy equals the probability that it is a girl. Use a tree diagram to find the probability that
a. the youngest child is a girl.
b. the two youngest children are girls.
c. the two youngest children are of opposite sex.
d. all three children are the same sex.
e. the first two children are girls and the third is a boy.
f. the first two are boys and the third is a girl.
g. two are girls or all are the same sex.
h. two are girls or the youngest is a girl.
i. all are girls or the youngest is a boy.
j. all are the same sex or the youngest is a girl.

35. Mortality. The probability that John will live at least 20 more years is $\frac{1}{3}$, and the probability that Maria will live at least 20 more years is $\frac{1}{4}$. Find the probability that
a. both will live at least 20 more years.
b. at least one will live at least 20 more years.
c. only John will live at least 20 more years.
d. neither will live at least 20 more years.

Social Sciences **36. Voting.** In a certain community 55% of those registered to vote are registered as Democrats and 45% are registered as Republicans. It is believed that 60% of the Democrats favor the new tax to be voted on, and 30% of the Republicans favor the tax. If all registered voters vote, what is the probability that the tax will pass?

37. Vandalism. In one neighborhood, one of every two cars parked on the streets is vandalized. In an adjacent neighborhood in the same city, one of every three cars parked on the streets is vandalized. A visitor to the city randomly parks her car on the street in one of the two neighborhoods. What is the probability that the car will be vandalized?

38. Government. A five-member city council is voting on the establishment of an inner-city trade school. Two members are definitely for the establishment of the school; the other three are indifferent and will vote randomly. A majority is required. What is the probability that the school will be established?

In this section we are given conditional probabilities in one direction, and we need to find conditional probabilities in the opposite direction. That is, $P(A|B)$ may be given or computed, when the objective is to find $P(B|A)$. Typical problems involve looking at the outcome of an experiment and then asking for the probability that the outcome was due to a particular cause. Such problems are usually solved by using **Bayes' Formula** (introduced in this section). We introduce the problem with two boxes, B_1 and B_2, each containing some red balls and some white balls. Suppose the probabilities of selecting box B_1 and box B_2 are given. A ball is randomly selected. If it is red, what is the probability it came from box B_1?

To solve the problem proposed in the introduction, let's consider the following example. Colored balls are distributed in two boxes as follows. The first box contains three red balls and one white ball, while the second box contains two white balls and one red ball. A box is selected in such a manner that the probability of selecting B_1 is $\frac{2}{3}$ and the probability of selecting B_2 is $\frac{1}{3}$. Figure 5.29 summarizes these facts.

Figure 5.29

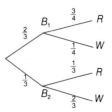

In the previous section we learned that

$$P(R \cap B_1) = P(R) \cdot P(B_1|R)$$

or

$$P(B_1|R) = \frac{P(R \cap B_1)}{P(R)}$$

From Figure 5.29 it is easily seen that

$$P(R \cap B_1) = \frac{2}{3} \cdot \frac{3}{4} = \frac{1}{2}$$
$$P(R) = \frac{2}{3} \cdot \frac{3}{4} + \frac{1}{3} \cdot \frac{1}{3} = \frac{11}{18}$$

Therefore,

$$P(B_1|R) = \frac{\frac{1}{2}}{\frac{11}{18}} = \frac{9}{11}$$

Now let's consider the same problem without a specific number of red and white balls and without specific probabilities for drawing each box. The corresponding tree diagram is seen in Figure 5.30.

Figure 5.30

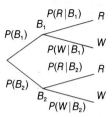

The formula for finding the probability that if a red ball is drawn it came from box B_1 can be formulated in the following manner. First note that in Figure 5.30 $P(R) = P(B_1)P(R|B_1) + P(B_2)P(R|B_2)$. Also,

$$P(R \cap B_1) = P(R) \cdot P(B_1|R) \quad \text{or} \quad P(R \cap B_1) = P(B_1) \cdot P(R|B_1)$$

$$P(B_1|R) = \frac{P(R \cap B_1)}{P(R)}$$

$$= \frac{P(R \cap B_1)}{P(B_1) \cdot P(R|B_1) + P(B_2) \cdot P(R|B_2)}$$

$$= \frac{P(B_1) \cdot P(R|B_1)}{P(B_1) \cdot P(R|B_1) + P(B_2) \cdot P(R|B_2)}$$

In a similar manner,

$$P(B_2|R) = \frac{P(B_2) \cdot P(R|B_2)}{P(B_1) \cdot P(R|B_1) + P(B_2) \cdot P(R|B_2)}$$

We now use these formulas to compute again the probability that, if a red ball is drawn in the preceding example, it is drawn from the first box. It is given or can be easily reasoned that

$P(R|B_1) = \frac{3}{4}$ (probability of drawing a red ball from box 1)

$P(R|B_2) = \frac{1}{3}$ (probability of drawing a red ball from box 2)

$P(B_1) = \frac{2}{3}$ (probability of selecting box 1)

$P(B_2) = \frac{1}{3}$ (probability of selecting box 2)

Thus,

$$P(B_1|R) = \frac{P(B_1) \cdot P(R|B_1)}{P(B_1) \cdot P(R|B_1) + P(B_2) \cdot P(R|B_2)}$$

$$= \frac{\frac{2}{3} \cdot \frac{3}{4}}{\frac{2}{3} \cdot \frac{3}{4} + \frac{1}{3} \cdot \frac{1}{3}} = \frac{9}{11}$$

This interpretation can be extended to three boxes containing red and white balls:

$$P(B_1|R) = \frac{P(B_1) \cdot P(R|B_1)}{P(B_1) \cdot P(R|B_1) + P(B_2) \cdot P(R|B_2) + P(B_3) \cdot P(R|B_3)}$$

Likewise,

$$P(B_2|R) = \frac{P(B_2) \cdot P(R|B_2)}{P(B_1) \cdot P(R|B_1) + P(B_2) \cdot P(R|B_2) + P(B_3) \cdot P(R|B_3)}$$

and

$$P(B_3|R) = \frac{P(B_3) \cdot P(R|B_3)}{P(B_1) \cdot P(R|B_1) + P(B_2) \cdot P(R|B_2) + P(B_3) \cdot P(R|B_3)}$$

In general we have the following formula:

Bayes' Formula

Let B_i $(i = 1, 2, \ldots, n)$ with probabilities $P(B_i)$ be a finite set of disjoint events whose union is the sample space. Let A be an event that has occurred when the experiment was performed, where A is a subset of the union of the B_i. Then

$$P(B_i|A) = \frac{P(B_i) \cdot P(A|B_i)}{P(B_1) \cdot P(A|B_1) + P(B_2) \cdot P(A|B_2) + \cdots + P(B_n) \cdot P(A|B_n)}$$

EXAMPLE 76 Suppose

$$P(A|B) = \tfrac{1}{2} \qquad P(A|C) = \tfrac{2}{5} \qquad P(A|D) = \tfrac{2}{3}$$

and

$$P(B) = \tfrac{1}{4} \qquad P(C) = \tfrac{5}{8} \qquad P(D) = \tfrac{1}{8}$$

Then

$$P(C|A) = \frac{P(C) \cdot P(A|C)}{P(B) \cdot P(A|B) + P(C) \cdot P(A|C) + P(D) \cdot P(D|C)}$$

$$= \frac{\tfrac{5}{8} \cdot \tfrac{2}{5}}{\tfrac{1}{4} \cdot \tfrac{1}{2} + \tfrac{5}{8} \cdot \tfrac{2}{5} + \tfrac{1}{8} \cdot \tfrac{2}{3}} = \frac{6}{11}$$

EXAMPLE 77 A business executive is allowed to make one of three choices for a decision. After a study of the choices, she figures the probability of making these choices could be approximated by .3, .3, and .4, respectively. It is known that the probability of a profit after each decision is .6, .3, and .2, respectively. A profit was realized after the decision was made. What is the probability that the business executive selected the third decision?

Solution Let D_i $(i = 1, 2, 3)$ represent the three possible decisions and E represent the profit. Then

$$P(D_3|E) = \frac{P(D_3) \cdot P(E|D_3)}{P(D_1) \cdot P(E|D_1) + P(D_2) \cdot P(E|D_2) + P(D_3) \cdot P(E|D_3)}$$

as shown in Figure 5.31.

$$P(D_3|E) = \frac{.4(.2)}{.3(.6) + .3(.3) + .4(.2)} = \frac{8}{35}$$

Figure 5.31

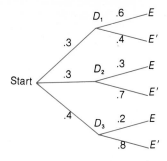

EXAMPLE 78 All employees of the XYZ Corporation are required to complete a human relations course and take a test. At the end of the next 6 months, 80% of the employees are classified as satisfactory. It was found that 90% of those classified as satisfactory had passed the test and only 40% of those classified as unsatisfactory had passed the test. The company now wants to know the probability that an employee who has taken and passed the test will be a satisfactory employee. And, if an employee fails the test, what is the probability that this person will be a satisfactory employee?

Solution We want to find the probability that an employee, after taking and passing the personality test (P), will be a satisfactory employee (S); that is, we want to find $P(S|P)$. Now

$$P(S|P) = \frac{P(S) \cdot P(P|S)}{P(S) \cdot P(P|S) + P(U) \cdot P(P|U)}$$

$$= \frac{(.80)(.90)}{(.80)(.90) + (.20)(.40)}$$

$$= .90$$

So the probability that an employee who has passed the test will be a satisfactory employee is .90. Likewise, the probability that one who has failed the test will be satisfactory is

$$P(S|F) = \frac{P(S) \cdot P(F|S)}{P(S) \cdot P(F|S) + P(U) \cdot P(F|U)}$$

$$= \frac{(.80)(.10)}{(.80)(.10) + (.20)(.60)}$$

$$= .40$$

EXAMPLE 79 Of the people in a given area, 10% are known to have some kind of cancer. A new method of detecting cancer is developed that gives a positive result 95% of the time when a person has cancer and gives a positive result 10% of the time when a person does not have cancer. John Weaklin's test is positive. What is the probability that John has cancer?

$$P(\text{test positive}|\text{person with cancer}) = P(T|C) = .95$$
$$P(\text{test positive}|\text{person without cancer}) = P(T|C') = .10$$
$$P(\text{person has cancer}) = P(C) = .10$$
$$P(\text{person does not have cancer}) = P(C') = .90$$

$$P(\text{person has cancer}|\text{test positive}) = \frac{P(C) \cdot P(T|C)}{P(C) \cdot P(T|C) + P(C') \cdot P(T|C')}$$

$$= \frac{(.10)(.95)}{(.10)(.95) + (.90)(.10)}$$

$$= .51$$

EXAMPLE 80 The teacher of a college history course estimates that an average student who has read the textbook has an 80% chance of answering a quiz question correctly. An average student who has not read the textbook has a 30% chance of answering this question correctly. If we assume it is equally likely that a student will or will not read the textbook, what is the probability that a student has read the textbook if he or she answers this quiz question correctly?

Solution

$$P(A|R) = .80 \text{ (the probability of answering correctly, } A, \text{ after having read the textbook, } R)$$

$$P(A|R') = .30 \text{ (the probability of answering correctly, } A, \text{ when the textbook has not been read, } R')$$

We wish to compute

$$P(R|A) = \frac{P(R) \cdot (A|R)}{P(R) \cdot P(A|R) + P(R') \cdot P(A|R')}$$

Since $P(R) = P(R')$,

$$P(R|A) = \frac{P(A|R)}{P(A|R) + P(A|R')} = \frac{.80}{.80 + .30} = \frac{8}{11} = .73$$

In Bayes' Formula, if the events of getting a $B_1, B_2, \ldots, B_n$ are equally likely, then

$$P(B_1) = P(B_2) = \cdots = P(B_n) = P$$

P will divide from the numerator and denominator, giving the following:

If it is known or can be assumed that the events $B_1, B_2, \ldots, B_n$ are equally likely—that is, that

$$P(B_1) = P(B_2) = \cdots = P(B_n)$$

then

$$P(B_i|A) = \frac{P(A|B_i)}{P(A|B_1) + P(A|B_2) + \cdots + P(A|B_n)}$$

EXAMPLE 81 Consider the two boxes of colored balls discussed in the first example of this section. Consider the case where we do not know the various probabilities of selecting a box. In this case we will assume that the events of selecting the boxes are equally likely. Now find the probability that, if a red ball is drawn, it is drawn from the first box.

Solution

$$P(B_1 | R) = \frac{P(R|B_1)}{P(R|B_1) + P(R|B_2)}$$

$$= \frac{\frac{3}{4}}{\frac{3}{4} + \frac{1}{3}} = \frac{9}{13}$$

Exercise Set 5.8

A   **1.** Find the following probabilities by referring to the given tree diagram.

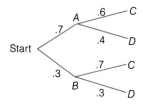

a. $P(C|A)$ **b.** $P(C|B)$ **c.** $P(D|A)$
d. $P(A \cap C)$ **e.** $P(A \cap D)$ **f.** $P(B \cap C)$
g. $P(C) = P(A \cap C) + P(B \cap C) = P(A) \cdot P(C|A) + P(B) \cdot P(C|B)$
h. $P(A|C) = \dfrac{P(A \cap C)}{P(C)} = \dfrac{P(A) \cdot P(C|A)}{P(A) \cdot P(C|A) + P(B) \cdot P(C|B)}$

2. Use the following tree diagram and Bayes' Formula to find each probability.

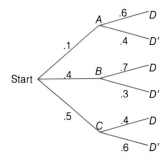

a. $P(A|D)$ **b.** $P(B|D')$ **c.** $P(C|D)$

3. Given that $P(A|B_1) = \frac{1}{4}$, $P(A|B_2) = \frac{1}{3}$, and $P(A|B_3) = \frac{2}{3}$, find $P(B_1|A)$, $P(B_2|A)$, and $P(B_3|A)$ under each of the following sets of conditions.
   a. $P(B_1) = P(B_2) = P(B_3) = \frac{1}{3}$
   b. $P(B_1) = \frac{1}{4}$, $P(B_2) = \frac{1}{3}$, $P(B_3) = \frac{5}{12}$
   c. $P(B_1) = \frac{1}{5}$, $P(B_2) = \frac{2}{5}$, $P(B_3) = \frac{2}{5}$
   d. $P(B_1) = P(B_2) = \frac{1}{5}$, $P(B_3) = \frac{3}{5}$

4. Box I contains six red and four white balls, and box II contains five red, three white, and two green balls. An experiment consists of selecting a box (equally likely) and then randomly drawing a ball from the box selected.
   a. Find the probability of getting a red ball.
   b. Find the probability of getting a white ball.
   c. Find the probability of getting a green ball.
   d. If a red ball is drawn, find the probability that it came from box I.
   e. If a white ball is drawn, find the probability that it came from box I.
   f. If a green ball is drawn, find the probability that it came from box I.

5. Use exercise 4 to find the following.
   a. If a red ball is drawn, find the probability that it came from box II.
   b. If a white ball is drawn, find the probability that it came from box II.
   c. If a green ball is drawn, find the probability that it came from box II.

B

6. An urn contains three coins; two of them are fair, and the other has heads on both sides. A coin is selected at random and tossed twice, coming up heads both times. What is the probability that the coin selected has two heads?

7. Box A contains three red and five black chips, box B has two red and three black chips, and box C has one red and two black chips. A box is selected at random and a chip is drawn. If the chip is red, what is the probability that it came from box B?

Business

8. **Salaries.** Of the employees of the JNT Corporation, 5% of the men and 7% of the women have salaries in excess of $10,000. Furthermore, 60% of the employees are men. If an employee who is selected at random earns more than $10,000, what is the probability that the employee is a man?

9. **Unions.** A proposal to accept or reject a union is submitted to all employees of the RJW Corporation. Of the employees, 30% are laborers, 35% are white-collar workers, and 35% are blue-collar workers. In the response, 80% of the laborers, 15% of the white-collar workers, and 5% of the blue-collar workers vote to reject the union. What is the probability that a person selected at random who has voted against the union is
   a. a laborer?   b. a blue-collar worker?

10. **Unions.** Sixty percent of the workers at the CFB plant are men. Seventy-five percent of the men and fifty percent of the women belong to a union. A union card is found. What is the probability that it belongs to a woman? A man?

11. **Marketing.** A given area is divided into submarkets according to the percentage of prospective customers: area I is 30%; area II, 45%; and area III, 25%. From a sampling of the customers it is found in area I that 23% favor a given detergent. In area II 20% favor the detergent, and in area III, 16%. If a customer is selected at random and favors the detergent, what is the probability that the customer came from area I? Area III?

Economics

12. **Quality Control.** A dealer reports a major defect in a TV set. The set could have been manufactured at any one of three plants, A, B, or C. For the week in which the given set was manufactured, plant A made 30% of the sets, B made 45%, and C, 25%. During this week quality control located 2% defects at A, 3% defects at B, and 5% defects at C. What is the probability that the TV set came from C? From A?

13. Stock Trends. Three proposed economic theories about the future have probabilities of .2, .5, and .3 of occurring. If the first economic situation occurs, the probability that the common stock of the Investors Corporation will increase by 5 points is .6; if the second economic theory occurs, the probability of the increase is .7; and if the third theory occurs, the probability is .8. During the next year the common stock of the Investors Corporation does increase by 5 points. What is the probability that the first economic theory has occurred?

Life Sciences

14. Medicine. The probability that a person has disease D is $P(D) = .1$. The probability that a medical examination will indicate the disease if a person has the disease is $P(I|D) = .8$, and the probability that the examination will indicate the disease if a person does not have it is $P(I|D') = .02$. What is the probability that Patty has the disease if the medical examination indicates that she has the disease?

Social Sciences

15. Lie Detection. Suppose that a lie-detector test is 90% accurate for guilty people and 95% accurate for innocent people. If T stands for the test indicating guilt, G stands for a person being guilty, and I stands for a person being innocent, $P(T|G) = .90$ and $P(T'|I) = .05$, or $P(T|I) = .95$. One of five people in an office is guilty of stealing money. A person is selected and given the lie-detector test.
a. If the test indicates he is guilty, what is the probability that he is guilty?
b. If the test indicates he is guilty, what is the probability that he is innocent?

Summary and Review

Review to ensure that you understand the following terms as applied to probability:

Experiment	Bayes' Formula
Outcome	Probability of an event
Sample space	A priori probability
Relative frequency interpretation of probability	$A \cup B$ (A or B)
	$A \cap B$ (A and B)
Probability rule on a sample space	Complement
Uniform sample space	Mutually exclusive events
Event	Conditional probability
Simple event	Dependent events
Compound event	Independent events

Review the following concepts used in counting:

Tree diagrams	Permutations of n things taken
Fundamental Principle of Counting	r at a time
Permutations	Combinations of n things taken
Combinations	r at a time

Success in solving probability problems depends on the ability to use the correct formula. Do you know the conditions that allow you to use each of the following formulas?

$$P(A) = \frac{\text{number of times } A \text{ occurs}}{N}$$

$$0 \le P(A) \le 1$$

$$P(A) = \frac{1}{n(S)}$$

$$P(A) = \frac{n(A)}{n(S)}$$

$$n! = n(n-1)(n-2) \cdot \cdots \cdot 3 \cdot 2 \cdot 1$$

$$P(n, r) = \frac{n!}{(n-r)!}$$

$$P(n, n) = n!$$

$$C(n, r) = \frac{n!}{r!(n-r)!}$$

$$P = \frac{n!}{n_1! n_2! \cdot \cdots \cdot n_k!}$$

$$P(A \cup B) = P(A) + P(B)$$
$$P(A \cup B) = P(A) + P(B) - P(A \cap B)$$
$$P(A \cup B \cup C)$$
$$= P(A) + P(B) + P(C)$$
$$- P(A \cap B) - P(A \cap C)$$
$$- P(B \cap C) + P(A \cap B \cap C)$$
$$P(A') = 1 - P(A)$$

$$P(A \mid B) = \frac{P(A \cap B)}{P(B)}$$

$$P(A \cap B) = P(A) \cdot P(B \mid A)$$
$$P(A \cap B) = P(B) \cdot P(A \mid B)$$
$$P(A \cap B) = P(A) \cdot P(B)$$

$$P(B_i \mid A) = \frac{P(B_i) \cdot (A \mid B_i)}{P(B_1) \cdot P(A \mid B_1) + P(B_2) \cdot P(A \mid B_2) + \cdots + P(B_n) \cdot P(A \mid B_n)}$$

Review Exercise Set **5.9**

A   1. In a certain town, 40% of the families have incomes exceeding $25,000 a year, 30% of the families have two or more automobiles, and 15% have both two or more automobiles and incomes exceeding $25,000 a year. A family is selected at random from this town.
     a. What is the probability that a family has an income exceeding $25,000 a year or has two or more automobiles?
     b. What is the probability that a family has neither two or more automobiles nor an income exceeding $25,000 a year?

   2. A bag contains six red balls, four black balls, and three green balls. Tabulate a sample space for the following experiments.
     a. A single ball is drawn (a sample space with three outcomes).
     b. A single ball is drawn (a uniform sample space).
     c. A ball is drawn and pocketed. A second ball is drawn. (A tree diagram might be helpful.)
     d. A ball is drawn, its color is recorded, and it is replaced. A second ball is drawn. (Try a tree diagram.)
     e. A ball is drawn and pocketed; a second ball is drawn and pocketed; a third ball is drawn and pocketed. (Try a tree diagram.)

   3. A ball is drawn from the bag in exercise 2. What is the probability that it is
     a. red or black?   **b.** blue?
     c. red or black or green?   **d.** not red and not green?

e. not black?　　　　　**f.** green?

g. not red or not black?　　**h.** red and black?

i. not red or not green?　　**j.** not green?

4. A ball is drawn from the bag in exercise 2, its color is recorded, and the ball is replaced. A second ball is drawn. What is the probability of
   a. two red balls?
   b. a red ball followed by a green ball?
   c. two black balls?

5. At the Fresh Air Farm Charity Bazaar, one booth sells 60 identically wrapped surprise packages, where 8 of the packages contain tape players, 12 contain electric razors, 16 contain rubber galoshes, and 24 contain a box of Kleenex.
   a. What is the probability of getting a tape player or an electric razor?
   b. What is the probability of getting something other than the Kleenex?

6. Suppose $P(A) = .35$, $P(B) = .51$, and $P(A \cap B) = .17$. Compute
   a. $P(A')$　　**b.** $P(A \cup B)$

7. Find the probability of drawing a king from a deck of cards if you know that the card drawn is a face card.

8. An experiment involves two urns. Urn A contains four red chips and three black chips, urn B contains five red and two black chips. One of the urns is selected at random, and a chip is drawn. Suppose we know only that a red chip was drawn. What is the probability that it was drawn from urn A?

9. A die is tossed three times. If the throws are assumed to be independent, what is the probability that, on the first throw, the die will show an even number; on the second throw, a number divisible by 3; and on the third throw, a 1?

10. Suppose sample space S has four outcomes, $\{a_1, a_2, a_3, a_4\}$. Suppose that the probabilities of these outcomes are

$$P(a_1) = .6 \qquad P(a_2) = .2 \qquad P(a_3) = .1 \qquad P(a_4) = .1$$

   a. What is the probability of event $E = \{a_1, a_3\}$?
   b. What is the probability of event $F = \{a_1, a_2\}$?
   c. What is the probability of $E \cap F$?
   d. What is the probability of $E \cup F$?

B 11. Use a tree diagram to list the sample space showing the possible arrangements when three coins are tossed.
   a. Find the probability that all three coins show heads.
   b. Find the probability that at least one coin shows a head.
   c. Find the probability that no coins show heads.

12. **a.** What is the probability of drawing four hearts from an ordinary deck of cards?
   b. What is the probability of drawing the ace, king, queen, and jack, where all are hearts?
   c. What is the probability of drawing any four cards of the same suit?

13. A hand of five cards is dealt from a standard deck. Which of the following pairs of events are mutually exclusive? If a pair of events is not mutually exclusive, list at least one outcome they have in common.
   a. {exactly two aces}, {exactly three aces}
   b. {at least two aces}, {at least two red cards}
   c. {at least three aces}, {at least three tens}
   d. {five red cards}, {exactly three diamonds}
   e. {exactly two 2s}, {exactly two 4s}

C **14.** Marna holds 4 tickets for a raffle in which three clock radios are offered as prizes. If 200 tickets are sold and three winners drawn, what is the probability that Marna will have at least one clock radio?

15. Box 1 contains 10 chips with 5 marked A, 4 marked B, and 1 marked C. Box 2 contains 4 chips: 2 As, 1 B, and 1 C. Urn A contains 3 red balls and 2 black balls, urn B contains 2 red and 2 black balls, and urn C contains 1 red and 4 black balls. A coin is tossed. If the coin shows heads, a chip is drawn from box 1; if it shows tails, a chip is drawn from box 2. When a chip is drawn from either box, a ball is drawn from the urn denoted on the chip. The experiment is performed. What is the probability of getting a red ball?

16. Consider the experiment in exercise 15 with the following changes. If a black ball is drawn from urn A, it is placed in urn B, and a second ball is drawn from urn B. What is the probability of getting a red ball?

17. Consider the experiment in exercise 15 with the following changes. If a black ball is drawn from urn B (at the time the chip indicates drawing from urn B), it is placed in urn A and a second ball is drawn from urn A. What is the probability of getting a red ball?

18. If two cards are drawn without replacement from a deck of cards, what is the probability that
  a. both cards are red?
  b. the two cards are the king of spades and then the queen of hearts?
  c. both cards will be aces?

19. The letters f, o, u, and r are written on four cards and placed in a hat. They are drawn one at a time and arranged according to the order drawn.
  a. Count the number of possible arrangements (without tabulating them).
  b. Tabulate all possible arrangements of these letters.
  c. What is the probability that the arrangement drawn will have the two vowels adjacent to one another?

20. A 13-card bridge hand is drawn from a standard deck. What is the probability that it consists of
  a. all hearts?
  b. first 6 red cards and then 7 black cards?
  c. all face cards (jack, king, queen)?
  d. first 4 hearts, then 6 diamonds, and then 3 other cards?

21. In exercise 18 find the probability that one card is red and one is black.

22. Three men go duck hunting. One hunter usually makes four hits out of five shots; the second hunter, two hits out of three shots; and the third hunter, one hit out of two shots. All shoot simultaneously at the same duck. What is the probability that
  a. the duck is hit?   **b.** the duck is missed?
  c. the duck is hit exactly once?   **d.** all three hit the duck?

Business **23.** **Board of Directors.** The board of directors of a company consists of 6 women and 10 men. A committee of 3 is chosen at random from the board. What is the probability that
  a. exactly 3 men are selected?   **b.** at least 1 man is selected?
  c. exactly 2 women are selected?   **d.** exactly 2 men are selected?

24. **Management.** After finishing her course, a management trainee for a chain of shoe stores will be assigned to a store in Boston, New York, or Denver. The probability that she will be assigned to Denver is $\frac{1}{6}$, to New York is $\frac{1}{2}$, and to Boston is $\frac{1}{3}$.

a. What is the probability that she will be assigned to either Boston or Denver?

b. What is the probability that she will be assigned to the East Coast?

25. **Purchasing.** A store requests 3 models each week for 52 weeks. In no 2 consecutive weeks will the same 3 models be used. What is the minimum number of models necessary to fill this request?

Economics

26. **Quality Control.** A shipment contains 96 good items and 4 defective items. Three items are drawn, one at a time, from the shipment.

a. What is the probability of 3 defective items?

b. What is the probability of 2 good items and 1 defective item?

Life Sciences

27. **Vaccines.** A vaccine for measles protects 92% of those who take it. In Homewood 10% of the people have been vaccinated for measles. The probability that a person will get measles (without protection) any given year is .18. What is the probability that a randomly selected person in Homewood will have measles this year?

Social Sciences

28. **Voting.** From a study of voting patterns exhibited by the voters in a region comprising a number of counties in northern Florida, the following results were obtained.

		Age of Voter			
		Below 30	30–49	50–59	Above 59
Black	Democrat	180	160	150	170
	Republican	130	80	90	200
White	Democrat	250	210	180	230
	Republican	160	150	160	210

If a voter is chosen at random, what is the probability that the voter is

a. a white Republican?

b. a black voter below 30 years of age?

c. between 30 and 59 years of age, inclusive?

d. either a black Republican or a white Democrat?

e. either a black Democrat or in the age group 30–49?

f. black, a Republican, and in the age group 50–59?

29. **Anthropology.** An anthropologist notes in a region study that there are two large tribes, R and S, and three small tribes, u, v, and w. R and S are always hostile. Each of the small tribes, u, v, and w, may or may not form a military alliance with one large tribe. If a large tribe has an alliance with two or more small tribes, there is always war. Under any other circumstances, there is a feeling of a balance of power, and war is averted. If alliances are formed randomly, what is the probability of war?

CHAPTER **6**

Data Description and Probability Distributions

When Aunt Jane asserts that smoking is not harmful to one's health because Uncle Joe lived to be 88 years of age and smoked two packs of cigarettes every day of his adult life, Aunt Jane is using a probability or statistical idea. That is, Aunt Jane organized the data of her experience (Uncle Joe) and then made a statement on the basis of her data. However, she lacked understanding of what data were needed, how the data should be organized, and what conclusions were appropriate or inappropriate relative to the data. This chapter should help you avoid making the same types of mistakes that Aunt Jane made.

If people on the street were asked for their interpretations of statistics, they might answer "Statistics is a hodgepodge of numbers." Or they might comment that statistical statements are used in an attempt to "prove" a statement that may be only partly true. These reactions are normal. We have been bombarded with so many misuses of statistics that many people have doubts about the field; yet when we lack adequate information to defend our position, we often respond with a mumbo jumbo of statistical facts. These tactics would not be possible if everyone had an adequate knowledge of statistics.

Statistics can be divided into two subdivisions: *descriptive statistics* and *inferential statistics.* **Descriptive statistics** includes those techniques used to summarize and describe the main characteristics of a set of data. Most of the material in this chapter can be classified as descriptive statistics.

In **inferential statistics,** a small sample is selected from a large population. Then the information from the sample is used to draw inferences about the population. For the purposes of this discussion, **a population** is any predetermined set of elements or items upon which we make observations or measurements. Since most populations are too large for the examination of every element, we examine a part of the population, called a *sample*. A **sample** is a group of measurements, observations, or objects selected from a larger group called the population. In much of statistics, a sample is used in which each element of a population has equally likely probability of being in the sample. Such a sample is called a **random sample.**

This book is not devoted to statistics, so not all of your questions will be answered in this short chapter. In fact, we introduce only those statistical concepts that are needed to define two important probability distributions, the **normal distribution** and the **binomial distribution.** However, it is true that the concepts introduced are also statistical measures encountered in various education, sociology, psychology, and business models, and we show how these measures are used and interpreted. In addition, we use both the normal distribution and binomial distribution in different applications in order to develop an appreciation of these distributions.

1 Summarizing Data with Frequency Distributions

We are immersed daily in a torrent of numbers flowing in bubbling splendor from our televisions, our radios, our newspapers, our hair stylist, and our favorite Uncle Al. Although data are a part of our daily life-style, it is evident that we often do not know how to organize, interpret, or understand the message being conveyed. In this section we learn to organize and summarize data for better understanding.

Sets of data that are numerical in nature are called **quantitative data.** Throughout your studies and in everyday experience you will encounter quantitative data: price to earnings stock ratios, grade point averages, life spans in different civilizations, weights of members of Obesity Anonymous, salaries of employees, and so on.

From a table of data we obtain **relative frequencies,** and we use relative frequencies to introduce the concept of a **probability distribution.**

The first objective of a would-be statistician is to make sense out of a large amount of data. Suppose you have collected the numbers in Table 6.1. The table contains your tabulation of the number of colds experienced during a winter by a group of 30 elementary school children.

Table 6.1

7	1	1	0	3	4	5	5	3	2	3	3	6	6	2
4	2	1	0	0	3	4	5	6	3	1	4	1	3	4

A quick glance at this array of numbers tells us very little about what the data imply about the group of people represented. Closer observation indicates that the largest number of colds experienced was 7, while the smallest number experienced was 0. *The difference between the largest and smallest entry in the data is called the* **range** *of the data.* In this case, the range is $7 - 0 = 7$. To understand better the significance of this list of numbers, we might summarize it in a **frequency distribution.** To make this summary, we record the number of students who reported each number of colds.

EXAMPLE 1 Make a frequency distribution for the data in Table 6.1.

Solution From the summary in Table 6.2 it is easily seen that three colds was the number most often reported. The summary also shows how the number of colds was distributed among the 30 students.

Table 6.2

Number of Colds	Tally	Frequency
0					3
1	ﷻ	5
2					3
3	ﷻ ||	7
4	ﷻ	5
5					3
6					3
7			1
	Total	30

A consumer interest group surveyed 35 drugstores in a metropolitan area to determine the cost of a certain prescription drug. The results of the survey are given in Table 6.3.

Table 6.3

$4.65	$5.10	$5.05	$4.70	$5.20
3.85	4.90	4.75	4.90	4.85
5.05	4.55	3.90	4.75	5.00
4.70	3.75	4.05	5.20	4.30
5.25	3.95	4.35	4.60	4.35
4.20	4.50	4.40	4.20	4.40
5.10	4.55	4.65	3.55	5.40

A frequency distribution for this data is given in Table 6.4. We observe, however, that this frequency distribution is not much more comprehensible than the original data. We have 24 entries in the table, and none appears more than twice. When there are so many distinct values in the collection of data, it is more informative to arrange the data in a **grouped frequency distribution.**

Table 6.4

$3.55	|	1
3.75	|	1
3.85	|	1
3.90	|	1
3.95	|	1
4.05	|	1
4.20	||	2
4.30	|	1
4.35	||	2
4.40	||	2
4.50	|	1
4.55	||	2
4.60	|	1
4.65	||	2
4.70	||	2
4.75	||	2
4.85	|	1
4.90	||	2
5.00	|	1
5.05	||	2
5.10	||	2
5.20	||	2
5.25	|	1
5.40	|	1

In a grouped frequency distribution, we cover the range of data by intervals of equal length and record the number of pieces of data that fall in each interval. There are three main steps in the construction of a grouped frequency distribution:

Steps in Making a Grouped Frequency Distribution

1. Choose the number and size of the classes into which the information will be grouped.
2. Make a record of the data in a given class; that is, tabulate the data into the selected classes.
3. Count the data in each class. This number is the **frequency** of the class.

EXAMPLE 2 Make a grouped frequency distribution of the data in Table 6.3.

Solution The range is $\$5.40 - 3.55 = 1.85$. In Table 6.5 we choose to cover the range by eight intervals of length \$0.25.

Observe that there is no mystical significance to the fact that we covered the range by eight intervals of length 0.25. We could also have used six intervals of length 0.35 or ten intervals of length 0.20. All that is required in choosing the length and number of the intervals is a little common sense. Remember that we wish to reduce the number of pieces of data that must be considered, so we do not want to use too many intervals. As a practical matter, there are few occasions requiring fewer than six or more than twenty classes.

The class limits (of equal length) may be chosen as 3.50–3.75, 3.75–4.00, 4.00–4.25, and so on. If this choice is made, in which interval do we place 3.75? To avoid confusion, we will write the **class boundaries** with one more decimal place than appears in raw data. Thus, the class boundaries can be written as 3.495–3.745, 3.745–3.995, 3.995–4.245, and so on, so each score can be assigned to only one class interval as seen in Table 6.5. Sometimes the class limits are written 3.50–3.74, 3.75–3.99, 4.00–4.24, and so on (with gaps); however, the class boundaries and the frequency distribution are still the same. Note that the class boundaries now are halfway between class limits.

Table 6.5

Class Boundaries	Tally	Frequency
3.495–3.745	|	1
3.745–3.995	||||	4
3.995–4.245	||	2
4.245–4.495	|||||	5
4.495–4.745	||||| |||	8
4.745–4.995	|||||	5
4.995–5.245	||||| ||	7
5.245–5.495	||	2

The total of the tallies for each class is called the **frequency** for the class. The set of all classes and corresponding frequencies is called a **frequency distribution** or a **grouped frequency distribution**. The length of the class interval is the difference in class boundaries, and the middle of a class interval is called a **class mark**.

Table 6.6

		Lengths of Engagements		
10	2	9	6	11
17	4	10	7	3
1	4	11	6	3
8	15	12	9	12
8	18	12	6	10
8	18	12	6	9

EXAMPLE 3 Table 6.6 gives the lengths of engagements (by the number of months) of 30 newly married students. Construct a grouped frequency distribution.

Solution The range of the data is

$$18 - 1 = 17$$

We arbitrarily select six classes for our grouping. Since $17 \div 6$ is 2.833, the length of the classes (if the classes are of equal length) must be more than 2.833 in order to include all the data in six classes. Whenever feasible, it is desirable to have classes of equal length. Thus, we arbitrarily select (with equal lengths) the following class limits: 1–3, 4–6, 7–9, 10–12, and so on. The class boundaries (halfway between class limits) are 0.5–3.5, 3.5–6.5, 6.5–9.5, and so on. The grouped frequency distribution is shown in Table 6.7.

Table 6.7

Class Boundaries	Mark	Tally	Frequency	Relative Frequency
0.5–3.5	2	||||	4	$\frac{4}{30} =$ .13
3.5–6.5	5	|||| |	6	$\frac{6}{30} =$ .20
6.5–9.5	8	|||| ||	7	$\frac{7}{30} =$ .24
9.5–12.5	11	|||| ||||	9	$\frac{9}{30} =$ .30
12.5–15.5	14	|	1	$\frac{1}{30} =$ .03
15.5–18.5	17	|||	3	$\frac{3}{30} =$ .10
Total			30	1.00

If in the preceding example we divide each frequency by the total number of items in the original data (in our case, 30), we obtain the **relative frequency** of each interval. From Chapter 5, we can interpret relative frequency to be the probability that a score falls in a given interval. That is, the probability that a score falls in the interval 9.5 to 12.5 is .30. The set of relative frequencies, interpreted as probabilities and associated with given intervals, is called a **probability distribution.**

The relative frequencies, which we interpreted as probabilities, were obtained from a *sample* of 30 newly married students from a **population** consisting of all newly married students. Let p_i be the probability that the length of engagement occurs in interval e_i in the population. If p_i satisfies the properties

1. $0 \leq p_i \leq 1$

2. Sum of all $p_i = 1$

we have described generally the probability distribution of a variable (in this case, length of engagement).

It is much easier to describe a probability distribution of a **discrete variable.** A variable is **discrete** if it is defined only for integral values such as $0, 1, 2, \ldots, n$.

EXAMPLE 4 Consider the experiment of tossing a die, and let the variable x represent the number of dots facing up. Tabulate the discrete probability distribution.

Solution   Of course, x can take on values 1, 2, 3, 4, 5, or 6.

x	1	2	3	4	5	6
P(x)	$\frac{1}{6}$	$\frac{1}{6}$	$\frac{1}{6}$	$\frac{1}{6}$	$\frac{1}{6}$	$\frac{1}{6}$

EXAMPLE 5   Let x be the discrete variable representing the number of tails that can appear on a toss of three coins. x can assume values 0, 1, 2, or 3. Find a discrete probability distribution.

Solution

Table 6.8

x	0	1	2	3
P(x)	$\frac{1}{8}$	$\frac{3}{8}$	$\frac{3}{8}$	$\frac{1}{8}$

Exercise Set **6.1**

A   **1.** In a transportation survey, bus riders on the Friday evening run were asked how many times they had ridden the bus that week. Summarize the data in a frequency distribution.

4	8	6	4
7	2	2	8
2	5	8	1
7	9	8	3
8	2	4	8
10	3	3	9

2. Park officials want to understand the use of a municipal park. One evening the officials interviewed 36 people and recorded their ages.
   a. Summarize the resulting data in a grouped frequency distribution with seven intervals. Let the first interval be 4.5–14.5.
   b. What trend can you see in the data?

7	18	35	73	18	28
15	19	41	61	16	24
51	65	12	65	61	26
16	62	14	73	72	48
17	59	16	62	43	68
21	16	17	19	32	72

3. The following is a tabulation of the ages of mothers of the first babies born in Morningside Hospital in 1984.

Class	Tallies	Frequency
15–19	||||	4
20–24	|||| ||	7
25–29	||||	5
30–34	||	2
35–39	||	2

a. Find class boundaries.
b. Find class marks.
c. Can you determine the number of mothers in the tabulation?
d. Find the number of mothers younger than 30.
e. Find the number of mothers who were at least 19.5 years of age.
f. Find the number of mothers whose ages were between 19.5 and 34.5.

4. An agricultural researcher investigating the growth of fruit trees recorded the following data about 40 young trees. The data are the heights of the trees measured in centimeters. Make a grouped frequency distribution using five intervals where the first interval is 99.65 to 103.85 (class boundaries).

102.6	106.7	101.3	100.2
107.4	109.3	104.2	102.6
105.2	111.2	105.7	110.5
109.4	101.6	120.4	104.2
104.3	106.6	116.6	105.1
109.8	99.8	112.9	101.3
119.2	104.2	111.1	112.7
112.6	107.8	104.3	117.9
101.3	111.6	106.2	107.2
111.1	117.2	102.1	109.6

5. The grades of 66 students in a mathematics course were recorded as follows. Make a frequency distribution, starting the first class boundary at 43.5 and using seven intervals of minimum integral length.

97	73	44	78	75	74	88	82	92	80	73
79	73	83	82	88	94	96	54	65	67	87
84	72	59	98	54	75	62	69	68	64	62
56	82	63	88	77	75	72	66	94	72	47
75	72	78	84	86	85	95	57	64	66	95
76	49	90	85	76	77	76	62	92	91	81

6. Roswell College has 1500 students. The following table is a tabulation of their ages. Use relative frequencies to construct a probability distribution.

Age	Number of Students
14.5–19.5	500
19.5–24.5	400
24.5–29.5	300
29.5–34.5	200
34.5–39.5	100

    a. What is the probability that the age of a student at Roswell College is between 19.5 and 24.5?

    b. What is the probability that an age is less than 34.5?

    c. What is the probability that an age is more than 19.5?

    d. What is the probability that an age is less than 39.5?

    e. What is the probability that an age is greater than 14.5?

7. Let a variable represent the number where a spinner stops in each of the following diagrams. Tabulate a discrete probability distribution for each.

(a) 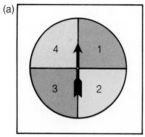 (b) 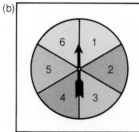 (c)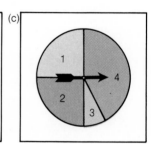

B   8. Let a variable represent the number of dots that appear face up in the toss of two dice. Tabulate a discrete probability distribution.

9. The following two spinners are spun simultaneously. Let the variable be the sum of the numbers where the two spinners stop. Tabulate a discrete probability distribution.

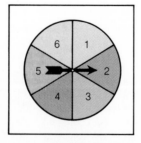 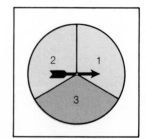

C   10. The following table lists the amounts rounded to the nearest $1 that a sample of 50 students spent on textbook supplements during a fall semester.

33	41	35	53	42	47	41	31	38	37
30	38	37	33	41	35	42	50	41	38
39	42	41	40	40	38	37	41	45	48
35	36	35	38	33	39	40	40	47	38
37	38	37	34	35	44	44	46	40	39

Use six intervals (of minimum integral length) to make a frequency distribution, with the first class boundary beginning at 29.5.

11. The grades of 60 students in a mathematics course were recorded as follows:

96	71	43	77	74	73	87	81	91	79
78	72	82	81	87	93	95	53	64	66
83	71	58	97	53	74	61	68	67	63
55	81	62	87	76	74	71	65	93	71
74	71	77	83	85	84	94	56	63	65
75	48	89	84	75	76	75	61	91	90

Make a frequency distribution, starting the first class boundary at 42.5 and using seven intervals of minimum integral length.

12. Tabulate a probability distribution for the data in exercise 10.

13. Tabulate a probability distribution for the data in exercise 11.

Business **14. Exports.** A small foreign country each year exports 20 main products, ranging from iron ore to toy medical kits to surgical instruments. The value of each export in millions of dollars is given in the table below. Group the values into six intervals of minimum integral length, starting the first class boundary at 59.5.

86	62	239	290	207
285	232	214	131	195
424	343	476	140	398
363	348	156	222	370

15. Sales. Tabulate a discrete probability distribution from the table below, where the variable is the number of units sold per day.

Units Sold	Days
0	20
1	80
2	120
3	250
4	260
5	190
6	80

16. **Common Stocks.** The following table gives the price-earnings ratio of 100 common stocks listed on the New York Stock Exchange. Let the variable be the price-earnings ratio and tabulate a probability distribution.

Interval	Frequency
−0.5–4.5	6
4.5–9.5	46
9.5–14.5	30
14.5–19.5	10
19.5–24.5	4
24.5–29.5	2
29.5–34.5	2

a. What is the probability that a price-earnings ratio is in the interval 9.5–14.5?
b. What is the probability of a price-earnings ratio of less than 19.5?
c. What is the probability of a price-earnings ratio of less than 34.5?
d. What is the probability of a price-earnings ratio between 14.5 and 29.5?

17. **Pollution.** The daily air-particulate count per cubic meter of air in a smog-laden city for the months of July and August is given below. Make the frequency distribution, starting the first boundary at 99.5 and using 10 intervals of minimum integral length.

156	195	420	465	191	225	159	171
205	145	461	407	163	275	101	223
225	159	508	395	159	255	114	191
185	210	509	388	175	235	151	223
160	265	565	388	151	220	163	227
149	307	593	305	184	254	171	229
145	333	535	263	198	240	172	
187	393	515	207	202	234	171	

18. **IQs.** The following are the IQ scores of 30 first-grade students in one classroom.

128	133	100	115	82	99
107	142	98	112	152	100
105	78	114	84	86	110
96	93	101	94	86	124
120	100	102	107	94	128

Group these scores into six intervals (of minimum integral length), starting the first class boundary at 77.5.

19. **Education.** The 25 scores on the next page were achieved by a group of high school seniors on a mathematics placement test. Tabulate this information into five groups of minimum integral length, the first beginning with the class boundary of 449.5.

477	485	527	483	582
567	513	609	596	525
566	540	451	519	530
576	656	525	621	603
648	555	535	528	546

2 Summarizing Data with Graphs

> Tables and distributions are useful in summarizing data; however, many times they are not as useful as graphs. In fact, one of the best ways to summarize data for public consumption is through the use of visual displays or **graphs.**
>
> In this section, we consider **bar graphs** (or **histograms**), **line graphs, circle charts,** and **frequency polygons.** These graphs enable us to present most data visually.

We have seen throughout this text that if we can draw a graph, picture, or diagram, much is gained in terms of understanding. There are several ways to graphically represent a conglomeration of data. One such representation is a **bar graph.** To construct a bar graph, we first construct a frequency distribution or a grouped frequency distribution, whichever is appropriate. Then we plot the frequencies on the y-axis and the data values or intervals on the x-axis. A bar is then drawn showing the relationship between the values and the frequencies.

EXAMPLE 6   Draw a bar graph representing the number of graduates shown in Table 6.9.

Table 6.9

Year	1968	1969	1970	1971	1972	1973	1974	1975	1976	1977	1978	1979
Number of Graduates	152	163	197	185	201	196	210	189	195	205	200	180

Solution   Figure 6.1 is a bar graph of the data in Table 6.9. Notice that the number of graduates is measured on the vertical axis and that the years are given on the horizontal axis. The break in the vertical axis, denoted by ⩷, indicates that the scale is not accurate from 0 to 150. The height of each bar represents the number of students who graduated in a given year. To determine from the bar graph the number of students who graduated in 1971, locate the bar labeled 1971 and draw a horizontal line from the top of the bar to the vertical axis. The point where this horizontal line meets the vertical axis gives the number of graduating students. We see that about 185 students graduated in 1971.

Figure 6.1

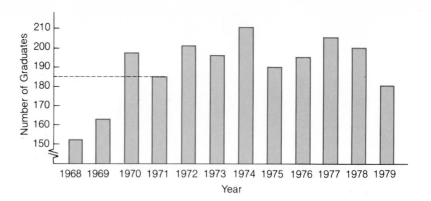

A **line graph** shows the fluctuations and emphasizes the changes that have taken place better than a bar graph. The line graph in Figure 6.2 represents the data in Table 6.9. By looking at this graph, we can readily see the changes that occur from year to year in the number of graduates.

Figure 6.2

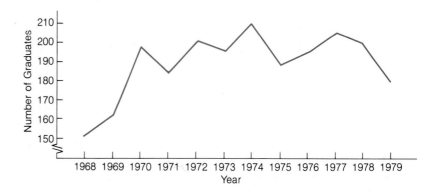

A bar graph representing a grouped frequency distribution is called a **histogram.** To construct a histogram, we first construct a grouped frequency distribution. Then we represent each interval by marking its upper and lower class boundaries on the x-axis. We draw the sides of the rectangles (or bars) at the class boundaries; the height of a rectangle represents the frequency of an interval.

E X A M P L E 7   Draw a histogram of the data in Table 6.10.

Table 6.10

Class	Tallies	Frequency
15–19	‖‖	4
20–24	‖‖‖ ‖	7
25–29	‖‖‖	5
30–34	‖	2
35–39	‖	2

Solution   Figure 6.3 is the histogram that corresponds to the data in Table 6.10.

Figure 6.3

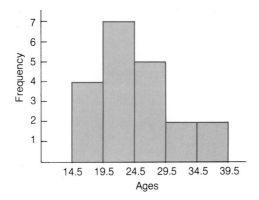

EXAMPLE 8   The length of engagements for 30 students is given in Table 6.11. Draw a histogram for this data.

Table 6.11

Class	Tallies	Frequency
1–3	‖‖‖	4
4–6	‖‖‖ ‖	6
7–9	‖‖‖ ‖‖	7
10–12	‖‖‖ ‖‖‖‖	9
13–15	‖	1
16–18	‖‖‖	3

Solution   First change the class limits to class boundaries so that there will be no gaps when drawing the histogram. The solution is given in Figure 6.4.

Figure 6.4

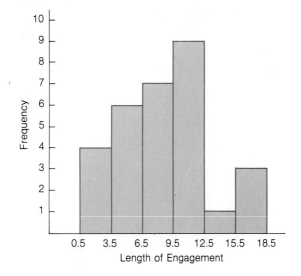

A line graph used to represent a grouped frequency distribution is sometimes called a **frequency polygon.** To draw a frequency polygon, we plot the midpoints (class marks) of the intervals versus the frequency of the intervals, and then connect the resulting points by straight-line segments. Finally, we connect the first and last points to points on the horizontal axis located one-half of an interval from the last class boundary.

EXAMPLE 9   Draw a frequency polygon for the data in Table 6.10.

Solution   Figure 6.5 presents a frequency polygon for the grouped frequency distribution of Table 6.10.

Figure 6.5

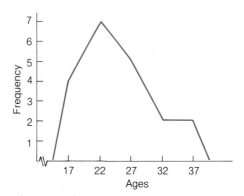

EXAMPLE 10   The class marks for the lengths of engagements (Table 6.11) are 2, 5, 8, 11, 14, and 17. Figure 6.6 presents a frequency polygon for these data.

Figure 6.6

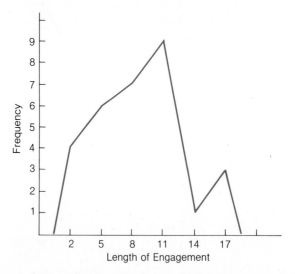

Many times a **cumulative frequency polygon** (called an **ogive**) is of more value than other graphs. To form this graph, the **cumulative frequency** (the total of a frequency and all preceding frequencies) is plotted against the upper boundary of the corresponding class.

EXAMPLE 11 Make a table showing the cumulative frequency and the cumulative relative frequency, and then draw a cumulative frequency polygon for the data.

Solution

Table 6.12

Intervals	Frequency	Cumulative Frequency	Cumulative Relative Frequency
14.5–19.5	4	4	.20
19.5–24.5	7	11	.55
24.5–29.5	5	16	.80
29.5–34.5	2	18	.90
34.5–39.5	2	20	1.00

Notice in Figure 6.7 that we can easily see that 75% of the data are below 24.5, that 90% are below 34.5, and that only 20% are below 19.5. Thus, we can estimate that in a random sample of this data, the probability of a selected entry being less than 34.5 is .90, and being less than 19.5 is .20.

Figure 6.7

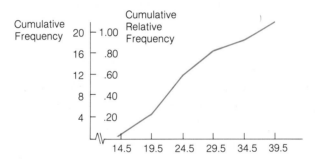

One of the simplest types of graphs is the **circle graph,** sometimes called a **pie chart.** In consists of a circle partitioned into sections, where each section represents a percentage of the whole.

EXAMPLE 12 Table 6.13 records the final-examination grades in a class. Represent the data by a circle graph.

Table 6.13

Final-Examination Grades	Frequency
A	4
B	15
C	36
D	3
F	2
	Total = 60

Solution The circle graph in Figure 6.8 is a visual representation of the data. We see that the largest percentage of the class made Cs. In fact, more than half of the class made Cs.

Figure 6.8

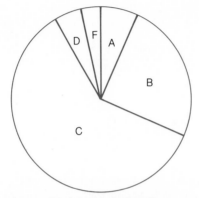

Final-Examination Grades

In constructing the circle graph shown in Figure 6.8, we use a protractor to obtain angle measurement. Since 36 out of 60 or $\frac{36}{60}$ or 60% of the students made Cs, the section representing Cs has an angle of 0.60(360°) = 216°. Similarly, $\frac{1}{15}$ of the grades were As; so the section representing As encompasses $(\frac{1}{15}) \cdot (360°) =$ 24°. The remaining sections are constructed similarly.

Exercise Set **6.2**

A   **1.** In the given pie chart or circle graph,
   a. what percent are professionals?
   b. what percent are craftsmen?
   c. what percent are managers or clerical?
   d. what percent are neither managers nor professionals?

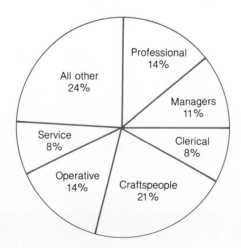

2. The following table gives the number of students who had a specific number of absences in a given semester.

Number of Absences	Frequency
0	25
1	18
2	20
3	31
4	34
5	14
6	13
7	12
8	8
9	3
10	1

a. Display the data with a bar graph.
b. Represent the data with a line graph.

3. Consider a grouped frequency distribution defined by the given table.
a. Find the class marks.
b. Construct a histogram.
c. Construct a frequency polygon.
d. Construct a cumulative frequency polygon.

Class	Frequency
20–29	1
30–39	2
40–49	4
50–59	5
60–69	9
70–79	6
80–89	3

4. Alabaster College has 1426 students. The table below presents a tabulation of their ages.
a. Present the data as a frequency polygon.
b. Present the data as a histogram.

Age	Number of Students
15–19	562
20–24	450
25–29	350
30–34	58
35–39	6

5. a. Indicate on a bar graph a comparison of the number of students in mathematics courses who are majoring in the following academic fields.

Academic Fields	Number of Students
Business administration	110
Social sciences	100
Life sciences	60
Humanities	30
Physical sciences	60
Elementary education	140

b. Display the data with a circle graph.
c. Draw a line graph for these data.

B   *In the next two exercises (a) draw a histogram, (b) draw a frequency polygon, and (c) draw a cumulative frequency polygon.*

6. Use the data given in exercise 10 of Exercise Set 6.1.

7. Use the data given in exercise 11 of Exercise Set 6.1.

C   **8.** Given the histogram below, tabulate a frequency distribution and find the class marks.

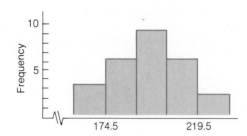

9. Given the frequency polygon below, tabulate a grouped frequency distribution.

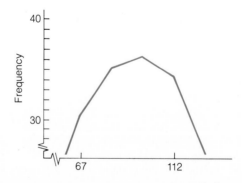

Business   **10. Production.** The new vice president of the Seashore Oil Company claims that production has doubled during the first 12 months of her tenure. To present this fact to the board of directors, she has the following graph prepared.

What is misleading about this graph? (*Hint:* The viewer mentally compares volumes. What happens to the volume of a cylinder if you double its height and its radius?)

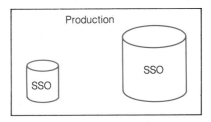

11. **Classification of Occupations.** Use a protractor to construct a pie chart showing the percentage of women who work in the various occupations. These percents are given below.

Professional	16%
Managers	4%
Clerical	35%
Craftspeople	2%
Operative	14%
Service	17%
All other	12%

Economics   12. **Income per Capita.** This line graph shows personal per capita income for Americans during the years 1940–1978. Use the graph to answer the questions as accurately as possible.

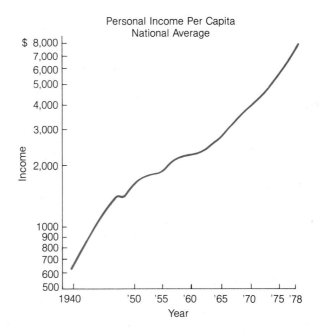

a. What was per capita income in 1960?

b. What was the increase in per capita income from 1958 to 1968?

c. What was the increase in per capita income from 1968 to 1975?

d. Examine the vertical axis carefully. What distortion did the graph makers introduce?

Life Sciences **13. Pollution.** Draw a cumulative frequency distribution for the data in exercise 17 of Exercise Set 6.1.

Social Sciences **14. Politics.** These circle graphs record the contributions to candidates for federal office in the late 1970s.

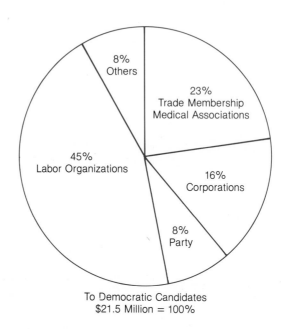

8%
Others

23%
Trade Membership
Medical Associations

45%
Labor Organizations

16%
Corporations

8%
Party

To Democratic Candidates
$21.5 Million = 100%

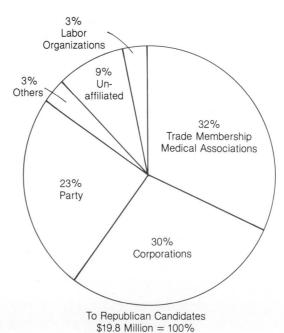

3%
Labor
Organizations

3%
Others

9%
Un-
affiliated

32%
Trade Membership
Medical Associations

23%
Party

30%
Corporations

To Republican Candidates
$19.8 Million = 100%

a. Compare the percent of contributions to Democratic and Republican candidates that came from labor organizations; from corporations.

b. What dollar amount of support for Democratic candidates came from the party?

c. What dollar amount of support for Republican candidates came from corporations?

3 What Is Average?

Sandra receives 69, 71, 78, 82, and 73 on her five tests in Math 102, Mathematics for Business. She gives her average grade as 74.6, but her friend Sam claims her average is 73. Which average is correct? In this section we learn that both averages are correct.

One common use of statistics is comparing sets of data by means of averages (or, more accurately, **measures of central tendency**). Three measures are in general use—the **arithmetic mean,** the **median,** and the **mode.** The fact that there are these three (as well as others) often leads to misuses of statistics. One measure may be quoted and the reader automatically thinks of another. When a measure is quoted, immediately ask the question, "Which one?"

In the preceding section we discussed grouping data and the graphical techniques for describing and analyzing data. However, there are occasions when even these tools are too cumbersome. Often all that is needed is a single number that estimates the location of the center of a set of data. Such a number is called a **measure of central tendency** (or an *average*). In this section we discuss the **mean,** the **median,** and the **mode,** three measures of central tendency.

The most widely used measure of central tendency is the *arithmetic mean* (sometimes called *arithmetic average*). The arithmetic mean of a set of n measurements is the sum of the measurements divided by n.

Arithmetic Mean

Consider n measurements $x_1, x_2, x_3, \ldots, x_n$. The formula for the arithmetic mean, denoted by $\bar{x}$, is

$$\bar{x} = \frac{x_1 + x_2 + x_3 + \cdots + x_n}{n} = \frac{\sum\limits_{i=1}^{n} x_i}{n} = \frac{\sum x}{n}$$

EXAMPLE 13   Find the arithmetic mean of 8, 16, 4, 12, and 10.

Solution
$$\bar{x} = \frac{8 + 16 + 4 + 12 + 10}{5} = 10$$

EXAMPLE 14 During the 8 days that the British crown jewels were exhibited in San Antonio, Texas, the following numbers of people viewed the exhibit each day: 464, 598, 742, 643, 1026, 1500, 800, 875. Find the mean number of people who viewed the exhibit.

Solution
$$\bar{x} = \frac{464 + 598 + 742 + 643 + 1026 + 1500 + 800 + 875}{8} = 831$$

EXAMPLE 15 Find the arithmetic mean of 25, 25, 25, 25, 30, 30, 30, 40, 40, 40, 40, 50.

Solution
$$\bar{x} = \frac{25 + 25 + 25 + 25 + 30 + 30 + 30 + 40 + 40 + 40 + 40 + 50}{12}$$

$$= \frac{25(4) + 30(3) + 40(4) + 50(1)}{4 + 3 + 4 + 1}$$

$$= \frac{400}{12} = 33\tfrac{1}{3}$$

In the preceding example, observe that the 4, 3, 4, and 1 are the frequencies of the 25, 30, 40, and 50, respectively. Note that the mean is obtained by multiplying each value by the frequency of occurrence of the value and by dividing the sum of these products by the sum of the frequencies. Let us now generalize the formula for finding the arithmetic mean to include frequencies of the observations.

$$\bar{x} = \frac{x_1 f_1 + x_2 f_2 + x_3 f_3 + \cdots + x_m f_m}{f_1 + f_2 + f_3 + \cdots + f_m} = \frac{\displaystyle\sum_{i=1}^{m} x_i f_i}{\displaystyle\sum_{i=1}^{m} f_i} = \frac{\sum xf}{\sum f}$$

where f_i is the frequency of x_i for $i = 1, 2, 3, \ldots, m$.

If data are presented in a frequency table, we may have no way of knowing the distribution of the data within a class. We therefore assume that the data are uniformly distributed within a class interval around the class mark or that all of the data within a class interval are located at the class mark. Thus, we use the formula for $\bar{x}$ given above, where x represents the class mark, f the frequency of each class, and m the number of class intervals.

EXAMPLE 16 Find the arithmetic mean for the data in Table 6.14.

Solution
$$\bar{x} = \frac{495}{20} = 24.75$$

Table 6.14

Class Mark (x)	Frequency (f)	xf
17	4	68
22	7	154
27	5	135
32	2	64
37	2	74
Total	20	495

A small company has four employees, with annual salaries of $5,500, $6,053, $7,144, and $7,553. The president of the company has an annual salary of $35,000. The mean of the five salaries is $12,250. This is a true average as given by the arithmetic mean; yet most people would not accept it as a meaningful average salary. The median salary would be more representative.

The median of a set of observations is the middle number when the observations are ranked according to size.

Median | If $x_1, x_2, x_3, \ldots, x_n$ is a set of data placed in increasing or decreasing order, the median is the middle entry if n is odd. If n is even, the median is the mean of the two middle entries.

EXAMPLE 17   Consider the set of five measurements 7, 1, 2, 1, 3. Arranged in increasing order, they may be written as 1, 1, 2, 3, 7. Hence, the median is 2.

EXAMPLE 18   The array

$$25, 2, 5, 6, 5, 23, 7, 10, 22, 15, 21, 23$$

can be arranged in decreasing order as

$$25, 23, 23, 22, 21, 15, 10, 7, 6, 5, 5, 2$$

so the median is

$$\frac{15 + 10}{2} = 12.5$$

The median for data expressed as a frequency distribution is a bit more involved. When the distribution is represented by a histogram, the median is a point such that the areas enclosed by the histograms on each side of the point are equal. Analytically, the process involves assuming that the values in the class that contains the median are uniformly distributed across the interval. Then the class interval is divided into two parts so that each part contains the frequency necessary for the frequency above and the frequency below the dividing point to be $\frac{1}{2}$ of the total frequency.

EXAMPLE 19 Find the median of the data in Table 6.15, which gives the results of a survey of weekly take-home pay (denoted by x) for 100 employees.

Table 6.15

x	f
60–69	4
70–79	10
80–89	18
90–99	24
100–109	14
110–119	10
120–129	9
130–139	7
140–149	4
	N = 100

Solution The first step in finding the median is to find $\frac{1}{2}$ of the total frequency. In this case $\frac{1}{2}$ of the total frequency is $(\frac{1}{2})(100) = 50$. The total frequency in the first three classes is $4 + 10 + 18 = 32$, and the total frequency in the first four classes is $4 + 10 + 18 + 24 = 56$. Thus, the class 90–99 contains the median.

There are 32 weekly wages below this class. Therefore, $50 - 32 = 18$ wages are needed from this class below the median in order to have 50% of the wages below the median. The class boundaries of the interval containing the median are 89.5–99.5. Since 18 wages are needed from the 24 in this class (assumed to be spread uniformly throughout the interval), these 18 wages should be in the first $\frac{18}{24}$ of the interval. The interval is of width 10; hence, the length of the interval below the median should be $(\frac{18}{24})10 = 7.5$. Thus, the median, m, is

$$m = 89.5 + 7.5 = 97.0$$

The **median for a grouped frequency distribution** can be expressed by the formula

$$m = L + \left(\frac{N/2 - F_b}{F_i}\right)i$$

where

$L =$ the lower boundary of the class containing the median

$N =$ the total frequency

$F_i =$ the frequency of the class containing the median

$F_b =$ the total frequency below the class containing the median

$i =$ the length of the class interval

Thus, in the preceding example,

$$m \approx 89.5 + \left(\frac{\frac{100}{2} - 32}{24} \right) 10$$

$$= 89.5 + (\tfrac{18}{24})10$$

$$= 89.5 + 7.5 = 97.0$$

The third average we present is called the *mode* and is the measurement that appears most often in a given set of data.

Mode

The mode of a set of measurements is the observation that occurs most often. If every measurement occurs only once, then there is no mode. If two measurements occur with the same frequency, the set of data is **bimodal.** There may be cases where there are three or more modes.

EXAMPLE 20 Baseball caps with the following head sizes were sold in a week by the Glo-Slo Sporting Goods Store: 7, $7\frac{1}{2}$, 8, 6, $7\frac{1}{2}$, 7, $6\frac{1}{2}$, $8\frac{1}{2}$, $7\frac{1}{2}$, 8, $7\frac{1}{2}$. Find the mode head size.

Solution The mode is $7\frac{1}{2}$ since it occurs four times, more times than any other size.

EXAMPLE 21 In one series of games against the Dodgers, the Reds won six of seven games by the following scores (see Table 6.16). Find the mean, median, and mode of these scores.

Table 6.16

Dodgers	2	6	1	15	4	2	2
Reds	4	7	2	1	5	3	3

Solution When the mean scores are computed, the following results are obtained:

Dodgers' mean score = 4.57

Reds' mean score = 3.57

Although the Reds won the series impressively, the Dodgers' mean score was substantially higher. In this case, the mean is not a good average to use because the Dodgers had one game whose extraordinarily high score biased the mean. In such cases it is often better to use the median.

Reds' scores (placed in order):   1 2 3 ③ 4 5 7

median

Dodgers' scores (placed in order):   1 2 2 ② 4 6 15

In this case, then, the median offers a better measure with which to make a comparison of the scores. The median score for the Reds is 3, and the median score for the Dodgers is 2. It is interesting to note that the mode scores are also 3 and 2.

The decision as to which "average" to use in a given situation is not always easy to make. When extraordinarily large or small values are included in the data set, the median is usually better than the mean. However, the mean is the most-used average since it gives equal weight to the value of each measurement. The mode is used when the "most common" measurement is desired.

Unfortunately, people use the average that is suitable to the objectives they hope to accomplish. A factory might report an average income of $15,000, while the union representative might report only $12,000. Don't be misled. Determine whether the average is the mean, median, or mode.

Exercise Set **6.3**

A
1. Compute the arithmetic mean, the median, and the mode (or modes if any) for the given sets of data.

   a. 3, 4, 5, 8, 10   **b.** 4, 6, 6, 8, 9, 12

   c. 3, 6, 2, 6, 5, 6, 4, 1, 1   **d.** 7, 1, 3, 1, 4, 6, 5, 2

   e. 21, 13, 12, 6, 23, 23, 20, 19   **f.** 18, 13, 12, 14, 12, 11, 16, 15, 21

2. An elevator has a capacity of 15 people and a load limit of 2250 pounds. What is the mean weight of the passengers if the elevator is loaded to capacity with people and weight?

3. Find the mean of the given distribution.

x	Frequency
10	2
20	6
30	8
40	4

4. Make up a set of data with four or more measurements, not all of which are equal, with each of the following characteristics.

   a. The mean and median are equal.

   b. The mean and mode are equal.

   c. The mean, median, and mode are equal.

   d. The mean and median have values of 8.

   e. The mean and mode have values of 6.

   f. The mean, median, and mode have values of 10.

5. The mean score of a set of eight scores is 65. What is the sum of the eight scores?

6. The mean score of nine of ten scores is 81. The tenth score is 100. What is the mean of the ten scores?

7. Which of the three averages should be used for the following data?
  a. The average salary of four salespeople and the owner of a small store
  b. The average height of all male students in We-Fail High School
  c. The average dress size sold at Acme Apparel

8. At the initial meeting of the candidates for defensive linemen of the Hard College football team, the weights of the players were found to be 220, 275, 199, 246, 302, 333, 401, 190, 286, 254, 302, 232, and 221 pounds.
  a. Compute the mean and median of these data.
  b. Which measure is most representative of the data?

B **9.** The weights in kilograms of the members of the Lo-Ho football squad are as follows: 75, 60, 62, 94, 78, 80, 72, 74, 76, 89, 95, 98, 97, 80, 98, 91, 96, 90, 84, 73, 80, 92, 94, 96, 99, 84, 60, 68, 74, 80, 92, 96, 88, 74, 84, 94, 72, 76, 64, 80.
  a. What is the mean weight of the "small" football squad?
  b. What is the median weight?
  c. What is the modal weight?
  d. If you were a sportswriter assigned to do a story on this squad, how would you describe the (average) weight?

10. The grades below were recorded for a test on Chapter 4. Find the arithmetic mean.

Score	Frequency
100	3
90	5
80	7
70	15
60	14
50	3
40	3

C **11.** The following is the distribution of scores on a test administered to juniors at Laneville College.

Score	Frequency
140–149	3
130–139	4
120–129	8
110–119	13
100–109	4
90–99	2
80–89	0
70–79	1

  a. Find the arithmetic mean. (*Hint:* Use the class marks.)
  b. Find the median.

12. Consider the following data.

Class	Frequency
100–119	2
120–139	3
140–159	4
160–179	6
180–199	21
200–219	18
220–239	20
240–259	18
260–279	20
280–299	8

a. Compute the arithmetic mean.
b. Compute the median.

13. A student has an average of 85 on nine tests. What will she need to make on the tenth test to have an average of 90?

14. An interesting property of the mean is that the sum of the differences in the mean and each observation (deviations of each score from the mean, considered as signed numbers) is 0. Show that this statement is true for the following data: 5, 8, 10, 12, 15.

15. a. What is the median of the data given by the histogram below?
  b. What is the mean?

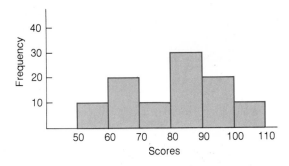

16. The following data have been collected on the expenses (excluding travel and lodging) of six trips made by teachers in the mathematics department at Snelling College.

Number of Days on Trip	Total Expenses	Expenses per Day
0.5	$13.50	$27.00
2.5	12.00	4.80
3	21.00	7.00
1	9.50	9.50
8	32.00	4.00
5	60.00	12.00
20	$148.00	$64.30

Let

$$\bar{x} = \frac{\$64.30}{20} = \$3.22 \text{ average expense per day}$$

or

$$\bar{x} = \frac{\$148.00}{20} = \$7.40 \text{ average expense per day}$$

or

$$\bar{x} = \frac{\$64.30}{5} = \$12.86 \text{ average expense per day}$$

Which average is realistic?

Business   **17. Salaries.** The president of We-Work Factory draws a salary of $100,000 per year. Four supervisors have salaries of $20,000 each. Twenty blue-collar workers have salaries of $10,000 each. Discuss each of the following.

a. The president says the average salary is $15,200.

b. The union says the average salary is $10,000.

c. Which average is more representative of the factory salaries?

18. Salaries. If 99 people have a mean income of $8,000, how much is the mean income increased by the addition of a man with an income of $150,000?

19. Salaries. The following frequency distribution gives the weekly salaries by title of the employees of the Glo-Worm Light Bulb Factory. Frank examined this list and concluded that the mean salary is

$$\frac{550 + 450 + 350 + 250 + 150}{5} = \$350$$

Title	Number	Weekly Salary, $
Manager	1	550
Supervisors	3	450
Inspectors	3	350
Line workers	21	250
Clerks	5	150

a. Is he correct?

b. If he is not correct, find what the mean should be.

Economics   **20. Price-Earnings Ratio.** Find the mean and median price-earnings ratio of the data in exercise 16 of Exercise Set 6.1.

Life Sciences   **21. Pollution.** A study of the number of oil spills into the nation's waterways in recent years gives the number of spills of various sizes:

Millions of Gallons of Oil	Number of Spills
1–3	6
4–6	9
7–9	13
10–12	10
13–15	7
16–18	3

Find:

a. the arithmetic mean.   **b.** the median of the sizes of the spills.

22. **Life Span.** An ethnologist investigated the life span of a tribe of natives on a remote South Pacific island. During the year he lived with the tribe, a total of 35 deaths occurred. He developed the following table giving the age in years of each person at the time of death. Find the mean age of death. (*Hint:* Before finding the arithmetic mean, divide the table into five classes of minimum integral length, starting the first class at -0.5.)

39	39	1	10	43	2	21
45	4	45	52	1	18	35
47	33	45	18	26	58	22
50	18	26	63	15	$\frac{1}{2}$	39
6	3	1	$\frac{1}{2}$	39	14	41

Social Sciences   23. **IQs.** Find the mean and median IQ scores for the data in exercise 18 of Exercise Set 6.1.

4 Expected Value

> Probabilities by themselves do not always supply all the information that is useful when making a decision in an uncertain situation. Equally important is information about what the decision-maker stands to gain or lose in the transaction. The tool that is used to discuss such expected gain or loss is **expected value.**
>
>   To understand intuitively the meaning of expected value, we begin with the arithmetic mean, discussed in the previous section.

Table 6.17 gives the number of students who had a specific number of absences in a given semester. The third column is the product of the number of absences and the frequency. The last column is the product of the number of absences and the relative frequency. Now by definition the arithmetic mean of the number of absences of 200 students is

$$\bar{x} = \frac{800}{200} = 4$$

Note that this mean is the exact sum of the column consisting of the products of the relative frequencies (or probabilities) and the number of absences. Thus,

$$\bar{x} = x_1 p_1 + x_2 p_2 + \cdots + x_n p_n$$

When probabilities are used, the average is often called the **expected value** instead of the arithmetic mean. When the arithmetic mean is used for discrete probability distributions, it is denoted by μ_x instead of $\bar{x}$. The preceding discussion leads to the following definitions.

   A variable x whose values are determined by the outcomes of an experiment is called a **random variable.** The events to which the values of the random vari-

Table 6.17

Number of Absences x	Frequency f	x · f	Relative Frequency P	x · P
0	22	0	.110	0
1	18	18	.090	.090
2	20	40	.100	.200
3	31	93	.155	.465
4	34	136	.170	.680
5	17	85	.085	.425
6	17	102	.085	.510
7	16	112	.080	.560
8	14	112	.070	.560
9	8	72	.040	.360
10	3	30	.015	.150
	200	800	1.000	4.000

able x are associated are both mutually exclusive and exhaustive. From these characteristics, we can deduce the following properties of $P(x)$, called the **probability function** associated with the random variable x.

1. $0 \leq P(x) \leq 1$

2. Sum of all $P(x) = 1$

Expected Value

> To compute the expected value of a random variable x with probabilities $P(x)$, we multiply each value x of the random variable by the probability that the variable will occur and then find the sum of the products.

One interpretation of the expected value is that it is the average payoff per experiment when the experiment is performed a large number of times.

EXAMPLE 22   Let x be a variable representing the number of tails that can appear in the toss of three coins. Of course x can assume values 0, 1, 2, or 3. Tabulating the results as in Table 6.18 assists in computing the expected value of x. The expected number of tails is $\frac{3}{2}$.

Table 6.18

x	P(x)	xP(x)
0	$\frac{1}{8}$	0
1	$\frac{3}{8}$	$\frac{3}{8}$
2	$\frac{3}{8}$	$\frac{6}{8}$
3	$\frac{1}{8}$	$\frac{3}{8}$
Total		$E(x) = \frac{12}{8} = \frac{3}{2}$

Since the expected value for this example is the expected value of a discrete probability distribution, it can be denoted as the mean of the discrete probability distribution or

$$\mu_x = \tfrac{3}{2}$$

EXAMPLE 23 In one version of the game of roulette the equipment consists of a wheel with 38 compartments and a ball. Of the 38 compartments, 18 are red, 18 are black, and 2, labeled 0 and 00, are neither red nor black. The player bets $1 on a color, either red or black. The wheel is spun, and if the ball lands on the selected color, the player collects $2. Otherwise, the player collects nothing.

    a. What is the expected value of this game?
    b. What is the expected loss if someone plays roulette 1000 times?

Solution   **a.** There are two payoffs. Either the ball lands on the player's color and the payoff is $1 ($2 collected − $1 bet), or the ball lands off the player's color and the payoff is −$1.

$$P(\$1) = \tfrac{18}{38} \qquad P(-\$1) = \tfrac{20}{38}$$

$$\text{Expected value} = \$1 \cdot P(\$1) + (-\$1) \cdot P(-\$1)$$

$$= \$1 \cdot \tfrac{18}{38} + (-\$1) \cdot \tfrac{20}{38} = -\$\tfrac{2}{38}$$

$$= -\$0.05263 = -5.263\text{¢}$$

    b. $1000(-\$0.05263) = -\$52.63$. A loss of $52.63 is expected.

It must be understood that expected value deals with averages, with what happens in the long run. Hence, in any given game a player could very well win a dollar. It is after several games that the accumulated gains and losses will approach −5.263¢ per game.

EXAMPLE 24 A nationwide promotion promises a first prize of $25,000, two second prizes of $5,000, and four third prizes of $1,000. A total of 950,000 persons enter the lottery.

    a. What is the expected value if the lottery costs nothing to enter?
    b. Is it worth the stamp required to mail the lottery form?

Solution   **a.** Since

$$P(\$25,000) = \frac{1}{950,000} \qquad P(\$5,000) = \frac{2}{950,000}$$

and

$$P(\$1,000) = \frac{4}{950,000}$$

the expected value is

$$(\$25,000)\frac{1}{950,000} + (\$5,000)\frac{2}{950,000} + (\$1,000)\frac{4}{950,000} = 4.1\text{¢}$$

    b. Hardly!

The expected value of an experiment need not be a sum of money, as indicated by the following example.

EXAMPLE 25 Consider a variable defined as the sum of dots on two dice. In the toss of two dice, the expected value of the number of dots is

$$E(x) = 2\left(\frac{1}{36}\right) + 3\left(\frac{2}{36}\right) + 4\left(\frac{3}{36}\right) + 5\left(\frac{4}{36}\right) + 6\left(\frac{5}{36}\right) + 7\left(\frac{6}{36}\right)$$
$$+ 8\left(\frac{5}{36}\right) + 9\left(\frac{4}{36}\right) + 10\left(\frac{3}{36}\right) + 11\left(\frac{2}{36}\right) + 12\left(\frac{1}{36}\right)$$
$$= 7$$

Note again that expected value is not something to be expected in the ordinary sense of the word. It is a long-run average of repeated experimentation. Thus, if we were to perform the experiment of tossing two dice, we should not expect a sum of 7 to appear. The fact that the expected value is equal to 7 has the meaning that, in repeated experimentation, the average of the number of dots on the upper faces of two dice would approach 7.

Expected value is useful in studying games of chance. In a **fair game,** the expected value of the game is 0. Casinos understandably do not operate fair games; instead, they operate games in which the player has an expected value that is negative. That is, the player can expect to lose money on repeated playing of the game. Of course, there are moral, social, and legal reasons for refusing to gamble. However, we emphasize here the mathematical or financial reasons.

EXAMPLE 26 Consider a game in which the player pays $2 for the privilege of playing. Suppose her probability of winning is $\frac{1}{10}$ and her probability of losing is $\frac{9}{10}$. The game is set up so that when she wins, she receives $10. What is the expected value of the game?

Solution If a player wins, she will gain $8 (the $10 she wins minus the $2 charge for playing the game). If the player loses, she will lose the $2 charge for playing the game. The expected value of the game is

$$E(x) = \$8(\tfrac{1}{10}) - \$2(\tfrac{9}{10}) = -\$1$$

Thus, if the player should continue to play the game, her average earnings per game would be $-$1. That is, she would lose, on the average, $1 per game.

It should be clear that expected value would be helpful in making decisions involving uncertainty. One method in choosing a course of action is to choose the action that gives the largest expected value. We will see throughout the remainder of this chapter how expected value plays a role in monetary situations and in various social science problems.

EXAMPLE 27 A company has the privilege of bidding on two contracts, which we call A and B. It is estimated that, if the company should win contract A, a profit of $14,000 would be realized; however, it costs $500 to prepare a proposal in order to submit a bid. Contract B would give a profit of only $10,000, but the cost of preparing a proposal would be only $200. It is estimated that the probability that the company will win contract A is $\frac{1}{4}$, and the probability of winning contract B is $\frac{1}{3}$. If the company can submit a proposal for only one contract, which proposal should be submitted?

Solution

$$E(A) = \$14,000(\tfrac{1}{4}) - \$500(\tfrac{3}{4}) = \$3,125$$
$$E(B) = \$10,000(\tfrac{1}{3}) - \$200(\tfrac{2}{3}) = \$3,200$$

If the expected value is considered as an appropriate criterion for a decision, the proposal should be for contract B.

EXAMPLE 28 Students over the years have observed that Professor Ab Stract is never on time and yet never misses class. Records kept by malcontents in the back row indicate the probabilities shown in Table 6.19.

Table 6.19

Minutes Late	Probability
1	.1
2	.4
3	.3
4	.1
5	.05
6	.05

a. What is the expected number of minutes that Professor Stract will be late?
b. If a class is to meet 45 times in a semester, what is the expected number of minutes of enlightenment to be denied the students?

Solution

a. $1 \cdot P(1) + 2 \cdot P(2) + 3 \cdot P(3) + 4 \cdot P(4) + 5 \cdot P(5) + 6 \cdot P(6) =$
$1(.1) + 2(.4) + 3(.3) + 4(.1) + 5(.05) + 6(.05) = 2.75$ minutes
b. $45(2.75) = 123.75$ minutes

A good example of a business decision made under conditions of uncertainty is the purchase of stock for inventory. The uncertainty is magnified for purchases of perishable items that lose most or all of their value if they remain in stock a long time. Since it usually is not known how many items will be sold in a given period, the decision to purchase any number of items is made under conditions of uncertainty.

Consider the case of a fruit dealer who buys a shipment of strawberries for $15 a crate and sells the strawberries to yield a profit of $10 a crate. Since the product has no value at the end of the fifteenth day after purchase, the fruit dealer faces a decision on how many crates to order. An observation of sales of previous shipments of strawberries is given in Table 6.20. The first column lists the different number of crates sold in 15 days, and the second column shows the frequency of these sales as recorded from 40 shipments.

Table 6.20

Number of Crates Sold (x)	Frequency	Relative Frequency
4	4	$\frac{4}{40} = .10$
5	8	$\frac{8}{40} = .20$
6	16	$\frac{16}{40} = .40$
7	10	$\frac{10}{40} = .25$
8	2	$\frac{2}{40} = .05$
	Total 40	

Let's consider the relative frequencies as probabilities and the number of crates of strawberries sold as a discrete variable x. Then the expected value $E(x)$ may be computed as

$$E(x) = 4(.10) + 5(.20) + 6(.40) + 7(.25) + 8(.05)$$
$$= 5.95$$

If we assume that the fruit dealer has no reason to think that selling conditions for strawberries today are any different from those in the past, the expected number of crates of strawberries that will be sold from the next shipment is 5.95 crates. However, there are other contingencies to be considered before the fruit dealer makes a decision about the number of crates of strawberries to purchase.

For example, an analysis should be made of prospective profit and loss. If the demand is for more crates of strawberries than are available in stock, the fruit dealer misses a possible $10 profit on each crate not in stock. On the other hand, if the dealer overstocks, he will have a loss of $15 on each crate of strawberries not sold. Should the dealer take a risk in order to make a possible profit, or should he purchase conservatively?

Table 6.21 tabulates the possible profits for several possible purchases and sales. Each entry in the table is computed as profit realized from crates sold minus the loss due to unsold stock at the end of the period. The table does not reflect profit denied the fruit dealer because of inability of fill all requests for purchases.

Table 6.21

Estimated Demand (Crates)	Possible Profits from Number of Crates in Stock				
	4	5	6	7	8
4	$40	$25	$10	−$5	−$20
5	40	50	35	20	5
6	40	50	60	45	30
7	40	50	60	70	55
8	40	50	60	70	80

If no fewer than the four estimated crates of strawberries are sold, and if there are four crates of strawberries in stock, then the profit remains fixed at $40. If seven crates of strawberries are purchased for stock, then the possible profit varies from a $5 loss when the demand is for only four crates to a $70 profit when the demand is for seven or eight crates.

Table 6.21 does not indicate the number of crates of strawberries that should be purchased in order to maximize profit or minimize loss. However, if the probability of a given number of sales from Table 6.20 is combined with the data in Table 6.21, the expected profit for each possible purchase decision can be computed. Thus,

Four crates in stock:

$$E(\text{Profit}) = .10(40) + .20(40) + .40(40) + .25(40) + .05(40)$$
$$= \$40.00$$

Five crates in stock:

$$E(\text{Profit}) = .10(25) + .20(50) + .40(50) + .25(50) + .05(50)$$
$$= \$47.50$$

Six crates in stock:

$$E(\text{Profit}) = .10(10) + .20(35) + .40(60) + .25(60) + .05(60)$$
$$= \$50.00$$

Seven crates in stock:

$$E(\text{Profit}) = .10(-5) + .20(20) + .40(45) + .25(70) + .05(70)$$
$$= \$42.50$$

Eight crates in stock:

$$E(\text{Profit}) = .10(-20) + .20(5) + .40(30) + .25(55) + .05(80)$$
$$= \$28.75$$

The maximum expected profit is attained by stocking six crates of strawberries. The purchase of stock that maximizes expected profit is called an **optimum decision.**

If the fruit dealer decides to purchase the number of crates of strawberries that provides a maximum expected profit, he has not eliminated risk from his decision. In fact, if the fruit dealer purchases six crates of strawberries, the probability is small that he will make a profit of exactly $50. The $50 is the long-run average of his expected profit if he continues to make this decision under similar conditions. There is also uncertainty about whether sales will continue in the future in the same manner as in the past.

So far we have assumed that the strawberries are completely worthless after 15 days. This assumption that the strawberries have no salvage value after 15 days may not be realistic. Suppose that in the past the fruit dealer has been able to sell the 15-day-old strawberries at a salvage value of $5 a crate. The results of Table 6.21 are revised to take into consideration the added assets of salvage value, and the new values are given in Table 6.22.

Table 6.22

Estimated Demand (Crates)	Possible Profits (with Salvage Value) from Number of Crates in Stock				
	4	5	6	7	8
4	$40	$30	$20	$10	$0
5	40	50	40	30	20
6	40	50	60	50	40
7	40	50	60	70	60
8	40	50	60	70	80

This table will be used in exercise 16 of the following exercise set.

Exercise Set 6.4

A 1. Consider the probability function of the random variable x defined by the following table.

x	1	2	3	4	5	6
P(x)	.05	.12	.23	.27	.22	.11

Find the expected value of x.

2. Consider the probability function of the variable x defined by the following table.

x	8	12	16	20	24
P(x)	.11	.13	.49	.15	.12

Find the expected value of x.

3. A highway engineer knows that her crew can repair 4 miles of road a day in dry weather and 2 miles of road a day in wet weather. If the weather in her region is rainy 25% of the time, what is the average number of miles of repairs per day that she can expect?

B 4. In a lottery, 200 tickets are sold for $1 each. There are four prizes, worth $50, $25, $10, and $5. What is the expected value for someone who purchases one ticket?

5. In one version of the game of roulette, the wheel has 37 slots numbered 0–36. The player bets $1 on a number from 1 to 36. If the ball comes to rest on his number, the player receives $36 including his stake. Otherwise, he loses his dollar.
   a. What is the expected value for the player?
   b. How much can he expect to lose in 100 games?

6. Several students decide to play the following game for points. A single die is rolled. If it shows an even number, the student receives points equal to twice the number of dots showing. If it shows an odd number, the student loses points equal to 3 times the number of dots showing. What is the expected value of the game?

7. A man who rides a bus to work each day determines that the probability that the bus will be on time is $\frac{7}{16}$. The probability that the bus will be 5 minutes late is $\frac{3}{16}$; 10 minutes late, $\frac{1}{4}$; and 15 minutes late, $\frac{1}{8}$. What is his expected waiting time if the man arrives at the bus stop at the scheduled time?

8. Two coins, each biased (or weighted) $\frac{1}{3}$ heads and $\frac{2}{3}$ tails, are tossed. The payoff is $5 for matching heads, $3 for matching tails, and $-$2 if they don't match. What is the expected value of the game?

C 9. Find the expected value of the number of dots that appear in the toss of three dice.

Business 10. **Contracts.** The Ronco Corporation prepares a bid on a job at a cost of $7,000. They estimate that if they get the job, they will make $250,000 in profits. If the probability of getting the job is .4, what is their expected profit or loss?

11. **Contracts.** Find the expected values for the following contracts.
   a. estimated profit $5,000, cost of proposal $500, probability of winning $\frac{1}{8}$
   b. estimated profit $1,000, cost of proposal $200, probability of winning $\frac{1}{5}$
   c. estimated profit $10,000, cost of proposal $600, probability of winning $\frac{1}{3}$

12. **Sales.** During a sale, an appliance dealer offers a chance on a $1,200 motorcycle for each refrigerator sold. If he sells his refrigerators at $25 more than other dealers, and if he sells 120 units during the sale, what is the expected value of a purchase to the consumer?

13. **Optimum Decisions.** Consider the following table of monthly sales of an article at a department store, as accumulated over a period of 5 years.

Number of Sales	20	25	30	35	40
Frequency	8	10	20	16	6

The cost of the article is $1.00, and it sells for $1.50. At the end of the month, the article has depreciated by $\frac{1}{4}$ of the cost, or has a value of $0.75.
   a. If there are 20 units of this article on inventory, what is the expected profit from the sales of this article for the next month?
   b. If there are 30 units in stock, what is the expected profit for the next month?
   c. If there are 40 units in stock, what is the expected profit for the next month?
   d. Find the maximum expected profit.

14. **Optimum Decisions.** A candy store has been ordering candy bars that cost fifteen cents each and sell for twenty-five cents each. A record has been kept of the number of sales per month for the past 5 years.

Number of Bars of Candy Sold	40	41	42	43	44	45	46	47	48	49	50
Frequency	1	1	6	10	12	10	8	8	3	1	0

   a. Tabulate a profit table, letting the inventory vary from 40 to 50.
   b. How many bars should be purchased for maximum expected profit?
   c. What is the maximum expected profit if the store can sell all stale candy bars for five cents each?

15. **Optimum Decisions.** A grocery store can purchase a case of a perishable commodity for $4.50 and retail the case for $8.00. The commodity is purchased on Wednesday,

and anything that remains at the end of the day on Saturday is thrown away. The store determines the following probabilities of the number of cases sold between Wednesday and Saturday.

Number of Cases Sold	100	110	120	130	140
P(x)	.2	.2	.3	.2	.1

a. Make a possible profit table varying by tens from 100 to 140 for the number of cases purchased.
b. How many cases should be purchased for maximum expected profit?
c. Repeat **a** if the salvage value of the commodity is $1.
d. Repeat **b** if the salvage value of the commodity is $1.

16. a. Use Tables 6.20 and 6.22 to compute the expected profits for 4, 5, 6, 7, and 8 crates of strawberries in stock.
b. Select the inventory that gives the maximum expected profit.
c. How does this answer compare with the inventory that afforded the maximum profit for the data in Table 6.20?

17. Optimum Decisions. The possible demand for the sale of a machine in a month is 10, 11, 12, 13, and 14. When a machine is sold, the profit is $500. When a machine is not sold, it depreciates in 1 month by $100.
a. If 10 machines are placed in stock for the month, what would be the profit for each of the possible demands?
b. Find **a** for 11 machines.
c. Find **a** for 12 machines.
d. Find **a** for 13 machines.
e. Find **a** for 14 machines.
f. Make a profit table.

Life Sciences

18. Mortality Table. According to a mortality table, the probability that a 20-year-old woman will live 1 year is .994; the probability that she will die is, of course, .006. She buys a $1,000 1-year term life insurance policy for $20. What is the expected loss or gain of the insurance company?

19. Mortality Table. The probability that a man age 40 will live for 1 year is .906. How large a premium should he be willing to pay for a 1-year, $2,000 term policy?

Social Sciences

20. Polls. A public-opinion pollster finds that, in a mailing process costing 50¢ per questionnaire, she gets a 40% return. Her follow-up procedure to assure a reply for most of the questionnaires is $3 per questionnaire. She devises a scheme that costs $1 per questionnaire, but she thinks she will get an 80% return. Which scheme should she use for minimum expected cost?

21. Unemployment. The probability that a steel worker will remain employed during the next year is .866. Each steel worker who loses his job is eligible for $2,000 in unemployment benefits from his state. How much money should the state have in its budget for each steel worker?

22. Testing Techniques. A psychology professor notes that a systematized review increases her students' scores on final examinations. Of the number of times she has given final examinations after systematized reviews, scores increased $\frac{1}{4}$ of the time by 20%, $\frac{1}{2}$ of the time by 10%, $\frac{1}{8}$ of the time by 8%, and $\frac{1}{8}$ of the time by 4%. What is the expected increase in final-examination scores if the professor gives her students a systematized review?

How to Measure Scattering

Misuses of statistics frequently involve a disregard for the **dispersion** or **scattering** of the observations. The fact that the average salary of the Do-Good Company exceeds the average salary of the We-Fix-Um Company does not mean that the salaries of the Do-Good Company are superior to those of the We-Fix-Um Company. To illustrate, compare four salaries: $3,000, $3,100, $3,100, and $20,000, with a mean of $7,300, and four salaries. $6,800, $6,900, $7,000, and $7,200, with a mean of $6,975. The mean salary of the first company exceeds the mean salary of the second company, but the lowest salary of the second company is better than all the salaries except the largest salary of the first company.

José Lopez has a score of 450 on an intelligence test. By some this score is considered exceptional because it is well above the mean of 400. Is it? The answer is no because, on this test, 50% of the scores are between 450 and 550. To be exceptional on this test, one must score above 500.

The average depth of the Cahaba River is 1 foot. This river should be a nice river in which to go wading. Wait a minute! There are many shallow areas, but there are also a number of potholes 15 to 16 feet deep.

The preceding misuses of statistics should emphasize the need for a measure for dispersion or scattering of data. There are several ways to measure dispersion or scattering of observations. The easiest measurement to calculate is the **range** (defined to be the difference between the largest and smallest values in a set of observations). For example, for the set of data, 7, 3, 1, 15, 41, 74, 35, the range is $74 - 1 = 73$. However, the range is not usually a good measure of dispersion because it often varies with the number of observations in a set of observations. Note also that the range can change greatly if just one observation at either end is changed. For example, suppose the 74 in the set of observations listed above were miscopied and listed as 24 instead. The range would change from 73 to 40.

Since the range is affected significantly by extreme values, other measures of dispersion are preferable. **Variance,** the average of the squares of the deviations from the arithmetic mean, is one such measure. In this section we define variance, denoted by s_x^2 for a sample and by σ_x^2 for a probability distribution, and **standard deviation,** which is the positive square root of the variance.

Variance

The variance for a set of data can be obtained in three easy steps:

1. Compute the difference of each observation from the arithmetic mean.
2. Square each difference.
3. Divide the sum of the differences squared by $n - 1$, where n is the number of observations.

EXAMPLE 29   Compute the variance of 112, 108, 114, 100, and 116.

Solution   **a.** Compute the mean of the data.

$$\bar{x} = \frac{x_1 + x_2 + \cdots + x_n}{n}$$

$$\frac{112 + 108 + 114 + 100 + 116}{5} = 110$$

b. Determine how much each piece of data x deviates from the mean; that is, compute $x - \bar{x}$.

Table 6.23

Data	Deviation from the Mean
112	$112 - 110 = 2$
108	$108 - 110 = -2$
114	$114 - 110 = 4$
100	$100 - 110 = -10$
116	$116 - 110 = 6$

c. Square the deviation of each data value; that is, compute $(x - \bar{x})^2$.

Table 6.24

Data	Square of the Deviation
112	4
108	4
114	16
100	100
116	36

d. Divide the sum of the squares of the deviations by $n - 1$.

$$s_x^2 = \frac{(x_1 - \bar{x})^2 + (x_2 - \bar{x})^2 + \cdots + (x_n - \bar{x})^2}{n - 1}$$

$$= \frac{4 + 4 + 16 + 100 + 36}{4} = 40$$

These computations are indicated by the following formula for variance:

Formula for Variance

Variance, denoted by s_x^2, is

$$s_x^2 = \frac{(x_1 - \bar{x})^2 + (x_2 - \bar{x})^2 + (x_3 - \bar{x})^2 + \cdots + (x_n - \bar{x})^2}{n - 1}$$

where $\bar{x}$ is the mean of the observations.

Another measure of dispersion or variation is the **standard deviation.** The standard deviation is the square root of the variance and has the advantage that it is expressed in the same units as the original data.

Standard Deviation

The *standard deviation* of the data $x_1, x_2, \ldots, x_n$, with the mean $\bar{x}$, is given by

$$s_x = \sqrt{\frac{(x_1 - \bar{x})^2 + (x_2 - \bar{x})^2 + \cdots + (x_n - \bar{x})^2}{n - 1}}$$

Standard deviation, denoted by s_x, is the positive square root of the variance.

EXAMPLE 30 Find the standard deviation for the data 5, 7, 1, 2, 3, and 6, using Table 6.25.

Table 6.25

x	$x - \bar{x}$	$(x - \bar{x})^2$
5	1	1
7	3	9
1	-3	9
2	-2	4
3	-1	1
6	2	4
Total 24		28

Solution

$$\bar{x} = \tfrac{24}{6} = 4$$
$$s_x^2 = \tfrac{28}{5} = 5.60$$

The standard deviation is $\sqrt{5.60}$, which is approximately 2.37.

Again, a more general formula can be used when the observations are repeated with given frequencies.

Variance

Suppose $x_1, x_2, \ldots, x_m$ have respective frequencies $f_1, f_2, \ldots, f_m$. Then

$$s_x^2 = \frac{(x_1 - \bar{x})^2 f_1 + (x_2 - \bar{x})^2 f_2 + \cdots + (x_m - \bar{x})^2 f_m}{n - 1}$$

where $n = f_1 + f_2 + \cdots + f_m$.

EXAMPLE 31 Find the variance and standard deviation of the distribution as tabulated in Table 6.26.

Table 6.26

x	f	xf	$x - \bar{x}$	$(x - \bar{x})^2$	$(x - \bar{x})^2 f$
2	3	6	-4	16	48
4	4	16	-2	4	16
6	6	36	0	0	0
8	4	32	2	4	16
10	3	30	4	16	48
	20	120			128

Solution

$$\bar{x} = \tfrac{120}{20} = 6$$
$$s_x^2 = \tfrac{128}{19} = 6.74$$
$$s_x = \sqrt{6.74} = 2.60$$

To find the variance of probability distributions, the squared deviations are multiplied by the probability that the variable occurs. Remember for probability distribution functions that the mean is denoted by μ_x.

Variance of a Discrete Probability Distribution

Variance, denoted by σ_x^2, is

$$\sigma_x^2 = (x_1 - \mu_x)^2 p_1 + (x_2 - \mu_x)^2 p_2 + \cdots + (x_n - \mu_x)^2 p_n$$

Standard deviation $= \sqrt{\text{variance}} = \sigma_x$

To illustrate this theory we return to Example 31 for a discussion of the standard deviation of x, a variable representing the number of tails that can appear in the toss of three coins.

EXAMPLE 32 Find the standard deviation of the variable representing the number of tails that can appear in the toss of three coins.

Solution From Table 6.18 we have the data, and the mean was computed as $\mu_x = \tfrac{3}{2}$. In Table 6.27 we compute the variance.

Table 6.27

x	$p(x)$	$x - \mu_x$	$(x - \mu_x)^2$	$(x - \mu_x)^2 p(x)$
0	$\tfrac{1}{8}$	$-\tfrac{3}{2}$	$\tfrac{9}{4}$	$\tfrac{9}{32}$
1	$\tfrac{3}{8}$	$-\tfrac{1}{2}$	$\tfrac{1}{4}$	$\tfrac{3}{32}$
2	$\tfrac{3}{8}$	$\tfrac{1}{2}$	$\tfrac{1}{4}$	$\tfrac{3}{32}$
3	$\tfrac{1}{8}$	$\tfrac{3}{2}$	$\tfrac{9}{4}$	$\tfrac{9}{32}$
Total				$\sigma_x^2 = \tfrac{24}{32} = \tfrac{3}{8}$

Thus,

$$\sigma_x = \sqrt{\tfrac{3}{8}} = \tfrac{1}{4}\sqrt{6} = .61$$

One of the most common misuses of statistics is the making of inappropriate comparisons.

EXAMPLE 33   Juan made scores of 90, 82, 70, 61, and 94 on five tests. Of course, Juan did his best work relative to the rest of the class on the last test.

Or did he? What do we know about the rest of the class? Maybe everyone in the class made a higher score than 90 on the last test.

The preceding example illustrates a need for what are called **z scores.**

z Scores   A score or measurement, denoted by x, from a population with mean μ_x and standard deviation σ_x has a corresponding **z score** given by

$$z = \frac{x - \mu_x}{\sigma_x}$$

the number of standard deviations from the mean.

The z score is a measurement in **standard units** or without units since, for example, if x and μ_x are in feet, then σ_x is in feet, and the division eliminates the units. Consequently, z scores are of value in comparing two sets of data with different units. In many comparisons the mean and standard deviation of the population are not known, and the z score is approximated by using the mean and standard deviation of a sample.

EXAMPLE 34   Teresa scores a 76 on the entrance test at school X and an 82 at school Y. At which school did she have the best score?

Solution   To answer this question, we need to know that the mean score at school X was 70 with a standard deviation of 12 and the mean score at school Y was 76 with a standard deviation of 16. The z scores are then as follows:

$$\text{School X:} \quad z = \frac{76 - 70}{12} = 0.5$$

$$\text{School Y:} \quad z = \frac{82 - 76}{16} = 0.375$$

Since 0.5 is greater than 0.375, Teresa's score at school X was superior in comparison with others who took the test.

Exercise Set **6.5**

A   **1.** For the given sets of observations, find the range, the variance, and the standard deviation.
   a. 6, 8, 8, 14   **b.** 10, 12, 13, 14, 16
   c. 1, 4, 5, 7, 13   **d.** 80, 75, 80, 70, 80
   e. 15, 17, 19, 23, 26
   f. 16, 14, 12, 13, 15, 18, 24, 8, 10, 4

Find the standard deviation of the data in exercises 2–4.

2. 18, 47, 64, 32, 41, 92, 84, 27, 14, 12

3. 9, 7, 16, 14, 12, 13, 14, 18, 24, 8, 10, 4

4. 10, 17, 18, 47, 64, 32, 41, 92, 84, 27, 14, 12

5. Compute s_x^2 for the frequency distribution below.

x	10	14	18	22
f	4	6	8	2

6. The mean of a population is 100 with a standard deviation of 10. Convert the following to z scores.
   a. 110   **b.** 80   **c.** 71   **d.** 120   **e.** 140   **f.** 40

7. Compute the variance for this frequency distribution.

x	11	13	18	21
f	5	6	7	2

8. Find the standard deviation of the given data.

x	Frequency
1	10
4	20
7	30
10	40

B   **9.** Find the standard deviation of the following data.

Class	Frequency
0–2	10
3–5	20
6–8	30
9–11	40

10. The following data show the miles per gallon reported by owners of five eight-cylinder automobiles from different manufacturers.

	Manufacturer				
	A	B	C	D	E
	18	18	24	21	18
	19	18	16	18	18
Miles per Gallon	20	20	18	19	19
	21	21	20	18	27
	22	24	22	20	18
	22	19	24	21	18

a. Which sample suggests the best gasoline mileage?
b. Which sample has the lowest standard deviation?

C **11.** It can be shown that, for any set of data, most of the values lie within two standard deviations on either side of the mean. Examine the data from the following table in view of this fact.

Heights in Centimeters					
Class I			Class II		
156	158	182	168	180	183
178	159	176	180	187	190
160	176	174	176	176	178
166	160	172	188	186	174
189	187	154	179	192	188
153	180	198	176	179	181
159	162	176	173	174	180
180	166	192	178	176	175

a. How many of the values from class I lie within two standard deviations on either side of the mean? What percent of class I is this on either side?
b. How many of the values from class II lie within two standard deviations on either side of the mean? What percent of class II is this?

12. Two instructors gave the same test to their classes. Both classes had a mean score of 72 but the scores of class A showed a standard deviation of 4.5 while class B showed a standard deviation of 9. Discuss the difference in the two classes.

Business **13. Salaries.** When Tran entered his profession in 1965, the average salary in the profession was $11,500, with a standard deviation of $1,000. In 1975 the average salary in the profession was $21,000 with a standard deviation of $3,000. Tran made $11,000 in 1965 and $20,000 in 1975. In which year did he do better in comparison to the rest of the profession?

Economics **14. Price-Earnings Ratio.** Find the standard deviation of the price-earnings ratio given in exercise 16 of Exercise Set 6.1.

15. Vitamins. A pollster tabulated the ages of 30 users of a vitamin pill designed to make one feel young. The results are shown in the table below. Find the standard deviation.

Age	Frequency
20–29	1
30–39	2
40–49	4
50–59	5
60–69	9
70–79	6
80–89	3

16. Test Scores. The following table shows the distribution of scores on a test administered to first-year students at Laneville College. Find the standard deviation.

Score	Frequency
140–149	3
130–139	4
120–129	8
110–119	13
100–109	4
90–99	2
80–89	0
70–79	1

17. Test Scores. Joan decides to join the New Army to seek her fortune. She takes a battery of tests to determine placement into the appropriate corps. She makes 75 on the bazooka shooting test and 80 in the potato peeling test. The bazooka shooting test has a mean of 60 and a standard deviation of 20 while the potato peeling test has a mean of 75 and a standard deviation of 10. Into which corps should Joan be placed?

Bernoulli Trials and the Binomial Distribution

A new drug is being tested that causes side effects in 6% of the patients. What is the probability of no side effects if the drug is tested on 20 patients?

Experiments of this nature lead to our discussion of **Bernoulli trials** in this section and to the discussion of the probability of r successes in n Bernoulli trials. These probabilities are then considered the probabilities associated with n values $(1, 2, 3, 4, \ldots, n)$ of a discrete probability distribution function called the **binomial distribution.** To conclude the section, we consider the mean and standard deviation of the binomial distribution.

In this section we are interested in an outcome that can be classified as a success or as a failure. For example, in tossing a coin either a tail occurs or does not occur. In tossing a die we either get or do not get a 6. What do these outcomes have in common? In each experiment there are only two outcomes—what we call a success and its complement, which we call a failure.

EXAMPLE 35   Suppose we toss a coin four times and are interested in the probability of exactly two tails. Discuss the circumstances of this experiment.

Solution   First note that in one toss (sometimes called one trial) we either get a tail (called a success) or we get a head (complement of a tail and called a failure). Note also that in the second toss the probability of a tail (namely, $\frac{1}{2}$) is the same as in the first toss. Finally, note that each toss is completely independent of the other tosses. This discussion leads to the following definition:

<table>
<tr><td>Bernoulli Trials</td><td>

Repeated trials of an experiment are called *Bernoulli trials* if

1. There are only two possible outcomes on each trial.
2. The probability of success p remains constant from trial to trial. (The probability of failure is $q = 1 - p$.)
3. All trials are independent.

</td></tr>
</table>

EXAMPLE 36   Consider the experiment of tossing a die four times. Getting a 6 will be a success. What is the probability that the die will fall failure, success, success, success (*FSSS*)?

Solution $p = \frac{1}{6}$, $q = 1 - p = \frac{5}{6}$. The trials are independent. Thus,

$$P(FSSS) = \frac{5}{6} \cdot \frac{1}{6} \cdot \frac{1}{6} \cdot \frac{1}{6} = \frac{5}{1296}$$

EXAMPLE 37   Consider the experiment in Example 36, but this time find $P(SFSS)$.

Solution $$P(SFSS) = \frac{1}{6} \cdot \frac{5}{6} \cdot \frac{1}{6} \cdot \frac{1}{6} = \frac{5}{1296}$$

We note from the two preceding examples that, for two of the possibilities for obtaining three 6s out of four tosses of a die, the probability remains constant as $\frac{5}{1296}$. Since these possibilities are mutually exclusive, to find the probability of three 6s in four tosses, we add the probabilities of the individual possibilities. How many possibilities are there? This problem is equivalent to taking four things three at a time or $C(4, 3)$. Therefore

$$P(\text{three 6s in 4 tosses}) = C(4, 3) \cdot \frac{5}{1296}$$

$$= \frac{4 \cdot 5}{1296} = \frac{5}{324}$$

In general, the preceding reasoning can be used to prove the following theorem:

Probability of x Successes in n Bernoulli Trials	The probability of exactly x successes in a sequence of n Bernoulli trials is given by $$P(x \text{ successes}) = C(n, x)p^x q^{n-x}$$

EXAMPLE 38 An advertising agency believes that two out of every three people who read their advertisement will purchase the product involved. To test this assertion, five people who have read the advertisement are selected at random. What is the probability that exactly three will purchase the product?

Solution $P(\text{exactly 3 out of 5}) = C(5, 3)(\frac{2}{3})^3(\frac{1}{3})^2 = \frac{10}{1} \cdot \frac{8}{243} = \frac{80}{243}$

EXAMPLE 39 In the production of radio parts, it is found that 1 out of 100 is defective. A sample of 8 parts is selected. What is the probability that 2 or fewer are defective?

Solution
$$
\begin{aligned}
P(\text{2 or fewer defects}) &= P(\text{no defects}) + P(\text{1 defect}) + P(\text{2 defects}) \\
&= C(8, 0)p^8 q^0 + C(8, 1)p^7 q^1 + C(8, 2)p^6 q^2 \\
&= (.99)^8 + 8(.99)^7(.01) + 28(.99)^6(.01)^2 \\
&= .99
\end{aligned}
$$

EXAMPLE 40 A coin is tossed six times. What is the probability of obtaining more than one head?

Solution
$$
\begin{aligned}
P(\text{more than 1 head}) &= 1 - P(\text{no heads}) - P(\text{1 head}) \\
&= 1 - (\tfrac{1}{2})^6 - 6(\tfrac{1}{2})^6 \\
&= \tfrac{57}{64}
\end{aligned}
$$

The sequence of Bernoulli trials considered in the preceding discussion is often called the **binomial experiment** because $C(n, x)$ also represents the coefficients in the binomial expansion $(a + b)^n$.

Let's now consider a discrete probability distribution with variable x that represents the number of successes in n trials with corresponding probabilities $C(n, x)p^x q^{n-x}$. This probability distribution is called the **binomial distribution**. Since it is a discrete probability distribution, we can obtain a mean and standard deviation for it.

EXAMPLE 41 Consider again rolling a die four times where getting a 6 is a success. Find the probability of getting x successes, and tabulate the values of the variable and corresponding probabilities of a discrete probability distribution.

Solution $P(x \text{ successes in 4 tosses}) = C(4, x)(\tfrac{1}{6})^x(\tfrac{5}{6})^{4-x}$

The probability distribution is defined by the following table:

Table 6.28

x	P(x)	
0	$C(4, 0)(\tfrac{1}{6})^0(\tfrac{5}{6})^4$	.482
1	$C(4, 1)(\tfrac{1}{6})^1(\tfrac{5}{6})^3$	.386
2	$C(4, 2)(\tfrac{1}{6})^2(\tfrac{5}{6})^2$	.116
3	$C(4, 3)(\tfrac{1}{6})^3(\tfrac{5}{6})^1$	.015
4	$C(4, 4)(\tfrac{1}{6})^4(\tfrac{5}{6})^0$	.001
	Total	1.000

Now we use the data in Example 41 to compute the mean and standard deviation for this discrete probability distribution.

Table 6.29

x	P(x)	$x \cdot P(x)$	$(x - .667)^2 \cdot P(x)$
0	.482	0.000	.214
1	.386	.386	.043
2	.116	.232	.206
3	.015	.045	.082
4	.001	.004	.011
Total		.667	.556

Note that np and npq for the preceding example are

$$np = 4(\tfrac{1}{6}) = .667$$
$$npq = 4(\tfrac{1}{6})(\tfrac{5}{6}) = .556$$

What are these quantities in Table 6.29? This discussion suggests the following property of the binomial distribution.

Binomial Distribution

For the **binomial distribution** obtained from Bernoulli trials with constant probability of success p:

a. The mean μ is np.
b. The variance σ^2 is npq, where $q = 1 - p$.
c. The standard deviation σ is $\sqrt{npq}$.

EXAMPLE 42   Two-thirds of the participants at a state Republican convention are conservatives. If 12 people are chosen at random to be the rules committee, how many conservatives can you expect to be on this committee? What is the standard deviation of this distribution?

Solution   The probabilities satisfy the requirements of a binomial distribution: therefore, the expected number of conservatives (or the mean number of conservatives) is np.

$$\mu = np = 12(\tfrac{2}{3}) = 8$$

$$\sigma = \sqrt{npq} = \sqrt{12(\tfrac{2}{3})(\tfrac{1}{3})} = \frac{\sqrt{24}}{3}$$

$$= 1.63$$

EXAMPLE 43   During inspection of 1000 welded joints produced by a certain machine, 100 defective joints are found. Consider the random variable to be the number of defective joints that result when 5 joints are welded. Compute the mean value of x, the standard deviation, and the probability of getting more than $\mu_x + 3\sigma_x$ defective parts, where $\mu_x + 3\sigma_x$ stands for 3 standard deviations above the expected value.

Solution $p = \frac{100}{1000} = \frac{1}{10}$

Thus,

$$\mu_x = 5(\tfrac{1}{10}) = \tfrac{1}{2}$$
$$\sigma_x = \sqrt{5(\tfrac{1}{10})(\tfrac{9}{10})} = \sqrt{\tfrac{45}{100}} = .67$$
$$\mu_x + 3\sigma_x = 2.51$$

Therefore, $P(x > 2.51) = P(3) + P(4) + P(5)$, since 3, 4, and 5 defective parts are greater than 2.51.

$$P(3) = C(5, 3)(\tfrac{1}{10})^3(\tfrac{9}{10})^2 = \tfrac{810}{100,000}$$
$$P(4) = C(5, 4)(\tfrac{1}{10})^4(\tfrac{9}{10}) = \tfrac{45}{100,000}$$
$$P(5) = C(5, 5)(\tfrac{1}{10})^5 = \tfrac{1}{100,000}$$

Thus,

$$P(x > 2.51) = \frac{810 + 45 + 1}{100,000} = .00856$$

Exercise Set **6.6**

A   **1.** Assume there are four independent repetitions of a Bernoulli experiment with the probability of success on a single trial equal to $\frac{1}{3}$. Find the following probabilities.
   a. No successes   **b.** Exactly one success
   c. Exactly two successes   **d.** Exactly three successes
   e. Exactly four successes   **f.** Exactly five successes

2. What is the probability of obtaining exactly three heads if a coin is tossed six times?

3. An ordinary die is tossed six times. What is the probability of obtaining exactly three 5s?

4. Records show that 0.2% of the taxicabs in a firm have accidents each day. If five taxicabs are operating on a given day, what is the probability of exactly one accident?

5. The output of an automatic machine at Anderson Corporation is analyzed and found to be a binomial process with a probability of a defect of .04. Consider a sample of six units to be tested.
  a. What is the expected number of defects?
  b. What is the standard deviation of the distribution?
  c. What is the probability that the first three units tested are defective?
  d. What is the probability of exactly three defects?

B

6. In its training program, a company has a drop-out rate of .20. If eight trainees start the program, what is the probability that six or more would finish?

7. A baseball player has a batting average of .200. What is the probability that he will get exactly two hits in the next five official times at bat?

8. On a true-false test consisting of five questions, what is the probability of passing (60% or better) by guessing?

C

9. Sam Selpeep is noted for his ability to sleep through an entire class. Following a psychology lecture during which he performed admirably by sleeping throughout the class period, he was given a 10-question, true-false test. What is his expected number of correct answers? What is his probability of getting better than 75% of the answers correct by guessing?

10. Let x be the number of successes in 10 independent repetitions of a Bernoulli experiment where the probability of success on a single trial is .4. Find each of the following.
  a. $P(x = 6)$ **b.** $P(x = 0)$ **c.** $P(x > 8)$
  d. $P(x < 6)$ **e.** $P(x > 9)$ **f.** $P(x \leq 2)$

Business

11. Sales. A company has found that 25% of all customers contacted will buy its product. If 20 customers are contacted, how many sales could be expected? What is the probability of more than two sales? How many standard deviations below the mean are two sales?

Economics

12. Quality Control. Suppose that 10% of the items produced by a factory are defective. If six items are chosen at random, what is the probability that
  a. exactly one is defective?   **b.** exactly three are defective?
  c. at least one is defective?   **d.** fewer than three are defective?

13. Quality Control. In the manufacture of a certain item, under normal conditions 4% of the items have a defect. If 10 items are selected from an assembly line, what is the probability that exactly 9 would be defective?

Life Sciences

14. Fertility Drug. The probability of multiple births for women using a certain fertility drug is 20%. Ten women take the fertility drug. What is the probability of more than two but fewer than six of the women having multiple births?

15. Drug Effectiveness. A drug manufacturer claims that a particular drug is effective 90% of the time. A physician prescribes the drug to 10 patients and 6 respond to this treatment. What is the probability of 6 or fewer successes if $p = .9$? What conclusion is the physician apt to draw? How many standard deviations below the mean are 6 or fewer?

Social Sciences

16. Politics. Two-thirds of the participants at a state Republican convention are conservatives. If seven members of the convention are chosen at random to serve on a committee, what is the probability that the conservatives would be the majority?

17. Divorce. The probability that a couple in state X will get a divorce within the next 10 years is $\frac{1}{5}$. Six couples living in state X form a dinner club. What is the probability that there will be a broken home in the club within the next 10 years?

You may have heard the statement that a given variable is normally distributed. What does this statement mean? To introduce the normal probability distribution we consider it as an approximation to the binomial distribution.

If n is large, to find the binomial probabilities $P(x) = C(n, x)p^x q^{n-x}$ becomes exceedingly tedious. It would be helpful to have another distribution that approximates the binomial distribution so that probabilities are easy to obtain. The **normal distribution** serves this purpose.

Let's consider the histogram of the binomial probabilities in the following example.

EXAMPLE 44 Draw a histogram showing the binomial probabilities in tossing a die 10 times where getting a 3 is considered a success.

Solution

Table 6.30

x	$P(x) = C(10, x)(\frac{1}{6})^x(\frac{5}{6})^{n-x}$
0	.16
1	.32
2	.29
3	.16
4	.06
5	.01
6	.00
7	.00
8	.00
9	.00
10	.00
Total	1.00

In Figure 6.9 a continuous distribution curve, called the **normal distribution curve,** is used to approximate the histogram of the binomial distribution of Example 44. A study of this approximation leads to the following observations.

Note that the normal distribution is a *continuous* (smooth curve) probability distribution—defined for all real values—whereas all other probability distributions studied have been discrete (defined only for positive integer values). It is bell-shaped, and the area between the curve and the x-axis is 1. The mean and standard deviation completely define the distribution. When σ_x is large, the curve is flat; when σ_x is small, the curve is steep. These properties and others are

Figure 6.9

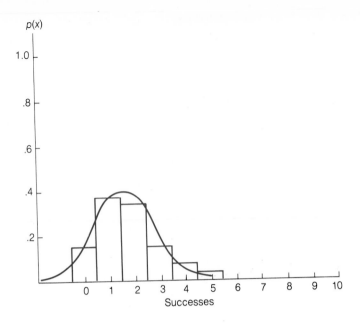

described as follows:

**Properties of a
Normal Curve**

1. The area under a normal curve is 1.
2. The normal curve is symmetric about a vertical line through the mean of the set of data.
3. The interval extending from 2 standard deviations to the left of the mean to 2 standard deviations to the right of the mean contains approximately 95% of the area; the corresponding interval extending 1 standard deviation on each side of the mean contains approximately 68% of the area; the corresponding interval extending 3 standard deviations on each side of the mean contains 99% of the area.
4. If x is a data value from a set of data that is normally distributed, then the probability that x is greater than a and less than b is the area under the normal curve between a and b.

In Section 6.5 we discussed the process of converting data to standard units. Recall that to express x in standard units, we subtract the mean and then divide by the standard deviation, or $z = (x - \mu)/\sigma$. When a data value from a normal distribution is standardized, the resulting data value lies in the **standard normal distribution**. The standard normal distribution has a mean of 0 and a standard deviation of 1.

The curve in Figure 6.10 is the standard normal distribution. We use z to represent the standard normal variable and y to represent the frequency. The maximum value of the curve is attained at $z = 0$. The standard normal curve has perfect symmetry. Because of this characteristic, the mean and median of the distribution have the same value, namely, 0. The range is not defined because there are values occurring as far out as you wish to go—that is, the curve never intersects the axis.

Figure 6.10

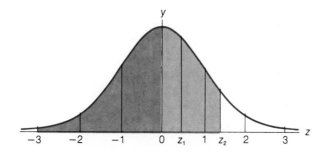

Standard deviation is very important relative to the normal curve: 68% of the values lie between -1 and 1 (1 standard deviation on each side of the mean), 95% between -2 and 2 (2 standard deviations), and 99% between -3 and 3 (3 standard deviations). Since the total area under the curve is 1, these percentages or probabilities can be shown as areas in Figure 6.11.

Figure 6.11

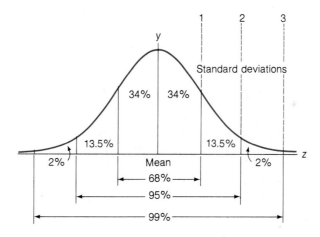

The area under the standard normal curve is 1; thus, to find the probability that z is between z_1 and z_2, we obtain the area under the curve between z_1 and z_2 (the region in Figure 6.10). Table 6.31 gives the area under the normal curve less than or equal to $z = z_1$, and greater than or equal to $z = 0$. That is, the area indicated by the light shading in Figure 6.10 is given in Table 6.31 at $z = z_1$. The area from $z = 0$ to $z = z_1$ is the same as the probability that z is less than or equal to z_1 and greater than or equal to 0. The table stops at $z = 3.09$ because the area under the curve beyond $z = 3.09$ is negligible.

Table 6.31

z	.00	.01	.02	.03	.04	.05	.06	.07	.08	.09
0.0	.0000	.0040	.0080	.0120	.0160	.0199	.0239	.0279	.0319	.0359
0.1	.0398	.0438	.0478	.0517	.0557	.0596	.0636	.0675	.0714	.0753
0.2	.0793	.0832	.0871	.0910	.0948	.0987	.1026	.1064	.1103	.1141
0.3	.1179	.1217	.1255	.1293	.1331	.1368	.1406	.1443	.1480	.1517
0.4	.1554	.1591	.1628	.1664	.1700	.1736	.1772	.1808	.1844	.1879
0.5	.1915	.1950	.1985	.2019	.2054	.2088	.2123	.2157	.2190	.2224
0.6	.2257	.2291	.2324	.2357	.2389	.2422	.2454	.2486	.2517	.2549
0.7	.2580	.2611	.2642	.2673	.2704	.2734	.2764	.2794	.2823	.2852
0.8	.2881	.2910	.2939	.2967	.2995	.3023	.3051	.3078	.3106	.3133
0.9	.3159	.3186	.3212	.3238	.3264	.3289	.3315	.3340	.3365	.3389
1.0	.3413	.3438	.3461	.3485	.3508	.3531	.3554	.3577	.3599	.3621
1.1	.3643	.3665	.3686	.3708	.3729	.3749	.3770	.3790	.3810	.3830
1.2	.3849	.3869	.3888	.3907	.3925	.3944	.3962	.3980	.3997	.4015
1.3	.4032	.4049	.4066	.4082	.4099	.4115	.4131	.4147	.4162	.4177
1.4	.4192	.4207	.4222	.4236	.4251	.4265	.4279	.4292	.4306	.4319
1.5	.4332	.4345	.4357	.4370	.4382	.4394	.4406	.4418	.4429	.4441
1.6	.4452	.4463	.4474	.4484	.4495	.4505	.4515	.4525	.4535	.4545
1.7	.4554	.4564	.4573	.4582	.4591	.4599	.4608	.4616	.4625	.4633
1.8	.4641	.4649	.4656	.4664	.4671	.4678	.4686	.4693	.4699	.4706
1.9	.4713	.4719	.4726	.4732	.4738	.4744	.4750	.4756	.4761	.4767
2.0	.4772	.4778	.4783	.4788	.4793	.4798	.4803	.4808	.4812	.4817
2.1	.4821	.4826	.4830	.4834	.4838	.4842	.4846	.4850	.4854	.4857
2.2	.4861	.4864	.4868	.4871	.4875	.4878	.4881	.4884	.4887	.4890
2.3	.4893	.4896	.4898	.4901	.4904	.4906	.4909	.4911	.4913	.4916
2.4	.4918	.4920	.4922	.4925	.4927	.4929	.4931	.4932	.4934	.4936
2.5	.4938	.4940	.4941	.4943	.4945	.4946	.4948	.4949	.4951	.4952
2.6	.4953	.4955	.4956	.4957	.4959	.4960	.4961	.4962	.4963	.4964
2.7	.4965	.4966	.4967	.4968	.4969	.4970	.4971	.4972	.4973	.4974
2.8	.4974	.4975	.4976	.4977	.4977	.4978	.4979	.4979	.4980	.4981
2.9	.4981	.4982	.4982	.4983	.4984	.4984	.4985	.4985	.4986	.4986
3.0	.4987	.4987	.4987	.4988	.4988	.4989	.4989	.4989	.4990	.4990

The fact that the standard normal curve is symmetric about $z = 0$ means that the area under the curve on either side of 0 is 0.5. This symmetry allows us to compute the probabilities that do not specifically occur in the table.

EXAMPLE 45 Find $P(z \leq 1.84)$.

Solution Since the area under either half of the curve in Figure 6.12 is 0.5000,

$$P(z \leq 1.84) = .5000 + P(0 \leq z \leq 1.84)$$
$$= .5000 + .4671$$
$$= .9671$$

Figure 6.12

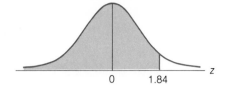

For the normal curve, $P(z \leq a) = P(z < a)$, and $P(z \geq a) = P(z > a)$, for all a. In general, for distributions (called *continuous distributions*) like the standard normal curve, the probability that z is less than or equal to a number is the same as the probability that z is less than the number.

E X A M P L E 46 $P(z < 2.67) = .5000 + .4962 = .9962$

E X A M P L E 47 Find $P(z \leq 1.2)$.

Solution From Table 6.31 we read that the value for $z = 1.2$ is .3849. Thus,

$$P(z \leq 1.2) = .3849 + .5000 = .8849$$

Recall that the normal curve is symmetrical about $z = 0$. This fact is important as we discuss areas under the curve. The fact that the standard normal curve is symmetric about the origin means that the area under the curve on either side of 0 is the same. For example.

$$P(-1.05 \leq z \leq 1.05) = 2P(0 \leq x \leq 1.05)$$
$$= 2(.3531)$$
$$= .7062$$

E X A M P L E 48 Use Table 6.31 to verify that $P(-2 \leq z \leq 2) = .9544$. Note that in the table,

$$P(-2 \leq z \leq 2) = 2P(0 \leq z \leq 2)$$
$$= 2(.4772)$$
$$= .9544$$

Since the standard normal curve is symmetrical about the mean, the area under the curve to the right of $z = -2.5$ is the same as the area under the curve to the left of $z = 2.5$ (see Figure 6.13). That is,

$$P(z \geq -2.5) = P(z \leq 2.5)$$
$$= .5000 + P(0 \leq z \leq 2.5)$$
$$= .5000 + .4938$$
$$= .9938$$

Figure 6.13

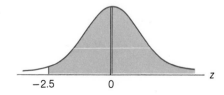

Since the total area under the curve is 1, the area to the right of $z = 1.66$ is 1 minus the area to the left of 1.66. That is,

$$
\begin{aligned}
P(z \geq 1.66) &= 1 - P(z \leq 1.66) \\
&= 1 - [.5000 + P(0 \leq z \leq 1.66)] \\
&= 1 - [.5000 + .4515] \\
&= 1 - .9515 \\
&= .0485
\end{aligned}
$$

Sometimes we need to compute the probability that z is in a certain range, say, between 0.4 and 1.4 (see Figure 6.14). This probability is indicated by $P(0.4 < z < 1.4)$. It can be obtained by finding the probability that z is less than 1.4 and subtracting from this the probability that z is less than 0.4.

$$
\begin{aligned}
P(0.4 < z < 1.4) &= P(z < 1.4) - P(z < 0.4) \\
&= .9192 - .6554 \\
&= .2638
\end{aligned}
$$

Figure 6.14

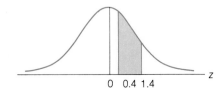

EXAMPLE 49   Find $P(-1.2 \leq z \leq 2)$.

Solution   This time the area is on both sides of the line of symmetry. Therefore, let's divide the total area into two areas.

$$
\begin{aligned}
P(-1.2 \leq z \leq 2) &= P(-1.2 \leq z \leq 0) + P(0 \leq z \leq 2) \\
&= P(0 \leq z \leq 1.2) + P(0 \leq z \leq 2) \\
&= .3849 + .4772 \\
&= .8621
\end{aligned}
$$

EXAMPLE 50   Find the probability that the normal variable x, with mean 175 and standard deviation 20, is less than or equal to 215.

Solution
$$
z = \frac{215 - 175}{20} = 2
$$

$$
P(x \leq 215) = P(z \leq 2) = .9772
$$

EXAMPLE 51   The grades on a certain test are known to be normally distributed with mean 74 and standard deviation 8. What is the probability that a student will make less than 58 on this test?

Solution
$$
z = \frac{58 - 74}{8} = -2
$$

$$P(x < 58) = P(z < -2)$$
$$= P(z > 2)$$
$$= 1 - P(z \leq 2)$$
$$= 1 - .9772$$
$$= .0228$$

Thus, 2.28% of the students will make less than 58 on the test. Equivalently, the probability that a student chosen at random will make less than 58 is .0228.

EXAMPLE 52 The Iron Fist Security Agency has uniforms to fit men ranging in height from 68 to 74 inches. The heights of adult males are normally distributed with a mean of 70 inches and a standard deviation of 2.5 inches. What percentage of male applicants to Iron Fist can be fitted in their existing uniforms?

Solution The z values that correspond to 68 and 74 are

$$z = \frac{68 - 70}{2.5} = -0.8 \quad \text{and} \quad z = \frac{74 - 70}{2.5} = 1.6$$

$$P(68 \leq x \leq 74) = P(-0.8 \leq z \leq 1.6)$$
$$= P(-0.8 \leq z \leq 0) + P(0 \leq z \leq 1.6)$$
$$= P(0 \leq z \leq 0.8) + .4452$$
$$= .2881 + .4452$$
$$= .7333$$

Hence, the probability that a given applicant can be fitted in a uniform is .73, or 73% of the applicants can be fitted.

By reversing our thinking we can find the z values that determine a certain percentage of the data.

EXAMPLE 53 At the very exclusive Rochester Academy, the faculty wishes to admit only the top 30% of those applying for entrance. The scores on the entrance exam are normally distributed with mean 60 and standard deviation 10. What cut-off score does Rochester wish to use for admissions?

Solution If 30% of the applicants are to exceed the cut-off score, 70% are below the cut-off score. Looking in Table 6.31, we see that approximately 20% of the z scores are between 0 and 0.52, and 50% are below 0. Hence, 70% of the z scores are below 0.52. If x is the test score corresponding to z = 0.52, then

$$\frac{x - 60}{10} = 0.52$$

$$x - 60 = 5.2$$

$$x = 65.2$$

The cut-off score should be 65.2.

If x lies between $\mu_x - \sigma_x$ and $\mu_x + \sigma_x$, then, since

$$\frac{\mu_x - \sigma_x - \mu_x}{\sigma_x} = -1 \qquad \text{and} \qquad \frac{\mu_x + \sigma_x - \mu_x}{\sigma_x} = 1$$

we have

$$P(-1 \leq z \leq 1) = 2P(0 \leq z \leq 1)$$
$$= 2(.3413)$$
$$= .6826$$

Since $P(-2 \leq z \leq 2) = .9544$ and $P(-3 \leq z \leq 3) = .9974$, the following summary may be made for any normal distribution.

If measurements are normally distributed with mean μ_x and standard deviation σ_x, then

68.26% of the measurements deviate less than $1\sigma_x$ from μ_x

95.44% of the measurements deviate less than $2\sigma_x$ from μ_x

99.74% of the measurements deviate less than $3\sigma_x$ from μ_x

---

Exercise Set 6.7

A 1. Find the area under the standard normal curve that lies between the following pairs of values of z.

    a. $z = 0$ to $z = 2.40$ **b.** $z = 0$ to $z = 0.41$

    c. $z = 0$ to $z = 1.67$ **d.** $z = -0.36$ to $z = 0.36$

2. Assuming these sketches represent the standard normal curve, compute the shaded areas.

a.

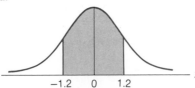

b.

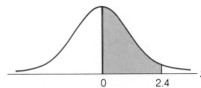

c.

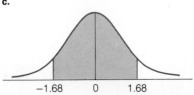

d.

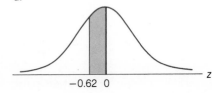

3. Find the following probabilities from Table 6.31.
   a. $P(z \le -2.1)$ b. $P(z \ge -1.4)$ c. $P(z \le 0.1)$
   d. $P(z < -1.6)$ e. $P(z > 1.5)$ f. $P(z > 2.4)$
   g. $P(z > -2.1)$ h. $P(z > -1.8)$ i. $P(1.3 \le z \le 2.4)$
   j. $P(2.1 < z < 2.8)$ k. $P(-1.2 \le z \le 0.3)$ l. $P(-2.6 \le z \le 1.4)$

4. Find the probability that a piece of data picked at random from a normal distribution
   will have a standard z score that lies between the following pairs of z values. Sketch
   the region that represents this probability.
   a. $z = 0$ to $z = 1.16$ b. $z = -1.01$ to $z = 1.01$
   c. $z = -2.41$ to $z = 2.41$ d. $z = -0.66$ to $z = 0.66$

5. Find the following probabilities from Table 6.31.
   a. $P(z \le 1.5)$ b. $P(z \le 2.6)$
   c. $P(-1.6 \le z \le 1.6)$ d. $P(-0.6 \le z \le 0.6)$

6. If x is a variable having a normal distribution with $\mu_x = 12$ and $\sigma_x = 4$, find the probability that x assumes the following values.
   a. $x \le 16$ b. $x \ge 10$ c. $10 \le x \le 14$
   d. $8 \le x \le 16$ e. $x \ge -4$

7. Given that x is normally distributed with mean 50 and standard deviation 10, find the
   following probabilities.
   a. $P(x \ge 50)$ b. $P(x \le 50)$ c. $P(x \ge 60)$
   d. $P(x \le 70)$ e. $P(x \le 40)$ f. $P(x \ge 46)$
   g. $P(38 \le x \le 54)$ h. $P(32 \le x \le 61)$

B
8. Given that x is normally distributed with mean 6 and standard deviation 1.4, find the
   following probabilities.
   a. $P(6 \le x \le 7)$ b. $P(6 \le x \le 8)$ c. $P(6 \le x \le 9)$
   d. $P(6 \le x \le 10)$ e. $P(4.6 \le x \le 7.4)$ f. $P(5.2 \le x \le 6.8)$

9. The mean of a normal distribution is 35 with a standard deviation of 4. What percentage of the data should be in the following intervals?
   a. 31.5 to 38.5   b. 24.5 to 45.5
   c. 17.5 to 52.5   d. 35 to 38.5
   e. 35 to 45.5   f. 35 to 52.5

10. Let x be normally distributed with mean 100 and standard deviation 10. Find the
    probability that x lies in the following ranges.
    a. $x = 100$ to 120 b. $x = 100$ to 300
    c. $x = 100$ to 150 d. $x = 100$ to 110

11. A large set of measurements is closely approximated by a normal curve with mean 30
    and standard deviation 4.
    a. What percentage of the measurements can be expected to lie in the interval from
       20 to 32?
    b. Find the probability that a measurement will differ from the mean by more than 5.

C
12. In exercise 9 compute the percent of the data that should be in the following intervals.
    a. 38.5 to 45.5   b. 45.5 to 52.5   c. 17.5 to 24.5   d. 24.5 to 31.5

In each of the following problems assume that the data are normally distributed.

Business 13. **Sales.** It is known from experience that the number of telephone orders made daily
    to a company approximates a normal curve with mean 350 and standard deviation 20.
    What percentage of the time will there be more than 400 telephone orders per day?

14. Radar. Radar is used to check the speed of traffic on Interstate 75 north of Atlanta. If the mean speed of the traffic is 60 miles per hour with a standard deviation of 4 miles per hour, what percentage of the cars are exceeding the legal speed of 55 miles per hour?

15. Diets. Young rabbits placed on a certain high-protein diet for a month show a weight gain with a mean of 120 grams and a standard deviation of 12 grams.
   a. What is the probability that a given rabbit will gain at least 100 grams in weight?
   b. If 15,000 rabbits are placed on this diet, how many can be expected to gain at least 140 grams?

16. Heights. The heights of men in a certain army regiment are normally distributed with mean 177 centimeters and standard deviation 4 centimeters.
   a. What percentage of the men are between 173 and 181 centimeters in height?
   b. What percentage of the men are between 169 and 185 centimeters in height?

17. Tests. The scores on the entrance exam for the Kentucky Police Academy are normally distributed with a mean of 60 and a standard deviation of 6. What is the probability that a randomly selected test score will lie between 60 and 75?

18. Grades. The grades in a certain class are normally distributed with mean 76 and standard deviation 6. The lowest D is 61, the lowest C is 70, the lowest B is 82, and the lowest A is 91. What percentage of the class will make As? What percentage will make Bs? Cs? Ds? Fs?

19. Achievement Tests. A nationally administered achievement test is known to have a mean score of 500 and a standard deviation of 100. What is the probability that a score is less than 300?

20. Aptitude Tests. The average time required for completing an aptitude test is 80 minutes with a standard deviation of 10 minutes. Assuming that the lengths of times necessary for completing the test are normally distributed, when should you stop the test to make certain that 90% of the people taking it have had time to complete the test?

8 Summary and Review

As you read the following review list, be sure you understand the meaning (or definition) of each of the terms. If you are not completely satisfied with your knowledge of the term, find the relevant discussion in the chapter and review it.

Frequency	Frequency polygon
Frequency distribution	Circle graph
Grouped frequency distribution	Mean
Class boundaries	Median
Class marks	Mode
Bar graph	Expected value
Histogram	Bernoulli probability
Line graph	Binomial distribution

No explanation is given for the following formulas. If you do not immediately recognize a formula, then you need to look it up and review how to use it.

$$\bar{x} = \frac{x_1 + x_2 + x_3 + \cdots + x_n}{n}$$

$$s_x^2 = \frac{(x_1 - \bar{x})^2 + (x_2 - \bar{x})^2 + \cdots + (x_n - \bar{x})^2}{n-1}$$

$$\bar{x} = \frac{x_1 f_1 + x_2 f_2 + \cdots + x_m f_m}{f_1 + f_2 + \cdots + f_m}$$

$$s_x^2 = \frac{(x_1 - \bar{x})^2 f_1 + (x_2 - \bar{x})^2 f_2 + \cdots + (x_m - \bar{x})^2 f_m}{n-1}$$

$$\mu_x = x_1 p_1 + x_2 p_2 + \cdots + x_m p_m$$

$$s_x = \sqrt{\text{variance}}$$

$$m = L + \left(\frac{N/2 + F_b}{F_i}\right) i$$

$$\sigma_x^2 = (x_1 - \mu_x)^2 p_1 + (x_2 - \mu_x)^2 p_2 + \cdots + (x_n - \mu_x)^2 p_n$$

$$P(x) = C(n, x) p^x q^{n-x}$$

$$z = \frac{x - \mu_x}{\sigma_x}$$

$$\mu_x = np$$

$$\sigma_x = \sqrt{npq}$$

Review Exercise Set 6.8

A
1. Consider the set of scores 1, 8, 16, 18, 20, 20, 21, 23, 24, 29. Find the following.
    a. Mean   **b.** Median   **c.** Mode
    d. Range   **e.** Standard deviation

2. Find the mean, median, and standard deviation for the following observations: 104, 106, 101, 102, 110, 108, 111, 116.

3. The mean salary of all employees at the Brown Corporation is $30,000. Make up an example to show how this statistic may be misleading.

4. Find the mean, median, and standard deviation for the following frequency distribution.

x	10	20	30	40	50
f	4	6	8	4	3

5. For the data in exercise 4 draw a
    a. histogram.   **b.** frequency polygon.

B
6. The following test scores were received by 24 students: 63, 71, 85, 96, 94, 90, 75, 72, 77, 71, 62, 84, 81, 76, 61, 54, 87, 94, 32, 81, 94, 77, 63, 60. Find the following.
    a. Mean   **b.** Median   **c.** Mode
    d. Range   **e.** Standard deviation

7. Group the test scores in exercise 6 into classes 95–99, 90–94, and so on. Then compute each part of exercise 6.

8. For the data in exercise 7, construct a
    a. histogram.   **b.** frequency polygon.

9. On a test, the grades are distributed as shown below. Show these grades on a pie chart.

   A 20%
   B 25%
   C 35%
   D 10%
   F 10%

10. Eight poker chips are numbered 10, 11, 12, 13, 14, 15, 16, and 17 respectively. Suppose a chip is drawn and its number recorded as x. Find $E(x)$.

11. Eight poker chips are numbered 1, 2, 3, 4, 5, 6, 7, and 8, respectively. If x is the random variable denoting the sum of numbers on two chips drawn at random, tabulate the probability function; find $E(x)$.

Business 12. **Maximum Expected Profit.** An article costs $2.00 and sells for $2.50 with a salvage value of $0.50. The following distribution describes the sales of the article.

Sales	100	125	150	175	200	225	250
Probability	.1	.3	.2	.2	.1	.05	.05

Find the maximum expected profit.

13. **Maximum Expected Profit.** The following tabulation is given for the daily purchases of a given dish in a cafeteria line rounded to the nearest twenty-fifth purchase.

Number of Dishes Sold	Number of Days
200	34
225	67
250	180
275	194
300	170
325	40
350	30
375	25
400	10

The cost of 25 dishes is $6.00, and the selling price is $10. The food is considered to be no good at the end of the day.
a. Make a probability table.
b. Make a profit table.
c. What is the maximum expected profit?

Economics 14. **Quality Control.** A shipment contains 96 good items and 4 defective items. Three items are drawn from the shipment. What is the probability
a. that all 3 are defective?
b. of exactly 2 defective items?
c. of exactly 1 defective item?
d. of no defective items?

Life Sciences

15. Mortality Table. According to a mortality table, the probability John Salls will live for 1 year is .992. He buys a $10,000 1-year term life insurance policy for $40. What is the expected gain or loss of the insurance company?

Social Sciences

16. IQs. The following are the IQ scores of 30 first-grade students in one classroom.

128	133	100	115	82	99
107	142	98	112	152	100
105	78	114	84	86	110
96	93	101	94	86	124
120	100	102	107	94	128

What is the median IQ score?

7 Applications of Probability

In this chapter we focus on applications of probability theory. Matrix theory and probability are combined to introduce and discuss the theory of **Markov chains.** We conclude the chapter with three sections on **game theory.** The **optimum strategy** for a strictly determined game is defined, and, for 2×2 games that are not strictly determined, the formulas for optimum strategy and the **value of the game** are developed.

All the topics in this chapter are used in applications found in business, economics, the natural sciences, and social science.

1 Markov-Chain Models

In this section we apply matrix theory to problems involving probability. A **stochastic matrix** whose elements are probabilities is defined and illustrated. We examine the product of two stochastic matrices and in particular the product of a stochastic matrix with itself.

Also, we are interested in a sequence of experiments with an unusual property. The probability of any outcome in this experiment depends only on the outcome of the preceding experiment. That is, the probability of, for example, moving from state S to a new state depends only on the current state and in no way depends on the historical background leading to the given state. Stochastic matrices will be used to show this transition. Such probability models are useful in the discussion of population flows, voting trends, market analysis, and many other applications.

A stochastic matrix is defined as follows.

A square matrix

$$\begin{bmatrix} p_{11} & p_{12} & \cdots & p_{1n} \\ p_{21} & p_{22} & \cdots & p_{2n} \\ \vdots & \vdots & & \vdots \\ p_{n1} & p_{n2} & \cdots & p_{nn} \end{bmatrix}$$

is called a *stochastic matrix* if each element p_{ij} is a probability and if the sum of the probabilities in each row of the matrix is 1.

EXAMPLE 1 The following matrices are stochastic matrices:

$$\begin{bmatrix} \frac{2}{3} & \frac{1}{3} \\ \frac{1}{2} & \frac{1}{2} \end{bmatrix} \quad \begin{bmatrix} 0 & 1 \\ \frac{1}{4} & \frac{3}{4} \end{bmatrix} \quad \begin{bmatrix} 1 & 0 & 0 \\ \frac{1}{3} & \frac{1}{3} & \frac{1}{3} \\ \frac{1}{2} & \frac{1}{4} & \frac{1}{4} \end{bmatrix}$$

Any 2×2 matrix

$$\begin{bmatrix} x & 1-x \\ y & 1-y \end{bmatrix}$$

is a stochastic matrix if $0 \le x \le 1$ and $0 \le y \le 1$.

A very important property of stochastic matrices is given below:

The product of two stochastic matrices is a stochastic matrix. As a special case, if **A** is a stochastic matrix, then so is $\mathbf{A}^n$, where n is any positive integer.

Before we use stochastic matrices in the next topic (Markov chains), let's look at an example using stochastic matrices.

EXAMPLE 2 The following stochastic matrix represents the various probabilities of smoking or nonsmoking fathers having smoking or nonsmoking sons.

Sons

		Smoking	Nonsmoking
Fathers	Smoking	.8	.2
	Nonsmoking	.4	.6

We obtain the desired probabilities by locating the appropriate row and column. For example, the probability of a smoking father having a nonsmoking son is only .2. Once again note that the sum of the probabilities in each row totals 1.

Consider now an experiment that consists of a finite number of possible outcomes, $S_1, S_2, \ldots, S_n$. In this section these outcomes are called **states.** Let the experiment be repeated many times. Under the circumstances specified below, the sequence of experiments is said to form a **Markov chain**:

Markov Chain

A sequence of experiments is a Markov chain if

1. the outcome of each experiment is one of a finite number of states, $S_1, S_2, S_3, \ldots, S_n$.

2. the probability of any outcome depends only on the outcome of the preceding experiment.

Suppose the latest performance of an experiment has just resulted in outcome S_i. We say the experiment is "in the state S_i." If the next experiment results in outcome S_j (note that i and j are not necessarily different), we say that the experiment has resulted in a **transition** from state S_i to state S_j. The probability that after outcome S_i the next outcome will be S_j is denoted by p_{ij}, the transition probability from state S_i to state S_j.

We illustrate a Markov chain by a simple experiment having only two possible outcomes, S_1 and S_2. If the present state is S_1 and the experiment is performed, then the next state can be either S_1 or S_2. Likewise, if the present state is S_2, then the next state can be S_1 or S_2. Note that there are four transition probabilities involved:

p_{11}, probability of going from S_1 to S_1 (staying in S_1)

p_{12}, probability of going from S_1 to S_2

p_{21}, probability of going from S_2 to S_1

p_{22}, probability of going from S_2 to S_2 (staying in S_2)

The tree diagram in Figure 7.1 shows the possibilities of this experiment.

Figure 7.1

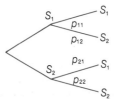

As shown, at S_1 it is possible to go to only S_1 or S_2. Therefore,

$$p_{11} + p_{12} = 1$$

Likewise,

$$p_{21} + p_{22} = 1$$

Thus, the matrix

$$\begin{bmatrix} p_{11} & p_{12} \\ p_{21} & p_{22} \end{bmatrix}$$

is a stochastic matrix, and for Markov chains it is called a **transition matrix.**

EXAMPLE 3 A basketball player has discovered a very interesting fact about his free-throw accuracy. When he makes a free throw, he is 80% accurate on his next attempt. When he misses a free throw, he is only 60% accurate on the next attempt. Identify appropriate states for a Markov chain, and find the transition matrix.

Solution Let S_1 represent making a free throw and S_2 represent missing one. Assume that only the present state influences the next attempt. The transition matrix for this Markov chain is, thus,

$$\mathbf{A} = \begin{bmatrix} .80 & .20 \\ .60 & .40 \end{bmatrix}$$

Recall that when we introduced Markov chains we suggested that an experiment might very well be repeated many times. That is, we might be interested in the probability of going from state S_i and ending in state S_j when an experiment has been repeated three times. We denote this probability as $p_{ij}(3)$.

EXAMPLE 4 Use the data of Example 3 to find the transition probabilities when two free throws have been shot. Then, find these probabilities when three free throws have been shot.

Solution The transition probabilities are listed in Figure 7.2 where S_1 represents the state of having made a free throw and S_2 represents the state of having missed one.

We now calculate the probabilities of going from state S_i to S_j (i and j = 1 and 2) in two free-throw tosses:

$$p_{11}(2) = .80(.80) + .20(.60) = .76 \quad S_1 \text{ to } S_1$$
$$p_{12}(2) = .80(.20) + .20(.40) = .24 \quad S_1 \text{ to } S_2$$
$$p_{21}(2) = .60(.80) + .40(.60) = .72 \quad S_2 \text{ to } S_1$$
$$p_{22}(2) = .60(.20) + .40(.40) = .28 \quad S_2 \text{ to } S_2$$

Let's note what happens when we square the transition matrix $\mathbf{A}$:

$$\mathbf{A}^2 = \begin{bmatrix} .80 & .20 \\ .60 & .40 \end{bmatrix}^2 = \begin{bmatrix} .76 & .24 \\ .72 & .28 \end{bmatrix}$$

A comparision of the probabilities within the square of the transition matrix and the transition probabilities after two free throws indicates that

$$\mathbf{A}^2 = \begin{bmatrix} p_{11}(2) & p_{12}(2) \\ p_{21}(2) & p_{22}(2) \end{bmatrix}$$

Let's compute $\mathbf{A}^3$ and the transition probabilities after three free throws and see if the same relationship holds. From Figure 7.2,

$$p_{11}(3) = .80(.80)(.80) + .80(.20)(.60) + .20(.60)(.80) + .20(.40)(.60) = .752$$
$$p_{12}(3) = .80(.80)(.20) + .80(.20)(.40) + .20(.60)(.20) + .20(.40)(.40) = .248$$
$$p_{21}(3) = .60(.80)(.80) + .60(.20)(.60) + .40(.60)(.80) + .40(.40)(.60) = .744$$
$$p_{22}(3) = .60(.80)(.20) + .60(.20)(.40) + .40(.60)(.20) + .40(.40)(.40) = .256$$

Figure 7.2

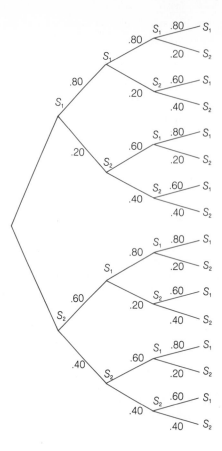

Likewise,

$$\mathbf{A}^3 = \mathbf{A} \cdot \mathbf{A}^2 = \begin{bmatrix} .80 & .20 \\ .60 & .40 \end{bmatrix} \begin{bmatrix} .76 & .24 \\ .72 & .28 \end{bmatrix} = \begin{bmatrix} .752 & .248 \\ .744 & .256 \end{bmatrix}$$

Thus,

$$\mathbf{A}^3 = \begin{bmatrix} p_{11}(3) & p_{12}(3) \\ p_{21}(3) & p_{22}(3) \end{bmatrix}$$

The preceding example illustrates the following theory:

Power of a **Transition** **Matrix**	If a transition matrix of a Markov chain is raised to the nth power, the element $p_{ij}(n)$ of the nth power of the matrix gives the probability that an experiment in state S_i will be in state S_j after n repetitions of the experiment.

EXAMPLE 5   Given the transition matrix $\begin{bmatrix} \frac{1}{2} & \frac{1}{2} \\ \frac{1}{3} & \frac{2}{3} \end{bmatrix}$, suppose an experiment is in state 1. Find the probability it is in state 2

a. one step later,   **b.** two steps later, and

c. three steps later

Solution
$$A^2 = \begin{bmatrix} \frac{5}{12} & \frac{7}{12} \\ \frac{7}{18} & \frac{11}{18} \end{bmatrix} \quad \text{and} \quad A^3 = \begin{bmatrix} \frac{29}{72} & \frac{43}{72} \\ \frac{43}{108} & \frac{65}{108} \end{bmatrix}$$

a. From A, $p_{12}(1) = \frac{1}{2}$

b. From A^2, $p_{12}(2) = \frac{7}{12}$

c. From A^3, $p_{12}(3) = \frac{43}{72}$

Exercise Set 7.1

A   **1.** Which of the following are stochastic matrices?

a. $\begin{bmatrix} 0 & 1 \\ 1 & 0 \end{bmatrix}$
  b. $\begin{bmatrix} \frac{3}{4} & \frac{1}{4} \\ \frac{1}{2} & \frac{1}{2} \end{bmatrix}$
  c. $\begin{bmatrix} \frac{1}{6} & \frac{5}{6} \\ \frac{2}{3} & \frac{3}{4} \end{bmatrix}$

d. $\begin{bmatrix} 1 & 1 & 1 \\ 0 & 0 & 1 \\ 1 & 0 & 0 \end{bmatrix}$
  e. $\begin{bmatrix} \frac{1}{3} & \frac{1}{3} & \frac{1}{3} \\ \frac{1}{2} & \frac{1}{2} & 0 \\ 1 & 0 & 1 \end{bmatrix}$
  f. $\begin{bmatrix} -\frac{1}{2} & \frac{1}{2} & 0 \\ 1 & 0 & 0 \\ 0 & 0 & 1 \end{bmatrix}$

g. $\begin{bmatrix} .2 & .7 & .1 \\ .3 & .5 & .2 \\ .8 & -.2 & .4 \end{bmatrix}$
  h. $\begin{bmatrix} \frac{1}{3} & \frac{2}{3} & 0 \\ 0 & \frac{1}{2} & \frac{1}{2} \end{bmatrix}$
  i. $\begin{bmatrix} .6 & .4 & 0 \\ 0 & 1 & 0 \end{bmatrix}$

2. A Markov chain has the transition matrix

$$A = \begin{bmatrix} .7 & .3 \\ 0 & 1 \end{bmatrix}$$

a. What is the probability of starting in state 1 and going to state 2?

b. What is the probability of being in state 2 and staying in state 2?

3. A Markov chain has the transition matrix

$$A = \begin{bmatrix} .3 & .3 & .4 \\ .2 & .2 & .6 \\ .1 & .5 & .4 \end{bmatrix}$$

a. What is the probability of starting in state 1 and going to state 3?

b. What is the probability of being in state 3 and going to state 2?

c. What is the probability of being in state 3 and staying in state 3?

4. A Markov chain has the following transition matrix. Draw a tree diagram to represent it.

$$A = \begin{bmatrix} .2 & .8 \\ .7 & .3 \end{bmatrix}$$

5. Repeat exercise 4 for the transition matrix

$$A = \begin{bmatrix} .2 & .3 & .5 \\ .5 & .5 & 0 \\ 1 & 0 & 0 \end{bmatrix}$$

6. A Markov chain has the transition matrix

$$A = \begin{bmatrix} \frac{1}{4} & \frac{3}{4} \\ \frac{2}{3} & \frac{1}{3} \end{bmatrix}$$

Find

a. A^2 **b.** A^3

7. In exercise 6 find the following probabilities.
  a. What is the probability of starting in state 1 and being in state 2 two steps later?
  b. What is the probability of being in state 2 and remaining in state 2 two steps later? (Two repetitions of the experiment.)
  c. What is the probability of being in state 2 and being in state 1 three steps later?
  d. What is the probability of being in state 1 and remaining in state 1 three steps later?

B   **8.** Using the transition matrices in the following exercises, assume that the experiment is in state 2 on the first step, and find the probability that it is in state 1 two steps later.
  a. Exercise 2   **b.** Exercise 4
  c. Exercise 3   **d.** Exercise 5

9. Draw a tree diagram and find the probabilities of the transition matrix in exercise 4 after two steps. Then find A^2 and show that they are the same.

C   **10.** Determine the first row of A^2 for A in exercise 5 by using a tree diagram.

11. If the experiment begins in state 2 of exercise 5, find the probability it is in states 1, 2, 3 in that order.

12. A Markov chain has the transition matrix given below. If the chain starts in state 2, what is the probability that it is still in state 2 after three steps?

$$\begin{bmatrix} 0 & 1 & 0 & 0 \\ \frac{1}{2} & 0 & 0 & \frac{1}{2} \\ 0 & 0 & 1 & 0 \\ 0 & 0 & 0 & 1 \end{bmatrix}$$

13. In exercise 12, if the chain starts in state 1, what state is it most likely to be in after three steps?

Business   **14. Occupational Probabilities.** The following transition matrix gives occupational change probabilities:

Sons

		White Collar	Blue Collar
Fathers	White Collar	.7	.3
	Blue Collar	.2	.8

  a. If the father is a blue-collar worker, what is the probability that a son is a white-collar worker?
  b. If a man is a blue-collar worker, what is the probability that his grandson is also a blue-collar worker?
  c. If a man is a blue-collar worker, what is the probability that his great-grandson is a white-collar worker?

15. Advertising. After an intensive advertising campaign, it was found that 90% of the people contacted continued to use product X and 10% changed brands. Of those not using product X, it was found that 40% switched to product X and 60% continued to use what they had been using.

a. Write a transition matrix for this Markov chain.

b. After two intensive advertising campaigns, what percentage of people changed to product X from other brands?

c. After two campaigns, what percentage of those using product X decided not to use product X?

Economics 16. **Quality Control.** In a manufacturing plant, machines have a tendency to get out of adjustment when stopped at the end of a day. Eight times out of ten, a machine in adjustment one day will be in adjustment the next day. One time out of ten, a machine out of adjustment one day will be in adjustment the next day.

a. Write a transition matrix for this Markov chain.

b. What is the probability that a machine in adjustment today will be in adjustment at the beginning of the third day?

c. What is the probability that a machine out of adjustment today will be out of adjustment two days hence?

Life Sciences 17. **Genetics.** A basic assumption in a simple genetics problem is that the offspring inherits one gene from each parent and that these genes are selected at random. Suppose an inheritance trait is governed by a pair of genes, each of which is of type G or g. The possible combinations are gg, gG (same genetically as Gg), and GG. Those possessing the gg combination are called **recessive** (denoted by R); **hybrid** (denoted by H) is used to indicate those possessing gG; and **dominant** (denoted by D) indicates those possessing GG. Note that in the mating of two dominant parents the offspring must be dominant. In the mating of two recessive parents, the offspring must be recessive. In the mating of a dominant parent with a recessive parent, the offspring must be hybrid. Suppose a person of unknown genetic character is crossed with a hybrid, the offspring is again crossed with a hybrid, and the process is continued, hence forming a Markov chain; the transition matrix is

$$
\begin{array}{cc}
 & \textbf{Offspring} \\
 & \begin{array}{ccc} R & H & D \end{array} \\
\textbf{Parents} \begin{array}{c} R \\ H \\ D \end{array} &
\begin{bmatrix}
\frac{1}{2} & \frac{1}{2} & 0 \\
\frac{1}{4} & \frac{1}{2} & \frac{1}{4} \\
0 & \frac{1}{2} & \frac{1}{2}
\end{bmatrix}
\end{array}
$$

a. What is the probability that a recessive parent will have a dominant child?

b. What is the probability that a hybrid parent will have a recessive child?

c. What is the probability that a recessive parent will have a hybrid grandchild?

18. **Communications.** A system transmits the digits 0 and 1. A digit must pass through several stages before reaching its destination. The probability that the digit 1 entering a stage will be unchanged is .80, and that the digit 0 will be unchanged is .90.

a. Write a transition matrix for this system.

b. What is the probability that 0 will be unchanged through two stages?

Social Sciences 19. **Population Movement.** The transition matrix of a population movement model is as follows:

	City	Suburb	Nonmetro Area
City	.86	.10	.04
Suburb	.02	.97	.01
Nonmetro Area	.005	.005	.99

a. What is the probability of moving from the city to the suburbs?

b. What is the probability of moving from the suburbs to a nonmetro area?

c. What is the probability of moving from the suburbs to the city in 2 years?

d. What is the probability of staying in the city for 2 years?

20. Political Party Change. The transition matrix for changing political parties in a given election is:

$$
\begin{array}{c}
\\
\text{Democrats} \\
\text{Republicans} \\
\text{Independents}
\end{array}
\begin{array}{ccc}
\text{Democrats} & \text{Republicans} & \text{Independents} \\
\left[\begin{array}{ccc}
.7 & .2 & .1 \\
.1 & .8 & .1 \\
.4 & .2 & .4
\end{array}\right]
\end{array}
$$

a. What is the probability of a Democrat voting Republican?

b. What is the probability of a Republican voting Republican?

c. What is the probability of a Republican voting Democratic in a second election?

d. What is the probability of a Democrat voting for a Democrat in a second election?

Regular Markov Chains

In the preceding section we introduced stochastic matrices and considered transition matrices of Markov chains as a subset of stochastic matrices. In this section we continue our study of Markov chains by writing what happens at a given stage or step as a **probability vector.** A probability vector at one step times the transition matrix gives the probability vector at the next step.

Also in this section we study a special type of Markov chain. **Regular Markov chains** are especially useful in applications. This special type and the one considered in the next section illustrate the extremes of behavior of Markov chains.

Since Markov chains are stochastic processes, it seems reasonable to express the initial state in terms of probabilities. For example, if the transition matrix

$$
\begin{array}{c}
\\
\text{Brand I} \\
\text{Brand II}
\end{array}
\begin{array}{cc}
\text{Brand I} & \text{Brand II} \\
\left[\begin{array}{cc}
.6 & .4 \\
.3 & .7
\end{array}\right]
\end{array}
$$

represents the probability that a person now using one brand (possibly brand I) will switch to another brand (say, brand II), .6 represents the probability that a person using brand I will stay with brand I, and .4 the probability that the person will switch to brand II.

Many times in examples such as the preceding one, we are given an initial-state matrix (since it has only one row it is called a **vector**). A stochastic matrix with only one row is called a **probability vector.** Suppose in the preceding example brand I has 80% of the market, and brand II has 20%. This idea can be illustrated with the state vector (or probability vector)

$$[.80 \quad .20]$$

After one transition period the new probability vector is the old vector multiplied by the transition matrix:

$$[.80 \quad .20] \begin{bmatrix} .6 & .4 \\ .3 & .7 \end{bmatrix} = [.54 \quad .46]$$

Thus, brand I now has only 54% of the market, and brand II now has 46%.

Note that if we let X_i be a state vector and A be the transition matrix, we have the following result:

$$X_1 = X_0 A$$
$$X_2 = X_1 A$$
$$\quad = (X_0 A)A$$
$$\quad = X_0 A^2$$
$$X_3 = X_2 A$$
$$\quad = (X_0 A^2)A$$
$$\quad = X_0 A^3$$

In general, $X_n = X_0 A^n$ and $X_{i+n} = X_i A^n$.

EXAMPLE 6 A Markov chain has the transition matrix

$$A = \begin{bmatrix} .5 & .5 \\ .3 & .7 \end{bmatrix}$$

If the initial state X_0 is $[.4 \quad .6]$, what is the state 2 vector?

Solution

$$A^2 = \begin{bmatrix} .40 & .60 \\ .36 & .64 \end{bmatrix}$$

$$X_2 = X_0 A^2$$

$$\quad = [.4 \quad .6] \begin{bmatrix} .40 & .60 \\ .36 & .64 \end{bmatrix}$$

$$\quad = [.376 \quad .624]$$

Let us now consider the primary idea of this section. We are interested in classifying Markov chains on the basis of their long-run behavior. That is, we are interested in the nature of the state vector after many transitions. We want to know whether the sequence of state vectors

$$X_0, X_1, X_2, X_3, \ldots$$

approaches an equilibrium situation in which the numbers in the various states do not change. Such a state would have to satisfy $X = XA$.

Fixed or Steady-State Vector

A state vector X such that

$$XA = X$$

is called a **fixed** or **steady-state vector** for the transition matrix A.

When we reach the state where $\mathbf{XA} = \mathbf{X}$, or is very close to it, the system is said to be in **equilibrium**; further states either will not change or will not change very much.

We now investigate the situation that might lead to a system in equilibrium.

Regular Markov Chain

A transition matrix is said to be regular if some power of it contains only positive elements. The chain is then called a *regular Markov chain*.

EXAMPLE 7 The following matrix is regular because the first power contains all positive elements.

$$\begin{bmatrix} .7 & .3 \\ .4 & .6 \end{bmatrix}$$

Likewise,

$$\mathbf{A} = \begin{bmatrix} .1 & .9 & .0 \\ .3 & .3 & .4 \\ .8 & .1 & .1 \end{bmatrix}$$

is regular since

$$\mathbf{A}^2 = \begin{bmatrix} .28 & .36 & .36 \\ .44 & .40 & .16 \\ .19 & .76 & .05 \end{bmatrix}$$

contains all positive elements. However,

$$\mathbf{A} = \begin{bmatrix} 1 & 0 \\ .7 & .3 \end{bmatrix}$$

is not regular because the element in the upper right corner will be 0 for all $\mathbf{A}^n$.

The following theorem, which we present without proof, contains important properties of regular transition matrices.

If $\mathbf{A}$ is a **regular transition matrix,** then

1. $\mathbf{A}$ has a unique fixed probability vector $\mathbf{P}$.
2. The sequence $\mathbf{A}, \mathbf{A}^2, \mathbf{A}^3, \ldots$ approaches a steady-state matrix $\mathbf{M}$. The rows of $\mathbf{M}$ are identical. The elements of a row are equal to the elements of $\mathbf{P}$, the fixed probability vector.
3. If $\mathbf{X}_i$ is any vector, the sequence

$$\mathbf{X}_i\mathbf{A}, \mathbf{X}_i\mathbf{A}^2, \mathbf{X}_i\mathbf{A}^3, \ldots$$

approaches a fixed or steady-state vector $\mathbf{X}$.

This theorem states that no matter what the initial-state vector, a regular Markov chain will tend to stabilize, and thus the long-term behavior will become predictable. Powers of the transition matrix approach a matrix in which the elements in a column are identical. Thus, no matter what the initial state, the long-term probability of being in state S_i from any state is constant.

EXAMPLE 8   Find the fixed probability vector for the matrix $\begin{bmatrix} 0 & 1 \\ \frac{3}{5} & \frac{2}{5} \end{bmatrix}$.

Solution   We first show that this matrix is regular. Multiplying

$$\begin{bmatrix} 0 & 1 \\ \frac{3}{5} & \frac{2}{5} \end{bmatrix}\begin{bmatrix} 0 & 1 \\ \frac{3}{5} & \frac{2}{5} \end{bmatrix} = \begin{bmatrix} \frac{3}{5} & \frac{2}{5} \\ \frac{6}{25} & \frac{19}{25} \end{bmatrix}$$

gives a matrix with only positive elements and proves that the original matrix is regular. Now let the fixed probability vector be $[x_1 \quad x_2]$. Then, by definition,

$$[x_1 \quad x_2]\begin{bmatrix} 0 & 1 \\ \frac{3}{5} & \frac{2}{5} \end{bmatrix} = [x_1 \quad x_2]$$

Multiplying the two matrices on the left side of the equation gives

$$[\tfrac{3}{5}x_2 \quad x_1 + \tfrac{2}{5}x_2] = [x_1 \quad x_2]$$

Hence, the corresponding elements must be equal:

$$\tfrac{3}{5}x_2 = x_1 \quad \text{and} \quad x_1 + \tfrac{2}{5}x_2 = x_2$$

Now these two equations are dependent. Since the fixed probability vector is a probability vector, we must also satisfy the condition that $x_1 + x_2 = 1$. Solving these three equations in two unknowns gives $x_1 = \frac{3}{8}$ and $x_2 = \frac{5}{8}$. Hence, the fixed probability vector is $[\frac{3}{8} \quad \frac{5}{8}]$, as can be proved by multiplying:

$$[\tfrac{3}{8} \quad \tfrac{5}{8}]\begin{bmatrix} 0 & 1 \\ \frac{3}{5} & \frac{2}{5} \end{bmatrix} = [\tfrac{3}{8} \quad \tfrac{5}{8}]$$

EXAMPLE 9   Use Example 8 to find the matrix $\mathbf{M}$ that $\mathbf{A}, \mathbf{A}^2, \mathbf{A}^3, \mathbf{A}^4, \ldots$ approaches; then find for the initial-state vector $\mathbf{X}_0 = [100 \quad 200]$, the steady-state vector $\mathbf{X}$; and show that $\mathbf{X}\mathbf{A} = \mathbf{X}$.

Solution   In the previous example we found that the fixed probability vector is $[\frac{3}{8} \quad \frac{5}{8}]$. Thus, we can form $\mathbf{M}$ as $\begin{bmatrix} \frac{3}{8} & \frac{5}{8} \\ \frac{3}{8} & \frac{5}{8} \end{bmatrix}$. Note that the long-term probability of being in state 1 is $\frac{3}{8}$ regardless of whether the initial state is 1 or 2. Likewise, the long-term probability of being in state 2 is $\frac{5}{8}$.

Now the steady-state vector for $\mathbf{X}_0 = [100 \quad 200]$ is

$$\mathbf{X}_0\mathbf{M} = [100 \quad 200]\begin{bmatrix} \frac{3}{8} & \frac{5}{8} \\ \frac{3}{8} & \frac{5}{8} \end{bmatrix} = [\tfrac{900}{8} \quad \tfrac{1500}{8}]$$

Hence, $\mathbf{X}_0\mathbf{A}, \mathbf{X}_0\mathbf{A}^2, \mathbf{X}_0\mathbf{A}^3, \ldots$ approaches $[\frac{900}{8} \quad \frac{1500}{8}]$. Note also that for steady-state vector $\mathbf{X}$,

$$\mathbf{XA} = \mathbf{X}$$

$$[\tfrac{900}{8} \quad \tfrac{1500}{8}]\begin{bmatrix} 0 & 1 \\ \frac{3}{5} & \frac{2}{5} \end{bmatrix} = [\tfrac{900}{8} \quad \tfrac{1500}{8}]$$

EXAMPLE 10   Find the fixed probability vector for the regular transition matrix

$$\begin{bmatrix} \frac{3}{4} & \frac{3}{20} & \frac{1}{10} \\ \frac{3}{10} & \frac{3}{5} & \frac{1}{10} \\ \frac{1}{20} & \frac{3}{20} & \frac{4}{5} \end{bmatrix}$$

Solution   Let the fixed probability vector be $[x_1 \quad x_2 \quad x_3]$. Then, by definition,

$$[x_1 \quad x_2 \quad x_3]\begin{bmatrix} \frac{3}{4} & \frac{3}{20} & \frac{1}{10} \\ \frac{3}{10} & \frac{3}{5} & \frac{1}{10} \\ \frac{1}{20} & \frac{3}{20} & \frac{4}{5} \end{bmatrix} = [x_1 \quad x_2 \quad x_3]$$

This matrix equation with the condition that $x_1 + x_2 + x_3 = 1$ gives the following system of equations:

$$-\tfrac{1}{4}x_1 + \tfrac{3}{10}x_2 + \tfrac{1}{20}x_3 = 0$$
$$\tfrac{3}{20}x_1 - \tfrac{2}{5}x_2 + \tfrac{3}{20}x_3 = 0$$
$$\tfrac{1}{10}x_1 + \tfrac{1}{10}x_2 - \tfrac{1}{5}x_3 = 0$$
$$x_1 + x_2 + x_3 = 1$$

The solution is $x_1 = \frac{13}{33}$, $x_2 = \frac{3}{11}$, $x_3 = \frac{1}{3}$. This can be verified by multiplying:

$$[\tfrac{13}{33} \quad \tfrac{3}{11} \quad \tfrac{1}{3}]\begin{bmatrix} \frac{3}{4} & \frac{3}{20} & \frac{1}{10} \\ \frac{3}{10} & \frac{3}{5} & \frac{1}{10} \\ \frac{1}{20} & \frac{3}{20} & \frac{4}{5} \end{bmatrix} = [\tfrac{13}{33} \quad \tfrac{3}{11} \quad \tfrac{1}{3}]$$

EXAMPLE 11   Suppose a woman is trying to determine whether to invest in company I or company II. From a survey, she learns that company I has 130,000 customers out of a possible 150,000, while company II has only 20,000 customers. The survey also tells her that 15% of I's customers switch to II each month, while only 5% of II's customers switch to I each month.

The transition matrix for this Markov chain is found as follows. By stating that 15% of I's customers switch to II, the survey tells us that 85% of I's customers remain customers of I. Similarly, the fact that 5% of II's customers switch to I means that 95% of II's customers remain customers of II. Writing this information as a matrix gives

$$\begin{matrix} & \begin{matrix} \text{I} & \ \ \text{II} \end{matrix} \\ \begin{matrix} \text{I} \\ \text{II} \end{matrix} & \begin{bmatrix} .85 & .15 \\ .05 & .95 \end{bmatrix} \end{matrix} = \begin{matrix} & \begin{matrix} \text{I} & \ \text{II} \end{matrix} \\ \begin{matrix} \text{I} \\ \text{II} \end{matrix} & \begin{bmatrix} \frac{85}{100} & \frac{15}{100} \\ \frac{5}{100} & \frac{95}{100} \end{bmatrix} \end{matrix} = \begin{matrix} & \begin{matrix} \text{I} & \ \text{II} \end{matrix} \\ \begin{matrix} \text{I} \\ \text{II} \end{matrix} & \begin{bmatrix} \frac{17}{20} & \frac{3}{20} \\ \frac{1}{20} & \frac{19}{20} \end{bmatrix} \end{matrix}$$

By definition, the fixed probability vector for this matrix is found to be $[\frac{1}{4} \quad \frac{3}{4}]$. (Prove this.) Hence, the customers would be divided $\frac{1}{4}$ to $\frac{3}{4}$, or 37,500 for I and 112,500 for II, after a period of time. This result would indicate that the woman should invest in company II, but the amount of time required for the division to reach this fixed vector may affect her decision.

$$[130,000 \quad 20,000] \begin{bmatrix} \frac{17}{20} & \frac{3}{20} \\ \frac{1}{20} & \frac{19}{20} \end{bmatrix} = [111,500 \quad 38,500]$$

This product indicates that at the end of 1 month, company I will have 111,500 customers and company II will have 38,500 customers. Multiplying again gives

$$[111,500 \quad 38,500] \begin{bmatrix} \frac{17}{20} & \frac{3}{20} \\ \frac{1}{20} & \frac{19}{20} \end{bmatrix} = [96,700 \quad 53,300]$$

We find that at the end of 2 months, company I will have 96,700 customers and company II will have 53,300 customers. Another multiplication yields

$$[96,700 \quad 53,300] \begin{bmatrix} \frac{17}{20} & \frac{3}{20} \\ \frac{1}{20} & \frac{19}{20} \end{bmatrix} = [84,860 \quad 65,140]$$

for the customer distribution after 3 months. After 4 months, it becomes [75,388 $\quad$ 74,612], at which point the customers are almost equally divided. After 16 months, it becomes approximately 40,000 for I and 109,900 for II. This indicates that the fixed vector is approached fairly quickly in this case.

Exercise Set **7.2**

A   **1.** The transition matrix of a Markov chain is

$$A = \begin{bmatrix} .7 & .3 \\ .4 & .6 \end{bmatrix}$$

Possible initial-state vectors are

$$\mathbf{X}_0 = [1000 \quad 2000]$$
$$\mathbf{X}'_0 = [1 \quad 0]$$
$$\mathbf{X}''_0 = [\frac{1}{5} \quad \frac{4}{5}]$$

Compute the following:

a. $\mathbf{X}_0 A$ b. $\mathbf{X}'_0 A$ c. $\mathbf{X}''_0 A$
d. $\mathbf{X}_0 A^2$ e. $\mathbf{X}'_0 A^2$ f. $\mathbf{X}''_0 A^2$

2. Which of the following transition matrices are regular?

a. $\begin{bmatrix} \frac{1}{2} & \frac{1}{2} \\ 0 & 1 \end{bmatrix}$ b. $\begin{bmatrix} 0 & 1 \\ \frac{1}{2} & \frac{1}{2} \end{bmatrix}$ c. $\begin{bmatrix} 1 & 0 \\ \frac{1}{2} & \frac{1}{2} \end{bmatrix}$

d. $\begin{bmatrix} 0 & 1 \\ 1 & 0 \end{bmatrix}$ e. $\begin{bmatrix} \frac{1}{3} & \frac{2}{3} \\ 1 & 0 \end{bmatrix}$ f. $\begin{bmatrix} \frac{1}{3} & \frac{2}{3} \\ 0 & 1 \end{bmatrix}$

g. $\begin{bmatrix} 1 & 0 \\ \frac{1}{3} & \frac{2}{3} \end{bmatrix}$ h. $\begin{bmatrix} 0 & 1 \\ \frac{1}{3} & \frac{2}{3} \end{bmatrix}$ i. $\begin{bmatrix} 1 & 0 \\ \frac{3}{4} & \frac{1}{4} \end{bmatrix}$

$$\textbf{j.} \begin{bmatrix} 0 & 1 \\ \frac{3}{4} & \frac{1}{4} \end{bmatrix} \qquad \textbf{k.} \begin{bmatrix} \frac{2}{3} & \frac{1}{3} \\ \frac{3}{4} & \frac{1}{4} \end{bmatrix} \qquad \textbf{l.} \begin{bmatrix} 1 & 0 & 0 \\ \frac{1}{3} & \frac{1}{3} & \frac{1}{3} \\ 0 & \frac{3}{4} & \frac{1}{4} \end{bmatrix}$$

$$\textbf{m.} \begin{bmatrix} \frac{1}{3} & \frac{2}{3} & 0 \\ \frac{1}{2} & 0 & \frac{1}{2} \\ 0 & 1 & 0 \end{bmatrix} \qquad \textbf{n.} \begin{bmatrix} 0 & 1 & 0 \\ \frac{1}{2} & 0 & \frac{1}{2} \\ \frac{1}{3} & \frac{2}{3} & 0 \end{bmatrix}$$

3. For each of the regular matrices of exercise 2, find the fixed probability vector. Also, find the matrix that each regular matrix approaches as it is raised to higher powers.

4. Do any of the matrices in exercise 2 that are not regular have fixed probability vectors?

5. Determine the steady-state vector **X** and the long-term transition matrix **M** for the Markov chains having the following initial states $\mathbf{X_0}$ and transition matrices **A**.

   a. [50 70] $\qquad \mathbf{A} = \begin{bmatrix} 1 & 0 \\ \frac{1}{2} & \frac{1}{2} \end{bmatrix}$

   b. [60 30] $\qquad \mathbf{A} = \begin{bmatrix} .7 & .3 \\ .5 & .5 \end{bmatrix}$

   c. [100 200 300] $\qquad \mathbf{A} = \begin{bmatrix} 0 & .5 & .5 \\ .8 & .1 & .1 \\ .2 & .2 & .6 \end{bmatrix}$

B 6. Find the steady-state matrix for each transition matrix below.

   a. $\begin{bmatrix} .7 & .3 \\ .4 & .6 \end{bmatrix}$ $\qquad$ **b.** $\begin{bmatrix} .5 & .5 \\ .3 & .7 \end{bmatrix}$

   c. $\begin{bmatrix} 0 & .5 & .5 \\ .8 & .1 & .1 \\ .2 & .2 & .6 \end{bmatrix}$ $\qquad$ **d.** $\begin{bmatrix} .3 & .7 & 0 \\ .6 & .3 & .1 \\ .3 & .2 & .5 \end{bmatrix}$

C 7. Compute the first five powers of the following transition matrix.

$$\mathbf{A} = \begin{bmatrix} .30 & .70 \\ .80 & .20 \end{bmatrix}$$

   Can you guess the steady-state vector?

8. For the following transition matrices, in which state is the system most likely to be found in the long run?

   a. $\begin{bmatrix} .6 & .4 \\ .2 & .8 \end{bmatrix}$ $\qquad$ **b.** $\begin{bmatrix} .5 & .5 \\ .4 & .6 \end{bmatrix}$

   c. $\begin{bmatrix} \frac{1}{3} & \frac{1}{3} & \frac{1}{3} \\ \frac{1}{4} & \frac{1}{4} & \frac{1}{2} \\ \frac{1}{5} & \frac{1}{5} & \frac{3}{5} \end{bmatrix}$ $\qquad$ **d.** $\begin{bmatrix} .3 & .7 & 0 \\ .8 & .1 & .1 \\ .3 & .2 & .5 \end{bmatrix}$

Business 9. **Marketing.** Two newspapers in town, the *Star* and the *Times*, are competing for customers. A study shows the following: At the beginning of the study, the *Star* had $\frac{2}{3}$ of the customers; at the end of a year, it is found that the *Star* kept 60% of its customers and lost 40% to the *Times*. The *Times* kept 70% of its customers and lost 30% to the *Star*. What will be the customer distribution
   a. at the end of next year?
   b. 2 years after the study was made?
   c. What is the long-range distribution prediction?

10. **Marketing.** Three hair tonic companies, Stickemdown, Standemup, and Greasy, are competing for customers. A study reveals the following: At the beginning of the study, Stickemdown had $\frac{1}{4}$ of the customers, Standemup had $\frac{1}{4}$, and Greasy had $\frac{1}{2}$. At the end of a year, Stickemdown kept 75% of its customers, lost 20% to Standemup, and lost 5% to Greasy; Standemup kept 50% of its customers, lost 30% to Stickemdown, and lost 20% to Greasy; Greasy kept 60% of its customers, lost 30% to Stickemdown, and lost 10% to Standemup. Find the transition matrix.

a. What is the customer distribution at the end of the year in which the study was made?

b. What will it be a year after the study was made?

c. What will be the long-range distribution prediction?

11. **Marketing.** Redo exercise 10 if the distribution at the beginning of the study is Stickemdown, $\frac{1}{8}$; Standemup, $\frac{3}{8}$; and Greasy, $\frac{1}{2}$.

12. **Demographics.** Over a given year, the following shifts in employment are recorded.

From business (or industry) to business (or industry)	75%
From business (or industry) to unemployment	15%
From business (or industry) to self-employment	10%
From unemployment to business (or industry)	25%
From unemployment to unemployment	60%
From unemployment to self-employment	15%
From self-employment to business (or industry)	5%
From self-employment to unemployment	5%
From self-employment to self-employment	90%

How will people be distributed in the various employment categories in the long run?

13. **Genetics.** Assume that the transition matrix for an inheritance trait is given by the following matrix:

$$
\begin{array}{c}
\textbf{Offspring} \\
\begin{array}{ccc} R & H & D \end{array} \\
\textbf{Parents}\ \begin{array}{c} R \\ H \\ D \end{array}
\begin{bmatrix}
\frac{1}{4} & \frac{3}{4} & 0 \\
\frac{1}{4} & \frac{1}{2} & \frac{1}{4} \\
0 & \frac{3}{4} & \frac{1}{4}
\end{bmatrix}
\end{array}
$$

Find the fixed probability vector, and interpret your results.

14. **Genetics.** Assume that research indicates the following transition matrix for an inheritance trait:

$$
\begin{array}{c}
\textbf{Offspring} \\
\begin{array}{ccc} R & H & D \end{array} \\
\textbf{Parents}\ \begin{array}{c} R \\ H \\ D \end{array}
\begin{bmatrix}
\frac{1}{2} & \frac{1}{2} & 0 \\
\frac{1}{8} & \frac{5}{8} & \frac{1}{4} \\
0 & \frac{1}{2} & \frac{1}{2}
\end{bmatrix}
\end{array}
$$

Find the fixed probability vector, and interpret your results.

15. **Political Parties.** In a town three political parties are competing for members. A survey shows that party I has 50,000 members, party II has 120,000 members, and party III

has 30,000 members. The survey predicts the following transition matrix:

$$
\begin{array}{c}
 \\
\text{I} \\
\text{II} \\
\text{III}
\end{array}
\begin{array}{ccc}
\text{I} & \text{II} & \text{III} \\
\left[\begin{array}{ccc}
.7 & .1 & .2 \\
.2 & .5 & .3 \\
.2 & .2 & .6
\end{array}\right]
\end{array}
$$

How will the members be distributed in the long run?

3 Absorbing Markov Chains

> One of the distinct properties of regular Markov chains is that for a large enough number of transitions there is a positive probability that a system will move from a given state to any other state.
>
> In this section we observe one way for this to fail. That is, we observe a state from which transitions are impossible and introduce a type of chain called an **absorbing Markov chain.**
>
> Absorbing Markov chains are useful tools in many fields of study. They are especially useful in the designing of models by research scientists.

We now discuss a class of Markov chains that have very different characteristics from any discussed in the preceding sections. We introduce this new concept with the definition of an **absorbing state**:

Absorbing State	A state of a Markov chain is an absorbing state if it is impossible to leave it.

Let $p_{ii} = 1$ and $p_{ij} = 0$ when $i \neq j$ in the ith row of a transition matrix. When this is true we have an absorbing state of a Markov chain.

EXAMPLE 12 In

$$
\left[\begin{array}{ccc}
\frac{1}{2} & \frac{1}{4} & \frac{1}{4} \\
1 & 0 & 0 \\
0 & 0 & 1
\end{array}\right]
$$

note that in the third row $p_{33} = 1$ and $p_{3j} = 0$ when $j \neq 3$. Thus, we have an absorbing state. Note in the second row that [1, 0, 0] does not represent an absorbing state because it has $p_{21} = 1$ and not $p_{22} = 1$.

Now, absorbing Markov chains must have absorbing states, but this is not sufficient to assure that a chain is absorbing. In absorbing Markov chains it must be possible to go from a nonabsorbing state to an absorbing state.

Absorbing Markov Chain

A Markov chain is an absorbing Markov chain if

1. it has at least one absorbing state, and
2. it is possible to go from any nonabsorbing state to an absorbing state in one or more steps.

The second part of this requirement may be written as follows. For every nonabsorbing state i and absorbing state j, there is a probability ($\neq 0$) of the transition from state i to state j in one or more steps.

EXAMPLE 13 Classify the following transition matrices as representing absorbing Markov or nonabsorbing Markov chains and explain.

$$\textbf{a.} \begin{bmatrix} \frac{1}{4} & \frac{1}{4} & \frac{1}{2} \\ 0 & 1 & 0 \\ \frac{3}{10} & \frac{3}{10} & \frac{4}{10} \end{bmatrix} \qquad \textbf{b.} \begin{bmatrix} \frac{1}{2} & \frac{1}{2} & 0 \\ \frac{4}{10} & \frac{6}{10} & 0 \\ 0 & 0 & 1 \end{bmatrix}$$

Solution
a. This is an absorbing Markov chain because [0 1 0] represents an absorbing state; also, because $p_{12} = \frac{1}{4}$ and $p_{32} = \frac{3}{10}$, it is possible to go from state 1 and state 3 to state 2.

b. This is not an absorbing Markov chain. [0 0 1] represents an absorbing state, but it is impossible to go from either state 1 to state 3 or from state 2 to state 3 since $p_{13} = 0$ and $p_{23} = 0$.

EXAMPLE 14 Show that

$$\begin{bmatrix} 1 & 0 & 0 \\ 0 & .5 & .5 \\ .3 & .3 & .4 \end{bmatrix}$$

is an absorbing Markov chain.

Solution At first it seems impossible to go from state 2 to state 1 (the absorbing state) since $p_{21} = 0$. However, $p_{23} \neq 0$, so it is possible to go from state 2 to state 3. Then, since $p_{31} \neq 0$, it is possible to go to state 1. Therefore, this transition matrix represents an absorbing Markov chain.

It is often easier to discuss absorbing Markov chains when the transition matrix is written in **canonical form.** In canonical form the absorbing states are collected together. The states are renamed so that 1s appear down the diagonal of the part representing absorbing states. The other states will change automatically to accommodate the preceding change.

EXAMPLE 15 Write in canonical form the transition matrix of the following absorbing Markov chain.

$$
\begin{array}{c}
 & \begin{array}{ccc} S_1 & S_2 & S_3 \end{array} \\
\begin{array}{c} S_1 \\ S_2 \\ S_3 \end{array} &
\left[\begin{array}{ccc}
.3 & .3 & .4 \\
0 & 1 & 0 \\
.5 & .2 & .3
\end{array}\right]
\end{array}
$$

Solution In canonical form, the 1 should appear in the upper left corner of the transition matrix.

$$
\begin{array}{c}
 & \begin{array}{ccc} S_2 & S_1 & S_3 \end{array} \\
\begin{array}{c} S_2 \\ S_1 \\ S_3 \end{array} &
\left[\begin{array}{ccc}
1 & 0 & 0 \\
.3 & .3 & .4 \\
.2 & .5 & .3
\end{array}\right]
\end{array}
$$

EXAMPLE 16 Write in canonical form the transition matrix of the following absorbing Markov chain

$$
\begin{array}{c}
 & \begin{array}{cccc} S_1 & S_2 & S_3 & S_4 \end{array} \\
\begin{array}{c} S_1 \\ S_2 \\ S_3 \\ S_4 \end{array} &
\left[\begin{array}{cccc}
.2 & .2 & .2 & .4 \\
0 & 1 & 0 & 0 \\
.3 & .2 & 0 & .5 \\
0 & 0 & 0 & 1
\end{array}\right]
\end{array}
$$

Solution

$$
\begin{array}{c}
 & \begin{array}{cccc} S_4 & S_2 & S_3 & S_1 \end{array} \\
\begin{array}{c} S_4 \\ S_2 \\ S_3 \\ S_1 \end{array} &
\left[\begin{array}{cccc}
1 & 0 & 0 & 0 \\
0 & 1 & 0 & 0 \\
.5 & .2 & 0 & .3 \\
.4 & .2 & .2 & .2
\end{array}\right]
\end{array}
$$

In canonical form an $n \times n$ transition matrix can be written as

$$
\left[\begin{array}{cc}
\mathbf{C} & \mathbf{S} \\
\mathbf{R} & \mathbf{M}
\end{array}\right]
$$

where $\mathbf{C}$ is a $k \times k$ identity matrix, $\mathbf{M}$ is a $(n - k) \times (n - k)$ matrix, $\mathbf{R}$ is an $(n - k) \times k$ matrix, and $\mathbf{S}$ is a zero matrix. We form the matrix $\mathbf{I} - \mathbf{M}$, where $\mathbf{I}$ is the $(n - k) \times (n - k)$ identity matrix. The inverse of $\mathbf{I} - \mathbf{M}$ is defined as follows:

Fundamental Matrix

The fundamental matrix ($\mathbf{F}$) for an absorbing Markov chain is

$$
\mathbf{F} = (\mathbf{I} - \mathbf{M})^{-1}
$$

where $\mathbf{M}$ is obtained from the canonical form of the transition matrix.

EXAMPLE 17   Find the fundamental matrix for the transition matrix

$$\begin{bmatrix} .2 & .2 & .2 & .4 \\ 0 & 1 & 0 & 0 \\ .3 & .2 & 0 & .5 \\ 0 & 0 & 0 & 1 \end{bmatrix}$$

Solution   **M** is obtained from Example 16; thus,

$$\mathbf{I} - \mathbf{M} = \begin{bmatrix} 1 & 0 \\ 0 & 1 \end{bmatrix} - \begin{bmatrix} 0 & .3 \\ .2 & .2 \end{bmatrix} = \begin{bmatrix} 1 & -.3 \\ -.2 & .8 \end{bmatrix}$$

$$\mathbf{F} = (\mathbf{I} - \mathbf{M})^{-1} = \begin{bmatrix} \frac{80}{74} & \frac{30}{74} \\ \frac{20}{74} & \frac{100}{74} \end{bmatrix}$$

The main characteristic of an absorbing Markov chain is that in the long run the absorbing states will gradually absorb the other states. However, we do not know when a system will reach an absorbing state. The expected number of transitions is given by the following theorem:

Use of the Fundamental Matrix

> **1.** The sum of the entries in the ith row of the fundamental matrix gives the expected number of transitions of a system that begins in the ith state before reaching an absorbing state.
> **2.** The entry in the i, j position of the fundamental matrix gives the expected number of times that a system that begins in the ith nonabsorbing state will be in the jth nonabsorbing state before reaching an absorbing state.

EXAMPLE 18   Consider the following maze:

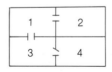

A mouse is just as likely to leave a state as to stay in the state. The mouse can enter state 4 but cannot get out. Set up a transition matrix and find the expected number of transitions, or states the mouse will occupy, with the mouse starting in each state before reaching absorbing state 4. If the mouse is released in state 2, in state 1, or in state 3, find the expected number of times it will be in each of the nonabsorbing states.

Solution   The probability of staying in state 1 is $\frac{1}{2}$; the probability of leaving is $\frac{1}{2}$. The probability of going to state 2 or state 3 is then $\frac{1}{4}$. Therefore, we have the first line of the transition matrix. Can you verify the remaining probabilities of the transition matrix?

$$
\begin{array}{c}
\begin{array}{cccc} S_1 & S_2 & S_3 & S_4 \end{array} \\
\begin{array}{c} S_1 \\ S_2 \\ S_3 \\ S_4 \end{array}
\begin{bmatrix}
\frac{1}{2} & \frac{1}{4} & \frac{1}{4} & 0 \\
\frac{1}{2} & \frac{1}{2} & 0 & 0 \\
\frac{1}{4} & 0 & \frac{1}{2} & \frac{1}{4} \\
0 & 0 & 0 & 1
\end{bmatrix}
\end{array}
$$

In canonical form this matrix can be written as

$$
\begin{array}{c}
\begin{array}{cccc} S_4 & S_2 & S_3 & S_1 \end{array} \\
\begin{array}{c} S_4 \\ S_2 \\ S_3 \\ S_1 \end{array}
\begin{bmatrix}
1 & 0 & 0 & 0 \\
0 & \frac{1}{2} & 0 & \frac{1}{2} \\
\frac{1}{4} & 0 & \frac{1}{2} & \frac{1}{4} \\
0 & \frac{1}{4} & \frac{1}{4} & \frac{1}{2}
\end{bmatrix}
\end{array}
$$

Thus,

$$
\mathbf{I} - \mathbf{M} =
\begin{bmatrix}
1 & 0 & 0 \\
0 & 1 & 0 \\
0 & 0 & 1
\end{bmatrix}
-
\begin{bmatrix}
\frac{1}{2} & 0 & \frac{1}{2} \\
0 & \frac{1}{2} & \frac{1}{4} \\
\frac{1}{4} & \frac{1}{4} & \frac{1}{2}
\end{bmatrix}
=
\begin{bmatrix}
\frac{1}{2} & 0 & -\frac{1}{2} \\
0 & \frac{1}{2} & -\frac{1}{4} \\
-\frac{1}{4} & -\frac{1}{4} & \frac{1}{2}
\end{bmatrix}
$$

$$
\mathbf{F} = (\mathbf{I} - \mathbf{M})^{-1} =
\begin{array}{c}
\begin{array}{ccc} S_2 & S_3 & S_1 \end{array} \\
\begin{array}{c} S_2 \\ S_3 \\ S_1 \end{array}
\begin{bmatrix}
6 & 4 & 8 \\
2 & 4 & 4 \\
4 & 4 & 8
\end{bmatrix}
\end{array}
$$

If the mouse is released in state 2, the expected number of times it will occupy state 3 before reaching the absorbing state is four; for state 1, eight; and for state 2, six.

If the mouse is released in state 1, the expected number of times it will be in state 2 is four; in state 3, four; and in state 1, eight.

If the mouse is released in state 3, the expected number of times it will be in state 2 is two; in state 1, four; and in state 3, four.

If the mouse starts in state 2, it is expected to be in 18 different states before reaching the absorbing state; starting in state 1, 16 transitions are expected; and starting in state 3, 10 are expected.

Exercise Set 7.3

A 1. Consider the Markov chains defined by the following transition matrices. Give all the absorbing states in each chain, and state whether or not the chain is absorbing.

a.
$$
\begin{bmatrix}
.1 & .5 & .4 \\
0 & 1 & 0 \\
.6 & .4 & 0
\end{bmatrix}
$$

b.
$$
\begin{bmatrix}
.4 & .6 & 0 \\
.2 & .7 & .1 \\
0 & 0 & 1
\end{bmatrix}
$$

c.
$$
\begin{bmatrix}
0 & .6 & .4 \\
0 & 1 & 0 \\
\frac{1}{3} & \frac{1}{3} & \frac{1}{3}
\end{bmatrix}
$$

d.
$$
\begin{bmatrix}
\frac{1}{3} & 0 & \frac{2}{3} \\
0 & 1 & 0 \\
\frac{1}{2} & \frac{1}{2} & 0
\end{bmatrix}
$$

$$\text{e.}\begin{bmatrix} 1 & 0 & 0 & 0 \\ 0 & 1 & 0 & 0 \\ \frac{2}{5} & 0 & \frac{3}{5} & 0 \\ 0 & \frac{1}{3} & \frac{1}{3} & \frac{1}{3} \end{bmatrix} \quad \text{f.}\begin{bmatrix} 1 & 0 & 0 & 0 \\ 0 & \frac{1}{3} & \frac{1}{3} & \frac{1}{3} \\ 0 & 0 & 1 & 0 \\ 0 & \frac{1}{2} & 0 & \frac{1}{2} \end{bmatrix} \quad \text{g.}\begin{bmatrix} 1 & 0 & 0 & 0 \\ .1 & .1 & .7 & .1 \\ 0 & 1 & 0 & 0 \\ .6 & .3 & .1 & 0 \end{bmatrix}$$

$$\text{h.}\begin{bmatrix} .9 & .1 & 0 & 0 \\ 0 & 1 & 0 & 0 \\ 0 & 0 & 1 & 0 \\ 0 & .2 & .5 & .3 \end{bmatrix} \quad \text{i.}\begin{bmatrix} .4 & .4 & .2 & 0 \\ .1 & .6 & 0 & .3 \\ 0 & 0 & 1 & 0 \\ .2 & .1 & 0 & .7 \end{bmatrix} \quad \text{j.}\begin{bmatrix} 0 & .1 & .7 & .2 \\ 0 & .6 & .4 & 0 \\ 0 & 0 & .3 & .7 \\ 0 & 0 & 0 & 1 \end{bmatrix}$$

B **2.** Write in canonical form the transition matrix for each absorbing Markov chain in exercise 1.

3. Use the canonical forms in exercise 2 to label the rows and columns in terms of the original states. (See Example 16.)

C **4.** In exercise 2, find the fundamental matrix for each absorbing Markov chain.

5. For each part of exercise 1, find the expected number of transitions before each non-absorbing state reaches an absorbing state for the absorbing Markov chains.

6. Use exercise 4 to find the expected number of times that a system starting in one non-absorbing state will be in another nonabsorbing state before it goes to an absorbing state.

Business **7. Product Analysis.** A new company is so sure of its product that it believes that once a customer tries the product the customer will never change to another product. A study of customer satisfaction indicates the following:

	A	B	C	D
A	.70	.20	.05	.05
B	.20	.60	.12	.08
C	.04	.05	.90	.01
D	0	0	0	1

The first row implies that 70% of those who use the product of company A will stay with A the next year, 20% will switch to B's product, 5% will switch to C's product, and 5% will switch to D's product.

a. Under the given circumstances, can company D expect to attain all customers at some future date?

b. If the distribution of sales now is A, $10,000,000; B, $8,000,000; C, $6,000,000; and D, $250,000, what will be the distribution of sales in 4 years?

c. Find the expected number of years before D has all of A's sales.

d. All of B's sales.

e. All of C's sales.

Life Sciences **8. Genetics.** The following transition matrix shows a rose cross-fertilization.

	Red	Pink	White
Red	1	0	0
Pink	$\frac{1}{2}$	$\frac{1}{2}$	0
White	1	0	0

Why is this an absorbing Markov chain? What is the long-term result of such cross-fertilization?

9. Psychology. A mouse moves randomly in the following maze:

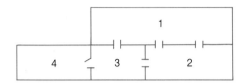

A mouse in room 1 has the probabilities $p_{11} = 0$, $p_{12} = \frac{2}{3}$, and $p_{13} = \frac{1}{3}$ of moving to the various rooms. Room 4 is a trap door, so that when the mouse goes to room 4, it cannot return.

a. Form a transition matrix for this model.

b. Does this transition matrix represent an absorbing Markov chain?

c. If the mouse is placed in room 1, how many changes of rooms are expected before the mouse is trapped in room 4?

d. Repeat part **c** for room 2.

e. Repeat part **c** for room 3.

 Introduction to the Theory of Games

Most of us like to play games. From childhood games of hide-and-seek and London Bridge, we progress to baseball, football, and "post office." As we grow older, we compete in games such as poker, bridge, or chess. Have you realized that for many simple games a mathematical model can be constructed that will describe how you should play to win, or at least to keep from losing too much?

On a third-down play with 5 yards to go, the defensive football captain says, "I believe the quarterback will pass. Let's use our pass defense and rush." The offensive quarterback tries to guess what the defense is going to do. He says, "They're probably thinking I'll pass. I'll call the draw play up the middle." Notice that each opponent is trying to anticipate what the other will do and then act accordingly. This type of strategy is present in most games, but it also occurs in many daily activities and decisions. A student tries to determine what his professor considers important and then studies accordingly. A doctor tries to determine what illness will cause certain symptoms and then treats her patient accordingly. A sociologist tries to determine what causes certain social problems and then seeks to reduce the causes of these problems.

John Von Neumann, in the 1920s, was one of the first people to research the theory of games. Since the theory of games and linear programming are closely related, it was not until World War II, when linear programming was developed, that the theory of games was developed sufficiently to be recognized as a branch of mathematics.

In the preceding chapters we considered decision techniques such as linear programming in which we assumed a benign environment. That is, we have not considered problems in which a decision-maker faces active competition as she or he makes decisions. In this chapter the decision-maker faces an active opponent—a hostile, aggressive player who is trying to win. This type of problem is similar to many of our actual experiences. Recent development in mathematical modeling has brought many economic, political, and social games within the scope of present-day game theory.

To understand how game theory may be useful in helping to make decisions, consider the following example.

EXAMPLE 19 The board of education of a small community is planning to build a new school in location I or location II. The county board of education decides to counter this by building a new school in location III or location IV. Neither system wishes to lose students, but a careful study indicates the following outcomes.

If the community builds in location I and the county builds in location III, the community will gain 600 students from the county. If the community builds in location I and the county builds in location IV, the community will gain 800 students from the county. If the community builds in location II and the county builds in location III, the community will lose 400 students to the county. If the community builds in location II and the county builds in location IV, the community will gain 900 students from the county. Where should the boards build their schools in order to be assured of gaining the largest number or losing the smallest number of students?

Solution This information may be written as the following matrix

$$
\begin{array}{c}
\textbf{County Builds} \\
\begin{array}{cc}
\text{III} & \text{IV}
\end{array}
\end{array}
$$

$$
\textbf{Community Builds} \quad
\begin{array}{c}
\text{I} \\
\text{II}
\end{array}
\begin{bmatrix}
600 & 800 \\
-400 & 900
\end{bmatrix}
$$

where the entries represent the net change in students from the viewpoint of the community. Note from the first row of the matrix that the community will always gain students from the county if it builds in location I. Hence, the community should build in location I. Knowing this, the only choice left for the county is to minimize the number of students it will lose to the community. Hence, the county should build in location III.

The preceding example illustrates the type of problem encountered in game theory. We now introduce the notation, terminology, and theory for playing games. We refer to the participants as **players,** and the amounts that the players gain or lose as **payoffs.** A matrix of payoffs (sometimes called the **payoff matrix**) defines a game. The rows of the payoff matrix provide the options available to one player (called the **row player**), and the columns provide the options available to a second player (called the **column player**).

Let's assume there are two players, X and Y. A play of the game consists of X choosing a row of matrix **A** at the same time that Y chooses a column of matrix

A. After each play, X receives from Y the amount equal to the element in the chosen row and column if the element is positive. If the element is negative, Y receives this amount from X. For example, in the matrix

$$X \begin{array}{c} Y \\ \begin{bmatrix} 2 & -1 & 3 \\ 4 & -5 & 2 \end{bmatrix} \end{array}$$

if X should select the first row and Y the third column, then X would win three units. If Y selects the second column when X selects the first row, Y would win one unit.

Consider a two-person game defined by the matrix

$$X \begin{array}{c} Y \\ \begin{bmatrix} 2 & 5 \\ -1 & -2 \end{bmatrix} \end{array}$$

Notice that the game is biased against player Y since X would probably select the first row so that she would never lose; however, since Y is involved in the game, he will do his best to make his loss as small as possible. This is comparable to a situation in which a person, finding he must sustain a loss for a period of time, attempts to minimize this loss. X selects the first row, because she wins with this row regardless of Y's selection. To minimize his loss, Y must select the first column.

In each of the preceding examples each player has a fixed number of options available on each play, and on each play the gain of one player is the loss of the other player. Such games are called **two-person zero-sum games**.

Zero-Sum Game	A game is a **zero-sum game** if the sum of the gains and losses of the players is always equal to zero.

By the **strategy** of a game for X, we mean the decision to select the rows according to a probability distribution; the **strategy** for Y is the selection of the columns by a probability distribution. We indicate the strategy of X by a row vector $\mathbf{P} = [p_1 \quad p_2 \quad p_3 \quad \cdots \quad p_n]$, where $p_1 + p_2 + p_3 + \cdots + p_n = 1$. That is, X selects row 1 with a probability of p_1 or row 2 with a probability of p_2, and so forth. In a like manner, the strategy of Y is defined by the column vector

$$\mathbf{Q} = \begin{bmatrix} q_1 \\ q_2 \\ \vdots \\ q_m \end{bmatrix} \quad \text{where } q_1 + q_2 + \cdots + q_m = 1$$

Strategies	A strategy in which one p_i and one q_i are 1 and all other p_i and q_i are 0 is called a **pure strategy**; otherwise, it is called a **mixed strategy**.

Actually a pure strategy is one in which X plays the same row and Y plays the same column repeatedly. Of course, X would like to win as much as possible, and Y would like to keep X from winning.

Optimum Strategies	The strategies used when X and Y play their best are called **optimum strategies.**

By "playing their best" we mean that X plays so that she can win as much as possible, regardless of what Y does; similarly, Y plays so that he can keep X's winnings as small as possible, regardless of what X does.

Value of a Game	The value won by X (or by Y) when both X and Y play their optimum strategy is called the **value of the game.** If the value of the game is zero, the game is said to be **fair.**

Consider the matrix

$$\mathbf{A} = \begin{bmatrix} a_{11} & a_{12} \\ a_{21} & a_{22} \end{bmatrix}$$

as defining a game in which

$$\mathbf{P} = [p_1 \quad p_2] \quad \text{and} \quad \mathbf{Q} = \begin{bmatrix} q_1 \\ q_2 \end{bmatrix}$$

represent the strategies of X and Y, respectively. The probability that a_{12} will be the payoff is $p_1 q_2$. Likewise, the probabilities for a_{11}, a_{21}, and a_{22} are $p_1 q_1$, $p_2 q_1$, and $p_2 q_2$, respectively.

The **expected value** or **expectation** of the 2 × 2 matrix game is:

$$\text{Expectation} = p_1 a_{11} q_1 + p_1 a_{12} q_2 + p_2 a_{21} q_1 + p_2 a_{22} q_2$$

This definition can be written in matrix form as

$$\text{Expectation} = [p_1 \quad p_2] \cdot \begin{bmatrix} a_{11} & a_{12} \\ a_{21} & a_{22} \end{bmatrix} \cdot \begin{bmatrix} q_1 \\ q_2 \end{bmatrix}$$

In general, we have the following definition of expectation:

Expectation of a Game

> Expectation = **PAQ**
>
> where
>
> $$\mathbf{P} = [p_1 \quad p_2 \quad \cdots \quad p_n] \quad \text{and} \quad \mathbf{Q} = \begin{bmatrix} q_1 \\ q_2 \\ \vdots \\ q_m \end{bmatrix}$$
>
> and **A** is the $n \times m$ payoff matrix of the game.

EXAMPLE 20 Suppose that X decides to use the strategy $[\frac{1}{4} \quad \frac{1}{2} \quad \frac{1}{4}]$ and Y decides to use the strategy

$$\begin{bmatrix} \frac{1}{6} \\ \frac{1}{6} \\ \frac{2}{3} \end{bmatrix}$$

Find the expectation of the matrix game

$$\begin{bmatrix} -1 & 3 & 2 \\ 4 & -3 & -2 \\ 1 & -1 & 0 \end{bmatrix}$$

Solution The expectation of the game is defined to be **PAQ**.

$$\text{Expectation} = [\tfrac{1}{4} \quad \tfrac{1}{2} \quad \tfrac{1}{4}] \cdot \begin{bmatrix} -1 & 3 & 2 \\ 4 & -3 & -2 \\ 1 & -1 & 0 \end{bmatrix} \cdot \begin{bmatrix} \frac{1}{6} \\ \frac{1}{6} \\ \frac{2}{3} \end{bmatrix}$$

$$= [2 \quad -1 \quad -\tfrac{1}{2}] \cdot \begin{bmatrix} \frac{1}{6} \\ \frac{1}{6} \\ \frac{2}{3} \end{bmatrix}$$

$$= -\tfrac{1}{6}$$

If the strategies for a game are optimum, the expectation is the same as the value of the game. Otherwise, it is not.

EXAMPLE 21 For the game $\mathbf{A} = \begin{bmatrix} 2 & 5 \\ -1 & -2 \end{bmatrix}$, the strategies $\mathbf{P} = [1 \quad 0]$ and $\mathbf{Q} = \begin{bmatrix} 1 \\ 0 \end{bmatrix}$ are optimum.

$$\text{Expectation} = \mathbf{PAQ} = [1 \quad 0] \cdot \begin{bmatrix} 2 & 5 \\ -1 & -2 \end{bmatrix} \cdot \begin{bmatrix} 1 \\ 0 \end{bmatrix} = [2 \quad 5] \cdot \begin{bmatrix} 1 \\ 0 \end{bmatrix}$$

$$= 2 = \text{value of game}$$

The strategies $\mathbf{P} = [\frac{1}{2} \quad \frac{1}{2}]$ and $\mathbf{Q} = \begin{bmatrix} \frac{1}{3} \\ \frac{2}{3} \end{bmatrix}$ are not optimum.

$$\text{Expectation} = \mathbf{PAQ} = [\tfrac{1}{2} \quad \tfrac{1}{2}] \cdot \begin{bmatrix} 2 & 5 \\ -1 & -2 \end{bmatrix} \cdot \begin{bmatrix} \frac{1}{3} \\ \frac{2}{3} \end{bmatrix} = [\tfrac{1}{2} \quad \tfrac{3}{2}] \cdot \begin{bmatrix} \frac{1}{3} \\ \frac{2}{3} \end{bmatrix} = \tfrac{7}{6}$$

$\neq$ value of game

Some games are **strictly determined,** and some are not. The games discussed earlier, the school-boards game, $\begin{bmatrix} 600 & 800 \\ -400 & 900 \end{bmatrix}$, and the two-person game, $\begin{bmatrix} 2 & 5 \\ -1 & -2 \end{bmatrix}$, are examples of strictly determined games, defined as follows:

<table>
<tr><td>**Strictly Determined Game**</td><td>A matrix game is said to be strictly determined if the matrix has an entry that is the smallest element in its row and the largest element in its column. Such an entry is called a **saddle point.**</td></tr>
</table>

Of course, player X would like to select the row having an element that is the largest in its column so that she would win more if Y were to select this column. Likewise, Y would like to select a column having an element that is the smallest in its row. **It can be proved that, when a saddle point exists, the optimum strategy for both players is to select the row and the column containing the saddle point.** For this reason, the game is said to be strictly determined. This entry (the saddle point) is the value of the game.

EXAMPLE 22   Determine whether the following matrix has a saddle point. If it does, find the value of the game, and determine whether X or Y wins the game.

$$\begin{bmatrix} 1 & 0 & 1 & \boxed{-1} \\ 2 & 3 & \boxed{-4} & 7 \\ \boxed{3} & 4 & 6 & 5 \end{bmatrix}$$

Solution   First we circle the minimum value in each row. Then we inspect them to see if one of the circled numbers is the maximum value in a column. We note that 3 is the maximum value in the first column. Thus, the value of the game is 3, and X wins the game.

EXAMPLE 23   Determine whether the following matrix has a saddle point. If it does, find the value of the game, and determine whether X or Y wins the game.

$$\begin{bmatrix} 1 & 0 & 1 & \boxed{-1} \\ 2 & 1 & \boxed{-4} & 7 \\ \boxed{3} & \boxed{3} & 6 & 5 \end{bmatrix}$$

Solution   Again we circle the elements that are minimum in each row and look for circled numbers that are maximum in their columns. Note that there are two saddle points for this game, but their values are the same. The value of the game is 3, and X wins the game by selecting $\mathbf{P} = [0 \quad 0 \quad 1]$. Y selects

$$\begin{bmatrix} 1 \\ 0 \\ 0 \\ 0 \end{bmatrix} \quad \text{or} \quad \begin{bmatrix} 0 \\ 1 \\ 0 \\ 0 \end{bmatrix} \quad \text{or} \quad \begin{bmatrix} \frac{1}{2} \\ \frac{1}{2} \\ 0 \\ 0 \end{bmatrix}$$

or other strategies involving the first two columns. Hence, in this case Y's optimum strategy is not unique.

Exercise Set 7.4

A **1.** Which of the following matrix games have saddle points? Find all the saddle points.

a. $\begin{bmatrix} 0 & 3 \\ -2 & 2 \end{bmatrix}$ b. $\begin{bmatrix} 1 & 3 \\ -2 & 5 \end{bmatrix}$ c. $\begin{bmatrix} 1 & 3 & 4 \\ 3 & 3 & 4 \\ 3 & 3 & 3 \end{bmatrix}$

d. $\begin{bmatrix} 1 & -3 & 4 \\ 0 & 3 & -2 \\ 1 & -1 & 4 \end{bmatrix}$ e. $\begin{bmatrix} 0 & 4 & 1 \\ 5 & -1 & 0 \\ 4 & 5 & 4 \end{bmatrix}$ f. $\begin{bmatrix} 1 & 3 & 2 & 0 \\ -1 & 1 & -2 & 3 \\ 2 & 0 & -1 & -1 \\ 2 & 1 & -1 & 3 \end{bmatrix}$

2. For those games in exercise 1 that have saddle points, find the value of the game and the optimum strategies for X and Y.

3. Determine which of the following strictly determined games are fair. Find the optimum strategy for each player and the value of the game.

a. $\begin{bmatrix} 0 & 3 \\ -2 & 5 \end{bmatrix}$ b. $\begin{bmatrix} 5 & 2 \\ 6 & 0 \end{bmatrix}$ c. $\begin{bmatrix} 8 & -2 \\ 5 & 0 \end{bmatrix}$

d. $\begin{bmatrix} 2 & 1 \\ -2 & 0 \end{bmatrix}$ e. $\begin{bmatrix} 7 & 0 \\ 0 & -4 \end{bmatrix}$ f. $\begin{bmatrix} 5 & 2 \\ -4 & 0 \end{bmatrix}$

g. $\begin{bmatrix} -5 & 0 \\ 0 & 1 \end{bmatrix}$ h. $\begin{bmatrix} 0 & -2 & -3 \\ 2 & 0 & -4 \\ 3 & 4 & 0 \end{bmatrix}$ i. $\begin{bmatrix} 0 & 6 & 5 \\ -5 & 2 & -6 \\ -1 & -3 & 6 \end{bmatrix}$

j. $\begin{bmatrix} 0 & 3 \\ -4 & -5 \\ -3 & -2 \end{bmatrix}$ k. $\begin{bmatrix} 0 & -1 & 3 \\ 2 & -3 & 4 \end{bmatrix}$ l. $\begin{bmatrix} 2 & 3 & -1 \\ 3 & 4 & 5 \end{bmatrix}$

4. Calculate the expectations of the following matrix games for the given strategies. Are any of these games strictly determined?

a. $\begin{bmatrix} 6 & -1 \\ 5 & 7 \end{bmatrix}$, $[\frac{2}{9} \; \frac{7}{9}]$, $\begin{bmatrix} \frac{8}{9} \\ \frac{1}{9} \end{bmatrix}$ b. $\begin{bmatrix} 3 & -1 \\ -2 & 1 \end{bmatrix}$, $[\frac{3}{7} \; \frac{4}{7}]$, $\begin{bmatrix} \frac{2}{7} \\ \frac{5}{7} \end{bmatrix}$

c. $\begin{bmatrix} 4 & -5 \\ 1 & 4 \end{bmatrix}$, $[\frac{1}{4} \; \frac{3}{4}]$, $\begin{bmatrix} \frac{3}{4} \\ \frac{1}{4} \end{bmatrix}$ d. $\begin{bmatrix} 1 & 0 & 0 \\ 0 & 1 & 0 \\ 0 & 0 & 1 \end{bmatrix}$, $[\frac{1}{3} \; \frac{1}{3} \; \frac{1}{3}]$, $\begin{bmatrix} \frac{1}{3} \\ \frac{1}{3} \\ \frac{1}{3} \end{bmatrix}$

B **5.** For what values of x is the matrix strictly determined?

$$\begin{bmatrix} x & 10 & 3 \\ 0 & x & -8 \\ -4 & 6 & x \end{bmatrix}$$

C **6.** For the matrix game

$$\begin{bmatrix} x & y \\ x & z \end{bmatrix}$$

Show that this matrix game is strictly determined for all values of x, y, and z.

7. Find an example of a game that has exactly two saddle points.

Business **8.** Profits. Two companies are deciding where to locate stores in eastern Tennessee. If company A locates in city I and company B in city II, then company A can expect an annual profit of $100,000 more than company B's profit. If company A locates in city II and B in city I, then B's profits will exceed A's by $50,000. If both locate in city I, their profits will be equal. If both locate in II, then A's profits will exceed B's by $20,000. What are the optimum strategies (from the standpoint of competition) and what is the value of the game?

Social Sciences **9.** Political Parties. The Hats and the Wigs are engaged in a political campaign. Both parties are planning their strategies. The Hats have two plans, I and II, and the Wigs are countering with their plans, III and IV. A survey was conducted and obtained the following information. If the Hats choose I and the Wigs choose III, the Hats would gain 300 votes. If the Hats choose I and the Wigs choose IV, the Hats would lose 100 votes. If the Hats choose II and the Wigs choose III, the Hats would gain 400 votes. If the Hats choose II and the Wigs choose IV, the Hats would lose 150 votes. Write this survey as a matrix game, and then find the optimum strategies and value of the game.

Solving 2 × 2 Matrix Games

We have already discovered that the best strategy for two-person strictly determined games is found in the row and column that contain the saddle point. For games that are not strictly determined, a player may choose strategies according to given probabilities.

If the size of the matrix games is 2 × 2, the probabilities are easily computed. In fact, in this section there is a well-developed mathematical-model theory for finding the optimum strategies for the 2 × 2 matrix game.

Consider a 2 × 2 matrix game. If the game is strictly determined, the solution can be obtained from the saddle-point theory of the preceding section. If the game is not strictly determined, how can you find the optimum strategy for X, the optimum strategy for Y, and the value of the game?

EXAMPLE 24 Consider the nonstrictly determined game

$$\begin{bmatrix} -3 & 4 \\ 6 & -2 \end{bmatrix}$$

Find the optimum strategies of player X and player Y, and find the value of the game.

Solution   If player X chooses row 1 with a probability p, then row 2 is chosen with a probability of $1 - p$. If player Y chooses column 1, then player X expects to receive

$$E \text{ (Expectation)} = -3p + 6(1 - p) = 6 - 9p$$

If player Y chooses column 2, then player X expects to receive

$$E = 4p + (-2)(1 - p) = 6p - 2$$

We graph these expectations with E on the vertical axis and p on the horizontal.

Figure 7.3

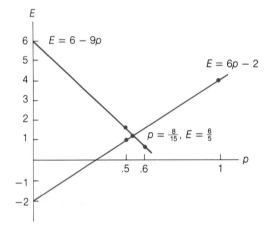

Player X wants to maximize expectations. This maximum occurs where the two lines intersect. For any other value of p, one of the two expectations is less. Solving these expectations simultaneously gives

$$6 - 9p = 6p - 2$$
$$p = \tfrac{8}{15}$$

Thus, the optimum strategy for player X is

$$[\tfrac{8}{15} \quad \tfrac{7}{15}]$$

Similarly, suppose player Y chooses column 1 with a probability of q and column 2 with a probability of $1 - q$. If player X chooses row 1, player Y expects

$$E = -3q + 4(1 - q) = 4 - 7q$$

If player X chooses row 2,

$$E = 6q + (-2)(1 - q) = 8q - 2$$

Setting $4 - 7q = 8q - 2$ gives

$$q = \tfrac{6}{15}$$

as seen in Figure 7.4.

Figure 7.4

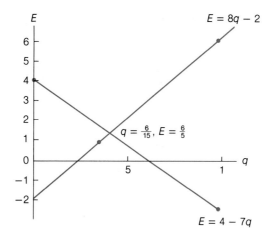

Note that E for p and E for q are identical. In fact, this value of E is the value of the game. The game is not fair but in favor of player X, who should use the strategy $[\frac{8}{15} \quad \frac{7}{15}]$ to win, $V = \frac{6}{5}$. To minimize X's expectations, player Y uses the strategy $[\frac{6}{15} \quad \frac{9}{15}]$. Note that

$$\mathbf{PAQ} = [\frac{8}{15} \quad \frac{7}{15}] \cdot \begin{bmatrix} -3 & 4 \\ 6 & -2 \end{bmatrix} \cdot \begin{bmatrix} \frac{6}{15} \\ \frac{9}{15} \end{bmatrix}$$

$$= [\frac{18}{15} \quad \frac{18}{15}] \cdot \begin{bmatrix} \frac{2}{5} \\ \frac{3}{5} \end{bmatrix}$$

$$= \frac{90}{75} = \frac{6}{5}$$

which is again the value of the game.

In general, let $\mathbf{P} = [p_1 \quad p_2]$ be the optimum strategy for X, and let $\mathbf{Q} = \begin{bmatrix} q_1 \\ q_2 \end{bmatrix}$ be the optimum strategy for Y. If V is the value of the matrix game $\mathbf{A} = \begin{bmatrix} a & b \\ c & d \end{bmatrix}$, then

$$\mathbf{PAQ} = [p_1 \quad p_2] \cdot \begin{bmatrix} a & b \\ c & d \end{bmatrix} \cdot \begin{bmatrix} q_1 \\ q_2 \end{bmatrix} = V$$

Since $p_1 + p_2 = 1$ and $q_1 + q_2 = 1$, then $p_2 = 1 - p_1$ and $q_2 = 1 - q_1$. Hence,

$$[p_1 \quad 1 - p_1] \cdot \begin{bmatrix} a & b \\ c & d \end{bmatrix} \cdot \begin{bmatrix} q_1 \\ 1 - q_1 \end{bmatrix} = V$$

Thus, $p_1 a q_1 - p_1 c q_1 - p_1 b q_1 - p_1 d - q_1 d + c q_1 + d + p_1 b + p_1 q_1 d = V$. Factoring gives

$$(a + d - b - c)\left(p_1 - \frac{d - c}{a + d - b - c}\right)\left(q_1 - \frac{d - b}{a + d - b - c}\right)$$

$$+ \frac{ad - bc}{a + d - b - c} = V$$

X wants to make the expectation as large as possible, and Y wants to make the expectation as small as possible. By making the first term zero, both players will be doing their best regardless of what the other does. X can make the first term zero by making

$$p_1 = \frac{d - c}{a + d - b - c}$$

Y can make the first term zero by making

$$q_1 = \frac{d - b}{a + d - b - c}$$

For these strategies

$$V = \frac{ad - bc}{a + d - b - c}$$

If

$$p_1 = \frac{d - c}{a + d - b - c}$$

then

$$p_2 = \frac{a - b}{a + d - b - c}$$

since

$$p_2 = 1 - p_1 = 1 - \frac{d - c}{a + d - b - c} = \frac{a - b}{a + d - b - c}$$

Optimum Strategies

For a 2 × 2 matrix game

$$\begin{bmatrix} a & b \\ c & d \end{bmatrix}$$

the **optimum strategy for X** is given by the row matrix $[p_1 \quad p_2]$, where

$$p_1 = \frac{d - c}{a + d - b - c} \qquad \text{and} \qquad p_2 = \frac{a - b}{a + d - b - c}$$

Similarly, the **optimum strategy for Y** is given by the column matrix

$$\begin{bmatrix} q_1 \\ q_2 \end{bmatrix}$$

where

$$q_1 = \frac{d - b}{a + d - b - c} \qquad \text{and} \qquad q_2 = \frac{a - c}{a + d - b - c}$$

The **value of the game** is given by

$$V = \frac{ad - bc}{a + d - b - c}$$

EXAMPLE 25 For the game defined by the following matrix, determine the optimum strategies and the value of the game.

$$\begin{bmatrix} -3 & 4 \\ 6 & -2 \end{bmatrix}$$

Solution We will solve this game this time by using formulas instead of graphs.

$$p_1 = \frac{-2-6}{-3+(-2)-4-6} = \frac{8}{15} \quad \text{and} \quad p_2 = \frac{-3-4}{-3+(-2)-4-6} = \frac{7}{15}$$

X's optimum strategy is $[\frac{8}{15} \quad \frac{7}{15}]$.

$$q_1 = \frac{-2-4}{-15} = \frac{6}{15} = \frac{2}{5} \quad \text{and} \quad q_2 = \frac{-3-6}{-15} = \frac{9}{15} = \frac{3}{5}$$

Y's optimum strategy is $\begin{bmatrix} \frac{2}{5} \\ \frac{3}{5} \end{bmatrix}$. The value of the game is given by

$$V = \frac{-3(-2)-4(6)}{-15} = \frac{-18}{-15} = \frac{6}{5}$$

The game is not fair but is in favor of player X, who should use the strategy $[\frac{8}{15} \quad \frac{7}{15}]$.

EXAMPLE 26 Add 4 to each element of the matrix given in the preceding example so that all the elements of the new matrix will be positive. Show that this adds 4 to the value of the game but does not change the optimum strategies.

Solution The new matrix is

$$\begin{bmatrix} 1 & 8 \\ 10 & 2 \end{bmatrix}$$

The value of this game is

$$V = \frac{1(2)-8(10)}{1+2-8-10} = \frac{-78}{-15} = \frac{26}{5}$$

Note that $\frac{26}{5} = \frac{6}{5} + 4$. For this game,

$$p_1 = \frac{2-10}{1+2-8-10} = \frac{8}{15} \quad \text{and} \quad p_2 = \frac{1-8}{1+2-8-10} = \frac{7}{15}$$

$$q_1 = \frac{2-8}{1+2-8-10} = \frac{2}{5} \quad \text{and} \quad q_2 = \frac{1-10}{1+2-8-10} = \frac{3}{5}$$

Hence, the optimum strategies are unchanged.

EXAMPLE 27 Multiply each element of the matrix given in Example 24 by 3. Show that this multiplies the value of the game by 3 but does not change the optimum strategies.

Solution When each element of $\begin{bmatrix} -3 & 4 \\ 6 & -2 \end{bmatrix}$ is multiplied by 3, the result is

$$\begin{bmatrix} -9 & 12 \\ 18 & -6 \end{bmatrix}$$

The value of this new game is

$$V = \frac{(-9)(-6) - (12)(18)}{(-9) + (-6) - 12 - 18} = \frac{-162}{-45} = \frac{18}{5}$$

Note that $\frac{18}{5} = 3\left(\frac{6}{5}\right)$.

$$p_1 = \frac{-6 - 18}{(-9) + (-6) - 12 - 18} = \frac{-24}{-45} = \frac{8}{15}$$

$$p_2 = \frac{-9 - 12}{(-9) + (-6) - 12 - 18} = \frac{-21}{-45} = \frac{7}{15}$$

$$q_1 = \frac{-6 - 12}{(-9) + (-6) - 12 - 18} = \frac{-18}{-45} = \frac{2}{5}$$

$$q_2 = \frac{-9 - 18}{(-9) + (-6) - 12 - 18} = \frac{-27}{-45} = \frac{3}{5}$$

Hence, the optimum strategies are unchanged.

The two examples illustrate the following theorem:

Value of a Game

> If to each element of a matrix game a constant is added (or multiplied), the value of the game is added to (or multiplied by) the constant, but the optimum strategies are unchanged.

There are times when games defined by larger matrices may be reduced to 2 × 2 games.

Dominated Row

> Sometimes each element of a row of a matrix is as large as or larger than the corresponding elements of another row. When this happens, the row with the larger elements is said to **dominate** the other row, and the row with the smaller elements is said to be **dominated by** the other row.

Of course, X would rather play the row with the larger elements because X would like to win as much as possible. Thus, the dominated row may be omitted without affecting the solution of the matrix game. Similarly, we say one column **dominates** another if the elements of the dominating column are as small as or are smaller than the corresponding elements of the dominated column. Since Y would always choose the column containing the smaller elements, the dominated column may be omitted from the game. The dominated rows and columns may be dropped in any order.

EXAMPLE 28 For the matrix game

$$\begin{bmatrix} 1 & 4 & -3 \\ -1 & -3 & -4 \\ -3 & 7 & 5 \end{bmatrix}$$

each element of the first row, [1 4 −3], is larger than the corresponding element of the second row, [−1 −3 −4]; hence, the second row may be omitted to obtain

$$\begin{bmatrix} 1 & 4 & -3 \\ -3 & 7 & 5 \end{bmatrix}$$

Each element of the first column, $\begin{bmatrix} 1 \\ -3 \end{bmatrix}$, is less than the corresponding element of the second column, $\begin{bmatrix} 4 \\ 7 \end{bmatrix}$, so the second column may be omitted, and we have

$$\begin{bmatrix} 1 & -3 \\ -3 & 5 \end{bmatrix}$$

The game is biased in favor of Y since the value of the game is

$$V = \frac{1(5) - (-3)(-3)}{1 + 5 - (-3) - (-3)} = -\frac{1}{3}$$

For the reduced 2 × 2 game, X's strategy should be [$\frac{2}{3}$ $\frac{1}{3}$], and Y's strategy should be $\begin{bmatrix} \frac{2}{3} \\ \frac{1}{3} \end{bmatrix}$. Relative to the original matrix, X's strategy should be [$\frac{2}{3}$ 0 $\frac{1}{3}$], and Y's strategy should be

$$\begin{bmatrix} \frac{2}{3} \\ 0 \\ \frac{1}{3} \end{bmatrix}$$

The zero probability indicates that X should never play the second row and Y should never play the second column.

Exercise Set **7.5**

A **1.** Find the value of each matrix game and the optimum strategy for each player. Be sure to check whether the game is strictly determined.

a. $\begin{bmatrix} 1 & 3 \\ 4 & -5 \end{bmatrix}$ b. $\begin{bmatrix} 2 & 0 \\ -3 & 3 \end{bmatrix}$ c. $\begin{bmatrix} 3 & 4 \\ 0 & 5 \end{bmatrix}$

d. $\begin{bmatrix} 12 & -3 \\ -2 & 2 \end{bmatrix}$ e. $\begin{bmatrix} 8 & -5 \\ 4 & 6 \end{bmatrix}$ f. $\begin{bmatrix} 4 & -12 \\ -2 & 9 \end{bmatrix}$

B   **2.** For the following matrix games, find the optimum strategies and the values of the games.

a.
$$\begin{bmatrix} 16 & 8 & -4 \\ 7 & 6 & 8 \\ -8 & 5 & 0 \end{bmatrix}$$

b.
$$\begin{bmatrix} 6 & 3 & -3 & -3 \\ 2 & 2 & 0 & 2 \\ 4 & 0 & -5 & 8 \end{bmatrix}$$

c.
$$\begin{bmatrix} 0 & 8 & 9 & -5 \\ 4 & -3 & 5 & 6 \\ 4 & 5 & 6 & 7 \\ 8 & 10 & 10 & -3 \end{bmatrix}$$

d.
$$\begin{bmatrix} 3 & 2 & 1 \\ 4 & 3 & 2 \\ -1 & 3 & -2 \end{bmatrix}$$

3. Find the optimum strategies and the values of the following matrix games by eliminating the dominated rows and columns.

a.
$$\begin{bmatrix} 4 & -1 & -2 \\ 5 & 2 & 3 \\ -4 & 3 & 4 \end{bmatrix}$$

b.
$$\begin{bmatrix} 4 & 1 & 1 \\ -1 & 4 & 2 \\ -3 & 1 & 0 \end{bmatrix}$$

c.
$$\begin{bmatrix} 1 & 0 & 2 \\ -1 & 4 & 0 \\ -2 & 0 & 1 \end{bmatrix}$$

d.
$$\begin{bmatrix} 1 & 3 & 2 \\ 0 & -4 & 1 \\ -1 & 2 & 2 \\ 0 & -5 & 0 \end{bmatrix}$$

e.
$$\begin{bmatrix} -1 & 4 & 0 & 5 \\ -3 & 6 & -2 & 7 \end{bmatrix}$$

f.
$$\begin{bmatrix} 3 & 2 & 4 \\ 4 & 3 & -2 \end{bmatrix}$$

4. To each matrix game given in exercise 1, add the smallest positive integer that will make every element of the game positive. Show that this increases the value of the game by this amount but does not change the optimum strategies.

5. Multiply each element of the matrix games in exercise 1 by 3. Show that this multiplies the values by 3 but does not change the optimum strategies.

C   **6.** Two college students, Rowe and Collum, play the following game. Collum is to conceal either a $1 bill or a $5 bill in his hand. If Rowe guesses correctly the denomination of the bill, he gets the bill. How much should Rowe pay for the game in order to have a fair game? (*Hint:* Find the value of the game.)

7. In one version of the two-finger game, each player shows one or two fingers simultaneously. If the sum of the number of fingers shown is odd, Katie gets the sum; if the sum is even, Jeannie gets the sum. Set up the matrix game, and find the value of the game and the optimum strategy of each player.

8. Suppose Katie and Jeannie are to show two or three fingers simultaneously. Let the game be played as in exercise 7. Find the value of the game and the optimum strategy of each player.

Business   **9.** **Competing Businesses.** Firms X and Y are competing in two cities, A and B. The elements of the matrix below indicate the differences in the possible sales of X and Y in hundred thousands of dollars if both firms were to focus their full sales force on either city.

$$\begin{array}{cc} & \text{Firm Y} \\ & \begin{array}{cc} \text{A} & \text{B} \end{array} \\ \text{Firm X} \begin{array}{c} \text{A} \\ \text{B} \end{array} & \begin{bmatrix} 2 & 6 \\ -8 & -4 \end{bmatrix} \end{array}$$

Find the optimum strategy for each firm and the value of the game.

Social Sciences   **10.** **Political Campaigns.** The Republicans and Democrats are making plans for their next campaign. The Republicans are considering making promises I and II in their speeches, and the Democrats are considering promises A and B. A telephone survey obtained the following information. If the Republicans promise I and the Democrats promise A, the Republicans will gain 2000 votes. If the Republicans promise I and the Democrats promise B, the Republicans will lose 1000 votes. If the Republicans promise II and the Democrats promise A, the Republicans will gain 500 votes. If the Republicans promise II and the Democrats promise B, the Republicans will gain 800 votes. Write this as a matrix game, and then determine the optimum strategies and the value of the game.

11. **Political Campaigns.** Redo exercise 10 using the following information. If the Republicans promise I and the Democrats promise A, the Republicans will gain 1800 votes. If the Republicans promise I and the Democrats promise B, the Republicans will lose 1200 votes. If the Republicans promise II and the Democrats promise A, the Republicans will gain 600 votes. If the Republicans promise II and the Democrats promise B, the Republicans will gain 700 votes.

 A Technique for Solving _n_ × 2 Games

> In the preceding sections we discussed the solution of 2 × m or n × 2 games when the games were strictly determined, or could be reduced to 2 × 2 games by eliminating the dominated rows and columns. We now utilize graphical means to solve 2 × m and n × 2 games that are not strictly determined and cannot be reduced to 2 × 2 games by dropping the dominated rows and columns.

In an n × 2 matrix game, player X has n strategies and player Y has two strategies. In a 2 × m game, player X has two strategies and player Y has m strategies. Both types of games can be solved graphically.

EXAMPLE 29 Find the optimum strategy for X, the optimum strategy for Y, and the value of the following matrix game by graphical means.

$$
\begin{array}{c}
 \quad Y \\
X \begin{bmatrix} 3 & -2 & -1 \\ -2 & 3 & 1 \end{bmatrix}
\end{array}
$$

Solution Recall that, if **P** is the optimum strategy for X and **Q** is the optimum strategy for Y, then **PAQ** = V, the value of the game. If Y should play a strategy **Q'**, which is not optimum, and X continues to play an optimum strategy, then X's winnings will be greater than or equal to V; that is, **PAQ'** ≥ V. Now denote by [p 1 − p] the optimum strategy for X. This is a suitable representation for the probability vector because the sum of the probabilities must equal 1, and p + (1 − p) = 1. If Y plays the first column, then the expectation, or expected winnings, for X would be

$$[p \quad 1-p] \cdot \begin{bmatrix} 3 & -2 & -1 \\ -2 & 3 & 1 \end{bmatrix} \cdot \begin{bmatrix} 1 \\ 0 \\ 0 \end{bmatrix} \geq V$$

$$[p \quad 1-p] \cdot \begin{bmatrix} 3 \\ -2 \end{bmatrix} \geq V$$

$$3p - 2(1-p) \geq V$$

$$5p - 2 \geq V$$

Similarly, if Y plays the second column,

$$[p \quad 1-p] \cdot \begin{bmatrix} 3 & -2 & -1 \\ -2 & 3 & 1 \end{bmatrix} \cdot \begin{bmatrix} 0 \\ 1 \\ 0 \end{bmatrix} \geq V \qquad \text{or} \qquad 3 - 5p \geq V$$

Figure 7.5

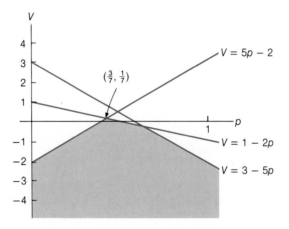

and if Y plays the third column, $1 - 2p \geq V$. The shaded region of Figure 7.5 represents the set of points satisfying these three inequalities. Note that the maximum value of V occurs at the intersection of

$$V = 1 - 2p \qquad \text{and} \qquad V = 5p - 2$$

$p = \frac{3}{7}$ and $V = \frac{1}{7}$ at this point. Thus, the optimum strategy for X is $[\frac{3}{7} \quad \frac{4}{7}]$, and the value of the game is $\frac{1}{7}$.

To find the optimum strategy for Y, note that the optimum strategy for X was determined by the intersection of lines computed from the first and third columns of the matrix. Omit the second column and consider the 2×2 matrix

$$\begin{bmatrix} 3 & -1 \\ -2 & 1 \end{bmatrix}$$

Y's strategy is computed to be

$$q_1 = \frac{1 - (-1)}{3 + 1 - (-2) - (-1)} = \frac{2}{7} \qquad \text{and} \qquad q_3 = \frac{3 - (-2)}{3 + 1 - (-2) - (-1)} = \frac{5}{7}$$

Thus, Y's optimal strategy is

$$\begin{bmatrix} \frac{2}{7} \\ 0 \\ \frac{5}{7} \end{bmatrix}$$

EXAMPLE 30 Find the optimum strategy for X and Y and the value of the following game.

$$\begin{bmatrix} 3 & 1 \\ 4 & -2 \\ -1 & 2 \\ -3 & 3 \end{bmatrix}$$

Solution Let Y's optimum strategy be $\begin{bmatrix} q \\ 1-q \end{bmatrix}$; then the expectation of Y will be less than or equal to V, and the expectation will be

$$[3 \quad 1] \cdot \begin{bmatrix} q \\ 1-q \end{bmatrix} \le V$$

$$[4 \quad -2] \cdot \begin{bmatrix} q \\ 1-q \end{bmatrix} \le V$$

$$[-1 \quad 2] \cdot \begin{bmatrix} q \\ 1-q \end{bmatrix} \le V$$

$$[-3 \quad 3] \cdot \begin{bmatrix} q \\ 1-q \end{bmatrix} \le V$$

depending on whether X plays the first, second, third, or fourth rows, respectively. Multiplying gives

$$3q + (1-q) \le V$$
$$4q - 2(1-q) \le V$$
$$-q + 2(1-q) \le V$$
$$-3q + 3(1-q) \le V$$

The shaded region of Figure 7.6 indicates the Vs that satisfy all inequalities, regardless of the value of q and X's strategy. The smallest V for the solution set of V occurs at the intersection of

$$V = 2q + 1 \quad \text{and} \quad V = -6q + 3$$

This point is $q = \frac{1}{4}$, $V = \frac{3}{2}$. Thus, the optimum strategy for Y is

$$\begin{bmatrix} \frac{1}{4} \\ \frac{3}{4} \end{bmatrix}$$

and the expected earnings for X are $\frac{3}{2}$. To find the optimum strategy for X, note that the optimum strategy for Y was determined by the intersection of lines computed from the first and fourth rows of the matrix. Omit the second and third

Figure 7.6

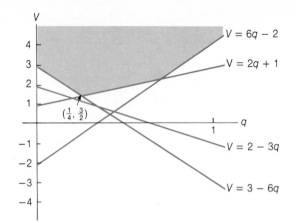

rows and consider the 2 × 2 matrix $\begin{bmatrix} 3 & 1 \\ -3 & 3 \end{bmatrix}$. Then

$$p_1 = \frac{3 - (-3)}{3 + 3 - (-3) - 1} = \frac{3}{4} \quad \text{and} \quad p_4 = \frac{3 - 1}{8} = \frac{1}{4}$$

Thus, the optimum strategy for X is $[\tfrac{3}{4} \quad 0 \quad 0 \quad \tfrac{1}{4}]$.

Exercise Set **7.6**

A **1.** For the following matrix games, find the optimum strategies for X and Y, and the values of the games. Be sure to check for saddle points.

a. $\begin{bmatrix} 5 & 0 \\ -3 & 4 \\ 8 & -5 \end{bmatrix}$
    b. $\begin{bmatrix} 8 & 5 & 3 & 7 \\ 10 & 3 & 2 & 5 \end{bmatrix}$
    c. $\begin{bmatrix} 2 & 0 & 1 \\ 0 & 2 & 1 \end{bmatrix}$

d. $\begin{bmatrix} 0 & 3 \\ 1 & 2 \\ -2 & 0 \\ 3 & 0 \end{bmatrix}$
    e. $\begin{bmatrix} 1 & 3 & 4 \\ 3 & 3 & 2 \end{bmatrix}$
    f. $\begin{bmatrix} 0 & 4 \\ 6 & 0 \\ -8 & 10 \\ 5 & 6 \end{bmatrix}$

g. $\begin{bmatrix} -2 & 5 & 0 & -2 \\ 2 & -3 & -2 & 5 \end{bmatrix}$
    h. $\begin{bmatrix} 2 & -2 & 3 \\ -4 & 0 & -1 \end{bmatrix}$

B **2.** Find the optimum strategy for each player and the value of the game for each of the following matrix games.

a. $\begin{bmatrix} 2 & 1 & -3 \\ -1 & -1 & 4 \\ -1 & -2 & 2 \end{bmatrix}$
    b. $\begin{bmatrix} 1 & 3 & 0 \\ 1 & -2 & 2 \\ -1 & 5 & 2 \\ -1 & 2 & 2 \end{bmatrix}$

c. $\begin{bmatrix} 0 & -2 & 1 & 4 \\ 3 & 2 & -1 & 0 \\ 1 & -1 & 2 & 4 \\ 2 & 1 & 0 & 1 \end{bmatrix}$
    d. $\begin{bmatrix} -1 & 0 & -2 & -3 \\ 1 & 0 & -2 & 1 \\ 2 & -3 & -2 & 3 \\ -4 & -4 & -3 & -5 \end{bmatrix}$

C *Solve the following two-person matrix games with the given payoffs.*

3. $\begin{bmatrix} l & m \\ n & o \end{bmatrix}$ where $l < m$ **4.** $\begin{bmatrix} x & y \\ y & -x \end{bmatrix}$ where $x > y$

5. Suppose two of the lines involving p obtained from the r row and the s row do not intersect for p between 0 and 1. What can you say about the r and s columns of the payoff matrix?

Business

6. Investments. An investor has designed a game for investing in stock or buying interest-bearing notes. She has set the average rate of gain as 8%, and all numbers in the matrix are above or below 8%.

	High Inflation	Tight Money Supply	Neither
Stocks	2	−1	6
Notes	1	3	−1

Calculate the investor's optimal strategy.

7. Optimum Purchases. Two companies are trying to secure the business of the XYZ Corporation. Company A is considering three bids classified as good profit, little profit, and at cost. Company B has only two bids, good profit and little profit. If company B bids good profit, credit company A with −4, 3, and 6 points for bids of good profit, little profit, and at cost, respectively. If company B bids little profit, credit company A with −6, −4, and 2 points. Disregarding profit, what strategy should each company use to obtain the bid, where the points indicate an index for obtaining the business of the XYZ Corporation?

Life Sciences

8. Medicine. Suppose there are two bacteria associated with a disease. Three antibiotics have been tested on each bacterium and the probability of destroying the bacterium is given. What should the strategy be for mixing the three antibiotics for the greatest probability of killing bacteria?

Bacteria

		A	B
Antibiotics	X	.4	.7
	Y	.5	.3
	Z	.6	.1

Social Sciences

9. Romance. A young man is planning a romantic campaign. He is considering sending his dream girl flowers, poems, or candies. He discusses her likes and dislikes with her friends and thereby learns that her response depends on whether she has allergic tendencies or is on a diet. He estimates her appreciation by the following matrix.

Girl's Response

		Allergic	On a Diet
He Sends	Flowers	−1	4
	Poems	1	2
	Candies	3	1

Find the optimum strategy and the value of the game.

> In the preceding section we were able to solve $n \times 2$ and $2 \times m$ matrix games that are not strictly determined by using a mixed strategies technique with graphical applications. In this section we expand our problem-solving ability to encompass $n \times m$ games. We find the optimal strategy for each player by setting up the problem as a linear programming problem and then applying the *simplex method* discussed in Chapter 3.

In the application of linear programming techniques to matrix game theory, we denote the strategy of player X

$$[p_1 \quad p_2 \quad \cdots \quad p_n]$$

where player X will play row i, p_i of the time, and $p_1 + p_2 + \cdots + p_n = 1$. Likewise, the strategy of player Y is

$$\begin{bmatrix} q_1 \\ q_2 \\ \vdots \\ q_m \end{bmatrix}$$

where player Y will play column j, q_j of the time, and $q_1 + q_2 + \cdots + q_m = 1$.

We want the payoff matrix to contain only positive numbers; thus, we add a large enough number to each element of the payoff matrix so that each element will be positive. It can be shown that if each element of a payoff matrix is positive, then the value of the game is positive.

To use our previous procedures for linear programming problems, we introduce variables $x_1, x_2, x_3, \ldots, x_m$ such that

$$x_1 = \frac{q_1}{V} \qquad x_2 = \frac{q_2}{V} \qquad \cdots \qquad x_m = \frac{q_m}{V}$$

where V is the value of the game. Since $q_1 + q_2 + \cdots + q_m = 1$,

$$x_1 + x_2 + \cdots + x_m = \frac{1}{V}$$

The objective function to be maximized is

$$\frac{1}{V} = f = x_1 + x_2 + \cdots + x_m$$

The constraint inequalities are

$$a_{11}x_1 + a_{12}x_2 + \cdots + a_{1m}x_m \leq 1$$
$$\vdots \qquad\quad \vdots \qquad\qquad \vdots$$
$$a_{m1}x_1 + a_{m2}x_2 + \cdots + a_{mm}x_m \leq 1$$
$$x_1 \geq 0 \cdots x_m \geq 0$$

EXAMPLE 31 Use linear programming techniques to find strategies for the matrix game

$$\begin{bmatrix} -3 & 4 \\ 6 & -2 \end{bmatrix}$$

Solution First note that not all the elements in the payoff matrix are positive. To make all the elements positive, add 4 to each element.

$$\begin{bmatrix} 1 & 8 \\ 10 & 2 \end{bmatrix}$$

The constraint equations are

$$x_1 + 8x_2 \leq 1$$
$$10x_1 + 2x_2 \leq 1$$
$$x_1 \geq 0 \qquad x_2 \geq 0$$

We desire to maximize

$$f = x_1 + x_2$$

To apply the simplex methods of linear programming, we introduce the slack variables y_1 and y_2 (each ≥ 0) such that

$$x_1 + 8x_2 + y_1 = 1$$
$$10x_1 + 2x_2 + y_2 = 1$$

Thus, the first tableau becomes

$$\begin{array}{c} \\ y_1 \\ y_2 \\ f \end{array} \begin{array}{cccc} x_1 & x_2 & y_1 & y_2 \\ \begin{bmatrix} 1 & \circledR{8} & 1 & 0 & 1 \\ \circledR{10} & 2 & 0 & 1 & 1 \\ -1 & -1 & 0 & 0 & 0 \end{bmatrix} \end{array}$$

The second tableau is

$$\begin{array}{c} \\ y_1 \\ x_1 \\ f \end{array} \begin{array}{cccc} x_1 & x_2 & y_1 & y_2 \\ \begin{bmatrix} 0 & \frac{78}{10} & 1 & -\frac{1}{10} & \frac{9}{10} \\ \circled{1} & \frac{2}{10} & 0 & \frac{1}{10} & \frac{1}{10} \\ 0 & -\frac{8}{10} & 0 & \frac{1}{10} & \frac{1}{10} \end{bmatrix} \end{array}$$

The third tableau is

$$\begin{array}{c} \\ x_2 \\ x_1 \\ \end{array} \begin{array}{cccc} x_1 & x_2 & y_1 & y_2 \\ \begin{bmatrix} 0 & 1 & \frac{10}{78} & -\frac{1}{78} & \frac{9}{78} \\ 1 & 0 & -\frac{2}{78} & \frac{8}{78} & \frac{6}{78} \\ 0 & 0 & \frac{8}{78} & \frac{7}{78} & \frac{15}{78} \end{bmatrix} \end{array}$$

Since all the elements in the last row are positive, we have

$$x_1 = \tfrac{6}{78}$$
$$x_2 = \tfrac{9}{78}$$

$$\frac{1}{V} = \frac{15}{78} \quad \text{or} \quad V = \frac{78}{15}$$

$$q_1 = x_1 V = (\tfrac{6}{78})(\tfrac{78}{15}) = \tfrac{6}{15}$$
$$q_2 = x_2 V = (\tfrac{9}{78})(\tfrac{78}{15}) = \tfrac{9}{15}$$

Thus, player Y has the strategy $\begin{bmatrix} \tfrac{6}{15} \\ \tfrac{9}{15} \end{bmatrix}$.

Recall that player X has the strategy

$$[p_1 \quad p_2 \quad p_3 \quad \cdots \quad p_n]$$

and we introduce variables

$$y_1 = \frac{p_1}{V} \qquad y_2 = \frac{p_2}{V} \qquad \cdots \qquad y_n = \frac{p_n}{V}$$

where

$$y_1 + y_2 + \cdots + y_n = \frac{1}{V}$$

You may need to review dual problems of linear programming in Section 6 in Chapter 3 before reading the value of y_i from the third tableau.

$$y_1 = \tfrac{8}{78}$$
$$y_2 = \tfrac{7}{78}$$

Thus,

$$p_1 = y_1 V = (\tfrac{8}{78})(\tfrac{78}{15}) = \tfrac{8}{15}$$
$$p_2 = y_2 V = (\tfrac{7}{78})(\tfrac{78}{15}) = \tfrac{7}{15}$$

Player X thus has the strategy $[\tfrac{8}{15} \quad \tfrac{7}{15}]$, player Y has the strategy $\begin{bmatrix} \tfrac{6}{15} \\ \tfrac{9}{15} \end{bmatrix}$, and the value of the game is

$$V = \tfrac{78}{15} - 4 = \tfrac{6}{5}$$

EXAMPLE 32 Use linear programming techniques to find the strategies for the matrix game

$$\begin{bmatrix} 2 & -2 & 1 \\ -1 & 1 & -1 \\ -3 & 4 & 0 \end{bmatrix}$$

Solution First note that not all the elements are positive. Let's add 4 to each element, getting

$$\begin{bmatrix} 6 & 2 & 5 \\ 3 & 5 & 3 \\ 1 & 8 & 4 \end{bmatrix}$$

The constraint equations are

$$6x_1 + 2x_2 + 5x_3 \le 1$$
$$3x_1 + 5x_2 + 3x_3 \le 1$$
$$x_1 + 8x_2 + 4x_3 \le 1$$
$$x_1 \ge 0 \qquad x_2 \ge 0 \qquad \text{and} \qquad x_3 \ge 0$$

We desire to maximize

$$f = x_1 + x_2 + x_3$$

To apply the simplex method, we introduce the slack variables y_1, y_2, y_3 (each ≥ 0) so that

$$6x_1 + 2x_2 + 5x_3 + y_1 = 1$$
$$3x_1 + 5x_2 + 3x_3 + y_2 = 1$$
$$x_1 + 8x_2 + 4x_3 + y_3 = 1$$

Thus, the first tableau becomes

	x_1	x_2	x_3	y_1	y_2	y_3	
y_1	⑥	2	5	1	0	0	1
y_2	3	5	3	0	1	0	1
y_3	1	8	4	0	0	1	1
f	-1	-1	-1	0	0	0	0

The second tableau is

	x_1	x_2	x_3	y_1	y_2	y_3	
x_1	1	$\frac{2}{6}$	$\frac{5}{6}$	$\frac{1}{6}$	0	0	$\frac{1}{6}$
y_2	0	4	$\frac{3}{6}$	$-\frac{3}{6}$	1	0	$\frac{3}{6}$
y_3	0	$\frac{46}{6}$	$\frac{19}{6}$	$-\frac{1}{6}$	0	1	$\frac{5}{6}$
f	0	$-\frac{4}{6}$	$-\frac{1}{6}$	$\frac{1}{6}$	0	0	$\frac{1}{6}$

The third tableau is

	x_1	x_2	x_3	y_1	y_2	y_3	
x_1	1	0	$\frac{34}{46}$	$\frac{8}{46}$	0	$-\frac{2}{46}$	$\frac{6}{46}$
y_2	0	0	$-\frac{55}{46}$	$-\frac{19}{46}$	1	$-\frac{24}{46}$	$\frac{3}{46}$
x_2	0	1	$\frac{19}{46}$	$-\frac{1}{46}$	0	$\frac{6}{46}$	$\frac{5}{46}$
f	0	0	$\frac{32}{46}$	$\frac{7}{46}$	0	$\frac{4}{46}$	$\frac{11}{46}$

Since all the elements in the last row are positive, we can read the answers for x from the right column.

$$x_1 = \tfrac{6}{46}$$
$$x_2 = \tfrac{5}{46}$$
$$x_3 = 0$$

$$\frac{1}{V} = \frac{11}{46} \qquad \text{or} \qquad V = \frac{46}{11}$$

or

$$q_1 = x_1 V = (\tfrac{6}{46})(\tfrac{46}{11}) = \tfrac{6}{11}$$
$$q_2 = x_2 V = (\tfrac{5}{46})(\tfrac{46}{11}) = \tfrac{5}{11}$$
$$q_3 = 0$$

The strategy of player Y is thus $\begin{bmatrix} \tfrac{6}{11} \\ \tfrac{5}{11} \\ 0 \end{bmatrix}$.

From the dual problem,

$$y_1 = \tfrac{7}{46}$$
$$y_2 = 0$$
$$y_3 = \tfrac{4}{46}$$

or

$$p_1 = y_1 V = (\tfrac{7}{46})(\tfrac{46}{11}) = \tfrac{7}{11}$$
$$p_2 = 0$$
$$p_3 = y_3 V = (\tfrac{4}{46})(\tfrac{46}{11}) = \tfrac{4}{11}$$

The strategy of player X is $[\tfrac{7}{11} \quad 0 \quad \tfrac{4}{11}]$, and the value of the game is $\tfrac{46}{11} - 4 = \tfrac{2}{11}$. To check this value, we look at

$$\mathbf{PAQ} = [\tfrac{7}{11} \quad 0 \quad \tfrac{4}{11}] \cdot \begin{bmatrix} 2 & -2 & 1 \\ -1 & 1 & -1 \\ -3 & 4 & 0 \end{bmatrix} \cdot \begin{bmatrix} \tfrac{6}{11} \\ \tfrac{5}{11} \\ 0 \end{bmatrix}$$

$$= [\tfrac{2}{11} \quad \tfrac{2}{11} \quad \tfrac{7}{11}] \cdot \begin{bmatrix} \tfrac{6}{11} \\ \tfrac{5}{11} \\ 0 \end{bmatrix} = \tfrac{2}{11}$$

Exercise Set 7.7

A 1. Use the techniques of linear programming to solve each part of exercise 1 in Exercise Set 7.6.

B 2. Use linear programming techniques to solve each part of exercise 2 in Exercise Set 7.6.

C 3. Solve the following matrix games.

a. $\begin{bmatrix} 1 & 0 & 1 \\ -1 & 1 & -1 \\ 0 & -1 & 2 \end{bmatrix}$ b. $\begin{bmatrix} 1 & -2 & 3 \\ 2 & 1 & -2 \\ -1 & 0 & 1 \end{bmatrix}$ c. $\begin{bmatrix} 3 & -2 & 1 \\ 1 & 2 & 1 \\ 1 & 3 & 2 \end{bmatrix}$

Use linear programming techniques to solve the following problems.

Business 4. Work exercise 6 in Exercise Set 7.6.

5. Work exercise 7 in Exercise Set 7.6.

Life Sciences 6. Work exercise 8 in Exercise Set 7.6.

Social Sciences 7. Work exercise 9 in Exercise Set 7.6.

Review to ensure you understand and can use the following concepts:

Finite stochastic processes
Stochastic matrix

Markov chains: transition matrix, initial state, Markov process, state matrix, state vector, steady-state matrix, regular Markov chain, regular transition matrix, absorbing Markov chain, absorbing state, canonical form of a transition matrix, fundamental matrix

Game theory: payoff matrix, zero-sum game, pure strategy, mixed strategy, optimum strategies, value of a game, expectation, saddle point, dominant rows and columns, solving $n \times 2$ and $2 \times m$ games, solving games using linear programming

Review Exercise Set **7.8**

A 1. Find the optimal strategies for the players and the values of the following matrix games.

a. $\begin{bmatrix} -1 & 0 \\ 1 & 2 \end{bmatrix}$ b. $\begin{bmatrix} 18 & 6 \\ 2 & 5 \end{bmatrix}$ c. $\begin{bmatrix} 7 & -7 \\ 5 & -2 \end{bmatrix}$

d. $\begin{bmatrix} 3 & 9 \\ -1 & -4 \end{bmatrix}$ e. $\begin{bmatrix} 16 & 3 & -3 \\ 6 & 5 & 8 \\ -8 & 4 & 1 \end{bmatrix}$ f. $\begin{bmatrix} -2 & 1 & -3 \\ -5 & 7 & 8 \end{bmatrix}$

g. $\begin{bmatrix} 1 & 0 & -1 \\ -2 & -3 & 1 \end{bmatrix}$ h. $\begin{bmatrix} 4 & -1 & 3 \\ 2 & -4 & 1 \\ 3 & -1 & -1 \end{bmatrix}$ i. $\begin{bmatrix} 4 & 0 \\ -2 & 3 \\ 6 & 4 \end{bmatrix}$

j. $\begin{bmatrix} 1 & 0 & 3 \\ 0 & -3 & 2 \end{bmatrix}$

2. Find the optimum strategies and the value of the game defined by $\begin{bmatrix} 5 & 0 & 6 \\ -3 & 4 & -1 \\ 8 & -5 & 10 \end{bmatrix}$.

3. A Markov chain has the transition matrix

$$\begin{bmatrix} \frac{1}{3} & \frac{1}{3} & \frac{1}{3} \\ \frac{1}{4} & \frac{1}{4} & \frac{1}{2} \\ 0 & \frac{1}{2} & \frac{1}{2} \end{bmatrix}$$

a. If the initial state is $[\frac{2}{3} \quad \frac{1}{6} \quad \frac{1}{6}]$, what is the state vector after one transition?
b. After two transitions?

4. A Markov chain with the transition matrix

$$\begin{bmatrix} .2 & .3 & .5 \\ .2 & .6 & .2 \\ .4 & .2 & .4 \end{bmatrix}$$

is initially in state 2. In what state is it most likely to be after two transitions?

5. Explain why

$$\begin{bmatrix} \frac{1}{3} & \frac{1}{3} & \frac{1}{3} \\ 0 & 1 & 0 \\ \frac{3}{4} & \frac{1}{2} & \frac{1}{4} \end{bmatrix}$$

cannot be a transition matrix.

6. A Markov process is defined by

$$\begin{bmatrix} .7 & .3 \\ .8 & .2 \end{bmatrix}$$

If the state matrix at a certain observation is [.66 .34], what is the state matrix of the next observation?

7. Find the steady-state matrix for the Markov process whose transition matrix is as follows.

a. $\begin{bmatrix} .70 & .30 \\ .75 & .25 \end{bmatrix}$ b. $\begin{bmatrix} .1 & .2 & .7 \\ .2 & .3 & .5 \\ .3 & .3 & .4 \end{bmatrix}$ c. $\begin{bmatrix} .3 & .3 & .4 \\ .4 & .4 & .2 \\ 0 & 0 & 1 \end{bmatrix}$

B   8. An absorbing Markov chain has the transition matrix

$$\begin{bmatrix} 1 & 0 & 0 & 0 \\ \frac{1}{3} & 0 & \frac{2}{3} & 0 \\ 0 & 1 & 0 & 0 \\ 0 & \frac{1}{4} & \frac{1}{4} & \frac{1}{2} \end{bmatrix}$$

Find the fundamental matrix.

9. A Markov chain has the transition matrix

$$\begin{bmatrix} .5 & 0 & .5 \\ 1 & 0 & 0 \\ .4 & .4 & .2 \end{bmatrix}$$

a. Determine whether this Markov chain is regular.
b. If it is regular, find the steady-state vector.
c. In which state is the system most likely to be found in the long run?

10. A Markov chain has the transition matrix

$$\begin{bmatrix} .2 & .2 & .4 \\ .3 & .1 & .6 \\ .5 & .3 & .2 \end{bmatrix}$$

It is initially in state 1. In what state is it most likely to be after two transitions? Three transitions?

11. A Markov chain has the transition matrix

$$\begin{bmatrix} \frac{1}{3} & \frac{1}{3} & \frac{1}{3} & 0 \\ \frac{1}{4} & \frac{1}{4} & \frac{1}{4} & \frac{1}{4} \\ 0 & 1 & 0 & 0 \\ 0 & 0 & 0 & 1 \end{bmatrix}$$

If the system is in state 2, determine the expected number of transitions before it reaches an absorbing state.

C **12.** Use the simplex method to solve the matrix game with payoff matrix

$$\begin{bmatrix} 2 & -1 & 3 \\ -3 & 2 & -5 \\ 4 & -3 & 5 \end{bmatrix}$$

Business **13. Consumer Choices.**

This Purchase

A B C

Previous
Purchase
$$\begin{matrix} A \\ B \\ C \end{matrix} \begin{bmatrix} .7 & .2 & .1 \\ .1 & .6 & .3 \\ .1 & .1 & .8 \end{bmatrix}$$

  a. If the distribution of people using brand A, B, or C is [.6 .3 .1] at this time, what will it be after all have made two purchases?
  b. What is the probability that a person who purchases brand A today will purchase brand B on his second purchase? Will purchase brand C on his third purchase?

Life Sciences **14. Forestry.** The following transition matrix demonstrates how trees are distributed in a forest after 20 years.

Pine Oak Hickory

$$\begin{matrix} \text{Pine} \\ \text{Oak} \\ \text{Hickory} \end{matrix} \begin{bmatrix} .8 & .1 & .1 \\ .3 & .6 & .1 \\ .3 & .2 & .5 \end{bmatrix}$$

Find the long-run composition of the forest.

Social Sciences **15. Compartment Maze.** The movement of a mouse in a compartment maze is defined by the transition matrix

$$\begin{bmatrix} .5 & .5 & 0 \\ .2 & .3 & .5 \\ .2 & .2 & .6 \end{bmatrix}$$

In what compartment is the mouse most likely to be found in the long run?

Functions and Graphs

This chapter discusses algebraic manipulations that are important in the study of calculus. First, we review manipulations that use exponents and radicals. Then we introduce an important mathematical concept called a **function.** Functions and functional notation are extremely important in the study of calculus. Some who study this book will need to review basic operations with algebraic expressions, including factoring.

In the last two sections of this chapter, we study two important functions and their graphs: **quadratic functions** (along with quadratic equations) and **rational functions.** These functions not only are important in the study of calculus but also serve as models in business, economics, the life sciences, and social science.

1 Exponents and Radicals

The demand for a certain commodity is given in terms of price x by

$$D = 500 - 100x^{1/2}$$

This example demonstrates the fact that many application models or equations involve an unknown raised to a power. Thus, this section is not only important for the study of calculus but is also important when real life situations are represented with models or equations. Undoubtedly your manipulative skills will be sharpened by reviewing in this section the basic definitions and properties of exponents and radicals.

Sometimes in writing algebraic expressions we use symbols such as x^2, x^3, or x^4, which represent $x \cdot x$, $x \cdot x \cdot x$, and $x \cdot x \cdot x \cdot x$, respectively. These symbols are defined as follows:

Exponents

Let x be any real number.

1. If n is any positive integer, then x^n is the product $x \cdot x \cdot x \cdot \cdots \cdot x$ consisting of n factors, each of which is x:

$$x^n = \underbrace{x \cdot x \cdot x \cdot \cdots \cdot x}_{n \text{ factors}}$$

2. $x^0 = 1 \qquad x \neq 0$

3. $x^{-n} = \dfrac{1}{x^n} \qquad x \neq 0$

The symbol x^n is read "the nth power of x" or "x to the nth power"; n is called the **exponent,** and the number x is called the **base.** Important properties of **exponentials** (numbers or variables with exponents) are discussed for positive integral exponents and defined later in this section for any real numbers. Since

$$x^3 = x \cdot x \cdot x \qquad \text{and} \qquad x^4 = x \cdot x \cdot x \cdot x$$

then

$$(x^3)(x^4) = (x \cdot x \cdot x)(x \cdot x \cdot x \cdot x) = x^7$$

In general, if m and n are any positive integers, then

$$(x^m)(x^n) = \underbrace{(x \cdot x \cdot x \cdot \cdots \cdot x)}_{m \text{ factors}} \cdot \underbrace{(x \cdot x \cdot x \cdot \cdots \cdot x)}_{n \text{ factors}} = x^{m+n}$$

Likewise,

$$\frac{x^5}{x^3} = \frac{x \cdot x \cdot x \cdot x \cdot x}{x \cdot x \cdot x} = x^2 \qquad x \neq 0$$

and, in general, if $x \neq 0$,

$$\frac{x^m}{x^n} = \frac{\overbrace{(x \cdot x \cdot x \cdot \cdots \cdot x)}^{m \text{ factors}}}{\underbrace{(x \cdot x \cdot x \cdot \cdots \cdot x)}_{n \text{ factors}}} = \begin{cases} x^{m-n} & \text{if } m \text{ is larger than } n \\ \dfrac{1}{x^{n-m}} & \text{if } n \text{ is larger than } m \end{cases}$$

Now

$$(x^2)^3 = x^2 \cdot x^2 \cdot x^2 = (x \cdot x)(x \cdot x)(x \cdot x) = x^6$$

and, in general, $(x^m)^n = x^{mn}$. Likewise,

$$(xyz)^3 = (xyz)(xyz)(xyz) = x^3y^3z^3$$

and $(xyz)^m = x^my^mz^m$ for any exponent m.

The fact that

$$\frac{x^m}{x^n} = x^{m-n} \qquad x \neq 0$$

provides a reason for property 2 of the preceding definition. Consider this property when m and n are equal and $x \neq 0$.

$$\frac{x^m}{x^m} = x^{m-m} = x^0$$

But any number, except 0, divided by itself equals 1. Therefore, x^0 is defined to be 1.

Now let's take a look at

$$x^n \cdot x^{-n} = x^{n+(-n)}$$
$$= x^{n-n}$$
$$= x^0$$
$$= 1$$

Divide both sides by x^n, where $x \neq 0$, to obtain

$$x^{-n} = \frac{1}{x^n}$$

Therefore, x^{-n} is defined to equal $\dfrac{1}{x^n}$ when $x \neq 0$. For example,

$$2^{-3} = \frac{1}{2^3} = \frac{1}{8}$$

Since any exponential with a negative exponent can be changed to one with a positive exponent, we can now list the following properties of exponentials.

Properties of Exponentials

For any integers m and n, and any nonzero real numbers x and y for which the following exist,

a. $x^m \cdot x^n = x^{m+n}$

b. $\dfrac{x^m}{x^n} = x^{m-n}$

c. $(x^m)^n = x^{mn}$

d. $(xy)^m = x^m \cdot y^m$

e. $\left(\dfrac{x}{y}\right)^m = \dfrac{x^m}{y^m}$

EXAMPLE 1 The five properties of exponentials are illustrated as follows:

a. $11^3 \cdot 11^{-5} = 11^{3+(-5)} = 11^{-2} = \frac{1}{11^2} = \frac{1}{121}$

b. $\frac{7^4}{7^{-2}} = 7^{4-(-2)} = 7^6 = 117,649$

c. $(2^3)^{-2} = 2^{3(-2)} = 2^{-6} = \frac{1}{2^6} = \frac{1}{64}$

d. $(3y)^2 = 3^2 \cdot y^2 = 9y^2$

e. $\left(\frac{2}{y}\right)^2 = \frac{2^2}{y^2} = \frac{4}{y^2}$

EXAMPLE 2 Use the properties described in this section to simplify each of the following. Leave the answers with positive exponents.

a. $\dfrac{x^5 y^2}{xy^4} = \dfrac{x^5}{x} \cdot \dfrac{y^2}{y^4} = x^4 \cdot \dfrac{1}{y^2} = \dfrac{x^4}{y^2}$

b. $\dfrac{3x^2}{y^2} \cdot \dfrac{y^2}{9x^3} = \dfrac{3x^2 y^2}{9x^3 y^2} = \dfrac{3}{9} \cdot \dfrac{x^2}{x^3} \cdot \dfrac{y^2}{y^2} = \dfrac{1}{3} \cdot \dfrac{1}{x} \cdot 1 = \dfrac{1}{3x}$

c. $\left(\dfrac{x^{-6}}{y^{-2}}\right)^{-2} = \dfrac{(x^{-6})^{-2}}{(y^{-2})^{-2}} = \dfrac{x^{12}}{y^4}$

Now let's extend the multiplicative property using integral exponents to include fractional exponents. For example,

$$x^{1/3} \cdot x^{1/3} \cdot x^{1/3} = x^{1/3+1/3+1/3} = x^{3/3} = x$$

The real number that is raised to the third power to yield a number x is called the **cube root** of x and is denoted by $\sqrt[3]{x}$. The symbol $\sqrt[3]{}$ is called a **radical.** $x^{1/3} = \sqrt[3]{x}$, and, in general,

$$x^{1/m} = \sqrt[m]{x} \qquad \text{if } \sqrt[m]{x} \text{ is defined}$$

If m is even and x is negative, then $\sqrt[m]{x}$ does not exist in the set of real numbers. If m is odd and x is negative, $x^{1/m} = \sqrt[m]{x}$ exists and is a negative number.

Properties of Radicals

Let x be any real number and m and n be any positive integers. Then

a. The **square root** of x is defined by

$$x^{1/2} = \sqrt{x} \qquad x \geq 0$$

b. The **cube root** of x is given by

$$x^{1/3} = \sqrt[3]{x}$$

c. The **nth root** of x is

$$x^{1/n} = \sqrt[n]{x} \qquad x \geq 0 \text{ if } n \text{ is even}$$

d. $x^{m/n} = \sqrt[n]{x^m} = (\sqrt[n]{x})^m \qquad x \geq 0 \text{ if } n \text{ is even}$

EXAMPLE 3 These properties are illustrated in the order listed.

    a. $25^{1/2} = \sqrt{25} = 5$

    b. $8^{1/3} = \sqrt[3]{8} = 2$

    c. $(32)^{1/5} = \sqrt[5]{32} = 2$

    d. $8^{2/3} \begin{cases} = \sqrt[3]{8^2} = \sqrt[3]{64} = 4 \\ = (\sqrt[3]{8})^2 = 2^2 = 4 \end{cases}$

We need to issue a word of caution concerning these definitions. Since $(-2)^2 = 4$ and $2^2 = 4$, a square root of 4 can be either -2 or 2. In order for the answer to be unique, we restrict

$$\sqrt[n]{a^n} = |a| \qquad \text{for n even}$$

Thus, $\sqrt{4}$ will always equal 2 in our discussion. If we want the two solutions of $y^2 = 4$, we need to write $y = \pm\sqrt{4} = \pm 2$ since otherwise $\sqrt{4}$ is taken to be 2.

EXAMPLE 4

    a. $(2x^{1/3})(3x^{1/2}) = 6x^{1/3 + 1/2}$
$$= 6x^{5/6}$$
$$= 6\sqrt[6]{x^5}$$

    b. $\left(\dfrac{4x^{1/2}}{x^{-2}}\right)^{1/2} = \dfrac{4^{1/2}x^{1/4}}{x^{-1}}$
$$= 4^{1/2}x^{5/4}$$
$$= 2 \cdot x \cdot x^{1/4}$$
$$= 2x\sqrt[4]{x}$$

The following example illustrates finding the odd root of a negative number.

EXAMPLE 5   **a.** $\sqrt[3]{-8} = \sqrt[3]{(-2)^3} = -2$ **b.** $\sqrt[5]{-243} = \sqrt[5]{(-3)^5} = -3$

We conclude this rapid review of exponents and radicals by summarizing the properties of radicals. These properties follow directly from the corresponding properties of exponents.

Properties of Radicals

Let m and n be positive integers and x and y be any real numbers for which the following exist. Then

    a. $(\sqrt[n]{x})^n = x$

    b. $\sqrt[n]{x^n} = \begin{cases} |x| & \text{if n is even} \\ x & \text{if n is odd} \end{cases}$

    c. $\sqrt[n]{xy} = \sqrt[n]{x} \cdot \sqrt[n]{y}$

    d. $\sqrt[n]{\dfrac{x}{y}} = \dfrac{\sqrt[n]{x}}{\sqrt[n]{y}} \qquad y \neq 0$

    e. $\sqrt[m]{\sqrt[n]{x}} = \sqrt[mn]{x}$

EXAMPLE 6 These five properties are illustrated as follows.

a. $(\sqrt[3]{5})^3 = 5$

b. $\sqrt[4]{y^8} = \sqrt[4]{(y^2)^4} = y^2;\quad \sqrt[3]{y^6} = \sqrt[3]{(y^2)^3} = y^2$

c. $\sqrt[4]{256x^4y^8} = \sqrt[4]{256} \cdot \sqrt[4]{x^4} \cdot \sqrt[4]{y^8} = \sqrt[4]{4^4} \cdot \sqrt[4]{x^4} \cdot \sqrt[4]{(y^2)^4} = 4|xy^2|$

d. $\sqrt[3]{\dfrac{-8y^6}{x^3}} = \dfrac{\sqrt[3]{-8y^6}}{\sqrt[3]{x^3}} = \dfrac{\sqrt[3]{-8} \cdot \sqrt[3]{y^6}}{\sqrt[3]{x^3}} = \dfrac{-2y^2}{x}$

e. $\sqrt[3]{\sqrt[2]{64}} = \sqrt[6]{64} = \sqrt[6]{2^6} = 2$

or

$\sqrt[3]{\sqrt[2]{64}} = \sqrt[3]{\sqrt{8^2}} = \sqrt[3]{8} = \sqrt[3]{2^3} = 2$

Properties **c** and **d** can be used in simplifying radicals. For example, $\sqrt{32} = \sqrt{16 \cdot 2} = \sqrt{16} \cdot \sqrt{2} = 4\sqrt{2}$.

EXAMPLE 7
$$\sqrt[3]{-16y^5x^4} = \sqrt[3]{-8y^3x^3 \cdot 2y^2x}$$
$$= -2yx\sqrt[3]{2y^2x}$$

A fraction involving radicals is said to be in simplest form if there is no radical in the denominator. Sometimes the procedure for placing a radical in simplest form is called **rationalizing the denominator.**

EXAMPLE 8 Put $2/\sqrt{x}$ in simplest form.

Solution
$$\frac{2}{\sqrt{x}} = \frac{2\sqrt{x}}{\sqrt{x} \cdot \sqrt{x}} = \frac{2\sqrt{x}}{x}$$

Exercise Set 8.1

A *Assume that all variables in the following problems represent positive real numbers.*

1. Write each of the following in radical form.
  a. $7^{1/2}$ **b.** $2x^{1/3}$ **c.** $(5y)^{1/2}$ **d.** $5y^{1/2}$
  e. $(xy)^{1/3}$ **f.** $x \cdot y^{1/3}$ **g.** $x^{3/5}$ **h.** $y^{3/4}$

2. Write each of the following in exponential form.
  a. $\sqrt[3]{x^4}$ **b.** $\sqrt{3y^2}$ **c.** $\sqrt[4]{x^2y^3}$ **d.** $\sqrt[5]{x^7y^4}$

3. Find the indicated root.
  a. $\sqrt[3]{-27}$ **b.** $\sqrt[4]{81}$ **c.** $\sqrt{100}$ **d.** $\sqrt[5]{-32}$

  e. $\sqrt{x^8y^4}$ **f.** $\sqrt[3]{x^9y^6}$ **g.** $\sqrt{9x^4y^2}$ **h.** $\sqrt[3]{\dfrac{125x^3}{8y^6}}$

4. Perform the indicated operations and leave each answer in simplest form with positive exponents.

  a. $(3x^3yz)(8xy^2z^4)$ **b.** $(x^2y^3)^4$ **c.** $\dfrac{10a^4b^3}{2a^5b^2}$

  d. $\left(\dfrac{a^4}{b^3}\right)^2$ **e.** $5x^3a^2z^4 \cdot \dfrac{1}{15x^4ay^2}$ **f.** $\left(\dfrac{x^2y^3}{x^4y}\right)^2$

5. Evaluate each of the following.

a. $(9)^{1/2}$ **b.** $(-27)^{1/3}$ **c.** $\sqrt{16}$ **d.** $100^{-1/2}$

e. $(16^{-2})^{-1/2}$ **f.** $(-27)^{2/3}$ **g.** $(25^{-1/2})^{-1}$ **h.** $(2^{-7/4})^{-4}$

6. Complete the following statements.

a. $x^n \cdot (\underline{\hspace{1cm}}) = x^{n+7}$ **b.** $\dfrac{6^4 \cdot \underline{\hspace{1cm}} \cdot y^6}{2x^4y} = \dfrac{6^4x^7y^5}{2} = 3 \cdot 6^3x^7y^5$

c. $x^{1/2} \div \underline{\hspace{1cm}} = x^0 = 1$ **d.** $x^{7/2} \cdot x^{3/2} = \underline{\hspace{1cm}}$

B

7. Simplify each of the following as much as possible and express the result without zero or negative exponents.

a. $\dfrac{x^{-7}y^0z^{-1}}{x^{-2}y^3z^2}$ **b.** $\left(\dfrac{4a^{-1}b^{-3}c}{2^0a^{-4}b^2c^{-2}}\right)^{-1}$ **c.** $(3)^{-3} \cdot \dfrac{9^{-3}}{9^{-5}}$

d. $\left(\dfrac{16x^{-2}y^3}{x^{-2}y^{-1}}\right)^{1/4}$ **e.** $\dfrac{(a^{-4}y^{-2})^{-1/2}}{(a^{-1}y^{-2})^2}$ **f.** $\left(\dfrac{25x^{-1}y^{1/2}}{16x^{-1/2}y}\right)^{1/2}$

8. Remove as much of the expression from the radical as possible.

a. $\sqrt{8x^5}$ **b.** $\sqrt{9x^5y^2}$ **c.** $\sqrt[3]{2x^3y^4}$ **d.** $\sqrt{x} \cdot \sqrt{xy}$

9. Rationalize the denominator of each expression.

a. $\dfrac{1}{\sqrt{2}}$ **b.** $\dfrac{2}{\sqrt{3}}$ **c.** $\dfrac{4}{\sqrt{2x}}$ **d.** $\dfrac{1}{\sqrt[3]{4}}$

e. $\dfrac{2}{\sqrt[3]{9}}$ **f.** $\dfrac{2}{\sqrt[3]{y^2}}$ **g.** $\dfrac{x}{\sqrt{xy}}$ **h.** $\dfrac{1}{\sqrt[3]{xy^2}}$

10. Put each of the following in simplest form.

a. $\sqrt{8x^3y^5}$ **b.** $\sqrt[3]{40a^7b^5}$ **c.** $\dfrac{6a^2}{\sqrt{3a}}$

d. $\dfrac{4y^2}{\sqrt{4y^3}}$ **e.** $\sqrt[3]{\dfrac{x}{2}}$ **f.** $\sqrt{\dfrac{4xy^5}{3x^2y}}$

C

11. Using exponents, rewrite each expression below. Remove all radicals and do not use negative exponents.

a. $(\sqrt{9/4})^3(\sqrt[3]{2^2/15})^4$ **b.** $\sqrt{\sqrt[3]{x^5/y^7}}$ **c.** $\dfrac{4x^3\sqrt{y}}{y^4\sqrt{x^4}}$

d. $\dfrac{(343x^6y^5)^{-1/3}}{(49x^6y^{16/3})^{-1/2}}$ **e.** $(2\sqrt{2}-2)^{-1}$ **f.** $\dfrac{\sqrt[3]{2a^2b^7}}{\sqrt[3]{ab^2}}$

g. $\dfrac{\sqrt{6a}\sqrt{5ab}}{\sqrt{15b}}$ **h.** $\dfrac{3}{\sqrt{2}-1}$

Business

12. Double-Declining Balance Depreciation. After k years the value of a machine that has a life of n years and an original cost of C dollars is given by

$$V = C\left(1 - \dfrac{2}{n}\right)^k$$

If a machine costs $10,000 and has a life of 10 years, find its value after

a. 1 year.   **b.** 2 years.   **c.** 3 years.

d. Use your calculator to find its value after 8 years.

13. **Sales Decay.** A company finds that sales begin to fall between November 1 and January 1 according to

$$S = \$1,000,000(2)^{-0.2t}$$

where t is the number of days after November 1. Find the sales volume on November 6, on November 11, and on November 16. Use your calculator to find the sales volume on December 10, December 14, and December 22.

Economics

14. **Exponential Growth.** The formula below indicates how money grows when compounded continuously. That is,

$$A = P(e)^{ni} \quad \text{(See Table III of the Appendix.)}$$

where P is the money deposited and A is the value after n years at $i\%$ per year (expressed as a decimal). Find the amount of $100 invested at 10% per year for 20 years.

Life Sciences

15. **Decay Models.** The pressure in the aorta of a human adult can be approximated by

$$P = 100(e)^{-0.5t}$$

where t is the number of seconds after the valves have closed. Find the aortic pressure when $t = 0, 1, 2, 4$. Notice how the pressure decays. Now use your calculator to find the pressure when $t = 6, 8, 10$.

Social Sciences

16. **Population Growth.** The formula

$$P = 40,000(e)^{0.02t}$$

predicts the population of a city in t years. Find the population of this city now; in 50 years; in 100 years. Use a calculator to find the population in 5, 10, and 30 years.

2 What Is a Function?

> An important concept that influences the study of mathematics from elementary grades through graduate work is the concept of a **function.** Its study is often introduced through a "function machine"; that is, a function is regarded as a machine that produces a unique output number for a given input number. Instead of a function machine, we use the concept of input–rule–output, along with numerous simple examples, to help you understand the meaning of a function.
>
> The concept of a function is used in just about every chapter in the remainder of this book. We study functional relationships between supply and demand, unit cost and production, age and the value of a piece of equipment, IQ and accomplishment, as well as many other examples.

Let's first think of a function as an operation that associates or assigns to each element of a first set A a unique element of the second set B. This way of thinking of a function can be demonstrated by what we call input–rule–output. The first set can be considered as the input, and then from a rule the second set, or some subset of it, can be obtained as the output.

EXAMPLE 9   Notice in Figure 8.1 that we insert an input, operate with the rule, and obtain an output. Suppose that the rule, or function, is "add a 4 to the input." This rule can be expressed as $x + 4$ when the input is x. When the input is 3, the rule operates to give $3 + 4$, and the output is 7.

In addition, notice that this function $x + 4$ is a rule or procedure that associates with each element of set A (the input) one and only one element of set B (the output).

Figure 8.1

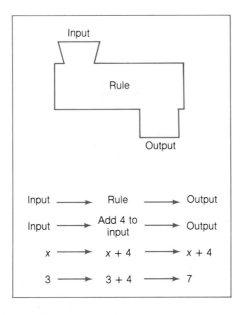

EXAMPLE 10   As a more complex example, consider the function described in Figure 8.2. By examining this concept closely, we see that each element of the input is paired with exactly one output element. This property defines a function.

Figure 8.2

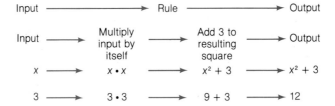

Function | A function is a rule that assigns to each element of the nonempty input set A (the **domain**) exactly one element of the output set B (the **range**).

If we let y be the output in Figure 8.1, "add 4 to x" or $x + 4$ is written as an equation

$$y = x + 4$$

This example illustrates another procedure for expressing a function. Use this equation and let x assume the value 2. Then $y = 2 + 4 = 6$. Also

$$x = 3, \quad y = 7$$
$$x = 4, \quad y = 8$$
$$x = 8, \quad y = 12$$

This suggests that a set of ordered pairs may describe a function. A set of ordered pairs defines a function if and only if no two of the ordered pairs have the same first element.

EXAMPLE 11 Consider the following sets of ordered pairs where $x \in \{2, 3, 4\}$ and $y \in \{3, 4, 5, 6\}$. Which of these sets of ordered pairs are functions?

a. $S = \{(2, 3), (3, 4), (4, 5)\}$
b. $S = \{(3, 3), (3, 4)\}$
c. $S = \{(2, 3), (3, 4), (4, 5), (2, 6)\}$
d. $S = \{(2, 5), (3, 5), (4, 5)\}$

Solution It is easy to verify, using the preceding definition, that **a** and **d** are functions. The set in **c** is not a function because 2 is paired with both 3 and 6, and the set in **b** is not a function because 3 is paired with both 3 and 4.

Sometimes the ordered pair relationship is shown as a correspondence. The relationship in Figure 8.3(a) is a function; the relationship in 8.3(b) isn't. Why not?

Figure 8.3(a) illustrates why a function is sometimes called a *mapping*. In each figure, set A is being "mapped" into set B. For the function in (a), set A is called the **domain** of the function, and set B is called the **range** of the function. When a variable represents an arbitrary element of set A, it is called the **independent variable.** Set B is called the **dependent variable** because it depends on the choice of the variable in A.

Figure 8.3

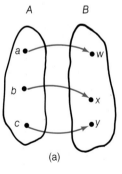

(a)

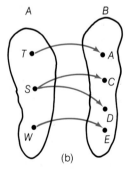

(b)

A table of values may also be used to represent a function. For example,

x	1	3	4	6
y	4	6	12	18

represents a function since to each x there corresponds only one y.

x	1	0	1	2
y	-2	3	4	5

does not represent a function because the two ordered pairs $(1, -2)$ and $(1, 4)$ have the same first element and different second elements.

EXAMPLE 12 For **a.** $y = \sqrt{9 - x^2}$ and **b.** $y = 2/(x + 3)$, specify a domain that would yield real numbers y.

Solution **a.** For what values of x is $9 - x^2 \geq 0$? The domain is

$$\{x \,|\, -3 \leq x \leq 3\}$$

b. For what values of x is $x + 3 \neq 0$? The domain is

$$\{x \,|\, x \text{ is real and } x \neq -3\}$$

In a graphical sense the fact that a function associates each element in its domain with one and only one element in the range implies that no two of the ordered pairs in a function graph into points on the same vertical line. That is, if a vertical line cuts the graph at more than one point, then the graph does not represent a function. Figure 8.4(a) and (c) show the graphs of functions. Figure 8.4(b) shows a graph that is not a function.

Figure 8.4

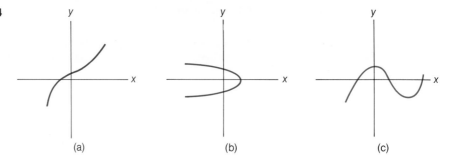

(a)   (b)   (c)

One way to test whether an equation represents a function is to solve the equation for the dependent variable in terms of the independent variable. This new equation will show whether more than one value of the dependent variable (in the range) is associated with a single value of the independent variable (in the domain).

EXAMPLE 13 Is the relation $y^2 = 2 + x^2$ a function?

Solution Since $y^2 = 2 + x^2$ implies that $y = \pm\sqrt{2 + x^2}$, the assignment of a real value to x will result in two different values of y, and hence the relation is not a function.

Often we write a function as $y = f(x)$, or possibly $y = F(x)$ or $y = h(x)$ (read "y equals a function of x" or "y equals the value of the function at x") to indicate that with each x there is associated a unique y. Suppose we write $y = f(x) = x + 7$. When $x = 2$, we substitute 2 for x to obtain

$$y = f(2) = 2 + 7 = 9$$

Likewise, when $x = 4$, $f(4) = 11$, and $f(6) = 13$.

The notation $y = f(x)$ actually states a rule for determining values of y when values are assigned to x. For example, if $y = f(x) = x^2$, where x is any real number, then $f(2) = 2^2 = 4$ or $y = 4$. If

$$f(x) = x^2 - 3x + 2$$

then

$$f(3) = 3^2 - 3(3) + 2 = 2$$

EXAMPLE 14 Given $f(t) = 6 + 3t$, find $f(-1)$, $f(2)$, and $f(0) - f(-4)$.

Solution

$$f(-1) = 6 + 3(-1) = 3$$
$$f(2) = 6 + 3(2) = 12$$
$$f(0) = 6 + 3(0) = 6 \quad \text{and} \quad f(-4) = 6 + 3(-4) = -6$$
$$f(0) - f(-4) = 6 - (-6) = 12$$

EXAMPLE 15 For the function in Example 14, find $f(1) \cdot f(3)$, $f(2z)$, and $f(t + 1)$.

Solution

$$f(1) \cdot f(3) = [6 + 3(1)] \cdot [6 + 3(3)] = 135$$
$$f(2z) = 6 + 3(2z) = 6 + 6z$$
$$f(t + 1) = 6 + 3(t + 1) = 6 + 3t + 3 = 9 + 3t$$

In our work in calculus, we will be using functions of functions. For example, if

$$g(x) = x^2 \quad \text{and} \quad f(x) = 2x$$

then

$$g[f(x)] = [f(x)]^2 = [2x]^2 = 4x^2$$

$g[f(x)]$ is called a **composite function.** This idea is illustrated in Figure 8.5.

Figure 8.5

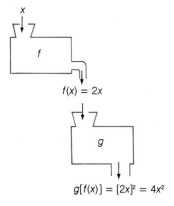

$$g[f(x)] = [2x]^2 = 4x^2$$

EXAMPLE 16   If $g(x) = 3x^2 + 1$ and $f(x) = x + 1$, then

$$g[f(x)] = 3[f(x)]^2 + 1 = 3(x + 1)^2 + 1$$

Note that $g[f(x)]$ is defined for all values of the range of $f(x)$ that are in the domain of g, as demonstrated by Figure 8.6.

Figure 8.6

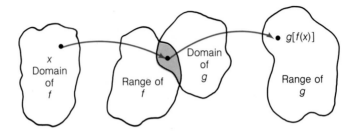

Exercise Set 8.2

A   **1.** Which of the following sets of ordered pairs are functions?
  a. $\{(1, 3), (3, 3), (5, 3)\}$ **b.** $\{(1, 3), (3, 3), (5, 7)\}$
  c. $\{(1, 3), (3, 5), (5, 1)\}$ **d.** $\{(1, 1), (3, 3), (5, 5)\}$
  e. $\{(3, 4), (5, 10), (6, 4), (7, 1)\}$ **f.** $\{(1, 5), (1, 6), (2, 5), (3, 10)\}$
  g. $\{(3, 7), (7, 3), (8, 3)\}$ **h.** $\{(4, 6), (5, 6)\}$
  i. $\{(5, 3), (5, 4)\}$ **j.** $\{(5, 5), (6, 6)\}$

2. Which of the following tables define functions? (x is the independent variable.)

a.

x	2	2
y	4	1

b.

x	1	3
y	−1	−1

c.

x	1	1
y	1	2

d.

x	0	0
y	0	1

e.

x	1	2
y	1	1

f.

x	0	2	3	4
y	2	4	7	2

g.

x	−2	1	3	2	1
y	1	2	4	3	4

h.

x	−1	2	4	2
y	3	4	6	5

3. If $y = f(x) = x^3 - 2x$, find $f(-2)$, $f(1)$, and $f(0) - f(3)$.

4. If $y = f(x) = (x + 2)(x - 1)$, find $f(3)$, $f(2)$, and $f(-1) - \dfrac{f(0)}{2}$.

5. Which of the following graphs represent functions?

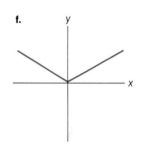

a.

b.

c.

d.

e.

f.

B **6.** If $y = f(x) = x^3 - 2x$, find $\dfrac{f(-1)}{f(1)}$, $f(2) \cdot f(4)$, $f(w)$, and $f(2z)$.

7. If $y = f(x) = (x + 2)(x - 1)$, find $f(-2) \cdot f(2)$, $f(z)$, $f(3w)$, and $f(t + 3)$.

Specify the domain that would yield real numbers y for elements in the range of the function defined by each equation.

8. $y = \dfrac{3}{x - 2}$

9. $y = \sqrt{3 - x}$

10. $y = \dfrac{1}{x}$

11. $y = \dfrac{3}{x(x - 2)}$

12. $y = \sqrt{9 - x^2}$

13. $y = \sqrt{x(x + 4)}$

C **14.** Given $f(x) = \dfrac{3x^2 - 6}{x - 1}$, find the following.

  a. $f(0.015)$ **b.** $f(-7.612)$ **c.** $f(\tfrac{4}{3})$
  d. $f(2t)$ **e.** $f(2t + 1)$ **f.** $f(0.1t + 0.005)$

15. If the domain of a function is not stated, we assume that it is the largest set of real numbers for which the rule or formula gives a real-valued function. State the domain for the following functions.
  a. $y = x + 7$ **b.** $y = x^2 + 6x + 4$ **c.** $y = \sqrt{x + 1}$

  d. $y = x + \sqrt{x - 4}$ **e.** $y = \sqrt{4x}$ **f.** $y = \dfrac{6}{4 - x}$

16. Let $g(x) = x^2 + 2x + 1$ and $f(x) = x - 2$. Find $g[f(x)]$.

17. Let $h(x) = \dfrac{x}{x - 1}$ and $l(x) = 2x^2 - 7$.

a. Find $h[l(x)]$. **b.** Find $l[h(x)]$.
c. Discuss the domain of $h[l(x)]$. **d.** Discuss the domain of $l[h(x)]$.

18. Can you determine a formula for the function denoted by the following table?

x	1	2	3	4	0	−1	−2
y	8	11	16	23	7	8	11

19. **a.** If $f(x) = 3x + 1$, does $f(ax + b) = f(ax) + f(b)$?
 b. If $g(x) = 2x^2 - x + 1$, does $g(ax + b) = g(ax) + g(b)$?

Business 20. A parking lot charges by the hour as follows:

$$f(x) = \$2.00 + \$1.50(x - 1) \quad \text{for } x \geq 1$$

Find the charge for 1 hour, 2 hours, 10 hours, and 24 hours.

Economics 21. **Revenue Functions.** A travel agency books a flight to Europe for a group of college students. The fare in a 200-passenger airplane will be $400 per student plus $2.00 per student for each vacant seat.
 a. Write the total revenue $R(x)$ as a function of empty seats, x.
 b. What is the domain of this function?
 c. Calculate $R(x)$ for 5 empty seats; 10 empty seats; 20 empty seats; 40 empty seats; and 100 empty seats.

22. **Demand Functions.** Suppose the demand for a certain item is given by

$$D(x) = \frac{50 - 5x}{4}$$

where $D(x)$ represents the demand as a function of price x.
 a. What is the demand when $x = 0$?
 b. What is the demand when $x = 4$?
 c. What happens to the demand when $x = 10$?
 d. Graph $D(x)$.

23. **Supply Functions.** Suppose the supply for the item in exercise 22 is given by

$$S(x) = \frac{5x}{6}$$

where $S(x)$ represents supply as a function of price.
 a. What is the supply when $x = 3$; when $x = 9$?
 b. Graph $S(x)$ on the same axis system as you used in exercise 22.
 c. Estimate from the intersection of the graphs the equilibrium price.
 d. Estimate the equilibrium demand; the equilibrium supply.
 e. When is supply greater than demand?

24. **Demand and Supply Functions.** Let the supply S and demand D functions for a certain commodity be given in terms of price x by

$$D(x) = \frac{400 - 5x}{2} \quad \text{and} \quad S(x) = \frac{5x}{2}$$

 a. Graph $D(x)$ and $S(x)$ on the same axes.
 b. Find the equilibrium price.
 c. Find the equilibrium demand; the supply.
 d. When is the supply less than the demand?

Life Sciences

25. **Bacteria Count.**

$$N(x) = 1000 - 150x \qquad 0 \le x \le 6$$

represents the number of bacteria in a culture x hours after an antibacterial treatment has been administered. Find $N(0)$, $N(2)$, $N(4)$, and $N(6)$.

26. **Temperature.** The functional relationship between Celsius temperature and Fahrenheit temperature is

$$C(F) = \frac{5(F - 32)}{9}$$

Find $C(0°)$, $C(32°)$, and $C(98.6°)$. $98.6°F$ is the normal body temperature. Draw a graph relating the Celsius and Fahrenheit temperatures.

Social Sciences

27. **Population.** From a study of the enrollment in elementary schools and the record of previous transfers, Vestavia High School estimates the size of the graduating class by the equation

$$N(t) = 200 - 12t + t^2 \qquad 0 \le t \le 15$$

with t representing the number of years after 1980. Find $N(5)$, $N(7)$, and $N(15)$. Can you locate the year with the smallest graduating class?

Basic Operations with Algebraic Expressions

In this section we review operations with algebraic expressions, operations that are used in each chapter in the remainder of this book. First we practice **combining** algebraic expressions. Then we practice **factoring**; that is, we write algebraic expressions as products of factors. Factoring is used in solving quadratic equations in this chapter and in various application problems in calculus.

The approach we use in factoring is to recognize a standard form for factoring and to put our problem in this form. This section is an easy but important section.

The rules for combining algebraic expressions have as their basis the basic properties of addition and multiplication of real numbers.

a. $2 + 3 = 3 + 2$ or $a + b = b + a$	**Commutative property of addition**
b. $2 \cdot 3 = 3 \cdot 2$ or $ab = ba$	**Commutative property of multiplication**
c. $2 + (3 + 4) = (2 + 3) + 4$ or $a + (b + c) = (a + b) + c$	**Associative property of addition**
d. $2(3 \cdot 4) = (2 \cdot 3) \cdot 4$ or $a(bc) = (ab)c$	**Associative property of multiplication**
e. $2(3 + 4) = 2 \cdot 3 + 2 \cdot 4$ or $a(b + c) = ab + ac$ also $(b + c)a = ba + ca$	**Distributive property of multiplication over addition**

We now use these properties to perform addition on algebraic expressions.

EXAMPLE 17   Perform the following addition, illustrating the properties listed.

$$3xy + 5xy.$$

Solution

$$3xy + 5xy = (3 + 5)xy \quad \text{Property e}$$
$$= 8xy$$

EXAMPLE 18   Add $(5x^2 + 7) + 6x^2$ using the appropriate properties.

Solution

$$(5x^2 + 7) + 6x^2 = 5x^2 + (7 + 6x^2) \quad \text{Property c}$$
$$= 5x^2 + (6x^2 + 7) \quad \text{Property a}$$
$$= (5x^2 + 6x^2) + 7 \quad \text{Property c}$$
$$= (5 + 6)x^2 + 7 \quad \text{Property e}$$
$$= 11x^2 + 7$$

The two preceding examples indicate that the procedure for combining like terms (terms with the same variable and exponent) that we have been using is correct.

EXAMPLE 19 $(3x^2 + 4xy + 7) + (6x^2 - xy - 4) = 9x^2 + 3xy + 3$

To multiply a polynomial by a one-term expression, we use a generalization of the distributive property of multiplication over addition (or subtraction), property **e**.

EXAMPLE 20 $3xy(2x^2 - 3xy + y^2) = 3xy(2x^2) + 3xy(-3xy) + 3xy(y^2)$
$$= 6x^3y - 9x^2y^2 + 3xy^3$$

(Are you aware that you used properties **b** and **d**?)

The distributive property of multiplication over addition is also the basis by which we multiply in the following example.

EXAMPLE 21   Multiply $(3x + 2)(6x + 1)$.

Solution

$$(3x + 2)(6x + 1) = (3x + 2)(6x) + (3x + 2)(1)$$
$$= (3x)(6x) + 2(6x) + 3x(1) + 2(1)$$
$$= 18x^2 + 12x + 3x + 2$$
$$= 18x^2 + 15x + 2$$

The following procedure may also be used.

$$\begin{array}{r} 3x + 2 \\ 6x + 1 \\ \hline 18x^2 + 12x \qquad \\ 3x + 2 \\ \hline 18x^2 + 15x + 2 \end{array}$$

6x times $(3x + 2)$

1 times $(3x + 2)$

Verify the following multiplications, which are useful in the next discussion.

EXAMPLE 22

a. $(a - b)(a + b) = a^2 - b^2$
b. $(a + b)^2 = a^2 + 2ab + b^2$
c. $(a + b)(a + c) = a^2 + a(b + c) + bc$
d. $(a + b)(c + d) = ac + ad + bc + bd$

The inverse process of multiplying polynomials is called **factoring**; that is, we write a polynomial as a product of polynomials. The easiest procedure of factoring involves using the distributive property over addition. For example, $6x + 3y$ is completely factored as

$$6x + 3y = 3 \cdot 2x + 3 \cdot y = 3(2x + y)$$

If there are several terms of a polynomial that have common factors, the common factors can be removed by the generalized distributive property.

EXAMPLE 23 Factor $4x^2y + 8x^3y^3 + 12x^4y$.

Solution

$$4x^2y + 8x^3y^3 + 12x^4y = 4x^2y(1) + 4x^2y(2xy^2) + 4x^2y(3x^2)$$

$$= 4x^2y(1 + 2xy^2 + 3x^2)$$

It is easy to recognize expressions of the form $a^2 - b^2$ as the difference of two squares, that is, $a^2 - b^2 = (a - b)(a + b)$, as seen in part **a** of Example 22.

EXAMPLE 24 Factor $4x^2 - 9y^4$.

Solution Note that

$$4x^2 = (2x)^2 \qquad \text{and} \qquad 9y^4 = (3y^2)^2$$

Thus,

$$4x^2 - 9y^4 = (2x)^2 - (3y^2)^2 = (2x - 3y^2)(2x + 3y^2)$$

It is somewhat more difficult to recognize and factor expressions of the form $a^2 + 2ab + b^2$, which, from part **b** of Example 22, equals $(a + b)^2$. First locate the two terms that are squared. Then determine if the product of these terms is multiplied by 2 to get the middle term.

EXAMPLE 25 Factor $9y^4 + 12y^2x + 4x^2$.

Solution Note that

$$9y^4 + 12y^2x + 4x^2 =$$
$$(3y^2)^2 + 12y^2x + (2x)^2 =$$
$$(3y^2)^2 + 2(3y^2)(2x) + (2x)^2 =$$
$$(3y^2 + 2x)^2$$

Now see if you can recognize and use

$$(a + b)(a + c) = a^2 + a(b + c) + bc \quad \text{Property c}$$

EXAMPLE 26 Factor $x^2 - 7x + 12$.

Solution Now 12 is not a perfect square so let's look at products that will give 12 and see what their possible sums will be.

$$12 = 1 \cdot 12 = 2 \cdot 6 = 3 \cdot 4 = -1(-12) = -2(-6) = -3(-4)$$

Since $-3 + (-4) = -7$, we have

$$x^2 - 7x + 12 = x \cdot x - 7x + (-3)(-4)$$
$$= x \cdot x + [-3 + (-4)]x + (-3)(-4)$$
$$= (x - 3)(x - 4)$$

The expression $(a + b)(c + d) = ac + ad + bc + bd$, property **d**, may occur with three terms or four terms.

EXAMPLE 27 Factor $6x^2 + 7x + 2$.

Solution Now

$$6x^2 = (x)(6x) = (2x)(3x) \quad \text{and} \quad 2 = (1)(2) = (-1)(-2)$$

By trial and error we multiply pairs of factors until the sum of the two products is the middle term $7x$.

$$6x^2 + 7x + 2 = (2x)(3x) + (2x)(2) + (3x)(1) + (1)(2)$$
$$= (2x + 1)(3x + 2)$$

EXAMPLE 28 Factor $3xy + 9x + 2y + 6$.

Solution A four-factor expression can often be factored by using a double application of the distributive property.

$$3xy + 9x + 2y + 6 = 3x(y + 3) + 2(y + 3)$$
$$= (3x + 2)(y + 3)$$

EXAMPLE 29   Factor $3x^2y + 2x + 3xy^2 + 2y$.

Solution $3x^2y + 2x + 3xy^2 + 2y = x(3xy) + 2(x) + y(3xy) + 2(y)$

$$= 3xy(x + y) + 2(x + y)$$

$$= (3xy + 2)(x + y)$$

EXAMPLE 30   Factor $2x^2 + 2x + 1$.

Solution   The factors of $2x^2$ are $2x$ and x. The factors of 1 are 1 and 1. Thus,

$$(2x + 1)(x + 1) = 2x^2 + 3x + 1 \neq 2x^2 + 2x + 1$$

Actually, $2x^2 + 2x + 1$ cannot be factored.

EXAMPLE 31   See if you agree that $x^2 + 1$ cannot be factored.

Exercise Set **8.3**

A   *Write each polynomial in standard form.*

1. $(3x^2 - 6x + 4) + (x^2 - 4x + 4) - (x^2 - 1)$

2. $(x^3 + 2x^2 - 4) + (2x^3 - x^2 + 2x) + (x - 1)$

3. $(2x^2 - 7x - 10) - 3(3x^2 - 2x + 5) - 5(x^2 - 2x)$

4. $(x^3 + 2x + 7) - 2(x^2 - 7x + 2) + 4(3x - 1)$

Simplify each product by combining all constants and all powers of each variable.

5. $6x(x^2 + 2x)$ **6.** $3xy(x^2y - 4x)$ **7.** $(x + 2)(x - 3)$

8. $(x - 1)(x + 5)$ **9.** $(3x - 1)(x + 2)$ **10.** $(x + 3)(2x + 1)$

11. $4(2x - 1)(3x + 7)$ **12.** $-5(x - 5)(2x - 1)$

Factor the following expressions completely into products.

13. $3x^2y - 12x^2$ **14.** $2x^3y^2 + 8x^2y + 16x^2y^2$

15. $x^2 + 10x + 25$ **16.** $x^2 + 14x + 49$

17. $4x^2 - 9$ **18.** $9y^4 - 25x^2$

19. $x^2 + 3x - 10$ **20.** $x^2 + 7x + 10$

21. $xy + 3y - x - 3$ **22.** $xy^2 - 2y^2 + 2xy - 4y$

B   *Simplify each polynomial by combining like terms.*

23. $(2xy + x^2 - 3y^2) + (xy - x^2) - 2(y^2 - 3xy)$

24. $(x^2y + x^2z) - z(xyz + 2x^2z + 3xz^2) - 3(x^2y - xyz + xz^2)$

Simplify by multiplying and combining terms.

EXAMPLE $(x + 1)(x^2 + 2x + 3)$

Solution

$$x^2 + 2x + 3$$
$$x + 1$$
$$\overline{x^3 + 2x^2 + 3x}$$
$$\phantom{x^3 + {}}x^2 + 2x + 3$$
$$\overline{x^3 + 3x^2 + 5x + 3}$$

25. $(x - 2)(3x^2 - x + 4)$

26. $(2x + 1)(x^2 - x + 1)$

27. $2x(x + 1)(x^2 - x + 1)$

28. $(x^2 + 1)(x^2 - 2x + 3)$

Factor completely each of the following.

29. $x^3 - 2x^2 - 8x$

30. $2x^2 + 6x + 4$

31. $xy^3 + 3y^3 - xy^2 - 3y^2$

32. $xy^2 + 5xy - 14x$

33. $x^2y - xy + 3x^2 - 3x$

34. $3x^2 + 12x - 15$

35. $3x^4y^2 - 48y^4$

36. $12x^2y - 9y$

C   Let $P(x) = 3x^2 - 2$, $Q(x) = 2x^2 - x + 1$, and $R(x) = -2x^2 + 3x + 4$. *Write each of the following in standard form.*

37. $2P(x) - 3Q(x) - 2R(x)$

38. $P(x) - 2Q(x) - 3R(x)$

39. $P(x) \cdot Q(x) - 5R(x)$

40. $P(x) - 3Q(x) \cdot R(x)$

Factor completely each of the following.

41. $6x^2y + 2xy^2 - 28y^3$

42. $20p^3 + 26p^2q - 6pq^2$

43. $3x^3 + yx^2 + 3xy^2 + y^3$

44. $2x^3 + z^2x^2 + 2xz + z^3$

Business   **45. Simple Interest.** The formula for simple interest is given by $I = Prt$ (principal times rate times time) and the amount owed A is given by $A = P + I$. Substitute for I and factor so that A equals P times some factor.

Economics   **46. Profit and Cost Functions.** As we learned, profit = revenue − cost, or

$$P(x) = R(x) - C(x)$$

Suppose a company's cost of manufacturing x units is $10,000 + 300x - 10^{-6}x^2$ and the revenue function is $(175 - x)x$. Express the profit as a simplified quadratic expression.

Life Sciences   **47. Blood Velocity.** The velocity of blood at x centimeters from the center of a given artery can be approximated by

$$v = 2 - 20,000x^2$$

where x is limited by the size of the artery. Write the velocity as 20,000 times some factor.

Social Sciences   **48. Response Function.** A sociologist noted in a study that she could relate the number of responses received per month (y) to the number of invitations (x) to fund-raising social occasions by

$$y = x - 0.004(x - 1)(x + 200) \qquad 0 < x \le 200$$

Simplify this expression.

Since prior to this chapter we considered mainly linear functions, you may have erroneously concluded that most application problems can be solved with linear models. Of course, there are a multitude of examples that demand nonlinear applications.

In this section we study the **quadratic function,** whose graph is a **parabola.** Radar dishes, reflectors or spotlights, components of microphones, and some cables of suspension bridges are all in the shape of parabolas. Likewise, quadratic function models are used in business, economics, and social science as well as in the life sciences. We illustrate the use of quadratic functions in finding equilibrium points in economics and in other examples in the exercise set. We also review how to solve quadratic equations.

You should find this section to be both interesting and useful.

All functions that can be written in the form

$$y = f(x) = ax^2 + bx + c$$

where $a \neq 0$ are called **quadratic functions.** The graphs of such functions are curves called **parabolas.**

The quadratic function is a special case (where $n = 2$) of a more general type of nonlinear function called the **polynomial function.** Polynomial functions are of the form

$$y = f(x) = a_n x^n + a_{n-1} x^{n-1} + \cdots + a_1 x + a_0$$

where n is a nonnegative integer, and $a_n, a_{n-1}, \ldots, a_0$ are real numbers.

We begin our discussion by examining the graphs of quadratic functions. If several pairs of coordinates that satisfy a given quadratic function are plotted on a coordinate system, the general shape of the curve can be obtained by drawing a smooth curve through the plotted points.

EXAMPLE 32 Find several solutions of the equation $y = f(x) = x^2 + 2x - 3$, plot these points, and draw the graph of the function.

Solution Assign to x the values $\{-5, -4, -3, -2, -1, 0, 1, 2, 3\}$ to obtain the following set of ordered pairs that satisfy $y = x^2 + 2x - 3$:

$$\{(-5, 12), (-4, 5), (-3, 0), (-2, -3), (-1, -4), (0, -3), (1, 0), (2, 5), (3, 12)\}$$

These points are then plotted on the coordinate system in Figure 8.7, and a smooth curve is drawn through the points, taking the shape of a parabola. Note that the curve seems to be symmetric about the dashed line (called the **line of symmetry** or **axis of symmetry**) shown in the figure, and the lowest point on the graph (called the **minimum**) seems to be attained on this line.

Figure 8.7

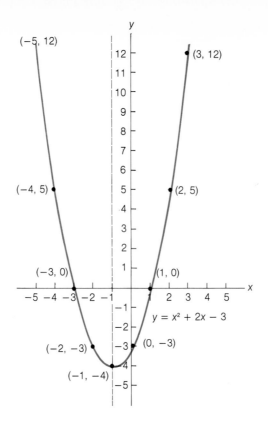

$$y = x^2 + 2x - 3$$

The graph of the function in this example opens upward. After you draw a number of graphs of quadratic functions, you should notice that **a parabola opens upward when the coefficient of x^2 is positive and downward when the coefficient of x^2 is negative, as seen in the next example.**

EXAMPLE 33   Draw the graph of $y = f(x) = -2x^2 + 4x - 2$ by first making a table of values.

Solution   Let x be -1, 0, 1, 2, and 3 to obtain

x	-1	0	1	2	3
y	-8	-2	0	-2	-8

In Figure 8.8 the graph has been sketched through the points listed in the table. Note again that the graph seems to be symmetric about the dashed line. Likewise, the **maximum value,** the highest point on the graph of the function, is attained on the line of symmetry. Also, note that the coefficient of x^2 is negative and that the curve turns downward.

Figure 8.8

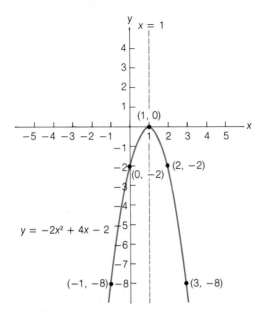

$y = -2x^2 + 4x - 2$

Graph of a Quadratic Function

The graph of a quadratic function turns **upward** and has a **minimum value** when a in

$$f(x) = ax^2 + bx + c$$

is a *positive* number. When a is *negative*, the graph turns **downward** and has a **maximum value.**

When a quadratic function is used to represent a profit or cost function, the point at which the maximum or minimum value occurs is often useful. To determine the value of x at which a maximum or minimum value occurs, we perform the following algebraic manipulations (called **completing the square**):

$$y = ax^2 + bx + c$$

Factor out the a:

$$y = a\left(x^2 + \frac{bx}{a} + \frac{c}{a}\right)$$

Add and subtract the square of one-half of the coefficient of the x term as follows:

$$y = a\left(x^2 + \frac{bx}{a} + \frac{b^2}{4a^2} - \frac{b^2}{4a^2} + \frac{c}{a}\right)$$

The first three terms can be written as

$$\left(x + \frac{b}{2a}\right)^2$$

Thus,

$$y = a\left[\left(x + \frac{b}{2a}\right)^2 - \frac{b^2}{4a^2} + \frac{c}{a}\right]$$

or

$$y = a\left(x + \frac{b}{2a}\right)^2 - \frac{b^2 - 4ac}{4a}$$

Note that the value of

$$\frac{b^2 - 4ac}{4a}$$

is constant. The only term involving x is

$$a\left(x + \frac{b}{2a}\right)^2$$

If $a > 0$, this term is always positive or zero. Thus, the minimum value the function can attain is $\frac{-b^2 + 4ac}{4a}$. If $a < 0$, $a\left(x + \frac{b}{2a}\right)^2$ is always negative or zero, and the maximum value the function can attain is $\frac{-b^2 + 4ac}{4a}$. When the maximum or minimum is attained, $a\left(x + \frac{b}{2a}\right)^2 = 0$, which means

$$x + \frac{b}{2a} = 0 \quad \text{or} \quad x = \frac{-b}{2a}$$

Maximum and Minimum Values

The function $y = f(x) = ax^2 + bx + c$ attains a **minimum value,** when $a > 0$, at $x = -b/2a$, and a **maximum value,** when $a < 0$, at $x = -b/2a$. The maximum or minimum value is

$$y = \frac{-b^2 + 4ac}{4a}$$

obtained by substituting $x = -b/2a$ in $y = f(x)$.

The point where the maximum or minimum value is attained is called the **vertex** of the parabola. The **line of symmetry** is given by $x = -b/2a$.

In the first example of this section the function $y = x^2 + 2x - 3$ assumes a minimum value at

$$x = \frac{-2}{2 \cdot 1} = -1 \qquad y = \frac{-2^2 + 4 \cdot 1(-3)}{4 \cdot 1} = -4$$

In the second example the maximum value of the function $y = -2x^2 + 4x - 2$ is attained at

$$x = \frac{-4}{2(-2)} = 1 \qquad y = \frac{-4^2 + 4(-2)(-2)}{4(-2)} = 0$$

EXAMPLE 34 Find the line of symmetry, the coordinates of the maximum or minimum value, several ordered pairs that satisfy the equation, and sketch the graph of

$$y = f(x) = x^2 - 4x + 3$$

Solution The line of symmetry is $x = -(-4)/2(1)$ or $x = 2$. Since $a > 0$, the minimum occurs at $(2, -1)$. (See Figure 8.9.)

Figure 8.9

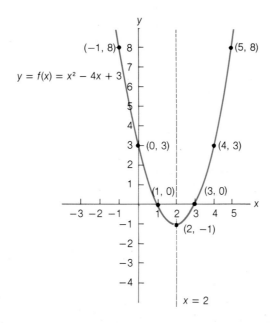

We assign to x the values $\{-1, 0, 1, 2, 3, 4, 5\}$ (note that some are larger than 2 and some are smaller than 2) to obtain the following set of ordered pairs:

$$\{(-1, 8), (0, 3), (1, 0), (2, -1), (3, 0), (4, 3), (5, 8)\}$$

The graph of the curve is shown in Figure 8.9.

It should be noted that the x-coordinates where the curve crosses the x-axis are the values where $f(x)$ is 0 and thus are the solutions of $f(x) = 0$. For example, in the preceding example, $x = 1$ and $x = 3$ are solutions of $x^2 - 4x + 3 = 0$.

Our first procedure for solving quadratic equations is by factoring. We need the following property of real numbers to find solutions by factoring: **If a and b are real numbers, then $ab = 0$ if and only if $a = 0$ or $b = 0$ or both.**

EXAMPLE 35 Find the solution set of $x^2 + x - 12 = 0$.

Solution The equation $x^2 + x - 12 = 0$ is equivalent to

$$(x + 4)(x - 3) = 0$$

Since $(x + 4)(x - 3) = 0$ is true if and only if $x + 4 = 0$ or $x - 3 = 0$, we can see by inspection that the only values of x that satisfy the original equation are -4 and 3. Hence, the solution set is $\{-4, 3\}$.

Ordinarily the solution set of a quadratic equation over real numbers contains two solutions. In order for this to be true for all quadratic equations, we must classify some quadratic equations as having **repeated solutions** or **solutions of multiplicity two** as seen in the following example.

EXAMPLE 36 Solve $3x^2 + 3 = 6x$.

Solution By applying the appropriate properties (including dividing both sides of the equation by 3), the equivalent equation in standard form is

$$x^2 - 2x + 1 = 0$$

This equation is equivalent to $(x - 1)^2 = 0$. Thus, $x = 1$ is said to be a solution of multiplicity two.

Sometimes it is not easy to factor quadratic equations. When we cannot factor a quadratic equation we sometimes use a procedure called completing the square introduced earlier in this section. Recall that

$$ax^2 + bx + c = 0 \qquad a \neq 0$$

can be written as

$$\left(x + \frac{b}{2a}\right)^2 - \frac{b^2 - 4ac}{4a^2} = 0$$

or as

$$x + \frac{b}{2a} = \pm\sqrt{\frac{b^2 - 4ac}{4a^2}}$$

$$x = \frac{-b \pm \sqrt{b^2 - 4ac}}{2a}$$

This result is called the **quadratic formula.**

The Quadratic Formula

$$ax^2 + bx + c = 0 \qquad a \neq 0$$

where a, b, and c are real numbers, has as solutions

$$x = \frac{-b + \sqrt{b^2 - 4ac}}{2a} \qquad \text{or} \qquad x = \frac{-b - \sqrt{b^2 - 4ac}}{2a}$$

EXAMPLE 37 Solve $2x^2 + 2x = 12$.

Solution In order to use the quadratic formula, we need to put the equation in the form $ax^2 + bx + c = 0$, or $2x^2 + 2x - 12 = 0$. Now $a = 2$, $b = 2$, and $c = -12$. The two solutions are

$$x = \frac{-2 + \sqrt{(2)^2 - 4(2)(-12)}}{2(2)} \quad \text{or} \quad x = \frac{-2 - \sqrt{(2)^2 - 4(2)(-12)}}{2(2)}$$

so

$$x = \frac{-2 + \sqrt{100}}{4} = 2 \quad \text{or} \quad x = \frac{-2 - \sqrt{100}}{4} = -3$$

EXAMPLE 38 Solve $x^2 - 6x + 25 = 0$.

Solution Now $a = 1$, $b = -6$, and $c = 25$, so

$$x = \frac{+6 \pm \sqrt{36 - 100}}{2} = \frac{6 \pm \sqrt{-64}}{2}$$

Since $\sqrt{-64}$ is not defined on the set of real numbers, this equation has no real solution. If you sketch the graph of $f(x) = x^2 - 6x + 25$, you will note that the curve does not cross the x-axis; hence, $f(x)$ cannot be 0.

The expression under the radical in the quadratic formula, $b^2 - 4ac$, is called the **discriminant** and may be used to determine whether a quadratic equation has real solutions, as seen in Table 8.1.

Table 8.1

$b^2 - 4ac$	$ax^2 + bx + c = 0 \quad a \neq 0$
Positive	Two real solutions
Zero	Two real equal solutions
Negative	No real solutions

First quadrant parts of parabolas are often used for supply and demand curves in economics. Often the demand for a product depends primarily on the price. As the price increases, the demand for the product decreases, as shown in Figure 8.10(a). As the price increases, the manufacturer produces more of the product, so the supply of the product increases, as shown in Figure 8.10(b).

Figure 8.10

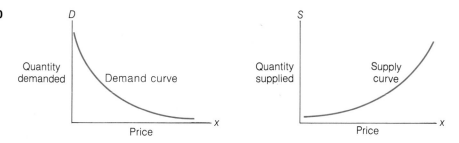

As you have learned previously, if the supply and demand graphs are placed on the same coordinate system, the point of intersection is called the point of **market equilibrium.** The **equilibrium price** of a product is the price found at the point where the supply and demand graphs intersect. Thus, the **equilibrium demand** and the **equilibrium supply** are equal and are obtained from where the graphs intersect.

EXAMPLE 39 If the supply function for a commodity is given by $S = 2x^2 + 30x$ and the demand function by $D = -15x + 5000$, find the point of market equilibrium and give the equilibrium price, the equilibrium supply, and the demand.

Solution See Figure 8.11.

Figure 8.11

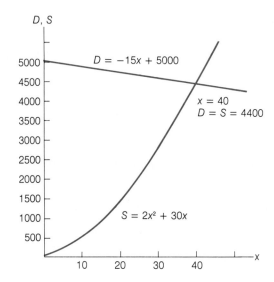

The market equilibrium is (40, 4400). The equilibrium price is $x = 40$, and the equilibrium supply and demand are equal to 4400.

Exercise Set **8.4**

A   **1.** For the graphs of the following functions, find the equations of the lines of symmetry.

    a. $f(x) = x^2 + x - 6$ **b.** $f(x) = 2x^2 - 9x - 5$
    c. $f(x) = -x^2 - 2x + 24$ **d.** $f(x) = -2x^2 + 7x - 3$
    e. $f(x) = 3x^2 + 9x - 12$ **f.** $f(x) = 2x^2 + 6x - 30$
    g. $f(x) = -6x^2 + 7x + 3$ **h.** $f(x) = 20x^2 + 11x - 3$
    i. $f(x) = -8x^2 + 5x + 3$ **j.** $f(x) = 6x^2 - 13x + 6$
    k. $f(x) = -x^2 - 3x + 5$ **l.** $f(x) = -2x^2 + 5x + 3$

2. Find the point at which a maximum or minimum value occurs for each function in exercise 1.

3. Without drawing the graphs, state whether the graphs of the functions in exercise 1 turn upward or downward.

4. Make a table of ordered pairs for each part of exercise 1.

5. Draw the graphs of each part of exercise 1, indicating with a dashed line the line of symmetry and plotting the extreme point (maximum or minimum).

Solve each equation below by factoring.

6. $x^2 - 5x = 0$ 7. $3x^2 - 7x = 0$

8. $3x^2 - 75 = 0$ 9. $4x^2 - 36 = 0$

10. $x^2 - 2x = 3$ 11. $x^2 - 2x = 15$

12. $2x^2 - 6x = 56$ 13. $x^2 + 2x = 24$

14. $x^2 + x = 2$ 15. $x^2 - 5x - 10 = 4$

16. $x^2 = 6 - x$ 17. $x^2 - 2x = -1 + 4$

Use the quadratic formula to solve each equation below.

18. $x^2 + 8x - 9 = 0$ 19. $x^2 - 4x = 4$

20. $x^2 + 11x = -30$ 21. $3x^2 = 5x + 2$

Use the discriminant to determine the nature of the solution of the following equations.

22. $3x^2 + 16x = 4x + 12$ 23. $x^2 = 2x - 2$

24. $3x^2 + 11x = 4$ 25. $x^2 + 10x = 4x - 13$

26. $-2x^2 + x = 5$ 27. $x^2 = 10x - 28$

B *Solve each equation below by factoring.*

28. $12x^2 - x - 1 = 0$ 29. $6x^2 - 5x + 1 = 0$

30. $2x^2 - 7x + 3 = 0$ 31. $3x^2 = 16x - 5$

32. $2(2x + 9) = -9$ 33. $x(2x - 1) = 1$

Solve each equation below by using the quadratic formula.

34. $3x^2 + 11x = 4$ 35. $5x^2 - 7x = 1$

36. $3x^2 + 8x + 1 = 9$ 37. $3x^2 = -x - 7$

C *For the following relations, answer the questions:*

a. Does the graph have a maximum or minimum value?
b. Does the graph have a line of symmetry?
c. Is the graph a function?

38. $x = y^2$ 39. $x = y^2 - 2y$ 40. $x = y^2 - 2y - 3$

Solve the following equations by using a calculator.

41. $3.1x^2 - 17.4x = 14.3$ 42. $1.01y = 1.74y^2 - 6.3$

43. Profit Functions. The following formula has been developed for predicting the outcome or profit of a pawnshop in terms of t, which represents the time before and after the first day of the month (payday).

$$P = -t^2 + t + 56$$

When does the pawnshop break even?

44. Profit Functions. Find the maximum profits for each function.
a. $P(x) = 10x - x^2$ **b.** $P(x) = 100x - 5x^2$ **c.** $P(x) = 70x - 8x^2$

45. Cost Functions. The daily cost $C(x)$ of producing x items per day at Trimbell Manufacturing Company is approximated by the quadratic expression $C(x) = 2x^2 - 12x + 35$. Graph the cost function, find x for the minimum cost, and find the minimum cost.

46. Equilibrium Point. Sketch the graph of the demand function $D(x) = (x - 6)^2$ and the supply function $S(x) = x^2 + x + 10$ on the same coordinate system and locate the equilibrium point. What is the demand at this point?

47. $D(x) = x^2 + 4$ and $S(x) = x^2 + 2x + 1$, where x represents 1000 items. Follow the instructions of exercise 46.

48. Now do exercise 47 with $D(x) = (x - 4)^2$ and $S(x) = x^2$.

49. Cost and Revenue Functions. The total cost of producing x items is $C(x) = 2026 + 20x + x^2$ and the total revenue is given by $R(x) = 100x - 1$. Sketch the two graphs on the same coordinate system and locate the break-even point.

50. Profit Functions. Use $P(x) = R(x) - C(x)$ to find $P(x)$ for exercise 49. Then draw the graph of $P(x)$, and find x for the maximum profit.

51. Laffer Curve. At the endpoints of the Laffer curve shown there is no revenue (R) for given tax rates (r). Suppose a Laffer curve is approximated by

$$R = \frac{r(50r - 5000)}{r - 110} \qquad \text{for } 0 \leq r < 110$$

What tax rates would provide no revenue?

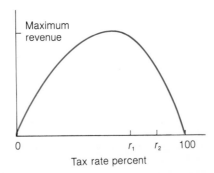

52. Blood Velocity.

$$V_r = V_m\left(1 - \frac{r^2}{R^2}\right)$$

where V_r is velocity of a blood corpuscle r units from the center of the artery, R is the constant radius of the artery, and V_m is the constant maximum velocity of the corpuscle. If $V_r = 2V_m$, solve for r in terms of R.

53. **Pollution.** An environmental study is used to approximate the annual growth of carbon monoxide in the air (parts per million) as a quadratic function. The approximating function is $M(t) = 0.01t^2 + 0.05t + 1.6$, where M is parts per million and t is measured in minutes starting at 7:00 A.M. ($0 \le t \le 180$). Show this relationship with a graph.

Social Sciences   54. **Population Growth.** A small city is expecting a decline in growth for a few years and then a rapid growth. This trend has been approximated by $P(t) = 2t^2 - 100t + 10,000$, ($t \ge 0$), where $P(t)$ is the population and t is time in years from now. Show this growth trend with a graph.

 Introduction to Graphs of Polynomial and Rational Functions

In this section we learn to graph certain special, but important, polynomials. In addition we will briefly introduce a rational function of the form

$$y = \frac{f(x)}{g(x)}$$

where $f(x)$ and $g(x)$ are polynomials and $g(x) \ne 0$.

These functions have many uses in application problems. They are also very useful in the study of calculus. The asterisk indicates that you may wish to postpone the study of this section until it is needed in the study of calculus.

In the preceding section, we discussed quadratic functions of the form $f(x) = ax^2 + bx + c$, which are polynomials of degree 2. We now look at polynomial functions of degree 3 or more. The simplest of these polynomial functions is $y = x^3$, which we graph in Example 40.

EXAMPLE 40   Make a table of values and graph $y = x^3$.

Solution   When $x = 0$, $y = 0$; when $x = 1$, $y = 1$; when $x = 2$, $y = 8$. In general, as x gets larger it is obvious that y gets larger as well. For $x = -1$, $y = -1$; for $x = -2$, $y = -8$; and as x decreases in size, y also decreases. These ordered pairs are listed in the following table.

x	-2	-1	0	1	2
y	-8	-1	0	1	8

When we plot these points and connect them with a smooth curve, we get the graph in Figure 8.12.

Figure 8.12

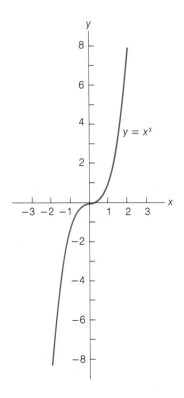

Note in Figure 8.13 that $y = x^4$ is very similar to $y = x^2$ except that the graph is much flatter at $x = 0$, and $y = x^5$ in Figure 8.15 is similar to $y = x^3$ (Figure 8.14) except that it is much flatter at $x = 0$.

It is fun to graph a polynomial where the zeros [values that make $f(x) = 0$] are easy to find.

Figure 8.13

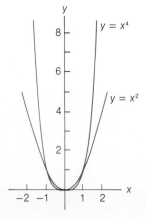

Figure 8.14

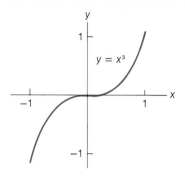

Figure 8.15

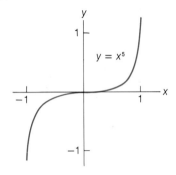

EXAMPLE 41 Graph $y = x^3 - x^2 - 4x + 4$.

Solution
$$y = x^3 - x^2 - 4x + 4$$
$$= x^2(x - 1) - 4(x - 1)$$
$$= (x - 1)(x^2 - 4)$$
$$= (x - 1)(x - 2)(x + 2)$$

Note that y becomes 0 as $x = 1$, 2, or -2. Therefore, the polynomial crosses the x-axis at $x = 1$, $x = 2$, and $x = -2$. Let's discuss the sign of y when x varies between these zeros. When $x < -2$, $x - 1$ is negative, $x - 2$ is negative, and $x + 2$ is negative. Thus, the sign of y is negative. See if you can verify the rest of the following table.

Table 8.2

Value of x	Sign of y
$x < -2$	Negative
$-2 < x < 1$	Positive
$1 < x < 2$	Negative
$x > 2$	Positive

You may wish to get exact points to obtain greater accuracy; however, the graph in Figure 8.16 utilizes the information we have already obtained.

Figure 8.16

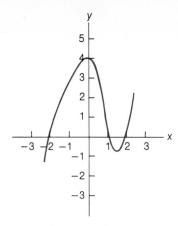

In the study of calculus we learn a procedure to determine the maximum and minimum points. This knowledge facilitates the graphing of simple polynomials such as cubics. For example, the graphs of cubics could take any of the forms shown in Figure 8.17. Without calculus, we need to find a large number of points and draw a smooth curve.

Figure 8.17

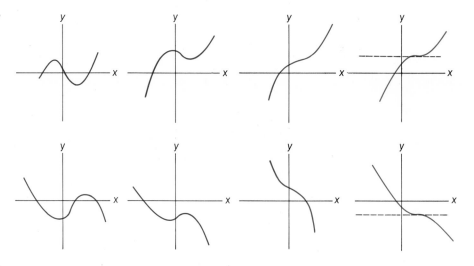

Let's now graph functions of the form

$$y = \frac{f(x)}{g(x)}$$

where $f(x)$ and $g(x)$ are polynomials and $g(x) \neq 0$. Such functions are called **rational functions.** If there are values of x that will make $g(x) = 0$, these values are excluded from the domain of the function since division by 0 is impossible.

EXAMPLE 42   Find a table of values and sketch the graph of

$$y = \frac{3}{x - 1}$$

Solution   Since $x = 1$ is excluded in the domain of the function, we examine a number of values close to 1 to see what happens.

x	-6	-2	-1	0	$\frac{1}{2}$	$\frac{3}{4}$	$\frac{7}{8}$	$\frac{9}{10}$	$\frac{99}{100}$
y	$-\frac{3}{7}$	-1	$-\frac{3}{2}$	-3	-6	-12	-24	-30	-300

x	8	4	3	2	$\frac{3}{2}$	$\frac{5}{4}$	$\frac{9}{8}$	$\frac{11}{10}$	$\frac{101}{100}$
y	$\frac{3}{7}$	1	$\frac{3}{2}$	3	6	12	24	30	300

This table suggests that as x gets closer and closer to 1 from the left, $y = 3/(x - 1)$ gets smaller and smaller. Likewise, as x gets closer and closer to 1 from the right, y gets larger and larger. The line $x = 1$ that the graph approaches is called a **vertical asymptote** and is drawn along with the graph in Figure 8.18.

Figure 8.18

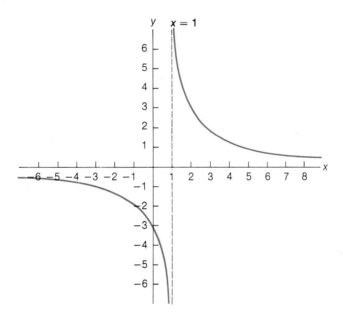

In general, an asymptote can be found by the following procedure:

Asymptotes

> 1. A **vertical asymptote** can be found by locating a value of x, say, c, which will make the denominator of a rational function equal to zero (provided the numerator is not zero also). Then $x = c$ is a vertical asymptote.
> 2. A **horizontal asymptote** can be found by assigning to x very large values and discovering if y seems to approach some number.

EXAMPLE 43   In the previous example,

$$y = \frac{3}{x - 1}$$

Now assign to x some very large values and some numerically large values in a negative direction and see if you can discover a horizontal asymptote.

Solution

x	10	100	1000	10,000	-8	-98	-998	-9998
y	$\frac{1}{3}$	$\frac{1}{33}$	$\frac{1}{333}$	$\frac{1}{3333}$	$-\frac{1}{3}$	$-\frac{1}{33}$	$-\frac{1}{333}$	$-\frac{1}{3333}$

It is evident that as x gets larger, y approaches 0; it is also evident that as x gets larger numerically in a negative direction, y again approaches 0. Thus, $y = 0$ is a horizontal asymptote, as seen in Figure 8.18.

The following theorem is also helpful in locating horizontal asymptotes.

Horizontal Asymptote

Except for very special cases, the graph of the rational function

$$y = \frac{a_0 x^n + a_1 x^{n-1} + \cdots + a_n}{b_0 x^m + b_1 x^{m-1} + \cdots + b_m}$$

where $a_0 \neq 0$, $b_0 \neq 0$, and m and n are nonnegative integers, has

1. a horizontal asymptote at $y = 0$ if $n < m$,
2. a horizontal asymptote at $y = a_0/b_0$ if $n = m$, and
3. no horizontal asymptote if $n > m$.

EXAMPLE 44   Find the horizontal asymptotes of

a. $y = \dfrac{2x - 1}{x - 2}$ **b.** $y = \dfrac{x + 1}{x^2 + 3}$

Solution **a.** $y = \dfrac{2x - 1}{x - 2}$ has a horizontal asymptote at $y = \frac{2}{1} = 2$.

b. $y = \dfrac{x + 1}{x^2 + 3}$ has a horizontal asymptote at $y = 0$.

Exercise Set 8.5

A **1.** Graph the following polynomials.
   a. $y = 3x^3$ **b.** $y = 3(x - 1)^3$ **c.** $y = 3(x + 2)^3$
   d. $y = 2x^4$ **e.** $y = 2(x + 1)^4$ **f.** $y = 2(x - 1)^4$

2. Locate the horizontal and vertical asymptotes for the graphs of the following functions.

a. $y = \dfrac{1}{x}$ **b.** $y = \dfrac{6}{x - 2}$ **c.** $y = \dfrac{3}{x + 4}$

d. $y = \dfrac{1}{2x - 6}$ **e.** $y = \dfrac{2x + 4}{x - 3}$ **f.** $y = \dfrac{4}{(x + 2)(x + 3)}$

g. $y = \dfrac{x^2}{x^2 - 4}$ **h.** $y = \dfrac{x^2}{x^2 - 3x + 2}$ **i.** $y = \dfrac{x^2 - 3x + 2}{x^2 - 3x - 4}$

B

3. Sketch the graphs of **a** through **e** of exercise 2.

4. Find the zeros, discuss the sign of y between the zeros, and graph the following polynomial functions.

a. $y = x(x - 1)(x + 2)$ **b.** $y = x(x + 2)(x - 2)$
c. $y = x^2(x - 4)$ **d.** $y = x(x + 1)^2$
e. $y = x(x + 1)(x^2 - 4)$ **f.** $y = x^2(x^2 - 9)$

5. Graph the functions in **f** through **i** of exercise 2.

6. Graph $xy = 9$.

C

7. Find the zeros, discuss the sign of y between the zeros, and graph each of the following.

a. $y = 3x^4 + x^3 - 2x^2$ **b.** $y = x^4 + x^3 - 2x^2$
c. $y = x^3 - 3x^2 - x + 3$ **d.** $y = x^4 - 13x^2 + 36$

Business

8. Stock Market. There is some evidence that the stock market varies inversely with the prime interest rate. One formula is

$$D = \frac{132}{i + 0.02}$$

Draw this graph as i varies from a prime of 0.08 to a prime of 0.20.

Economics

9. Profit Functions. A profit function for each 1000 cases of a product is given by

$$P(x) = 0.1x^3 - x^2 - 28x - 300$$

Sketch this graph. Are there values of x for which there is no profit but a loss?

10. Revenue Functions. A total revenue function is given by

$$R(x) = 5440x - 8x^2 - x^3$$

Locate approximately the value of x where $R(x)$ is a maximum.

11. Cost-Benefit Model. Sometimes cost becomes excessive in relation to a given benefit. For example, to remove all waste material in a sewage treatment plant would be impossible and the cost would be prohibitive as indicated by the formula

$$C(p) = \frac{7.1p}{1.00 - p}$$

where p is given in percent removed, and $C(p)$ is the cost per 100 liters. Show this result on a graph.

Life Sciences

12. Drug Concentration. The concentration $C(t)$ in milligrams per cubic centimeter of a drug in the bloodstream, where t is the number of hours since the drug was administered, is given by

$$C(t) = \frac{0.24t}{(t + 2.1)^2}$$

Sketch this curve from $t = 0$ to $t = 10$ hours.

13. Drug Response. The response of a drug seems to vary with the concentration c as

$$R = \frac{c}{a + bc}$$

Show this function with a graph when $a = 1.6$ and $b = 0.04$.

Social Sciences **14. Learning Curve.** The function

$$N(t) = 30t - 1.5t^2$$

approximates the number of concepts grasped in reading tedious material in t hours. In the graph of this function, is there a time at which someone forgets everything?

15. Population. The population (expressed in thousands) of a certain city is estimated to become $1000 + 30t + t^2$ at t years from now. In how many years will the population exceed 2,000,000?

Summary and Review

Review the following concepts to ensure that you understand and can use them: exponents and radicals, functions (domain, range, independent variable, dependent variable), function of a function, factoring, quadratic functions (graphs, line of symmetry, maximum or minimum value), polynomial functions, and rational functions (asymptotes).

Be sure you can use the following formulas.

$$x^m \cdot x^n = x^{m+n}$$

$$\frac{x^m}{x^n} = x^{m-n} = \frac{1}{x^{n-m}}$$

$$(x^m)^n = x^{mn}$$

$$(xy)^m = x^m \cdot y^m$$

$$x^{-m} = \frac{1}{x^m}$$

$$x^0 = 1$$

$$\sqrt[n]{x} = x^{1/n}$$

$$\sqrt[n]{x^n} = \begin{cases} x & \text{for } n \text{ odd} \\ |x| & \text{for } n \text{ even} \end{cases}$$

$$x^{m/n} = \sqrt[n]{x^m}$$

$$\sqrt[n]{x} \cdot \sqrt[n]{y} = \sqrt[n]{xy}$$

$$\frac{\sqrt[n]{x}}{\sqrt[n]{y}} = \sqrt[n]{\frac{x}{y}}$$

$$x = -\frac{b}{2a} \quad \begin{array}{l}\text{as a line of symmetry for} \\ y = ax^2 + bx + c\end{array}$$

$$x = \frac{-b \pm \sqrt{b^2 - 4ac}}{2a} \quad \begin{array}{l}\text{as solutions of} \\ ax^2 + bx + c = 0\end{array}$$

Review Exercise Set **8.6**

A
1. Let $B = \{10, 11, 12\}$. Which of the following sets of ordered pairs are functions of B?
a. $\{(10, 11), (11, 11), (12, 11)\}$　　**b.** $\{(10, 10), (11, 11), (12, 12)\}$
c. $\{(10, 11), (11, 12), (10, 12)\}$

2. If the domain for the function $f(x) = 2x^2 - x + 4$ is the set of real numbers, find the following.
a. $f(-1)$　　**b.** $f(2)$　　**c.** $f(0)$　　**d.** $f(\tfrac{1}{2})$　　**e.** $f(0.1)$　　**f.** $f(100)$

3. Simplify the following expressions.

a. $\dfrac{30x^2y^3z^4}{5xyz^3}$

b. $(x^2 - 5x + 1) - (2 - 3x - x^2)$

c. $3\{x^2 + 1 - 2[x^2 - 3(x^2 - 1)] + 1\}$

d. $(x + 2)(3x^2 + 2x + 1)$

e. $\dfrac{(x^2y)^{-2}}{x^0y^{-3}}$

f. $\dfrac{(x^{-1}y^0)^{-2}}{x^{-2}}$

4. Factor the following expressions.

a. $3x^2y^2 - 48z^4$

b. $3x^3y^2 - 12xy^3 + 6x^2y^4$

c. $2x^2y - 2xy^2 - 12y^3$

d. $xy^2 + 2yw + 2y^3 + xw$

5. Rationalize the denominator of $\dfrac{x^2}{\sqrt{2x}}$.

6. Simplify $\sqrt[3]{24x^5y^5}$.

7. Solve the following equations by factoring.

a. $x^2 - 3x = 4$ **b.** $2x^2 - 5x + 3 = 6$

8. Solve the following quadratic equations.

a. $3x^2 + x = 2$ **b.** $4x^2 - 5x = 7$

B

9. Find the equations of the lines of symmetry for the following quadratic functions.

a. $y = x^2 - x - 6$

b. $y = x^2 + 5x + 6$

c. $y = x^2 - 5x - 6$

d. $y = x^2 - 7x + 12$

e. $y = -x^2 + 4x + 12$

f. $y = x^2 + x - 12$

g. $y = 2x^2 - 5x - 2$

h. $y = -3x^2 + 10x - 3$

10. Find the point at which a maximum or minimum value occurs for each function in exercise 9.

11. Without drawing the graphs, state whether the graphs of the functions in exercise 9 turn upward or downward.

12. Make a table of ordered pairs for each function given in exercise 9.

13. Draw the graphs of the functions given in exercise 9, and indicate each line of symmetry, maximum or minimum values, and points at which the graphs cross the x-axis.

14. Graph the following functions.

a. $S = P(1 + rt)$,   for $t = 3$ and $P = 1000$

b. $t = I/Pr$,   for $P = \$1,000$ and $r = 0.06$

15. Does $y = \sqrt{x + 3}$ denote a function with x as the independent variable? Explain.

16. Suppose a bicyclist, in going up a hill, gains 4 feet vertically for each 100 feet of horizontal travel. Find the slope of the hill she is climbing.

17. Ralph Miller, the sales manager of a small corporation, is paid a salary of $900 per month plus a commission of 3% of the gross sales for the month. Determine the function that expresses Ralph's monthly earnings as a function of the gross sales.

C

18. Find all asymptotes, horizontal and vertical, and graph

$$y = \dfrac{x - 2}{(x + 3)(x - 3)}$$

19. Graph $y = 5(x - 2)^3$.

20. Factor the following algebraic expressions.

a. $40x^3 + 52x^2y - 12xy^2$ **b.** $6r^3 + 2sr^2 + 6rs^2 + 2s^3$

21. Find the zeros, discuss the sign between the zeros, and graph $y = x(x - 3)(x + 2)$.

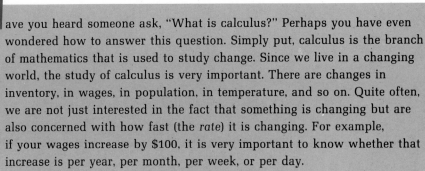

CHAPTER 9

Differential Calculus

Have you heard someone ask, "What is calculus?" Perhaps you have even wondered how to answer this question. Simply put, calculus is the branch of mathematics that is used to study change. Since we live in a changing world, the study of calculus is very important. There are changes in inventory, in wages, in population, in temperature, and so on. Quite often, we are not just interested in the fact that something is changing but are also concerned with how fast (the *rate*) it is changing. For example, if your wages increase by $100, it is very important to know whether that increase is per year, per month, per week, or per day.

We begin our study of differential calculus by explaining how the derivative is related to the slope of a curve. We then discuss **limits,** which are basic for calculus. This study is followed by a discussion of **continuous functions.** Next, we state the definition of a derivative and give several interpretations of the derivative. Formulas are then obtained to make our calculations easier.

1 Introduction to Differential Calculus

As just stated, calculus is the mathematics used to study change. Since change has not been studied in detail in our previous discussions, an entirely new mathematical concept is required. We need the concept of the **derivative of a function.** Instead of beginning by developing the theory of derivatives, we illustrate how the derivative is related to the slope of a curve. This informal explanation should motivate a more thorough study of the subject in later sections.

One interpretation of the derivative of a function at a point is that the value of the derivative at a point is the slope of the graph at the point. Later we give the formal definition of the derivative and additional interpretations. Since we are already familiar with slopes, we begin our study of derivatives by considering slopes of simple functions. The simplest function we have studied has a graph that is a straight line, and the simplest straight line is a horizontal line, as illustrated in Figure 9.1.

Figure 9.1

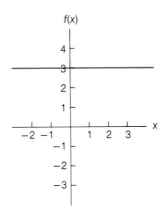

The function illustrated in Figure 9.1 is the constant function

$$f(x) = 3$$

Note that this function does not change, that is, it neither increases nor decreases. The slope of this function is 0, and we state that the derivative, denoted by $f'(x)$, of this function is 0. We write

$$f'(x) = 0$$

If a function is $f(x) = C$ for any constant C, the graph is a horizontal line $|C|$ units above or below the x-axis. Since such a function neither increases nor decreases, the slope is 0, and the derivative, $f'(x)$, is 0. We write $f'(x) = 0$.

The graph of $f(x) = 2x + 3$ is given in Figure 9.2. Note that as x gets larger, this function gets larger, or increases. The slope of this function is 2, and we define the derivative of this function to be 2; that is,

$$f'(x) = 2$$

The graph of $f(x) = -2x + 3$ is given in Figure 9.3. Note that as x increases, this function gets smaller, or decreases. The slope of this function is -2, and again the derivative of this function is defined to be -2; that is,

$$f'(x) = -2$$

Figure 9.2

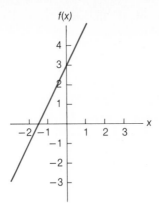

Figure 9.3

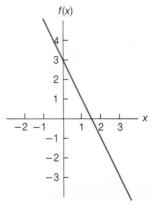

In general, the graph of the function $y = f(x) = mx + b$ is a straight line with y-intercept b, slope m, and derivative $f'(x) = m$. The function is increasing when the derivative is positive and decreasing when the derivative is negative. Note that the slope of a straight line is the same at all points on the line. For a function whose graph is not a straight line, the slope is not the same at all points. Let us now consider the meaning of the slope of a curve at a point on the graph of a function whose graph is not a straight line.

In geometry a tangent line at a point A on a circle is the limit of the secants AQ_1, AQ_2, AQ_3, and so forth, as the distance between A and Q_i approaches zero. (See Figure 9.4.)

Figure 9.4

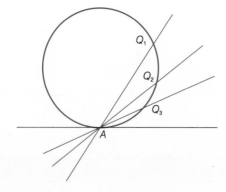

The tangent line at a point on the graph of any function is defined similarly. **The slope of the tangent line at any point A on the graph of a function is called the slope of the function at A or the slope of the curve at A. In accordance with our interpretation of the derivative, the derivative at a given point of a function is defined at this time to be the slope of the tangent line to the graph of the function at the given point.**

EXAMPLE 1 Graph the function $y = x^2 - 1$ and draw the tangent line to this curve at $(0, -1)$.
  a. Find the slope of the line from $(0, -1)$ to $(2, 3)$.
  b. Find the slope of the line from $(0, -1)$ to $(1, 0)$.
  c. Find the slope from $(0, -1)$ to $(\frac{1}{2}, -\frac{3}{4})$.
  d. As the point on the graph gets closer and closer to $(0, -1)$, what can you say about the slope of the secant?
  e. What is the value of the derivative at $(0, -1)$?
  The answers to these questions illustrate the previous theory.

Solution **a.** The slope of the line from $(0, -1)$ to $(2, 3)$ is

$$m = \frac{y_2 - y_1}{x_2 - x_1} = \frac{3 - (-1)}{2 - 0} = \frac{4}{2} = 2$$

b. The slope of the line from $(0, -1)$ to $(1, 0)$ is

$$m = \frac{y_2 - y_1}{x_2 - x_1} = \frac{0 - (-1)}{1 - (0)} = \frac{1}{1} = 1$$

c. The slope of the line from $(0, -1)$ to $(\frac{1}{2}, -\frac{3}{4})$ is

$$m = \frac{y_2 - y_1}{x_2 - x_1} = \frac{-(\frac{3}{4}) - (-1)}{\frac{1}{2} - 0} = \frac{-\frac{3}{4} + 1}{\frac{1}{2}} = \frac{\frac{1}{4}}{\frac{1}{2}} = \frac{1}{2}$$

d. The slope of the secant gets closer to the slope of the tangent.
e. The value of the derivative at $(0, -1)$ is the slope of the tangent line drawn to the curve at that point. Since the tangent line at $(0, -1)$ is parallel to the x-axis, the slope is 0, and, hence, the value of the derivative at $(0, -1)$ is 0. (See Figure 9.5.)

Figure 9.5

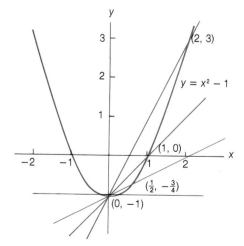

EXAMPLE 2 Find the slope of the line from the point $(2, 3)$ on the curve $y = x^2 - 1$ to the following points on the curve: $(\frac{5}{2}, \frac{21}{4})$, $(\frac{9}{4}, \frac{65}{16})$, $(\frac{11}{5}, \frac{96}{25})$, and $(\frac{13}{6}, \frac{133}{36})$. Use these values of the slopes of lines to nearby points to guess the slope of the tangent to the curve at $(2, 3)$.

Solution The slope of the line from $(2, 3)$ to $(\frac{5}{2}, \frac{21}{4})$ is

$$m_1 = \frac{y_2 - y_1}{x_2 - x_1} = \frac{\frac{21}{4} - 3}{\frac{5}{2} - 2} = \frac{\frac{9}{4}}{\frac{1}{2}} = \frac{9}{2} = 4\frac{1}{2}$$

The slope of the line from $(2, 3)$ to $(\frac{9}{4}, \frac{65}{16})$ is

$$m_2 = \frac{y_2 - y_1}{x_2 - x_1} = \frac{\frac{65}{16} - 3}{\frac{9}{4} - 2} = \frac{\frac{17}{16}}{\frac{1}{4}} = \frac{17}{4} = 4\frac{1}{4}$$

The slope of the line from $(2, 3)$ to $(\frac{11}{5}, \frac{96}{25})$ is

$$m_3 = \frac{y_2 - y_1}{x_2 - x_1} = \frac{\frac{96}{25} - 3}{\frac{11}{5} - 2} = \frac{\frac{21}{25}}{\frac{1}{5}} = \frac{21}{5} = 4\frac{1}{5}$$

The slope of the line from $(2, 3)$ to $(\frac{13}{6}, \frac{133}{36})$ is

$$m_4 = \frac{y_2 - y_1}{x_2 - x_1} = \frac{\frac{133}{36} - 3}{\frac{13}{6} - 2} = \frac{\frac{25}{36}}{\frac{1}{6}} = \frac{25}{6} = 4\frac{1}{6}$$

From these slopes, it appears that the slope of the tangent at $(2, 3)$ might be 4. We shall see later that this is indeed the case.

Since the slope of the line from the point (x_1, y_1) to (x_2, y_2) is given by the formula

$$m = \frac{y_2 - y_1}{x_2 - x_1}$$

the slope gives the average change of a function over the interval from x_1 to x_2. As (x_2, y_2) approaches (x_1, y_1), the slope of the secant approaches the slope of the tangent at (x_1, y_1) and the average rate of change approaches the instantaneous rate of change. Hence, another interpretation of the derivative at a point is that the derivative at a point is the **instantaneous rate of change** of a function at the point. To illustrate the instantaneous rate of change, we need to introduce one procedure for finding the derivative at a point. The derivative of many functions can be found by using what is called the **power rule.**

Power Rule

If

$$f(x) = Cx^n \qquad \text{where } C \text{ and } n \neq 0 \text{ are real numbers}$$

then

$$f'(x) = Cnx^{n-1}$$

Let's see if this new procedure is in agreement with our previous discussion that the derivative of a function at a point is the slope of the function at the point.

EXAMPLE 3   We learned previously that the derivative of $f(x) = 3x$ is $f'(x) = 3$ since 3 is the slope of the straight line. Using the power rule with $C = 3$ and $n = 1$,

$$f'(x) = (3)(1)x^{1-1} = 3$$

EXAMPLE 4   If $f(x) = 3x^2$, show that $f'(x) = 6x$.

Solution   Use the power rule with $C = 3$ and $n = 2$. Then

$$f'(x) = (3)(2)x^{2-1}$$
$$= 6x$$

EXAMPLE 5   Find the instantaneous rate of change of $f(x) = 4x^3$ at $(1, 4)$, and interpret this result.

Solution   Use the power rule with $C = 4$ and $n = 3$.

$$f'(x) = (4)(3)x^{3-1} = 12x^2$$

At $x = 1$,

$$f'(1) = 12(1)^2 = 12$$

So the instantaneous rate of change of the functions at $x = 1$ is 12. This result means that at $x = 1$ the function is increasing 12 units for each unit increase in x.

There are many functions that are sums or differences of terms of the form Cx^n. For such functions the power rule is applied to each term. Remember that the derivative of a constant term is 0.

EXAMPLE 6   If $f(x) = 4x^3 - 3x^2 + 2x - 3$, show that

$$f'(x) = 12x^2 - 6x + 2$$

Solution   For the first term, use the power rule with $C = 4$ and $n = 3$. For the second term, use the power rule with $C = -3$ and $n = 2$. For the third term, use the power rule with $C = 2$ and $n = 1$. For the fourth term, remember that the derivative of a constant is 0. When the derivatives of all the terms are combined, we obtain

$$f'(x) = (4)(3)x^{3-1} + (-3)(2)x^{2-1} + (2)(1)x^{1-1} + 0$$
$$= 12x^2 - 6x + 2$$

EXAMPLE 7   Show that the slope of the tangent line to $f(x) = x^2 - 1$ at $(2, 3)$ is 4, as guessed in Example 2.

Solution   The slope of the tangent line to a curve at a point on the curve is the value of the derivative at the point. Using the power rule gives

$$f'(x) = 2x$$

At the point (2, 3), the value of the derivative is

$$f'(2) = 2(2) = 4$$

EXAMPLE 8 Find the average rate of change of the function $f(x) = 4 - x^2$ from
- **a.** $x = 1$ to $x = 2$.
- **b.** $x = 1$ to $x = 1.5$.
- **c.** $x = 1$ to $x = 1.1$.
- **d.** $x = 1$ to $x = 1.01$.

Solution **a.** The average rate of change from $x = 1$ to $x = 2$ is the slope of the line from (1, 3) to (2, 0):

$$m = \frac{f(2) - f(1)}{2 - 1} = \frac{0 - 3}{1} = -3$$

b. $m = \dfrac{f(1.5) - f(1)}{1.5 - 1} = \dfrac{1.75 - 3}{0.5} = -2.5$

c. $m = \dfrac{f(1.1) - f(1)}{1.1 - 1} = \dfrac{2.79 - 3}{0.1} = -2.1$

d. $m = \dfrac{f(1.01) - f(1)}{1.01 - 1} = -2.01$

EXAMPLE 9 Find the instantaneous rate of change of the function $f(x) = 4 - x^2$ at $x = 1$.

Solution
$$f'(x) = -2x$$
$$f'(1) = -2(1) = -2$$

Note again, as the second point gets closer and closer to the first point (1, 3) that the average rate of change $(-3, -2.5, -2.1, -2.01, \ldots)$ gets closer and closer to the instantaneous rate at (1, 3), namely, -2.

EXAMPLE 10 Find the instantaneous rate of change of $f(x) = 4 - x^2$ at $x = 2$.

Solution
$$f'(x) = -2x$$
$$f'(2) = -2(2) = -4$$

Exercise Set **9.1**

A **1.** Find $f'(x)$ for the following functions.
- **a.** $f(x) = 4$
- **b.** $f(x) = 6$
- **c.** $f(x) = -3$
- **d.** $f(x) = -5$
- **e.** $f(x) = \sqrt{2}$
- **f.** $f(x) = \sqrt{3}$

2. Find $f'(x)$ for the following functions.
- **a.** $f(x) = 4x$
- **b.** $f(x) = 6x$
- **c.** $f(x) = -3x$
- **d.** $f(x) = -5x$
- **e.** $f(x) = \frac{2}{3}x$
- **f.** $f(x) = -\frac{3}{4}x$

3. Find $f'(x)$ for the following functions.
   a. $f(x) = 4x^2$ b. $f(x) = 6x^2$ c. $f(x) = -3x^2$
   d. $f(x) = -5x^2$ e. $f(x) = \frac{2}{3}x^2$ f. $f(x) = -\frac{3}{4}x^2$

4. Find $f'(x)$ for the following functions.
   a. $f(x) = 4x^3$ b. $f(x) = 6x^3$ c. $f(x) = -3x^3$
   d. $f(x) = -5x^3$ e. $f(x) = \frac{2}{3}x^3$ f. $f(x) = -\frac{3}{4}x^3$

B

5. Find $f'(x)$ for the following functions.
   a. $f(x) = 5x + 3$ b. $f(x) = -2x + 4$
   c. $f(x) = 3x^2 - 5x + 2$ d. $f(x) = 4x^2 + 3x - 2$
   e. $f(x) = 6x^2 + 4x - 3$ f. $f(x) = -3x^2 + 4x - 3$
   g. $f(x) = \frac{1}{2}x^2 - 2x + 1$ h. $f(x) = \frac{1}{3}x^3 + 5x^2$
   i. $f(x) = \frac{2}{3}x^3 + \frac{1}{2}x^2 - 5x$ j. $f(x) = 2x^3 - 3x^2 + 7$

C

6. Find the average rate of change of $f(x) = 3x^2 + 2$ from
   a. $x = 1$ to $x = 2$ b. $x = 1$ to $x = 1.5$
   c. $x = 1$ to $x = 1.1$ d. $x = 1$ to $x = 1.01$

7. Find the instantaneous rate of change of $f(x) = 3x^2 + 2$ at $x = 1$.

8. Find the average rate of change of the function $f(x) = -2x^2 + 3$ from
   a. $x = 2$ to $x = 3$ b. $x = 2$ to $x = 2.5$
   c. $x = 2$ to $x = 2.1$ d. $x = 2$ to $x = 2.01$

9. Find the instantaneous rate of change of the function $f(x) = -2x^2 = 3$ at $x = 2$.

Business

10. **Profit Functions.** A company lists its profit function as
$$P(x) = 8x - 0.02x^2 - 500$$
   a. Find the average rate of change in profit from $x = 100$ to $x = 200$.
   b. Find the instantaneous rate of change in profit at $x = 100$.
   c. Find the instantaneous rate of change in profit at $x = 200$.
   d. Find the profit at $x = 200$.

Economics

11. **Cost Functions.** A cost function is given as
$$C(x) = 40{,}000 - 300x + x^2$$
Graph the function and find the instantaneous rate of change of cost when $x = 100$, when $x = 150$, and when $x = 200$.

Life Sciences

12. **Bacteria.** The number of bacteria, N in thousands, present x hours after being treated by a poison is
$$N(x) = x^2 - 6x + 10 \qquad 0 \leq x \leq 6$$
Find the average rate of change of the number present from $x = 1$ to $x = 3$. Find the instantaneous rate of change at $x = 1$.

Physical Sciences

13. **Velocity Functions.** A rock is dropped from the top of a 256-foot building. The distance D that the rock has fallen after t seconds is given by $D = 16t^2$.
   a. Find the time it will take the rock to strike the ground.
   b. What is the average rate of change of distance (velocity) during the time the rock is falling?
   c. What is the instantaneous rate of change of distance (velocity) of the rock at the time it strikes the ground?
   d. At what time is the rock falling at its average velocity?

14. Weight Functions. The approximate weight W of a person in pounds is related to height in feet by

$$W = \tfrac{108}{125}h^3$$

a. Find the average rate of change of weight when height changes from 5 to 6 feet.
b. Find the instantaneous rate of change of weight for a height of 5 feet.

Social Sciences

15. Language Functions. Suppose that the number N of foreign language phrases learned in t hours is given by

$$N = 12t - t^2 \qquad 0 \le t \le 6$$

a. Find the average rate of learning from $t = 2$ to $t = 5$.
b. Find the instantaneous rate of learning at $t = 2$.

16. Learning Functions. Suppose a person learns y items in t hours according to the function

$$y = 40t^{1/2} \qquad 0 \le t \le 10$$

a. Find the average rate of learning from $t = 4$ to $t = 9$.
b. Find the instantaneous rate of learning at $t = 4$.

2 The Concept of a Limit

The concept of a **limit of a function** is basic to the study of calculus. This concept helps us describe the behavior of a function $f(x)$ when x is close to a particular value a. In this section we slowly and carefully develop the concept of a limit in order to provide the necessary solid foundation for the understanding of calculus.

Some people feel that calculus is difficult to understand. The reason is that the mathematical development of calculus uses extensively the notion of limits. Thus, to understand the development of calculus, it is important to thoroughly understand this section.

If the values of x in the domain of a function $y = f(x)$ get closer and closer to some number a, what happens to the values of $f(x)$? A first guess would be that the values of $f(x)$ get closer to $f(a)$, but $f(a)$ may not even exist. Consider the function

$$y = f(x) = \frac{x^2 - 4}{x - 2}$$

Table 9.1

x	0	1	1.9	1.99	1.999	2.001	2.01	2.1	3
$y = f(x) = \dfrac{x^2 - 4}{x - 2}$	2	3	3.9	3.99	3.999	4.001	4.01	4.1	5

How does y behave as x gets closer and closer to 2? Values for this function are given in Table 9.1. The graph is given in Figure 9.6.

Figure 9.6

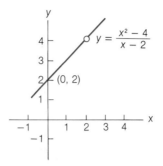

Note that this function is not defined when $x = 2$. Both the table and the graph indicate that as x approaches 2, the function $f(x)$ approaches 4. We write this in symbols as:

$$\lim_{x \to 2} f(x) = 4 \qquad \text{or} \qquad \lim_{x \to 2} \frac{x^2 - 4}{x - 2} = 4$$

This symbol is read "the limit of $\dfrac{x^2 - 4}{x - 2}$ as x approaches 2 is 4." Although this discussion intuitively gives the value of the limit, the actual proof that $\lim\limits_{x \to 2} f(x) = 4$ uses limit properties that are given later in this section.

Limit of a Function (Intuitive)

If the value of a function $f(x)$ gets closer and closer to some number L when x gets closer and closer to some number a, but $x \ne a$, we say that L is the limit of $f(x)$ as x approaches a and write

$$\lim_{x \to a} f(x) = L$$

Definition of Limit (Formal)

$\lim\limits_{x \to a} f(x) = L$ if for each $\varepsilon > 0$, there exists $\delta > 0$ such that $|f(x) - L| < \varepsilon$ whenever $0 < |x - a| < \delta$.

The formal definition will not be used in this book; it is given to illustrate how the intuitive terms "close to L" and "close to a" can be made mathematically rigorous.

Comments about Limits

EXAMPLE 11 Suppose $f(x) = 1$ when $x \leq 2$ and $f(x) = 3$ when $x > 2$. The graph of this function is given in Figure 9.7. Find intuitively

a. $\lim\limits_{x \to 0} f(x)$

b. $\lim\limits_{x \to 2} f(x)$

c. $\lim\limits_{x \to 4} f(x)$

Figure 9.7

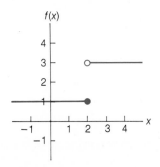

Solution **a.** From Figure 9.7, it is clear that as x approaches 0, $f(x)$ approaches 1. Hence.

$$\lim\limits_{x \to 0} f(x) = 1$$

b. From Figure 9.7, we see that as x approaches 2 from the left, $f(x)$ approaches 1; that is,

$$\lim\limits_{x \to 2^-} f(x) = 1 \qquad x \to 2^- \text{ means } x \to 2 \text{ from the left}$$

As x approaches 2 from the right, $f(x)$ approaches 3; that is,

$$\lim\limits_{x \to 2^+} f(x) = 3 \qquad x \to 2^+ \text{ means } x \to 2 \text{ from the right}$$

Since $f(x)$ does not approach the same number as x approaches 2 from the left as it does from the right, $f(x)$ does not approach a limit as $x \to 2$.

c. From Figure 9.7, we see that as x approaches 4, $f(x)$ approaches 3; that is,

$$\lim\limits_{x \to 4} f(x) = 3$$

The following properties of limits can be proved by using the formal definition. They are listed here for reference. It is easier to remember the properties by words; consequently, both the symbolic form and the statement of the property are given. An example illustrating each property follows the listing of properties.

Properties of Limits

Assume a and c are constants, n is a positive integer, and $\lim\limits_{x \to a} f(x) = L$ and $\lim\limits_{x \to a} g(x) = M$.

1. $\lim\limits_{x \to a} c = c$

The limit of a constant c as x approaches a is the constant c.

2. $\lim\limits_{x \to a} x^n = a^n$

The limit of x^n as x approaches a is a^n.

3. $\lim\limits_{x \to a} cf(x) = c \lim\limits_{x \to a} f(x) = cL$

The limit of a constant times a function is the constant times the limit of the function.

4. $\lim\limits_{x \to a} [f(x) \pm g(x)] = \lim\limits_{x \to a} f(x) \pm \lim\limits_{x \to a} g(x) = L \pm M$

The limit of a sum or difference is equal to the sum or difference of the limits.

5. $\lim\limits_{x \to a} [f(x) \cdot g(x)] = \left[\lim\limits_{x \to a} f(x) \right]\left[\lim\limits_{x \to a} g(x) \right] = LM$

The limit of a product is the product of the limits.

6. $\lim\limits_{x \to a} \dfrac{f(x)}{g(x)} = \dfrac{\lim\limits_{x \to a} f(x)}{\lim\limits_{x \to a} g(x)} = \dfrac{L}{M} \qquad M \neq 0$

The limit of a quotient is the quotient of the limits whenever the limit of the denominator is not zero.

7. $\lim\limits_{x \to a} [f(x)]^n = L^n$

The limit of a function to a power is the limit to the power.

8. $\lim\limits_{x \to a} \sqrt[n]{f(x)} = \sqrt[n]{\lim\limits_{x \to a} f(x)} = \sqrt[n]{L}$

[The domain of $f(x)$ is restricted so that $\sqrt[n]{f(x)}$ is always real.] The limit of the nth root is the nth root of the limit.

EXAMPLE 12

$\lim\limits_{x \to 2} 7 = 7$

EXAMPLE 13

$\lim\limits_{x \to 2} x^3 = 2^3 = 8$

EXAMPLE 14

$\lim\limits_{x \to 3} 9x^2 = 9 \lim\limits_{x \to 3} x^2 = 9 \cdot 3^2 = 81$

EXAMPLE 15

$$\lim_{x \to 2} (8x^3 - 3x) = \lim_{x \to 2} 8x^3 - \lim_{x \to 2} 3x$$

$$= 8 \cdot 2^3 - 3 \cdot 2 = 58$$

EXAMPLE 16

$$\lim_{x \to 4} (3x^2)(2x^3) = \left(\lim_{x \to 4} 3x^2 \right)\left(\lim_{x \to 4} 2x^3 \right)$$

$$= (48)(128) = 6144$$

EXAMPLE 17

$$\lim_{x \to 3} \frac{5x^3}{3x} = \frac{\lim_{x \to 3} 5x^3}{\lim_{x \to 3} 3x} = \frac{5 \cdot 3^3}{3 \cdot 3} = 15$$

EXAMPLE 18

$$\lim_{x \to 2} \sqrt{3x + 5} = \sqrt{\lim_{x \to 2} (3x + 5)} = \sqrt{3 \cdot 2 + 5} = \sqrt{11}$$

Besides being interested in what happens to a function as the independent variable approaches a number, we are often concerned about what happens as the independent variable gets larger and larger. For example, consider the function

$$f(x) = 1 - \frac{1}{x}$$

and determine what happens as x gets larger and larger. Values for $f(x)$ are tabulated in Table 9.2. The graph is given in Figure 9.8. It appears that $f(x) = 1 - 1/x$ approaches 1 as x gets larger and larger. To indicate this, we write

$$\lim_{x \to \infty} \left(1 - \frac{1}{x} \right) = 1$$

where $x \to \infty$ (read "x approaches infinity") means that x is getting larger and larger.

Table 9.2

x	1	2	3	5	10	100	1000	100,000
$f(x)$	0	$\frac{1}{2}$	$\frac{2}{3}$	$\frac{4}{5}$	0.9	0.99	0.999	0.99999

Figure 9.8

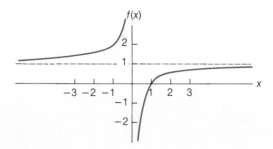

$\lim\limits_{x \to \infty} f(x) = L$ means that $f(x)$ is close to L as x gets larger and larger.

Similarly, as x becomes more negative, the function also approaches 1. We indicate this by writing $\lim\limits_{x \to -\infty} f(x) = 1$.

All the limit properties listed previously continue to hold when a is replaced by ∞, with the exception of property 2, which is replaced by the following property:

$$\lim_{x \to \infty} \frac{c}{x^n} = 0 \quad \text{and} \quad \lim_{x \to -\infty} \frac{c}{x^n} = 0$$

The limit, when x approaches infinity or minus infinity, of a constant divided by x^n, where n is a positive constant, is zero.

EXAMPLE 19

$$\lim_{x \to -\infty} \frac{5}{x^3} = 0$$

EXAMPLE 20 Find $\lim\limits_{x \to \infty} \dfrac{3x^2 - 5}{2x^2 + x - 3}$.

Solution Although this example is a quotient of two functions, we cannot use property 6 to find the limit because the numerator and denominator do not have limits as x approaches infinity. In this situation we use algebra to transform the quotient into a form where the numerator and denominator do have limits. The algebraic manipulation is to divide the numerator and the denominator by x raised to the largest power to which it is raised in the numerator or denominator. In this case we divide the numerator and the denominator by x^2 and then use property 6 for the limit of a quotient.

$$\lim_{x \to \infty} \frac{3x^2 - 5}{2x^2 + x - 3} = \lim_{x \to \infty} \frac{3 - \dfrac{5}{x^2}}{2 + \dfrac{1}{x} - \dfrac{3}{x^2}}$$

$$= \frac{\lim\limits_{x \to \infty} \left(3 - \dfrac{5}{x^2}\right)}{\lim\limits_{x \to \infty} \left(2 + \dfrac{1}{x} - \dfrac{3}{x^2}\right)} = \frac{3}{2}$$

EXAMPLE 21 Find $\lim\limits_{x \to \infty} \dfrac{3x^3 + x - 5}{2x^2 + 5}$.

Solution   Divide the numerator and denominator by x^3.

$$\lim_{x \to \infty} \frac{3x^3 + x - 5}{2x^2 + 5} = \lim_{x \to \infty} \frac{3 + \dfrac{1}{x^2} - \dfrac{5}{x^3}}{\dfrac{2}{x} + \dfrac{5}{x^3}}$$

The limit of the numerator is 3, and the limit of the denominator is 0; consequently, the quotient becomes very large and the limit as x approaches infinity does not exist.

EXAMPLE 22   Find $\lim\limits_{x \to 3} \dfrac{x^2 - 9}{x - 3}$.

Solution   Property 6 does not apply since the limit of the denominator is zero. We use algebra to factor the numerator to obtain

$$\lim_{x \to 3} \frac{x^2 - 9}{x - 3} = \lim_{x \to 3} \frac{(x + 3)(x - 3)}{x - 3}$$

Since the definition of limit rules out $x = 3$, we may divide the common factor $x - 3$ (which is not zero) out of the numerator and denominator to obtain

$$\lim_{x \to 3} \frac{(x + 3)(x - 3)}{(x - 3)} = \lim_{x \to 3} (x + 3) = 3 + 3 = 6$$

Exercise Set **9.2**

A   *Find the following limits.*

1. $\lim\limits_{x \to 4} 8$

2. $\lim\limits_{x \to 0} 8$

3. $\lim\limits_{x \to 3} 0$

4. $\lim\limits_{x \to 3} 2$

5. $\lim\limits_{x \to 2} -3$

6. $\lim\limits_{x \to 1} \dfrac{2}{3}$

7. $\lim\limits_{x \to 3} 2x$

8. $\lim\limits_{x \to 2} 5x$

9. $\lim\limits_{x \to -1} 3x$

10. $\lim\limits_{x \to 0} 4x$

11. $\lim\limits_{x \to 2} \dfrac{3x}{2}$

12. $\lim\limits_{x \to -1} \dfrac{-2}{3} x$

13. $\lim\limits_{x \to 3} (2x^2 - 4)$

14. $\lim\limits_{x \to 5} (3x + 5)$

15. $\lim\limits_{x \to 2} (3x^2 - 5)(x + 4)$

16. $\lim\limits_{x \to 2} (2x + 7)(3x^2 - 1)$

17. $\lim\limits_{x \to -3} \dfrac{7x}{2x + 3}$

18. $\lim\limits_{x \to 0} \dfrac{9x^2 - x + 1}{x^3 + 2x + 5}$

19. $\lim\limits_{x \to \infty} \dfrac{3}{x}$

20. $\lim\limits_{x \to \infty} \dfrac{5}{x^2}$

21. $\lim\limits_{x \to \infty} 7 - \dfrac{5}{x}$

22. $\lim\limits_{x \to \infty} \dfrac{2}{x^2} - \dfrac{3}{x} + 5$

23. Determine whether or not $\lim\limits_{x \to 2} f(x)$ exists for the following functions. If it exists, find it.

a.

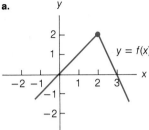

b.

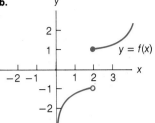

c.

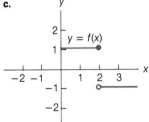

d.

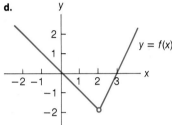

B *Find the following limits if they exist.*

24. $\lim\limits_{x \to 3} \dfrac{x^2 - x - 6}{x - 3}$

25. $\lim\limits_{x \to 0} \dfrac{4x^2 - 3x}{x}$

26. $\lim\limits_{x \to 0} \dfrac{3x^2 - 4x^3}{x^2}$

27. $\lim\limits_{x \to \infty} \dfrac{3x - 2}{3x + 5}$

28. $\lim\limits_{x \to \infty} \dfrac{4x - 2}{4x + 2}$

29. $\lim\limits_{x \to \infty} \dfrac{3x^2 - 5x + 7}{4x^2 + x + 1}$

30. $\lim\limits_{x \to \infty} \dfrac{5x^3 + 3x - 7}{6x^2 + 3x + 2}$

31. $\lim\limits_{x \to \infty} \dfrac{3x^3 - 2x + 5}{4x + 5}$

32. $\lim\limits_{x \to \infty} \dfrac{4x + 5}{3x^2 - 2x + 5}$

Use the following graphs to find the following limits if they exist.

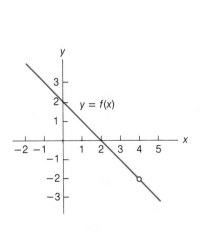

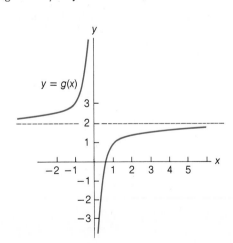

33. $\lim_{x \to -1} f(x)$ **34.** $\lim_{x \to 0} f(x)$ **35.** $\lim_{x \to 1} f(x)$ **36.** $\lim_{x \to 2} f(x)$

37. $\lim_{x \to 4} f(x)$ **38.** $\lim_{x \to 5} f(x)$ **39.** $\lim_{x \to -1} g(x)$ **40.** $\lim_{x \to 0} g(x)$

41. $\lim_{x \to 1/2} g(x)$ **42.** $\lim_{x \to \infty} g(x)$ **43.** $\lim_{x \to -\infty} g(x)$

C   *Complete the following tables to help find the limits if they exist. A calculator may be helpful.*

44. If $f(x) = \dfrac{x^3 - 8}{x - 2}$, find $\lim_{x \to 2} f(x)$.

x	1	1.5	1.9	1.99	1.999	2.001
f(x)						

45. If $f(x) = \dfrac{x^3 + 8}{x + 2}$, find $\lim_{x \to -2} f(x)$.

x	−1	−1.5	−1.9	−1.99	−1.999	−2.001
f(x)						

46. If $f(x) = \dfrac{x^3 - 27}{x - 3}$, find $\lim_{x \to 3} f(x)$.

x	2	2.5	2.9	2.99	2.999	3.001
f(x)						

47. If $f(x) = \dfrac{x^3 + 27}{x + 3}$, find $\lim_{x \to -3} f(x)$.

x	−2	−2.5	−2.9	−2.99	−2.999	−3.001
f(x)						

Find the following limits if they exist.

48. $\lim_{x \to \infty} \sqrt{\dfrac{27x^2 - 2x + 3}{3x^2 + x - 2}}$

49. $\lim_{x \to \infty} \sqrt[3]{\dfrac{27x + 2}{x - 3}}$

50. $\lim_{x \to \infty} \sqrt{\dfrac{32x^2 - 5x + 4}{3 + 2x^2}}$

51. $\lim_{x \to \infty} \sqrt[3]{\dfrac{24x^3 - 3x + 5}{3x^3 - 2x^2 + 7}}$

Business   **52. Demand Functions.** A demand, $D(x)$, for a product is given as a function of the price, $\$x$, per unit.

$$D(x) = \frac{900}{x^2} + \frac{800}{x}$$

Find

a. $\lim_{x \to 1} D(x)$ **b.** $\lim_{x \to 2} D(x)$ **c.** $\lim_{x \to 3} D(x)$ **d.** $\lim_{x \to \infty} D(x)$

Economics **53. Cost Functions.** A cost function C is given as

$$C(x) = 5 \quad \text{for} \quad 0 \le x \le 4$$
$$C(x) = 6 \quad \text{for} \quad 4 < x \le 6$$
$$C(x) = x \quad \text{for} \quad 6 < x \le 10$$

Find the following limits if they exist.

a. $\lim_{x \to 1} C(x)$ **b.** $\lim_{x \to 4} C(x)$ **c.** $\lim_{x \to 6} C(x)$ **d.** $\lim_{x \to 8} C(x)$

Life Sciences **54. Growth Functions.** A growth function is given as

$$N(x) = \frac{80{,}000x}{100 + x}$$

Find the value of each of the following

a. $\lim_{x \to 100} N(x)$ **b.** $\lim_{x \to 200} N(x)$ **c.** $\lim_{x \to 1000} N(x)$ **d.** $\lim_{x \to \infty} N(x)$

Social Sciences **55. Voting.** Suppose the probability P that a person will vote yes on ballot n is

$$P = \frac{1}{3} + \frac{1}{10}\left(-\frac{1}{2}\right)^n$$

Find the value of each of the following

a. $\lim_{n \to 1} P$ **b.** $\lim_{n \to 2} P$ **c.** $\lim_{n \to 3} P$ **d.** $\lim_{n \to \infty} P$

3 Continuous Functions

The intuitive concept of a **continuous function** is that it is a function whose graph does not have any breaks in it. Another way of stating this intuitive concept is to say that we can draw the graph of the function without taking our pen off the paper. Perhaps you are wondering why we are interested in continuous functions. If a function has a derivative at a point, the function is continuous at that point. Thus, if a function is not continuous at a point, the function does not have a derivative at the point. Continuous functions have many special properties. For this reason many theorems in calculus assume that the functions are continuous. Consequently, when functions are used to model real-world problems, continuous functions are chosen as often as possible. In this section we define a continuous function, give examples of continuous and discontinuous functions, and list some of the properties of continuous functions.

In our study of $\lim_{x \to a} f(x) = L$ we were not concerned with the value of the function at $x = a$. We were interested in what happens to the function as x approaches a. We now shift our interest to the value of the function at $x = a$. If the function is defined at $x = a$ and if the $\lim\limits_{x \to a} f(x) = f(a)$, then the function is **continuous** at $x = a$.

Continuous Function

A function $f(x)$ is **continuous** at $x = a$ if

    1. $f(x)$ is defined at $x = a$.

    2. $\lim\limits_{x \to a} f(x)$ exists.

    3. $\lim\limits_{x \to a} f(x) = f(a)$.

If any one of these conditions is not satisfied, the function $f(x)$ is **discontinuous** at $x = a$. A function is **continuous on an interval** if it is continuous at each point of the interval.

EXAMPLE 23   Graph

$$f(x) = \frac{1}{x - 2}$$

Is $f(x)$ continuous at $x = 2$?

Solution   The graph of $f(x) = 1/(x - 2)$ is given in Figure 9.9. Since $f(x)$ is not defined at $x = 2$, condition 1 of the definition is not satisfied. Thus, $f(x)$ is discontinuous at $x = 2$. It is continuous at all other values of x; hence, $f(x)$ is continuous on the interval $x < 2$ and on the interval $x > 2$.

Figure 9.9

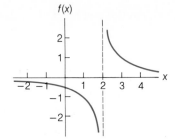

EXAMPLE 24   Graph

$$f(x) = \begin{cases} 1 & \text{if } x \le 2 \\ 2 & \text{if } x > 2 \end{cases}$$

Is $f(x)$ continuous at $x = 2$?

Solution   The graph is given in Figure 9.10. Note that $f(2) = 1$ but $\lim\limits_{x \to 2} f(x)$ does not exist. Since condition 2 of the definition is not satisfied, $f(x)$ is not continuous at $x = 2$. It is continuous at all other values of x; consequently, $f(x)$ is continuous on the open interval $x < 2$ and on the open interval $x > 2$.

Figure 9.10

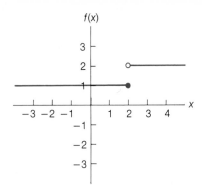

E X A M P L E 25   Graph

$$f(x) = \begin{cases} \dfrac{x - 2}{x - 2} & \text{if } x \neq 2 \\ 3 & \text{if } x = 2 \end{cases}$$

Is $f(x)$ continuous at $x = 2$?

Solution   The graph is given in Figure 9.11. Note that

$$\lim_{x \to 2} \frac{x - 2}{x - 2} = \lim_{x \to 2} 1 = 1$$

The value of $f(x)$ at $x = 2$ is 3. Since $\lim\limits_{x \to 2} f(x) \neq f(2)$, this function is discontinuous at $x = 2$ because it does not satisfy condition 3 of the definition. It is continuous at all other values of x; that is, $f(x)$ is continuous on the open interval $x < 2$ and on the open interval $x > 2$.

Figure 9.11

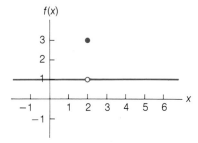

E X A M P L E 26   Graph

$$f(x) = \begin{cases} \dfrac{x^2 - 4}{x - 2} & \text{if } x \neq 2 \\ 4 & \text{if } x = 2 \end{cases}$$

Is this function continuous at $x = 2$?

Solution   The graph of this function is given in Figure 9.12. Note that

$$\lim_{x \to 2} \frac{x^2 - 4}{x - 2} = \lim_{x \to 2} \frac{(x + 2)(x - 2)}{x - 2} = \lim_{x \to 2} (x + 2) = 4$$

Since $f(2) = 4$ and $\lim_{x \to 2} f(x)$ exists and $\lim_{x \to 2} f(x) = f(2)$, this function is continuous at $x = 2$. It is also continuous at all other values of x.

Figure 9.12

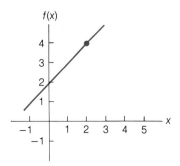

EXAMPLE 27   The cost of transporting a truckload of an item is given by

$$C(x) = \begin{cases} \$1.00x & \text{if} & 0 \le x \le 200 \\ \$0.90x & \text{if} & 200 < x \le 500 \\ \$0.80x & \text{if} & 500 < x \le 700 \end{cases}$$

where x is distance measured in miles. Is this function continuous at

a. $x = 100$?
b. $x = 200$?
c. $x = 300$?
d. $x = 500$?

Solution   The graph is given in Figure 9.13. Note the breaks at $x = 200$ and $x = 500$.

a. Since $\lim_{x \to 100} f(x) = f(100)$, $f(x)$ is continuous at $x = 100$.
b. Since $\lim_{x \to 200} f(x)$ does not exist, $f(x)$ is not continuous at $x = 200$.

Figure 9.13

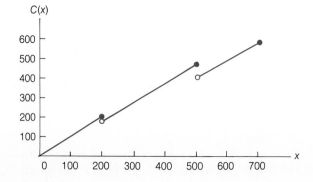

c. Since $\lim\limits_{x \to 300} f(x) = f(300)$, $f(x)$ is continuous at $x = 300$.

d. Since $\lim\limits_{x \to 500} f(x)$ does not exist, $f(x)$ is not continuous at $x = 500$.

Hence, $f(x)$ is continuous on the open interval $0 < x < 200$, on the open interval $200 < x < 500$, and on the open interval $500 < x < 700$.

As we try to find derivatives of functions, it is important to remember that if a function is not continuous at a point, the function does not have a derivative at that point. Continuous functions have many special properties. The following box summarizes some of these properties:

Properties of Continuous Functions

1. $f(x) = C$ is continuous for all real values of x.
2. $f(x) = x^n$, where n is a positive integer, is continuous for all real values of x.

Assume that $f(x)$ and $g(x)$ are continuous functions; then

3. $f(x) \pm g(x)$ is continuous.
4. $f(x) \cdot g(x)$ is continuous.

5. $\dfrac{f(x)}{g(x)}$ is continuous except where $g(x) = 0$.

6. $\sqrt[n]{f(x)}$ is continuous when x is restricted to those values that make $\sqrt[n]{f(x)}$ real.

From these properties it is easy to see that all polynomials are continuous functions and that rational functions of polynomials are continuous except where the denominators are zero.

Exercise Set 9.3

A *Determine whether the following functions are continuous at the given points.*

1. $f(x) = 5$ at $x = -1$, $x = 0$, $x = 2$

2. $f(x) = -3$ at $x = 1$, $x = 2$

3. $f(x) = 3x$ at $x = -2$, $x = 0$, $x = 1$

4. $f(x) = -2x$ at $x = -1$, $x = 3$

5. $f(x) = 2x^2$ at $x = -1$, $x = 0$, $x = 2$

6. $f(x) = -2x^2$ at $x = -2$, $x = 3$

7. $f(x) = \dfrac{1}{x}$ at $x = -1$, $x = 0$, $x = 2$

8. $f(x) = \dfrac{2}{x}$ at $x = 0$, $x = 1$

9. $f(x) = \dfrac{1}{x + 2}$ at $x = -2$, $x = 0$, $x = 1$

10. $f(x) = \dfrac{2}{x + 2}$ at $x = -2$, $x = 1$

11. $f(x) = \dfrac{x - 1}{x - 2}$ at $x = -1$, $x = 0$, $x = 2$

12. $f(x) = \dfrac{1-x}{x-2}$ at $x = 1$, $x = 2$

13. $f(x) = 2x^2 - x$ at $x = \frac{1}{2}$, $x = 0$, $x = 1$

14. $f(x) = 2x^2 + x$ at $x = -\frac{1}{2}$, $x = 0$

15. $f(x) = \dfrac{x^2 - 9}{x - 3}$ at $x = -3$, $x = 0$, $x = 3$

16. $f(x) = \dfrac{x^2 - 9}{x + 3}$ at $x = -3$, $x = 3$

17. $f(x) = \dfrac{1}{x(x-1)}$ at $x = -1$, $x = 0$, $x = 1$

18. $f(x) = \dfrac{1}{2x(x-1)}$ at $x = 0$, $x = 1$

19. $f(x) = \dfrac{x+2}{(2-x)(2+x)}$ at $x = -2$, $x = 0$, $x = 2$

20. $f(x) = \dfrac{3x}{(x+2)(2x+1)}$ at $x = -\frac{1}{2}$, $x = -2$

Are the following functions continuous or discontinuous at $x = 2$? Explain your answer.

21. a.

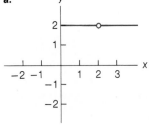

b.

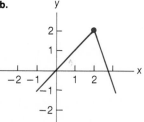

22. a.

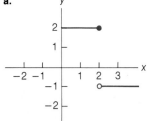

b.

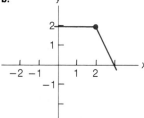

B Explain why the given function is continuous or discontinuous at the indicated points.

23. $g(x) = -\dfrac{2}{x}$ at $x = -1$, $x = 0$

24. $g(x) = \dfrac{3}{x}$ at $x = 0$, $x = 1$

25. $h(x) = \dfrac{x^2 - x - 6}{x + 2}$ at $x = -2$, $x = 2$

26. $h(x) = \dfrac{x^2 - x - 6}{x + 2}$ at $x = -3$, $x = 3$

27. $p(x) = (3x + 2)(2x - 3)$ at $x = -\frac{2}{3}$, $x = -\frac{3}{2}$

28. $p(x) = \dfrac{5x - 2}{3x + 2}$ at $x = -\frac{2}{3}, x = \frac{2}{5}$ **29.** $g(x) = 3x^2 - 2x + 5$ at $x = 0, x = 1$

30. $g(x) = \dfrac{1}{x^2 - x - 6}$ at $x = 2, x = 3$

C   *Draw the graphs and find all points of discontinuity for each function below.*

31. $f(x) = 3x^2$ **32.** $g(x) = \dfrac{1}{3x}$

33. $f(x) = \dfrac{1}{x - 3}$ **34.** $g(x) = \dfrac{x}{x + 2}$

35. $f(x) = \dfrac{1}{x(x - 2)}$ **36.** $g(x) = \dfrac{x + 2}{x^2 - 4}$

37. $f(x) = \begin{cases} x^2 & \text{if } -1 \le x < 1 \\ 3x & \text{if } \qquad x \ge 1 \end{cases}$ **38.** $f(x) = \dfrac{x - 2}{x^2 - 4}$

39. $g(x) = \sqrt[3]{x}$ **40.** $f(x) = \begin{cases} \sqrt{x} & \text{if } 0 \le x \le 4 \\ 2 & \text{if } \qquad x > 4 \end{cases}$

Business   **41. Sales.** A store charges \$5 per pound for orders under 25 pounds of an item. For orders between 25 and 50 pounds, the store charges \$4 per pound. For orders of 50 to 100 pounds, inclusive, the store charges \$3 per pound. For all orders over 100 pounds, the store charges \$2.75 per pound. Let $C(x)$ represent the cost of x pounds of the item.
  a. Find $C(10)$.   **b.** Find $C(40)$.
  c. Find $C(80)$.   **d.** Find $C(100)$.
  e. Find $C(200)$.   **f.** Draw the graph of $C(x)$.
  g. Where is $C(x)$ discontinuous?

42. Cost Functions. A cost function $C(x)$ has the following graph for $0 \le x \le 8$.

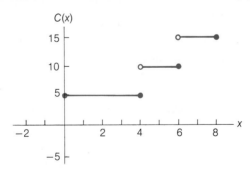

  a. Where is the cost function discontinuous?
  b. Find $\lim\limits_{x \to 2} C(x)$.   **c.** Find $C(2)$.   **d.** Find $\lim\limits_{x \to 4} C(x)$.
  e. Find $C(4)$.   **f.** Find $\lim\limits_{x \to 7} C(x)$.   **g.** Find $C(7)$.

Economics   **43. Revenue Functions.** A revenue function, $R(x)$, is found to be

$$R(x) = 10x - \frac{x^2}{100} \qquad 0 \le x \le 1000$$

  a. Find $R(10)$.   **b.** Find $R(100)$.
  c. Find $R(500)$.   **d.** Draw the graph of $R(x)$.
  e. Is $R(x)$ continuous on $0 < x < 1000$?

44. Demand Functions. The demand function for an item is given by

$$D(x) = \frac{80}{x - 16} \qquad \text{for } 16 < x \le 96$$

Draw the graph of the demand function and discuss the continuity of $D(x)$.

Life Sciences **45. Agronomy.** The height of a plant is given by

$$h(t) = 3\sqrt{t}$$

where h is measured in inches and t in days. Graph this function and find any points of discontinuity.

46. Laboratory Experiment. A laboratory uses mice in its experiments. The number N of mice available is a function of time t, and the following chart was drawn for 6 days.

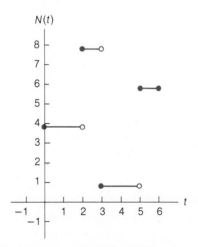

a. Where is this function discontinuous?
b. Find $N(1)$.   **c.** Find $\lim\limits_{t \to 2^-} N(t)$.   **d.** Find $\lim\limits_{t \to 2^+} N(t)$.

47. Pollution. Suppose the concentration $C(x)$ of a pollutant in the air is given by

$$C(x) = \frac{0.2}{x^2}$$

a. Find $C(1)$ **b.** Find $C(2)$.
c. Draw the graph of $C(x)$.   **d.** Discuss the continuity of $C(x)$.

Social Sciences **48. Learning Functions.** A person learns $l(x)$ items in x hours according to the function

$$l(x) = 40\sqrt{x} \qquad 0 \le x \le 16$$

a. Find $l(4)$.   **b.** Find $l(9)$.
c. Find $l(16)$.   **d.** Draw the graph of $l(x)$.
e. Discuss the continuity of $l(x)$.

49. Learning Functions. Suppose a learning function is given as

$$l(x) = 30x^{2/3} \qquad 0 \le x \le 8$$

a. Find $l(x) = 30x^{2/3}$.   **b.** Find $l(8)$.
c. Draw the graph of $l(x)$.   **d.** Discuss the continuity of $l(x)$.

50. Voting. The voting population, $P(t)$, in thousands is given as

$$P(t) = 40 + 9t^2 - t^3 \qquad 0 \le t \le 8$$

a. Find $P(2)$.　　**b.** Find $P(4)$.
c. Find $P(6)$.　　**d.** Draw the graph of $P(t)$.
e. Discuss the continuity of $P(t)$.

4　What Is a Derivative?

> In this section we define the derivative of a function and give some of the possible interpretations of the derivative. The first interpretation of the derivative at a point on the graph is that the derivative gives the value of the *slope of the function* at the point on the graph. The **slope of the function** is the slope of the tangent line to the graph at the point. The derivative at a point can also be interpreted as the *instantaneous rate of change* of the function at the point. When distance is given as a function of time, the derivative of distance with respect to time gives the *velocity of a particle at a particular time*. In economics, if $C(x)$ represents a cost function, the derivative of $C(x)$ is the *marginal cost function*. If $P(x)$ represents a profit function, the derivative of $P(x)$ is the *marginal profit function*. If $D(x)$ represents a demand function, the derivative of $D(x)$ is the *marginal demand function*. If $S(x)$ represents a supply function, the derivative of $S(x)$ is the *marginal supply function*. In medicine, if $P(x)$ represents the systolic pressure, the derivative of $P(x)$ is the *sensitivity* of the patient.

As just stated, the derivative at a point on the graph of a function is the value of the slope of the function at the point on the graph. If the function is a straight line, the slope is the same at each point of the graph. We have shown earlier that the slope of the line $y = mx + b$, is m. In order to develop a way of finding the derivative of any function, we shall use the more general functional notation for y, that is, $y = f(x)$.

Let Δx (read "delta x") represent a change in x and Δy represent the corresponding change in y. Thus, if x is replaced by $x + \Delta x$, then y is replaced by $y + \Delta y$. In the equation of a straight line

$$f(x) = y = mx + b$$

replacing x by $x + \Delta x$ and y by $y + \Delta y$ gives

$$f(x + \Delta x) = y + \Delta y = m(x + \Delta x) + b$$

Subtracting $f(x) = y = mx + b$ gives

$$f(x + \Delta x) - f(x) = y + \Delta y - y = m(x + \Delta x) - mx$$
$$= \Delta y = m\,\Delta x$$

Dividing by $\Delta x \neq 0$ gives

$$\frac{f(x + \Delta x) - f(x)}{\Delta x} = \frac{\Delta y}{\Delta x} = \frac{m\,\Delta x}{\Delta x} = m$$

Thus, the slope of a straight line can be found from the expression

$$\frac{f(x + \Delta x) - f(x)}{\Delta x}$$

which is called the **difference quotient.** This difference quotient gives the average rate of change of a function $f(x)$ between the point $(x, f(x))$ and a "near" point $(x + \Delta x, f(x + \Delta x))$. In general, it will be the slope of the secant line joining these two points, as indicated in Figure 9.14, and not the slope of the tangent line at the point $(x, f(x))$.

Figure 9.14

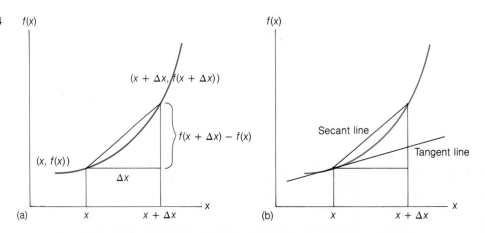

Geometrically, it appears that as Δx becomes smaller, the point $(x + \Delta x, f(x + \Delta x))$ approaches the point $(x, f(x))$ on the curve, and the slope of the line joining these two points appears to approach the slope of the tangent line to the curve at $(x, f(x))$. Thus, it seems natural to define the **derivative of $f(x)$ with respect to x** to be the quantity that the difference quotient approaches as Δx approaches 0, if such a quantity exists.

Definition of the Derivative of a Function $f(x)$

For $y = f(x)$, the *derivative of $f(x)$ at x* is

$$\lim_{\Delta x \to 0} \frac{f(x + \Delta x) - f(x)}{\Delta x}$$

If the limit exists, dy/dx, y', and $f'(x)$ are used as symbols to denote the derivative of $f(x)$ at x; thus,

$$\frac{dy}{dx} = y' = f'(x) = \lim_{\Delta x \to 0} \frac{f(x + \Delta x) - f(x)}{\Delta x}$$

A derivative $f'(x)$ expresses the slope of the tangent line to the graph of $y = f(x)$ as a function of the x-coordinate of the point of tangency.

Since the difference quotient gives the *average* rate of change of a function between two points, the derivative gives, by definition, the **instantaneous rate of change of a function at a point** $(x, f(x))$.

EXAMPLE 28 Use the definition of the derivative to prove that if $f(x) = x^2 - 1$, then $f'(x) = 2x$.

Solution To find the derivative, we must compute the difference quotient,

$$\frac{f(x + \Delta x) - f(x)}{\Delta x}$$

To find $f(x + \Delta x)$, we simply replace x by $x + \Delta x$ to obtain

$$f(x + \Delta x) = (x + \Delta x)^2 - 1 = x^2 + 2x\,\Delta x + (\Delta x)^2 - 1$$

Subtract

$$f(x) = x^2 - 1$$

to obtain

$$f(x + \Delta x) - f(x) = 2x\,\Delta x + (\Delta x)^2$$

Dividing by Δx gives

$$\frac{f(x + \Delta x) - f(x)}{\Delta x} = 2x + \Delta x$$

Now as Δx approaches zero, $2x + \Delta x$ approaches $2x$. Hence,

$$f'(x) = \lim_{\Delta x \to 0} \frac{f(x + \Delta x) - f(x)}{\Delta x} = 2x$$

**Procedure for
Finding a
Derivative of a
Function $f(x)$**

1. Given $f(x)$, find $f(x + \Delta x)$.

2. Subtract $f(x)$ from $f(x + \Delta x)$ to obtain $f(x + \Delta x) - f(x)$.

3. Divide by Δx to obtain $\dfrac{f(x + \Delta x) - f(x)}{\Delta x}$.

4. Take the limit of this quotient as $\Delta x \to 0$.

$$\lim_{\Delta x \to 0} \frac{f(x + \Delta x) - f(x)}{\Delta x} = f'(x)$$

EXAMPLE 29   Given $f(x) = x^3$, compute $f'(x)$.

Solution   **1.** $f(x + \Delta x) = (x + \Delta x)^3 = x^3 + 3x^2\,\Delta x + 3x(\Delta x)^2 + (\Delta x)^3$

Subtract

$$f(x) = x^3$$

to obtain

2. $f(x + \Delta x) - f(x) = 3x^2\,\Delta x + 3x(\Delta x)^2 + (\Delta x)^3$

Dividing by Δx gives

3. $\dfrac{f(x + \Delta x) - f(x)}{\Delta x} = 3x^2 + 3x\,\Delta x + (\Delta x)^2$

Now as Δx approaches zero, $3x^2 + 3x\,\Delta x + (\Delta x)^2$ approaches $3x^2$; hence,

4. $f'(x) = \lim\limits_{\Delta x \to 0} \dfrac{f(x + \Delta x) - f(x)}{\Delta x} = 3x^2$

Economists make use of the derivative of a function in determining what they call *marginal cost* and *marginal revenue*. The rate of change of cost as output changes is called **marginal cost** and is denoted by *MC*. It is described by economists as the additional cost of producing an additional unit of output. Thus,

$$MC = \lim_{\Delta x \to 0} \frac{\Delta C}{\Delta x} = C'(x)$$

Likewise, **marginal revenue**, *MR*, is defined as

$$MR = \lim_{\Delta x \to 0} \frac{\Delta R}{\Delta x} = R'(x)$$

EXAMPLE 30   The cost function $C(x)$ for manufacturing an item is given in units of 1000 to be

$$C(x) = 3 + 10x - x^2 \qquad 0 \le x \le 4$$

a. Find the *marginal cost, $C'(x)$,* which is the rate of change in the cost per unit increase in production.
b. Find $C'(1)$.
c. Find $C'(2)$.
d. Find $C'(3)$.
e. Interpret these results and draw the graph of the cost function.

Solution   **a. 1.** $C(x + \Delta x) = 3 + 10(x + \Delta x) - (x + \Delta x)^2$
$= 3 + 10x + 10\,\Delta x - x^2 - 2x\,\Delta x - (\Delta x)^2$
$C(x) = 3 + 10x - x^2$
2. $\Delta C = C(x + \Delta x) - C(x) = 10\,\Delta x - 2x\,\Delta x - (\Delta x)^2$
3. $\dfrac{\Delta C}{\Delta x} = \dfrac{C(x + \Delta x) - C(x)}{\Delta x} = 10 - 2x - \Delta x$

4. $C'(x) = \lim\limits_{\Delta x \to 0} \dfrac{\Delta C}{\Delta x} = \lim\limits_{\Delta x \to 0} \dfrac{C(x + \Delta x) - C(x)}{\Delta x} = 10 - 2x$

Hence, the rate of change in the cost per unit increase in production is $10 - 2x$. This is the marginal cost, $C'(x)$.

b. The marginal cost for $x = 1$ is

$$C'(1) = 10 - 2(1) = 8$$

c. For $x = 2$, the marginal cost is

$$C'(2) = 10 - 2(2) = 6$$

d. For $x = 3$, the marginal cost is

$$C'(3) = 10 - 2(3) = 4$$

e. Since the units for the given cost function were thousands, the marginal costs can be interpreted as follows:

When production is at $x = 1000$, it costs \$8,000 to increase production an additional unit (an additional 1000). When production is at $x = 2000$, it costs \$6,000 to increase production an additional unit. When production is at $x = 3000$, it costs only \$4,000 to increase production another unit. Thus, as production increases, marginal cost goes down for this example. The graph of this function is given in Figure 9.15. Note that the slope, which is the marginal cost, decreases.

Figure 9.15

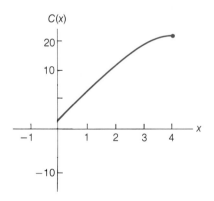

EXAMPLE 31 A doctor administers x milligrams of a drug and records a patient's blood pressure 1 hour later. The doctor finds the systolic pressure to be closely approximated by the following function. The pressure is in millimeters of mercury.

$$P(x) = 138 + 12x - 6x^2 \qquad 0 \le x \le 4$$

What is the sensitivity of the patient to this drug? What is the sensitivity when 2 milligrams are used?

Solution Let us find the sensitivity, which is dP/dx.

1. $P(x + \Delta x) = 138 + 12(x + \Delta x) - 6(x + \Delta x)^2$
$$= 138 + 12x + 12\,\Delta x - 6x^2 - 12x\,\Delta x - 6(\Delta x)^2$$
$$P(x) = 138 + 12x + 6x^2$$

2. $\Delta P = P(x + \Delta x) - P(x) = 12\,\Delta x - 12x\,\Delta x - 6(\Delta x)^2$

3. $\dfrac{\Delta P}{\Delta x} = \dfrac{P(x + \Delta x) - P(x)}{\Delta x} = 12 - 12x - 6\,\Delta x$

4. $\dfrac{dP}{dx} = \lim\limits_{\Delta x \to 0} \dfrac{\Delta P}{\Delta x} = \lim\limits_{\Delta x \to 0} \dfrac{P(x + \Delta x) - P(x)}{\Delta x} = 12 - 12x$

Hence, the sensitivity is $12 - 12x$. When $x = 2$, the sensitivity is $12 - (12)(2) = -12$. This means that the administration of 2 milligrams of the drug will cause the blood pressure to drop at the rate of 12 millimeters of mercury per milligram of drug.

Exercise Set 9.4

A *Find the derivative of the following functions, and then find $f'(0)$, $f'(1)$, and $f'(2)$.*

1. $f(x) = 3x$ **2.** $f(x) = 2x$ **3.** $f(x) = 3x + 5$

4. $f(x) = -2x + 5$ **5.** $f(x) = 4x - 3$ **6.** $f(x) = -4x + 3$

7. $f(x) = 5x - 2$ **8.** $f(x) = -3x - 5$

Find all points where the graphed functions do not have derivatives.

9.

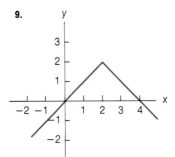

10.

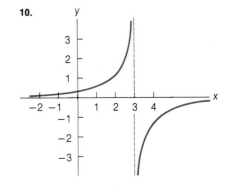

11.

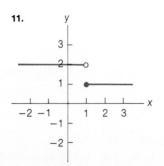

12.

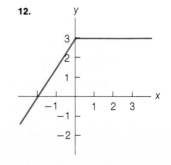

B *Find the derivative of each function below, and then find $f'(0)$, $f'(1)$, and $f'(-1)$.*

13. $f(x) = 3x^2$

14. $f(x) = -3x^2$

15. $f(x) = 7x + x^2$

16. $f(x) = 6x - 2x^2$

17. $f(x) = 4x - 3x^2$

18. $f(x) = 4x - 4x^2$

19. $f(x) = x^2 + x - 2$

20. $f(x) = x^2 - x + 2$

21. $f(x) = -3x^2 + 2x + 3$

22. $f(x) = -2x^2 - 3x + 5$

C **23.** For the function $f(x) = x^2 + 1$,
  a. find the slope of this curve.
  b. find the slope at $x = 1$ and $x = 2$.
  c. find the equations of the tangent lines drawn to this curve at $x = 1$ and $x = 2$.
  d. graph the function and draw the tangent lines at $x = 1$ and $x = 2$.

24. A rock is dropped from the top of a building. If its distance from the ground is

$$S(t) = -16t^2 + 144$$

  a. find its velocity, $S'(t)$, in terms of t.
  b. How high is the building?
  c. How long does it take the rock to reach the ground?
  d. What is the velocity of the rock when it strikes the ground?

Business **25.** **Cost Functions.** A cost function is given as

$$C(x) = 900 + 300x + x^2$$

  a. Find the marginal cost function, $C'(x)$.
  b. Find $C'(2)$.   **c.** Find $C'(3)$.

Economics **26.** **Demand Functions.** A demand function, $D(x)$, is given as

$$D(x) = 144 - x^2, \qquad 1 \le x \le 12$$

  a. Find the instantaneous rate of change, $D'(x)$.
  b. Find $D'(2)$.   **c.** Find $D'(6)$.

27. **Demand Functions.** A demand function, $D(x)$, is given as

$$D(x) = 169 - x^2, \qquad 1 \le x \le 13$$

  a. Find the instantaneous rate of change, $D'(x)$.
  b. Find $D'(3)$.   **c.** Find $D'(5)$.

Life Sciences **28.** **Human Sensitivity.** The systolic blood pressure of a patient an hour after receiving a drug is given by

$$P(x) = 136 + 18x - 8x^2, \qquad 0 \le x \le 3$$

  a. What is the sensitivity of the patient to this drug?
  b. What is the sensitivity when $x = 2$?

29. **Human Sensitivity.** A doctor administers x milligrams of a drug and records a patient's blood pressure. The systolic pressure is approximated by

$$P(x) = 140 + 10x - 5x^2, \qquad 0 \le x \le 4$$

  a. What is the sensitivity of the patient to the drug?
  b. What is the sensitivity when 2 milligrams are administered?
  c. What is the sensitivity when 3 milligrams are administered?

Social Sciences **30. Learning Functions.** A learning function is given as

$$N(t) = 15t - t^2, \qquad 0 \le t \le 8$$

  a. Find the rate of change of this function.
  b. Find $N'(2)$ and $N'(4)$.

Some Formulas for Derivatives

In Section 9.4 we found the derivative by using the definition and following a four-step procedure. The four-step procedure becomes tedious when it is repeated over and over again. Because the procedure is hard to use and may lead to algebraic errors, we now introduce some shortcuts or formulas for finding derivatives. The development of the formulas may appear complicated, but remember that our aim in developing the formulas is to eliminate the use of the tedious four-step procedure. The formulas will make the derivatives of many functions easy to obtain.

As just stated, we shall now develop formulas for derivatives of many often-used functions. Let us begin with the simplest possible function, $f(x) = C$. To develop the formula for the derivative of $f(x) = C$, we return to our four-step procedure:

  1. $f(x + \Delta x) = C$
        $f(x) = C$
  2. $f(x + \Delta x) - f(x) = C - C = 0$
  3. $\dfrac{f(x + \Delta x) - f(x)}{\Delta x} = \dfrac{0}{\Delta x} = 0$
  4. $\lim\limits_{\Delta x \to 0} \dfrac{f(x + \Delta x) - f(x)}{\Delta x} = f'(x) = 0$

Hence, we have proved that the derivative of a constant with respect to a variable is zero.

Derivative of a Constant Function

If $y = f(x) = C$, then

$$\frac{dy}{dx} = f'(x) = 0$$

E X A M P L E   32 If $f(x) = -5$, then $f'(x) = 0$.
If $y = \sqrt{3}$, then $dy/dx = 0$.

Functions of the form $y = x^n$ occur often in application problems. We will examine some special cases for this type of function and then state intuitively the **power rule.** The general power rule will be derived in Section 9.6. To develop the formula for the special case $f(x) = x^2$, we use our four-step procedure:

1. $f(x + \Delta x) = (x + \Delta x)^2$

   $\quad f(x) = x^2$

2. $f(x + \Delta x) - f(x) = (x + \Delta x)^2 - x^2$

   $\qquad\qquad\qquad = x^2 + 2x\,\Delta x + (\Delta x)^2 - x^2$

3. $\dfrac{f(x + \Delta x) - f(x)}{\Delta x} = \dfrac{2x\,\Delta x + (\Delta x)^2}{\Delta x} = 2x + \Delta x$

4. $\displaystyle\lim_{\Delta x \to 0} \dfrac{f(x + \Delta x) - f(x)}{\Delta x} = f'(x) = 2x$

Similarly, the special case $f(x) = x^3$ gives $f'(x) = 3x^2$. These are special cases of the power rule, which is stated for any real number n:

Power Rule

Let $y = x^n$, where n is any real number. Then

$$\frac{dy}{dx} = f'(x) = nx^{n-1}$$

E X A M P L E   33   If $f(x) = x^3$, then $f'(x) = 3x^2$.

E X A M P L E   34   If $f(x) = x^4$, then $f'(x) = 4x^3$.

E X A M P L E   35   If $y = x^{-3}$, then $dy/dx = -3x^{-4}$.

E X A M P L E   36   If $f(x) = x$, then $f'(x) = 1 \cdot x^{1-1} = 1 \cdot x^0 = 1$.

The next rule presents a formula for finding the derivative of a constant times a function.

Derivative of a Constant Times a Function

Let C be any real number and $y = f(x)$ be any function that has a derivative. The derivative of

$$y = C \cdot f(x) \qquad \text{is} \qquad y' = C \cdot f'(x)$$

That is, the derivative of a constant times a function is the constant times the derivative of the function.

EXAMPLE 37   Find the derivative of $y = 7x^3$.

Solution   Consider y as a product of 7 and x^3, or

$$y = 7f(x) = 7x^3$$
$$f(x) = x^3$$
$$f'(x) = 3x^2$$
$$y' = 7f'(x) = 7(3x^2) = 21x^2$$

The notation $\dfrac{d}{dx} [f(x)]$ means "find the derivative of the function inside the brackets."

EXAMPLE 38   Find

$$\frac{d}{dx}\left[\frac{x^3}{4}\right]$$

Solution $\dfrac{x^3}{4}$ can be written as $\frac{1}{4}x^3$. Thus,

$$\frac{d}{dx}\left[\frac{x^3}{4}\right] = \frac{1}{4}\cdot\frac{d}{dx}[x^3] = \frac{1}{4}[3x^2] = \frac{3x^2}{4}$$

Now that you've used the formula for the derivative of a constant times a function, you may want to follow our four-step procedure to help you understand how it is derived. Given

$$y = C \cdot f(x)$$

1. $y + \Delta y = C \cdot f(x + \Delta x)$

2. $y + \Delta y - y = C \cdot f(x + \Delta x) - C \cdot f(x)$
$$\Delta y \quad\quad = C \cdot [f(x + \Delta x) - f(x)]$$

3. $\dfrac{\Delta y}{\Delta x} = C \cdot \left[\dfrac{f(x + \Delta x) - f(x)}{\Delta x}\right]$

4. $\displaystyle\lim_{\Delta x \to 0} \frac{\Delta y}{\Delta x} = \lim_{\Delta x \to 0} C \cdot \left[\frac{f(x + \Delta x) - f(x)}{\Delta x}\right]$

$$= C \cdot \lim_{\Delta x \to 0} \left[\frac{f(x + \Delta x) - f(x)}{\Delta x}\right]$$

$$\frac{dy}{dx} = C \cdot f'(x)$$

The next rule is a great timesaver, especially when taking the derivative of a large polynomial. To differentiate the sum of two functions, differentiate each function individually and sum the two derivatives. That is, the derivative of a sum (or difference) is the sum (or difference) of the derivatives.

**Derivative
of a Sum of
Two Functions**

Let $f(x)$ and $g(x)$ be two functions whose derivatives exist. The derivative of their sum (or difference) is the sum (or difference) of their derivatives:

$$\frac{d}{dx}[f(x) + g(x)] = \frac{d[f(x)]}{dx} + \frac{d[g(x)]}{dx}$$

To prove this theorem we apply our four-step procedure. Let

$$y = f(x) + g(x)$$

1. $y + \Delta y = f(x + \Delta x) + g(x + \Delta x)$

2. $y + \Delta y - y = f(x + \Delta x) + g(x + \Delta x) - f(x) - g(x)$

$$\Delta y = f(x + \Delta x) - f(x) + g(x + \Delta x) - g(x)$$

3. $\dfrac{\Delta y}{\Delta x} = \dfrac{f(x + \Delta x) - f(x)}{\Delta x} + \dfrac{g(x + \Delta x) - g(x)}{\Delta x}$

4. $\displaystyle\lim_{\Delta x \to 0} \frac{\Delta y}{\Delta x} = \lim_{\Delta x \to 0} \left[\frac{f(x + \Delta x) - f(x)}{\Delta x} + \frac{g(x + \Delta x) - g(x)}{\Delta x} \right]$

$$\frac{dy}{dx} = \lim_{\Delta x \to 0} \left[\frac{f(x + \Delta x) - f(x)}{\Delta x} \right] + \lim_{\Delta x \to 0} \left[\frac{g(x + \Delta x) - g(x)}{\Delta x} \right]$$

$$= f'(x) + g'(x)$$

EXAMPLE 39 Find the derivative of $5x^3 + 3x^2$.

Solution Let $f(x) = 5x^3$ and $g(x) = 3x^2$. Then

$$\frac{d}{dx}[f(x) + g(x)] = \frac{d[f(x)]}{dx} + \frac{d[g(x)]}{dx}$$

$$\frac{d}{dx}[5x^3 + 3x^2] = \frac{d[5x^3]}{dx} + \frac{d[3x^2]}{dx}$$

$$= 15x^2 + 6x$$

By the repeated application of the sum formula, we see that the derivative of a polynomial is simply the sum of the derivatives of each term.

EXAMPLE 40 Find the derivative of $f(x) = 7x^4 - 5x^3 + 3x^2 - 2$.

Solution $f'(x) = 28x^3 - 15x^2 + 6x$

EXAMPLE 41 Find the derivative of $f(x) = 5x^3 - \frac{2}{3}x^2 + x - 3$.

Solution $f'(x) = 15x^2 - \frac{4}{3}x + 1$

Often it is possible to find the derivative of the derivative function. When this is true, the new derivative is called the **second derivative** of the original function.

EXAMPLE 42 If $f(x) = 2x^3 + 5x^2 + x - 3$, then $f'(x) = 6x^2 + 10x + 1$. Now it is possible to find the derivative of $f'(x)$, which is called the second derivative of $f(x)$ and is written $f''(x)$.

$$f''(x) = 12x + 10$$

When the derivative of the second derivative is obtained, it is called the **third derivative**. Similarly, the **fourth, fifth, sixth,** and **nth derivatives** can be defined. Many different notations are used to indicate derivatives and higher-order derivatives. Some of the different notations are given in Table 9.3.

Table 9.3

Function	First Derivative	Second Derivative	Third Derivative	Fourth Derivative		nth Derivative
$y = f(x)$	y'	y''	y'''	y^{IV}	$\cdots$	$y^{[n]}$
$y = f(x)$	$f'(x)$	$f''(x)$	$f'''(x)$	$f^{IV}(x)$	$\cdots$	$f^{[n]}(x)$
$y = f(x)$	$D_x f(x)$	$D_x^2 f(x)$	$D_x^3 f(x)$	$D_x^4 f(x)$	$\cdots$	$D_x^n f(x)$
$y = f(x)$	$\dfrac{dy}{dx}$	$\dfrac{d^2 y}{dx^2}$	$\dfrac{d^3 y}{dx^3}$	$\dfrac{d^4 y}{dx^4}$	$\cdots$	$\dfrac{d^n y}{dx^n}$
$y = f(x)$	$\dfrac{d}{dx}[f(x)]$	$\dfrac{d^2}{dx^2}[f(x)]$	$\dfrac{d^3}{dx^3}[f(x)]$	$\dfrac{d^4}{dx^4}[f(x)]$	$\cdots$	$\dfrac{d^n}{dx^n}[f(x)]$

EXAMPLE 43 Given $y = 3x^4 + 2x^3 + 5x^2 - x + 2$, find dy/dx, d^2y/dx^2, d^3y/dx^3, d^4y/dx^4, d^5y/dx^5, and d^ny/dx^n for $n > 5$.

Solution

$$\frac{dy}{dx} = 12x^3 + 6x^2 + 10x - 1$$

$$\frac{d^2 y}{dx^2} = 36x^2 + 12x + 10$$

$$\frac{d^3 y}{dx^3} = 72x + 12$$

$$\frac{d^4 y}{dx^4} = 72$$

$$\frac{d^5 y}{dx^5} = 0$$

$$\frac{d^n y}{dx^n} = 0 \qquad \text{(for } n > 5\text{)}$$

EXAMPLE 44 Given $y = 3x^{2/3}$, find dy/dx, d^2y/dx^2, and d^3y/dx^3.

Solution

$$\frac{dy}{dx} = 3(\tfrac{2}{3})x^{-1/3} = 2x^{-1/3}$$

$$\frac{d^2y}{dx^2} = 2(-\tfrac{1}{3})x^{-4/3} = -\tfrac{2}{3}x^{-4/3}$$

$$\frac{d^3y}{dx^3} = (-\tfrac{2}{3})(-\tfrac{4}{3})x^{-7/3} = \tfrac{8}{9}x^{-7/3}$$

Exercise Set 9.5

A Find the derivative $f'(x)$, and then find $f'(0)$, $f'(2)$, and $f'(-3)$ for the following functions.

1. $f(x) = 12$ **2.** $f(x) = -7$ **3.** $f(x) = \tfrac{2}{3}$

4. $f(x) = \sqrt{2}$ **5.** $f(x) = 0$ **6.** $f(x) = \sqrt[3]{5}$

7. $f(x) = x + 2$ **8.** $f(x) = -x + 3$ **9.** $f(x) = 2x - 3$

10. $f(x) = -2x + 3$ **11.** $f(x) = -3x + 2$ **12.** $f(x) = 3x - 4$

13. $f(x) = 2x^2$ **14.** $f(x) = -2x^2$ **15.** $f(x) = 3x^2 - 2$

16. $f(x) = 3x^2 + 5$ **17.** $f(x) = 4x^2 + 3x$ **18.** $f(x) = 5x^2 - 3x$

19. $f(x) = 2x^2 - 4x + 3$ **20.** $f(x) = -2x^2 + 3x - 2$

21. $f(x) = 5x^3 - 3x^2 + 7$ **22.** $f(x) = -3x^3 + 2x^2 - x$

23. $f(x) = 6x^4 - 3x^2$ **24.** $f(x) = 5x^4 - 3x^3 + 2x^2$

25. $f(x) = 3x^{-1} + 4x$ **26.** $f(x) = -3x^{-1} - 4x$

27. $f(x) = 4x^{-2} - 4x^2$ **28.** $f(x) = -3x^{-2} + 4x^2$

29. $f(x) = 4x^{1/2}$ **30.** $f(x) = 6x^{2/3}$

B Find dy/dx, d^2y/dx^2, and d^3y/dx^3 for the following functions.

31. $y = 25$ **32.** $y = -5$

33. $y = 3x + 5$ **34.** $y = 3x^2 - 5$

35. $y = 35x^2 - 27x + 5$ **36.** $y = -3x^2 + 4x + 2$

37. $y = 2x^3 + 3x^2 - x + 2$ **38.** $y = 4x^3 - 3x^2 + 5x - 3$

39. $y = 2x^6 + 3x^3 - 2x + 7$ **40.** $y = -3x^8 + 2x^5 - 3x^2$

41. $y = \tfrac{1}{2}x^4 + \tfrac{1}{3}x^3$ **42.** $y = -\tfrac{2}{3}x^3 + \tfrac{1}{2}x^2$

43. $y = 3x^{1/3}$ **44.** $y = 3x^{2/3}$

C **45.** $y = 6x^{2/3} + 4x^{1/2}$ **46.** $y = 9x^{-2/3} - 4x^{-1/2}$

47. $y = 3x^2 - 4x^{-1/2}$ **48.** $y = 3x^4 - 6x^{-1/3}$

49. $y = 7\sqrt{x} + 9\sqrt[3]{x}$ **50.** $y = \dfrac{6}{\sqrt{x}} + \dfrac{3}{\sqrt[3]{x}}$

Business **51. Profit Functions.** A profit curve is given by

$$P = \frac{x^2}{2} + 4x$$

a. Find the first derivative.
b. What values of x make the first derivative positive?
c. What value of x makes the first derivative zero?
d. What values of x make it negative?

52. Cost Functions. A cost function is given as

$$C(x) = 800 + 400x + x^2$$

a. Find the marginal cost function, $C'(x)$.
b. Find $C'(1)$.   **c.** Find $C'(2)$.

Economics

53. Demand Functions. A demand function is given as

$$D(x) = 138 - x^2 \qquad 1 \le x \le \sqrt{138}$$

a. Find the instantaneous rate of change, $D'(x)$.
b. Find $D'(2)$.   **c.** Find $D'(5)$.

54. Revenue Functions. A revenue function is given as

$$R(x) = 20x - \frac{x^2}{500} \qquad 0 \le x \le 10,000$$

a. Find the marginal revenue function.
b. Find the value of x that makes the marginal revenue equal to zero.
c. Find the value of the revenue at the value of x found in **b.**

Life Sciences

55. Pulse Rates. A doctor has found the relation between the pulse rate, y, and a person's height, x, to be approximately

$$y = \frac{600}{\sqrt{x}} \qquad 34 \le x \le 74$$

Find the rate of change of the pulse rate at the following heights.
a. 36   **b.** 49   **c.** 64

56. Rate of Pollution Change. Suppose the concentration of a pollutant in the air is given in parts per million by

$$P(x) = 0.2x^{-2}$$

where x is the distance in miles from a factory.
a. Find the instantaneous rate of change of pollutant.
b. Find $P'(1)$.   **c.** Find $P'(2)$.

Social Sciences

57. Learning Functions. Suppose a person learns according to the function

$$f(x) = 48\sqrt{x} \qquad 0 \le x \le 10$$

a. Find the instantaneous rate of change of learning.
b. Find $f'(1)$.   **c.** Find $f'(4)$.   **d.** Find $f'(9)$.

58. Learning Functions. Suppose the learning function in exercise 57 is changed to

$$f(x) = 72\sqrt[3]{x} \qquad 0 \le x \le 10$$

a. Find the instantaneous rate of change of learning.
b. Find $f'(1)$.
c. Find the instantaneous rate of change of learning at the end of 8 hours, that is, find $f'(8)$.
d. Find the number of items learned at the end of 8 hours, $f(8)$.

In many practical situations the item or quantity of interest is given as a function of one variable, which in turn is considered as a function of another variable. In this section we develop a formula for the derivative of the quantity with respect to the second variable. The formula we develop for such derivatives is called the **chain rule.** The chain rule is important because it describes how the derivative of a function of a function is obtained.

For example, a company may know

$$\frac{dC}{dp} = \text{rate of change of cost with respect to production}$$

$$\frac{dp}{dt} = \text{rate of change of production with respect to time}$$

Since cost varies with respect to time, we would like to know dC/dt. We will learn in this section how to find dC/dt in terms of dC/dp and dp/dt.

This section involves the composite functions discussed in Chapter 8. If y is a function of u (that is, $y = f(u)$), and u is a function of x (that is, $u = g(x)$) such that the range of $g(x)$ is in the domain of f, then y is a function of x (that is, $y = f[g(x)]$). Such a function of a function is called a **composite function.**

EXAMPLE 45   Suppose $y = 5u^2 + 2u - 1$ and $u = 3x + 2$; then by substitution,

$$y = 5(3x + 2)^2 + 2(3x + 2) - 1$$

and, hence, y is a function of x.

The function found for y in terms of x in Example 45 could be simplified, and the derivative of y with respect to x could be found in the manner used in Section 9.5. Sometimes, however, it is difficult or even impossible to substitute and find the derivative by this means. In this case the **chain rule** is used. The proof of the chain rule is beyond the scope of this book; consequently, the rule is simply stated below and its use illustrated in the remainder of this section.

The Chain Rule

If y is a function of u and u is a function of x, whose range is in the domain of y, and if dy/du and du/dx exist, then y is a function of x and

$$\frac{dy}{dx} = \left(\frac{dy}{du}\right)\left(\frac{du}{dx}\right)$$

EXAMPLE 46   If $y = 5u^2 + 2u - 1$ and $u = 3x + 2$, then

$$\frac{dy}{du} = 10u + 2 \quad \text{and} \quad \frac{du}{dx} = 3$$

Thus, by the chain rule,

$$\frac{dy}{dx} = \left(\frac{dy}{du}\right)\left(\frac{du}{dx}\right) = (10u + 2)(3)$$

Hence, $dy/dx = 30u + 6$. Notice that if $u = 3x + 2$ is substituted, we obtain

$$\frac{dy}{dx} = 30(3x + 2) + 6 = 90x + 66$$

If the function given for y in terms of x in the preceding example is simplified, we obtain

$$y = 5(3x + 2)^2 + 2(3x + 2) - 1$$
$$= 5(9x^2 + 12x + 4) + 6x + 4 - 1$$
$$= 45x^2 + 60x + 20 + 6x + 3$$
$$= 45x^2 + 66x + 23$$

Now if dy/dx is found by the method of Section 9.5,

$$\frac{dy}{dx} = 90x + 66$$

which agrees with the derivative found by using the chain rule.

EXAMPLE 47   If $P = s^{3/4}$ and $s = 2t^3 - t + 1$, find dP/dt.

Solution

$$\frac{dP}{dt} = \left(\frac{dP}{ds}\right)\left(\frac{ds}{dt}\right) = \tfrac{3}{4}s^{-1/4}(6t^2 - 1)$$

EXAMPLE 48   Find dy/dx if $y = (3x^2 + 2x - 5)^5$.

Solution   This derivative could be found by raising the expression to the fifth power and then differentiating term by term. Let's use the chain rule instead. Let

$$u = 3x^2 + 2x - 5$$

Then $y = u^5$. Now by the chain rule,

$$\frac{dy}{dx} = \left(\frac{dy}{du}\right)\left(\frac{du}{dx}\right) = 5u^4(6x + 2) = 5(3x^2 + 2x - 5)^4(6x + 2)$$

Example 48 motivates our development of the **generalized power rule**, which is given next. Suppose

$$y = [f(x)]^n$$

Letting $u = f(x)$ gives $y = u^n$. Then, using the chain rule,

$$\frac{dy}{dx} = \left(\frac{dy}{du}\right)\left(\frac{du}{dx}\right)$$

note that

$$\frac{dy}{du} = n \cdot u^{n-1} \qquad \text{and} \qquad \frac{du}{dx} = f'(x)$$

Substituting these values gives

$$\frac{dy}{dx} = n \cdot u^{n-1} f'(x) \qquad \text{or} \qquad \frac{dy}{dx} = n[f(x)]^{n-1} f'(x)$$

which is called the *generalized power rule*.

The Generalized Power Rule

Let $f(x)$ be a function of x whose derivative exists. If $y = [f(x)]^n$, where n is a real number, then the derivative, dy/dx, exists and

$$\frac{dy}{dx} = n[f(x)]^{n-1} f'(x)$$

EXAMPLE 49   If $y = (4x^3 - 3x^2 + x - 2)^3$, find dy/dx.

Solution   Now

$$f(x) = 4x^3 - 3x^2 + x - 2 \qquad \text{and} \qquad f'(x) = 12x^2 - 6x + 1$$

Using

$$\frac{d}{dx}[f(x)]^n = n[f(x)]^{n-1} f'(x)$$

gives

$$\frac{dy}{dx} = 3(4x^3 - 3x^2 + x - 2)^2 f'(x)$$

Hence,

$$\frac{dy}{dx} = 3(4x^3 - 3x^2 + x - 2)^2 (12x^2 - 6x + 1)$$

EXAMPLE 50   If $y = 7(x^3 - 3x^2 + 2x + 1)^6$, find dy/dx.

Solution
$$\frac{dy}{dx} = 7(6)(x^3 - 3x^2 + 2x + 1)^5 (3x^2 - 6x + 2)$$

EXAMPLE 51   If $y = (3x^2 - 2)^{1/2}$, find dy/dx.

Solution
$$\frac{dy}{dx} = \tfrac{1}{2}(3x^2 - 2)^{-1/2}(6x) = \frac{3x}{(3x^2 - 2)^{1/2}}$$

A Use the chain rule to find dy/dx. To check your results, find y as a function of x and then find dy/dx by the method of Section 9.5.

1. $y = 3u, \quad u = 2x + 5$

2. $y = 4u, \quad u = 3x - 2$

3. $y = 2u + 3, \quad u = 3x - 4$

4. $y = 3u - 2, \quad u = 4x + 3$

5. $y = 3u + 4, \quad u = 3x + 2$

6. $y = 4u - 3, \quad u = 2x + 3$

7. $y = 3u, \quad u = 4x^2$

8. $y = 2u + 4, \quad u = 3x^2$

9. $y = -4u, \quad u = 3x^2$

10. $y = -3u, \quad u = 5x^2$

11. $y = -2u + 3, \quad u = 2x^2$

12. $y = -4u + 3, \quad u = 3x^2$

13. $y = 3u^2, \quad u = 2x$

14. $y = -3u^2, \quad u = 2x$

15. $y = 4u^2, \quad u = 3x + 5$

16. $y = -5u^2, \quad u = 3x - 2$

17. $y = -3u^2 + 2, \quad u = 2x - 3$

18. $y = 4u^2 - 3, \quad u = 2x + 5$

19. $y = 2u^2 - 3u, \quad u = 2x^2$

20. $y = 3u^2 + 2u + 3, \quad u = 3x^2$

B Use the chain rule to find dy/dx for the following functions.

21. $y = 4u^2 - 3u + 2, \quad u = 3x + 7$

22. $y = 3u^2 - 2u + 5, \quad u = x^2 + x - 1$

23. $y = 2u^3 + 5, \quad u = x^2 - 3$

24. $y = u^3 + 2u - 1, \quad u = 3x - 2$

25. $y = 5u^4 - 2u^2 + 1, \quad u = 2x + 3$

26. $y = 2u^2 + 3u - 2, \quad u = 3x^2 - x + 2$

27. $y = 3u^2 - 2u + 3, \quad u = 2x^2 - x - 3$

28. $y = 4u^2, \quad u = 3x^2 - 2x + 1$

29. $y = u^3, \quad u = 3x + 4$

30. $y = 5u^2 + 2u - 3, \quad u = x^2 - 2x + 3$

Use the generalized power rule to find dy/dx.

31. $y = (3x^2 - 2x + 1)^3$

32. $y = (2x^2 - x + 1)^4$

33. $y = 5(x^2 + 2x - 1)^2$

34. $y = 7(3x - 2)^5$

35. $y = (x^2 + x - 1)^{1/2}$

36. $y = 2(x^2 - 3)^{3/2}$

37. $y = 3(x^2 - 2x + 1)^4$

38. $y = \frac{1}{2}(x - 3)^{1/2}$

39. $y = \frac{2}{3}(x - 4)^{2/3}$

40. $y = \frac{3}{2}(x - 4)^{2/3}$

C Write the following composite functions in the form $y = f(u), \quad u = g(x)$, as in exercises 1–20, and find their derivatives by the chain rule. Then work the problems using the generalized power rule. Do you get the same answers?

41. $y = 3(2x + 5)^2$

42. $y = 4(3x - 2)^2 - 5$

43. $y = 2(3x - 2)^2 + (3x - 2)$

44. $y = 3(2x + 3)^3$

45. $y = 4(3x + 2)^3 + 5$

46. $y = -3(3x - 2)^3$

47. $y = -5(2x + 1)^3 - 7$

48. $y = 4(3x + 4)^2 - 3(3x + 4)$

49. $y = 3(2x - 3)^2 - 2(2x - 3) + 4$

50. $y = -3(2x + 3)^2 + 3(2x + 3) + 5$

51. For the function $f(x) = (2x^2 + x + 1)^2$, find the slope function, $f'(x)$. Use the slope function to find the slope at $x = 1$ and $x = 3$.

Business **52. Cost Functions.** A cost function is found to be

$$C(x) = (3x - 10)^2 + 24$$

a. Find the marginal cost function.

b. Find $C'(3)$.

c. Find $C'(\frac{10}{3})$.

d. Find $C'(4)$.

Economics   **53. Revenue Functions.** A revenue function for the sale of stereo sets is

$$R(x) = 4608 - 372\left(12 - \frac{x}{3}\right) - \left(12 - \frac{x}{3}\right)^2 \qquad 0 \leq x \leq 36$$

a. Find the marginal revenue function.

b. Find $R'(9)$.   **c.** Find $R'(18)$.

Life Sciences   **54. Pollution.** The pollution from a factory is given by

$$P = 0.4(2x + 3)^{-2}$$

where x is measured in miles. Find the rate of change of the pollution. What is the rate of change of pollution at

a. 1 mile?   **b.** 3 miles?

Social Sciences   **55. Learning Functions.** For the learning function

$$L = 36(2x - 1)^{2/3} \qquad \tfrac{1}{2} \leq x \leq 15$$

find the rate of learning at the end of

a. 1 hour.   **b.** 14 hours.

Products and Quotients

Since the derivative of the sum of two functions is the sum of their derivatives, we might expect the derivative of the product of two functions to be the product of their derivatives. In this section we show that this statement is not true. Formulas are developed for the product of two functions and for the quotient of two functions. When these formulas are combined with formulas already obtained, the derivatives of many new functions can be obtained.

In terms easy to remember, the **product formula** states that **the derivative of a product is the first factor times the derivative of the second plus the second factor times the derivative of the first.** After some practice in using this formula, we show why it is true.

Product Formula

Let $f(x)$ and $g(x)$ be two functions whose derivatives with respect to x exist. Then

$$\frac{d}{dx}[f(x) \cdot g(x)] = f(x)g'(x) + g(x)f'(x)$$

EXAMPLE 52   If $y = (x^2 + x - 1)(3x + 2)$, find dy/dx.

Solution
$$\frac{dy}{dx} = \text{(first factor)(derivative of second)}$$
$$+ \text{(second factor)(derivative of first)}$$
$$= (x^2 + x - 1)(3) + (3x + 2)(2x + 1)$$
$$= 3x^2 + 3x - 3 + 6x^2 + 7x + 2$$
$$= 9x^2 + 10x - 1$$

To verify this result, multiply the factors to get

$$y = 3x^3 + 5x^2 - x - 2$$

and differentiate

$$\frac{dy}{dx} = 9x^2 + 10x - 1$$

EXAMPLE 53   If $y = (4x^3 - 3x + 2)(3x^2 - x + 1)$, find dy/dx.

Solution
$$\frac{dy}{dx} = (4x^3 - 3x + 2)(6x - 1) + (3x^2 - x + 1)(12x^2 - 3)$$

$$= 24x^4 - 4x^3 - 18x^2 + 15x - 2 + 36x^4 - 12x^3 + 3x^2 + 3x - 3$$
$$= 60x^4 - 16x^3 - 15x^2 + 18x - 5$$

EXAMPLE 54   If $y = (x^2 + 3)^{1/2}(3x + 2)$, find dy/dx.

Solution
$$\frac{dy}{dx} = (x^2 + 3)^{1/2}(3) + (3x + 2)[\tfrac{1}{2}(x^2 + 3)^{-1/2}(2x)]$$

$$= 3(x^2 + 3)^{1/2} + \frac{x(3x + 2)}{(x^2 + 3)^{1/2}} = \frac{3(x^2 + 3) + 3x^2 + 2x}{(x^2 + 3)^{1/2}}$$

$$= \frac{6x^2 + 2x + 9}{(x^2 + 3)^{1/2}}$$

To derive the product formula we return to our four-step procedure. Let

$$y = f(x) \cdot g(x)$$

then

1. $y + \Delta y = f(x + \Delta x) \cdot g(x + \Delta x)$
2. $y + \Delta y - y = f(x + \Delta x) \cdot g(x + \Delta x) - f(x) \cdot g(x)$

Before dividing by Δx, we subtract and then add $f(x + \Delta x) \cdot g(x)$ to the right side of the equation:

$$\Delta y = f(x + \Delta x) \cdot g(x + \Delta x) - f(x + \Delta x) \cdot g(x) + f(x + \Delta x) \cdot g(x) - f(x)g(x)$$

3. $\dfrac{\Delta y}{\Delta x} = f(x + \Delta x)\left[\dfrac{g(x + \Delta x) - g(x)}{\Delta x}\right] + \left[\dfrac{f(x + \Delta x) - f(x)}{\Delta x}\right] \cdot g(x)$

$$4. \ \lim_{\Delta x \to 0} \frac{\Delta y}{\Delta x} = \lim_{\Delta x \to 0} f(x + \Delta x) \left[\frac{g(x + \Delta x) - g(x)}{\Delta x} \right]$$

$$+ \lim_{\Delta x \to 0} \left[\frac{f(x + \Delta x) - f(x)}{\Delta x} \right] g(x)$$

$$\frac{dy}{dx} = f(x)g'(x) + f'(x)g(x)$$

Similarly, the derivative of the quotient of two functions is not the quotient of their derivatives.

Quotient Formula

Let $f(x)$ and $g(x)$ be two functions whose derivatives with respect to x exist and $g(x) \neq 0$. Then

$$\frac{d}{dx} \left[\frac{f(x)}{g(x)} \right] = \frac{g(x)f'(x) - f(x)g'(x)}{[g(x)]^2}$$

In other words, the quotient formula states that **the derivative of a quotient is: the denominator times the derivative of the numerator minus the numerator times the derivative of the denominator, all divided by the denominator squared.**

EXAMPLE 55   If

$$y = \frac{3x - 2}{5x + 3}$$

find dy/dx.

Solution

$$\frac{dy}{dx} = \frac{(5x + 3)(3) - (3x - 2)(5)}{(5x + 3)^2} = \frac{15x + 9 - 15x + 10}{(5x + 3)^2} = \frac{19}{(5x + 3)^2}$$

Notice that this function could be written as a product and its derivative obtained by the use of the product formula. That is,

$$y = \frac{3x - 2}{5x + 3} = (3x - 2)(5x + 3)^{-1}$$

$$\frac{dy}{dx} = (3x - 2)[-1(5x + 3)^{-2}(5)] + (5x + 3)^{-1}(3)$$

$$= -\frac{5(3x - 2)}{(5x + 3)^2} + \frac{3}{5x + 3} = \frac{-5(3x - 2)}{(5x + 3)^2} + \frac{3(5x + 3)}{(5x + 3)^2}$$

$$= \frac{-15x + 10 + 15x + 9}{(5x + 3)^2}$$

$$= \frac{19}{(5x + 3)^2}$$

EXAMPLE 56   If

$$y = \frac{3x^2 + 2x - 1}{2x^2 - 3x + 2}$$

find dy/dx.

Solution

$$\frac{dy}{dx} = \frac{(2x^2 - 3x + 2)(6x + 2) - (3x^2 + 2x - 1)(4x - 3)}{(2x^2 - 3x + 2)^2}$$

$$= \frac{12x^3 - 14x^2 + 6x + 4 - (12x^3 - x^2 - 10x + 3)}{(2x^2 - 3x + 2)^2}$$

$$= \frac{-13x^2 + 16x + 1}{(2x^2 - 3x + 2)^2}$$

EXAMPLE 57   If

$$y = \frac{3x + 4}{(2x - 3)^{1/2}}$$

find dy/dx.

Solution

$$\frac{dy}{dx} = \frac{(2x - 3)^{1/2}(3) - (3x + 4)(\tfrac{1}{2})(2x - 3)^{-1/2}(2)}{2x - 3}$$

$$= \frac{3(2x - 3) - (3x + 4)}{(2x - 3)^{3/2}} = \frac{3x - 13}{(2x - 3)^{3/2}}$$

Exercise Set 9.7

A Multiply the following functions and then obtain their derivatives by previous formulas. Check your results by using the product formula.

1. $y = (3x + 2)(x - 3)$ **2.** $y = (2x - 3)(x + 2)$

3. $y = (4x - 3)(2x + 1)$ **4.** $y = (3x - 2)(2x - 1)$

5. $y = (5x + 3)(2x - 3)$ **6.** $y = (2x - 3)(2x + 3)$

7. $y = (x^2 - 1)(x^2 + 1)$ **8.** $y = (3x^2 - 2)(3x^2 + 2)$

9. $y = (x^2 + x + 1)(x - 1)$ **10.** $y = (x^2 - x + 1)(x + 1)$

Find the derivatives of the following functions by using the product or the quotient formula.

11. $y = \dfrac{5}{2x - 3}$ **12.** $y = \dfrac{3x - 2}{5}$

13. $y = \dfrac{3x + 2}{2x - 3}$ **14.** $y = \dfrac{3x + 4}{5x - 1}$

15. $y = (3x^2 - 2x + 1)(4x + 5)$ **16.** $y = (4x^2 - 3x + 2)(3x - 2)$

17. $y = \dfrac{5}{x^2 + 1}$

18. $y = \dfrac{7}{2x^2 - 1}$

19. $y = \dfrac{3x - 2}{x^2 - 3}$

20. $y = \dfrac{2x + 3}{x^2 - 2}$

B Find dy/dx for the following functions.

21. $y = \dfrac{2x + 5}{(x - 1)^{1/2}}$

22. $y = \dfrac{x + 3}{(x - 1)^{1/3}}$

23. $y = (3x + 2)^{1/2}(2x - 3)$

24. $y = (x^2 + x - 1)(3x + 2)^{1/3}$

25. $y = (x + 2)(x - 1) - \dfrac{5}{x - 3}$

26. $y = 3x^2 - 2x + \dfrac{6}{x - 2}$

27. $y = 2x^{-2} + \dfrac{3}{x - 2}$

28. $y = (x^2 + 3x + 2)(x - 1)^2$

29. $y = 5(x - 2)^{1/2} + \dfrac{4}{x + 1}$

30. $y = (3x + 2)^{1/2}(2x + 7)$

31. $y = (3x - 2)^2(x + 2)^3$

32. $y = (2x - 3)^4(3x + 2)^3$

33. $y = 3(2x + 5)^3 + 2x(3x - 5)^2$

34. $y = \dfrac{(2x - 3)^2}{(3x + 2)^3}$

35. $y = \dfrac{(2x^2 - 1)^2}{(x^3 + 1)^2}$

C **36.** Find the equation in slope-intercept form of the tangent line to the graph of

$$y = \frac{5}{(x^2 - 2x)^{1/3}} \quad \text{at} \quad (-2, \tfrac{5}{2})$$

Business **37. Average Cost.** The average cost, $\bar{C}(x)$, is found by dividing the total cost by the number of items:

$$\bar{C}(x) = \frac{C(x)}{x}$$

a. If $C(x) = 7x^2 - 3x + 10$, find the average cost.
b. Find the marginal cost, $C'(x)$.
c. Find the marginal average cost, $\bar{C}'(x)$.
d. Find $\bar{C}'(5)$.

Economics **38. Demand Functions.** A demand function is given by

$$D(x) = \frac{4000(25 - x)}{x^2} \quad (1 \le x \le 25)$$

a. Find the marginal demand function.
b. Find the marginal demand when $x = 2$.
c. What is the demand when $x = 2$?

Life Sciences **39. Rate of Change of Drug Concentration.** The concentration of a drug in a person's bloodstream t hours after injection is

$$C(t) = \frac{t}{16t^2 + 10t + 63}$$

a. Find the rate of change of the concentration.
b. What is the concentration after 1 hour?

c. What is the rate of change of the concentration after 1 hour?

d. What is $\lim\limits_{t \to \infty} C(t)$?

Social Sciences   **40. Learning Functions.** A learning function is given as

$$L = \frac{80t}{90t + 85}$$

a. Find the instantaneous rate of learning.

b. Find the rate of learning at $t = 1$.

c. Find the rate of learning at $t = 8$.

8 Summary and Review

Review the following definitions and formulas to ensure that you understand and can use them.

Slope of function

$$\frac{d}{dx}[Cx^n] = Cnx^{n-1}$$

Derivative at a point

$$\frac{dC}{dx} = 0$$

Instantaneous rate of change

Limit of a function

$$\frac{d}{dx}[Cf(x)] = C \cdot \frac{d}{dx}[f(x)]$$

Continuous function

Velocity

$$\frac{d}{dx}[f(x) + g(x)] = \frac{d}{dx}[f(x)] + \frac{d}{dx}[g(x)]$$

Marginal cost function

$$\frac{dy}{dx} = \frac{dy}{du} \cdot \frac{du}{dx}$$

Marginal demand function

Marginal profit function

$$\frac{d}{dx}[f(x)]^n = n[f(x)]^{n-1}f'(x)$$

Marginal supply function

$$\frac{d}{dx}[f(x)g(x)] = f(x)g'(x) + g(x)f'(x)$$

Sensitivity

Difference quotient

$$\frac{d}{dx}\left[\frac{f(x)}{g(x)}\right] = \frac{g(x)f'(x) - f(x)g'(x)}{[g(x)]^2}$$

Review Exercise Set 9.8

A   Find dy/dx for the following functions.

1. $y = 7x^2 - 3x + 2$

2. $y = 10x^2 - 5x + 3$

3. $y = 3x^2 - x^3 + 2x^4$

4. $y = 5 - 3x + 6x^2$

5. $y = 5x^3 - 2x^{-1}$

6. $y = 4x^3 - 6x^{-2}$

7. $y = 6x^4 - 5x^{-2} + 3$ **8.** $y = 7x^{-3} + 2x^2 - 3$

9. $y = (3x + 7)(2x - 5)$ **10.** $y = (4x + 5)(3x - 2)$

11. $y = \dfrac{2x + 5}{3x - 2}$ **12.** $y = \dfrac{4x + 3}{2x - 3}$

13. $y = (4x^2 - 2)(3x + 2)$ **14.** $y = (5x^2 + 2)(3x + 5)$

15. $y = \dfrac{3x - 7}{2x + 3}$ **16.** $y = \dfrac{4x - 5}{3x + 4}$

17. $y = 3(2x + 5)^3$ **18.** $y = 4(3x - 2)^2$

19. $y = 5(3x - 2)^2$ **20.** $y = 6(2x + 3)^3$

B   *Find dy/dx for the following functions.*

21. $y = 2x^{1/2} + 3x^2$ **22.** $y = 3x^{1/3} - 5x^3$

23. $y = 2x^{1/2} - 4x^{-1/2}$ **24.** $y = 3x^{1/3} - 3x^{-1/3}$

25. $y = 4x^{-1/2} - 6x^{-2/3}$ **26.** $y = 9x^{-2/3} + 8x^{-3/4}$

27. $y = (3x + 5)(2x - 3)^2$ **28.** $y = (3x - 2)^2(2x + 3)$

29. $y = 4(2x^2 + x - 1)^{1/2}$ **30.** $y = 9(3x^2 - x + 1)^{1/3}$

31. $y = 4x^{1/2}(3x - 2)^2$ **32.** $y = 6x^{-1/2}(4x - 3)^2$

33. $y = \dfrac{4x^2}{(2x - 3)^2}$ **34.** $y = \dfrac{3x^2 - 2}{(2x + 3)^2}$

35. $y = 3x^2(3x - 5)^2 - 2x$ **36.** $y = 4x^2(3x - 5)^3 - 4x^2$

37. $y = (3x^2 + 2x + 5)(2x + 5)^2$ **38.** $y = (4x^2 - 3x + 2)(3x - 2)^2$

39. $y = \dfrac{3x^2 + 2x + 1}{3x - 2}$ **40.** $y = \dfrac{4x^2 - 3x + 2}{2x - 3}$

C   **41.** Find the equation in slope-intercept form of the tangent to the graph of

$$y = 6(3x^2 - 2x)^3 \quad \text{at } (1, 6)$$

Business   **42. Cost Functions.** If a cost function is given as

$$C(x) = 4(3x - 2)^2$$

     a. Find the marginal cost, $C'(x)$.
     b. Find the average cost function $\bar{C}(x)$.
     c. Find the marginal average cost $\bar{C}'(x)$.
     d. Find $\bar{C}'(3)$.

Economics   **43. Demand Functions.** A demand function is given as

$$D(x) = \frac{6000(20 - x)}{x^2} \quad (1 \le x \le 20)$$

     a. Find the marginal demand function.
     b. Find the demand when $x = 2$.
     c. Find the marginal demand when $x = 2$.

Life Sciences   **44. Drug Concentration.** The concentration of a drug in a person's bloodstream t hours after injection is

$$C(t) = \frac{t}{18t^2 + 8t + 61}$$

a. Find the instantaneous rate of change of concentration.

b. What is the concentration after 2 hours?

c. What is the instantaneous rate of change of concentration after 2 hours?

d. What is $\lim\limits_{t \to \infty} C(t)$?

Social Sciences   **45. Learning Functions.** Find the instantaneous rate of learning for the learning function

$$L = 32(3x - 1)^{2/3} \qquad \tfrac{1}{3} \text{ hour} \le x \le 10 \text{ hours}$$

Find the instantaneous rate of learning at the end of

a. $\tfrac{2}{3}$ hour   **b.** $\tfrac{28}{3}$ hours.

10

Additional
Derivative Topics

he previous chapter introduced the use of calculus to study change. Historically, the first application of calculus was to study motion—motion of the planets, motion of projectiles, motion of particles, motion of vehicles. Motion is an example of continuous change, but it is not the only example. Other changing quantities include growth, supply, demand, vibration, decay, pressure, inflation, pollution, and so forth. Some changes are slow while others are very, very fast. In this chapter we continue the study of the derivative and particularly the applications of the derivative to changing quantities.

1 Implicit Differentiation

The functions whose derivatives we have obtained have been given in the form

$$y = f(x)$$

and are called **explicit functions.** Some relations of the form $f(x, y) = 0$ are difficult or even impossible to solve explicitly for y in terms of x; yet the relation may define y as a function of x. In such cases we may wish to find the derivative of y with respect to x without solving for y in terms of x. We introduce in this section **implicit differentiation,** which allows us to do this.

Suppose we wish to find dy/dx for $4x^3 + y - 3 = 0$. We can solve this function for y in terms of x as

$$y = -4x^3 + 3$$

The derivative is found by methods of Chapter 9 to be

$$\frac{dy}{dx} = -12x^2$$

Sometimes it may be difficult or even impossible to express the relation as an **explicit function,** and yet the relation may still be such that it defines one or more functions of x. Such a function is called an **implicit function.** The derivative of an implicit function may be found by differentiating both sides of the equation. Let's differentiate with respect to x both sides of the equation

$$4x^3 + y - 3 = 0$$

$$\frac{d}{dx}(4x^3 + y - 3) = \frac{d0}{dx}$$

By using the fact that the derivative of a sum is the sum of the derivatives, we find

$$\frac{d}{dx}(4x^3) + \frac{dy}{dx} + \frac{d}{dx}(-3) = 0$$

$$12x^2 + \frac{dy}{dx} + 0 = 0$$

Solving for dy/dx gives

$$\frac{dy}{dx} = -12x^2$$

Note that this result is the same as that obtained by differentiating the explicit function. The procedure for finding a derivative by implicit differentiation is summarized below:

Procedure for the Implicit Differentiation of $f(x, y) = 0$

1. Differentiate both sides of the equation with respect to x.
2. Solve for the derivative, dy/dx, in terms of x and y.

Many times in implicit differentiation we encounter terms such as y^3. How do we differentiate such terms, or what is $\frac{d}{dx}(y^3)$? To take the derivative with respect to x of y^3, we use the chain rule, When y is a function of x, recall that

$$\frac{d}{dx}(y^3) = \frac{d}{dy}(y^3)\left(\frac{dy}{dx}\right)$$

Thus,

$$\frac{d}{dx}(y^3) = 3y^2\left(\frac{dy}{dx}\right)$$

In general,

$$\frac{d}{dx}(y^n) = ny^{n-1}\left(\frac{dy}{dx}\right)$$

EXAMPLE 1 Find dy/dx for the function defined implicitly by

$$y^2 - x^2 - 3 = 0$$

Solution Differentiate both sides with respect to x to obtain

$$\frac{d}{dx}(y^2 - x^2 - 3) = \frac{d0}{dx}$$

Using the theorem that the derivative of a sum is the sum of the derivatives gives

$$\frac{d}{dx}(y^2) + \frac{d}{dx}(-x^2) + \frac{d}{dx}(-3) = 0$$

Now we use the differentiation formulas to obtain

$$2y\frac{dy}{dx} - 2x + 0 = 0$$

Solving for $\frac{dy}{dx}$ gives $\frac{dy}{dx} = \frac{x}{y}$.

Note that the derivative found in Example 1 is obtained as a function of both x and y. In order to take the derivative of y with respect to x, y must be considered as a function of x. If the original relation is solved for y^2, we obtain $y^2 = x^2 + 3$. Solving for y then gives

$$y = \sqrt{x^2 + 3} \qquad \text{or} \qquad y = -\sqrt{x^2 + 3}$$

Both of these expressions define y as a function of x; hence, there are two choices for y in this relation. If the first choice, $y = \sqrt{x^2 + 3}$, is chosen,

$$\frac{dy}{dx} = \frac{1}{2}(x^2 + 3)^{-1/2}2x$$

$$= \frac{x}{\sqrt{x^2 + 3}} = \frac{x}{y}$$

If the second choice, $y = -\sqrt{x^2 + 3}$, is chosen,

$$\frac{dy}{dx} = -\frac{1}{2}(x^2 + 3)^{-1/2}2x$$

$$= \frac{x}{-\sqrt{x^2 + 3}} = \frac{x}{y}$$

When the value of the derivative at a point on the graph is desired, the coordinates of the point are substituted for x and y in the expression for the derivative. **Caution!** Be sure that the coordinates satisfy the equation, that is, be sure that the point is on the graph before substituting the coordinates of the point for x and y. Remember that the value of the derivative at a point on the graph of a function is the slope of the tangent line to the graph at that point and is also defined to be the slope of the function at that point. The symbol

$$\left.\frac{dy}{dx}\right|_{(a,\,b)} \qquad \text{or} \qquad y'|_{(a,b)}$$

is used to denote the evaluation of the derivative at the point (a, b).

EXAMPLE 2 Find dy/dx and the slope of the function

$$y^3 + y + 3x^2 + 2x + 1 = 0 \quad \text{at } (-1, -1)$$

Solution Differentiating both sides with respect to x gives

$$\frac{d}{dx}(y^3 + y + 3x^2 + 2x + 1) = 0$$

$$3y^2\frac{dy}{dx} + \frac{dy}{dx} + 6x + 2 = 0$$

$$3y^2\frac{dy}{dx} + \frac{dy}{dx} = -6x - 2$$

$$(3y^2 + 1)\frac{dy}{dx} = -6x - 2$$

$$\frac{dy}{dx} = \frac{-6x - 2}{3y^2 + 1}$$

By substituting $(-1, -1)$,

$$\left.\frac{dy}{dx}\right|_{(-1,\,-1)} = \frac{-6(-1) - 2}{3(-1)^2 + 1} = \frac{6 - 2}{3 + 1} = \frac{4}{4} = 1$$

EXAMPLE 3 Find dy/dx and the slope of

$$y^2 - 3xy - 7 = 0 \quad \text{at } (-2, 1)$$

Solution Differentiate both sides with respect to x but remember to use the product formula on $-3xy$.

$$\frac{d}{dx}(y^2 - 3xy - 7) = 0$$

$$\frac{d}{dx}(y^2) - \frac{d}{dx}(-3xy) + \frac{d}{dx}(-7) = 0$$

$$2y\frac{dy}{dx} - 3\left(x\frac{dy}{dx} + y\right) + 0 = 0$$

$$2y\frac{dy}{dx} - 3x\frac{dy}{dx} - 3y = 0$$

$$(2y - 3x)\frac{dy}{dx} = 3y$$

$$\frac{dy}{dx} = \frac{3y}{2y - 3x}$$

$$\frac{dy}{dx}\Big|_{(-2,\,1)} = \frac{3(1)}{2(1) - 3(-2)} = \frac{3}{2 + 6} = \frac{3}{8}$$

EXAMPLE 4 Find dy/dx and the equations of the tangent lines to the graph of

$$xy^2 - y + 4x^2 + 2 = 0$$

at the points where $x = -1$.

Solution Differentiate implicitly to obtain

$$\frac{d}{dx}(xy^2 - y + 4x^2 + 2) = \frac{d0}{dx}$$

$$\frac{d}{dx}(xy^2) + \frac{d}{dx}(-y) + \frac{d}{dx}(4x^2) + \frac{d(2)}{dx} = 0$$

$$x\left(2y\frac{dy}{dx}\right) + y^2 - \frac{dy}{dx} + 8x + 0 = 0$$

$$2xy\frac{dy}{dx} - \frac{dy}{dx} = -8x - y^2$$

$$(2xy - 1)\frac{dy}{dx} = -8x - y^2$$

$$\frac{dy}{dx} = \frac{-8x - y^2}{2xy - 1}$$

To evaluate the derivative where $x = -1$, we need to find the value or values of y when $x = -1$. We substitute $x = -1$ into the original equation to find y.

$$xy^2 - y + 4x^2 + 2 = 0$$
$$-1y^2 - y + 4(-1)^2 + 2 = 0$$
$$-y^2 - y + 4 + 2 = 0$$
$$y^2 + y - 6 = 0$$
$$(y + 3)(y - 2) = 0$$

Thus,

$$y = -3 \quad \text{or} \quad y = 2$$

Hence, there are two points on the graph where $x = -1$: $(-1, -3)$ and $(-1, 2)$.

To find the equation of the tangent to the graph at $(-1, -3)$, we need the slope at $(-1, -3)$.

$$m = \frac{dy}{dx}\Big|_{(-1, -3)} = \frac{-8(-1) - (-3)^2}{2(-1)(-3) - 1} = \frac{8 - 9}{5} = -\frac{1}{5}$$

We substitute into the point-slope form using $m = -\frac{1}{5}$ and $(x_1, y_1) = (-1, -3)$.

$$y - y_1 = m(x - x_1)$$
$$y + 3 = -\frac{1}{5}(x + 1)$$
$$y = -\frac{1}{5}x - \frac{16}{5}$$

Similarly, to find the equation of the tangent to the graph at $(-1, 2)$, we need the slope at $(-1, 2)$.

$$m = \frac{dy}{dx}\Big|_{(-1, 2)} = \frac{-8(-1) - (2)^2}{2(-1)(2) - 1} = \frac{8 - 4}{-4 - 1} = \frac{4}{-5} = -\frac{4}{5}$$

Substituting into the point-slope form gives the equation of the tangent at $(-1, 2)$.

$$y - y_1 = m(x - x_1)$$
$$y - 2 = -\frac{4}{5}(x + 1)$$
$$y = -\frac{4}{5}x + \frac{6}{5}$$

Exercise Set 10.1

A *Find dy/dx by implicit differentiation. Solve for the explicit function $y = f(x)$, and then differentiate to check your results.*

1. $y - 4x^2 + 3x = 0$

2. $x - y + 3x^3 = 0$

3. $x + 2y + 3x^2 = 0$

4. $3x - 2y + 5x^3 = 0$

5. $4x^2 - 3x + 7y = 2$

6. $9y - 3x + 4x^3 - 2 = 0$

7. $x^2 - 3x + 2 + 5y = 0$

8. $x^2 + 4x - 3y = 7$

9. $x^2 - 3x^3 + x - 2y = 0$

10. $2x^2 - 4x - 7y = 5$

11. $3xy - 4x^2 = 0$

12. $4xy + 5x^2 = 0$

13. $2x^2y - 3x + 5 = 0$

14. $3x^2y + 4x^2 - 2 = 0$

15. $y + 3xy - 4 = 0$

16. $y + 2xy - 3x^3 = 0$

17. $y + 2x^2y + 3x = 0$

18. $y + 3x^2y - 4x = 0$

19. $y - 3x^2y - 2x = 0$

20. $y - 4x^2y + 5x = 0$

B *Find dy/dx by implicit differentiation.*

21. $y^2 + y - 3x = 0$

22. $y^3 + y + 4x = 0$

23. $3y^2 - y + 4x^2 = 0$

24. $4y^2 - 2y + 3x = 0$

25. $y^2 + xy - 4x = 5$

26. $y^2 + 3xy - x^3 = 4$

27. $3xy^2 - 2y - 3 = 0$

28. $4x^2y^2 - 3y + 6 = 0$

29. $2xy^2 - 3xy + x^3 = 0$

30. $3xy^2 - 2xy + 4x^2 = 0$

C *Find the equation(s) of the tangent(s) to the graphs at the indicated value of x.*

31. $3xy - x - 2 = 0$ at $x = 1$

32. $y^2 + 2y - x = 0$ at $x = 0$

33. $y + 3xy - 7 = 0$ at $x = 2$

34. $y^2 - 2xy - 8 = 0$ at $x = -1$

35. $x^3y + 3x^2 + 4 = 0$ at $x = -2$

Find dy/dx and the value of the slope of the graph at the indicated point.

36. $(1 + y)^3 + y = 2x + 7$ at $(1, 1)$

37. $(y - 2)^2 + x = y$ at $(2, 3)$

38. $(x + y)^2 + 3y = -3$ at $(1, -1)$

39. $(2x + y)^2 + 2x = -1$ at $(-1, 3)$

40. $(x + 2y)^3 - x^2 + 8 = 0$ at $(3, -1)$

Draw the graphs of the following relations. Find dy/dx and the equation of the tangent line at the indicated point.

41. $x^2 - y^2 = 9$ at $(5, 4)$

42. $x^2 + y^2 = 25$ at $(4, 3)$

43. $4x^2 + y^2 = 40$ at $(3, 2)$

44. $x^2 - 9y^2 = 144$ at $(15, 3)$

45. $xy = 8$ at $(4, 2)$

Business **46. Instantaneous Change in Sales.** Suppose a company's sales S, in hundreds of thousands of dollars, is related to the amount x, in thousands of dollars spent on training, by

$$Sx + S = 900 + 40x$$

a. Find dS/dx, the instantaneous rate of change of S.

b. Find $\left. \dfrac{dS}{dx} \right|_{(1, 470)}$

Economics **47. Instantaneous Demand.** If x is the number of items that can be sold at a price of p dollars in the demand equation

$$x^3 + p^3 = 1200$$

find dp/dx.

48. Redo exercise 47 for the demand equation

$$p^3 - 3p^2 - x + 300 = 0$$

Life Sciences **49. Pollution.** Suppose that pollution P, in parts per million, x yards away is given by

$$P + 2xP + x^2P = 600$$

Find the instantaneous rate of pollution 10 yards away.

50. Learning Functions. A learning function L is given in terms of t hours as

$$L^2 - 256t = 0$$

  a. Find the instantaneous rate of learning.
  b. Find the instantaneous rate of learning at the end of 1 hour.
  c. Find the instantaneous rate of learning at the end of 9 hours.

2 Derivatives and Related Rates

> In this section we define **related rates,** outline a procedure for finding related rates, and apply such related rates to physical quantities. For example, the rate of increase of the radius of a balloon is related to the rate of pumping helium into the balloon. If the bottom of a ladder is pulled from the wall, the rate of descent of the top is related to the rate at which the bottom is pulled away.

Often two or more variables may be differentiable functions of another variable, such as time, and yet the explicit functions may not be given. Suppose x and y are related by the equation $x^2 + y^2 = 36$ and that both x and y are functions of t. If we differentiate both sides with respect to t, we obtain

$$\frac{d}{dt}(x^2 + y^2) = \frac{d}{dt}(36)$$

$$2x\frac{dx}{dt} + 2y\frac{dy}{dt} = 0$$

Since dx/dt and dy/dt are related by an equation, they are called **related rates.** The equation can be used to find the value of one of the rates when values are known for x and y and the other rate.

A procedure to help solve problems involving rates is given in the following box.

Procedure for Solving Related Rate Problems

  1. Identify carefully all the variables involved. This step is one of the most important steps in the procedure and is the one that is most often neglected or only partly done.
  2. Relate the variables by some equation that holds generally and not just at some particular time. A sketch will often help find this equation.
  3. List all the rates involved in the problem, those that are known and those that are to be found.
  4. If the variables are functions of time, then differentiate with respect to time both sides of the equation relating the variables.
  5. Substitute the values of the known rates and the known variables at the given time, and solve for the unknown rate.

EXAMPLE 5   Given $x^2 + y^2 = 169$ and $dy/dt = 2$, find

$$\frac{dx}{dt} \quad \text{at (5, 12)}$$

Solution   The equation relating the variables is

$$x^2 + y^2 = 169$$

The rate dy/dt is known, and the rate dx/dt is to be found. Differentiate both sides of the given equation with respect to t:

$$\frac{d}{dt}(x^2 + y^2) = \frac{d}{dt}(169)$$

$$2x\frac{dx}{dt} + 2y\frac{dy}{dt} = 0$$

Substitute $x = 5$, $y = 12$, and $dy/dt = 2$:

$$2(5)\frac{dx}{dt} + 2(12)(2) = 0$$

$$10\frac{dx}{dt} + 48 = 0$$

$$\frac{dx}{dt} = -\frac{48}{10} = -\frac{24}{5}$$

EXAMPLE 6   A particle travels along the curve $y = x^3$ in such a way that $dx/dt = 3$ centimeters per second. How fast is y changing
a. when $x = 1$ centimeter?   **b.** when $x = 2$ centimeters?

Solution   The variables and the equation are given: That is, $y = x^3$ and $dx/dt = 3$ are given, and dy/dt is unknown. Differentiate both sides of the equation with respect to t:

$$\frac{dy}{dt} = \frac{d}{dt}(x^3)$$

$$= 3x^2\frac{dx}{dt}$$

a. $\dfrac{dy}{dt} = 3(1)^2(3) = 9$ cm/sec   when $x = 1$

b. $\dfrac{dy}{dt} = 3(2)^2(3) = 36$ cm/sec   when $x = 2$

EXAMPLE 7   Suppose the radius of a circular oil slick is increasing at the rate of 12 yards per hour. Find the rate at which the area is increasing when $r = 40$ yards.

Solution Let r = the radius and A = the area. We know that the area of a circle is $A = \pi r^2$, that $dr/dt = 12$, and that dA/dt is unknown. Then

$$\frac{dA}{dt} = \frac{d}{dt}(\pi r^2)$$

$$= 2\pi r \frac{dr}{dt}$$

$$= 2\pi(40)(12) = 960\pi \ \text{yd}^2/\text{hr} \qquad \text{when } r = 40 \text{ yd}$$

EXAMPLE 8 A toy manufacturer has found that its cost, revenue, and profit functions can be expressed as functions of production. If x is the production (number) of toys produced in a week, and C, R, and P represent cost, revenue, and profit, respectively, then

$$C = 6000 + 2x$$

$$R = 20x - \frac{x^2}{2000}$$

$$P = R - C$$

Suppose production is increasing at the rate of 200 toys per week from a production level of 1000 toys. Find the rate of increase in

a. cost.　　**b.** revenue.　　**c.** profit.

Solution Since production is changing with respect to time, production must be a function of time. Hence, cost, revenue, and profit are all functions of time. To find their rate of increase, we differentiate each with respect to time.

a.　$C = 6000 + 2x$

$$\frac{dC}{dt} = \frac{d}{dt}(6000) + \frac{d}{dt}(2x)$$

$$= 0 + 2\frac{dx}{dt}$$

Since $dx/dt = 200$,

$$\frac{dC}{dt} = 2(200) = \$400 \text{ per week}$$

Thus, cost is increasing at a rate of $400 per week.

b.　$R = 20x - \dfrac{x^2}{2000}$

$$\frac{dR}{dt} = \frac{d}{dt}(20x) - \frac{d}{dt}\left(\frac{x^2}{2000}\right)$$

$$= 20\frac{dx}{dt} - \left(\frac{x}{1000}\right)\frac{dx}{dt}$$

$$= 20(200) - \tfrac{1000}{1000}(200)$$

$$= 3800$$

Thus, revenue is increasing at a rate of $3,800 per week.

c. $P = R - C$

$$\frac{dP}{dt} = \frac{dR}{dt} - \frac{dC}{dt}$$

$$= 3800 - 400$$

$$= 3400$$

Thus, profit is increasing at a rate of $3,400 per week.

EXAMPLE 9   The amount of time A, in minutes, required to perform an operation on an assembly line is given as a function of the number of trials x, by the equation

$$A = 9 + 9x^{-1/2}$$

Find dA/dt if $dx/dt = 4$ when $x = 25$.

Solution $A = 9 + 9x^{-1/2}$

$$\frac{dA}{dt} = \frac{d}{dt}(9) + \frac{d}{dt}(9x^{-1/2})$$

$$= 0 + 9\frac{d}{dt}(x^{-1/2})$$

$$= 9(-\tfrac{1}{2})x^{-3/2}\frac{dx}{dt}$$

$$= -\tfrac{9}{2}(25)^{-3/2}(4)$$

$$= -\tfrac{9}{2}\cdot\tfrac{1}{125}(4) = -\tfrac{18}{125}$$

Exercise Set 10.2

A   *For the following relations assume that x and y are functions of t. Find dy/dt given that dx/dt = 3 when x = 2.*

1. $x + y = 3$

2. $2x + y = 5$

3. $3x - 2y = 4$

4. $4x - 3y = 2$

5. $y - 2\sqrt{x} = 0$

6. $x^2 - 2y = 0$

7. $y - 3\sqrt{x} = 0$

8. $y - 2\sqrt[3]{x} = 0$

9. $y - x^2 = 4$

10. $y - 2x^2 + x = 0$

B   **11.** $xy = 4$

12. $3xy = 1$

13. $x + xy = 6$

14. $2x - xy = 4$

15. $y + xy = 5$

16. $y - 2xy = 3$

17. $y - xy + x^2 = 5$

18. $y + 2xy - x^2 = 3$

19. $y + x^2y - 3x = 2$

20. $y - x^2y - 4x = 4$

C   **21.** A particle travels along the curve $y = \sqrt{x}$ so that $dx/dt = 4$ centimeters per second. How fast is y changing when
   a. $x = 2$?   **b.** $x = 9$?

22. The radius of a circle is increasing at the rate of 2 centimeters per second. At what rate is the area of the circle increasing when the radius is
    a. 10 centimeters? **b.** 15 centimeters?

23. The length of a rectangle is 4 times the width. If the length is increasing at the rate of 8 centimeters per second, how fast is the area changing when the width is
    a. 1 centimeter? **b.** 2 centimeters?

24. The edges of a cube are increasing at the rate of 2 centimeters per second. At what rate is the volume changing when the edge is 3 centimeters?

25. At what rate is the surface area of the cube in exercise 24 increasing when the edge is 3 centimeters?

Business

26. **Revenue Functions.** Suppose the revenue from the sale of x stereos is given by $R(x) = 500x - x^2$ and the cost is given by $C(x) = 2000 + 30x$. If the company is selling six stereos per day, then, when 50 stereos are sold, find
    a. the rate of change of revenue.
    b. the rate of change of cost.
    c. the rate of change of profit.

Economics

27. **Demand Equations.** For the demand equation $p^2 + p + 3x = 39$, find dp/dt if $dx/dt = 3$ when $p = 2$.

Life Sciences

28. **Pollution.** Oil is leaking from a tanker and has formed a circular oil slick 3 centimeters thick. To estimate the rate of leakage, the radius was measured and found to be 100 meters and increasing at the rate of 5 centimeters per minute. Assume that the depth is constant.
    a. Use these results to find the rate of leakage.
    b. After finding the rate of leakage, assume that the rate of leakage is constant and find how fast the radius is changing 5 hours after the leakage began.
    c. Find how fast the radius is changing 20 hours after the leakage began.

29. **Pollution.** Suppose the oil slick in exercise 28 does not have constant depth but instead varies linearly from 3 centimeters at the point of leakage to 1 centimeter at the outside edge of the slick. If the tanker is leaking at a rate of 60π liters per minute, how fast is the radius of the slick increasing 5 hours after the leaking began?

Social Sciences

30. **Learning Function.** A learning function is given as required time R after x tries.
    $$R = 7 + 7x^{-1/2}$$
    Find dR/dt if $dx/dt = 5$ when $x = 49$.

How Derivatives Are Related to Graphs

We know that if a function has a derivative at a point, then the function is continuous at that point. The theory that is developed in this section concerns continuous functions. Recall that the slope of a curve at a point is the slope of the tangent line to the curve at the point. The slope can be found by evaluating the first derivative of the function at the point. This idea is useful in sketching the graphs of complicated functions. In this section we examine where a function is increasing, where it is decreasing, and where it has a maximum or a minimum. All of these ideas are helpful as we draw the graphs of functions.

We note that the tangent line to a curve at a point is horizontal when the slope is zero—that is, when the first derivative evaluated at the point is zero. When the first derivative of the function $y = f(x)$ is positive at a point, the slope of the tangent line to the curve is a positive number, and the function is said to be **increasing.** See Figure 10.1(a). That is, y increases as x increases. Similarly if at a point on the graph the slope of the tangent line is negative [that is, $f'(x)$ at the point is negative], the function is said to be **decreasing.** See Figure 10.1(b). This means that y decreases as x increases. This discussion is summarized below:

Increasing and Decreasing Functions

If $f'(x_1) > 0$ for all x_1 in an interval, then the function defined by $y = f(x)$ is **increasing** for all x_1 in the interval. If $f'(x_2) < 0$ for all x_2 in an interval, then the function is **decreasing** for all x_2 in the interval.

Figure 10.1

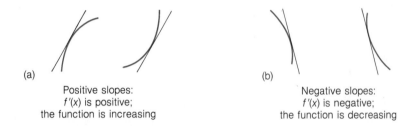

(a)

Positive slopes:
$f'(x)$ is positive;
the function is increasing

(b)

Negative slopes:
$f'(x)$ is negative;
the function is decreasing

Thus, a function is increasing (the graph is rising) when its derivative is positive and decreasing (the graph is falling) when its derivative is negative. In general to change from positive to negative or from negative to positive, $f'(x)$ must assume the value of 0.

EXAMPLE 10 Determine the intervals in which the function is increasing or decreasing, find where $f'(x) = 0$, and sketch of graph of

$$y = f(x) = x^3 + 3x^2 - 9x + 3$$

Solution Now $f'(x) = 3x^2 + 6x - 9$. If $f'(x) > 0$, the graph is increasing; and if $f'(x) < 0$, the graph is decreasing. As stated, to change from positive to negative or from negative to positive, usually $f'(x)$ must assume the value of 0. Thus, we examine $f'(x) = 0$.

$$3x^2 + 6x - 9 = 3(x + 3)(x - 1) = 0$$

$f'(x) = 0$ only when $x = -3$ or $x = 1$. Consider the set of all x's as the union of five disjoint sets: $x < -3$, $x = -3$, $-3 < x < 1$, $x = 1$, and $x > 1$. At $x = -3$ and at $x = 1$ the slope of the graph is 0. The function is either increasing or decreasing for all $x < -3$. It cannot do both because there are no values of x in the set $x < -3$ for which the first derivative is 0. It is easy to determine whether or not the function is increasing or decreasing throughout this interval: merely substitute any value of x in the interval; for example, substitute $x = -5$. Now

$$f'(-5) = 3(-5)^2 + 6(-5) - 9 = 36$$

Since the derivative is positive at x = −5, the derivative is positive at all x < −3, and the function is increasing in this interval.

Select x = 0 as a point in the interval −3 < x < 1. At x = 0, f'(0) = −9; thus, the function is decreasing in the interval −3 < x < 1. Select x = 2 as a point in the interval x > 1. At x = 2,

$$f'(2) = 3(2)^2 + 6(2) - 9 = 15$$

and the function is increasing in the interval x > 1.

The table below shows selected ordered pairs of (x, y). It is not necessary to find a large number of ordered pairs in order to sketch the graph because we know where the graph is increasing and decreasing.

x	−5	−3	0	1	3
y	−2	30	3	−2	30

The graph, as sketched in Figure 10.2, is increasing when x < −3 and when x > 1, and decreasing for −3 < x < 1.

Figure 10.2

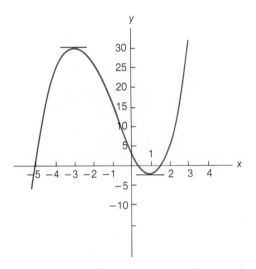

At the point (−3, 30) in Figure 10.2 the tangent line to the curve is parallel to the x-axis, and the functional value at x = −3 is larger than at other nearby points on the curve. The function is said to have a **relative maximum** at (−3, 30). Note the word *relative*. The function does not have an **absolute maximum** at x = −3 because there are larger values of the function, namely, at x's where x > 3.

The absolute maximum is the largest value that a function attains. A relative maximum is the largest value the function attains in the immediate neighborhood of a point.

In a similar manner, the function has a relative minimum at x = 1. Again, this is not an absolute minimum because the function assumes smaller values for x < −5.

<table>
<tr><td>

Relative
Maximum and
Relative
Minimum

</td><td>

$f(c)$ is a *relative maximum* if there exists an interval, $a < c < b$, such that

$$f(x) \leq f(c) \qquad \text{for all x in } a < x < b$$

$f(c)$ is a *relative minimum* if there exists an interval, $a < c < b$, such that

$$f(x) \geq f(c) \qquad \text{for all x in } a < x < b$$

</td></tr>
</table>

Note the graph in Figure 10.3. The points where x has each of the values c_1, c_2, c_3, c_4, c_5, and c_6 are important in drawing the graph. For this reason they are called **critical points.**

Figure 10.3

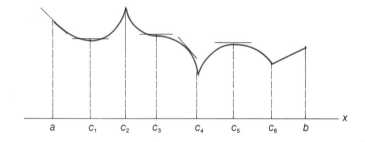

<table>
<tr><td>

Critical Points

</td><td>

The critical points $(c, f(c))$ on the graph of a function $y = f(x)$ are points for which $f'(c) = 0$ or for which $f'(c)$ does not exist.

</td></tr>
</table>

On the graph illustrated in Figure 10.3, relative minima occur at $x = c_1$, $x = c_4$, and $x = c_6$. Relative maxima occur at $x = c_2$ and $x = c_5$. We will discuss later what occurs at the other critical points.

EXAMPLE 11   Find all critical points for

$$y = 7x^2 - 14x + 3$$

Solution   Critical points occur where the derivative is 0 or does not exist. To find the critical points we first compute the derivative:

$$\frac{dy}{dx} = 14x - 14$$

Note that the derivative exists for all real values of x; hence, the only critical value occurs when the derivative is 0:

$$0 = 14x - 14$$

By solving this equation we obtain x = 1. When x = 1,

$$y = 7(1)^2 - 14(1) + 3 = -4$$

The only critical point for this function is (1, −4).

Relative maxima and relative minima are helpful when sketching the graph of a function. To determine the relative maxima or relative minima of a function, find the critical points of the function and then apply the tests shown in Table 10.1.

Table 10.1 First-Derivative Test for Relative Maxima or Relative Minima
(For y = f(x) continuous on a < x < b)

$f'(c)$	Algebraic sign of $f'(x)$ for $a < x < c$	Algebraic sign of $f'(x)$ for $c < x < b$	$f(c)$	Graph
0	−	+	**Relative minimum**	∨
0	+	−	**Relative maximum**	∧
Does not exist	−	+	**Relative minimum**	Y
Does not exist	+	−	**Relative maximum**	⅄

If the slope is positive at the immediate left of a critical point (curve increasing) and the slope is negative at the immediate right (curve decreasing), the critical point is a relative maximum. That is, the slope changes from positive to negative as the curve crosses a relative maximum.

In a like manner, at a relative minimum the slope changes from negative to positive. At the immediate left of a relative minimum, the slope is negative, and at the immediate right, it is positive.

E X A M P L E 12   Test $y = 3x^2 - 6x$ for relative maxima or minima.

Solution   The derivative of the function is

$$\frac{dy}{dx} = 6x - 6$$

To determine the critical values of x, if such exist, we solve

$$6x - 6 = 0$$
$$6x = 6$$
$$x = 1$$

Hence, x = 1, $y = 3(1)^2 - 6(1) = -3$ is a critical point. To determine whether this critical point is a relative maximum or minimum, we find out whether the function is increasing or decreasing to the right and to the left of x = 1. The set of x's can be considered as the union of x < 1, x = 1, and x > 1 since x = 1 is the only zero of $f'(x) = 0$. At x = 0, $f'(0) = -6$, so f(x) is decreasing. At x = 2, $f'(2) = 6$, so f(x) is increasing. Thus, the point (1, −3) is a relative minimum.

Exercise Set 10.3

A   *Find all critical points for the following functions.*

1. $y = 5$

2. $y = -3x$

3. $f(x) = 3x + 5$

4. $f(x) = -5x + 3$

5. $f(x) = x^2$

6. $f(x) = -3x^2$

7. $y = x^2 + 2x$

8. $y = -3x^2 + 2$

9. $y = 4x^2 + 3x - 2$

10. $y = -5x^2 - 3x + 8$

11. $y = 3x^2 + 12x - 5$

12. $y = 6x^2 + 3x - 2$

13. $y = 5x^2 - 4x + 3$

Exercises 14–20 refer to the function $f(x)$ represented by the following graph. Answer the questions from your observation of the graph.

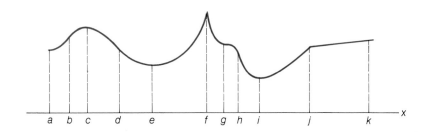

14. Find all intervals over which $f(x)$ is increasing.

15. Find all intervals over which $f(x)$ is decreasing.

16. Find all critical points on $a < x < f$.

17. Find all relative maxima on $a < x < d$.

18. Find all relative minima on $d < x < f$.

19. Find all relative maxima on $e < x < g$.

20. Find all relative minima on $g < x < k$.

B   *Sketch the graphs of the following functions. Find the critical points, relative maxima, relative minima, intervals over which they are increasing, and intervals over which they are decreasing.*

21. $y = 2x^2$

22. $y = 3x^2$

23. $y = -2x^2 + 3$

24. $y = -2x^2 + 4x$

25. $y = 3x^2 + 3x + 2$

26. $y = -3x^2 - 3x + 2$

27. $y = x^3$

28. $y = -x^3$

C   *Sketch the graphs of the following functions. Find the critical points, relative maxima, relative minima, intervals over which they are increasing, and intervals over which they are decreasing.*

29. $y = x^3 + 3x$

30. $y = x^3 - 3x$

31. $y = x^3 + 6x^2$

32. $y = x^3 - 6x^2$

33. $y = 2x^3 - 6x^2$

34. $y = 2x^3 + 6x^2$

35. $y = x^3 - 6x^2 + 9x$

36. $y = x^3 + 6x^2 + 9x$

37. $f(x) = x^3 - 3x^2 + 3x - 5$

38. $f(x) = x^3 + 6x^2 + 3x - 5$

39. $f(x) = 2x^2 - x^4$

40. $f(x) = 2x^2 + x^4$

Business **41. Profit Functions.** Profit P is related to selling price S by the formula

$$P = 10,000S - 250S^2$$

a. Is the profit increasing or decreasing when $S = 5$?
b. For what range of values of S is the profit increasing?
c. At what selling price is the profit a maximum?

Economics **42. Demand Functions.** A demand, $D(x)$, for a product is given as a function of the price x by

$$D(x) = \$800x^{-2} + 400x^{-1} \qquad \text{for } x > 0$$

a. Draw the graph of this function.
b. Does this function have any relative maxima or relative minima? (*Caution!* Note the domain of this function, $x > 0$.)
c. Is this function increasing or decreasing?

Physical Sciences **43. Velocity.** A rock is thrown upward from the top of a building, and its distance s from the ground in feet is given as a function of time t in seconds as

$$s = 80 + 64t - 16t^2 \qquad 0 \le t \le 5$$

a. How high is the building?
b. Find the velocity as a function of time.
c. How high does the rock go?
d. When does the rock strike the ground?
e. How fast is the rock going when it strikes the ground?

Social Sciences **44. Population.** A population study has been made for 8 years in a community, and the following population function P has been obtained:

$$P = 1000t^2 - 6000t + 29,000$$

where t is time measured in years from the beginning date of the study.
a. Was the population increasing or decreasing at the end of 2 years?
b. When was the population a minimum?
c. What was the minimum population?

45. Graph the population function given in exercise 44 for the first 8 years.
a. Was the population increasing or decreasing at the end of the fifth year?
b. What was the maximum population for the 8 years?

4 Concavity, Inflection Points, and Absolute Extrema

In this section we discuss several other useful tools in the drawing of graphs: **concavity, inflection points,** and **absolute maxima** and **minima**. In addition we show how the second derivative can be used to determine if a critical point is a relative maximum or a relative minimum. Procedures are developed for finding each of these, and the concepts are used to draw graphs.

In the preceding section the first-derivative test was given for relative maxima or relative minima (sometimes called **relative extrema**). Another test for relative maxima and relative minima uses the *second derivative,* and this test is used when the second derivative is easy to obtain. The second derivative is evaluated at the critical point. If the second derivative is negative at the critical point, the graph has points near the critical point whose y-coordinates are less than the y-coordinate at the critical point, and the critical point is a relative maximum. If the second derivative is positive at the critical point, the graph has points near the critical point whose y-coordinates are greater than the y-coordinate at the critical point, and, hence, the critical point is a relative minimum. If the second derivative is 0 at the critical point, the test fails, and the first-derivative test must be used. These statements describing the second-derivative test are summarized in Table 10.2.

Table 10.2   Second-Derivative Test for Relative Maxima or Relative Minima

$f'(c)$	$f''(c)$	$f(c)$	Graph
0	−	**Relative maximum**	∧
0	+	**Relative minimum**	∨
0	0	Test fails; use first-derivative test	

EXAMPLE 13   Find the points of $f(x) = x^3 - 3x^2 - 9x + 5$ that are relative maxima or minima.

Solution
$$f(x) = x^3 - 3x^2 - 9x + 5$$
$$f'(x) = 3x^2 - 6x - 9$$

To determine the critical values of x, set the first derivative equal to 0:

$$3x^2 - 6x - 9 = 0 \quad \text{or} \quad 3(x - 3)(x + 1) = 0$$

Then

$$x = 3 \quad \text{or} \quad x = -1$$

We test these critical values by the second-derivative test:

$$f''(x) = 6x - 6$$
$$f''(3) = 18 - 6 = 12 > 0$$
$$f''(-1) = -6 - 6 = -12 < 0$$

Thus, $(3, -22)$ is a relative minimum, and $(-1, 10)$ is a relative maximum.

EXAMPLE 14   Test $y = 2x^3 - 12x^2 + 24x + 12$ for relative maxima or minima.

Solution   The derivative of the function is

$$\frac{dy}{dx} = 6x^2 - 24x + 24$$

To determine the critical values of x, if such exist, we solve

$$6x^2 - 24x + 24 = 0$$
$$x^2 - 4x + 4 = 0$$
$$(x - 2)^2 = 0$$
$$x = 2$$

Hence, the point at which

$$x = 2 \quad \text{and} \quad y = 2(2)^3 - 12(2)^2 + 24(2) + 12 = 28$$

is a critical point. To test the critical point by the second-derivative test, we compute

$$\frac{d^2y}{dx^2} = 12x - 24$$

$$\left.\frac{d^2y}{dx^2}\right|_{(2,\,28)} = 12(2) - 24 = 0$$

Hence, the second-derivative test fails, and we must use the first-derivative test.

To determine whether this critical point is a maximum or a minimum, we find out whether the function is increasing or decreasing to the left and to the right of x = 2:

$$f'(1) = 6(1)^2 - 24(1) + 24 = 6$$

Thus, f(x) is increasing for x < 2.

$$f'(3) = 6(3)^2 - 24(3) + 24 = 6$$

So f(x) is increasing for x > 2. Hence, (2, 28) is neither a relative maximum nor a relative minimum.

The graph of $y = 2x^3 - 12x^2 + 24x + 12$ is given in Figure 10.4. A curve that is below its tangent line at each point of an interval is **concave downward** on the interval. The graph in Figure 10.4 is concave downward on 0 < x < 2. If a curve is above its tangent line at each point of an interval, the curve is **concave upward.** The graph in Figure 10.4 is concave upward for x > 2. A point at which

Figure 10.4

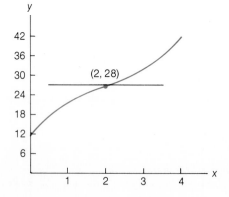

the curve changes concavity is called an **inflection point.** An inflection point occurs at (2, 28) in Figure 10.4. To prove that (2, 28) is an inflection point, we compute the second derivative at a value of $x < 2$ and at a value of $x > 2$:

$$\left. \frac{d^2y}{dx^2} \right|_{x=1} = 12(1) - 24 = -12 < 0$$

$$\left. \frac{d^2y}{dx^2} \right|_{x=3} = 12(3) - 24 = 12 > 0$$

Since the second derivative changes sign at $x = 2$, the concavity changes and (2, 28) is an inflection point.

| The Concavity of a Function | When $f''(c) > 0$, the graph is **concave upward** at $x = c$: | $\vee$ |
| | When $f''(c) < 0$, the graph is **concave downward** at $x = c$: | $\wedge$ |

Inflection Point

A point $(c, f(c))$ is defined to be an *inflection point* for the graph of $f(x)$ if there exists an interval $a < x < b$ such that

1. $f(x)$ is concave upward on $a < x < c$ and concave downward on $c < x < b$; or
2. $f(x)$ is concave downward on $a < x < c$ and concave upward on $c < x < b$.

We can prove that if $(c, f(c))$ is an inflection point and $f''(x)$ is continuous at $x = c$, then $f''(c) = 0$. Hence, to find inflection points, we seek values of x that make the second derivative equal to zero. We test these values by substituting smaller and larger values into the second derivative to see if the sign changes.

EXAMPLE 15 Find the inflection points for the graph of $f(x) = x^3 - 6x^2 + 8$.

Solution

$$f(x) = x^3 - 6x^2 + 8$$
$$f'(x) = 3x^2 - 12x$$
$$f''(x) = 6x - 12$$

To find possible inflection points, we seek values of x that make $f''(x) = 0$:

$$0 = 6x - 12$$
$$x = 2$$
$$f(2) = (2)^3 - 6(2)^2 + 8$$
$$= 8 - 24 + 8 = -8$$

Hence, $(2, -8)$ is a possible inflection point. To test to determine whether the graph changes concavity at this point, we try values smaller and larger than 2 in the second derivative:

$$f''(1) = 6(1) - 12 = -6 < 0$$
$$f''(3) = 6(3) - 12 = 6 > 0$$

Since the second derivative changes sign at x = 2, the function changes concavity at (2, −8), and thus (2, −8) is an inflection point. Because x = 2 is the only value that makes the second derivative equal zero, the point (2, −8) is the only inflection point.

If we wish to find relative maxima or relative minima for the function given in Example 15, we find the critical points by setting the first derivative equal to zero:

$$f'(x) = 3x^2 - 12x = 0$$
$$3x(x - 4) = 0$$

$$x = 0 \quad \text{or} \quad x = 4$$

$$f(0) = 0^3 - 6(0)^2 + 8 = 8$$
$$f(4) = 4^3 - 6(4)^2 + 8 = 64 - 96 + 8 = -24$$

The critical points are (0, 8) and (4, −24). We test these critical points by using the second-derivative test:

$$f''(x) = 6x - 12$$
$$f''(0) = 6(0) - 12 = -12 < 0$$
$$f''(4) = 6(4) - 12 = 12 > 0$$

Since $f''(0) < 0$, the graph is concave downward at (0, 8), and, hence, (0, 8) is a relative maximum. Since $f''(4) > 0$, the graph is concave upward at (4, −24), and, hence, (4, −24) is a relative minimum.

Now let's determine how to find the absolute maximum or absolute minimum of a function.

Definition of Absolute Maximum or Absolute Minimum	If $f(c) \geq f(x)$ for all x in the domain of the function $f(x)$, then $f(c)$ is called an **absolute maximum** of the function. If $f(c) \leq f(x)$ for all x in the domain of the function $f(x)$, then $f(c)$ is called an **absolute minimum** of the function.

For *continuous functions*, we can prove the following theorem.

If a function $f(x)$ is continuous on a closed interval $a \leq x \leq b$, then the function has *both an absolute maximum and an absolute minimum* on that interval.

To determine where the absolute maximum and the absolute minimum occur, study Figure 10.5. Note that for values between the endpoints and the critical points a continuous function is either increasing or decreasing. Hence, to find the absolute maximum and the absolute minimum of a continuous function on a closed interval, we evaluate the function at each endpoint and at each critical point and simply choose the largest value for the absolute maximum and the smallest value for the absolute minimum.

Figure 10.5

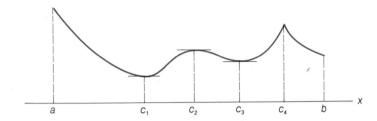

Procedure for Finding Absolute Maximum and Absolute Minimum

For $f(x)$ defined on $a \leq x \leq b$:

1. Find all critical values $c_1, c_2, \ldots, c_n$ for $a \leq x \leq b$.
2. Evaluate $f(a)$, $f(b)$, $f(c_1)$, $f(c_2)$, $\ldots$, $f(c_n)$.
3. The largest value found in step 2 is the absolute maximum on $a \leq x \leq b$. The smallest value found in step 2 is the absolute minimum on $a \leq x \leq b$.

EXAMPLE 16 Draw the graph of $f(x) = x^3 - 6x^2 + 8$, and find the absolute maximum and the absolute minimum
a. on the interval $-1 \leq x \leq 3$.
b. on the interval $-1 \leq x \leq 5$.
c. on the interval $-3 \leq x \leq 7$.

Solution The graph of $f(x) = x^3 - 6x^2 + 8$ is given in Figure 10.6.

Figure 10.6

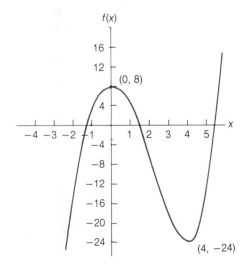

a. For the interval $-1 \leq x \leq 3$, $a = -1$ and $b = 3$. The critical point in the interval is at $x = 0$.

$$f(-1) = (-1)^3 - 6(-1)^2 + 8 = 1$$
$$f(0) = (0)^3 - 6(0)^2 + 8 = 8$$
$$f(3) = (3)^3 - 6(3)^2 + 8 = -19$$

Hence, for the interval $-1 \leq x \leq 3$, the absolute maximum occurs at $x = 0$ and is 8. The absolute minimum occurs at $x = 3$ and is -19.

b. For the interval $-1 \leq x \leq 5$, $a = -1$ and $b = 5$. The critical points are at $x = 0$ and $x = 4$.

$$f(-1) = (-1)^3 - 6(-1)^2 + 8 = 1$$
$$f(0) = 8$$
$$f(4) = -24$$
$$f(5) = (5)^3 - 6(5)^2 + 8 = -17$$

Hence, for the interval $-1 \leq x \leq 5$, the absolute maximum occurs at $x = 0$ and is 8. The absolute minimum occurs at $x = 4$ and is -24.

c. For the interval $-3 \leq x \leq 7$, $a = -3$ and $b = 7$. The critical points are at $x = 0$ and $x = 4$.

$$f(-3) = -73$$
$$f(0) = 8$$
$$f(4) = -24$$
$$f(7) = 57$$

Hence, for the interval $-3 \leq x \leq 7$, the absolute maximum occurs at $x = 7$ and is 57. The absolute minimum occurs at $x = -3$ and is -73. Note that for the function defined for all real numbers there is no absolute maximum and no absolute minimum because the function becomes infinitely large in both directions. This example illustrates the importance of the interval for which an absolute maximum or an absolute minimum is desired.

If there is only one critical point on $a \leq x \leq b$, the following second-derivative test is often used.

Table 10.3 Second-Derivative Test for Absolute Maximum or Absolute Minimum (Use only when c is the only critical value.)

$f'(c)$	$f''(c)$	$f(c)$	Graph
0	$-$	**Absolute maximum**	
0	$+$	**Absolute minimum**	

EXAMPLE 17 Find the absolute maximum and the absolute minimum of $f(x) = 3x^2 - 6x$ on $0 \le x \le 4$.

Solution $$f'(x) = 6x - 6 = 6(x - 1)$$

Set

$$f'(x) = 6(x - 1) = 0$$

Hence, $x = 1$ is the only critical value, and the second-derivative test can be used:

$$f''(x) = 6$$

Since $f''(1)$ is positive, the absolute minimum of $f(x)$ occurs at $x = 1$ and is

$$f(1) = 3(1)^2 - 6(1) = -3$$

The absolute maximum is found by evaluating $f(x)$ at the two endpoints of the interval $x = 0$ and $x = 4$:

$$f(0) = 3(0)^2 - 6(0) = 0$$
$$f(4) = 3(4)^2 - 6(4) = 48 - 24 = 24$$

Thus, the absolute maximum of $f(x)$ occurs at $x = 4$ and is $f(4) = 24$.

Exercise Set 10.4

A *Find the intervals on which the graph of the given function is concave downward and concave upward, and find any inflection points.*

1. $y = x^2$ **2.** $y = -x^2$ **3.** $y = 3x^2$

4. $y = -2x^2$ **5.** $y = 4x^2 + 3x$ **6.** $y = -3x^2 + 2x$

7. $y = x^3$ **8.** $y = -x^3$ **9.** $y = x^3 - 3x^2$

10. $y = x^3 + 4x^2$ **11.** $y = x^4 - 2x^2$ **12.** $y = x^4 + x^2$

13. $y = x^4 + x^3$ **14.** $y = x^4 - x^3$ **15.** $y = x + x^{-1}$

16. $y = x^2 + x^{-2}$ **17.** $y = \dfrac{x}{1 + x}$ **18.** $y = \dfrac{2x}{1 - x}$

19. $f(x) = (x^2 - 4)^2$ **20.** $y = (x - 1)^2(x + 2)^2$

Find the critical points, relative extrema, absolute extrema, and inflection points of the following functions.

21. $y = 4x^2 - x$ **22.** $y = x^2 + 2x$ **23.** $y = 2x^3$

24. $y = -2x^3$ **25.** $y = x^3 - 3x^2$ **26.** $y = x^3 + 3x^2$

B   **27.** $y = x^4 + 2x^2$ **28.** $y = x^4 - 2x^2$ **29.** $y = 2x + x^{-1}$

    30. $y = 3x - x^{-1}$

Find the critical points, relative extrema, absolute extrema, and inflection points, and then graph the function.

31. $y = x^3 - 6x^2 + 9x - 2$ **32.** $y = x^3 + 3x^2 + 3x + 1$

33. $f(x) = x(x - 1)^2$ **34.** $f(x) = x^2(x - 1)$

C **35.** $f(x) = \sqrt{x}$ **36.** $f(x) = \sqrt[3]{x}$

37. $f(x) = \dfrac{2x}{1 + x}$ **38.** $f(x) = \dfrac{x}{1 - x}$

39. $f(x) = (x^2 - 3)^2$ **40.** $f(x) = (x - 1)(2x + 1)^2$

41. Prove that if $a > 0$, $y = ax^2 + bx + c$ has a relative minimum at $x = -b/2a$. What is the relative minimum value of y? Does this function have an absolute maximum or absolute minimum? If so, find it.

42. Prove that if $a < 0$, $y = ax^2 + bx + c$ has a relative maximum at $x = -b/2a$. What is the maximum value of y?

43. Prove that $y = ax^2 + bx + c$ cannot have a point of inflection.

44. Prove that $y = ax^3 + bx^2 + cx + d$ has exactly one point of inflection if $a \neq 0$.

Business   **45. Maximum Profit.** Find the output x that maximizes profit P, if P is given as

$$P = 200 + 480x - 2x^2$$

Economics   **46. Minimum Cost of Production.** Find the production amount $x \geq 1$ for which the cost C is minimum.

$$C = x^3 - 6x^2 + 9x + 3$$

Life Sciences   **47. Drug Concentration.** The concentration $c(t)$ of a drug in a patient's bloodstream t hours after a drug is taken is given by

$$c(t) = \frac{0.2t}{t^2 + 4t + 9}$$

a. When will the concentration be a maximum?
b. What is the maximum concentration?

Social Sciences   **48. Learning Curves.** Suppose a learning curve is given by

$$f(x) = \frac{Lx + Lp}{x + p + r}$$

where L is the limit of practice, x is the amount of formal practice, and hence, is greater than or equal to zero, p is equivalent previous practice, and r is the rate of learning. If $L = 70$, $p = 15$, and $r = 5$, sketch this curve from $x = 0$ to $x = 25$. Find $f'(x)$. Does this curve have any relative maxima or relative minima? If so, find them. Where is the function increasing or decreasing?

 5   **Optimization Problems**

Many practical problems require determining maximum or minimum values. For example, businesspeople wish to maximize profit and minimize cost. Travelers wish to minimize travel time. Builders wish to maximize the strength of their structures. Such problems are called **optimization problems.** They require the determination of absolute maxima or absolute minima. We apply the theory developed in the preceding section to help determine the absolute maximum or absolute minimum.

Although it is impossible to describe mathematical procedures that can solve all optimization problems, it is possible to state some general rules: We should study the problem carefully, analyze the data, and attempt to set up a functional relationship between the variable to be optimized and the other variables. In this discussion we will use only one independent variable. Thus, if two or more independent variables arise, it will be necessary to eliminate all but one. Once the functional relationship between the variable to be optimized and the one independent variable has been formulated, it is easy to determine the critical values. Often the nature of the problem makes it unnecessary to test the critical values to determine if they are maxima or minima.

The four examples in this section suggest methods of setting up the functional relationships to be optimized.

EXAMPLE 18   A school is planning to build a rectangular playground that must contain 320,000 square feet. Find the minimum length of fence required and the dimensions of the playground if a fence has already been constructed by the state along one side of the site, which is bounded by a freeway.

Solution   Let x = the length of the playground along the freeway and y = the width of the playground. Since no additional fencing is needed along the freeway, the length of fence required is $L = x + 2y$. The area must contain 320,000 square feet; therefore, $x > 0$ and $y > 0$ must satisfy $x \cdot y = 320,000$. Solving this equation for y gives $y = 320,000x^{-1}$. Substituting this value of y into the expression for the length gives

$$L = x + 2(320,000x^{-1})$$
$$= x + 640,000x^{-1}$$

To make the length a minimum, the derivative of L with respect to x is computed:

$$\frac{dL}{dx} = 1 - 640,000x^{-2}$$

Setting $dL/dx = 0$ gives

$$\frac{640,000}{x^2} = 1$$

$$x = \pm 800$$

Since x represents the length along the freeway, choosing the positive value for x and solving for y give

$$y = \frac{320,000}{x} = \frac{320,000}{800} = 400$$

Hence, the playground should be 800 feet by 400 feet, and the minimum amount of fence required is 1600 feet.

EXAMPLE 19   A group of students are arranging a dance on the following basis. The charge for a couple will be $5.00 if 40 or fewer couples attend the dance. If more than 40 couples attend the dance, the charge for each couple will be reduced by an amount equal to 10 cents times the number of couples above 40. The promoters of the dance wish to limit the number of couples to the number that will provide maximum revenue. What limitation should be imposed?

Solution   Let x be the number of couples who attend the dance. Then $x - 40$ will be the number in excess of 40. The reduction in the cost for each couple will be $0.10(x - 40)$. Thus, the cost per couple is $5.00 - 0.10(x - 40)$. Since there are x couples attending the dance, the total revenue will be

$$R = x[5.00 - 0.10(x - 40)] \qquad 40 \le x \le 90$$
$$= x(5.00 - 0.10x + 4)$$
$$= 9.00x - 0.10x^2$$

Let's consider this as a continuous function with the understanding that it has a practical meaning only when x is a positive integer. That is, $1\frac{1}{3}$ couples does not have a practical meaning. The first-derivative condition for a maximum is

$$\frac{dR}{dx} = 9.00 - 0.20x = 0$$

or $x = 45$ couples. Thus, for maximum revenue, the dance should be limited to 45 couples.

EXAMPLE 20   Suppose it costs $1,000 to prepare a factory to produce a certain item. After the preparation is complete, it costs $40 to produce each item. After the items are produced, it costs an average of $10 per year for each item held in inventory. If a company needs 5000 items per year, how many units should be run off in each batch in order to minimize cost?

Solution   Let $x > 0$ be the number of items produced in each run or batch. Then

$$\text{Number of production runs per year} = \frac{5000}{x}$$

$$\text{Cost to prepare factory for production} = 1000 \left(\frac{5000}{x} \right)$$

$$\text{Cost for 5000 items} = 40(5000)$$

We assume that all of a production, or run, is put in inventory, that the items are withdrawn at a uniform rate, and that the inventory is depleted before a second run is made. Thus, the average number in inventory would be $x/2$. Cost for inventory storage is then $10(x/2)$. The total cost for the 5000 items is

$$C = 1000 \left(\frac{5000}{x} \right) + 40(5000) + \frac{10x}{2}$$

$$\frac{dC}{dx} = -\frac{5,000,000}{x^2} + \frac{10}{2} = 0$$

$$x = 1000$$

Thus, the minimum cost occurs when 1000 items are produced in each batch.

EXAMPLE 21   A firm sells a product for $1,000 per set of 100 units. The cost of making x sets of 100 units in 1 year is

$$C = 6 + 2x + 0.01x^2$$

Write an expression for profit in terms of x. Find the number of sets of 100 units that would give a maximum profit.

Solution   The revenue for x sets of 100 units would be $1,000x. Since profit equals selling price, or revenue, less cost ($P = S - C$), the profit on x sets of 100 units would be

$$P = 1000x - (6 + 2x + 0.01x^2)$$
$$= 1000x - 6 - 2x - 0.01x^2$$
$$= 998x - 6 - 0.01x^2$$

The first-derivative conditions for a maximum yield

$$\frac{dP}{dx} = 998 - 0.02x = 0$$

Thus, x = 49,900; or 49,900 sets of 100 units would yield a maximum profit.

Recall that the first derivative of C with respect to x is known as **marginal cost.** That is, the rate of change of cost when one more set of 100 units is produced is marginal cost. For the given example,

$$\frac{dC}{dx} = 2 + 0.02x$$

In a like manner, the rate of change of revenue with respect to the number of sets of units produced may be interpreted as **marginal revenue:**

$$\frac{dR}{dx} = 1000$$

Note that the marginal cost increases with increasing x, whereas the marginal revenue is a constant. If production is continued until marginal cost equals marginal revenue, the number of sets of 100 units would be obtained from

$$1000 = 2 + 0.02x$$
$$x = 49,900$$

which is the same answer we obtained previously.
This example illustrates the following condition:

Maximum Profit

Maximum profit occurs when

Marginal cost = marginal revenue

A For the given cost functions, find the production amount $x \geq 1$ for which the cost is minimum.

1. $C = x^2 - 2x + 4$

2. $C = x^2 - 4x + 8$

3. $C = x^2 - 8x + 20$

4. $C = x^2 - 6x + 10$

5. $C = x^2 - 10x + 30$

6. $C = x^2 - 12x + 40$

For the given profit functions, find the output x that maximizes profit P, and find the maximum profit.

7. $P = 600x - 2x^2$

8. $P = 800x - x^2$

9. $P = 1000x - 5x^2$

10. $P = 700x - 7x^2$

B For the given cost functions, find the production amount $x \geq 1$ for which the cost is minimum.

11. $C = x^3 - 3x^2 + 6$

12. $C = x^3 - 5x^2 + 3x + 12$

13. $C = x^3 - 6x^2 + 9x + 15$

14. $C = 2x^3 - 12x^2 + 30x$

For the given profit functions, find the output x that maximizes profit P, and find the maximum profit.

15. $P = x^3 - 40x^2 + 500x$

16. $P = x^3 - 50x^2 + 825x$

17. $P = x^3 - 70x^2 + 1600x$

18. $P = x^3 - 20x^2 + 125x$

19. $P = 2x^3 - 25x^2 + 104x$

20. $P = 2x^3 - 35x^2 + 200x$

C **21.** Find two numbers whose sum is 52 and whose product is a maximum.

22. Find the number that exceeds its square by the largest amount.

23. Find a positive number that when added to its reciprocal gives the smallest sum.

24. Find a positive number that when added to 4 times the square of its reciprocal gives the smallest sum.

25. From a piece of cardboard 60 centimeters by 60 centimeters square corners are cut out so that the sides can be folded up to form a box. What size square should be cut out to give a box of maximum volume? What is the maximum volume?

26. Redo exercise 25 for a piece of cardboard 50 centimeters by 50 centimeters.

27. Redo exercise 25 for a piece of cardboard 9 centimeters by 24 centimeters.

28. A rectangular plot of ground containing 576 square feet is to be fenced. Find the dimensions that require the least amount of fence.

29. A rectangular plot of ground containing 1350 square feet is to be fenced, and an additional fence is to be constructed in the middle to divide the plot into two equal parts. Find the dimensions that require the least amount of fence.

30. Suppose the fence used to enclose the plot in exercise 29 costs $12 per foot, and the fence used to divide the plot costs $6 per foot. Find the dimensions that make the cost a minimum.

31. Find the dimensions of a rectangular playground that is to be built along a freeway, as explained in Example 18, if the playground must contain 500,000 square feet and the cost of the fence is to be a minimum.

32. Cost Functions. A cost function is given as

$$C(x) = 10x + 30 + 0.01x^3$$

a. Find the marginal cost, $C'(x)$.

b. Find the average cost

$$\bar{C}'(x) = \frac{C(x)}{x}$$

c. Find the marginal average cost, $\bar{C}'(x)$.

d. Show that the average cost $\bar{C}(x)$ is a minimum when the marginal cost is the same as the average cost.

33. For a charter boat to operate, a minimum of 75 people paying $125 each is necessary. For each person in excess of 75, the fare is reduced $1 per person. Find the number of people that will make the revenue a maximum. What is the maximum revenue?

34. A rectangular building must contain 405,000 square feet of floor space. The front is to be all glass, and block construction is to be used for the other three walls. Assume that glass construction costs twice as much per linear foot as block construction, and find the dimensions of the building that will make the cost a minimum.

35. If a crop of oranges is harvested now, the average yield of 80 pounds per tree can be sold at 40 cents per pound. From past experience, the owners expect the crop yield to increase at a rate of 10 pounds per week per tree and the price to decrease at a rate of 2 cents per pound per week. When should the oranges be picked in order to attain maximum sale?

36. A restaurant is being planned on the basis of the following information. For a seating capacity of 50–100 persons, the weekly profit is approximately $6 per seat. As the seating capacity increases beyond 100 chairs, the weekly profit on each chair in the restaurant decreases by 5 cents times the excess above 100 chairs. What seating capacity would yield the maximum profit?

37. A rental agency has a problem of determining the rent to charge for each of 100 apartments in order to attain a maximum income. It is estimated that if the rent is set at $100 a month, all units will be occupied. On the average, one unit will remain vacant for each $5 per month increase in rent. What should the rent be in order to maximize the income?

38. A company has a contract to supply 500 units per month at a uniform daily rate. Since it costs $100 to start production and the production cost is $5 per unit, it is decided to produce a large quantity at one time, storing the excess units until time for delivery. Storage costs run 10 cents per item per month. How many items should be made per run in order to minimize the total average cost?

39. Revenue Functions. The cost and revenue from sales are

$$C = x^3 - 15x^2 + 76x + 25 \qquad \text{and} \qquad R = 55x - 3x^2$$

Find the number of units for which the profit will be a maximum.

40. Verify for exercise 39 that the marginal cost and marginal revenue are equal when the profit is a maximum.

41. Bacteria. Suppose the bacteria count t days after a treatment is given by

$$C(t) = 30t^2 - 180t + 700$$

a. When will the count be a minimum?

b. What is the minimum count?

42. Mosquitoes. Assume that the number of mosquitoes, $N(x)$ in thousands, depends on the rainfall in inches, according to the function

$$N(x) = 60 - 45x + 12x^2 - x^3 \qquad 0 \le x \le 6$$

a. Find the amount of rainfall that will produce the minimum number of mosquitoes.
b. Find the amount of rainfall that will produce the maximum number of mosquitoes.

Social Sciences **43. Class Attendance.** A professor has found that the attendance in her classes depends on the number of hours the student center is open. She gives her attendance function as

$$A = -x^2 + 16x + 70 \qquad 0 \le x \le 24$$

Find the number of hours she should request the center to remain open in order to maximize her attendance.

44. Voter Registration. The number of registered voters, in thousands, is estimated to grow according to the function of time in years as

$$N = 12 + 3t^2 - t^3 \qquad 0 \le t \le 3$$

a. Find the rate of increase.
b. When is the number a maximum?
c. When is the rate of increase a maximum?

 Summary and Review

Review the following concepts to ensure that you understand and can use them.

Implicit differentiation   Related rates
Inflection points   Curve sketching
Relative maxima   Relative minima
Absolute maxima   Absolute minima

The procedure for implicit differentiation uses the formula

$$\frac{d(y^n)}{dx} = ny^{n-1}\frac{dy}{dx}$$

in addition to the formulas from Chapter 9.

Review Exercise Set 10.6

A *Find the critical points, relative maxima, relative minima, and inflection points, and sketch the graph of the following functions.*

1. $y = x^2 - 2x + 3$ **2.** $y = x^2 - 4x + 3$

3. $y = 2x^2 - 4x + 3$ **4.** $y = 3x^2 - 3x + 2$

B **5.** $y = x^3 + 3x^2$ **6.** $y = x^3 - 3x^2$

7. $y = x^3 - 3x + 2$ **8.** $y = x^3 + x - 1$

9. $y = x^4 - 4x + 1$ **10.** $y = x^4 - 2x^2 + 1$

11. $y = x^{-1} + x^{-2}$

12. $y = x + x^{2/3}$

13. $y = \dfrac{x^3}{9(x + 2)}$

14. $y = \frac{1}{7}(2x^3 - 9x^2 + 12x + 3)$

C **15.** $y = \dfrac{x}{2}(16 - x^2)^{1/2}$

16. $y = (4 - x^{2/3})^{3/2}$

17. $y = \frac{1}{3}(x^4 - 4x^3)$

18. $y = x + x^{-1}$

19. $y = 2x(x - 2)^2$

20. $y = 2x\sqrt{x - 1}$

21. Given $y = ax^{-1} + bx$, find values for a and b so that $\sqrt{2}$ is a critical value for x and $y = 4\sqrt{2}$ when $x = \sqrt{2}$. Is $y = 4\sqrt{2}$ a maximum or a minimum value for y?

22. Given $y = x^3 + ax^2 + bx + c$, find values for a, b, and c so that $(1, 10)$ is a critical point and so that the graph goes through the origin. [That is, $(0, 0)$ is on the graph.] Is $y = 10$ a maximum or minimum value for y?

Business **23.** **Maximum Profit.** Profit P is related to selling price S by the formula

$$P = 15{,}000S - 500S^2$$

a. Is the profit increasing or decreasing when $S = 7$?
b. For what range of values of S is the profit increasing?
c. At what selling price is the profit a maximum?

24. **Maximum Profit.** The cost and revenue from sales curves are given by

$$C = 2x^2 - x \quad \text{and} \quad R = x^2 + 5x$$

Find the number of units for which the profit will be a maximum.

25. **Depreciation.** Suppose the value v of a car depreciates so that after n years its value is

$$v = \dfrac{\$8{,}000}{1 + (n/2)} + \$75$$

a. What is the car's value at the end of 1 year?
b. Differentiate with respect to n and find the change in the value of the car per year at the end of 2 years.
c. What is the scrap value of the car?

Life Sciences **26.** **Drug Concentration.** The concentration of a drug in a person's blood x hours after administration is

$$C = \dfrac{x}{20(x^2 + 6)}$$

a. When is the concentration a maximum?
b. What is the maximum concentration?

Physical Sciences **27.** **Beam Strength.** Assume that the strength of a rectangular beam is jointly proportional to its width and the square of its height. Find the dimensions of the strongest beam that can be cut from a cylindrical log of 12 inch diameter.

28. **Can Construction.** If a tin can is to hold a volume of 64 cubic inches, find the dimensions so that the amount A of tin is a minimum. [*Hint:* $A = 2\pi r^2 + 2\pi rh$ and $64 = \pi r^2 h$. Hence, $h = 64/\pi r^2$ and $A = 2\pi r^2 + 2\pi r(64/\pi r^2) = 2\pi r^2 + 128/r$. Now differentiate.]

Social Sciences **29.** **Maximum Work.** A psychiatrist has found that for $t \geq 0$, the equation $y(t) = c_0 + c_1 t + c_2 t^2 + c_3 t^3$, where c_0, c_1, c_2, and c_3 are constants, describes the relationship between amount of work output $y(t)$ and elapsed time t. Find any relative maxima or relative minima, and sketch the curve when $c_0 = 0$, $c_1 = 72$, $c_2 = -21$, and $c_3 = 2$.

30. Redo exercise 29 for $c_0 = 0$, $c_1 = 36$, $c_2 = -15$, and $c_3 = 2$.

11

Integral Calculus

The last two chapters involved the study of differential calculus. We introduce now the branch of mathematics, called **integral calculus,** which deals with the inverse or opposite operation to differentiation. This chapter begins with a discussion of **antiderivative** problems in which information about the derivative of a function is given and the function is unknown. This discussion is followed by a section on **integration formulas.** The theory that has been developed is then applied to **marginal analysis.**

Next we define the **definite integral** in a manner very similar to the definition given by the famous eighteenth century mathematician, Georg Friedrich Bernhard Riemann. Riemann worked in several branches of mathematics. He published papers on the theory of complex functions, on geometry, on number theory, and on the foundations of analysis. After studying conditions for a function to be integrable, Riemann gave the definition that has come to be known as the **Riemann integral.**

The definition of the definite integral is tedious to apply; consequently, the **fundamental theorem of calculus** is presented to show how the definite integral and the indefinite integral are related. The fundamental theorem is then applied to solve three types of problems: (1) antiderivative problems in which information about the rate of change of a function is given and the function must be determined, (2) area problems, and (3) problems involving the average value of a continuous function.

1 Antiderivatives

Many of the operations we have studied so far have inverse operations. For example, subtraction is the inverse operation for addition, division is the inverse operation for multiplication, and taking the square root is an inverse operation for squaring. In the same manner, many functions have inverse functions. Many matrices have multiplicative inverses. It seems natural to consider the inverse operation for differentiation. If the derivative of a function is known, can the function be found?

We learned in preceding chapters that the derivative of x^3 is $3x^2$. Suppose we start with $3x^2$ as the derivative of some function and see if we can determine what function or functions have $3x^2$ as the derivative. These functions are called **antiderivatives** of $3x^2$.

Antiderivative

A function $F(x)$ is called an **antiderivative** of a function $f(x)$ if and only if

$$f(x) = F'(x)$$

EXAMPLE 1 x^3 is an antiderivative of $3x^2$ since the derivative of x^3 is $3x^2$. Since the derivative of $x^3 + 1$ is also $3x^2$, it too is an antiderivative of $3x^2$. Similarly, $x^3 + 2$, $x^3 - 17$, $x^3 + \sqrt{34}$, and, in general, $x^3 + C$ for any number C are antiderivatives of $3x^2$.

Notice that, since the derivative of a constant is zero, once an antiderivative is found, another antiderivative can be found by adding a nonzero constant to the first antiderivative. The whole family of antiderivatives can be written as an antiderivative plus an arbitrary constant. Such a general expression is called the **indefinite integral** and is denoted by the symbol $\int f(x)\, dx$.

Definition of the Indefinite Integral

Let $F(x)$ be an antiderivative of the function $f(x)$. The indefinite integral of $f(x)$ is defined to be

$$F(x) + C = \int f(x)\, dx$$

The symbol $\int dx$ indicates that the operation of antidifferentiation is to be performed with respect to the variable x. $f(x)$ is called the **integrand,** and the arbitrary constant C is called the **constant of integration.**

EXAMPLE 2   Find the indefinite integral $\int 2x\,dx$.

> **Solution**   Since the derivative of x^2 is $2x$, x^2 is an antiderivative of $2x$, and so $x^2 + C$ is the indefinite integral of $2x$.
>
> $$\int 2x\,dx = x^2 + C$$

EXAMPLE 3   Find the indefinite integral $\int 5x^4\,dx$.

> **Solution**   Since the derivative of x^5 is $5x^4$, x^5 is an antiderivative of $5x^4$, and, hence, $x^5 + C$ is the indefinite integral of $5x^4$.
>
> $$\int 5x^4\,dx = x^5 + C$$

EXAMPLE 4   Find the indefinite integral $\int 2x^3\,dx$.

> **Solution**   The derivative of x^4 is $4x^3$ and not $2x^3$. Since $2x^3$ is one-half of $4x^3$, we should try $\frac{1}{2}x^4$ as an antiderivative of $2x^3$. The derivative of $\frac{1}{2}x^4$ is $2x^3$; therefore, $\frac{1}{2}x^4 + C$ is the indefinite integral of $2x^3$.
>
> $$\int 2x^3\,dx = \tfrac{1}{2}x^4 + C$$

EXAMPLE 5   Find the indefinite integral $\int \dfrac{3}{x^2}\,dx$.

> **Solution**   From our knowledge of algebra, $3/x^2 = 3x^{-2}$. We are now seeking a function whose derivative is $3x^{-2}$. Remember that when we take a derivative we decrease the exponent by 1. Suppose we try x^{-1} as an antiderivative. The derivative of x^{-1} is $-x^{-2}$ and not $3x^{-2}$. Since $3x^{-2} = -3(-x^{-2})$, we should try $-3x^{-1}$ as an antiderivative of $3x^{-2}$. The derivative of $-3x^{-1}$ is $3x^{-2}$; therefore, $-3x^{-1} + C$ is the indefinite integral of $3/x^2$.
>
> $$\int \frac{3}{x^2}\,dx = -3x^{-1} + C = -\frac{3}{x} + C$$

EXAMPLE 6   Find the indefinite integral $\int [5x^4 + 2x^3 + (3/x^2)]\,dx$.

> **Solution**   In Examples 3, 4, and 5, we found the antiderivatives of each of these terms. Remembering that the derivative of a sum is the sum of the derivatives, we test to see if the antiderivative of a sum is the sum of the antiderivatives. The derivative of $x^5 + \frac{1}{2}x^4 - (3/x)$ is $5x^4 + 2x^3 + (3/x^2)$; therefore, $x^5 + \frac{1}{2}x^4 - (3/x) + C$ is the indefinite integral of $5x^4 + 2x^3 + (3/x^2)$.
>
> $$\int \left(5x^4 + 2x^3 + \frac{3}{x^2}\right)dx = x^5 + \frac{1}{2}x^4 - \frac{3}{x} + C$$

EXAMPLE 7 Find the indefinite integral $\int \dfrac{5x^6 + 3}{x^2}\,dx$.

Solution Use algebra to express $(5x^6 + 3)/x^2$ as $5x^4 + (3/x^2)$. From the previous examples we know an antiderivative of $5x^4 + (3/x^2)$ is $x^5 - (3/x)$; thus, $x^5 - (3/x) + C$ is the indefinite integral of $(5x^6 + 3)/x^2$.

$$\int \left(\frac{5x^6 + 3}{x^2} \right) dx = \int \left(5x^4 + \frac{3}{x^2} \right) dx = x^5 - \frac{3}{x} + C$$

EXAMPLE 8 Find the function that passes through $(2, 7)$ and has a slope of $3x$ at each point x.

Solution Since the derivative of $\frac{3}{2}x^2 + C$ is $3x$, the indefinite integral $\int 3x\,dx = \frac{3}{2}x^2 + C$. Hence, $y = \frac{3}{2}x^2 + C$ is a set of functions such that each of the functions has slope $3x$. We need to pick out of this set the function that passes through $(2, 7)$. If we substitute this point into the equation, we obtain

$$y = \tfrac{3}{2}x^2 + C$$
$$7 = \tfrac{3}{2}(2)^2 + C$$
$$1 = C$$

Thus, the function we seek is

$$y = \tfrac{3}{2}x^2 + 1$$

EXAMPLE 9 The rate of sales of an item is given by $dS/dt = 10 + 6t$. Find the sales function and the number of sales when $t = 5$, if the number of sales $S = 0$ when $t = 0$.

Solution Since $dS/dt = 10 + 6t$, we take the antiderivative with respect to t and not S. The indefinite integral of $10 + 6t$ is

$$\int (10 + 6t)\,dt = 10t + 3t^2 + C$$

Since the integrand represents the rate-of-sales function, this indefinite integral represents all possible sales functions for this item. When $t = 0$, the number of sales is zero. Substituting $t = 0$ and $S = 0$ gives

$$S = 10t + 3t^2 + C$$
$$0 = 10(0) + 3(0)^2 + C$$
$$0 = C$$

Hence, the sales function is

$$S(t) = 10t + 3t^2$$

To find the number of sales when $t = 5$, we find $S(5)$:

$$S(5) = 10(5) + 3(5)^2 = 50 + 75 = 125$$

Exercise Set 11.1

A Find the indefinite integral in exercises 1–36.

1. $\int 5\,dx$ **2.** $\int 3\,dx$ **3.** $\int 0\,dx$ **4.** $\int -2\,dx$

5. $\int \sqrt{3}\,dx$ **6.** $\int \frac{4}{5}\,dx$ **7.** $\int -2x\,dx$ **8.** $\int 7x\,dx$

9. $\int \sqrt{2}x\,dx$ **10.** $\int \sqrt{3}x\,dx$ **11.** $\int x^2\,dx$ **12.** $\int 2x^2\,dx$

13. $\int 6x^2\,dx$ **14.** $\int 9x^2\,dx$ **15.** $\int x^3\,dx$ **16.** $\int 2x^3\,dx$

17. $\int 3x^3\,dx$ **18.** $\int 5x^3\,dx$

B **19.** $\int x^{1/2}\,dx$ **20.** $\int x^{-1/2}\,dx$ **21.** $\int x^{-3}\,dx$ **22.** $\int 2x^{1/3}\,dx$

23. $\int 3x^{-3}\,dx$ **24.** $\int x^{2/3}\,dx$ **25.** $\int x^{-2}\,dx$ **26.** $\int 3x^{-2}\,dx$

27. $\int \left(\frac{1}{x^2} - 2x \right) dx$ **28.** $\int (x + 3)\,dx$

C **29.** $\int (3x - 2)\,dx$ **30.** $\int (4x^{1/2} - 3)\,dx$

31. $\int \frac{x^4 - 7x^3 + x + 3}{x^2}\,dx$ **32.** $\int \frac{x^3 + 7}{\sqrt{x}}\,dx$

33. $\int \frac{x^2 - x}{x^{4/3}}\,dx$ **34.** $\int \frac{2x^3 - 3x}{\sqrt[3]{x}}\,dx$

35. $\int \frac{3x^2 - 5}{\sqrt[4]{x}}\,dx$ **36.** $\int \frac{x^2 - 2x + 3}{\sqrt[3]{x}}\,dx$

Business **37. Sales Functions.** The rate of sales of an item is

$$\frac{dS}{dt} = 8t + 6$$

Find the sales function and the number of sales at $t = 2$ if $S = 0$ when $t = 0$.

Life Sciences **38. Flu Epidemic.** Big City has a flu epidemic that the health department has been studying. The health department gives the rate of change of the number of people without flu to be

$$\frac{dN}{dt} = 500t - 10{,}000$$

If $N(0) = 600{,}000$, find a function $N(t)$ for the number of people without flu in terms of t. Use this function to find the number of people without flu 20 days after the epidemic began.

39. Bacteria. Find the bacteria growth function that passes through $(1, 5)$ and that has a slope of $3x^2 + 2x + 1$ at each point x.

Social Sciences **40. Population.** The change in the population of a certain area is estimated as

$$\frac{dP}{dt} = 600 + 500\sqrt{t} \qquad 0 \le t \le 5$$

If the current population is 8000, what will the population be in 4 years?

> The antiderivatives found in the preceding section were obtained from our knowledge of derivatives. We tried to guess a function whose derivative would be a given quantity, and then we tested our guess by actually taking the derivative. This method of guessing and testing is tedious and becomes more difficult with more complicated functions. To make the process easier we now develop formulas to help us find antiderivatives.

Let us now develop some formulas to aid in finding indefinite integrals. Actually, many of these integration formulas are easily obtained from the corresponding theorems concerning derivatives given in Chapter 10. In fact, we illustrated most of these formulas in finding antiderivatives in the preceding exercise set. We list in the box below some of these formulas and will demonstrate how they can be obtained from properties of derivatives by using the definition of the indefinite integral.

Integration Formulas (*k* and *n* are constants)

$$\int k \, dx = kx + C$$

$$\int x^n \, dx = \frac{x^{n+1}}{n+1} + C \qquad n \neq -1$$

$$\int k f'(x) \, dx = k \int f'(x) \, dx + C = k f(x) + C$$

$$\int [f(x) + g(x)] \, dx = \int f(x) \, dx + \int g(x) \, dx$$

Since $d(kx)/dx = k$, then $\int k \, dx = kx + C$. Notice that, although an antiderivative of k with respect to x is kx, the indefinite integral is $kx + C$ since it is the general expression for all functions whose derivatives are k.

EXAMPLE 10

$$\int 5 \, dx = 5x + C$$

EXAMPLE 11

$$\int -3 \, dx = -3x + C$$

Since

$$\frac{d\left(\dfrac{x^{n+1}}{n+1}\right)}{dx} = \left(\frac{1}{n+1}\right)\frac{d(x^{n+1})}{dx} = \left(\frac{1}{n+1}\right)[(n+1)x^{n+1-1}] = x^n$$

then

$$\int x^n \, dx = \frac{x^{n+1}}{n+1} + C \qquad n \neq -1$$

Note that this formula cannot be used when n = −1. (A special formula for the case n = −1 is given in Chapter 13.) The present formula states that **to find the indefinite integral of x^n with respect to x, you must increase the exponent on x by 1 and divide by the increased exponent.**

EXAMPLE 12
$$\int x^4 \, dx = \frac{x^5}{5} + C$$

EXAMPLE 13
$$\int x^{2/3} \, dx = \frac{x^{5/3}}{\frac{5}{3}} + C = \tfrac{3}{5}x^{5/3} + C$$

Since
$$\frac{d[kf(x)]}{dx} = kf'(x)$$

when k is a constant,
$$\int kf'(x) \, dx = kf(x) + C$$

EXAMPLE 14   Find $\int 10x^3 \, dx$.

Solution
$$\int 10x^3 \, dx = 10 \int x^3 \, dx = 10\left(\frac{x^4}{4}\right) + C = \frac{5x^4}{2} + C$$

EXAMPLE 15   Find $\int 30x^5 \, dx$.

Solution
$$\int 30x^5 \, dx = 30 \int x^5 \, dx = 30\left(\frac{x^6}{6}\right) + C = 5x^6 + C$$

Let's now consider a formula that states that the indefinite integral of the sum of two functions is the sum of their indefinite integrals. Since
$$\frac{d}{dx}[f(x) + g(x)] = \frac{d[f(x)]}{dx} + \frac{d[g(x)]}{dx}$$

therefore,
$$\int [f(x) + g(x)] \, dx = \int f(x) \, dx + \int g(x) \, dx$$

EXAMPLE 16
$$\int (x^3 + x^{1/2}) \, dx = \int x^3 \, dx + \int x^{1/2} \, dx = \frac{x^4}{4} + \tfrac{2}{3}x^{3/2} + C$$

EXAMPLE 17
$$\int (x^3 + x^2 + 2x + 3) \, dx = \int x^3 \, dx + \int (x^2 + 2x + 3) \, dx$$
$$= \int x^3 \, dx + \int x^2 \, dx + \int (2x + 3) \, dx$$
$$= \int x^3 \, dx + \int x^2 \, dx + \int 2x \, dx + \int 3 \, dx$$
$$= \frac{x^4}{4} + \frac{x^3}{3} + x^2 + 3x + C$$

This example shows that by repeated application of the sum formula, the indefinite integral of a function that is the sum of a finite number of functions can be obtained by taking the sum of the indefinite integrals of the functions. After this has been observed, it is not necessary to go through all of the steps of the example. The work can be simplified to

$$\int (x^3 + x^2 + 2x + 3)\, dx = \int x^3\, dx + \int x^2\, dx + \int 2x\, dx + \int 3\, dx$$

$$= \frac{x^4}{4} + \frac{x^3}{3} + x^2 + 3x + C$$

EXAMPLE 18

$$\int (3x^4 - 2x^3 + x - 3)\, dx = \int 3x^4\, dx + \int (-2)x^3\, dx + \int x\, dx + \int (-3)\, dx$$

$$= \frac{3x^5}{5} + \frac{(-2)x^4}{4} + \frac{x^2}{2} + (-3)x + C$$

$$= \frac{3x^5}{5} - \frac{x^4}{2} + \frac{x^2}{2} - 3x + C$$

To illustrate indefinite integrals, assume that the XYZ Company has the following information:

Input	Marginal Output
1	4
2	6
3	6
4	4
5	0
6	-6

By graphing this information, the company finds the marginal output function MO to be $MO = 5x - x^2$, where x is the number of input units. The total output TO is the antiderivative of the marginal output function; that is,

$$TO = \int (5x - x^2)\, dx = \frac{5x^2}{2} - \frac{x^3}{3} + C$$

The question now arises as to how C may be determined. Since TO represents the total output obtained when x units of input are used, the total output should be 0 when the input is 0 (you cannot produce items without input). Thus, setting $TO = 0$ when $x = 0$ gives

$$0 = \frac{5(0)^2}{2} - \frac{(0)^3}{3} + C$$

$$0 = C$$

Hence, the total output function is

$$TO = \frac{5x^2}{2} - \frac{x^3}{3}$$

If the company wishes to determine the input for the maximum output and the value of the maximum, remember that the marginal output must be 0 at this point. The input is 5 when the marginal output is 0. Substituting this value into the total output function gives $\frac{125}{6}$ as the maximum total output.

The importance of **marginal analysis** to management was stressed in Chapter 9 where we computed marginal functions when total functions were given. In this section we consider the problem of finding a total function when the marginal function is known. We have just seen how the total output function can be obtained when the marginal output function is known. Similarly, the total revenue function can be obtained from the marginal revenue function; the total cost function can be obtained from the marginal cost function; and the total profit function can be obtained from the marginal profit function.

EXAMPLE 19   Find the total revenue function TR if the marginal revenue is

$$MR = 500 - 0.6x$$

Find the total revenue for a sale of 800 items.

Solution   Since the marginal revenue is the derivative of the total revenue function, the total revenue function is an antiderivative of the marginal revenue function.

$$TR = \int (500 - 0.6x)\, dx$$

$$= 500x - 0.3x^2 + C$$

The constant C is found by setting $TR = 0$ when $x = 0$. (The total revenue is 0 when the number of items sold is 0.)

$$0 = 500(0) - 0.3(0)^2 + C$$

$$0 = C$$

Hence, the total revenue function is

$$TR = 500x - 0.3x^2$$

Setting $x = 800$ gives

$$TR = 500(800) - 0.3(800)^2$$

$$= 208{,}000$$

EXAMPLE 20   Find the total profit function if the marginal profit function is

$$MP = 600 - 4x$$

and x is the output. Assume there is a loss of $100 when no items are produced. Find the maximum profit.

Solution $$TP = \int (600 - 4x)\, dx$$

$$= 600x - 2x^2 + C$$

Substituting $TP = -100$ when $x = 0$ gives

$$-100 = 600(0) - 2(0)^2 + C$$

$$-100 = C$$

Hence,

$$TP = 600x - 2x^2 - 100$$

Since $MP = d(TP)/dx$, the critical points are found by setting $MP = 0$.

$$MP = 600 - 4x$$
$$0 = 600 - 4x$$
$$x = 150$$

Since

$$\frac{d^2(TP)}{dx^2} = \frac{d(MP)}{dx} = -4 < 0$$

the graph is concave downward and the absolute maximum occurs at $x = 150$. The absolute maximum value of the total profit function is then

$$TP = 600x - 2x^2 - 100$$
$$= 600(150) - 2(150)^2 - 100$$
$$= 90{,}000 - 45{,}000 - 100$$
$$= 44{,}900$$

Exercise Set **11.2**

A   *Find the following indefinite integrals.*

1. $\displaystyle\int (3x + 4x^2)\, dx$ $\qquad$ **2.** $\displaystyle\int (3 - 4x^2)\, dx$

3. $\displaystyle\int (4 + 2x - x^2)\, dx$ $\qquad$ **4.** $\displaystyle\int (3 - 4x + 6x^2)\, dx$

5. $\displaystyle\int (2 - 4x - 3x^2 + x^3)\, dx$ $\qquad$ **6.** $\displaystyle\int (3 + 2x + 9x^2 - 4x^3)\, dx$

B   **7.** $\displaystyle\int \frac{x^2 + x}{x}\, dx$ $\qquad$ **8.** $\displaystyle\int (3x^2 + x + x^{-3})\, dx$

9. $\displaystyle\int (2x^3 + 3x^2 - 2x + 4)\, dx$ $\qquad$ **10.** $\displaystyle\int (4x^3 - 6x^2 + x - 3)\, dx$

11. $\displaystyle\int (5x^4 + 4x^3 - 3x + 2)\, dx$ $\qquad$ **12.** $\displaystyle\int (10x^4 - 5x^3 - 3x^{-2})\, dx$

C   **13.** $\displaystyle\int (3x^4 - 2x^3 + x^2 + x - 1)\, dx$ $\qquad$ **14.** $\displaystyle\int (4x^5 - 3x^2 + x^{-3} - 3x^{-4})\, dx$

15. $\displaystyle\int (3x - 5)(2x + 3)\, dx$ $\qquad$ **16.** $\displaystyle\int (4x - 3)(2x + 5)\, dx$

Given the following marginal output functions, determine the total output functions, draw the graphs, and find the maximum outputs.

17. $MO = 7x - x^2$ $\qquad$ **18.** $MO = 8x - x^2$

19. $MO = 10x - x^2$ $\qquad$ **20.** $MO = 9x - x^2$

Business   **21. Total Sales Functions.** Find the total sales function TS if the marginal sales function is

$$MS = 5x + 3$$

where x is the number of units produced. Assume that $S = 0$ when $x = 0$. Draw the graph of the total sales function, and find its maximum value on $0 \le x \le 100$.

22. **Total Sales Functions.** Find the total sales TS if the marginal sales function is

$$MS = 50 - 5x$$

where x is the number of units produced. Assume that $S = 0$ when $x = 0$. Draw the graph of the total sales function, and find its minimum value on $0 \le x \le 20$.

Economics 23. **Total Revenue.** A marginal revenue function is given by

$$MR = 800 - 0.4x$$

Find the total revenue function and the revenue for a sale of 1000 items. What is the maximum revenue?

24. **Total Revenue.** If a marginal revenue function is given by

$$MR = 400 - 0.8x$$

find the total revenue function and the revenue for a sale of 300 items. What is the maximum revenue?

25. **Total Profit.** The marginal profit for producing x items is given by

$$MP = 500 - 4x$$

Find the total profit function if $TP = 0$ when $x = 0$. What is the maximum profit?

26. **Total Profit.** ABC Company has determined its marginal profit function to be

$$MP = 200 - 5x$$

If ABC Company loses $50 when no items are produced, find the company's total profit function. What is ABC Company's profit when 30 items are produced? What number of items should ABC Company produce in order to have maximum profit? What is the maximum profit?

Life Sciences 27. **Bacteria.** After introducing a bactericide into a culture, a biologist gives the rate of change of the number of bacteria present as

$$\frac{dN}{dt} = 60 - 12t$$

If $N(0) = 1200$, find $N(t)$, $N(5)$, and $N(8)$. When will the number of bacteria be 0?

Physical Sciences 28. **Velocity.** A rock is thrown up from the top of a building 128 feet high. If the velocity of the rock is

$$v = \frac{ds}{dt} = 32 - 32t$$

find the height of the rock above the ground as a function of t; that is, find $s(t)$. How high does the rock go? When does the rock strike the ground?

Social Sciences 29. **Learning Rate.** A learning rate is given by

$$\frac{dL}{dt} = 0.06t - 0.0006t^2$$

where L is the number of words learned and t is time in minutes. Find $L(30)$ and $L(40)$, if $L = 0$ when $t = 0$.

30. **Population.** The rate of change of a population function is given in thousands by

$$\frac{dP}{dx} = 60 - 0.06x$$

If $P(0) = 100$, find $P(x)$ and $P(60)$.

> Often functions are given in forms that do not appear suitable for our integration formulas. Sometimes, though, substitutions may be made that make possible the use of an integration formula. Such substitutions are referred to as **changes of variables.**

Find the indefinite integral of the function $y = (2x + 3)^2$. This function does not appear in a form suitable for our integration formulas. It is typical of many such functions. To find the indefinite integral, we could use algebraic properties to yield

$$y = (2x + 3)^2 = 4x^2 + 12x + 9$$

and then express the integral of the sum as the sum of the integrals. That is, $\int (2x + 3)^2 \, dx$ can be found by expressing it as

$$\int (4x^2 + 12x + 9) \, dx = \int 4x^2 \, dx + \int 12x \, dx + \int 9 \, dx$$

$$= \frac{4x^3}{3} + \frac{12x^2}{2} + 9x + C$$

$$= \frac{4x^3 + 18x^2 + 27x}{3} + C$$

This indefinite integral can also be obtained by substituting u for $2x + 3$. Such a substitution is called a **change of variable.** To illustrate a change of variable, let $u = 2x + 3$. Then $du/dx = 2$. If a change in variable is to be made, the integration must be done with respect to the new variable. Thus, it would be necessary to determine dx in terms of du, which is called the **differential** of u and is defined as

$$du = \left(\frac{du}{dx}\right) dx$$

Hence, for this example, $du = 2 \, dx$, and dividing by 2 gives $dx = \frac{1}{2} du$. Thus, substituting $2x + 3 = u$ and $dx = \frac{1}{2} du$ gives

$$\int (2x + 3)^2 \, dx = \int u^2 \left(\frac{1}{2}\right) du$$

in terms of u. Now by applying the integration formulas to $\int u^2 \frac{1}{2} \, du$, we get

$$\int u^2 \left(\frac{1}{2}\right) du = \frac{1}{2} \int u^2 \, du = \left(\frac{1}{2}\right)\left(\frac{u^3}{3}\right) + C' = \frac{u^3}{6} + C'$$

$$= \frac{(2x + 3)^3}{6} + C' = \frac{8x^3 + 36x^2 + 54x + 27}{6} + C'$$

$$= \frac{4x^3 + 18x^2 + 27x}{3} + \frac{9}{2} + C'$$

which is the same as we obtained earlier except for the constant term. Since the constant term is arbitrary, $\frac{9}{2} + C'$ may be made equal to C to obtain exactly the same indefinite integral.

EXAMPLE 21 Find $\int (2x + 3)^{1/2} \, dx$.

Solution This indefinite integral cannot be found by expanding it. It is possible to find its value, however, by a change of variable. Let $u = 2x + 3$. Then

$$\frac{du}{dx} = 2 \quad \text{and} \quad du = \left(\frac{du}{dx}\right) dx = 2 \, dx$$

Hence, again $dx = (\frac{1}{2}) \, du$. Thus,

$$\int (2x + 3)^{1/2} \, dx = \int u^{1/2} \left(\frac{1}{2}\right) du = \frac{1}{2} \int u^{1/2} \, du$$

$$= \frac{\frac{1}{2} u^{3/2}}{\frac{3}{2}} + C = \tfrac{1}{3} u^{3/2} + C = \tfrac{1}{3}(2x + 3)^{3/2} + C$$

EXAMPLE 22 Find $\int \sqrt{5 - x} \, dx$.

Solution Recall that $\sqrt{5 - x} = (5 - x)^{1/2}$, so that $\int \sqrt{5 - x} \, dx = \int (5 - x)^{1/2} \, dx$. Let $u = 5 - x$. Then $du/dx = -1$. Hence,

$$du = \left(\frac{du}{dx}\right) dx = (-1) \, dx \quad \text{or} \quad dx = -du$$

Substituting gives

$$\int (5 - x)^{1/2} \, dx = \int u^{1/2}(-1) \, du = -\int u^{1/2} \, du$$

$$= \frac{-u^{3/2}}{\frac{3}{2}} + C = -\tfrac{2}{3} u^{3/2} + C = -\tfrac{2}{3}(5 - x)^{3/2} + C$$

EXAMPLE 23 Find $\int \dfrac{dx}{(5 - 3x)^2}$.

Solution Let $u = 5 - 3x$. Then

$$\frac{du}{dx} = -3 \quad \text{and} \quad du = \left(\frac{du}{dx}\right) dx = (-3) \, dx$$

Hence, $dx = -\tfrac{1}{3} \, du$. Substitution gives

$$\int \frac{dx}{(5 - 3x)^2} = \int \frac{-\tfrac{1}{3} \, du}{u^2} = -\frac{1}{3} \int \frac{du}{u^2} = -\frac{1}{3} \int u^{-2} \, du$$

$$= \left(-\frac{1}{3}\right)\left(\frac{u^{-1}}{-1}\right) + C = \frac{1}{3u} + C = \frac{1}{3(5 - 3x)} + C$$

EXAMPLE 24 Find $\int (4 + 3x)^{2/3} \, dx$.

Solution   Let $u = 4 + 3x$. Then

$$\frac{du}{dx} = 3 \quad \text{and} \quad du = \left(\frac{du}{dx}\right) dx = 3\, dx$$

Hence, $dx = \frac{1}{3}\, du$. Substitution gives

$$\int (4 + 3x)^{2/3}\, dx = \int u^{2/3} \frac{1}{3}\, du = \frac{1}{3} \int u^{2/3}\, du = \frac{1}{3}\left(\frac{u^{5/3}}{\frac{5}{3}}\right) + C$$

$$= \tfrac{1}{5} u^{5/3} + C = \tfrac{1}{5}(4 + 3x)^{5/3} + C$$

EXAMPLE 25   Find $\int 2x^2 \sqrt{3 + 5x^3}\, dx$.

Solution   Let $u = 3 + 5x^3$. Then

$$\frac{du}{dx} = 15x^2 \quad \text{and} \quad du = \left(\frac{du}{dx}\right) dx = 15x^2\, dx$$

Hence, $dx = \dfrac{1}{15x^2}\, du$. Substitution gives

$$\int 2x^2 \sqrt{3 + 5x^3}\, dx = \int 2x^2 (\sqrt{u}) \frac{1}{15x^2}\, du$$

$$= \int \tfrac{2}{15} u^{1/2}\, du$$

$$= \tfrac{2}{15} \int u^{1/2}\, du$$

$$= \left(\tfrac{2}{15}\right)\left(\tfrac{2}{3}\right) \cdot u^{3/2} + C$$

$$= \tfrac{4}{45}(3 + 5x^3)^{3/2} + C$$

Exercise Set **11.3**

A   Use a change of variable to find the following indefinite integrals.

1. $\displaystyle\int (x - 3)^2\, dx$ 2. $\displaystyle\int (x + 4)^2\, dx$

3. $\displaystyle\int (2x - 3)^2\, dx$ 4. $\displaystyle\int (2x + 4)^2\, dx$

5. $\displaystyle\int (3x + 2)^2\, dx$ 6. $\displaystyle\int (2x - 11)^2\, dx$

7. $\displaystyle\int (3x - 7)^2\, dx$ 8. $\displaystyle\int (4x - 3)^2\, dx$

9. $\displaystyle\int (x - 2)^{-2}\, dx$ 10. $\displaystyle\int (x + 3)^{-2}\, dx$

B   11. $\displaystyle\int (4x + 5)^{-3}\, dx$ 12. $\displaystyle\int (3x + 7)^{-3}\, dx$

13. $\displaystyle\int (3x + 2)^{-4}\, dx$ 14. $\displaystyle\int (2x - 3)^{-4}\, dx$

15. $\displaystyle\int (3x + 5)^5\,dx$

16. $\displaystyle\int (4x + 3)^5\,dx$

17. $\displaystyle\int (2x - 5)^{-5}\,dx$

18. $\displaystyle\int (3x + 5)^{-5}\,dx$

19. $\displaystyle\int \sqrt{4 + x}\,dx$

20. $\displaystyle\int \sqrt{5 + x}\,dx$

21. $\displaystyle\int \sqrt{5 - x}\,dx$

22. $\displaystyle\int \sqrt{6 - x}\,dx$

23. $\displaystyle\int \sqrt{3 + 4x}\,dx$

24. $\displaystyle\int \sqrt{4 + 3x}\,dx$

25. $\displaystyle\int \sqrt{5 - 2x}\,dx$

26. $\displaystyle\int \sqrt{6 - 3x}\,dx$

27. $\displaystyle\int 6\sqrt{x + 3}\,dx$

28. $\displaystyle\int 5\sqrt{x - 4}\,dx$

29. $\displaystyle\int 6\sqrt{4 - 3x}\,dx$

30. $\displaystyle\int 5\sqrt{2x - 3}\,dx$

31. $\displaystyle\int \sqrt[3]{3 + 7x}\,dx$

32. $\displaystyle\int \sqrt[3]{x + 3}\,dx$

C   **33.** $\displaystyle\int \sqrt[3]{2x + 3}\,dx$

34. $\displaystyle\int \sqrt[3]{5 - 2x}\,dx$

35. $\displaystyle\int \sqrt[4]{3 + 2x}\,dx$

36. $\displaystyle\int \sqrt[4]{3 - 5x}\,dx$

37. $\displaystyle\int \frac{3\,dx}{(4x - 3)^2}$

38. $\displaystyle\int \frac{5\,dx}{(2x - 7)^2}$

39. $\displaystyle\int (4x - 5)^{2/3}\,dx$

40. $\displaystyle\int (3x + 2)^{2/3}\,dx$

41. $\displaystyle\int x(2x^2 - 7)^{3/4}\,dx$

42. $\displaystyle\int x\sqrt{x^2 + 1}\,dx$

43. $\displaystyle\int x\sqrt{x^2 + 4}\,dx$

44. $\displaystyle\int 2x(3x^2 - 4)^{2/3}\,dx$

45. $\displaystyle\int x^2\sqrt{1 + x^3}\,dx$

46. $\displaystyle\int x^2\sqrt[3]{1 + x^3}\,dx$

47. $\displaystyle\int 2x^2\sqrt[3]{5 + x^3}\,dx$

48. $\displaystyle\int 4x^2\sqrt[3]{3 + 2x^2}\,dx$

49. $\displaystyle\int 2x^3\sqrt{5 + 3x^4}\,dx$

50. $\displaystyle\int 3x^3\sqrt[3]{4 + 5x^4}\,dx$

Business   **51. Total Sales Functions.** A marginal sales function is given by

$$MS = x\sqrt{x^2 + 16}$$

Find the total sales function. Find the sales for a production of three items.

Economics   **52. Total Revenue Functions.** Suppose a marginal revenue function is given by

$$MR = \frac{x}{\sqrt{x^2 + 16}}$$

Find the total revenue function. Find the revenue for a production of three items.

Life Sciences   **53. Pollution.** Suppose the radius R, in feet, of an oil slick is increasing at the rate

$$\frac{dR}{dt} = 80(t + 16)^{-1/2}$$

where t is time in minutes. If $R = 0$ when $t = 0$, find the radius of the slick after 20 minutes.

Social Sciences   **54. University Enrollment.** New University has an enrollment of 3000, but its projected rate of increase in number of students is

$$\frac{dN}{dt} = 6000(1 + t)^{-3/2}$$

Find the projected number of students after t years. What is the projected number of students after 8 years?

Definite Integrals

> In the preceding sections we studied ways for obtaining the indefinite integral. We now define the **definite integral.** The definite integral was first studied by Georg Riemann. Because of his work the definite integral is sometimes called the **Riemann integral.**

In the application problems of the two preceding chapters it was necessary to know the value of the antiderivative at a given point in order to find the value of the constant of integration. An interesting result is obtained by taking the difference in an antiderivative evaluated at two points. Consider the indefinite integral

$$H(x) = \int 3x^2 \, dx$$

$$= x^3 + C$$

Now let's evaluate the indefinite integral at $x = 6$ and $x = 2$ and take the difference:

$$H(6) = 6^3 + C$$
$$H(2) = 2^3 + C$$
$$H(6) - H(2) = 6^3 - 2^3$$

Note that the difference in the indefinite integral at two points is independent of the constant of integration. Note also that

$$H(6) - H(2) = x^3 \Big|_2^6$$

where the symbol $x^3 \big|_2^6$ means subtract the value of x^3 at $x = 2$ from the value at $x = 6$. Finally note that x^3 is the antiderivative of $3x^2$ with $C = 0$ as the constant of integration.

In general, we write

$$F(b) - F(a) = F(x) \Big|_a^b$$

where $F(x)$ is obtained from $\int F'(x) \, dx$. This statement is written in symbols as

$$F(b) - F(a) = \int_a^b F'(x) \, dx$$

This integral form is called a **definite integral.** In the next section we show that it can be defined as a limit of a sum and at the same time show that it represents the area under a curve.

Definite Integral

The definite integral of a continuous function $f(x)$ over the interval from $x = a$ to $x = b$ is the difference in the antiderivative of $f(x)$ at $x = b$ and at $x = a$. This fact is symbolized by

$$\int_a^b f(x)\, dx = F(a) - F(b)$$

where $F(x)$ is any antiderivative of $f(x)$ over $a \le x \le b$; that is, $F'(x) = f(x)$.

The following definite integral properties can be proved for continuous functions.

Definite Integral Properties

Assume that $f(x)$ and $g(x)$ are continuous functions on the indicated intervals and k is a constant. Then

1. $\displaystyle \int_a^b kf(x)\, dx = k \int_a^b f(x)\, dx$

2. $\displaystyle \int_a^b [f(x) + g(x)]\, dx = \int_a^b f(x)\, dx + \int_a^b g(x)\, dx$

3. $\displaystyle \int_a^b f(x)\, dx = -\int_b^a f(x)\, dx$

4. $\displaystyle \int_a^a f(x)\, dx = 0$

5. $\displaystyle \int_a^b f(x)\, dx = \int_a^c f(x)\, dx + \int_c^b f(x)\, dx$

These definite integral properties are illustrated in the following examples.

EXAMPLE 26 Illustrate the definite integral properties.

Solution

1. $\displaystyle \int_2^3 6x\, dx = 6 \int_2^3 x\, dx = 6 \left(\frac{x^2}{2} \right) \Big|_2^3 = 6 \left(\frac{9}{2} - \frac{4}{2} \right) = 15$

2. $\displaystyle \int_2^3 (6x + 4)\, dx = \int_2^3 6x\, dx + \int_2^3 4\, dx = \left(\frac{6x^2}{2} \right) \Big|_2^3 + (4x) \Big|_2^3 = 15 + 4 = 19$

3. $\displaystyle \int_2^3 6x\, dx = -\int_3^2 6x\, dx$

$$3x^2 \Big|_2^3 = -3x^2 \Big|_3^2$$

$$27 - 12 = -(12 - 27)$$

$$15 = -(-15)$$

4. $\int_3^3 6x\,dx = 3x^2\Big|_3^3 = 12 - 12 = 0$

5. $\int_1^3 6x\,dx = \int_1^2 6x\,dx + \int_2^3 6x\,dx$

$$3x^2\Big|_1^3 = 3x^2\Big|_1^2 + 3x^2\Big|_2^3$$

$$27 - 3 = 12 - 3 + 27 - 12$$

$$24 = 9 + 15$$

EXAMPLE 27   Find $\int_1^3 (x^2 - 2x + 4)\,dx$.

Solution

$$\int_1^3 (x^2 - 2x + 4)\,dx = \left(\frac{x^3}{3} - x^2 + 4x\right)\Bigg|_1^3$$

$$= \frac{3^3}{3} - 3^2 + 4(3) - \frac{1^3}{3} + 1^2 - 4(1)$$

$$= 9 - 9 + 12 - \tfrac{1}{3} + 1 - 4 = \tfrac{26}{3}$$

EXAMPLE 28   Find $\int_0^3 (x^2 - 2x + 4)\,dx$.

Solution

$$\int_0^3 (x^2 - 2x + 4)\,dx = \left(\frac{x^3}{3} - x^2 + 4x\right)\Bigg|_0^3$$

$$= \frac{3^3}{3} - 3^2 + 4(3) - \frac{0^3}{3} + 0^2 - 4(0)$$

$$= 9 - 9 + 12 = 12$$

The definite integral can also be used to find the change in a function, as illustrated by the next example.

EXAMPLE 29   Suppose a company's marginal cost, marginal revenue, and marginal profit are given in thousands of dollars in terms of the number x of units produced as

$$C'(x) = 1$$
$$R'(x) = 12 - 2x \qquad \text{for } 0 \le x \le 12$$
$$P'(x) = R'(x) - C'(x)$$

If production changes from 3 units to 6 units, find the change in **(a)** cost, **(b)** revenue, and **(c)** profit.

Solution   **a.** The change in cost is

$$\int_3^6 C'(x)\,dx = \int_3^6 1\,dx = x\Big|_3^6 = 6 - 3 = 3$$

b. The change in revenue is

$$\int_3^6 R'(x)\,dx = \int_3^6 (12 - 2x)\,dx = (12x - x^2)\Big|_3^6$$

$$= (72 - 36) - (36 - 9) = 9$$

c. The change in profit is

$$\int_3^6 P'(x)\,dx = \int_3^6 [R'(x) - C'(x)]\,dx$$

$$= \int_3^6 (12 - 2x - 1)\,dx$$

$$= \int_3^6 (11 - 2x)\,dx$$

$$= (11x - x^2)\Big|_3^6$$

$$= (66 - 36) - (33 - 9) = 6$$

Exercise Set 11.4

A   Find the values of the following definite integrals.

1. $\int_1^5 dx$

2. $\int_5^{30} dx$

3. $\int_2^3 7\,dx$

4. $\int_2^5 3\,dx$

5. $\int_1^3 3x\,dx$

6. $\int_2^5 4x\,dx$

7. $\int_2^5 (2x + 3)\,dx$

8. $\int_1^3 (4x - 1)\,dx$

9. $\int_0^2 (6x + 1)\,dx$

10. $\int_0^2 (x^2 + x)\,dx$

11. $\int_2^5 (x^2 - x + 1)\,dx$

12. $\int_1^4 (x^2 - x + 1)\,dx$

13. $\int_0^3 (x^3 - 2x + 3)\,dx$

14. $\int_0^2 (x^3 - 2x + 3)\,dx$

15. $\int_2^5 (x^2 - x + 2)\,dx$

16. $\int_1^3 (2x^2 - 3x + 1)\,dx$

B   **17.** $\int_1^3 (x - 3)^2\,dx$

18. $\int_1^2 (x - 3)^2\,dx$

19. $\int_1^3 (x - 3)^3\,dx$

20. $\int_1^2 (x - 3)^3\,dx$

21. $\int_3^4 \sqrt{x - 3}\,dx$

22. $\int_3^5 \sqrt{x - 3}\,dx$

23. $\int_{-1}^3 (2x + 3)^3\,dx$

24. $\int_{-2}^3 (x + 3)^3\,dx$

25. $\int_{-2}^2 x^{2/3}\,dx$

26. $\int_{-1}^2 3x^{2/3}\,dx$

C   Evaluate the following definite integrals. (Hint: You may need to make a change of variable. Return to the original variable or change limits of integration before evaluating antiderivative.)

27. $\int_0^1 x\sqrt{x^2 + 1}\,dx$

28. $\int_0^1 x\sqrt[3]{x^2 + 2}\,dx$

29. $\int_1^2 x\sqrt{3x^2 - 1}\,dx$

30. $\int_0^3 2x\sqrt[3]{3x^2 + 2}\,dx$

31. $\int_0^2 3x\sqrt{3x^2 + 1}\,dx$

32. $\int_0^3 4x^2\sqrt[3]{3x^3 + 2}\,dx$

The application problems for this section are given in Section 11.6.

In this section we interpret a definite integral to be the area under the graph of a function from a to b. In fact, we explain why the definite integral gives the area under a curve. We also study a theorem that has come to be known as the **fundamental theorem of calculus** because it states how a definite integral and an indefinite integral are related.

Suppose we wish to find the area of the region under the curve $f(x) = 3x^2$ and above the x-axis from the origin to an arbitrary x. This region is shaded in Figure 11.1. The area of the shaded region could be approximated by finding the sum of the areas of the two rectangles illustrated in Figure 11.2. But note that the sum of the areas of these two rectangles would be greater than the area we seek. Computing the sum of the areas of the two rectangles (one has zero height) illustrated in Figure 11.3 shows that it is less than the area we seek. Let us call the sum of the areas of the two rectangles in Figure 11.2 the upper sum $\bar{S}$, and the sum of the areas of the two rectangles in Figure 11.3 the lower sum $\underline{S}$. Then if the area we seek (the shaded region in Figure 11.1) is represented by A,

Figure 11.1

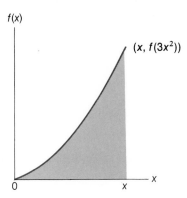

Figure 11.2

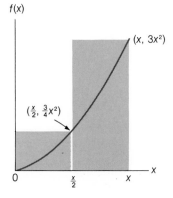

Figure 11.3

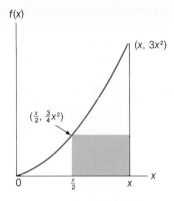

we have $\underline{S} < A < \bar{S}$. Now, from Figure 11.3,

$$\underline{S} = \text{area of first rectangle} + \text{area of second rectangle}$$

$$\underline{S} = 0\left(\frac{x}{2} - 0\right) + \frac{3}{4}x^2\left(x - \frac{x}{2}\right)$$

$$= 0 + \frac{3}{4}x^2\left(\frac{x}{2}\right) = \frac{3}{8}x^3$$

Similarly, from Figure 11.2,

$$\bar{S} = \text{area of first rectangle} + \text{area of second rectangle}$$

$$\bar{S} = \frac{3}{4}x^2\left(\frac{x}{2} - 0\right) + 3x^2\left(x - \frac{x}{2}\right)$$

$$= \tfrac{3}{8}x^3 + \tfrac{3}{2}x^3 = \tfrac{15}{8}x^3$$

Since $\underline{S} < A < \bar{S}$,

$$\tfrac{3}{8}x^3 < A < \tfrac{15}{8}x^3$$

Suppose the number of rectangles is doubled, as illustrated in Figures 11.4 and 11.5. From Figure 11.4 we obtain

$$\bar{S} = \text{area of first rectangle} + \text{area of second rectangle}$$
$$+ \text{area of third rectangle} + \text{area of fourth rectangle}$$

$$\bar{S} = 3\left(\frac{x}{4}\right)^2\left(\frac{x}{4} - 0\right) + 3\left(\frac{x}{2}\right)^2\left(\frac{x}{2} - \frac{x}{4}\right) + 3\left(\frac{3x}{4}\right)^2\left(\frac{3x}{4} - \frac{x}{2}\right)$$

$$+ 3x^2\left(x - \frac{3x}{4}\right)$$

$$= \frac{3x^2}{16}\left(\frac{x}{4}\right) + \frac{3x^2}{4}\left(\frac{x}{4}\right) + \frac{27x^2}{16}\left(\frac{x}{4}\right) + 3x^2\left(\frac{x}{4}\right)$$

$$= \frac{3x^3}{64} + \frac{12x^3}{64} + \frac{27x^3}{64} + \frac{48x^3}{64} = \frac{90x^3}{64} = \frac{45x^3}{32}$$

Figure 11.4

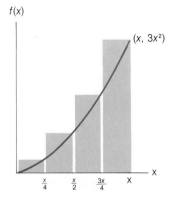

From Figure 11.5 we obtain

$$\underline{S} = \text{area of first rectangle} + \text{area of second rectangle}$$
$$+ \text{area of third rectangle} + \text{area of fourth rectangle}$$

$$\underline{S} = 3(0)^2 \left(\frac{x}{4} - 0 \right) + 3 \left(\frac{x}{4} \right)^2 \left(\frac{x}{2} - \frac{x}{4} \right) + 3 \left(\frac{x}{2} \right)^2 \left(\frac{3x}{4} - \frac{x}{2} \right)$$
$$+ 3 \left(\frac{3x}{4} \right)^2 \left(x - \frac{3x}{4} \right)$$

$$= 0 + \frac{3x^2}{16} \left(\frac{x}{4} \right) + \frac{3x^2}{4} \left(\frac{x}{4} \right) + \frac{27x^2}{16} \left(\frac{x}{4} \right)$$

$$= 0 + \frac{3x^3}{64} + \frac{12x^3}{64} + \frac{27x^3}{64}$$

$$= \frac{42x^3}{64} = \frac{21x^3}{32}$$

Figure 11.5

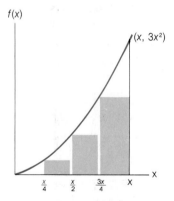

Thus, we now have the following inequality:

$$\underline{S} < A < \bar{S}$$

$$\frac{21x^3}{32} < A < \frac{45x^3}{32}$$

If the number of rectangles is doubled again, we obtain

$$\underline{S} < A < \bar{S}$$

$$\frac{105x^3}{128} < A < \frac{153x^3}{128}$$

Doubling again gives $\underline{S} < A < \bar{S}$,

$$\frac{465x^3}{512} < A < \frac{561x^3}{512}$$

Continuing this process leads us to suspect that A may equal x^3, and such is indeed the case. (Note that x^3 is an antiderivative of $3x^2$.)

The solution just given leads to the following formal definition of the definite integral:

The Definite Integral (Formal)

Assume that $y = f(x)$ is a function defined on $a \le x \le b$ and that

1. $a = x_0 \le x_1 \le \cdots \le x_{n-1} \le x_n = b$
2. $\Delta x_i = x_i - x_{i-1}$ for $i = 1, 2, \ldots, n$
3. $\Delta x_i \to 0$ as $n \to \infty$
4. $x_{i-1} \le c_i \le x_i$ for $i = 1, 2, \ldots, n$

If

$$\lim_{n \to \infty} [f(c_1)\Delta x_1 + f(c_2)\Delta x_2 + \cdots + f(c_n)\Delta x_n]$$

exists, then this limit is called **the definite integral** of $f(x)$ from a to b. In symbols this is written

$$\lim_{n \to \infty} [f(c_1)\Delta x_1 + f(c_2)\Delta x_2 + \cdots + f(c_n)\Delta x_n] = \int_a^b f(x)\,dx$$

Now let's consider the difference in two areas under a curve from x to $x + \Delta x$. Let $F(x)$ be the area under a curve from $x = 0$ to x, as illustrated in Figure 11.6.

Figure 11.6

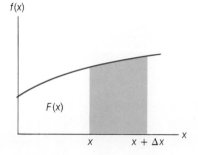

The area of the shaded region can be written as $F(x + \Delta x) - F(x)$, provided $f(x) \geq 0$. This difference can be approximated by $f(x)\,\Delta x$. Hence.

$$F(x + \Delta x) - F(x) \approx f(x)\,dx$$

$$\frac{F(x + \Delta x) - F(x)}{\Delta x} \approx f(x)$$

$$\lim_{\Delta x \to 0} \frac{F(x + \Delta x) - F(x)}{\Delta x} = \lim_{\Delta x \to 0} f(x)$$

$$F'(x) = f(x)$$

By definition, $F(x)$ is then an antiderivative of $f(x)$ and

$$F(b) - F(a) = \int_a^b f(x)\,dx$$

Note that $F(b) - F(a)$ represents the area under a curve from $x = a$ to $x = b$.
Since

$$\lim_{n \to \infty} [f(c_1)\,\Delta x_1 + f(c_2)\,\Delta x_2 + \cdots + f(c_n)\,\Delta x_n]$$

also represents the area under a curve from $x = a$ to $x = b$, these results can be combined to give the **fundamental theorem of calculus**:

Fundamental Theorem of Calculus

If $F(x)$ is any antiderivative of $f(x)$ over $a \leq x \leq b$, then

$$\lim_{n \to \infty} [f(c_1)\,\Delta x_1 + f(c_2)\,\Delta x_2 + \cdots + f(c_n)\,\Delta x_n] = \int_a^b f(x)\,dx$$

$$= F(b) - F(a)$$

The fundamental theorem provides the connecting link between a definite integral and an indefinite integral.

EXAMPLE 30 Find the area of the region bounded by $f(x) = 3x^2$, the x-axis, and the lines $x = 2$ and $x = 4$. This region is illustrated in Figure 11.7.

Figure 11.7

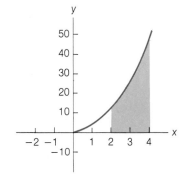

Solution By the fundamental theorem of calculus, this area is

$$\int_a^b f(x)\,dx = \int_2^4 3x^2\,dx = 3\int_2^4 x^2\,dx = 3\left(\frac{x^3}{3}\right)\Big|_2^4 = x^3\Big|_2^4$$

$$= 4^3 - 2^3 = 64 - 8 = 56$$

If the graph of the function $y = f(x)$ between $x = a$ and $x = b$ is below the x-axis, the value of the definite integral will be negative.

EXAMPLE 31 Find the definite integral of $f(x) = x^2 - 4$ from $x = 0$ to $x = 2$. The graph of the region bounded by this function, the x-axis, and the lines $x = 0$ and $x = 2$ is shaded in Figure 11.8.

Figure 11.8

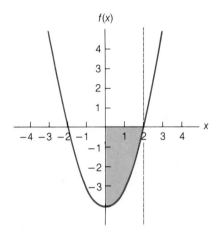

Solution By the fundamental theorem of calculus, the definite integral is

$$\int_a^b f(x)\,dx = \int_0^2 (x^2 - 4)\,dx = \left(\frac{x^3}{3} - 4x\right)\Big|_0^2$$

$$= \left[\frac{2^3}{3} - 4(2)\right] - \left[\frac{0^3}{3} - 4(0)\right]$$

$$= \tfrac{8}{3} - 8 = -\tfrac{16}{3}$$

Thus, the area of this region is $\left|-\tfrac{16}{3}\right|$.

EXAMPLE 32 Find the definite integral of $f(x) = x^2 - 4$ from $x = 0$ to $x = 4$.

Solution

$$\int_0^4 (x^2 - 4)\,dx = \left(\frac{x^3}{3} - 4x\right)\Big|_0^4 = \left[\frac{4^3}{3} - 4(4)\right] - \left[\frac{0^3}{3} - 4(0)\right]$$

$$= \tfrac{64}{3} - 16 = \tfrac{64}{3} - \tfrac{48}{3} = \tfrac{16}{3}$$

EXAMPLE 33 Find the value of the definite integral of $f(x) = x^2 - 4$ from $x = 2$ to $x = 4$.

Solution

$$\int_2^4 (x^2 - 4)\, dx = \left(\frac{x^3}{3} - 4x\right)\Bigg|_2^4 = \left[\frac{4^3}{3} - 4(4)\right] - \left[\frac{2^3}{3} - 4(2)\right]$$

$$= (\tfrac{64}{3} - 16) - (\tfrac{8}{3} - 8)$$

$$= \tfrac{16}{3} + \tfrac{16}{3} = \tfrac{32}{3}$$

EXAMPLE 34 Find the total area of the region bounded by $f(x) = x^2 - 4$, the x-axis, and the lines $x = 0$ and $x = 4$. This region is shaded in Figure 11.9.

Figure 11.9

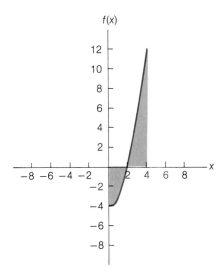

Solution Since part of this region is below the x-axis and part is above, the area of the total region must be found by finding the area of the region below the axis and the area of the region above the axis and adding their values. The area of the region below the axis was found earlier to be $\left|-\frac{16}{3}\right|$. The area of the region above the x-axis was found to be $\frac{32}{3}$. The total area is thus

$$\left|-\tfrac{16}{3}\right| + \left|\tfrac{32}{3}\right| = \tfrac{16}{3} + \tfrac{32}{3} = \tfrac{48}{3} = 16$$

Note that this answer cannot be found by evaluating the definite integral

$$\int_0^4 (x^2 - 4)\, dx = \tfrac{16}{3}$$

since the definite integral simply combines the values $-\frac{16}{3} + \frac{32}{3} = \frac{16}{3}$.

Exercise Set 11.5

A *Find the area under the curve from* $x = 1$ *to* $x = 3$ *for the following functions.*

1. $f(x) = 5$ **2.** $f(x) = 7$

3. $f(x) = 6x$ **4.** $f(x) = 10x$

5. $f(x) = 6x + 5$

6. $f(x) = 10x + 5$

7. $f(x) = x^2$

8. $f(x) = 6x^2$

9. $f(x) = 3x^2 + 6x$

10. $f(x) = 3x^2 + 5$

B   For exercises 11–20, find the area under the curve from $x = 2$ to $x = 4$ for each of the functions given in exercises 1–10.

C   Find the total area of the regions bounded by the following functions from $x = 0$ to $x = 4$.

21. $f(x) = x^2 - 9$

22. $f(x) = x^2 - 16$

23. $f(x) = 4x^2 - 9$

24. $f(x) = 9x^2 - 16$

Explain why the fundamental theorem of calculus cannot be used to evaluate the following integrals. (Hint: The function must exist at each point of the interval in order to have an antiderivative at each point of the interval.)

25. $\displaystyle\int_{-1}^{1} \frac{dx}{x^3}$

26. $\displaystyle\int_{0}^{3} \frac{dx}{(x-2)^2}$

27. $\displaystyle\int_{1}^{3} \frac{(2x-1)\,dx}{(x^2-x-2)^2}$

28. $\displaystyle\int_{0}^{1} \frac{dx}{(3x-2)^3}$

The application problems for this section are given in Section 11.6.

Applications of Integral Calculus

> There are many problems that can be solved by using integral calculus. In this section we demonstrate how calculus can be applied to solve three types of problems: (1) antiderivative problems in which we are given information about the rate of change of a function from which the function is to be determined, (2) area problems, and (3) problems involving the average value of a continuous function. These types of problems certainly do not exhaust the applications of integral calculus. Integrals are used to compute volumes of solids, cost functions, sales functions, profit functions, consumer's surplus, and producer's surplus. We have already discussed antiderivative problems in which the indefinite integral is used. In Section 11.5 we emphasized that the fundamental theorem of calculus provides the connecting link between the indefinite integral and the definite integral. In this section we show how the fundamental theorem of calculus leads in a natural way from a study of antiderivative problems to a study of area problems.

Suppose the ABC Factory obtains the marginal cost function $MC = 4x + 10$, where x represents the number of units produced. If the fixed cost is $10, can the total cost function be found? This question is typical of antiderivative problems in which information is given about the rate of change of a function from which the function is to be determined. The total cost function TC is the antiderivative of the marginal cost function. That is,

$$TC = \int (4x + 10)\,dx = \frac{4x^2}{2} + 10x + C$$

Since the fixed cost is \$10, setting $x = 0$ and $TC = \$10$ gives $C = \$10$. Hence,

$$TC = 2x^2 + 10x + 10$$

Now suppose the factory plans to sell the product for \$34 per unit. The marginal revenue function is $MR = \$34$. To find the total revenue function, integrate the marginal revenue function:

$$TR = \int 34\,dx = 34x + C_1$$

Since $TR = 0$ when $x = 0$, substituting these values gives $C_1 = 0$. Hence, the total revenue function is

$$TR = 34x$$

The profit function, $P(x)$, is

$$P(x) = TR - TC = 34x - (2x^2 + 10x + 10)$$
$$= 34x - 2x^2 - 10x - 10 = -2x^2 + 24x - 10$$

To find the number of units to produce a maximum profit, differentiate $P(x)$:

$$P'(x) = -4x + 24$$

Setting $P'(x) = 0$ gives $-4x + 24 = 0$, or

$$x = 6$$

The fact that $P''(x) = -4$ means that $x = 6$ will make $P(x)$ a maximum. Substituting $x = 6$ gives

$$P(6) = -2(6)^2 + 24(6) - 10$$
$$= -2(36) + 144 - 10$$
$$= 62$$

Thus, the maximum profit is \$62. Notice that setting the derivative equal to 0 to find the value of x that makes $P(x)$ a maximum is equivalent to setting the marginal cost function equal to the marginal revenue function.

$$MC = MR$$
$$4x + 10 = 34$$
$$4x = 24$$
$$x = 6$$

Suppose the factory wishes now to find the increase in profit as the number of units produced increases from 3 to 5 units. After the profit function $P(x)$ has been obtained, the increase can be found by subtracting $P(3)$ from $P(5)$:

$$P(5) = -2(5)^2 + 24(5) - 10$$
$$= -50 + 120 - 10 = 60$$
$$P(3) = -2(3)^2 + 24(3) - 10$$
$$= -18 + 72 - 10 = 44$$
$$P(5) - P(3) = 60 - 44 = 16$$

Recall that, by the fundamental theorem of calculus,

$$P(5) - P(3) = \int_3^5 (-4x + 24)\, dx = \int_3^5 [34 - (4x + 10)]\, dx$$

Thus, the increase in profit can be found by finding the value of the definite integral of the marginal revenue function minus the marginal cost function:

$$\int_3^5 [34 - (4x + 10)]\, dx = \int_3^5 (-4x + 24)\, dx = \left(\frac{-4x^2}{2} + 24x \right) \Big|_3^5$$
$$= (-2x^2 + 24x) \Big|_3^5$$
$$= [-2(5)^2 + 24(5)] - [-2(3)^2 + 24(3)]$$
$$= (-50 + 120) - (-18 + 72) = 70 - 54 = 16$$

EXAMPLE 35 From assembling 100 units of a product, the production manager obtained the following rate-of-assembly function:

$$f(x) = 1000x^{-1/2}$$

where $f(x)$ represents the rate of labor hours required to assemble the x units. The company plans to bid on a new order of 125 additional units. Help the manager estimate the total labor requirements for assembling the additional 125 units.

Solution The total labor, TL, requirement is the value of the following definite integral:

$$TL = \int_{100}^{225} 1000x^{-1/2}\, dx = \frac{1000x^{1/2}}{\frac{1}{2}} \Big|_{100}^{225}$$
$$= 2000x^{1/2} \Big|_{100}^{225} = 2000(225)^{1/2} - 2000(100)^{1/2}$$
$$= 2000(15) - 2000(10) = 30,000 - 20,000 = 10,000$$

Hence, the total labor requirement for assembling the additional 125 units is 10,000 hours.

The next example illustrates how the definite integral can be used to express certain important economic concepts. Recall from the study of break-even analysis that the intersection of the cost function and the revenue function gives the break-even point. Similarly, if $D(x)$ represents a demand function and $S(x)$ represents a supply function, the intersection of $S(x)$ and $D(x)$, denoted by $(x^*, D(x^*))$, is called the **equilibrium point** and is illustrated in Figure 11.10. The

Figure 11.10

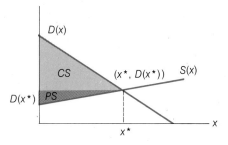

area of the shaded region above $D(x^*)$ and below $D(x)$ represents the **consumer's surplus** CS. It can be found by subtracting the area $x^*D(x^*)$ of the rectangular region from the area under the demand function:

$$CS = \int_0^{x^*} D(x)\,dx - x^*D(x^*)$$

Similarly, the area of the shaded region under $D(x^*)$ and above $S(x)$ represents the **producer's surplus** PS. It can be found by subtracting the area under the supply function from the area of the rectangular region, $x^*D(x^*)$:

$$PS = x^*D(x^*) - \int_0^{x^*} S(x)\,dx$$

To interpret these terms, remember that the demand function $p = D(x)$ gives the price per unit that the consumer is willing to pay for x units. The supply function $p = S(x)$ gives the price per unit for which the supplier is willing to supply x units. The equilibrium point is the price at which the supply is equal to the demand. If the price is less than $D(x^*)$, the demand will exceed the supply. If the price is greater than $D(x^*)$, the supply will exceed the demand. If the price stabilizes at $D(x^*)$, the people who are willing to pay a higher price benefit by having only to pay the equilibrium price. The total of their benefits over the closed interval from 0 to x^* is the consumer's surplus. Similarly, the suppliers who are willing to supply at a lower price than the equilibrium price benefit by receiving the equilibrium price. The total of their benefits over the closed interval from 0 to x^* is the producer's surplus.

EXAMPLE 36   Graph the demand function $D(x) = 10 - 5x/6$ and the supply function $S(x) = x/2 + 2$. Find the equilibrium point and then shade the region whose area is the consumer's surplus and the region whose area is the producer's surplus. Find the value of the consumer's surplus and the value of the producer's surplus. See Figure 11.11.

Figure 11.11

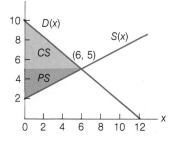

Solution To find the equilibrium point, set $D(x) = S(x)$:

$$10 - \frac{5x}{6} = \frac{x}{2} + 2$$

$$x = 6$$

Substituting $x = 6$ into $D(x)$ or $S(x)$ gives

$$D(x) = 10 - \frac{5x}{6}$$

$$D(6) = 10 - \frac{5(6)}{6} = 10 - 5 = 5$$

Hence, the equilibrium point is $(6, 5) = (x^*, D(x^*))$.

$$CS = \int_0^{x^*} D(x)\, dx - x^* D(x^*)$$

$$= \int_0^6 \left(10 - \frac{5x}{6}\right) dx - 6(5)$$

$$= \left(10x - \frac{5x^2}{12}\right)\Big|_0^6 - 30$$

$$= 60 - \tfrac{5}{12}(36) - 30 = 15$$

Similarly,

$$PS = x^* D(x^*) - \int_0^{x^*} S(x)\, dx$$

$$= 6(5) - \int_0^6 \left(\frac{1}{2}x + 2\right) dx$$

$$= 30 - (\tfrac{1}{4}x^2 + 2x)\Big|_0^6$$

$$= 30 - (9 + 12) = 9$$

The definite integral can be used to find the area of the region bounded by two curves, as the next example illustrates.

EXAMPLE 37 Find the area of the region bounded by $y = 4 - x^2$ and $y = 3x^2$. This region is illustrated in Figure 11.12.

Figure 11.12

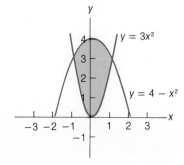

Solution Note that these graphs seem to intersect at (1, 3) and (−1, 3). To prove that the intersection contains these points, show that the coordinates of each of the points satisfy both equations. If the intersection is not apparent from the graph, the substitution method can be used. Substituting $y = 3x^2$ into the equation $y = 4 - x^2$ gives

$$3x^2 = 4 - x^2$$
$$x^2 = 1$$
$$x = 1 \quad \text{or} \quad x = -1$$

Then find y by substituting each of these values of x into the equation that gives y as a function of x. From the graph it is easy to see that the area of the regions bounded by the two functions can be found by finding the area bounded by the first function, the x-axis, and the lines $x = -1$ and $x = 1$, and then subtracting the area bounded by the second function, the x-axis, and the lines $x = -1$ and $x = 1$:

$$A = \int_{-1}^{1} (4 - x^2)\, dx - \int_{-1}^{1} 3x^2\, dx$$
$$= \int_{-1}^{1} (4 - x^2 - 3x^2)\, dx = \int_{-1}^{1} (4 - 4x^2)\, dx$$
$$= (4x - \tfrac{4}{3}x^3)\Big|_{-1}^{1} = 4 - \tfrac{4}{3} - (-4 + \tfrac{4}{3})$$
$$= 4 - \tfrac{4}{3} + 4 - \tfrac{4}{3} = \tfrac{16}{3}$$

The third type of problem we consider in this section involves finding the average value of a function over a closed interval. Let $y = f(x)$ and $\bar{y}$ denote the average of $y_1, y_2, \ldots, y_n$. That is,

$$\bar{y} = \frac{y_1 + y_2 + y_3 + \cdots + y_n}{n} = \frac{1}{n}[f(x_1) + f(x_2) + \cdots + f(x_n)]$$

This expression for $\bar{y}$ gives the average value of the function for n values. To find the average value of a function over a closed interval, it seems natural to generalize this expression for $\bar{y}$ by taking the limit of the expression as n approaches infinity:

$$\bar{y} = \lim_{n \to \infty} \frac{1}{n}[f(x_1) + f(x_2) + \cdots + f(x_n)]$$

To use a definite integral to evaluate this limit, we multiply the numerator and denominator by $b - a$ and then use summation and limits properties to put the expression in the following form:

$$\bar{y} = \lim_{n \to \infty} \left(\frac{1}{n}\right)\left(\frac{b - a}{b - a}\right)[f(x_1) + f(x_2) + \cdots + f(x_n)]$$
$$= \frac{1}{b - a} \lim_{n \to \infty} [f(x_1) + f(x_2) + \cdots + f(x_n)]\left(\frac{b - a}{n}\right)$$
$$= \frac{1}{b - a} \int_{a}^{b} f(x)\, dx$$

Average Value

> If $y = f(x)$ is a continuous function over $a \leq x \leq b$, then the **average value** $\bar{y}$ of the function over $a \leq x \leq b$ is
>
> $$\bar{y} = \frac{1}{b-a} \int_a^b f(x)\, dx$$

E X A M P L E 38   Find the average value of $y = f(x) = 8 - x^2$ over the interval $0 \leq x \leq 2$.

Solution

$$\bar{y} = \frac{1}{b-a} \int_a^b f(x)\, dx = \frac{1}{2-0} \int_0^2 (8 - x^2)\, dx$$

$$= \frac{1}{2}\left[8x - \frac{x^3}{3} \right]_0^2 = \frac{1}{2}\left[8(2) - \frac{2^3}{3} \right] - \frac{1}{2}\left[8(0) - \frac{0^3}{3} \right]$$

$$= \tfrac{1}{2}(16 - \tfrac{8}{3}) - \tfrac{1}{2}(0 - 0) = \tfrac{1}{2}(\tfrac{48}{3} - \tfrac{8}{3}) - 0$$

$$= \tfrac{1}{2}(\tfrac{40}{3}) = \tfrac{20}{3}$$

E X A M P L E 39   A temperature function, $C(t)$, in Celsius degrees was found to be

$$C(t) = t^3 - 3t + 15 \qquad 0 \leq t \leq 3$$

a. What was the average temperature over this period?
b. What was the average temperature over $1 \leq t \leq 3$?

Solution

a. $\displaystyle \bar{C} = \frac{1}{b-a} \int_a^b f(x)\, dx = \frac{1}{3-0} \int_0^3 (t^3 - 3t + 15)\, dt$

$$= \frac{1}{3}\left[\frac{t^4}{4} - \frac{3t^2}{2} + 15t \right]_0^3 = \frac{1}{3}\left[\frac{3^4}{4} - \frac{3}{2}(3)^2 + 15(3) \right]$$

$$= \tfrac{1}{3}(\tfrac{81}{4} - \tfrac{27}{2} + 45) = \tfrac{1}{3}(\tfrac{27}{4} + \tfrac{180}{4}) = \tfrac{1}{3}(\tfrac{207}{4}) = \tfrac{69}{4}$$

b. $\displaystyle \bar{C} = \frac{1}{b-a} \int_a^b f(x)\, dx = \frac{1}{3-1} \int_1^3 (t^3 - 3t + 15)\, dt$

$$= \frac{1}{2}\left[\frac{t^4}{4} - \frac{3t^2}{2} + 15t \right]_1^3$$

$$= \frac{1}{2}\left[\frac{3^4}{4} - \frac{3}{2}(3)^2 + 15(3) \right] - \frac{1}{2}\left[\frac{1^4}{4} - \frac{3}{2}(1)^2 + 15(1) \right]$$

$$= \tfrac{1}{2}(\tfrac{81}{4} - \tfrac{27}{2} + 45) - \tfrac{1}{2}(\tfrac{1}{4} - \tfrac{3}{2} + 15)$$

$$= \tfrac{207}{8} - \tfrac{1}{2}(\tfrac{1}{4} - \tfrac{6}{4} + \tfrac{60}{4}) = \tfrac{207}{8} - \tfrac{1}{2}(\tfrac{55}{4})$$

$$= \tfrac{207}{8} - \tfrac{55}{8} = \tfrac{152}{8} = 19$$

Exercise Set 11.6

A   *Find the area of the region bounded by the following curves.*

1. $f(x) = 5$, $f(x) = 0$, $x = 2$, and $x = 5$

2. $f(x) = x$, $f(x) = 1$, $x = 1$, and $x = 3$

3. $f(x) = 2x$, $f(x) = 0$, $x = 2$, and $x = 4$

4. $f(x) = 3x$, $f(x) = 1$, $x = 1$, and $x = 4$

5. $f(x) = 7x$, $f(x) = 2$, $x = 2$, and $x = 3$

B *Find the average value of each of the following functions over the indicated interval.*

6. $f(x) = 5 \qquad 1 \le x \le 4$

7. $f(x) = x \qquad 2 \le x \le 4$

8. $f(x) = 10 - 2x \qquad 3 \le x \le 4$

9. $f(t) = 3t^2 \qquad 0 \le t \le 4$

10. $c(t) = t^2 - t + 3 \qquad 0 \le t \le 2$

11. $f(x) = 3x^2 - 2x + 1 \qquad 1 \le x \le 3$

C *Find the area of the region bounded by the following curves.*

12. $f(x) = x^2$, $f(x) = x$

13. $y^2 = x$, $x = 9$

14. $y = x^2$, $y^2 = x$

15. $y = 16 - x^2$, $y = 6x$

Business **16. Assembly Functions.** From assembling 49 units of a product, the production manager obtained the following rate-of-assembly function:

$$f(x) = 1200x^{-1/2}$$

where $f(x)$ represents the rate of labor hours required to assemble x units. The company plans to bid on a new order of 32 additional units. Help the manager estimate the total labor requirements for assembling the additional 32 units.

17. Redo exercise 16 if the company now plans to bid on a new order of 72 additional units.

18. Cost Functions. The Good Coal Company gives the cost of producing coal as

$$C(x) = 15x + 100x^{1/2}$$

Find the average cost of producing
a. 2500 tons.   **b.** 6400 tons.

Economics **Marginal Functions.** *Given the following marginal cost and marginal revenue functions, find the total cost functions, the total revenue functions, and the profit functions. Assume a fixed cost of \$10.*

19. $MC = 3x + 8$, $MR = 23$

20. $MC = 2x + 5$, $MR = 19$

21. $MC = 4x + 9$, $MR = 37$

22. $MC = 3x + 7$, $MR = 19$

23. $MC = 4x + 7$, $MR = 19$

24. $MC = 2x + 7$, $MR = 23$

Graph the following demand and supply functions. Find the equilibrium points and shade the consumer's surplus regions and the producer's surplus regions. Compute the values of the consumer's surplus and the values of the producer's surplus.

25. $D(x) = 9 - x$, $S(x) = x + 3$

26. $D(x) = 8 - 2x$, $S(x) = x + 2$

27. $D(x) = 6 - x$, $S(x) = \frac{1}{4}x + 1$

28. $D(x) = 7 - x$, $S(x) = \frac{1}{4}x + 2$

29. $D(x) = 8 - \frac{1}{4}x^2$, $S(x) = \frac{1}{8}x^2 + 2$

30. $D(x) = 9 - \frac{1}{12}x^2$, $S(x) = \frac{1}{12}x^2 + 3$

Life Sciences **31. Temperature.** The rate of change of temperature 1 hour after x milligrams of a drug is administered is

$$\frac{dT}{dx} = 3x - \frac{x^2}{4} \qquad 0 \le x \le 8$$

What total change of temperature occurs when the dosage changes from
a. 0 to 3 milligrams?   **b.** 1 to 4 milligrams?

32. **Blood Flow.** Suppose V represents the total flow in cubic units per second of blood through an artery whose radius is R, and suppose r is the distance of a particle of blood from the center of the artery. Assume that

$$\frac{dV}{dr} = 2\pi C(Rr - r^2)\, dr$$

where C is a constant that depends on the units used.

  a. Compute

$$V = \int_{R}^{1.1R} 2\pi C(Rr - r^2)\, dr$$

  to find the increase in blood flow when the radius of the artery is increased by 10%.

  b. Find the increase in blood flow when the radius of the artery is increased by 20%.

Social Sciences   33. **Learning Functions.** A person's learning rate is given by

$$\frac{dL}{dt} = 30t^{-1/2} \qquad 1 \le t \le 16$$

Find the number of words learned (that is, find L) from $t = 4$ to $t = 9$.

7 Summary and Review

Review to ensure your understanding of the definitions of antiderivative and indefinite integral. Make sure you know how to solve rate problems and to find the total output, total cost, and total revenue when the marginal output, marginal cost, and marginal revenue functions are given.

The integration formulas presented include:

$$\int x^n\, dx = \frac{x^{n+1}}{n+1} + C \qquad n \ne -1$$

$$\int kf'(x)\, dx = k \int f'(x)\, dx + C = kf(x) + C$$

$$\int [f(x) + g(x)]\, dx = \int f(x)\, dx + \int g(x)\, dx$$

The **fundamental theorem of calculus** provides the connecting link between the indefinite integral and the definite integral. It is given as: If $F(x)$ is any antiderivative of $f(x)$ over $a \le x \le b$, then

$$\int_{a}^{b} f(x)\, dx = F(b) - F(a)$$

The **average value of a function** over $a \le x \le b$ is defined as

$$\bar{y} = \frac{1}{b - a} \int_{a}^{b} f(x)\, dx$$

Integral calculus is applied to solve problems in marginal analysis, in consumer and producer surplus problems, in rate problems, and in average value problems.

Review Exercise Set 11.7

A *Find the following indefinite integrals.*

1. $\int 5x^{1/2}\,dx$

2. $\int \left(\dfrac{2}{x^2} - 3x\right) dx$

3. $\int (3x - 5)\,dx$

4. $\int 6x^{-2}\,dx$

5. $\int (3x^2 + 5x - 7)\,dx$

6. $\int (2x^3 - 3x + 5)\,dx$

B **7.** $\int (x + 3)^{-2}\,dx$

8. $\int (x^2 + 3)^{-2}2x\,dx$

9. $\int (x^3 + 3)^{-2}x^2\,dx$

10. $\int 3x^{1/3}\,dx$

11. $\int x(x^2 - 5)\,dx$

12. $\int x^2(x + 3)\,dx$

13. $\int \sqrt{3x - 7}\,dx$

14. $\int \sqrt[3]{2x + 3}\,dx$

15. $\int (x + 2)3x^2\,dx$

16. $\int (x^2 - 2)x\,dx$

C *Find the value of the following definite integrals.*

17. $\int_0^3 (9x - x^3)\,dx$

18. $\int_2^3 \dfrac{2x\,dx}{(1 + x^2)^2}$

19. $\int_0^7 \sqrt[3]{x + 1}\,dx$

20. $\int_0^3 \sqrt{4 - x}\,dx$

Business **21. Inflation.** Inflation has caused the Good Coal Company's cost function to change to

$$C(x) = 16x + 100x^{1/2}$$

Find the average cost of producing
a. 2500 tons. **b.** 6400 tons.

Economics **22. Supply Functions.** Everlite has produced a new flashlight. If the supply function is

$$S(x) = x^2 + 13x$$

and the demand function is

$$D(x) = 169 - x^2$$

find the equilibrium point. Graph the functions and shade the consumer's surplus region and the producer's surplus region. Compute the values of the consumer's surplus and the producer's surplus.

23. Marginal Revenue Functions. A marginal revenue function is given by

$$MR = 900 - 0.6x$$

Find the total revenue function and the revenue for 1200 items. What is the maximum revenue?

Life Sciences **24. Temperature.** The rate of change of temperature 1 hour after x milligrams of a drug is administered is

$$\frac{dT}{dx} = 2x - \frac{x^2}{5} \qquad 0 \le x \le 7$$

What total change of temperature occurs when the dosage changes from
a. 0 to 2 milligrams? **b.** 1 to 3 milligrams?

Social Sciences   **25. Learning Functions.** A rate of learning is given by

$$\frac{dL}{dt} = 36t^{-1/2} \qquad 1 \le t \le 16$$

Find the number of words learned from $t = 1$ to $t = 16$.

Physical Sciences   **26.** Find the area of the region bounded by $f(x) = 4$ and $f(x) = x^2$.

12

The Calculus of Exponential and Logarithmic Functions

In the preceding chapters we have usually discussed algebraic functions. **Algebraic functions** are functions that can be defined in terms of the algebraic operations of addition, subtraction, multiplication, division, raising to powers, and taking roots of the variable. When the variable appears as an exponent, the function is called an **exponential function.** To solve for a variable in an exponential function, the inverse function is needed. The inverse function of an exponential function is called a **logarithmic function.** Many problems involving growth use exponential or logarithmic functions. For this reason we introduce and study the calculus of exponential and logarithmic functions.

1 Exponential Functions

In earlier discussions we have considered functions involving a variable raised to a power, such as x^2. We now consider functions involving exponential terms where the base is a constant and the exponent is a variable, such as 3^x. Although this type of function may seem rather strange, economists use such functions to study the growth of the money supply, businesspeople use them to study decay in sales, biologists to study the growth of organisms in a laboratory culture, and social scientists to study population growth and the dating of fossils.

When the base used in the function is $e = 2.71828\ldots$, the exponential function is then written in the form e^x. This function is very useful in the study of calculus.

In this section we consider mathematical models or equations of the form

$$y = a^x$$

where the variable occurs as an exponent.

Exponential Function

A function $f(x) = a^x$, where $a > 0$ and $a \neq 1$ and the exponent x is any real number, is called an *exponential function*.

Note that a must be positive; if a were negative, then x could not be any real number because the function would not have meaning when $x = \frac{1}{2}$ or $\frac{1}{4}$, and so forth.

The following examples illustrate several properties of exponential functions.

EXAMPLE 1 Compute some points of the exponential function $y = 2^x$, and use these points to draw the graph.

Solution Some points of this graph are given in Table 12.1, and the graph is shown in Figure 12.1. Note that the graph of the function $y = 2^x$ is completely above the x-axis. The curve crosses the y-axis at $y = 1$ and gets close to but never crosses the x-axis for negative values of x. These characteristics hold for any exponential function of the form $y = a^x$, where $a > 1$. Note that the graph increases very rapidly with increasing x, for $a > 1$.

Table 12.1

x	-5	-4	-3	-2	-1	0	1	2	3	4
2^x	2^{-5}	2^{-4}	2^{-3}	2^{-2}	2^{-1}	2^0	2^1	2^2	2^3	2^4
y	$\frac{1}{32}$	$\frac{1}{16}$	$\frac{1}{8}$	$\frac{1}{4}$	$\frac{1}{2}$	1	2	4	8	16

Figure 12.1

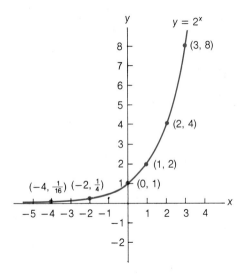

The characteristics of exponential functions discovered in the preceding example may be summarized as follows:

Properties of Exponential Functions

For the exponential function

$$y = f(x) = a^x \qquad a > 0, \qquad a \neq 1$$

1. Its graph lies above the x-axis for all x.
2. If $x = 0$, then $a^x = 1$ or $f(0) = 1$.
3. For $a > 1$, the function increases as x increases; as x decreases, $f(x)$ decreases, getting closer and closer to 0 but never becoming 0.
4. There are no x-intercepts; the graph does not cross the x-axis.

Figure 12.2 illustrates the steepness of the graph of an exponential function for various bases. Of course, a negative coefficient would change a positive exponential function to a negative function. Likewise, when $c > 0$ and $a > 1$, the graph

Figure 12.2

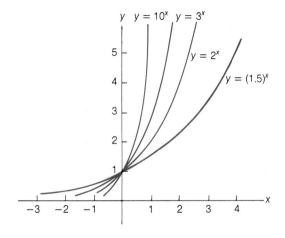

of $y = ca^x$ is above the x-axis and has a shape similar to the graph of $y = a^x$ except that the curve crosses the y-axis at $y = c$. When $c < 0$ and $a > 1$, the graph is below the x-axis and crosses the y-axis at $y = c$ (negative in this case).

EXAMPLE 2 Compute several points of the exponential function

$$y = -3(2)^x$$

and use these points, along with the preceding discussion, to draw the graph.

Solution Values of the function are computed for several selected values of x in Table 12.2, and the graph is given in Figure 12.3.

Table 12.2

x	-5	-4	-3	-2	-1	0	1	2	3	4
$-3(2)^x$	$-3(2)^{-5}$	$-3(2)^{-4}$	$-3(2)^{-3}$	$-3(2)^{-2}$	$-3(2)^{-1}$	$-3(2)^0$	$-3(2)^1$	$-3(2)^2$	$-3(2)^3$	$-3(2)^4$
y	$-\frac{3}{32}$	$-\frac{3}{16}$	$-\frac{3}{8}$	$-\frac{3}{4}$	$-\frac{3}{2}$	-3	-6	-12	-24	-48

Figure 12.3

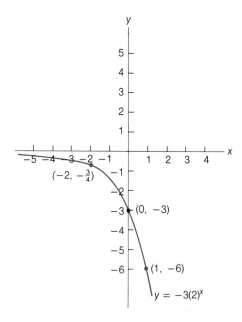

Likewise, a negative exponent changes an increasing function to a decreasing function.

EXAMPLE 3 Graph $y = 2^{-x}$ or $y = (\frac{1}{2})^x$.

Solution   Note in Figure 12.4 that $y = 2^{-x}$ is the mirror image of $y = 2^x$ across the y-axis.

Figure 12.4

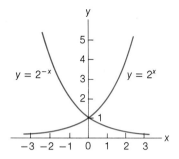

Sometimes enough information is given so that the equation of an exponential function can be found when only a graph is given. Let's consider the following simple example.

EXAMPLE 4   Find an exponential function with the graph shown in Figure 12.5.

Figure 12.5

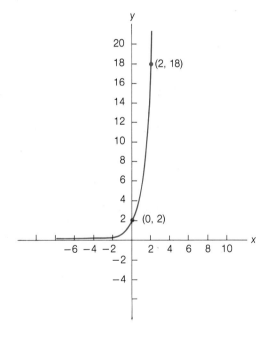

Solution   Assume that the exponential function is $y = ca^x$. Since (0, 2) is on the graph, its coordinates must satisfy the equation. Substitution gives $2 = ca^0$ and, since $a^0 = 1$, $c = 2$. Therefore, $y = 2a^x$. Since (2, 18) is also on the graph, its coordinates must also satisfy the equation. Substitution gives $18 = 2a^2$ or $9 = a^2$. Therefore, $a = +3$ or $a = -3$. Since the value of the function is always positive, $a = 3$, and an exponential function representing the graph of Figure 12.5 is $y = 2 \cdot 3^x$.

Undoubtedly, the most useful exponential function is the function

$$y = ce^{bx}$$

where e is an irrational number that occurs often in mathematics. Actually,

$$e = \lim_{n \to \infty} \left(1 + \frac{1}{n}\right)^n$$

or, equivalently.

$$\lim_{x \to 0} (1 + x)^{1/x}$$

In this chapter we will consider a rational number approximation for e accurate to seven decimal places:

$$e = 2.7182818$$

If you have a hand calculator that evaluates e to given powers, you can easily verify the approximate values of e^x for given values of x. If your hand calculator does not evaluate powers of e, you can compute integral powers of e by using $e = 2.7182818$. If you do not have a hand calculator, Table III in the Appendix can be used to evaluate e^x and e^{-x} for given values of x. However, since the

Table 12.3

x	-3	-2	-1	0	1	2	3
e^x	e^{-3}	e^{-2}	e^{-1}	e^0	e^1	e^2	e^3
y	0.05	0.14	0.37	1	2.7	7.4	20.1

Figure 12.6

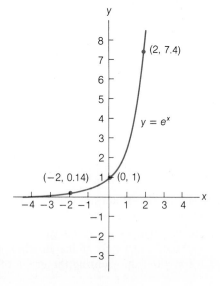

table of values will not be available at all times, it is suggested that you make use of a hand calculator if you have one. Let's now look at a table of values (Table 12.3) and the graph of $y = e^x$ (Figure 12.6).

EXAMPLE 5 Joe wishes to place \$10,000 in a savings account for $2\frac{1}{2}$ years. The XYZ Savings and Loan Association advertises that the interest rate is 12% compounded continuously. To what amount will Joe's \$10,000 accumulate in $2\frac{1}{2}$ years?

Solution To assist Joe in solving this problem, we recall the formula introduced in Chapter 4 for continuously compounding. This formula involves exponential functions and has applications in population growth, epidemic spread, mechanical failure, and radioactive decay. It is of the form $y = be^{ct}$.

Recall that the compound amount A of a principal P compounded *continuously* at an effective rate i per year for t years is given by

$$A = Pe^{it}$$

Thus, Joe's \$10,000 will accumulate as follows:

$$A = 10{,}000e^{(0.12)(5/2)}$$
$$= 10{,}000e^{(0.30)}$$
$$= 10{,}000(1.3498588)$$
$$= \$13{,}498.59$$

Exercise Set **12.1**

A *Find the values of y when x = 0, 1, −1, 2, and −2.*

1. $y = 2^x$ **2.** $y = -2^x$ **3.** $y = 2^{-x}$

4. $y = (\frac{1}{2})^x$ **5.** $y = 2^x - 2$ **6.** $y = 10^x - 1$

7. $y = 4(3)^{-2x} + 5$ **8.** $y = 3(2)^{-x} + 7$

9. Find the value of y when $t = 0, 0.5, 1,$ and 2.
    a. $y = e^{-t} + e^t$ **b.** $y = 3e^{-2t}$ **c.** $y = e^{0.05t}$
    d. $y = 500e^{-0.01t}$ **e.** $y = 4e^{0.005t}$ **f.** $y = 4e^{0.04t} - 6e^{-0.01t}$

10. Find some points of the following exponential functions and use these points to draw the graphs.
    a. $y = 2^{-x}$ **b.** $y = 3^x$ **c.** $y = 2^x + 1$
    d. $y = 3^{-x}$ **e.** $y = 2^{-x} + 2$ **f.** $y = 3^x + 1$

11. Graph the following exponential functions.
    a. $y = 3e^{-t}$ **b.** $y = 4e^t$ **c.** $y = 6e^{-0.2t}$

B **12.** Find some points of the following exponential functions, and use these points to draw the graphs.
    a. $y = 2^x - 2$ **b.** $y = 3^x - 2$ **c.** $y = 10^x - 1$

13. Find an exponential function having each of the following graphs.

a.

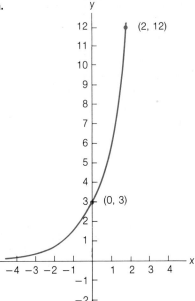

b.

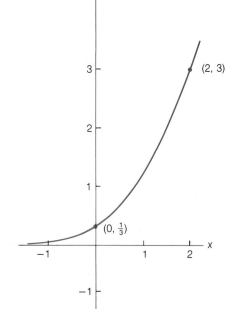

c.

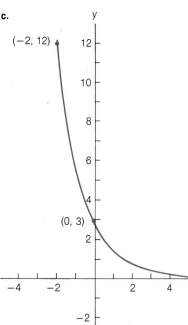

d.

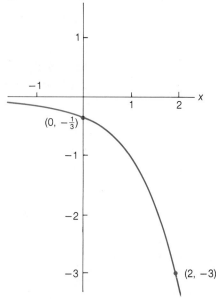

C **14.** Find some points of the following exponential functions, and use these points to draw the graphs.

a. $y = 3(2)^{-x} + 7$ **b.** $y = 5(3)^x - 4$ **c.** $y = 4(2)^{-x} + 7$

d. $y = 6(3)^{2x} - 10$ **e.** $y = 4(3)^{-2x} + 5$ **f.** $y = 8(2)^{-3x} + 4$

15. Graph the following exponential functions.
   a. $y = 4e^{-0.05t} - 6$ **b.** $y = 5 - 3e^{2t}$ **c.** $y = 6 - 4e^{-0.2t}$

16. Represent the following exponential functions by graphs.
   a. $y = 2^{x^2 - 1}$ **b.** $y = 3^{-x^2}$ **c.** $y = 4(2)^{-x}$
   d. $y = 5(3)^{2x^2}$ **e.** $y = 1 - 7e^{-2x^2}$ **f.** $y = 2 - 6e^{-3x}$

Business

17. Compound Interest. $6,000 is compounded continuously at a rate of 8% for 4 years. Find the sum to which it accumulates.

18. Compound Interest. What investment compounded continuously at 7% for 10 years will amount to $4,000?

19. Depreciation. A machine is depreciated by a given amount each year. The value of the machine (usually designated by S) at the end of n years, when the machine depreciates r% per year and C is the original cost, is

$$S = C\left(1 - \frac{r}{100}\right)^n$$

Find the value at the end of 8 years of a machine costing $100,000 at an annual rate of depreciation of 12%.

20. Depreciation. Find the value at the end of 12 years of a $30,000 machine depreciating at a rate of 15% per year.

21. Scrap Value. The scrap value of a machine is the value at the end of its useful life. If the scrap value of an $80,000 machine is $10,000 at the end of 10 years, what is the annual rate of depreciation?

22. Scrap Value. A house costing $120,000 is thought to have a scrap value at the end of 40 years of $20,000. What is the annual rate of depreciation?

Economics

23. Sales Functions. The sales for a product are represented by the following exponential function, where t represents the number of years the product has been on the market:

$$S(t) = 600 - 200e^{-t}$$

Graphically represent sales as a function of time t. From the graph describe how sales change with time.

Life Sciences

24. Radioactive Decay. Suppose that the amount in grams of a radioactive material present at a time t is given by

$$A(t) = 100e^{-0.2t}$$

where t is measured in days. Find the half-life of the substance. (The *half-life* is the time it takes for half of the substance to decay.)

25. Radioactive Decay. The half-life of an isotope is 200,000 years. How long will it take it to decay by 80%?

Social Sciences

26. Population. The population of Our Town was 60,000 in 1968 and 200,000 in 1978.
   a. Use an exponential growth curve to estimate the population in 1980.
   b. In 1985.
   c. Draw a graph of this function.

27. Learning Curves. The graph of an equation of the form

$$y = k - ke^{-ct}$$

is called a *learning curve*. Learning increases rapidly with time and then levels out and tends to an upper limit. Suppose $k = 300$ and $y = 200$ when $t = 10$.
   a. Find c.   **b.** Find y when $t = 5$.
   c. Find y when $t = 20$.   **d.** Draw the graph of the function you found for y.

28. Learning Curves. A special learning curve is found to be represented by

$$R = 100(1 - e^{-ct})$$

where R is the number of responses and t is the time involved. Suppose $R = 50$ when $t = 10$.

a. What is R when $t = 0$? Explain. **b.** Find c.

c. Find R when $t = 5$. **d.** Find R when $t = 30$.

e. Draw the graph of the function.

2 Logarithmic Functions

The inverse of an exponential function is called a **logarithmic function.** Because of this relationship the logarithmic function is very important. In this section we learn:

1. how to convert from logarithmic functions to exponential functions and vice versa,
2. how to evaluate logarithmic functions for certain values,
3. how to graph logarithmic functions, and
4. properties of logarithmic functions.

Since the logarithmic function is the inverse of the very useful growth function and decay function, you should expect it to have many applications. Perhaps its most useful application is in the solution of exponential equations.

We introduce this section with the exponential function discussed in the preceding section. However, this time we write

$$x = b^y$$

The exponent in this function can be written in terms of another function called a *logarithm*.

Logarithm

If b is a positive number not equal to 1, then the logarithm of x to the base b is equal to y, written as

$$\log_b x = y \qquad x > 0$$

if and only if $x = b^y$.

From this definition we see that **the logarithm of a number x to the base b is the power to which b must be raised to get x.** Observe in this definition that x must be greater than 0 in order for this definition to have meaning because there is no real number y for which b^y is not positive.

Log_b x is read "the logarithm to the base b of x" or "the logarithm of x to the base b." The function defined is called the logarithmic function; its domain is the set of positive real numbers and its range is the set of all real numbers. (See Figure 12.7.)

$$\log_b x \begin{cases} < 0 & \text{for } 0 < x < 1 \\ = 0 & \text{for } x = 1 \\ > 0 & \text{for } x > 1 \end{cases}$$

Figure 12.7

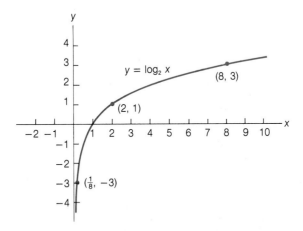

EXAMPLE 6   Table 12.4 compares the form of exponential statements with equivalent logarithmic statements.

Table 12.4

Exponential Statement	Equivalent Logarithmic Statement
$2^0 = 1$	$\log_2 1 = 0$
$2^1 = 2$	$\log_2 2 = 1$
$2^2 = 4$	$\log_2 4 = 2$
$2^{-1} = \frac{1}{2}$	$\log_2 \frac{1}{2} = -1$
$2^{-4} = \frac{1}{16}$	$\log_2 \frac{1}{16} = -4$
$2^{1/2} = \sqrt{2}$	$\log_2 \sqrt{2} = \frac{1}{2}$

EXAMPLE 7   Find $\log_5 125$.

Solution   Let $\log_5 125 = x$. Then, by the definition, $5^x = 125$. Since $5^3 = 125$, then $x = 3$; therefore, $\log_5 125 = 3$.

EXAMPLE 8   Write $27^{-2/3} = \frac{1}{9}$ in logarithmic notation.

Solution   Since $27^{-2/3} = \frac{1}{9}$, then $\log_{27} \frac{1}{9} = -\frac{2}{3}$.

From the definition we note that

$$\log_b b^4 = 4 \qquad \text{and} \qquad \log_b b^{-3} = -3$$

EXAMPLE 9   **a.** $\log_5 5^3 = 3$
                b. $\log_{10} 10^{-4} = -4$
                c. $\log_{10} 10 = 1$
                d. $\log_b 1 = \log_b b^0 = 0$

The graphs of logarithmic functions can be obtained easily by changing the functions to exponential form. For example, to graph $y = \log_2 x$, write the equation as $x = 2^y$ and obtain the values as given in Table 12.5.

Table 12.5

x	$\frac{1}{8}$	1	2	8
y	-3	0	1	3

Notice that this function is not defined when $x \leq 0$ and that the value of the function increases as x increases. (See Figure 12.7.)

When $b = 10$, we have $y = \log_{10} x$, which is called the **common logarithm** of x. In this case we write "log x" without indicating the base 10.

EXAMPLE 10   Write some equivalent exponential and common logarithmic statements.

Solution

Exponential Statement	Equivalent Logarithmic Statement
$10^0 = 1$	$\log 1 = 0$
$10^1 = 10$	$\log 10 = 1$
$10^2 = 100$	$\log 10^2 = 2$
$10^3 = 1000$	$\log 10^3 = 3$
$10^{-1} = \frac{1}{10}$	$\log 10^{-1} = -1$
$10^{-2} = \frac{1}{100}$	$\log 10^{-2} = -2$
$10^{1/2} = \sqrt{10}$	$\log 10^{1/2} = \frac{1}{2}$

Now let $N = b^x$ so that $\log_b N = x$, and let $M = b^y$ so that $\log_b M = y$. Then

$$NM = b^x \cdot b^y = b^{x+y}$$

Therefore,

$$\log_b NM = x + y = \log_b N + \log_b M$$

Likewise,

$$\frac{N}{M} = \frac{b^x}{b^y} = b^{x-y}$$

Thus,

$$\log_b \left(\frac{N}{M}\right) = x - y = \log_b N - \log_b M$$

Also note that

$$N^m = (b^x)^m = b^{mx}$$

and

$$\log_b N^m = mx = m \log_b N$$

These characteristics are summarized by the following properties, where $b > 0$, $b \neq 1$, and M and N are positive.

Properties of Logarithms

a. $\log_b (N \cdot M) = \log_b N + \log_b M$
b. $\log_b (N/M) = \log_b N - \log_b M$
c. $\log_b N^m = m \log_b N$
d. $\log_b M = \log_b N$ if and only if $M = N$
e. $\log_b b = 1$
f. $\log_b 1 = 0$

Let's apply these rules to common logarithms.

EXAMPLE 11

a. $\log 30 = \log (5 \cdot 6) = \log 5 + \log 6$
b. Given that $\log 2 = 0.3010$, find $\log 5$.

$$\log 5 = \log \tfrac{10}{2} = \log 10 - \log 2$$

$$= 1 - 0.3010 = 0.6990$$

c. Find $\log 4$.

$$\log 4 = 2 \log 2 = 2(0.3010) = 0.6020$$

d. If $\log x = \log 3$, then $x = 3$.
e. $\log 10 = 1$
f. $\log 1 = 0$

EXAMPLE 12 Given that $\log 3 = 0.4771$, find $\log 9$.

Solution Since $9 = 3^2$, property **c** of logarithms yields

$$\log 9 = 2 \log 3 = 2(0.4771) = 0.9542$$

EXAMPLE 13 Use $\log 4 = 0.6020$ and $\log 9 = 0.9542$ to find $\log 36$.

Solution Since $36 = (4)(9)$, property **a** of logarithms yields

$$\log 36 = \log 4 + \log 9$$
$$= 0.6020 + 0.9542$$
$$= 1.5562$$

EXAMPLE 14 Solve the exponential equation $3^x = 4$.

Solution Take the logarithm of both sides to obtain

$$\log 3^x = \log 4$$

Property **c** of logarithms gives

$$x \log 3 = \log 4$$

$$x = \frac{\log 4}{\log 3}$$

$$x = \frac{0.6020}{0.4771} = 1.26$$

Suppose we are interested in the exponential form $x = e^y$, and have a need to solve for y as

$$y = \log_e x$$

which is read "the **natural logarithm** of x." This logarithm is expressed as either

$$\log_e x \quad \text{or} \quad \ln x$$

EXAMPLE 15 Find the natural logarithm of $N = e^3$.

Solution Let $\ln e^3 = x$. Then $e^3 = e^x$, so $x = 3$. Thus, $\ln e^3 = 3$.

Exercise Set 12.2

A 1. Write the following equations in logarithmic notation.
   a. $3^4 = 81$ **b.** $2^7 = 128$ **c.** $3^{-2} = \frac{1}{9}$
   d. $5^4 = 625$ **e.** $8^{1/3} = 2$ **f.** $16^{1/4} = 2$

2. Write the following in exponential notation.
   a. $\log_7 49 = 2$ **b.** $\log_6 36 = 2$ **c.** $\log_3 \frac{1}{9} = -2$
   d. $\log_3 \frac{1}{27} = -3$ **e.** $\log_{10} \frac{1}{100} = -2$ **f.** $\log_{10} 1000 = 3$

3. Find the following logarithms.
   a. $\log_2 16$ **b.** $\log_2 \frac{1}{8}$ **c.** $\log_{1/2} \frac{1}{8}$ **d.** $\log_3 27$
   e. $\log_{10} 10$ **f.** $\log_{10} 1$ **g.** $\log_{10} 0.1$ **h.** $\log_{10} 0.01$

4. Find the base for the following logarithms.
   a. $\log_b 2 = \frac{1}{2}$ **b.** $\log_b 2 = -1$ **c.** $\log_b \frac{1}{8} = -3$ **d.** $\log_b 100 = 2$

5. Determine the solution for x by inspection or by first writing the equation in exponential form.
   a. $\log_3 9 = x$ **b.** $\log_4 x = 3$ **c.** $\log_{10} x = -3$ **d.** $\log_3 27 = x$

Express as the sum or difference of simpler logarithmic quantities.

EXAMPLE $\log_b \dfrac{x^2 y^{1/2}}{z^3}$

Solution $\log_b \dfrac{x^2 y^{1/2}}{z^3} = \log_b x^2 + \log_b y^{1/2} - \log_b z^3$

$$= 2 \log_b x + \tfrac{1}{2} \log_b y - 3 \log_b z$$

6. $\log_{10} x^2 y^3 z^4$ 　　　　　　 **7.** $\log_b \sqrt[3]{\dfrac{x^2}{y}}$ 　　　　　　 **8.** $\log_{10} \sqrt{\dfrac{xy^3}{z}}$

Express the following as a single logarithm with coefficient 1.

9. $2 \log_b x - \tfrac{1}{2} \log_b y$ 　　　　　　　　 **10.** $3 \log_b x + 2 \log_b y - 2 \log_b z$

11. $\log (x - 1) - \tfrac{1}{2} \log x$ 　　　　　　　　 **12.** $\tfrac{1}{2}(\log x + 2 \log y - 5 \log z)$

13. Use the properties of logarithms to write the following as sums or differences of logarithms, where $x > 0$ and $y > 0$.

　　a. $\ln \dfrac{x}{y}$ 　　**b.** $\ln xy$ 　　**c.** $\ln x^2 y$ 　　**d.** $\ln \dfrac{x^2}{y}$

B 　**14.** Graph the following logarithmic curves.
　　a. $y = \log_2 x$ 　　**b.** $y = \log_{10} (x + 10)$

15. Graph the following functions involving natural logarithms.
　　a. $y = \ln (2x + 1)$ 　　**b.** $y = 5 \ln 6x$

C 　**16.** Given that $\log_{10} 2 = 0.3010$, compute the following logarithms.
　　a. $\log_{10} 8$ 　　**b.** $\log_{10} 16$ 　　**c.** $\log_{10} 128$ 　　**d.** $\log_{10} 4$

17. Given that $\log_{10} 2 = 0.3010$ and $\log_{10} 3 = 0.4771$, compute the following logarithms.
　　a. $\log_{10} 9$ 　　**b.** $\log_{10} 6$ 　　**c.** $\log_{10} 18$ 　　**d.** $\log_{10} 12$

18. Given that $\ln 2 = 0.6931$ and $\ln 3 = 1.0986$, compute the following natural logarithms.
　　a. $\ln 9$ 　　**b.** $\ln 6$ 　　**c.** $\ln 18$ 　　**d.** $\ln 12$

19. Graph the following logarithmic curves.
　　a. $y = 8 \log_4 x^2$ 　　**b.** $y = \log_{10} (x^2 + 2x)$

20. Graph the following functions involving natural logarithms.
　　a. $y = 2 \ln 2x^2$ 　　**b.** $y = 10 \ln (x^2 + 2x)$

21. Solve each of the following equations.
　　a. $\log_6 1 = y$ 　　　　　　　 **b.** $\log_4 x = 1$
　　c. $\log x + \log (x + 1) = \log 2$ 　　**d.** $\ln (y + 2) - \ln 3 = \ln 4y$
　　e. $e^{-x} = \dfrac{1}{e^2}$ 　　　　　　　 **f.** $\ln (y + 1) + \ln 2 = \ln (y + 10)$

Business 　**22. Cost Functions.** The cost function for the manufacturing of a certain commodity is given as

$$C(x) = 10{,}000 + 600 \ln (2x^2 + 1)$$

where x is the number of items to be manufactured.
　a. What is the fixed cost (the cost when $x = 0$)?
　b. What is the average cost per item of manufacturing 100 items?
　c. Of manufacturing 1000 items?
　d. Of manufacturing 10,000 items?

Economics   **23. Demand Functions.** The demand function for a product is given by

$$x = \frac{500}{\ln(D+1)}$$

a. Find the price when the demand is for 999 articles.
b. Find the demand when the price is $300.
c. Draw the graph of the function.

Life Sciences   **24. pH Factor.** The pH of a solution is defined to be

$$pH = \log\frac{1}{H^+}$$

where H^+ represents the concentration of hydrogen ions per liter. Draw the graph of this function, letting pH be the dependent variable. Let H^+ take on values such as $6(10)^{-2}$, $4(10)^{-3}$, $8(10)^{-4}$, and so on.

Physical Sciences   **25. Earthquake.** A Richter scale measurement of the intensity of an earthquake is given as

$$RS = \log cI$$

Draw a graph of this function, letting I take on values $1000/c$, $10{,}000/c$, and $100{,}000/c$.

26. Carbon-14 Dating. A method of dating objects (called carbon-14 dating) has been developed based on the fact that the radioactive isotope of carbon has a half-life of 5600 years. Let R be the ratio of carbon-14 to nonradioactive carbon in the atmosphere, and let r be the ratio as found in the specimen. The formula

$$R = re^{(t\ln 2)/5600}$$

gives the relationship between R and r, where t is the age of the specimen in years.
a. What is the relationship between r and R when $t = 0$?
b. If $r = \frac{1}{2}R$, what is t?
c. If $r = \frac{1}{3}R$, what is t?
d. Draw the graph of the curve for $r = Re^{(-t\ln 2)/5600}$.

Social Sciences   **27. Archaeology.** In archaeology the following formula is used to relate the population of a site to the area of the site

$$\log P = c\log A$$

Let $c = 0.5$, and draw the graph of this function.

Finding Derivatives of Logarithmic Functions

After becoming familiar with exponential and logarithmic functions, it seems natural to study how the derivatives of these functions may be found. We begin our study of these derivatives by considering the derivative of a logarithmic function. As stated in the previous section, logarithmic functions are very useful in solving exponential equations. The properties of logarithms make finding the derivatives of some functions much easier.

To understand why e is a natural base for logarithmic functions we compute the derivative of

$$f(x) = \log_e x = \ln x$$

by the four-step procedure of Chapter 9:

1. $f(x + \Delta x) = \ln (x + \Delta x)$
$\qquad f(x) = \ln x$

2. $f(x + \Delta x) - f(x) = \ln (x + \Delta x) - \ln x$

3. $\dfrac{f(x + \Delta x) - f(x)}{\Delta x} = \dfrac{\ln (x + \Delta x) - \ln x}{\Delta x}$

4. $\displaystyle\lim_{\Delta x \to 0} \dfrac{f(x + \Delta x) - f(x)}{\Delta x} = \lim_{\Delta x \to 0} \dfrac{\ln (x + \Delta x) - \ln x}{\Delta x}$

$$f'(x) = \lim_{\Delta x \to 0} \frac{1}{\Delta x} \ln \left(\frac{x + \Delta x}{x} \right)$$

$$= \lim_{\Delta x \to 0} \left(\frac{1}{x} \right) \left(\frac{x}{\Delta x} \right) \ln \left(1 + \frac{\Delta x}{x} \right)$$

$$= \frac{1}{x} \lim_{\Delta x \to 0} \ln \left(1 + \frac{\Delta x}{x} \right)^{x/\Delta x}$$

$$= \frac{1}{x} \ln \left[\lim_{\Delta x \to 0} \left(1 + \frac{\Delta x}{x} \right)^{x/\Delta x} \right]$$

$$= \frac{1}{x} \ln e$$

Since $\ln e = 1$, the formula for the derivative of $f(x) = \ln x$ is

$$f'(x) = \frac{1}{x}$$

If any base other than e is used, then $\log_b e \neq 1$, and the constant $\log_b e$ would have to be part of the derivative of $f(x) = \log_b x$. That is,

$$f'(x) = \frac{1}{x} \log_b e$$

Thus, it is natural to choose e to be the base of our exponential or logarithmic functions whenever differentiation or integration is to be performed. Then, by using the chain rule (see page 461), the following formula is obtained.

Derivative of Logarithmic Functions

If $y = f(x) = \ln u(x)$, where $u(x)$ has a derivative with respect to x, then $y = f(x)$ has a derivative with respect to x, and

$$\frac{dy}{dx} = f'(x) = \frac{1}{u} \frac{du}{dx} = \frac{u'(x)}{u(x)}$$

EXAMPLE 16   If $f(x) = \ln(2x + 5)$, find $f'(x)$.

Solution   Let $u(x) = 2x + 5$. Then $u'(x) = 2$, and

$$f'(x) = \frac{u'(x)}{u(x)} = \frac{2}{2x + 5}$$

EXAMPLE 17   If $f(x) = \ln(3x^2 + x - 2)$, find $f'(x)$.

Solution   Let $u(x) = 3x^2 + x - 2$. Then $u'(x) = 6x + 1$, and

$$f'(x) = \frac{u'(x)}{u(x)} = \frac{6x + 1}{3x^2 + x - 2}$$

EXAMPLE 18   If $f(x) = \ln(x^3 + 2x^2 - x + 1)$, find $f'(x)$.

Solution   Let $u(x) = x^3 + 2x^2 - x + 1$. Then $u'(x) = 3x^2 + 4x - 1$, and

$$f'(x) = \frac{u'(x)}{u(x)} = \frac{3x^2 + 4x - 1}{x^3 + 2x^2 - x + 1}$$

Sometimes the properties of logarithms are useful in finding derivatives of complicated functions. Note how the properties of logarithms are used in the next examples.

EXAMPLE 19   Use logarithms to find the derivative of

$$y = (3x + 2)^2(4x^2 - 3x + 2)^3$$

Solution   Take the logarithm of both sides:

$$\ln y = \ln(3x + 2)^2(4x^2 - 3x + 2)^3$$

Since the logarithm of a product is the sum of the logarithms,

$$\ln y = \ln(3x + 2)^2 + \ln(4x^2 - 3x + 2)^3$$

Since the logarithm of a function to a power is the power times the logarithm of the function,

$$\ln y = 2\ln(3x + 2) + 3\ln(4x^2 - 3x + 2)$$

Now differentiate both sides with respect to x:

$$\left(\frac{1}{y}\right)\frac{dy}{dx} = 2\left(\frac{3}{3x + 2}\right) + 3\left(\frac{8x - 3}{4x^2 - 3x + 2}\right)$$

$$\frac{dy}{dx} = y\left(\frac{6}{3x + 2} + \frac{24x - 9}{4x^2 - 3x + 2}\right)$$

EXAMPLE 20   Use logarithms to find the derivative of

$$y = \frac{(3x + 2)^3(2x - 5)^{1/2}}{(2x^2 - x + 4)^2}$$

Solution   Take the logarithm of both sides,

$$\ln y = \ln \frac{(3x + 2)^3(2x - 5)^{1/2}}{(2x^2 - x + 4)^2}$$

$$= 3 \ln (3x + 2) + \frac{1}{2} \ln (2x - 5) - 2 \ln (2x^2 - x + 4)$$

Differentiate both sides with respect to x,

$$\left(\frac{1}{y}\right)\frac{dy}{dx} = 3\left(\frac{3}{3x + 2}\right) + \frac{1}{2}\left(\frac{2}{2x - 5}\right) - 2\left(\frac{4x - 1}{2x^2 - x + 4}\right)$$

$$\frac{dy}{dx} = y\left(\frac{9}{3x + 2} + \frac{1}{2x - 5} + \frac{-8x + 2}{2x^2 - x + 4}\right)$$

Exercise Set 12.3

A   *Find dy/dx for the following functions.*

1. $y = 3 \ln x$

2. $y = \ln x^2$

3. $y = \ln (2x + 3)$

4. $y = \ln (3x + 10)$

5. $y = 4 \ln (3x + 2)$

6. $y = 7 \ln (2x + 5)$

7. $y = \ln (3x^2 + 2x + 5)^2$

8. $y = 3 \ln (2x^2 + x + 3)^2$

9. $y = 3x^2 + 2x + \ln (2x + 5)$

10. $y = 2x \ln (3x + 7)$

B   *Use logarithms to find dy/dx.*

11. $y = (3x + 5)^3(2x - 3)^5$

12. $y = (3x^2 + 4x - 3)^4$

13. $y = \dfrac{(3x - 2)^4}{(2x + 3)^3}$

14. $y = \dfrac{(5x + 7)^3}{(3x^3 + 2x + 1)^2}$

C   *Find dy/dx for the following functions.*

15. $y = \ln [3\sqrt{x}(2x + 1)^3]$

16. $y = \ln [2x^3 \sqrt{3x + 2}]$

17. $y = [\ln (3x^2 - 2x + 5)]^2$

18. $y = \ln \left[\dfrac{3x^2 + 4x + 5}{(2x + 3)^4}\right]$

19. $y = \dfrac{(3x + 2)^{1/3}}{(2x - 4)^2}$

20. $y = \dfrac{3x^2(2x + 3)^{1/3}}{(4x^3 - 3x + 1)^2}$

Business   **21. Cost Functions.** The cost function for selling a product is given as

$$C(x) = 100 + 60 \ln (2x^2 - 2x + 1)$$

where x is the number of pounds sold. Find the number of pounds that should be sold to keep cost at a minimum.

Economics   **22. Demand Functions.** The demand function for a product is

$$p = \frac{600}{\ln (D + 1)}$$

Prove that the derivative of this function, with respect to D, is negative for $D > 0$ and, hence, that this function is a decreasing function for $D > 0$.

Life Sciences   23. **pH Factor.** Recall that the pH of a solution is defined to be

$$\text{pH} = \log \frac{1}{\text{H}^+}$$

where H^+ represents the concentration of hydrogen ions per liter. Compute the derivative of pH with respect to H^+, and show that this function is decreasing for $\text{H}^+ > 0$.

Social Sciences   24. **Archaeology.** The formula

$$\log P = \tfrac{1}{2} \log A$$

relates the population of a site to the area of the site. Find the rate of change of the population with respect to the area.

4   Finding Derivatives of Exponential Functions

In Section 12.1 we found that an exponential function is a function of the type $y = a^x$ where $a > 0$ and $a \neq 1$. In this section we obtain formulas for differentiating exponential functions. Since exponential functions are so very important in problems of growth, derivatives of these functions are needed by economists to study the growth rate of the money supply; are needed by businesspeople to study the rate of decline in sales; are needed by biologists to study the rate of growth of organisms; and are needed by social scientists to study the rate of population growth.

To develop a formula for the derivative of an exponential function, we could return to our four-step procedure for finding a derivative. This time we choose to use the logarithmic differentiation method developed in the preceding section. Given the exponential function $y = a^x$, we take the natural logarithm of both sides with respect to x:

$$\ln y = \ln a^x$$
$$= x \ln a$$

Then we differentiate both sides with respect to x:

$$\left(\frac{1}{y}\right) \frac{dy}{dx} = \ln a$$

$$\frac{dy}{dx} = y \ln a$$

or

$$\frac{dy}{dx} = a^x \ln a$$

Note that if $a = e$, then $\ln e = 1$, and the differentiation formula becomes

$$\frac{dy}{dx} = e^x$$

If y is a composite function, $y = e^u$, where $u = u(x)$ is a differentiable function of x, the chain rule yields

$$\frac{dy}{dx} = \left(\frac{dy}{du}\right)\left(\frac{du}{dx}\right)$$

$$= e^u\left(\frac{du}{dx}\right)$$

The derivative formulas for exponential functions are summarized below:

Differentiation Formulas for Exponential Functions	$\dfrac{d(e^x)}{dx} = e^x$ $\dfrac{d}{dx}(e^u) = e^u\dfrac{du}{dx}$ $\dfrac{d}{dx}(a^x) = a^x \ln a$ $\dfrac{d}{dx}(a^u) = a^u (\ln a)\dfrac{du}{dx}$

The following examples illustrate how these formulas are used.

EXAMPLE 21   If $y = e^{3x}$, find dy/dx.

Solution   Let $u(x) = 3x$. Then $u'(x) = 3$, and

$$\frac{dy}{dx} = u'(x)e^{u(x)} = 3e^{3x}$$

EXAMPLE 22   If $y = e^{3x^2}$, find dy/dx.

Solution   Let $u(x) = 3x^2$. Then $u'(x) = 6x$, and

$$\frac{dy}{dx} = u'(x)e^{u(x)} = 6xe^{3x^2}$$

EXAMPLE 23   If $y = e^{3x^3}$, find dy/dx.

Solution   Let $u(x) = 3x^3$. Then $u'(x) = 9x^2$, and

$$\frac{dy}{dx} = u'(x)e^{u(x)} = 9x^2e^{3x^3}$$

EXAMPLE 24   If $y = e^{3x^2 + x - 2}$, find dy/dx.

Solution   Let $u(x) = 3x^2 + x - 2$. Then $u'(x) = 6x + 1$, and

$$\frac{dy}{dx} = u'(x)e^{u(x)} = (6x + 1)e^{3x^2 + x - 2}$$

EXAMPLE 25   If $y = e^x$, find d^2y/dx^2.

Solution   Since $dy/dx = e^x$, then $d^2y/dx^2 = e^x$, and, in general,

$$\frac{d^n y}{dx^n} = e^x$$

EXAMPLE 26   If $y = xe^x$, find dy/dx.

Solution   Notice that y is a product of two functions, $u = x$ and $v = e^x$. Hence, by the derivative formula for a product,

$$\frac{dy}{dx} = u\frac{dv}{dx} + v\frac{du}{dx}$$

$$= xe^x + e^x(1)$$

$$= xe^x + e^x$$

EXAMPLE 27   If $y = 7(5^x)$, find dy/dx.

Solution $$\frac{dy}{dx} = 7(5^x) \ln 5$$

EXAMPLE 28   If $y = 7(5^{3x^2 + 2x + 1})$, find dy/dx.

Solution $$\frac{dy}{dx} = 7(5^{3x^2 + 2x + 1})(\ln 5)(6x + 2)$$

Exercise Set **12.4**

A   *Find dy/dx for the following functions.*

1. $y = e^{4x}$
2. $y = 4e^{3x}$
3. $y = 5 + e^{2x}$
4. $y = 3x^2 - 2e^{4x}$
5. $y = 4x - e^{-3x}$
6. $y = 8x^2 + e^{-5x}$
7. $y = 4x - 5^{3x}$
8. $y = 2^{3x} + e^{4x}$

B   9. $y = (3 + e^x)(2 - e^{-x})$
10. $y = \dfrac{3 + e^x}{3 - e^{-x}}$
11. $y = 3x^2 e^{4x}$

12. $y = (3 + 5x)e^{2x}$

13. $y = \ln x + 3e^{2x}$

14. $y = e^x \ln x$

15. $y = 7^{3x} - e^x$

16. $y = 4^{3x} + e^{4x}$

C **17.** $y = (e^{2x} + 5) \ln (3x - 5)$

18. $y = \dfrac{\ln (x^2 + 2x + 3)}{e^x - 5}$

19. $y = xe^{2x} + 5 \ln (3x + 2)$

20. $y = e^{3x} \ln (2x - 5)$

21. $y = 5^{7x} + e^x \ln x$

22. $y = 4^{5x} + e^{-x} \ln x$

23. a. Find the derivative of $y = e^{-x^2}$.

    b. Where does this function have a maximum?

    c. What is the maximum value?

    d. Find the two inflection points.

    e. Draw the graph.

Business **24. Salvage Value.** The salvage value of an airplane after t years is

$$V(t) = 400{,}000e^{-0.1t}$$

What is the rate of depreciation, dV/dt, after

a. 1 year?   **b.** 3 years?   **c.** 10 years?

Economics **25. Marginal Revenue Functions.** The price demand function for x units of an item is

$$p(x) = 100e^{-0.06x}$$

The revenue function for the item is

$$R(x) = xp(x) = 100xe^{-0.06x}$$

Find the marginal revenue function. What number of units gives the maximum revenue?

Social Sciences **26. Learning Functions.** A learning function is given by

$$N(t) = 100(1 - e^{-0.03t})$$

Find the rate of learning, $N'(t)$. What is the rate

a. after 10 hours?   **b.** after 20 hours?

Antiderivatives Containing e^u or $\ln |u|$

In this section we study antiderivatives that contain e^u or $\ln |u|$. In particular we show that the indefinite integral of $\int u^n \, du$ for the special case where $n = -1$ is $\ln |u| + C$, and the indefinite integral of $\int e^u \, du$ is $e^u + C$. The antiderivatives of this section follow directly from their corresponding derivative formulas.

In Section 12.3 we found that

$$\frac{d}{dx} (\ln u) = \frac{1}{u} \frac{du}{dx}$$

Since ln u was only defined when u > 0, the condition u > 0 was always assumed. If u < 0, then −u > 0 and

$$\frac{d}{dx} \ln (-u) = \frac{1}{-u}\left(\frac{d(-u)}{dx}\right)$$

$$= \frac{-1}{-u}\left(\frac{du}{dx}\right)$$

$$= \frac{1}{u}\left(\frac{du}{dx}\right)$$

Since $|u| = u$ if $u > 0$ and $|u| = -u$ if $u < 0$, we have proved that

$$\frac{d}{dx}(\ln |u|) = \frac{1}{u}\left(\frac{du}{dx}\right) \qquad \text{when } u \neq 0$$

This result is summarized by the indefinite integral given in the following box:

The Indefinite Integral $\int \dfrac{du}{u}$

$$\int \frac{du}{u} = \ln |u| + C \qquad u \neq 0$$

EXAMPLE 29 Find $\int 3x^{-1}\, dx$.

Solution

$$\int 3x^{-1}\, dx = 3 \int \frac{dx}{x} = 3 \ln |x| + C$$

EXAMPLE 30 Find $\int \dfrac{5\, dx}{3x + 2}$.

Solution Let

$$u(x) = 3x + 2$$
$$u'(x) = 3$$
$$du = u'(x)\, dx = 3\, dx$$

Hence,

$$dx = \tfrac{1}{3} du$$

Substituting gives

$$\int \frac{5\, dx}{3x + 2} = \int \frac{5(\tfrac{1}{3})\, du}{u} = \frac{5}{3} \int \frac{du}{u} = \frac{5}{3} \ln |u| + C = \frac{5}{3} \ln |3x + 2| + C$$

Since $d(e^x)/dx = e^x$, an antiderivative of e^x is e^x, and the indefinite integral $\int e^x\, dx = e^x + C$.

$$\int e^u \, du = e^u + C$$

EXAMPLE 31 Find $\int 5e^x \, dx$.

Solution

$$\int 5e^x \, dx = 5 \int e^x \, dx = 5e^x + C$$

EXAMPLE 32 Find $\int 5e^{3x+2} \, dx$.

Solution Let

$$u(x) = 3x + 2$$
$$u'(x) = 3$$
$$du = u'(x) \, dx = 3 \, dx$$

Hence,

$$dx = \tfrac{1}{3} \, du$$

Substituting gives

$$\int 5e^{3x+2} \, dx = \int 5e^u(\tfrac{1}{3}) \, du = \tfrac{5}{3} \int e^u \, du = \tfrac{5}{3}e^u + C = \tfrac{5}{3}e^{3x+2} + C$$

There are many quantities that change at a rate proportional to the amount of the quantity present. Some of these are population growth, money invested at continuously compounded interest, depletion of natural resources, and radioactive decay. These quantities are said to satisfy the **law of exponential growth.**

Suppose Q represents the amount of a quantity at time t and Q_0 represents the amount of the quantity at $t = 0$. Suppose r represents the rate of continuous growth. Then

$$\frac{dQ}{dt} = rQ$$

Multiplying both sides by dt/Q gives

$$\frac{dQ}{Q} = r \, dt$$

Now integrate both sides:

$$\int \frac{dQ}{Q} = \int r \, dt$$

$$\ln Q = rt + C$$

In exponential form this is equivalent to

$$Q = e^{rt+C} = e^C \cdot e^{rt}$$

Setting $Q = Q_0$ when $t = 0$ gives

$$Q_0 = e^C \cdot e^{r(0)} = e^C$$

Hence, the law of exponential growth is

$$Q = Q_0 e^{rt}$$

Law of Exponential Growth	Let Q represent the amount of a quantity at time t, Q_0 represent the amount of a quantity at $t = 0$, and r represent the rate of continuous growth. If $$\frac{dQ}{dt} = rQ$$ then $$Q = Q_0 e^{rt}$$

EXAMPLE 33 Assume a world population of 4 billion growing at the rate of 2% per year.

    a. Find a function that will represent the population as a function of time.
    b. How long will it take for the population to double if this rate continues?

Solution

    a. $P = P_0 e^{rt} = 4e^{0.02t}$
    b. To find how long it will take for the population to double, we replace P by 8 and solve for t:

$$8 = 4e^{0.02t}$$
$$2 = e^{0.02t}$$

From Table III in the Appendix we find approximately

$$0.02t = 0.69$$
$$t = 34.5 \text{ years}$$

EXAMPLE 34 The Good Share Company plans to introduce a new product to as many people as possible by an advertising program. Suppose that the rate of exposure to new people is proportional to those who have not seen the product out of P possible people. Suppose that no one is aware of the product at the start, and that after 10 days 30% of P are aware of the product. Solve

$$\frac{dN}{dt} = k(P - N)$$

for $N(t)$, the number of people who are aware of the product after t days of advertising.

Solution

$$\frac{dN}{dt} = k(P - N)$$

Multiply both sides by $dt/(P - N)$ to give

$$\frac{dN}{P - N} = k\,dt$$

Integrating both sides yields

$$\int \frac{dN}{P - N} = \int k\,dt$$

$$-\ln(P - N) = kt + C$$

$$\ln(P - N)^{-1} = kt + C$$

$$\ln\left(\frac{1}{P - N}\right) = kt + C$$

In exponential form this is equivalent to

$$\frac{1}{P - N} = e^{kt + C} = e^C \cdot e^{kt}$$

Setting $N = 0$ when $t = 0$ gives $1/P = e^C$; hence,

$$\frac{1}{P - N} = \frac{1}{P}\,e^{kt}$$

To find k, let $N = 0.30P$ when $t = 10$. Then

$$\frac{1}{P - 0.30P} = \frac{1}{P}\,e^{10k}$$

$$\frac{1}{0.7P} = \frac{1}{P}\,e^{10k}$$

$$\frac{1}{0.7} = e^{10k}$$

From Table III in the Appendix,

$$10k = 0.36 \text{ approximately}$$
$$k = 0.036 \quad \text{or} \quad 0.04$$

Thus,

$$\frac{1}{P - N} = \frac{1}{P}\,e^{0.04t}$$

$$P = (P - N)e^{0.04t}$$

$$Ne^{0.04t} = Pe^{0.04t} - P$$

$$N = P - Pe^{-0.04t}$$

Exercise Set **12.5**

A Find the following indefinite integrals.

1. $\int 6x^{-1}\,dx$ **2.** $\int 8x^{-1}\,dx$ **3.** $\int 4e^x\,dx$

4. $\int 10e^x\,dx$ **5.** $\int (6e^x + 2x)\,dx$ **6.** $\int (7e^x + 3x^2 - 5)\,dx$

7. $\int (2x^{-1} + e^x)\,dx$ **8.** $\int (5x^{-1} + x^2)\,dx$

Find the value of the following definite integrals. Do not evaluate powers of e or logarithms unless instructed to evaluate them by your instructor.

9. $\int_1^2 e^x\,dx$ **10.** $\int_2^5 3e^x\,dx$ **11.** $\int_2^4 3x^{-1}\,dx$

12. $\int_3^5 2x^{-1}\,dx$ **13.** $\int_1^3 (2x^{-1} + 5)\,dx$ **14.** $\int_1^4 (x^{-1} + 2e^x)\,dx$

B Find the following integrals but do not evaluate powers of e or logarithms unless instructed to evaluate them by your instructor.

15. $\int \dfrac{x^2 + 1}{x}\,dx$ **16.** $\int \dfrac{3x^2 + x + 2}{x}\,dx$

17. $\int_1^3 2xe^{x^2}\,dx$ **18.** $\int_1^2 3xe^{x^2}\,dx$

19. $\int_1^2 \dfrac{2x^2 + 1}{x}\,dx$ **20.** $\int_1^3 \dfrac{2x^2 + x + 3}{x}\,dx$

21. $\int \dfrac{3}{2x + 5}\,dx$ **22.** $\int \dfrac{3x\,dx}{4x^2 + 5}$

C **23.** $\int_1^2 \dfrac{(4x + 2)\,dx}{2x^2 + 2x + 3}$ **24.** $\int_1^3 \dfrac{(6x + 5)\,dx}{3x^2 + 5x + 2}$

Business **25. Advertising.** A company plans to introduce a product by an advertising program. The rate of exposure is proportional to those who have not seen the product. Suppose no one in a population of 500,000 is aware of the product at the start, and after 10 days 100,000 people are aware of the product. Find an expression for N(t), the number of people who are aware of the product after t days of advertising.

Economics **26. Price-Demand Equation.** The marginal price dp/dx at x units demand per month for a car is given by

$$\frac{dp}{dx} = -300e^{-0.05x}$$

Find the price-demand equation if at a price of $10,000 each, the demand is 10 cars per month.

Life Sciences **27. Blood Pressure.** Suppose the blood pressure P in the aorta changes with respect to time t, according to

$$\frac{dP}{dt} = -rP$$

Assume the pressure at time $t = 0$ is P_0, and find P(t).

28. **Rate of Decay.** Assume that the rate of decay of a radioactive element in a bone is given by

$$\frac{dQ}{dt} = -0.00012Q$$

If 60% of the original amount is found, estimate the age of the bone.

29. **Swimming.** Gerald is trying to improve his swimming ability. Let y represent the distance in feet he can swim in 1 minute after t hours of practice. Suppose his rate of improvement is proportional to the difference between y and 60.

$$\frac{dy}{dt} = k(60 - y)$$

Assume $y(0) = 0$, and solve for $y(t)$.

Social Sciences 30. **Population.** Assume that India had a population of 550 million in 1980 and a growth rate of 3% per year. Predict India's population in 1995.

Summary and Review

Review to ensure you understand the following concepts.

Exponential function Solutions of exponential functions
Logarithmic function Derivatives of logarithmic functions
Base of natural logarithms Properties of logarithms
Derivatives of exponential functions Logarithmic differentiation
Antiderivatives containing e^u or $\ln |u|$ Exponential growth

Review Exercise Set 12.6

A *Find the values of y when $x = 0, 1, -1, 2,$ and -2.*

1. $y = 2 + 3^x$ **2.** $y = 3 - 2x^{-x}$

3. $y = 2(3)^{-x} + 4$ **4.** $y = 3(2)^x - 3$

5. $y = 3e^{2x}$ **6.** $y = 4e^{-3x} - 1$

7. $y = 2 \ln (3x + 7)$ **8.** $y = 3 \ln (2x + 5)$

Write the following in logarithmic notation.

9. $3^{-3} = \frac{1}{27}$ **10.** $27^{-1/2} = \frac{1}{3}$

11. $2^{-6} = \frac{1}{64}$ **12.** $64^{-2/3} = \frac{1}{16}$

Solve the following exponential equations.

13. $3^x = 5$ **14.** $5^x = 7$

15. $4^{3x} = 7$ **16.** $e^{3x+2} = 3$

B *Find dy/dx for the following functions.*

17. $y = (4 + 2e^x)(3 - e^{-2x})$

18. $y = \dfrac{4 - 2e^{2x}}{3 + e^{-3x}}$

19. $y = 4x^3 e^{2x}$

20. $y = e^{3x}(2x + 3)$

21. $y = 3e^{2x} \ln (2x + 1)$

22. $y = 5^{3x} + e^{2x}$

23. $y = \dfrac{3 \ln (2x + 1)}{2 \ln (4x + 3)}$

24. $y = e^{3x} \ln (2x + 3)^2$

C **25.** $y = 3xe^{3x} + 2x^2 \ln (3x + 1)$

26. $y = \dfrac{3e^{2x} \ln x}{e^x - 4}$

Business **27. Profit Functions.** The profit function of a company is

$$P(x) = 500 \ln (x + 200) - 2x$$

a. Find the value of x that will make the profit a maximum.
b. What is the maximum profit?

28. Salvage Value. The salvage value of a piece of equipment after t years is

$$V(t) = 500,000e^{-0.2t}$$

What is the rate of depreciation dV/dt after
a. 2 years?   **b.** 10 years?

Economics **29. Marginal Revenue Functions.** The price-demand function for x units of an item is

$$p(x) = 200e - 0.05x$$

The revenue function for the item is

$$R(x) = xp(x) = 200xe - 0.05x$$

a. Find the marginal revenue function.
b. What number of units gives the maximum revenue?

Life Sciences **30. Sensed Sensation.** Let us assume from mathematical psychology that the rate of change of a sensed sensation S with respect to a stimulus T is inversely proportional to the strength of the stimulus. That is,

$$\frac{dS}{dt} = \frac{k}{T}$$

Find $S(T)$ if $S(T_0) = 0$.

Social Sciences **31. Learning Functions.** Suppose a learning function is given as a function of time in hours:

$$N(t) = 80(1 - e^{0.02t})$$

Find the rate of learning $N'(t)$. What is the rate of learning
a. after 6 hours?   **b.** after 20 hours?

13

Additional Integration Methods

A lthough we have studied many integration formulas in Chapters 11 and 12, there are still functions whose antiderivatives are not obtainable by those formulas. In this chapter we give additional integration methods for many of these functions. We begin by returning to the method of substitution. This method of substitution can be applied to more complicated problems than were previously treated. Next, we consider the problem of finding an antiderivative of a product. The integration-by-parts formula is derived and applied to product problems. Improper integrals are defined and used in probability problems. Finally, a short table of integrals is given and used to illustrate how other functions may be integrated.

1 Integration by Substitution

> Often we wish to find antiderivatives for functions that do not appear in a form suitable for our integration formulas. For some of these a substitution suggested by the nature of the problem may help. For example, functions involving $\sqrt{x}$ can sometimes be simplified for integration by substituting $u = \sqrt{x}$.

Consider the problem

$$\int \frac{dx}{\sqrt{x} + 5}$$

The $\sqrt{x}$ presents a difficulty when trying to use an integration formula for this problem. To simplify this problem, substitute $u = \sqrt{x}$. If $u = \sqrt{x}$, then $x = u^2$. Before substituting, we must find dx. Remember that

$$dx = \left(\frac{dx}{du}\right) du$$

Hence,

$$dx = 2u\,du$$

Now

$$\int \frac{dx}{\sqrt{x} + 5} = \int \frac{2u\,du}{u + 5}$$

Dividing $2u$ by $u + 5$ gives $2 + -10/(u + 5)$.

Hence,

$$\int \frac{2u\,du}{u + 5} = \int \left(2 + \frac{-10}{u + 5}\right) du$$

$$= 2u - 10 \ln |u + 5| + C$$

Since we substituted u for $\sqrt{x}$, we should replace u by $\sqrt{x}$. Thus,

$$\int \frac{dx}{\sqrt{x} + 5} = 2\sqrt{x} - 10 \ln |\sqrt{x} + 5| + C$$

This discussion illustrates a method that enables us to integrate many problems that do not appear to fit a formula. The method is called **integration by substitution.** The procedure is summarized below:

Integration by Substitution

1. Use a substitution that seems to simplify the function to be integrated.
2. Replace the old variables x and dx by their equals in terms of the new variable u. This is accomplished by solving for x in terms of u and then using $dx = (dx/du)\,du$.
3. Try to find an antiderivative for the new function of u.
4. If an antiderivative can be found in step 3, replace the new variable u by the substitution made in step 1.

Some substitutions may make the integration easier than others. If the integration is difficult after the substitution has been made, try another substitution.

EXAMPLE 1 Find

$$\int \frac{x\,dx}{\sqrt{x + 3}}$$

Solution   Let

$$u = \sqrt{x + 3}$$
$$u^2 = x + 3$$
$$x = u^2 - 3$$
$$dx = 2u\,du$$

Then

$$\int \frac{x\,dx}{\sqrt{x + 3}} = \int \frac{(u^2 - 3)2u\,du}{u}$$

$$= \int 2(u^2 - 3)\,du$$

$$= \tfrac{2}{3}u^3 - 6u + C$$
$$= \tfrac{2}{3}(x + 3)^{3/2} - 6(x + 3)^{1/2} + C$$

EXAMPLE 2   Find

$$\int \frac{e^x}{(4 + e^x)^2}\,dx$$

Solution   Let

$$u = 4 + e^x$$
$$e^x = u - 4$$
$$x = \ln |u - 4|$$

$$dx = \frac{du}{u - 4}$$

Then

$$\int \frac{e^x}{(4 + e^x)^2}\,dx = \int \left(\frac{u - 4}{u^2}\right) \frac{du}{u - 4}$$

$$= \int u^{-2}\,du$$

$$= -u^{-1} + C$$

$$= \frac{-1}{4 + e^x} + C$$

EXAMPLE 3   Find

$$\int \frac{\sqrt[3]{\ln x}}{x}\,dx$$

Solution   Let

$$u = \ln x$$
$$x = e^u$$
$$dx = e^u\,du$$

Then

$$\int \frac{\sqrt[3]{\ln x}}{x} dx = \int \frac{u^{1/3} e^u \, du}{e^u}$$

$$= \int u^{1/3} \, du$$

$$= \tfrac{3}{4} u^{4/3} + C$$

$$= \tfrac{3}{4} (\ln x)^{4/3} + C$$

EXAMPLE 4   Find

$$\int_0^2 \frac{6x^2}{\sqrt{x^3 + 1}} dx$$

Solution   Let

$$u = x^3 + 1$$

$$x^3 = u - 1$$

$$x = (u - 1)^{1/3}$$

$$dx = \tfrac{1}{3}(u - 1)^{-2/3} \, du$$

Since this is a definite integral, the limits should be changed when the variable is changed. When $x = 0$

$$u = 0^3 + 1 = 1$$

When $x = 2$

$$u = 2^3 + 1 = 9$$

$$\int_0^2 \frac{6x^2}{\sqrt{x^3 + 1}} dx = \int_1^9 \frac{6(u - 1)^{2/3}}{u^{1/2}} \frac{1}{3} (u - 1)^{-2/3} \, du$$

$$= \int_1^9 \frac{2 \, du}{u^{1/2}}$$

$$= \int_1^9 2u^{-1/2} \, du$$

$$= 2(\tfrac{2}{1}) u^{1/2} \Big|_1^9$$

$$= 4(9)^{1/2} - 4(1)^{1/2}$$

$$= 12 - 4 = 8$$

Exercise Set 13.1

A   Find the following integrals.

1. $\displaystyle\int \frac{3 \, dx}{\sqrt{x - 2}}$

2. $\displaystyle\int \frac{4 \, dx}{\sqrt[3]{x + 1}}$

3. $\displaystyle\int_3^6 \frac{4 \, dx}{\sqrt{x - 2}}$

4. $\displaystyle\int_0^7 \frac{2 \, dx}{\sqrt[3]{x + 1}}$

5. $\displaystyle\int \frac{2x\,dx}{\sqrt{x^2+2}}$

6. $\displaystyle\int \frac{3x\,dx}{\sqrt[3]{x^2+1}}$

7. $\displaystyle\int \frac{5e^{2x}}{e^{2x}+1}\,dx$

8. $\displaystyle\int \frac{4e^{-2x}}{e^{-2x}+2}\,dx$

9. $\displaystyle\int \frac{2x}{x+5}\,dx$

10. $\displaystyle\int_3^5 \frac{4x}{x+3}\,dx$

B **11.** $\displaystyle\int \frac{dx}{\sqrt{x+3}}$

12. $\displaystyle\int \frac{dx}{\sqrt[3]{x+2}}$

13. $\displaystyle\int_1^9 \frac{dx}{\sqrt{x+4}}$

14. $\displaystyle\int_1^8 \frac{dx}{\sqrt[3]{x+3}}$

15. $\displaystyle\int \frac{2x\,dx}{\sqrt{x+8}}$

16. $\displaystyle\int \frac{3x\,dx}{\sqrt{2x+1}}$

17. $\displaystyle\int \frac{3e^x}{\sqrt{e^x+4}}$

18. $\displaystyle\int_0^1 \frac{2e^x}{\sqrt[3]{e^x+1}}$

C **19.** $\displaystyle\int \frac{\sqrt{\ln x}}{x}\,dx$

20. $\displaystyle\int \frac{2\,dx}{x\ln x}$

21. $\displaystyle\int_2^7 3x\sqrt{x+2}\,dx$

22. $\displaystyle\int_0^5 \frac{3x\,dx}{\sqrt{x+4}}$

23. $\displaystyle\int \frac{\sqrt{x}-3}{\sqrt{x}+3}\,dx$

24. $\displaystyle\int \frac{2\,dx}{x+2\sqrt{x}}$

25. $\displaystyle\int \frac{1}{x^3}e^{1/x^2}\,dx$

26. $\displaystyle\int \frac{3\,dx}{4+\sqrt{x+2}}$

Business　**27. Cash Reserves.** The cash reserves C, in thousands, of a company are approximated by

$$C = 20 + t\sqrt{9-t} \qquad 0 \le t \le 9$$

where t is time in months. Find the average cash reserve for
a. the first 3 months.　　**b.** the last 3 months.

Economics　**28. Demand Equations.** The marginal price $p'(x)$ for x units per day of an item is

$$p'(x) = -24{,}000x(600 + x^2)^{-2}$$

Find the price-demand equation if at a price of \$15 the daily demand is 20.

Life Sciences　**29. Medicine.** The rate of change in temperature, dT/dx, is

$$\frac{dT}{dx} = \frac{1}{20}\,x\sqrt{10-x} \qquad 0 \le x \le 10$$

where x is the number of milligrams given. What is the total temperature change when the dosage changes from 0 to 4 milligrams?

Social Sciences　**30. Rate of Learning.** Suppose the rate of learning, dN/dt, is

$$\frac{dN}{dt} = \frac{16t}{\sqrt{2+t}} \qquad 0 \le t \le 8$$

where N is the number of items learned in t hours. Find the total number of items learned from $t = 2$ to $t = 7$.

2 Integration by Parts

> Recall that the derivative of a product is not the product of the derivatives. Hence, the antiderivative of a product is not the product of the antiderivatives. We have already considered the antiderivatives of some products, but in this section we give a method for finding antiderivatives of many additional products.

Suppose we want to find the indefinite integral $\int x e^x \, dx$. This problem is typical of many instances in which an antiderivative of a product is desired. Some of these antiderivatives can be found by the methods already given. Others, however, require an additional formula. Before deriving a formula for the antiderivative of a product, however, we use an example to illustrate that, in general, the antiderivative of a product is not the product of antiderivatives.

EXAMPLE 5 Show that $\int x^2(x+1) \, dx \neq \int x^2 \, dx \cdot \int (x+1) \, dx$.

Solution Now

$$\int x^2(x+1) \, dx = \int (x^3 + x^2) \, dx = \frac{x^4}{4} + \frac{x^3}{3} + C$$

Also,

$$\int x^2 \, dx = \frac{x^3}{3} + C_1 \qquad \text{and} \qquad \int (x+1) \, dx = \frac{x^2}{2} + x + C_3$$

Therefore,

$$\int x^2 \, dx \cdot \int (x+1) \, dx = \left(\frac{x^3}{3} + C_1 \right)\left(\frac{x^2}{2} + x + C_3 \right)$$

Since

$$\frac{x^4}{4} + \frac{x^3}{3} + C \neq \left(\frac{x^3}{3} + C_1 \right)\left(\frac{x^2}{2} + x + C_3 \right)$$

then

$$\int x^2(x+1) \, dx \neq \int x^2 \, dx \cdot \int (x+1) \, dx$$

To derive a formula for the antiderivative of a product, recall that

$$\frac{d(uv)}{dx} = u\frac{dv}{dx} + v\frac{du}{dx}$$

where u and v are functions of x. This formula can be written

$$\frac{d(uv)}{dx} = uv' + vu'$$

Taking antiderivatives of both sides of this equation gives

$$uv + C = \int (uv' + vu') \, dx$$

Hence,

$$uv + C = \int uv' \, dx + \int vu' \, dx$$

or

$$\int uv' \, dx = uv - \int vu' \, dx + C$$

<table>
<tr><td>**Integration-by-
Parts Formula**</td><td>If u(x) and v(x) are functions whose derivatives exist, then

$$\int uv' \, dx = uv - \int vu' \, dx + C$$</td></tr>
</table>

When an antiderivative is found by using the formula just derived, the process is called **integration by parts.** For some functions it does not matter which factor is chosen for u or which is selected for v'; but for other functions u and v' are chosen so that an antiderivative may be found for v'.

Now let us return to the problem of finding the indefinite integral $\int xe^x \, dx$. Notice that if u = x, then u' = 1, so it appears to be better to select the factors as u = x and v' = e^x. Then u' = 1 and v = e^x. Substitution in the integration-by-parts formula,

$$\int uv' \, dx = uv - \int vu' \, dx + C$$

gives

$$\int xe^x \, dx = xe^x - \int e^x \cdot (1) \, dx + C$$

Hence,

$$\int xe^x \, dx = xe^x - \int e^x \, dx + C$$

and

$$\int xe^x \, dx = xe^x - e^x + C$$

EXAMPLE 6   Find $\int x \ln x \, dx$.

Solution   Since we have not yet found an antiderivative for ln x, we cannot let v' = ln x. Hence, we select the factors as follows: Let u = ln x and v' = x. Then u' = 1/x and v = $x^2/2$. Substituting in the integration-by-parts formula,

$$\int uv' \, dx = uv - \int vu' \, dx + C$$

gives

$$\int (\ln x)x \, dx = (\ln x)\left(\frac{x^2}{2}\right) - \int \frac{x^2}{2} \cdot \frac{1}{x} \, dx + C$$

Hence,

$$\int x \ln x \, dx = \frac{x^2}{2} \ln x - \int \frac{x}{2} \, dx + C$$

and

$$\int x \ln x \, dx = \frac{x^2}{2} \ln x - \frac{x^2}{4} + C$$

EXAMPLE 7   Find $\int \ln x \, dx$.

Solution   We select the factors as follows: Let $u = \ln x$ and $v' = 1$. Then $u' = 1/x$ and $v = x$. Substitution in the integration-by-parts formula,

$$\int uv' \, dx = uv - \int vu' \, dx + C$$

gives

$$\int (\ln x) \cdot 1 \cdot dx = (\ln x)x - \int x \left(\frac{1}{x}\right) dx + C$$

Hence,

$$\int \ln x \, dx = x \ln x - \int dx + C$$

and

$$\int \ln x \, dx = x \ln x - x + C$$

EXAMPLE 8   Find $\int x\sqrt{1 + x} \, dx$.

Solution   Let $u = x$ and $v' = \sqrt{1 + x}$. Then $u' = 1$ and $v = \frac{2}{3}(1 + x)^{3/2}$. Substitution in the integration-by-parts formula,

$$\int uv' \, dx = uv - \int vu' \, dx + C$$

gives

$$\int x\sqrt{1 + x} \, dx = \frac{2}{3}x(1 + x)^{3/2} - \int \frac{2}{3}(1 + x)^{3/2} \, dx + C$$

Hence,

$$\int x\sqrt{1 + x} \, dx = \frac{2}{3}x(1 + x)^{3/2} - \frac{2}{3}\int (1 + x)^{3/2} \, dx + C$$

and

$$\int x\sqrt{1 + x} \, dx = \frac{2}{3}x(1 + x)^{3/2} - \frac{4}{15}(1 + x)^{5/2} + C$$

EXAMPLE 9   Find $\int x^2 e^x \, dx$.

Solution   Let $u = x^2$ and $v' = e^x$. Then $u' = 2x$ and $v = e^x$. Substitution in the integration-by-parts formula,

$$\int uv' \, dx = uv - \int vu' \, dx + C_1$$

gives

$$\int x^2 e^x \, dx = x^2 e^x - \int e^x (2x) \, dx + C_1$$

$$= x^2 e^x - 2 \int x e^x \, dx + C_1$$

Note that this gives the value of $\int x^2 e^x \, dx$ in terms of an integral that was previously found by the integration-by-parts formula. This example illustrates that some problems require the use of the integration-by-parts formula more than once. Recall that

$$\int x e^x \, dx = x e^x - e^x + C_2$$

Substituting this into the expression for $\int x^2 e^x \, dx$ gives

$$\int x^2 e^x \, dx = x^2 e^x - 2(x e^x - e^x + C_2) + C_1$$

$$= x^2 e^x - 2 x e^x + 2 e^x - 2C_2 + C_1$$

Let $C = -2C_2 + C_1$; then

$$\int x^2 e^x \, dx = x^2 e^x - 2 x e^x + 2 e^x + C$$

Exercise Set 13.2

A *Find the following indefinite integrals.*

1. $\int 3x e^x \, dx$ **2.** $\int x e^{3x} \, dx$ **3.** $\int 2x e^{-x} \, dx$

4. $\int x e^{-2x} \, dx$ **5.** $\int (x - 1) e^x \, dx$ **6.** $\int (x + 1) e^x \, dx$

7. $\int (2x - 1) e^{3x} \, dx$ **8.** $\int (3x + 2) e^{4x} \, dx$ **9.** $\int (3x + 1) e^{-2x} \, dx$

10. $\int (4x - 3) e^{-3x} \, dx$ **11.** $\int 5x \ln x \, dx$ **12.** $\int 3x^2 \ln x \, dx$

B **13.** $\int x^2 \ln x \, dx$ **14.** $\int 3x^2 \ln x \, dx$ **15.** $\int x^3 \ln x \, dx$

16. $\int 2x^3 \ln x \, dx$ **17.** $\int 3x \sqrt{1 + x} \, dx$ **18.** $\int 3x(1 + x)^{-1/2} \, dx$

19. $\int (3x - 1)(x + 2)^{-1/2} \, dx$ **20.** $\int (x e^{2x} - \ln x) \, dx$

The following exercises may require the use of the integration-by-parts formula more than once, or they may be integrable by previous methods.

C **21.** $\int x^2 e^{3x} \, dx$ **22.** $\int x e^{3x^2} \, dx$ **23.** $\int \dfrac{3 \ln x}{x} \, dx$

24. $\int \dfrac{2 \ln x}{x^2} \, dx$ **25.** $\int x^3 e^{x^2} \, dx$ **26.** $\int 4x^2 \sqrt{1 + x} \, dx$

Business **27.** **Production.** The rate of production per month of the ABC Company is given by

$$\frac{dP}{dt} = 20t e^{-0.2t}$$

Find the total production for a year.

28. Marginal Profit Functions. The ABC Company gives its marginal profit function as

$$MP = 3x - xe^{-x}$$

If $P(0) = 0$, find $P(x)$.

29. Medicine. The rate, dA/dt, of assimilation of a drug after t minutes is

$$\frac{dA}{dt} = te^{-0.3t}$$

Find the total amount assimilated after 8 minutes.

30. Population. Suppose the population P, in thousands, of a town is approximated by

$$P = 30 + 5t - 4te^{-0.1t}$$

where t is time in years after 1980. Find the average population from $t = 1$ to $t = 5$.

Improper Integrals

In previous sections we studied definite integrals in which the limits a and b on the integral $\int_a^b f(x)\,dx$ were real numbers. In this section we extend our study to integrals in which one or both of a and b may be infinite. Such integrals are important in finding the areas of some unbounded regions for certain functions and, especially, for probability density functions.

The study of calculus includes several types of integrals called **improper integrals.** Here we shall consider only those improper integrals that do not have bounds on one or both of their limits. Consider the graph of the function $f(x) = 1/x^2$ given in Figure 13.1. Suppose we want to know the area under this curve, above the x-axis, and to the right of the line $x = 1$. Notice that this region is not bounded. The integral that would represent this area would be the improper integral

$$\int_1^\infty \frac{dx}{x^2}$$

Figure 13.1

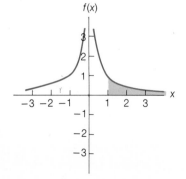

Now we must explain how to obtain the value of this integral, if indeed it even has a value. To evaluate this improper integral, we find the definite integral

$$\int_1^t \frac{dx}{x^2}$$

and then determine whether or not the value of this definite integral approaches a number as t becomes very large:

$$\int_1^t \frac{dx}{x^2} = -x^{-1}\Big|_1^t = -\frac{1}{t} + 1$$

Now as t becomes very large, $-1/t$ becomes very small and actually approaches 0. Since the definite integral $\int_1^t (1/x^2)\, dx$ approaches a limit, 1, as t becomes very large, we define

$$\int_1^\infty \frac{dx}{x^2} = 1$$

Hence, we see that the area of an unbounded region may be finite.

EXAMPLE 10 Find $\int_1^\infty e^{-x}\, dx$ if the value of this integral exists.

Solution $\int_1^\infty e^{-x}\, dx$ equals the value of $\int_1^t e^{-x}\, dx$ as t becomes very large. So

$$\int_1^t e^{-x}\, dx = -e^{-x}\Big|_1^t = -e^{-t} + e^{-1}$$

As t becomes very large, e^{-t} approaches 0; hence, $-e^{-t} + e^{-1}$ approaches e^{-1}. Thus,

$$\int_1^\infty e^{-x}\, dx = e^{-1} = \frac{1}{e}$$

EXAMPLE 11 Graph $f(x) = 1/x$ and find the area of the region under this curve and above the x-axis to the right of $x = 1$ if this area exists.

Solution

$$A = \int_1^\infty \frac{dx}{x}$$

$$\int_1^t \frac{dx}{x} = \ln x\Big|_1^t = \ln t - \ln 1$$

Now $\ln 1 = 0$; hence,

$$\int_1^t \frac{dx}{x} = \ln t$$

As t becomes very large, $\ln t$ becomes large. Since $\ln t$ does not approach a limit as t becomes very large,

$$\int_1^\infty \frac{dx}{x}$$

does not exist.

Figure 13.2

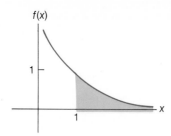

The previous examples suggest the following definitions for the improper integrals

$$\int_{-\infty}^{b} f(x)\,dx \qquad \int_{a}^{\infty} f(x)\,dx \qquad \int_{-\infty}^{\infty} f(x)\,dx$$

Improper Integrals

> If $f(x)$ is continuous over the interval and the limit exists, then
>
> $$\int_{a}^{\infty} f(x)\,dx = \lim_{t \to \infty} \int_{a}^{t} f(x)\,dx$$
>
> $$\int_{-\infty}^{b} f(x)\,dx = \lim_{t \to -\infty} \int_{t}^{b} f(x)\,dx$$
>
> $$\int_{-\infty}^{\infty} f(x)\,dx = \int_{-\infty}^{c} f(x)\,dx + \int_{c}^{\infty} f(x)\,dx$$
>
> where $-\infty < c < \infty$, provided that both improper integrals exist.

EXAMPLE 12 Find

$$\int_{2}^{\infty} \frac{dx}{(1+x)^{3/2}}$$

if it exists.

Solution

$$\lim_{t \to \infty} \int_{2}^{t} \frac{dx}{(1+x)^{3/2}} = \lim_{t \to \infty} \int_{2}^{t} (1+x)^{-3/2}\,dx$$

$$= \lim_{t \to \infty} \left[-2(1+x)^{-1/2} \Big|_{2}^{t} \right]$$

$$\lim_{t \to \infty} \left[-2(1+t)^{-1/2} + \frac{2}{\sqrt{3}} \right] = \lim_{t \to \infty} \left(\frac{-2}{\sqrt{1+t}} + \frac{2}{\sqrt{3}} \right) = 0 + \frac{2}{\sqrt{3}}$$

Hence,

$$\int_{2}^{\infty} \frac{dx}{(1+x)^{3/2}} = \frac{2}{\sqrt{3}} = \frac{2\sqrt{3}}{3}$$

EXAMPLE 13   Find

$$\int_1^\infty \frac{x\,dx}{(1 + x^2)^2}$$

if it exists.

Solution

$$\lim_{t \to \infty} \int_1^t \frac{x\,dx}{(1 + x^2)^2} = \lim_{t \to \infty} \int_1^t (1 + x^2)^{-2} x\,dx$$

Let us now find the indefinite integral $\int (1 + x^2)^{-2} x\,dx$, which can be obtained by a change of variable. Let $u = 1 + x^2$. Then

$$du = 2x\,dx \qquad \text{and} \qquad x\,dx = \tfrac{1}{2}\,du$$

Substituting gives

$$\int (1 + x^2)^{-2} x\,dx = \int u^{-2} \left(\frac{1}{2}\right) du = \frac{1}{2} \int u^{-2}\,du$$

$$= -\frac{1}{2} u^{-1} + C = -\frac{1}{2(1 + x^2)} + C$$

Hence,

$$\lim_{t \to \infty} \int_1^t (1 + x^2)^{-2} x\,dx = \lim_{t \to \infty} \frac{-1}{2(1 + x^2)} \bigg|_1^t = \lim_{t \to \infty} \left[\frac{-1}{2(1 + t^2)} + \frac{1}{4} \right]$$

Since $-\tfrac{1}{2}(1 + t^2)$ approaches 0 as t becomes very large,

$$\int_1^\infty \frac{x\,dx}{(1 + x^2)^2} = 0 + \frac{1}{4} = \frac{1}{4}$$

To illustrate how improper integrals are used in probability theory, we now relate them to distribution functions. Two types of distribution functions that play a leading role in statistics are characterized by the nature of the measurements. So far, we have been discussing **discrete distributions** such as the binomial distribution. In contrast, we wish now to discuss distribution functions of **continuous variables.**

Probability Density Function

For a continuous variable x, assume that a function $f(x)$ exists such that

$$P(a \le x \le b) = \int_a^b f(x)\,dx$$

and

$$\int_{-\infty}^\infty f(x)\,dx = 1 \qquad f(x) \ge 0$$

Any function $f(x)$ with these properties is called a **probability density function.** It should be noted that, when the variable is continuous,

$$P(a \le x \le b) = P(a < x < b)$$

EXAMPLE 14   Show that the function given by

$$f(x) = \begin{cases} 2e^{-2x} & \text{for } x > 0 \\ 0 & \text{for } x \le 0. \end{cases}$$

is a probability density function.

Solution   The graph of this function is shown in Figure 13.3.

Figure 13.3

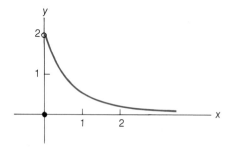

It is obvious in this example that the function is not continuous at $x = 0$ since there is a jump in the curve at this point. However, since the variable x is continuous and the function is integrable, and we show below that the integral from $-\infty$ to ∞ equals 1, the function is a probability density function.

$$\int_{-\infty}^{\infty} f(x)\,dx = \int_{-\infty}^{0} 0\,dx + \int_{0}^{\infty} 2e^{-2x}\,dx$$

$$\int_{0}^{t} 2e^{-2x}\,dx = -e^{-2x}\Big|_{0}^{t} = -e^{-2t} + 1$$

Since $-e^{-2t} + 1$ approaches 1 as t becomes very large,

$$\int_{0}^{\infty} 2e^{-2x}\,dx = 1$$

Hence,

$$\int_{-\infty}^{\infty} f(x)\,dx = 0 + 1 = 1$$

For this example, the probability that x assumes a value between 1 and 2 is given by

$$P(1 \le x \le 2) = \int_{1}^{2} 2e^{-2x}\,dx = e^{-2} - e^{-4}$$

Likewise, the probability that x assumes a value less than 2 is given by

$$P(x \le 2) = P(-\infty \le x \le 2)$$

$$= \int_{-\infty}^{2} f(x)\,dx = \int_{-\infty}^{0} 0\,dx + \int_{0}^{2} 2e^{-2x}\,dx$$

$$= \int_{0}^{2} 2e^{-2x}\,dx$$

$$= 1 - e^{-4}$$

In the application of statistics to problems in the physical, social, and biological sciences, as well as in economics and business, certain continuous probability density functions are extremely important. Probably the most important of these distributions is the **normal,** or **Gaussian, distribution.** The graph of this distribution is approximately bell-shaped (see Figure 13.4), and the probability density function is given by

$$f(x) = \frac{e^{-(x-\mu)^{2'}2\sigma^2}}{\sigma\sqrt{2\pi}}$$

Figure 13.4

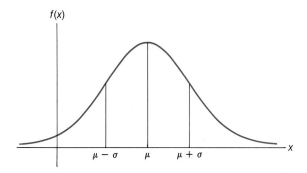

Where μ is the mean and σ is the standard deviation. To find $P(a \leq x \leq b)$, compute

$$P(a \leq x \leq b) = \int_a^b \frac{e^{-(x-\mu)^2/2\sigma^2}}{\sigma\sqrt{2\pi}}\, dx$$

Tables for finding the areas under the standard normal curve have been constructed and are available on page 322. Some hand calculators also give these values.

Exercise Set 13.3

A *Find the value of the following improper integrals if they exist.*

1. $\int_2^{\infty} \frac{dx}{x^2}$

2. $\int_{-\infty}^{-1} \frac{dx}{x^2}$

3. $\int_1^{\infty} \frac{dx}{x^{3/2}}$

4. $\int_{-\infty}^{-1} \frac{dx}{x^{3/2}}$

5. $\int_1^{\infty} \frac{dx}{(1+x)^{3/2}}$

6. $\int_{-\infty}^{-2} \frac{dx}{(1+x)^{3/2}}$

7. $\int_0^{\infty} e^x\, dx$

8. $\int_{-\infty}^0 e^x\, dx$

9. $\int_0^{\infty} e^{-x}\, dx$

10. $\int_{-\infty}^{-1} e^{-x}\, dx$

11. $\int_0^{\infty} e^{-2x}\, dx$

12. $\int_{-\infty}^0 e^{3x}\, dx$

B **13.** $\displaystyle\int_1^\infty \frac{x\,dx}{1+x^2}$ **14.** $\displaystyle\int_{-\infty}^{-1} \frac{x\,dx}{1+x^2}$ **15.** $\displaystyle\int_0^\infty xe^{-x^2}\,dx$

16. $\displaystyle\int_{-\infty}^0 xe^{-x^2}\,dx$ **17.** $\displaystyle\int_2^\infty \frac{x\,dx}{(1+x^2)^2}$ **18.** $\displaystyle\int_{-\infty}^{-1} \frac{x\,dx}{(1+x^2)^2}$

19. $\displaystyle\int_0^\infty x^2 e^{-x^3}\,dx$ **20.** $\displaystyle\int_{-\infty}^{-1} 2x^2 e^{x^3}\,dx$

C **21.** Suppose $f(x) = 0$ for $x < 0$, $f(x) = 0$ for $x > 2$, and $f(x) = x/2$ for $0 \le x \le 2$. Show that $f(x)$ satisfies the properties of a probability density function.

22. In exercise 21, find
  a. $P(x < 0)$ **b.** $P(x > 1)$ **c.** $P(.5 < x < 2.5)$
  d. $P(x < \frac{3}{2})$ **e.** $P(x > 2)$ **f.** $P(0 < x < \frac{3}{2})$

23. Given

$$f(x) = \begin{cases} kx^3 & \text{for } 0 < x < 2 \\ 0 & \text{elsewhere} \end{cases}$$

  a. find k so that $f(x)$ is a probability density function.
  b. find $P(.5 < x < 1.5)$. **c.** find $P(x > 1)$.
  d. find $P(x < .5)$ **e.** find $P(-2 < x < 2)$.

24. Given

$$f(x) = \begin{cases} ke^{-x/2} & \text{for } x > 0 \\ 0 & \text{otherwise} \end{cases}$$

  a. find k so that $f(x)$ is a probability density function.
  b. find $P(x > .5)$. **c.** find $P(x < 1)$.
  d. find $P(1 < x < 2)$. **e.** find $P(0 < x < 3)$.

Business **25. Production.** Suppose that the rate of production of an oil company per month is given in thousands of barrels as

$$\frac{dP}{dt} = 26te^{-0.04t}$$

How much oil is produced during the first 12 months of operation? If the production is continued indefinitely, what would be the total amount produced?

26. Investment. An investment gives

$$\frac{dA}{dt} = 2000e^{-0.12t}$$

dollars per year. Assume that the investment is continued indefinitely, and find the total amount A returned from this investment.

Life Sciences **27. Medicine.** A doctor finds that the rate of elimination of a drug in milliliters per minute, t, is given by

$$\frac{dE}{dt} = te^{-0.3t}$$

Assume that the eliminations continues indefinitely, and find the total amount eliminated, E.

Social Sciences   **28. Politics.** Suppose the length of time in minutes each voter spends on a candidate's campaign is represented by the probability density function

$$f(t) = \begin{cases} \dfrac{2}{(t+2)^2} & \text{for } t \geq 0 \\ 0 & \text{for } t < 0 \end{cases}$$

What is the probability that a voter chosen at random spends at least 8 minutes on the campaign?

4 Integration by the Use of Tables

> Although we have given many methods for finding antiderivatives, there are still a good number we have not considered. Some of these involve functions that we have not studied. Even courses in calculus do not study all of these functions. Consequently, tables of integrals have been developed that can be used to integrate many additional functions. Most of these integration formulas involve some substitution. This section illustrates how a table of integrals may be used. The table that we give is not long. For more complete tables we refer you to those found in other reference books, such as Schaum's *Mathematical Handbook* or CRC's *Mathematics Tables.**

This section gives a short list of integration formulas for finding more complicated antiderivatives. The list is short because there are many functions we have not studied and because we did not include in this table formulas already given. The table is presented to indicate how we may find antiderivatives by the use of more extensive integral tables. Note that the constant of integration has been omitted in the table but it should be added when obtaining an antiderivative.

EXAMPLE 15   Find

$$\int \frac{5\,dx}{x^2 - 36}$$

Solution

$$\int \frac{5\,dx}{x^2 - 36} = 5 \int \frac{dx}{x^2 - 36}$$

Using formula 1 from Table 13.1 with $u = x$ and $a = 6$ gives

$$\int \frac{5\,dx}{x^2 - 36} = \frac{5}{12} \ln \left| \frac{x-6}{x+6} \right| + C$$

Mathematical Handbook, Murray R. Spiegel. Schaum's Outline Series, McGraw-Hill Book Co., New York, 1968. *Standard Mathematics Tables*, 27TH Edition. CRC Press, Inc., 2000 Corporate Blvd., Northwest, Boca Raton, Fla. 33431.

Table 13.1 Table of Integrals ($a > 0$, $c \neq 0$, $bc - ad \neq 0$)

1. $\displaystyle\int \frac{du}{u^2 - a^2} = \frac{1}{2a} \ln \left| \frac{u - a}{u + a} \right| \qquad u^2 > a^2$

2. $\displaystyle\int \frac{du}{a^2 - u^2} = \frac{1}{2a} \ln \left| \frac{a + u}{a - u} \right| \qquad u^2 < a^2$

3. $\displaystyle\int \frac{du}{\sqrt{u^2 \pm a^2}} = \ln \left| u + \sqrt{u^2 \pm a^2} \right|$

4. $\displaystyle\int \frac{du}{u\sqrt{a^2 \pm u^2}} = -\frac{1}{a} \ln \left| \frac{a + \sqrt{a^2 \pm u^2}}{u} \right|$

5. $\displaystyle\int \frac{du}{u^2\sqrt{a^2 \pm u^2}} = -\frac{\sqrt{a^2 \pm u^2}}{a^2 u}$

6. $\displaystyle\int \frac{du}{u^2\sqrt{u^2 - a^2}} = \frac{\sqrt{u^2 - a^2}}{a^2 u}$

7. $\displaystyle\int \sqrt{u^2 \pm a^2}\, du = \tfrac{1}{2}(u\sqrt{u^2 \pm a^2} \pm a^2 \ln |u + \sqrt{u^2 \pm a^2}|)$

8. $\displaystyle\int u^2\sqrt{u^2 \pm a^2}\, du = \tfrac{1}{8}[u(2u^2 \pm a^2)\sqrt{u^2 \pm a^2} - a^4 \ln |u + \sqrt{u^2 \pm a^2}|]$

9. $\displaystyle\int \frac{\sqrt{a^2 \pm u^2}}{u}\, du = \sqrt{a^2 \pm u^2} - a \ln \left| \frac{a + \sqrt{a^2 \pm u^2}}{u} \right|$

10. $\displaystyle\int \frac{\sqrt{u^2 \pm a^2}}{u^2}\, du = -\frac{\sqrt{u^2 \pm a^2}}{u} + \ln |u + \sqrt{u^2 \pm a^2}|$

11. $\displaystyle\int \frac{u^2}{\sqrt{u^2 \pm a^2}}\, du = \tfrac{1}{2}(u\sqrt{u^2 \pm a^2} \pm a^2 \ln |u + \sqrt{u^2 \pm a^2}|)$

12. $\displaystyle\int \frac{1}{(au + b)(cu + d)}\, du = \frac{1}{bc - ad}(\ln |cu + d| - \ln |au + b|) \qquad bc - ad \neq 0$

EXAMPLE 16   Find

$$\int \frac{dx}{6x^2 + x - 15}$$

Solution   There does not appear to be a formula in the table for this expression. Note, however, that the denominator may be factored.

$$\int \frac{dx}{6x^2 + x - 15} = \int \frac{dx}{(3x + 5)(2x - 3)}$$

Now formula 12 may be used with $a = 3$, $b = 5$, $c = 2$, and $d = -3$:

$$\int \frac{dx}{(3x + 5)(2x - 3)} = \frac{1}{10 + 9}(\ln |2x - 3| - \ln |3x + 5|) + C$$

$$= \tfrac{1}{19}(\ln |2x - 3| - \ln |3x + 5|) + C$$

or, from the properties of logarithms,

$$\int \frac{dx}{6x^2 + x - 15} = \frac{1}{19}\left(\ln\left|\frac{2x - 3}{3x + 5}\right|\right) + C$$

Sometimes a substitution is needed to change the problem to a form where a formula can be used. We used this method previously, but it also applies to many more complicated problems than were considered at that time.

EXAMPLE 17 Find

$$\int \frac{2x^2}{\sqrt{25x^2 - 36}}\,dx$$

Solution To put this integral into a form involving $\sqrt{u^2 - a^2}$, let $u = 5x$. Then

$$x = \tfrac{1}{5}u \quad \text{and} \quad dx = \tfrac{1}{5}du$$

$$\int \frac{2x^2}{\sqrt{25x^2 - 36}}\,dx = \int \frac{2(\frac{1}{25})u^2}{\sqrt{u^2 - 36}}\,\tfrac{1}{5}\,du$$

$$= \tfrac{2}{125}\int \frac{u^2}{\sqrt{u^2 - 36}}\,du$$

Using formula 11 gives

$$\tfrac{2}{125}\int \frac{u^2}{\sqrt{u^2 - 36}}\,du = (\tfrac{2}{125})(\tfrac{1}{2})u\sqrt{u^2 - 36} + 36\ln\left|u + \sqrt{u^2 - 36}\right| + C$$

Thus,

$$\int \frac{2x^2}{\sqrt{25x^2 - 36}}\,dx = \tfrac{1}{125}(5x\sqrt{25x^2 - 36} + 36\ln\left|5x + \sqrt{25x^2 - 36}\right|) + C$$

EXAMPLE 18 Find

$$\int_9^{12} \frac{1}{x^2\sqrt{225 - x^2}}\,dx$$

Solution Use formula 5 with $u = x$ and $a = 15$. Then

$$\int_9^{12} \frac{1}{x^2\sqrt{225 - x^2}}\,dx = \int_9^{12} \frac{1}{u^2\sqrt{225 - u^2}}\,du$$

$$= -\frac{\sqrt{225 - u^2}}{225u}\,\Big|_{u=9}^{u=12}$$

$$= -\frac{\sqrt{225 - 144}}{(225)(12)} + \frac{\sqrt{225 - 81}}{(225)(9)}$$

$$= -\frac{9}{(225)(12)} + \frac{12}{(225)(9)}$$

$$= -\tfrac{1}{300} + \tfrac{4}{675}$$

$$= -\tfrac{9}{2700} + \tfrac{16}{2700} = \tfrac{7}{2700}$$

EXAMPLE 19   Solve

$$\frac{dy}{dx} = 3y(5 - y)$$

Solution   Multiply by dx to obtain $dy = 3y(5 - y) \, dx$. Assume that $y(5 - y) \neq 0$ and divide by it:

$$\frac{dy}{y(5 - y)} = dx$$

Integrate both sides:

$$\int \frac{dy}{y(5 - y)} = \int dx$$

Now use formula 12, with $a = 1$, $b = 0$, $c = -1$, and $d = 5$:

$$\frac{1}{0(-1) - (1)(5)} (\ln |5 - y| - \ln |y|) + C = x$$

Note that since C is arbitrary, it does not have to be added to both antiderivatives.

$$-\tfrac{1}{5}(\ln |5 - y| - \ln |y|) + C = x$$

If $y(5 - y) = 0$, then $y = 0$ or $y = 5$. Both of these values are also solutions, as can be seen from substituting them into the equation.

Exercise Set 13.4

A   *Use Table 13.1 to find the following antiderivatives.*

1. $\displaystyle\int \frac{dx}{x^2 - 25}$

2. $\displaystyle\int \frac{3\,dx}{x^2 - 36}$

3. $\displaystyle\int \frac{dx}{36 - x^2}$

4. $\displaystyle\int \frac{4\,dx}{16 - x^2}$

5. $\displaystyle\int \frac{dx}{\sqrt{x^2 + 36}}$

6. $\displaystyle\int \frac{dx}{\sqrt{x^2 - 36}}$

7. $\displaystyle\int \frac{dx}{x\sqrt{x^2 + 25}}$

8. $\displaystyle\int \frac{dx}{x\sqrt{25 - x^2}}$

9. $\displaystyle\int \frac{dx}{x^2\sqrt{49 + x^2}}$

10. $\displaystyle\int \frac{dx}{x^2\sqrt{49 - x^2}}$

11. $\displaystyle\int \frac{dx}{x^2\sqrt{x^2 - 49}}$

12. $\displaystyle\int \sqrt{x^2 - 49}\,dx$

13. $\displaystyle\int x^2\sqrt{x^2 + 25}\,dx$

14. $\displaystyle\int \frac{\sqrt{x^2 + 25}}{x^2}\,dx$

15. $\displaystyle\int \frac{\sqrt{x^2 + 25}}{x}\,dx$

16. $\displaystyle\int \frac{x^2}{\sqrt{x^2 - 16}}\,dx$

17. $\displaystyle\int \frac{x^2}{\sqrt{x^2 + 49}}\,dx$

18. $\displaystyle\int \frac{\sqrt{x^2 + 16}}{x^2}\,dx$

19. $\displaystyle\int \frac{dx}{(x + 3)(x - 2)}$

20. $\displaystyle\int \frac{dx}{(2x + 3)(3x - 2)}$

B **21.** $\int \dfrac{dx}{\sqrt{25x^2 + 16}}$ **22.** $\int \dfrac{3\,dx}{\sqrt{16x^2 - 25}}$ **23.** $\int \dfrac{8\,dx}{x\sqrt{25 - 4x^2}}$

24. $\int \dfrac{5\,dx}{x^2\sqrt{16 + 9x^2}}$ **25.** $\int 3x^2\sqrt{9x^2 + 16}\,dx$ **26.** $\int \dfrac{\sqrt{16 - 25x^2}}{3x}\,dx$

27. $\int \dfrac{\sqrt{16 + 25x^2}}{3x^2}\,dx$ **28.** $\int \dfrac{4x^2}{\sqrt{36x^2 - 9}}\,dx$ **29.** $\int \dfrac{dx}{6x^2 - 5x - 6}$

30. $\int \dfrac{2\,dx}{8x^2 + 10x - 3}$

Business **31. Cash Reserves.** The cash reserves of a company for a year are given in thousands of dollars by

$$C = 2 + \frac{x^2\sqrt{1 + x^2}}{144} \qquad 0 \le x \le 12$$

where x represents the number of months. Find the average cash reserve for
a. the first quarter.
b. the first half of the year.
c. the last quarter.

Economics **32. Consumer's Surplus.** Find the consumer's surplus for

$$D(x) = \frac{360}{x^2 + 2x - 3}$$

$$S(x) = \frac{5x}{x + 3}$$

Life Sciences **33. Pollution.** The radius R of an oil slick is increasing at the rate

$$\frac{dR}{dt} = \frac{144}{\sqrt{t^2 + 16}} \qquad t \ge 0$$

where t is time in minutes. Find the radius after 5 minutes if $R = 0$ when $t = 0$.

Social Sciences **34. Learning Rates.** A rate of learning is given by

$$\frac{dL}{dt} = \frac{64}{\sqrt{t^2 + 36}} \qquad t \ge 0$$

where L is the number of items learned in t hours. Find the number of items learned in 8 hours.

5 **Summary and Review**

Review to ensure your understanding of the following concepts:

Antiderivative of e^u
Integration by parts
Integration by use of tables

Antiderivative of $\ln |u|$
Improper integrals
Integration using substitutions

Review Exercise Set 13.5

A   Find the following integrals.

1. $\displaystyle\int_3^5 \frac{4\,dx}{\sqrt{2x-3}}$

2. $\displaystyle\int \frac{3\,dx}{\sqrt[3]{2x+1}}$

3. $\displaystyle\int \frac{3e^{2x}}{5e^{2x}+2}\,dx$

4. $\displaystyle\int \frac{4e^{-3x}}{3e^{-3x}+4}\,dx$

5. $\displaystyle\int \frac{3x}{2x+3}\,dx$

6. $\displaystyle\int_1^2 \frac{4x}{2x+5}\,dx$

B

7. $\displaystyle\int \frac{3\,dx}{\sqrt{x}+4}$

8. $\displaystyle\int \frac{4\,dx}{2\sqrt[3]{x}+3}$

9. $\displaystyle\int \frac{4x\,dx}{\sqrt{3x+1}}$

10. $\displaystyle\int \frac{5e^x\,dx}{\sqrt[3]{e^x+2}}$

11. $\displaystyle\int 3xe^{-2x}\,dx$

12. $\displaystyle\int (2x-3)e^{2x}\,dx$

13. $\displaystyle\int 4x^2 \ln x\,dx$

14. $\displaystyle\int x^4 \ln x\,dx$

C   Find the value of the following improper integrals if they exist.

15. $\displaystyle\int_2^\infty 3x^{-3/2}\,dx$

16. $\displaystyle\int_2^\infty \frac{4\,dx}{(1+x)^{3/2}}$

17. $\displaystyle\int_0^\infty 3e^{-2x}\,dx$

18. $\displaystyle\int_{-\infty}^\infty e^{2x}\,dx$

Use Table 13.1 to find the following antiderivatives.

19. $\displaystyle\int \frac{3x^2\,dx}{\sqrt{36x^2-25}}$

20. $\displaystyle\int_1^4 \frac{dx}{x^2\sqrt{144-4x^2}}$

21. $\displaystyle\int \frac{4\,dx}{6x^2-11x-10}$

22. $\displaystyle\int \frac{\sqrt{36x^2+16}}{3x^2}\,dx$

Business   **23. Production.** Suppose the rate of production of an oil company per month is given in thousands of barrels as

$$\frac{dP}{dt} = 24te^{-0.06t}$$

How much oil is produced during the first 6 months? If production is continued indefinitely, what would be the total amount produced?

24. Warranty. Suppose a product is guaranteed for 6 months. If the failure probability density function is

$$f(t) = \begin{cases} 0.02e^{-0.02t} & t \ge 0 \\ 0 & t < 0 \end{cases}$$

where t is in months, find the probability that an item will fail during the warranty period.

25. Investments. Assume an investment gives

$$\frac{dA}{dt} = 3000e^{-0.14t}$$

dollars per year. If the investment is continued indefinitely, what would be the total amount received?

Life Sciences

26. Medicine. Suppose the recovery time T, in days, for a particular disease can be represented by the probability density function

$$T = \begin{cases} 0.04e^{-0.04t} & t \geq 0 \\ 0 & t < 0 \end{cases}$$

What is the probability that a person who contracts the disease will take at least 8 days to recover?

Social Sciences

27. Politics. Suppose the length of time T, in minutes, each voter spends on a political campaign can be represented by the probability density function

$$T = \begin{cases} \dfrac{3}{(t+3)^2} & \text{for } t \geq 0 \\ 0 & \text{for } t < 0 \end{cases}$$

What is the probability that a voter chosen at random spends at least 7 minutes on the campaign?

14

Multivariable Calculus

T he study of calculus can proceed in several directions. Differentiation formulas and integration formulas can be obtained for many other functions, such as trigonometric functions, inverse trigonometric functions, hyperbolic functions, inverse hyperbolic functions, and vector functions. Additional methods of integration involving trigonometric substitution and partial fractions can be illustrated.

These different directions are followed in many calculus books. To explain these different directions in detail would make this book much longer than intended. Instead, we choose to present in these remaining few sections a generalization of many of the concepts already studied to functions of several variables. We present this material with the hope that this treatment will reveal some of the many possibilities for generalization in mathematics available for further study and application.

1 Functions of Several Variables

In an earlier exercise, the cost function $C(x)$ for the number x of items produced was given as

$$C(x) = \$0.25x + \$70$$

Suppose now that the producer decides to produce an additional, different item. Let y represent the number of these additional items produced. The cost function $C(x, y)$ for producing both items would depend upon both x

and y, and, hence, is a function of two variables. For example,

$$C(x, y) = \$130 + \$0.25x + \$0.30y$$

If the producer decides to produce more items, the cost function would involve more variables. We could define functions of three variables, four variables, or, in general, n variables. In the remainder of this chapter, however, we will usually restrict our discussion to functions of two independent variables.

We have already encountered many examples of functions of several variables. Most of the objective functions to be maximized or minimized in Chapter 3 were functions of two or more variables. The formula for the number of ways of selecting r objects from n objects without regard to order,

$$C(n, r) = \frac{n}{(n - r)!r!}$$

is a function of two variables. The formula for compound interest,

$$A = P\left(1 + \frac{r}{n}\right)^n$$

is a function of three variables.

Function of Two Independent Variables

An equation of the form $z = f(x, y)$ describes a **function of two independent variables** if for each ordered pair (x, y) from the domain of f there is one and only one value of z given by $f(x, y)$ in the range of f. Unless stated otherwise, the **domain** of $z = f(x, y)$ is the set of all ordered pairs of real numbers (x, y) such that $f(x, y)$ is also a real number.

Note that in many practical problems the domain may be further restricted; for example, in our producer's cost function since x and y represent number of items, x and y must be integers and greater than or equal to 0.

EXAMPLE 1   If $C(x, y) = \$130 + \$0.25x + \$0.30y$, find $C(4, 3)$.

Solution
$$C(4, 3) = \$130 + \$0.25(4) + \$0.30(3)$$
$$= \$130 + \$1.00 + \$0.90$$
$$= \$131.90$$

EXAMPLE 2   If $f(x, y, z) = 3x^2 - 2xy + y^2 - 3xyz + 2z^2$, find

    a. $f(1, 2, 3)$.
    b. $f(-1, 2, -3)$.

a. $f(1, 2, 3) = 3(1)^2 - 2(1)(2) + (2)^2 - 3(1)(2)(3) + 2(3)^2$

$\qquad = 3 - 4 + 4 - 18 + 18$

$\qquad = 3$

b. $f(-1, 2, -3) = 3(-1)^2 - 2(-1)(2) + (2)^2 - 3(-1)(2)(-3) + 2(-3)^2$

$\qquad = 3 + 4 + 4 - 18 + 18$

$\qquad = 11$

Suppose, now, we consider the graphs of functions of two variables. For each point (x, y) in the domain a unique value of z is determined by the function. To locate this value for z requires the use of three dimensions instead of two. A three-dimensional coordinate system was introduced in Section 2.5 of Chapter 2. It is recommended that you read again the first few paragraphs of that section before working the following example.

EXAMPLE 3 Find the coordinates of the vertices A, B, G, and H of the rectangular box illustrated in Figure 14.1.

Figure 14.1

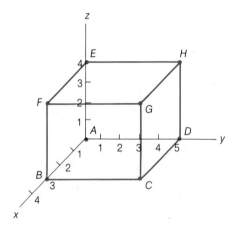

Solution The coordinates of A, B, G, and H are

$\qquad A(0, 0, 0) \qquad B(3, 0, 0) \qquad G(3, 5, 4) \qquad H(0, 5, 4)$

EXAMPLE 4 Draw the graph of $z = x^2 + y^2$.

Solution To help us draw this graph, we find the intersections of the graph with the coordinate planes. The x, z-plane is represented by the equation $y = 0$. To find the intersection of this plane with our graph, we substitute $y = 0$ into the equation of the graph and obtain

$\qquad z = x^2$

In the x, z-plane the graph of $z = x^2$ is the parabola illustrated in Figure 14.2.

Figure 14.2

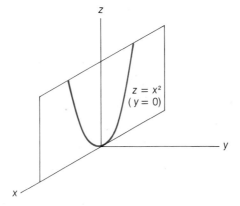

The y, z-plane is represented by the equation $x = 0$. To find the intersection of this plane with our graph, we substitute $x = 0$ into the equation and obtain

$$z = y^2$$

In the y, z-plane the graph of $z = y^2$ is the parabola illustrated by Figure 14.3.

Figure 14.3

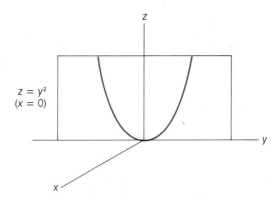

The x, y-plane is represented by the equation $z = 0$. To find the intersection of this plane with our graph, we substitute $z = 0$ into the equation and obtain

$$0 = x^2 + y^2$$

In the x, y-plane $0 = x^2 + y^2$ has only the real solution, $x = 0$ and $y = 0$. Hence, the only point of our graph in the x, y-plane is $(0, 0, 0)$. Since there is only one point of the graph in the x, y-plane, let us find the intersection of the graph with the plane $z = 4$. Substituting $z = 4$ into the equation gives

$$4 = x^2 + y^2$$

which is a circle. Our graph is illustrated in Figure 14.4. The graph is a surface and is called a **circular paraboloid**.

Figure 14.4

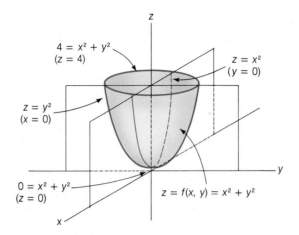

The previous example illustrates that the graph of a function $z = f(x, y)$ is the set of all ordered triples (x, y, z) that satisfy the equation and will, in general, be a surface. Graphing functions of two variables can be difficult, and we plan to do only enough of them to give a geometric interpretation to our generalizations.

As an introduction to the next section, we consider a limit of a function of two variables. In fact, we consider a particular limit that is part of a definition of a derivative in the next section.

EXAMPLE 5   If $f(x, y) = 2x^2 + y$, find

$$\lim_{\Delta x \to 0} \frac{f(x + \Delta x, y) - f(x, y)}{\Delta x}$$

Solution   To find this limit, we follow our usual four-step procedure for derivatives:

1. $f(x + \Delta x, y) = 2(x + \Delta x)^2 + y$
$$= 2x^2 + 4x\,\Delta x + 2(\Delta x)^2 + y$$
$$f(x, y) = 2x^2 \qquad\qquad\qquad y$$

2. $f(x + \Delta x, y) - f(x, y) = 4x\,\Delta x + 2(\Delta x)^2$

3. $\dfrac{f(x + \Delta x, y) - f(x, y)}{\Delta x} = 4x + 2\,\Delta x$

4. $\displaystyle\lim_{\Delta x \to 0} \dfrac{f(x + \Delta x, y) - f(x, y)}{\Delta x} = 4x$

Exercise Set 14.1

A   *Find the values of the following functions $f(x, y) = 3x^2 - 2xy + y^3$, $g(x, y) = 7 - 3x + 2y$, and $h(x, y) = 4x^3 - 3xy + 2y^2$ at the indicated points of their domain.*

1. $f(0, 1)$ **2.** $f(1, 0)$ **3.** $f(-1, 0)$ **4.** $f(-1, 1)$

5. $f(2, 1)$ **6.** $f(1, 2)$ **7.** $g(0, 0)$ **8.** $g(3, 2)$

9. $g(2, 3)$ **10.** $g(-3, -1)$ **11.** $h(1, 2)$ **12.** $h(2, -1)$

Locate the following points on a three-dimensional coordinate system.

13. $(1, 2, 3)$ **14.** $(-1, 2, 3)$ **15.** $(1, -2, 3)$ **16.** $(1, 2, -3)$

B   *Find*

a. $\lim\limits_{\Delta x \to 0} \dfrac{f(x + \Delta x, y) - f(x, y)}{\Delta x}$ **b.** $\lim\limits_{\Delta y \to 0} \dfrac{f(x, y + \Delta y) - f(x, y)}{\Delta y}$

for the following functions.

17. $f(x, y) = 2x^2 + y^2$ **18.** $f(x, y) = 3x + 4y - 2$

19. $f(x, y) = x^2 + 3y^2$ **20.** $f(x, y) = 4x^2 + y^2$

21. $f(x, y) = 3x^2 + 2y - y^2$ **22.** $f(x, y) = 2x^2 + 3y^2 + xy$

Draw the graphs of the following functions.

23. $z = x + y$ **24.** $z = 3x + y$

25. $z = 2x + 3y$ **26.** $z = 3x - 2y + 1$

C   *Draw the graphs of the following functions.*

27. $z = 2y^2$ **28.** $z = 3x^2$

29. $z = x^2 + 2y^2$ **30.** $z = -x^2 - y^2$

Business   **31. Profit Functions.** A profit function $P(x, y)$ is given by

$$P(x, y) = 2x^2 - xy + 3y^2 + 4x + 2y + 4$$

Find

a. $P(3, 2)$.   **b.** $P(4, 1)$.   **c.** $P(3, 4)$.

Economics   **32. Revenue and Cost Functions.** Suppose the revenue and cost functions for a firm producing two items are given in units of thousands by

$$R(x, y) = 3x + 4y$$
$$C(x, y) = x^2 - 3xy + 3y^2 + 2x + 4y + 7$$

Find

a. $P(x, y) = R(x, y) - C(x, y)$.   **b.** $R(3, 2)$.   **c.** $C(2, 3)$.   **d.** $P(3, 1)$.

Life Sciences   **33. Scuba Diving.** The time of a scuba dive is estimated by

$$T(v, d) = \frac{35v}{d + 35}$$

where v is the volume of air in the diver's tanks and d is the depth in feet of the dive. Find

a. $T(965, 30)$.   **b.** $T(75, 45)$.

Social Sciences   **34. Intelligence Quotient.** The function for determining the intelligence quotient is given as

$$I(M, C) = \frac{100M}{C}$$

where I represents intelligence quotient, M represents mental age, and C represents chronological age.

a. If $M = 14$ and $C = 10$, find $I(14, 10)$.
b. If $M = 11$ and $C = 10$, find $I(11, 10)$.
c. If $M = 10$ and $C = 10$, find $I(10, 10)$.

In Example 5, we found

$$\lim_{\Delta x \to 0} \frac{f(x + \Delta x, y) - f(x, y)}{\Delta x}$$

You probably notice the similarity of this limit to the limit that we defined to be a derivative. Because of this similarity this limit, when it exists, is called a **partial derivative.** Notice that y is kept fixed and the limit is taken as $\Delta x \to 0$. Such a limit is called the **partial derivative with respect to x.**

The definition of a partial derivative is given below:

Definition of
Partial Derivative
of z = f(x, y)

The **partial derivative of z with respect to x**—denoted by $\partial z/\partial x$, f_x, or $f_x(x, y)$—is defined to be

$$\frac{\partial z}{\partial x} = \lim_{\Delta x \to 0} \frac{f(x + \Delta x, y) - f(x, y)}{\Delta x}$$

The **partial derivative of z with respect to y**—denoted by $\partial z/\partial y$, f_y, or $f_y(x, y)$—is defined to be

$$\frac{\partial z}{\partial y} = \lim_{\Delta y \to 0} \frac{f(x, y + \Delta y) - f(y)}{\Delta y}$$

Since partial derivatives are simply ordinary derivatives with respect to one variable while keeping the other variable constant, partial derivatives can be found by using our previously obtained differentiation formulas instead of the four-step procedure.

EXAMPLE 6 If $z = f(x, y) = 2x^2 + y$, find $\partial z/\partial x$ and $\partial z/\partial y$.

Solution Differentiating with respect to x while holding y constant gives

$$\frac{\partial z}{\partial x} = 4x$$

Note that this is the same value obtained for

$$\lim_{\Delta x \to 0} \frac{f(x + \Delta x, y) - f(x, y)}{\Delta x}$$

in the previous section by using our four-step procedure. Differentiating the function with respect to y while holding x constant gives

$$\frac{\partial z}{\partial y} = 1$$

EXAMPLE 7 If $z = f(x, y) = 3x^2 - 2xy + 5xy^2 - 3y$, find

    a. $\partial z/\partial y$

    b. $f_y(3, 2)$

Solution   **a.** $\dfrac{\partial z}{\partial y} = -2x + 10xy - 3$

    b. $f_y(3, 2) = -2(3) + 10(3)(2) - 3$
$$= -6 + 60 - 3$$
$$= 51$$

EXAMPLE 8 If $z = \ln(3x^2 + 2y)$, find

    a. $\partial z/\partial x$

    b. $f_x(1, 0)$

    c. $\partial z/\partial y$

    d. $f_y(1, 0)$

Solution   **a.** $\dfrac{\partial z}{\partial x} = \dfrac{6x}{3x^2 + 2y}$

    b. $f_x(1, 0) = \dfrac{6(1)}{3(1)^2 + 2(0)} = \dfrac{6}{3 + 0} = 2$

    c. $\dfrac{\partial z}{\partial y} = \dfrac{2}{3x^2 + 2y}$

    d. $f_y(1, 0) = \dfrac{2}{3(1)^2 + 2(0)} = \dfrac{2}{3 + 0} = \dfrac{2}{3}$

The partial derivatives of $z = f(x, y)$ at a point (a, b) can be interpreted geometrically as illustrated in Figure 14.5. Note that $f_x(a, b)$ represents the slope of the tangent line drawn to the curve $z = f(x, b)$ at $x = a$. The curve $z = f(x, b)$ is the intersection of the surface and the plane $y = b$. The partial derivative $f_y(a, b)$ represents the slope of the tangent line drawn to the curve $z = f(a, y)$ at $y = b$. The curve $z = f(a, y)$ is the intersection of the surface and the plane $x = a$.

Figure 14.5

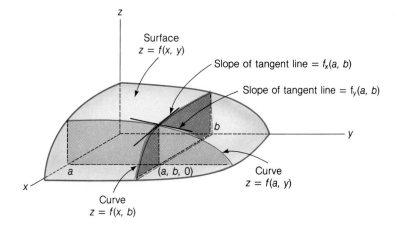

At this point you may be wondering if it is not possible to have higher-order partial derivatives just as there are higher-order ordinary derivatives. The answer is yes, and the second-order partial derivatives are indicated as follows.

Notation of Second-Order Partial Derivatives

Suppose $z = f(x, y)$; then

$$\frac{\partial^2 z}{\partial x^2} = \frac{\partial}{\partial x}\left(\frac{\partial z}{\partial x}\right) = f_{xx}(x, y) = f_{xx}$$

$$\frac{\partial^2 z}{\partial y\, \partial x} = \frac{\partial}{\partial y}\left(\frac{\partial z}{\partial x}\right) = f_{xy}(x, y) = f_{xy}$$

$$\frac{\partial^2 z}{\partial x\, \partial y} = \frac{\partial}{\partial x}\left(\frac{\partial z}{\partial y}\right) = f_{yx}(x, y) = f_{yx}$$

$$\frac{\partial^2 z}{\partial y^2} = \frac{\partial}{\partial y}\left(\frac{\partial z}{\partial y}\right) = f_{yy}(x, y) = f_{yy}$$

The meaning of $\partial^2 z/\partial x\, \partial y$, for example, is the partial derivative with respect to x of the partial derivative of z with respect to y. The other second-order partial derivatives are defined in a similar way.

EXAMPLE 9 If $z = f(x, y) = 2x^3 - 3xy^2 + y^3 - 2$, find

a. $\dfrac{\partial^2 z}{\partial x^2}$ b. $\dfrac{\partial^2 z}{\partial y\, \partial x}$ c. $\dfrac{\partial^2 z}{\partial x\, \partial y}$ d. $\dfrac{\partial^2 z}{\partial y^2}$

e. $f_{xx}(1, 2)$ f. $f_{xy}(1, 2)$ g. $f_{yx}(2, 1)$ h. $f_{yy}(5, 2)$

Solution

a. $\dfrac{\partial z}{\partial x} = 6x^2 - 3y^2$

   $\dfrac{\partial^2 z}{\partial x^2} = 12x$

b. $\dfrac{\partial z}{\partial x} = 6x^2 - 3y^2$

   $\dfrac{\partial^2 z}{\partial y\, \partial x} = -6y$

c. $\dfrac{\partial z}{\partial y} = -6xy + 3y^2$

   $\dfrac{\partial^2 z}{\partial x\, \partial y} = -6y$

d. $\dfrac{\partial z}{\partial y} = -6xy + 3y^2$

   $\dfrac{\partial^2 z}{\partial y^2} = -6x + 6y$

e. $f_x(x, y) = 6x^2 - 3y^2$
   $f_{xx}(x, y) = 12x$
   $f_{xx}(1, 2) = 12(1) = 12$

f. $f_x(x, y) = 6x^2 - 3y^2$
   $f_{xy}(x, y) = -6y$
   $f_{xy}(1, 2) = -6(2) = -12$

g. $f_y(x, y) = -6xy + 3y^2$
   $f_{yx}(x, y) = -6y$
   $f_{yx}(2, 1) = -6(1) = -6$

h. $f_y(x, y) = -6xy + 3y^2$
   $f_{yy}(x, y) = -6x + 6y$
   $f_{yy}(5, 2) = -6(5) + 6(2)$
   $\qquad\qquad = -30 + 12$
   $\qquad\qquad = -18$

Note that in finding the mixed partial $\partial^2 z/\partial y\, \partial x = f_{xy}$, we first differentiate with respect to x, keeping y constant, and then differentiate with respect to y, keeping x constant. Likewise, $\partial^2 z/\partial x\, \partial y = f_{yx}$. For most functions we consider,

$$f_{xy} = f_{yx}$$

Exercise Set 14.2

A Find $\partial z/\partial x$, $\partial z/\partial y$, $f_x(3, 2)$, and $f_y(3, 2)$ for the following functions.

1. $z = f(x, y) = 7 + 2x$

2. $z = f(x, y) = 7 - 3y$

3. $z = f(x, y) = 7 + 3x - 2y$

4. $z = f(x, y) = 5 - 2x + 3y$

5. $z = f(x, y) = 10 - 3x^2 - 2xy + y^3$

6. $z = f(x, y) = 4xy^2 - 3y^2$

7. $z = f(x, y) = 3e^x - 2e^y$

8. $z = f(x, y) = 3xy^2 - 2e^{xy}$

9. $z = f(x, y) = 3 \ln xy + x^2$

10. $z = f(x, y) = 2 \ln (3x^2 + 2y^2)$

B Find $\partial^2 z/\partial x^2$, $\partial^2 z/\partial y^2$, and $f_{xy}(1, 3)$ for the following functions.

11. $z = f(x, y) = 7 + 5x + 3y$

12. $z = f(x, y) = 5x^2 - 3y^3$

13. $z = f(x, y) = 10x^2 y^3$

14. $z = f(x, y) = 5x^3 y^2$

15. $z = f(x, y) = 5x^2 y - 3xy^3$

16. $z = f(x, y) = 4xy^2 - 3x^2 y^3$

17. $z = f(x, y) = 3e^x - 2e^y$

18. $z = f(x, y) = 4xe^x - 2xe^y$

19. $z = f(x, y) = 3e^{xy}$

20. $z = f(x, y) = \ln (3x + y)$

C Find $\partial^2 z/\partial x^2$, $\partial^2 z/\partial y^2$, and $f_{xy}(1, 3)$ for the following functions.

21. $z = f(x, y) = x \ln (3x^2 + 2y^2)$

22. $z = f(x, y) = 3e^{x^2} + y^2$

23. $z = f(x, y) = e^x \ln (3x + 2y)$

24. $z = f(x, y) = (e^x + e^y) \ln x$

25. $z = f(x, y) = \sqrt{2x + 3y}$

26. $z = f(x, y) = \sqrt[3]{x^2 + 3y^2}$

Business **27. Profit Functions.** A profit function is given in thousands of dollars as

$$P(x, y) = 3x^2 - xy + 2y^3 + 2x + 3y + 3$$

where x and y represent the number of items produced. Find

a. $P(1, 2)$.   **b.** $P(2, 1)$.   **c.** $P_x(1, 2)$.   **d.** $P_y(1, 2)$.

Economics **28. Revenue and Cost Functions.** The revenue and cost functions for the XYZ Company are given in units of thousands by

$$R(x, y) = 3x + 5y$$
$$C(x, y) = x^2 - 2xy + 3y^2 + 3x + 2y + 5$$

where x and y represent the number of items produced. Find

a. $P(x, y) = R(x, y) - C(x, y)$.   **b.** $R_x(3, 2)$.   **c.** $C_x(2, 3)$.
d. $C_y(2, 3)$.   **e.** $P_x(2, 3)$.

Life Sciences **29. Scuba Diving.** The time of a scuba dive is estimated by

$$T(v, d) = \frac{36v}{d + 36}$$

where v is the volume of air in the diver's tanks and d is the depth of the dive. Find **(a)** $T(65, 30)$, **(b)** $T_v(65, 30)$, **(c)** $T_d(65, 30)$, and interpret your results.

30. **Safety.** The length L of skid marks is given by

$$L(w, s) = 0.000014ws^2$$

where w is the weight of the car and s is the speed of the car. Find **(a)** $L(2000, 50)$, **(b)** $L(3000, 55)$, **(c)** $L_w(3000, 55)$, **(d)** $L_s(3000, 55)$, and interpret your results.

Social Sciences   31. **Intelligence Quotient.** IQ, represented by I, is given by the following equation

$$I = \frac{100M}{C}$$

where M represents mental age and C represents chronological age. Find **(a)** $I(13, 10)$, **(b)** $I(10, 13)$, **(c)** $I_M(13, 10)$, **(d)** $I_C(13, 10)$, and interpret your results.

3   Relative Maxima and Minima for Functions of Two Variables

In this section we show how partial derivatives may be used to find relative maxima or minima for functions of two variables. The development of the theory is similar to the development of the theory for functions of one variable. Since we have demonstrated that there are two first partial derivatives and possibly four second partial derivatives for functions of two variables, you may expect the procedure of finding and testing critical points to be more complicated. To simplify the discussion, we are going to assume that all higher-order partial derivatives of $z = f(x, y)$ exist in some circular region of the x, y-plane.

The following definition extends the definition of relative maximum and relative minimum to a function of two variables.

Relative Maximum and Relative Minimum for Functions of Two Variables

If there exists a circular region with (a, b) as the center in the domain of $z = f(x, y)$ such that

$$f(a, b) \geq f(x, y)$$

for all (x, y) in the region, then $f(a, b)$ is a **relative maximum.**

If there exists a circular region with (a, b) as the center in the domain of $z = f(x, y)$ such that

$$f(a, b) \leq f(x, y)$$

for all (x, y) in the region, then $f(a, b)$ is a **relative minimum.**

Recall that at a relative maximum or relative minimum for a function of one variable, the first derivative is 0. For a function of two variables, Figure 14.6 suggests that both partial derivatives must be 0 at a relative maximum or relative minimum. This is true and is stated as a necessary condition for a relative maximum or relative minimum.

Figure 14.6

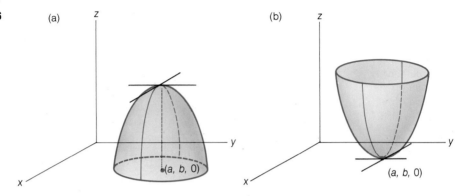

(a)

(b)

A Necessary Condition for a Relative Maximum or Relative Minimum

A necessary condition for $f(a, b)$ to be a relative maximum or a relative minimum is that both f_x and f_y exist at (a, b) and $f_x(a, b) = f_y(a, b) = 0$. The point (a, b) is called a **critical point** of the domain.

The converse of the theorem is not true. If $f_x(a,b) = f_y(a, b) = 0$, then $f(a,b)$ may or may not be a relative maximum or a relative minimum. Figure 14.7 illustrates a point (a, b) at which both partial derivatives equal 0, but the point is not a relative maximum or a relative minimum. The point illustrated in Figure 14.7 is called a **saddle point.**

Figure 14.7

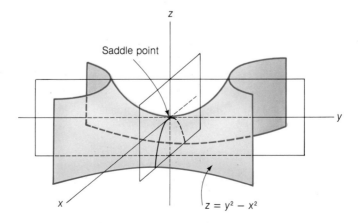

Saddle point

$z = y^2 - x^2$

The following theorem is similar to the second-derivative test and gives sufficient conditions for a relative minimum, a relative maximum, or a saddle point.

Sufficient Conditions for a Relative Minimum, a Relative Maximum, or a Saddle Point

Assume $z = f(x, y)$ and all higher-order partial derivatives exist in some circular region with (a, b) as the center. Suppose $f_x(a, b) = f_y(a, b) = 0$ and let

$$A = f_{xx}(a, b) \qquad B = f_{xy}(a, b) \qquad \text{and} \qquad C = f_{yy}(a, b)$$

1. If $AC - B^2 > 0$, and $A > 0$, then $f(a, b)$ is a relative minimum.
2. If $AC - B^2 > 0$, and $A < 0$, then $f(a, b)$ is a relative maximum.
3. If $AC - B^2 < 0$, then $f(x, y)$ has a saddle point at (a, b).
4. If $AC - B^2 = 0$, then the test fails.

Relative maxima, relative minima, or saddle points can often be found by using a three-step procedure.

Three-Step Procedure for Finding Relative Maxima, Relative Minima, or Saddle Points

1. Find each critical point (a, b) of the domain.
2. Compute $A = f_{xx}(a, b)$, $B = f_{xy}(a, b)$, and $C = f_{yy}(a, b)$.
3. Evaluate $AC - B^2$ and determine which sufficient condition applies.

EXAMPLE 10 Find all critical points and classify them for

$$z = f(x, y) = x^2 + y^2$$

Solution We follow our three-step procedure:

1. $f_x(x, y) = 2x$
   $f_y(x, y) = 2y$

Setting both of these equal to 0 gives

$$f_x(x, y) = 2x = 0$$
$$f_y(x, y) = 2y = 0$$

In this step we may obtain two equations in two unknowns in which we desire all common solutions. For this example the only common solution is $x = 0$ and $y = 0$. Hence, $(0, 0)$ is the only critical point of the domain.

2. $f_{xx}(x, y) = 2$

$f_{xy}(x, y) = 0$

$f_{yy}(x, y) = 2$

Hence,

$$A = f_{xx}(0, 0) = 2$$
$$B = f_{xy}(0, 0) = 0$$
$$C = f_{yy}(0, 0) = 2$$

3. $AC - B^2 = 2(2) - (0)^2 = 4 > 0$

and $A = 2 > 0$; hence, condition 1 applies and $f(0, 0)$ is a relative minimum. This fact agrees with the graph drawn in Figure 14.4 on page 600.

EXAMPLE 11   Find and classify all critical points of

$$z = f(x, y) = x^2 + xy + y^2 - 7x - 8y + 10$$

Solution   **1.** $f_x(x, y) = 2x + \ y - 7 = 0$

$f_y(x, y) = \ \ x + 2y - 8 = 0$

Solving this system gives $(2, 3)$ as the only critical point of the domain.

2. $f_{xx}(x, y) = 2 = f_{xx}(2, 3) = A$

$f_{xy}(x, y) = 1 = f_{xy}(2, 3) = B$

$f_{yy}(x, y) = 2 = f_{yy}(2, 3) = C$

3. $AC - B^2 = (2)(2) - (1)^2 = 3 > 0$

Since $A = 2 > 0$, condition 1 tells us that $f(2, 3)$ is a relative minimum.

EXAMPLE 12   Find all critical points and classify them for

$$z = f(x, y) = xy - \frac{x^4}{4} - \frac{y^2}{2} + 10$$

Solution   **1.** $f_x(x, y) = y - x^3 = 0$

$f_y(x, y) = x - y = 0$

To solve these two equations, we obtain $y = x$ from the second equation and substitute into the first equation to give

$$x - x^3 = 0$$
$$x(1 - x^2) = 0$$
$$x(1 + x)(1 - x) = 0$$

$x = 0$ or $x = -1$ or $x = 1$

$y = 0$ $y = -1$ $y = 1$

Hence, there are three critical points of the domain: $(0, 0)$, $(-1, -1)$, and $(1, 1)$. We test each of these.

2. $f_{xx}(x, y) = -3x^2$

$f_{xy}(x, y) = 1$

$f_{yy}(x, y) = -1$

For $(0, 0)$:

$$A = f_{xx}(0, 0) = -3(0)^2 = 0$$
$$B = f_{xy}(0, 0) = 1$$
$$C = f_{yy}(0, 0) = -1$$

3. $AC - B^2 = 0(-1) - (1)^2 = -1 < 0$

Condition 3 tells us that $f(x, y)$ has a saddle point at $(0, 0)$.

2. For $(-1, -1)$:

$$A = f_{xx}(-1, -1) = -3(-1)^2 = -3$$
$$B = f_{xy}(-1, -1) = 1$$
$$C = f_{yy}(-1, -1) = -1$$

3. $AC - B^2 = (-3)(-1) - (1)^2 = 2 > 0$

Since $A = -3 < 0$, condition 2 tells us that $f(-1, -1)$ is a relative maximum.

2. For $(1, 1)$:

$$A = f_{xx}(1, 1) = -3(1)^2 = -3$$
$$B = f_{xy}(1, 1) = 1$$
$$C = f_{yy}(1, 1) = -1$$

3. $AC - B^2 = (-3)(-1) - (1)^2 = 2 > 0$

Since $A = -3 < 0$, condition 2 tells us that $f(1, 1)$ is a relative maximum.

EXAMPLE 13 Find three numbers x, y, and z such that $x + y + z = 10$ and x^2yz is a maximum.

Solution Although x^2yz is not a function of two variables, we can solve $x + y + z = 10$ for z to obtain $z = 10 - x - y$. Substituting this value of z gives a function of two variables:

$$f(x, y) = x^2y(10 - x - y) = 10x^2y - x^3y - x^2y^2$$

1. $f_x(x, y) = 20xy - 3x^2y - 2xy^2 = xy(20 - 3x - 2y) = 0$

$f_y(x, y) = 10x^2 - x^3 - 2x^2y = x^2(10 - x - 2y) = 0$

Although $(0, y)$ is a critical point for any y, it is obvious that none of these yield a maximum because for each of these $f(0, y) = 10(0)^2y - (0)^3y - (0)^2y = 0$. An additional critical point, $(5, \frac{5}{2})$, is obtained from solving the system

$$20 - 3x - 2y = 0$$
$$10 - x - 2y = 0$$

2. $f_{xx}(x, y) = 20y - 6xy - 2y^2$

$\quad f_{xy}(x, y) = 20x - 3x^2 - 4xy$

$\quad f_{yy}(x, y) = -2x^2$

For $(5, \frac{5}{2})$:

$$A = f_{xx}(5, \tfrac{5}{2}) = 20(\tfrac{5}{2}) - 6(5)(\tfrac{5}{2}) - 2(\tfrac{5}{2})^2$$

$$= 50 - 75 - \tfrac{25}{2}$$

$$= -\tfrac{75}{2}$$

$$B = f_{xy}(5, \tfrac{5}{2}) = 20(5) - 3(5)^2 - 4(5)(\tfrac{5}{2})$$

$$= 100 - 75 - 50$$

$$= -25$$

$$C = f_{yy}(5, \tfrac{5}{2}) = -2(5)^2 = -50$$

3. $AC - B^2 = -\frac{75}{2}(-50) - (-25)^2 = 1250 > 0$

Since $A = -\frac{75}{2} < 0$, condition 2 tells us that

$$f(5, \tfrac{5}{2}) = 10(5)^2(\tfrac{5}{2}) - (5)^3(\tfrac{5}{2}) - (5)^2(\tfrac{5}{2})^2 = \tfrac{625}{4}$$

is a relative maximum.

Exercise Set **14.3**

A Find and classify all critical points for the following functions.

1. $f(x, y) = x^2 + 2y^2$ **2.** $f(x, y) = 3x^2 + y^2$

3. $f(x, y) = 4 - x^2 - y^2$ **4.** $f(x, y) = 9 - x^2 - y^2$

5. $f(x, y) = 10 - x^2 - 2y^2$ **6.** $f(x, y) = y + x^2 + 3y^2$

7. $f(x, y) = x^2 - y^2$ **8.** $f(x, y) = xy$

9. $f(x, y) = 5 - x^2 + 4x - y^2$ **10.** $f(x, y) = x^2 + y^2 - 6x + 2y + 10$

B Find and classify all critical points.

11. $f(x, y) = xy - 3x + 2y - 3$ **12.** $f(x, y) = xy + 5x - 3y + 7$

13. $f(x, y) = x^2 + y^2 - 6xy$ **14.** $f(x, y) = 8xy - x^2 - y^2$

15. $f(x, y) = x^2 + xy + 2y^2 - 3x + 2y + 2$

16. $f(x, y) = x^2 + 4xy + y^2 + 6y + 1$

17. $f(x, y) = -2x^2 + xy - y^2 + 10x + y - 3$

18. $f(x, y) = 3x^2 - 2xy + 2y^2 - 8x - 4y + 10$

C Find and classify all critical points.

19. $f(x, y) = 3xy - x^2y - xy^2$

20. $f(x, y) = e^{xy}$

21. $f(x, y) = x^3 + y^3 - 6x^2 - 3y^2 - 9y$

22. $f(x, y) = 2x^3 - x^2 - 4x + y^2 - 4y + 2$

23. Divide a straight line of length L into three parts such that the sum of the squares of their lengths is a minimum.

24. Find three numbers x, y, and z such that $x + y + z = 15$ and x^2y^2z is a maximum.

Business **25.** **Profit Functions.** The ABC Company has the following profit function:

$$P(x, y) = 2xy - x^2 - 2y^2 - 4x + 12y - 5$$

where x is the number of thousands of item I and y is the number of thousands of item II produced. How many of each type should be produced in order to maximize profit? What is the maximum profit?

Economics **26.** **Cost Functions.** A cost function is given by

$$C(x, y) = 3x^2 + 2xy + 2y^2 - 18x - 16y + 48$$

Find the critical point and the minimum cost if x and y represent the number of items produced.

Physical Sciences **27.** **Construction.** A rectangular parallelepiped tank is to be built so as to hold 4000 cubic feet. If the tank is to be open at the top, what should the dimensions be in order to use the least amount of material?

Lagrange Multipliers

In Example 13 we found three numbers, x, y, and z, which made $f(x, y, z) = x^2yz$ a maximum subject to the constraint $x + y + z = 10$. In the solution to that example we solved the constraint equation for z in terms of x and y, that is,

$$z = 10 - x - y$$

and substituted this value of z into the function x^2yz to obtain a function of two variables

$$x^2yz - x^2y(10 - x - y)$$

We then found the critical points for this function and used the critical points to find the relative maximum.

Sometimes it is difficult or even impossible to solve a constraint equation for one variable in terms of the others. In that case we may try a method called the **method of Lagrange multipliers.** In this method the introduction of another variable allows us to solve the constrained optimization problem without first solving the constraint equation for one of the variables. The method can be used for functions of two variables, three variables, four variables, or more; but for simplicity we state the method for two independent variables.

The method of Lagrange multipliers is outlined below:

The Method of Lagrange Multipliers

To find the relative maxima or relative minima of a function $f(x, y)$ subject to a constraint $g(x, y) = 0$, introduce a new variable, λ (called a **Lagrange multiplier**), and

1. Form
$$F(x, y, \lambda) = f(x, y) + \lambda \cdot g(x, y)$$

2. Form the system
$$F_x(x, y, \lambda) = 0$$
$$F_y(x, y, \lambda) = 0$$
$$F_\lambda(x, y, \lambda) = 0$$

We assume all indicated partial derivatives exist.
3. Solve the system found in step 2 for values of x, y, and λ that satisfy the system. The desired extrema will be found among the points (x, y) that satisfy the system.

The steps in solving a problem by the method of Lagrange multipliers are illustrated by the next example.

EXAMPLE 14   Find the minimum value of $f(x, y) = x^2 + y^2$ subject to $2x + y = 5$.

Solution   Note that $f(x, y) = x^2 + y^2$ and $g(x, y) = 2x + y - 5 = 0$.

Step 1.   Form
$$F(x, y, \lambda) = f(x, y) + \lambda \cdot g(x, y)$$
$$F(x, y, \lambda) = x^2 + y^2 + \lambda \cdot (2x + y - 5)$$

Step 2:
$$F_x(x, y, \lambda) = 2x + 2\lambda = 0$$
$$F_y(x, y, \lambda) = 2y + \lambda = 0$$
$$F_\lambda(x, y, \lambda) = 2x + y - 5 = 0$$

Step 3.   The system may be solved by any of our previous methods, but we choose to use the substitution method for this particular example. The first equation gives $x = -\lambda$. The second equation gives $y = -\frac{1}{2}\lambda$. Substituting these values into the third equation gives
$$2(-\lambda) + (-\tfrac{1}{2}\lambda) - 5 = 0$$
$$-\tfrac{5}{2}\lambda = 5$$
$$\lambda = -2$$

Hence,

$$x = -\lambda = -(-2) = 2$$

and

$$y = -\tfrac{1}{2}\lambda = -\tfrac{1}{2}(-2) = 1$$

The point $(x, y) = (2, 1)$ gives a relative minimum of $f(2, 1) = 2^2 + 1^2 = 5$ for the function subject to the constraint $2x + y = 5$.

In Example 14 we did not prove that $f(2, 1) = 5$ is a relative minimum subject to the constraint. Sufficient conditions may be found in textbooks on mathematical analysis, but you can usually tell from the problem whether the point leads to a maximum or minimum. In this book you may assume that the maxima or minima obtained are the desired extrema.

When solving the system obtained in step 2 of our procedure it is not necessary to actually obtain a numerical value for the Lagrange multiplier λ. However, in some problems you may want to compute λ because of the following interpretation.

<table>
<tr><td>**Interpretation of Lagrange Multiplier**</td><td>Suppose M is the maximum (or minimum) value of $f(x, y)$ subject to the constraint $g(x, y) - k = 0$. The Lagrange multiplier λ is the rate of change of M with respect to k:

$$\lambda = \frac{dM}{dk}$$

Thus, λ is approximately the change in M due to one unit increase in k.</td></tr>
</table>

EXAMPLE 15　Use the value $\lambda = -2$ found in Example 14 to estimate the change in the minimum value of $f(x, y) = x^2 + y^2$ when the constraint is changed to $2x + y = 6$.

Solution　The value of M is 5 subject to the constraint $2x + y = 5$. Under the new constraint k has changed from 5 to 6; therefore, k has increased by one unit. Since λ is approximately the change in M due to the one unit increase in k, M should decrease by approximately two units. Hence, M should equal approximately three units subject to the constraint $2x + y = 6$. Find the minimum of $f(x, y) = x^2 + y^2$ subject to $2x + y = 6$ to see how close your estimate is to the actual minimum subject to the new constraint.

EXAMPLE 16　Find two numbers whose sum is 76 and whose product is a maximum.

Solution　Let x represent the first number and y represent the second number. Then we want $P(x, y) = xy$ to be a maximum subject to $x + y = 76$.

1. Form

$$P(x, y, \lambda) = xy + \lambda(x + y - 76)$$

2.
$$P_x(x, y, \lambda) = y + \lambda = 0$$
$$P_y(x, y, \lambda) = x + \lambda = 0$$
$$P_\lambda(x, y, \lambda) = x + y - 76 = 0$$

3.
$$y = -\lambda \quad \text{and} \quad x = -\lambda$$

Hence,

$$-\lambda - \lambda - 76 = 0$$
$$2\lambda = -76$$
$$\lambda = -38$$
$$x = 38$$
$$y = 38$$

EXAMPLE 17 Use the method of Lagrange multipliers to find a maximum of $f(x, y, z) = x^2yz$ subject to the constraint $x + y + z = 10$. This is a Lagrange multiplier solution to the example given at the beginning of this section.

Solution **1.** Form

$$F(x, y, z, \lambda) = x^2yz + \lambda(x + y + z - 10)$$

2.
$$F_x(x, y, z, \lambda) = 2xyz + \lambda = 0$$
$$F_y(x, y, z, \lambda) = x^2z + \lambda = 0$$
$$F_z(x, y, z, \lambda) = x^2y + \lambda = 0$$
$$F_\lambda(x, y, z, \lambda) = x + y + z - 10 = 0$$

3. From the first equation,

$$\lambda = -2xyz$$

Substituting in the second equation gives

$$x^2z - 2xyz = 0$$

Hence,

$$xz(x - 2y) = 0$$
$$x = 0 \quad z = 0 \quad \text{or} \quad x = 2y$$

Substituting in the third equation gives

$$x^2y - 2xyz = 0$$

Hence,

$$xy(x - 2z) = 0$$

$$x = 0 \qquad y = 0 \qquad \text{or} \qquad x = 2z$$

From the fourth equation,

$$z = 10 - x - y$$

If $x = 0$, $y = 0$, or $z = 0$, the function $f(x, y, z)$ is 0, and, hence, not a maximum. Thus,

$$x = 2y$$

$$x = 2z$$

$$z = 10 - x - y$$

or

$$\frac{x}{2} = 10 - x - \frac{x}{2}$$

$$2x = 10$$

$$x = 5 \qquad y = \tfrac{5}{2} \qquad z = \tfrac{5}{2}$$

$f(5, \tfrac{5}{2}, \tfrac{5}{2}) = (5)^2(\tfrac{5}{2})(\tfrac{5}{2}) = \tfrac{625}{4}$ is a relative maximum subject to the constraint. This is the same value as obtained in Example 13.

Exercise Set 14.4

A Use the method of Lagrange multipliers to solve the following exercises.

1. Find a relative maximum of $f(x, y) = 3xy$ subject to $x + y = 10$.
2. Find a relative maximum of $f(x, y) = 4xy$ subject to $x + y = 8$.
3. Find a relative maximum of $f(x, y) = 4xy$ subject to $x + 2y = 6$.
4. Find a relative maximum of $f(x, y) = 2xy + 3$ subject to $x + y = 12$.
5. Find a relative maximum of $f(x, y) = 3xy + 2$ subject to $3x + y = 4$.
6. Find x and y such that $x + y = 22$ and xy^2 is a maximum.
7. Find x and y such that $x + y = 34$ and x^2y is a maximum.

B 8. Find a relative maximum of $f(x, y) = 3x^2y$ subject to $x + 2y = 5$.
9. Find a relative maximum of $f(x, y) = 2xy^2$ subject to $2x + 3y = 5$.
10. Find two numbers whose sum is 26 and whose product is a maximum.
11. Find two numbers whose sum is 94 and whose product is a maximum.

C 12. Find a relative minimum of $f(x, y) = 3x^2 + 2y^2 - xy$ subject to $x + y = 4$.
13. Find a relative minimum of $f(x, y) = x^2 + 3y^2 - 2xy$ subject to $2x + y = 5$.
14. Find three numbers whose sum is 80 and whose product is a maximum.
15. Find three numbers whose sum is 146 and whose product is a maximum.

Business **16. Production.** If x thousand dollars are spent on labor and y thousand dollars are spent on equipment, the production of a factory would be

$$P(x, y) = 40x^{1/3}y^{2/3}$$

How should $100,000 be allocated to obtain the maximum production?

17. Use the Lagrange multiplier λ to estimate the change in the maximum production that would occur if the money available was increased by $1,000 in exercise 16.

Economics **18. Cost Functions.** The cost function for x units of item I and y units of item II is

$$C(x, y) = 8x^2 + 14y^2$$

If it is necessary that $x + y = 99$, how many of each item should be produced for minimum cost? What is the minimum cost?

Life Sciences **19. Farming.** A farmer has 300 feet of fence. Find the dimensions of the rectangular field of maximum area he can enclose.

20. Redo exercise 19 if the farmer does not need to fence one side because of a building.

Physical Sciences **21. Construction.** A rectangular box with no top is to be built with 600 square feet of material. Find the dimensions of the box that would have maximum volume.

22. Redo exercise 21 if the box has a top.

Double Integrals

In Section 14.2 we discussed how the concept of differentiation could be generalized to functions of two or more variables by using partial differentiation. Recall that in finding a partial derivative we located all of the variables except one as a constant and differentiated with respect to that variable. Similarly, we can find antiderivatives of functions of several variables by treating all of the variables except one as a constant and finding an antiderivative with respect to that variable.

When finding an antiderivative of functions of several variables, we treat all variables as constant except one. To indicate which variable is to be used for antidifferentiation, we return to our integration notation. $\int f(x, y)\, dx$ means that we are to find an antiderivative of $f(x, y)$ with respect to x, keeping y fixed. To check to ensure that the operation has been done correctly, simply take the partial derivative with respect to x of the antiderivative. The result obtained by this partial differentiation should be $f(x, y)$. $\int f(x, y)\, dy$ means that an antiderivative of $f(x, y)$ with respect to y is to be found keeping x fixed.

EXAMPLE 18 Find

a. $\int (4x + 6xy^2)\, dx$

b. $\int (4x + 6xy^2)\, dy$

Solution

a. $\int (4x + 6xy^2)\,dx = \int 4x\,dx + \int 6xy^2\,dx$

$$= 4\int x\,dx + 6y^2\int x\,dx$$

$$= 4\left(\frac{x^2}{2}\right) + 6y^2\left(\frac{x^2}{2}\right) + C(y)$$

$$= 2x^2 + 3x^2y^2 + C(y)$$

Note that $C(y)$ can be any function of y since y is treated as a constant.

b. $\int (4x + 6xy^2)\,dy = \int 4x\,dy + \int 6xy^2\,dy$

$$= 4x\int dy + 6x\int y^2\,dy$$

$$= 4xy + 6x\left(\frac{y^3}{3}\right) + C(x)$$

$$= 4xy + 2xy^3 + C(x)$$

EXAMPLE 19 Verify that the solutions to the previous example are correct by performing partial differentiation.

Solution

a. $\dfrac{\partial}{\partial x}[2x^2 + 3x^2y^2 + C(y)] = 4x + 6xy^2 = f(x, y)$

b. $\dfrac{\partial}{\partial y}[4xy + 2xy^3 + C(x)] = 4x + 6xy^2 = f(x, y)$

The concept of a definite integral can also be extended to functions of two or more variables. The expression $\int_a^b f(x, y)\,dx$ means to find an antiderivative of $f(x, y)$ with respect to x keeping y fixed and then substitute b for x in the antiderivative and subtract a substituted for x in the antiderivative.

EXAMPLE 20 Evaluate

a. $\displaystyle\int_1^2 (4x + 6xy^2)\,dx$

b. $\displaystyle\int_1^2 (4x + 6xy^2)\,dy$

Solution

a. $\displaystyle\int_1^2 (4x + 6xy^2)\,dx = [2x^2 + 3x^2y^2 + C(y)]\Big|_{x=1}^{x=2}$

$$= [2(2)^2 + 3(2)^2y^2 + C(y)] - [2(1)^2 + 3(1)^2y^2 + C(y)]$$
$$= [8 + 12y^2 + C(y)] - [2 + 3y^2 + C(y)]$$
$$= 6 + 9y^2$$

b. $\displaystyle\int_3^4 (4x + 6xy^2)\,dy = [4xy + 2xy^3 + C(x)]\Big|_{y=3}^{y=4}$

$$= [4x(4) + 2x(4)^3 + C(x)] - [4x(3) + 2x(3)^3 + C(x)]$$
$$= [16x + 128x + C(x)] - [12x + 54x + C(x)]$$
$$= 78x$$

Note that $C(x)$ and $C(y)$ do not appear after the subtraction, so they may be chosen equal to 0 when a definite integral is to be found. Notice also that integrating a definite integral $f(x, y)$ with respect to x produces a function of y or a constant, and integrating a definite integral $f(x, y)$ with respect to y produces a function of x or a constant. The functions found can then be used as the integrand of a second definite integral.

EXAMPLE 21 Evaluate

a. $\int_3^4 \left[\int_1^2 (4x + 6xy^2) \, dx \right] dy$

b. $\int_1^2 \left[\int_3^4 (4x + 6xy^2) \, dy \right] dx$

Solution **a.** In the previous example we showed that

$$\int_1^2 (4x + 6xy^2) \, dx = 6 + 9y^2$$

Hence,

$$\int_3^4 \left[\int_1^2 (4x + 6xy^2) \, dx \right] dy = \int_3^4 (6 + 9y^2) \, dy$$

$$= (6y + 3y^3) \Big|_{y=3}^{y=4}$$

$$= [6(4) + 3(4)^3] - [6(3) + 3(3)^3]$$

$$= (24 + 192) - (18 + 81)$$

$$= 117$$

b. In the previous example we showed that

$$\int_3^4 (4x + 6xy^2) \, dy = 78x$$

Hence,

$$\int_1^2 \left[\int_3^4 (4x + 6xy^2) \, dy \right] dx = \int_1^2 78x \, dx$$

$$= 39x^2 \Big|_{x=1}^{x=2}$$

$$= 39(2)^2 - 39(1)^2$$

$$= 156 - 39$$

$$= 117$$

Note that the values in parts **a** and **b** are the same. This common value is called the **double integral** of $f(x, y)$ over the region

$$R = \{(x, y) \mid 1 \le x \le 2, \quad 3 \le y \le 4\}$$

and is written

$$\iint_R f(x, y) \, dx \, dy \quad \text{or} \quad \iint_R f(x, y) \, dy \, dx$$

$f(x, y)$ is called the **integrand,** and R is called the **region of integration.** $dx \, dy$ or $dy \, dx$ indicates that the double integral is over a two-dimensional region.

The integrals

$$\int_a^b \left[\int_c^d f(x, y) \, dy \right] dx \quad \text{and} \quad \int_c^d \left[\int_a^b f(x, y) \, dx \right] dy$$

are called **iterated integrals** and the order in which dy and dx are written indicates the order of integration. For simplification the brackets are often omitted but even then, if the expression is referred to as an iterated integral, the order in which dy and dx are written indicates the order of integration.

Double Integral over a Rectangular Region

The double integral of a function $f(x, y)$ over a rectangular region,

$$R = \{(x, y) \,|\, a \le x \le b, \quad c \le y \le d\}$$

is

$$\iint_R f(x, y) \, dy \, dx = \int_a^b \int_c^d f(x, y) \, dy \, dx = \int_c^d \int_a^b f(x, y) \, dx \, dy$$

EXAMPLE 22 Evaluate $\iint_R (x + 2y) \, dy \, dx$ over $R = \{(x, y) \,|\, 1 \le x \le 2, \quad 3 \le y \le 5\}$.

Solution The region R is illustrated in Figure 14.8.

Figure 14.8

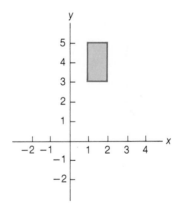

$$\iint_R (x + 2y) \, dy \, dx = \int_1^2 \int_3^5 (x + 2y) \, dy \, dx$$

$$= \int_1^2 (xy + y^2) \Big|_{y=3}^{y=5} \, dx$$

$$= \int_1^2 [(5x + 25) - (3x + 9)] \, dx$$

$$= \int_1^2 (2x + 16) \, dx$$

$$= (x^2 + 16x) \Big|_{x=1}^{x=2}$$

$$= (4 + 32) - (1 + 16)$$

$$= 19$$

This double integral can also be evaluated by using the other iterated integral.

$$\iint\limits_{R} (x + 2y)\, dy\, dx = \int_3^5 \int_1^2 (x + 2y)\, dx\, dy$$

$$= \int_3^5 \left(\frac{x^2}{2} + 2yx \right) \Bigg|_{x=1}^{x=2} dy$$

$$= \int_3^5 [(2 + 4y) - (\tfrac{1}{2} + 2y)]\, dy$$

$$= \int_3^5 (\tfrac{3}{2} + 2y)\, dy$$

$$= (\tfrac{3}{2}y + y^2) \Bigg|_{y=3}^{y=5}$$

$$= [\tfrac{3}{2}(5) + 25] - [\tfrac{3}{2}(3) + 9]$$

$$= 19$$

EXAMPLE 23   Evaluate

$$\iint\limits_{R} 3y^2 e^{2x+5}\, dx\, dy$$

over

$$R = \{(x, y) \,|\, 0 \leq x \leq 2, \quad 1 \leq y \leq 3\}$$

Solution

$$\iint\limits_{R} 3y^2 e^{2x+5}\, dx\, dy = \int_0^2 \left[\int_1^3 3y^2 e^{2x+5}\, dy \right] dx$$

$$= \int_0^2 \left[(y^3 e^{2x+5}) \Bigg|_{y=1}^{y=3} \right] dx$$

$$= \int_0^2 (27 e^{2x+5} - e^{2x+5})\, dx$$

$$= \int_0^2 26 e^{2x+5}\, dx$$

$$= 13 e^{2x+5} \Bigg|_{x=0}^{x=2}$$

$$= 13 e^9 - 13 e^5$$

Recall that the definite integral $\int_a^b f(x)\, dx$ could be interpreted as giving the area bounded by $y = f(x)$ and the x-axis between $x = a$ and $x = b$.

In a similar manner

$$\iint\limits_{R} f(x, y)\, dy\, dx$$

over the region

$$R = \{(x, y) \,|\, a \leq x \leq b, \quad c \leq y \leq d\}$$

can be interpreted as giving the volume of the solid under the surface $z = f(x, y)$, above the x,y-plane, and bounded by the planes $x = a$, $x = b$, $y = c$, $y = d$ as illustrated in Figure 14.9.

Figure 14.9

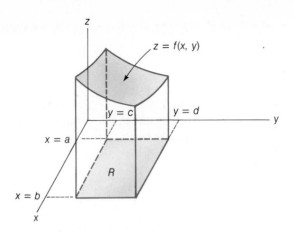

Volume under a Surface

If $f(x, y) \geq 0$ over the region $R = \{(x, y) \, | \, a \leq x \leq b, \quad c \leq y \leq d\}$, the volume V of the solid under the surface $z = f(x, y)$ above the x, y-plane, and bounded by the planes $x = a$, $x = b$, $y = c$, $y = d$ is

$$V = \iint_R f(x, y) \, dy \, dx$$

EXAMPLE 24   Find the volume of the solid under $z = 4$ and over

$$R = \{(x, y) \, | \, 0 \leq x \leq 2, \quad 0 \leq y \leq 1\}$$

illustrated in Figure 14.10.

Figure 14.10

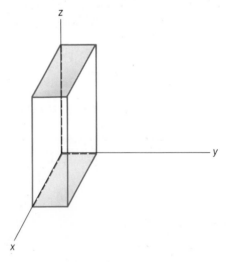

Solution   Note that this is a rectangular parallelepiped whose volume is the area of the base times the height:

$$V = A \cdot h = (2)(1)(4) = 8$$

Using the double integral validates our statement about the volume for this special case.

$$\iint_R 4\,dy\,dx = \int_0^2 \left[\int_0^1 4\,dy \right] dx$$

$$= \int_0^2 (4y)\Big|_{y=0}^{y=1} dx$$

$$= \int_0^2 (4-0)\,dx$$

$$= 4x\Big|_{x=0}^{x=2}$$

$$= 4(2) - 4(0)$$

$$= 8$$

EXAMPLE 25 Find the volume of the solid under $z = x^2 + y^2$ and over

$$R = \{(x, y)\,|\,0 \le x \le 2,\quad 0 \le y \le 1\}$$

illustrated in Figure 14.11.

Figure 14.11

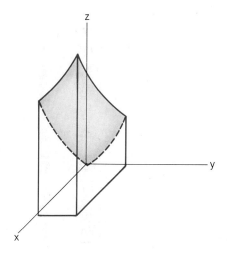

Solution

$$\iint_R (x^2 + y^2)\,dy\,dx = \int_0^2 \left[\int_0^1 (x^2 + y^2)\,dy \right] dx$$

$$= \int_0^2 \left(x^2 y + \frac{y^3}{3} \right)\Big|_{y=0}^{y=1} dx$$

$$= \int_0^2 \left[\left(x^2 + \frac{1}{3} \right) - (0 + 0) \right] dx$$

$$= \left(\frac{x^3}{3} + \tfrac{1}{3}x \right)\Big|_{x=0}^{x=2}$$

$$= (\tfrac{8}{3} + \tfrac{2}{3}) - (0 + 0)$$

$$= \tfrac{10}{3}$$

This brief treatment of multivariable calculus is presented to partly reveal the tremendous possibilities available for generalization and further study of the topics treated in this book. Mathematics can be applied to problems in electricity, fluid pressure, work, moment of inertia, astronomy, space exploration, meteorology, communications, pollution, political science, sociology, psychology, education, business, chemistry, biology, pharmacy, medicine, law, logistics, genetics, music, and numerous other fields. Some of these have been discussed briefly in this book.

For further information, we encourage you to take additional mathematics courses. It is hoped that this course will stimulate you to apply mathematics to the problems you face and to use mathematical methods as an aid in the decisions you make. Best wishes to you!

Exercise Set 14.5

A   *Find the following antiderivatives.*

1. $\int (3x + 2y)\, dx$

2. $\int (3x + 2y)\, dy$

3. $\int (4xy + 3y^2)\, dx$

4. $\int (4xy + 3y^2)\, dy$

5. $\int (5 + e^{3x} + e^{2y})\, dx$

6. $\int (5 + e^{3x} + e^2 y)\, dy$

Find the following definite integrals.

7. $\int_1^3 (3x + 2y)\, dx$

8. $\int_1^3 (3x + 2y)\, dy$

9. $\int_0^2 (3xy + 6y^2)\, dx$

10. $\int_1^2 (4xy + 6y^2)\, dy$

11. $\int_1^2 (4 + 2e^{3x} + 3e^{2y})\, dx$

12. $\int_0^3 (4 + 3e^{3x} + 2e^{2y})\, dy$

B   *Evaluate the following iterated integrals.*

13. $\int_0^2 \left[\int_0^1 6x^2 y^2\, dy \right] dx$

14. $\int_0^1 \left[\int_0^2 6x^2 y^2\, dx \right] dy$

15. $\int_1^2 \left[\int_1^3 (4x + 2y)\, dx \right] dy$

16. $\int_1^3 \left[\int_1^2 (4x + 2y)\, dy \right] dx$

17. $\int_0^1 \left[\int_0^2 e^{x+y}\, dx \right] dy$

18. $\int_0^2 \left[\int_0^1 e^{x+y}\, dy \right] dx$

C   *Use double integrals to find the volume under the given surface over the given region.*

19. $f(x, y) = 1$, $R = \{(x, y)\,|\,0 \le x \le 3,\ \ 0 \le y \le 2\}$

Note that since $f(x, y) = 1$, the volume under the surface over the region is numerically the same as the area of the region. This is not true for any other value of $f(x, y)$.

20. $f(x, y) = 3$, $R = \{(x, y)\,|\,0 \le x \le 3,\ \ 0 \le y \le 1\}$

21. $f(x, y) = x + 2$, $R = \{(x, y)\,|\,0 \le x \le 1,\ \ 0 \le y \le 2\}$

22. $f(x, y) = 2y + 3$, $R = \{(x, y)\,|\,0 \le x \le 2,\ \ 0 \le y \le 1\}$

23. $f(x, y) = 2x + 2y$, $R = \{(x, y)\,|\,0 \le x \le 1,\ \ 0 \le y \le 2\}$

24. $f(x, y) = x^2 + 3y^2$, $R = \{(x, y) | 0 \le x \le 2, \ 1 \le y \le 2\}$

25. $f(x, y) = e^x$, $R = \{(x, y) | 0 \le x \le 1, \ 0 \le y \le 2\}$

26. $f(x, y) = e^{x-y}$, $R = \{(x, y) | 0 \le x \le 3, \ 0 \le y \le 2\}$

27. $f(x, y) = 2xe^y$, $R = \{(x, y) | 0 \le x \le 3, \ 0 \le y \le 1\}$

28. $f(x, y) = 3ye^x$, $R = \{(x, y) | 1 \le x \le 3, \ 1 \le x < 2\}$

29. $f(x, y) = \dfrac{2xy^2}{1 + x^2}$, $R = \{(x, y | 0 \le x \le 2, \ 0 \le y \le 1\}$

30. $f(x, y) = \dfrac{6x}{1 + x^2}$, $R = \{(x, y) | 0 \le x \le 1, \ 1 \le y \le 2\}$

Business **31. Weekly Profit.** A producer finds her profit function to be given by

$$P(x, y) = 400x - x^2 + 200y - y^2 + 4000$$

for producing x units of one item and y units of a second item. For 1 week, x varied between 100 and 200 units while y varied from 60 to 80 units. The average profit for the week can be estimated by computing

$$\frac{1}{A} \iint_R P(x, y) \, dA$$

A is the area of the region $R = \{(x, y) | 100 \le x \le 200, \ 60 \le y \le 80\}$. For this week $A = (100)(20) = 2000$. Evaluate

$$\tfrac{1}{2000} \iint_R P(x, y) \, dy \, dx$$

to estimate the average profit for the week.

Social Sciences **32. Population.** If $f(x, y)$ is the population density function for a city, the population P can be found by

$$P = \iint_R f(x, y) \, dy \, dx$$

where R represents the city's limits. Suppose $R = \{(x, y) | 0 \le x \le 3, \ 0 \le y \le 4\}$ and $f(x, y) = 80{,}000/(x + y)$. Find the population of the city.

Summary and Review

Review to ensure you understand the following concepts.

Function of two variables	Function of several variables
Relative maxima	Relative minima
Critical point	Saddle point
Partial derivative	Second-order partial derivative
Lagrange multiplier	Lagrange method
Iterated integral	Double integral

Review Exercise Set 14.6

A   Find $\partial z/\partial x$, $\partial z/\partial y$, $f_x(1, 2)$, and $f_y(1, 2)$ for the following functions.

1. $z = 3x^2 + 2xy - 5y^2$

2. $z = 4x^2y - 3xy^3$

3. $z = 4x^2y + 2e^x$

4. $z = 4xy + 5e^{-y}$

5. $z = 3xy + \ln(x^2 + 2y^2)$

6. $z = e^{xy} + \ln(2x + y)$

Find the iterated integrals.

7. $\int_1^2 \left[\int_2^3 5x^2y^2 \, dy \right] dx$

8. $\int_1^3 \left[\int_1^2 4xy^3 \, dy \right] dx$

9. $\int_1^3 \left[\int_1^2 (6x + 8y) \, dx \right] dy$

10. $\int_1^2 \left[\int_1^3 e^{2x+y} \, dy \right] dx$

B   Find the relative maxima and relative minima for the following functions.

11. $f(x, y) = 4x^2 + y^2 - 4y$

12. $f(x, y) = 4x^2 + y^2 + 8x - 2y - 1$

13. $f(x, y) = x^2 + xy + y^2 - 6x - 2y$

14. $f(x, y) = x^3 - 3x - y^2$

C   Use double integrals to find the volume under the given surface over the given region.

15. $f(x, y) = 3x^2 + 6y^2$, $\quad R = \{(x, y) \,|\, 0 \le x \le 3, \ 1 \le y \le 3\}$

16. $f(x, y) = 6x^2 + e^{2y}$, $\quad R = \{(x, y) \,|\, 1 \le x \le 2, \ 0 \le y \le 3\}$

17. $f(x, y) = 3xe^{2y} + 4y^2$, $\quad R = \{(x, y) \,|\, 1 \le x \le 3, \ 1 \le y \le 2\}$

18. $f(x, y) = 4ye^{3x} + 2xy$, $\quad R = \{(x, y) \,|\, 0 \le x \le 2, \ 1 \le y \le 2\}$

19. $f(x, y) = \dfrac{2x}{1 + x^2}$, $\quad R = \{(x, y) \,|\, 1 \le x \le 2, \ 0 \le y \le 2\}$

20. $f(x, y) = \dfrac{2y}{3 + y^2}$, $\quad R = \{(x, y) \,|\, 0 \le x \le 2, \ 1 \le y \le 3\}$

Business   **21. Production.** The profit function for an automobile factory is given by

$$P(x, y) = 600x - 0.1x^2 - 0.02xy - 0.2y^2 + 800.28y - 800,000$$

where x is the number of model A produced and y is the number of model B. Find the number of each model that should be produced to maximize profit, and find the value of the maximum profit.

22. Minimum Cost. If the base of a rectangular box costs twice as much per square foot as the sides and top, find the most economical dimensions for a box with a volume of 12 cubic feet.

Physical Sciences   **23. Construction.** Find the shape of a covered rectangular box that will contain a given volume and yet have minimum surface area.

24. Redo exercise 23 for a box without a top.

Appendix

Table I Compound Interest

$i = 1\%$ (interest rate per period) n = number of periods

n	$(1 + i)^n$	$(1 + i)^{-n}$	n	$(1 + i)^n$	$(1 + i)^{-n}$
1	1.010000	0.990099	51	1.661078	0.602019
2	1.020100	0.980296	52	1.677689	0.596058
3	1.030301	0.970590	53	1.694466	0.590157
4	1.040604	0.960980	54	1.711410	0.584313
5	1.051010	0.951466	55	1.728525	0.578528
6	1.061520	0.942045	56	1.745810	0.572800
7	1.072135	0.932718	57	1.763268	0.567129
8	1.082857	0.923483	58	1.780901	0.561514
9	1.093685	0.914340	59	1.798710	0.555954
10	1.104622	0.905287	60	1.816697	0.550450
11	1.115668	0.896324	61	1.834864	0.545000
12	1.126825	0.887449	62	1.853212	0.539604
13	1.138093	0.878663	63	1.871744	0.534261
14	1.149474	0.869963	64	1.890462	0.528971
15	1.160969	0.861349	65	1.909366	0.523734
16	1.172579	0.852821	66	1.928460	0.518548
17	1.184304	0.844377	67	1.947745	0.513414
18	1.196147	0.836017	68	1.967222	0.508331
19	1.208109	0.827740	69	1.986894	0.503298
20	1.220190	0.819544	70	2.006763	0.498315
21	1.232392	0.811430	71	2.026831	0.493381
22	1.244716	0.803396	72	2.047099	0.488496
23	1.257163	0.795442	73	2.067570	0.483660
24	1.269735	0.787566	74	2.088246	0.478871
25	1.282432	0.779768	75	2.109128	0.474130
26	1.295256	0.772048	76	2.130220	0.469435
27	1.308209	0.764404	77	2.151522	0.464787
28	1.321291	0.756836	78	2.173037	0.460185
29	1.334504	0.749342	79	2.194767	0.455629
30	1.347849	0.741923	80	2.216715	0.451118
31	1.361327	0.734577	81	2.238882	0.446651
32	1.374941	0.727304	82	2.261271	0.442229
33	1.388690	0.720103	83	2.283884	0.437851
34	1.402577	0.712973	84	2.306723	0.433515
35	1.416603	0.705914	85	2.329790	0.429223
36	1.430769	0.698925	86	2.353088	0.424974
37	1.445076	0.692005	87	2.376619	0.420766
38	1.459527	0.685153	88	2.400385	0.416600
39	1.474122	0.678370	89	2.424389	0.412475
40	1.488864	0.671653	90	2.448633	0.408391
41	1.503752	0.665003	91	2.473119	0.404348
42	1.518790	0.658419	92	2.497850	0.400344
43	1.533978	0.651900	93	2.522829	0.396380
44	1.549318	0.645445	94	2.548057	0.392456
45	1.564811	0.639055	95	2.573537	0.388570
46	1.580459	0.632728	96	2.599273	0.384723
47	1.596263	0.626463	97	2.625266	0.380914
48	1.612226	0.620260	98	2.651518	0.377142
49	1.628348	0.614119	99	2.678033	0.373408
50	1.644632	0.608039	100	2.704814	0.369711

$i = 2\%$ (interest rate per period) n = number of periods

n	$(1 + i)^n$	$(1 + i)^{-n}$	n	$(1 + i)^n$	$(1 + i)^{-n}$
1	1.020000	0.980392	51	2.745420	0.364243
2	1.040400	0.961169	52	2.800328	0.357101
3	1.061208	0.942322	53	2.856335	0.350099
4	1.082432	0.923845	54	2.913461	0.343234
5	1.104081	0.905731	55	2.971731	0.336504
6	1.126162	0.887971	56	3.031165	0.329906
7	1.148686	0.870560	57	3.091788	0.323437
8	1.171659	0.853490	58	3.153624	0.317095
9	1.195093	0.836755	59	3.216697	0.310878
10	1.218994	0.820348	60	3.281031	0.304782
11	1.243374	0.804263	61	3.346651	0.298806
12	1.268242	0.788493	62	3.413584	0.292947
13	1.293607	0.773033	63	3.481856	0.287203
14	1.319479	0.757875	64	3.551493	0.281572
15	1.345868	0.743015	65	3.622523	0.276051
16	1.372786	0.728446	66	3.694973	0.270638
17	1.400241	0.714163	67	3.768873	0.265331
18	1.428246	0.700159	68	3.844250	0.260129
19	1.456811	0.686431	69	3.921135	0.255028
20	1.485947	0.672971	70	3.999558	0.250028
21	1.515666	0.659776	71	4.079549	0.245125
22	1.545980	0.646839	72	4.161140	0.240319
23	1.576899	0.634156	73	4.244363	0.235607
24	1.608437	0.621722	74	4.329250	0.230987
25	1.640606	0.609531	75	4.415835	0.226458
26	1.673418	0.597579	76	4.504152	0.222017
27	1.706886	0.585862	77	4.594235	0.217664
28	1.741024	0.574375	78	4.686120	0.213396
29	1.775845	0.563112	79	4.779842	0.209212
30	1.811362	0.552071	80	4.875439	0.205110
31	1.847589	0.541246	81	4.972948	0.201088
32	1.884541	0.530633	82	5.072407	0.197145
33	1.922231	0.520229	83	5.173855	0.193279
34	1.960676	0.510028	84	5.277332	0.189490
35	1.999889	0.500028	85	5.382878	0.185774
36	2.039887	0.490223	86	5.490536	0.182132
37	2.080685	0.480611	87	5.600347	0.178560
38	2.122299	0.471187	88	5.712354	0.175059
39	2.164745	0.461948	89	5.826601	0.171627
40	2.208040	0.452890	90	5.943133	0.168261
41	2.252200	0.444010	91	6.061995	0.164962
42	2.297244	0.435304	92	6.183235	0.161728
43	2.343189	0.426769	93	6.306900	0.158557
44	2.390053	0.418401	94	6.433038	0.155448
45	2.437854	0.410197	95	6.561699	0.152400
46	2.486611	0.402154	96	6.692933	0.149411
47	2.536343	0.394268	97	6.826791	0.146482
48	2.587070	0.386538	98	6.963327	0.143610
49	2.638812	0.378958	99	7.102594	0.140794
50	2.691588	0.371528	100	7.244645	0.138033

Table I Compound Interest (*continued*)

$i = 3\%$ (interest rate per period) $\quad n =$ number of periods

n	$(1 + i)^n$	$(1 + i)^{-n}$	n	$(1 + i)^n$	$(1 + i)^{-n}$
1	1.030000	0.970874	51	4.515423	0.221463
2	1.060900	0.942596	52	4.650886	0.215013
3	1.092727	0.915142	53	4.790412	0.208750
4	1.125509	0.888487	54	4.934125	0.202670
5	1.159274	0.862609	55	5.082148	0.196767
6	1.194052	0.837484	56	5.234613	0.191036
7	1.229874	0.813092	57	5.391651	0.185472
8	1.266770	0.789409	58	5.553401	0.180070
9	1.304773	0.766417	59	5.720003	0.174825
10	1.343916	0.744094	60	5.891603	0.169733
11	1.384234	0.722421	61	6.068351	0.164789
12	1.425761	0.701380	62	6.250402	0.159990
13	1.468534	0.680951	63	6.437914	0.155330
14	1.512590	0.661118	64	6.631051	0.150806
15	1.557967	0.641862	65	6.829982	0.146413
16	1.604706	0.623167	66	7.034882	0.142149
17	1.652848	0.605016	67	7.245928	0.138009
18	1.702433	0.587395	68	7.463306	0.133989
19	1.753506	0.570286	69	7.687205	0.130086
20	1.806111	0.553676	70	7.917822	0.126297
21	1.860295	0.537549	71	8.155356	0.122619
22	1.916103	0.521893	72	8.400017	0.119047
23	1.973586	0.506692	73	8.652017	0.115580
24	2.032794	0.491934	74	8.911578	0.112214
25	2.093778	0.477606	75	9.178925	0.108945
26	2.156591	0.463695	76	9.454293	0.105772
27	2.221289	0.450189	77	9.737922	0.102691
28	2.287928	0.437077	78	10.030060	0.099700
29	2.356565	0.424346	79	10.330961	0.096796
30	2.427262	0.411987	80	10.640890	0.093977
31	2.500080	0.399987	81	10.960117	0.091240
32	2.575083	0.388337	82	11.288920	0.088582
33	2.652335	0.377026	83	11.627588	0.086002
34	2.731905	0.366045	84	11.976416	0.083497
35	2.813862	0.355383	85	12.335708	0.081065
36	2.898278	0.345032	86	12.705779	0.078704
37	2.985227	0.334983	87	13.086953	0.076412
38	3.074783	0.325226	88	13.479561	0.074186
39	3.167027	0.315754	89	13.883948	0.072026
40	3.262038	0.306557	90	14.300466	0.069928
41	3.359899	0.297628	91	14.729480	0.067891
42	3.460696	0.288959	92	15.171365	0.065914
43	3.564517	0.280543	93	15.626506	0.063994
44	3.671452	0.272372	94	16.095301	0.062130
45	3.781596	0.264439	95	16.578160	0.060320
46	3.895044	0.256737	96	17.075505	0.058563
47	4.011895	0.249259	97	17.587770	0.056858
48	4.132252	0.241999	98	18.115403	0.055202
49	4.256219	0.234950	99	18.658865	0.053594
50	4.383906	0.228107	100	19.218631	0.052033

$i = 4\%$ (interest rate per period) n = number of periods

n	$(1 + i)^n$	$(1 + i)^{-n}$	n	$(1 + i)^n$	$(1 + i)^{-n}$
1	1.040000	0.961538	51	7.390950	0.135301
2	1.081600	0.924556	52	7.686588	0.130097
3	1.124864	0.888996	53	7.994052	0.125093
4	1.169859	0.854804	54	8.313814	0120282
5	1.216653	0.821927	55	8.646366	0.115656
6	1.265319	0.790315	56	8.992221	0.111207
7	1.315932	0.759918	57	9.351910	0.106930
8	1.368569	0.730690	58	9.725986	0.102817
9	1.423312	0.702587	59	10.115026	0.098863
10	1.480244	0.675564	60	10.519627	0.095060
11	1.539454	0.649581	61	10.940412	0.091404
12	1.601032	0.624597	62	11.378028	0.087889
13	1.665073	0.600574	63	11.833149	0.084508
14	1.731676	0.577475	64	12.306475	0.081258
15	1.800943	0.555265	65	12.798734	0.078133
16	1.872981	0.533908	66	13.310684	0.075128
17	1.947900	0.513373	67	13.843111	0.072238
18	2.025816	0.493628	68	14.396835	0.069460
19	2.106849	0.474642	69	14.972709	0.066788
20	2.191123	0.456387	70	15.571617	0.064219
21	2.278768	0.438834	71	16.194482	0.061749
22	2.369919	0.421955	72	16.842261	0.059374
23	2.464715	0.405726	73	17.515951	0.057091
24	2.563304	0.390121	74	18.216589	0.054895
25	2.665836	0.375117	75	18.945253	0.052784
26	2.772470	0.360689	76	19.703063	0.050754
27	2.883368	0.346817	77	20.491186	0.048801
28	2.998703	0.333477	78	21.310833	0.046924
29	3.118651	0.320651	79	22.163266	0.045120
30	3.243397	0.308319	80	23.049797	0.043384
31	3.373133	0.296460	81	23.971789	0.041716
32	3.508059	0.285058	82	24.930660	0.040111
33	3.648381	0.274094	83	25.927887	0.038569
34	3.794316	0.263552	84	26.965002	0.037085
35	3.946089	0.253415	85	28.043602	0.035659
36	4.103932	0.243669	86	29.165346	0.034287
37	4.268090	0.234297	87	30.331960	0.032969
38	4.438813	0.225285	88	31.545238	0.031701
39	4.616366	0.216621	89	32.807048	0.030481
40	4.801020	0.208289	90	34.119330	0.029309
41	4.993061	0.200278	91	35.484103	0.028182
42	5.192784	0.192575	92	36.903467	0.027098
43	5.400495	0.185168	93	38.379606	0.026056
44	5.616515	0.178046	94	39.914790	0.025053
45	5.841175	0.171198	95	41.511381	0.024090
46	6.074822	0.164614	96	43.171836	0.023163
47	6.317815	0.158283	97	44.898710	0.022272
48	6.570528	0.152195	98	46.694658	0.021416
49	6.833349	0.146341	99	48.562444	0.020592
50	7.106683	0.140713	100	50.504942	0.019800

Table I Compound Interest (*continued*)

$i = 5\%$ (interest rate per period) n = number of periods

n	$(1 + i)^n$	$(1 + i)^{-n}$	n	$(1 + i)^n$	$(1 + i)^{-n}$
1	1.050000	0.952381	51	12.040770	0.083051
2	1.102500	0.907029	52	12.642808	0.079096
3	1.157625	0.863838	53	13.274948	0.075330
4	1.215506	0.822702	54	13.938696	0.071743
5	1.276282	0.783526	55	14.635631	0.068326
6	1.340096	0.746215	56	15.367412	0.065073
7	1.407100	0.710681	57	16.135783	0.061974
8	1.477455	0.676839	58	16.942572	0.059023
9	1.551328	0.644609	59	17.789700	0.056212
10	1.628895	0.613913	60	18.679185	0.053536
11	1.710339	0.584679	61	19.613145	0.050986
12	1.795856	0.556837	62	20.593802	0.048558
13	1.885649	0.530321	63	21.623492	0.046246
14	1.979932	0.505068	64	22.704667	0.044044
15	2.078928	0.481017	65	23.839900	0.041946
16	2.182875	0.458112	66	25.031895	0.039949
17	2.292018	0.436297	67	26.283490	0.038047
18	2.406619	0.415521	68	27.597664	0.036235
19	2.526950	0.395734	69	28.977547	0.034509
20	2.653298	0.376889	70	30.426425	0.032866
21	2.785963	0.358942	71	31.947746	0.031301
22	2.925261	0.341850	72	33.545133	0.029811
23	3.071524	0.325571	73	35.222390	0.028391
24	3.225100	0.310068	74	36.983509	0.027039
25	3.386355	0.295303	75	38.832685	0.025752
26	3.555673	0.281241	76	40.774319	0.024525
27	3.733456	0.267848	77	42.813035	0.023357
28	3.920129	0.255094	78	44.953687	0.022245
29	4.116136	0.242946	79	47.201371	0.021186
30	4.321942	0.231377	80	49.561440	0.020177
31	4.538039	0.220359	81	52.039512	0.019216
32	4.764941	0.209866	82	54.641487	0.018301
33	5.003188	0.199873	83	57.373561	0.017430
34	5.253348	0.190355	84	60.242239	0.016600
35	5.516015	0.181290	85	63.254351	0.015809
36	5.791816	0.172657	86	66.417069	0.015056
37	6.081407	0.164436	87	69.737922	0.014339
38	6.385477	0.156605	88	73.224818	0.013657
39	6.704751	0.149148	89	76.886059	0.013006
40	7.039989	0.142046	90	80.730362	0.012387
41	7.391988	0.135282	91	84.766880	0.011797
42	7.761587	0.128840	92	89.005224	0.011235
43	8.149667	0.122704	93	93.455486	0.010700
44	8.557150	0.116861	94	98.128260	0.010191
45	8.985008	0.111297	95	103.034673	0.009705
46	9.434258	0.105997	96	108.186406	0.009243
47	9.905971	0.100949	97	113.595727	0.008803
48	10.401269	0.096142	98	119.275513	0.008384
49	10.921333	0.091564	99	125.239289	0.007985
50	11.467400	0.087204	100	131.501253	0.007604

$i = 6\%$ (interest rate per period) n = number of periods

n	$(1 + i)^n$	$(1 + i)^{-n}$	n	$(1 + i)^n$	$(1 + i)^{-n}$
1	1.060000	0.943396	51	19.525363	0.051215
2	1.123600	0.889996	52	20.696885	0.048316
3	1.191016	0.839619	53	21.938698	0.045582
4	1.262477	0.792094	54	23.255020	0.043001
5	1.338226	0.747258	55	24.650321	0.040567
6	1.418519	0.704961	56	26.129340	0.038271
7	1.503630	0.665057	57	27.697100	0.036105
8	1.593848	0.627412	58	29.358926	0.034061
9	1.689479	0.591898	59	31.120462	0.032133
10	1.790848	0.558395	60	32.987690	0.030314
11	1.898299	0.526788	61	34.966951	0.028598
12	2.012196	0.496969	62	37.064968	0.026980
13	2.132928	0.468839	63	39.288866	0.025453
14	2.260904	0.442301	64	41.646198	0.024012
15	2.396558	0.417265	65	44.144970	0.022653
16	2.540352	0.393646	66	46.793668	0.021370
17	2.692773	0.371364	67	49.601288	0.020161
18	2.854339	0.350344	68	52.577365	0.019020
19	3.025599	0.330513	69	55.732007	0.017943
20	3.207135	0.311805	70	59.075928	0.016927
21	3.399564	0.294155	71	62.620483	0.015969
22	3.603537	0.277505	72	66.377712	0.015065
23	3.819750	0.261797	73	70.360375	0.014213
24	4.048935	0.246979	74	74.581997	0.013408
25	4.291871	0.232999	75	79.056917	0.012649
26	4.549383	0.219810	76	83.800332	0.011933
27	4.822346	0.207368	77	88.828352	0.011258
28	5.111687	0.195630	78	94.158053	0.010620
29	5.418388	0.184557	79	99.807536	0.010019
30	5.743491	0.174110	80	105.795988	0.009452
31	6.088101	0.164255	81	112.143748	0.008917
32	6.453387	0.154957	82	118.872372	0.008412
33	6.840590	0.146186	83	126.004715	0.007936
34	7.251025	0.137912	84	133.564997	0.007487
35	7.686087	0.130105	85	141.578897	0.007063
36	8.147252	0.122741	86	150.073631	0.006663
37	8.636087	0.115793	87	159.078049	0.006286
38	9.154252	0.109239	88	168.622731	0.005930
39	9.703507	0.103056	89	178.740095	0.005595
40	10.285718	0.097222	90	189.464501	0.005278
41	10.902861	0.091719	91	200.832371	0.004979
42	11.557032	0.086527	92	212.882312	0.004697
43	12.250454	0.081630	93	225.655252	0.004432
44	12.985482	0.077009	94	239.194566	0.004181
45	13.764610	0.072650	95	253.546240	0.003944
46	14.590487	0.068538	96	268.759014	0.003721
47	15.465916	0.064658	97	284.884555	0.003510
48	16.393871	0.060998	98	301.977628	0.003312
49	17.377504	0.057546	99	320.096286	0.003124
50	18.420154	0.054288	100	339.302062	0.002947

Table I Compound Interest (*continued*)

$i = 8\%$ (interest rate per period) n = number of periods

n	$(1 + i)^n$	$(1 + i)^{-n}$	n	$(1 + i)^n$	$(1 + i)^{-n}$
1	1.080000	0.925926	51	50.653740	0.019742
2	1.166400	0.857339	52	54.706039	0.018280
3	1.259712	0.793832	53	59.082522	0.016925
4	1.360489	0.735030	54	63.809124	0.015672
5	1.469328	0.680583	55	68.913854	0.014511
6	1.586874	0.630170	56	74.426962	0.013436
7	1.713824	0.583490	57	80.381119	0.012441
8	1.850930	0.540269	58	86.811608	0.011519
9	1.999005	0.500249	59	93.756537	0.010666
10	2.158925	0.463193	60	101.257060	0.009876
11	2.331639	0.428883	61	109.357625	0.009144
12	2.518170	0.397114	62	118.106234	0.008467
13	2.719624	0.367698	63	127.554733	0.007840
14	2.937194	0.340461	64	137.759112	0.007259
15	3.172169	0.315242	65	148.779841	0.006721
16	3.425943	0.291890	66	160.682228	0.006223
17	3.700018	0.270269	67	173.536806	0.005762
18	3.996019	0.250249	68	187.419750	0.005336
19	4.315701	0.231712	69	202.413330	0.004940
20	4.660957	0.214548	70	218.606396	0.004574
21	5.033834	0.198656	71	236.094908	0.004236
22	5.436540	0.183941	72	254.982500	0.003922
23	5.871464	0.170315	73	275.381101	0.003631
24	6.341181	0.157699	74	297.411588	0.003362
25	6.848475	0.146018	75	321.204515	0.003113
26	7.396353	0.135202	76	346.900876	0.002883
27	7.988061	0.125187	77	374.652946	0.002669
28	8.627106	0.115914	78	404.625181	0.002471
29	9.317275	0.107328	79	436.995196	0.002288
30	10.062657	0.099377	80	471.954811	0.002119
31	10.867669	0.092016	81	509.711196	0.001962
32	11.737083	0.085200	82	550.488090	0.001817
33	12.676049	0.078889	83	594.527138	0.001682
34	13.690133	0.073045	84	642.089308	0.001557
35	14.785344	0.067635	85	693.456453	0.001442
36	15.968171	0.062625	86	748.932968	0.001335
37	17.245625	0.057986	87	808.847606	0.001236
38	18.625275	0.053690	88	873.555413	0.001145
39	20.115297	0.049713	89	943.439846	0.001060
40	21.724521	0.046031	90	1018.915031	0.000981
41	23.462483	0.042621	91	1100.428236	0.000909
42	25.339481	0.039464	92	1188.462491	0.000841
43	27.366640	0.036541	93	1283.539492	0.000779
44	29.555971	0.033834	94	1386.222649	0.000721
45	31.920449	0.031328	95	1497.120463	0.000668
46	34.474084	0.029007	96	1616.890095	0.000618
47	37.232011	0.026859	97	1746.241303	0.000573
48	40.210572	0.024869	98	1885.940604	0.000530
49	43.427418	0.023027	99	2036.815854	0.000491
50	46.901611	0.021321	100	2199.761119	0.000455

Table II Annuities

$i = 1\%$ (interest rate per period) $n = $ number of periods

$$s_{\overline{n}|i} = \frac{(1 + i)^n - 1}{i}$$

$$a_{\overline{n}|i} = \frac{(1 + i)^n - 1}{i(1 + i)^n}$$

n	$s_{\overline{n}|i}$	$a_{\overline{n}|i}$	n	$s_{\overline{n}|i}$	$a_{\overline{n}|i}$
1	1.000000	0.990099	51	66.107810	39.798135
2	2.010000	1.970395	52	67.768888	40.394193
3	3.030100	2.940985	53	69.446577	40.984349
4	4.060401	3.901965	54	71.141043	41.568663
5	5.101005	4.853431	55	72.852453	42.147191
6	6.152015	5.795476	56	74.580977	42.719991
7	7.213535	6.728194	57	76.326787	43.287120
8	8.285670	7.651677	58	78.090055	43.848633
9	9.368527	8.566017	59	79.870956	44.404587
10	10.462212	9.471304	60	81.669665	44.955037
11	11.566834	10.367628	61	83.486361	45.500037
12	12.682502	11.255077	62	85.321225	46.039640
13	13.809327	12.133740	63	87.174437	46.573901
14	14.947421	13.003702	64	89.046181	47.102872
15	16.096895	13.865052	65	90.936643	47.626606
16	17.257864	14.717873	66	92.846010	48.145155
17	18.430442	15.562251	67	94.774470	48.658569
18	19.614747	16.398268	68	96.722214	49.166900
19	20.810894	17.226008	69	98.689436	49.670198
20	22.019003	18.045552	70	100.676330	50.168513
21	23.239193	18.856982	71	102.683094	50.661894
22	24.471585	19.660379	72	104.709924	51.150390
23	25.716301	20.455820	73	106.757024	51.634049
24	26.973463	21.243386	74	108.824594	52.112920
25	28.243198	22.023155	75	110.912840	52.587050
26	29.525630	22.795203	76	113.021968	53.056485
27	30.820886	23.559607	77	115.152188	53.521272
28	32.129095	24.316442	78	117.303709	53.981457
29	33.450386	25.065784	79	119.476747	54.437087
30	34.784890	25.807707	80	121.671514	54.888205
31	36.132739	26.542284	81	123.888229	55.334856
32	37.494066	27.269588	82	126.127111	55.777085
33	38.869006	27.989691	83	128.388382	56.214936
34	40.257696	28.702665	84	130.672266	56.648451
35	41.660273	29.408579	85	132.978988	57.077674
36	43.076876	30.107504	86	135.308778	57.502648
37	44.507645	30.799509	87	137.661866	57.923414
38	45.952721	31.484662	88	140.038484	58.340014
39	47.412248	32.163032	89	142.438869	58.752489
40	48.886371	32.834685	90	144.863258	59.160880
41	50.375234	33.499688	91	147.311890	59.565228
42	51.878987	34.158107	92	149.785009	59.965572
43	53.397776	34.810007	93	152.282859	60.361952
44	54.931754	35.455452	94	154.805687	60.754408
45	56.481072	36.094507	95	157.353744	61.142978
46	58.045882	36.727235	96	159.927281	61.527701
47	59.626341	37.353698	97	162.526554	61.908615
48	61.222604	37.973958	98	165.151819	62.285758
49	62.834830	38.588077	99	167.803338	62.659166
50	64.463178	39.196116	100	170.481370	63.028877

Table II Annuities (*continued*)

$i = 2\%$ (interest rate per period) $n = $ number of periods

$$s_{\overline{n}|i} = \frac{(1 + i)^n - 1}{i}$$

$$a_{\overline{n}|i} = \frac{(1 + i)^n - 1}{i(1 + i)^n}$$

n	$s_{\overline{n}|i}$	$a_{\overline{n}|i}$	n	$s_{\overline{n}|i}$	$a_{\overline{n}|i}$
1	1.000000	0.980392	51	87.270984	31.787848
2	2.020000	1.941561	52	90.016403	32.144949
3	3.060400	2.883883	53	92.816731	32.495048
4	4.121608	3.807729	54	95.673065	32.838282
5	5.204040	4.713459	55	98.586527	33.174787
6	6.308121	5.601431	56	101.558257	33.504693
7	7.434283	6.471991	57	104.589422	33.828130
8	8.582969	7.325481	58	107.681210	34.145226
9	9.754628	8.162236	59	110.834834	34.456104
10	10.949720	8.982585	60	114.051531	34.760886
11	12.168715	9.786848	61	117.332562	35.059692
12	13.412089	10.575341	62	120.679212	35.352639
13	14.680331	11.348373	63	124.092797	35.639842
14	15.973937	12.106248	64	127.574652	35.921414
15	17.293416	12.849263	65	131.126145	36.197465
16	18.639284	13.577709	66	134.748668	36.468103
17	20.012070	14.291871	67	138.443642	36.733434
18	21.412311	14.992031	68	142.212514	36.993563
19	22.840558	15.678462	69	146.056764	37.248591
20	24.297369	16.351433	70	149.977899	37.498619
21	25.783316	17.011209	71	153.977457	37.743744
22	27.298982	17.658048	72	158.057006	37.984062
23	28.844962	18.292204	73	162.218146	38.219669
24	30.421861	18.913925	74	166.462508	38.450656
25	32.030298	19.523456	75	170.791759	38.677114
26	33.670904	20.121035	76	175.207593	38.899131
27	35.344322	20.706897	77	179.711746	39.116795
28	37.051208	21.281272	78	184.305980	39.330191
29	38.792232	21.844384	79	188.992100	39.539403
30	40.568077	22.396455	80	193.771941	39.744513
31	42.379438	22.937701	81	198.647380	39.945601
32	44.227027	23.468334	82	203.620327	40.142746
33	46.111568	23.988563	83	208.692734	40.336025
34	48.033799	24.498591	84	213.866588	40.525515
35	49.994475	24.998619	85	219.143920	40.711289
36	51.994364	25.488842	86	224.526798	40.893421
37	54.034251	25.969453	87	230.017333	41.071981
38	56.114936	26.440640	88	235.617680	41.247040
39	58.237235	26.902588	89	241.330033	41.418667
40	60.401979	27.355478	90	247.156633	41.586929
41	62.610019	27.799489	91	253.099766	41.751891
42	64.862219	28.234793	92	259.161761	41.913618
43	67.159464	28.661562	93	265.344996	42.072175
44	69.502653	29.079962	94	271.651895	42.227622
45	71.892706	29.490159	95	278.084933	42.380022
46	74.330560	29.892313	96	284.646631	42.529433
47	76.817171	30.286581	97	291.339564	42.675915
48	79.353514	30.673119	98	298.166354	42.819524
49	81.940584	31.052077	99	305.129682	42.960318
50	84.579396	31.423605	100	312.232275	43.098351

$i = 3\%$ (interest rate per period) $n =$ number of periods

$$s_{\overline{n}|i} = \frac{(1 + i)^n - 1}{i}$$

$$a_{\overline{n}|i} = \frac{(1 + i)^n - 1}{i(1 + i)^n}$$

n	$s_{\overline{n}|i}$	$a_{\overline{n}|i}$	n	$s_{\overline{n}|i}$	$a_{\overline{n}|i}$
1	1.000000	0.970874	51	117.180769	25.951227
2	2.030000	1.913470	52	121.696192	26.166240
3	3.090900	2.828611	53	126.347078	26.374990
4	4.183627	3.717098	54	131.137490	26.577660
5	5.309136	4.579707	55	136.071615	26.774427
6	6.468410	5.417191	56	141.153763	26.965464
7	7.662462	6.230283	57	146.388376	27.150935
8	8.892336	7.019692	58	151.780027	27.331005
9	10.159106	7.786109	59	157.333428	27.505830
10	11.463879	8.530203	60	163.053431	27.675564
11	12.807795	9.252624	61	168.945034	27.840353
12	14.192029	9.954004	62	175.013384	28.000343
13	15.617790	10.634955	63	181.263786	28.155672
14	17.086324	11.296073	64	187.701699	28.306478
15	18.598913	11.937935	65	194.332750	28.452891
16	20.156881	12.561102	66	201.162733	28.595040
17	21.761587	13.166118	67	208.197614	28.733049
18	23.414435	13.753513	68	215.443543	28.867038
19	25.116868	14.323799	69	222.906849	28.997124
20	26.870374	14.877475	70	230.594054	29.123421
21	28.676485	15.415024	71	238.511875	29.246040
22	30.536780	15.936916	72	246.667232	29.365087
23	32.452883	16.443608	73	255.067249	29.480667
24	34.426469	16.935542	74	263.719266	29.592881
25	36.459263	17.413147	75	272.630844	29.701826
26	38.553041	17.876842	76	281.809769	29.807598
27	40.709632	18.327031	77	291.264062	29.910290
28	42.930921	18.764108	78	301.001983	30.009990
29	45.218849	19.188454	79	311.032043	30.106786
30	47.575414	19.600441	80	321.363004	30.200763
31	50.002677	20.000428	81	332.003894	30.292003
32	52.502757	20.388765	82	342.964010	30.380586
33	55.077840	20.765792	83	354.252930	30.466588
34	57.730175	21.131836	84	365.880518	30.550085
35	60.462080	21.487220	85	377.856933	30.631151
36	63.275942	21.832252	86	390.192641	30.709855
37	66.174221	22.167235	87	402.898420	30.786267
38	69.159447	22.492461	88	415.985373	30.860454
39	72.234231	22.808215	89	429.464934	30.932479
40	75.401258	23.114772	90	443.348881	31.002407
41	78.663295	23.412400	91	457.649348	31.070298
42	82.023194	23.701359	92	472.378828	31.136212
43	85.483890	23.981902	93	487.550192	31.200206
44	89.048406	24.254274	94	503.176698	31.262336
45	92.719858	24.518712	95	519.271998	31.322656
46	96.501454	24.775449	96	535.850158	31.381219
47	100.396498	25.024708	97	552.925662	31.438077
48	104.408392	25.266706	98	570.513433	31.493279
49	108.540644	25.501657	99	588.628835	31.546872
50	112.796863	25.729764	100	607.287700	31.598905

Table II Annuities (*continued*)

$i = 4\%$ (interest rate per period) $n =$ number of periods

$$s_{\overline{n}|i} = \frac{(1 + i)^n - 1}{i} \qquad\qquad a_{\overline{n}|i} = \frac{(1 + i)^n - 1}{i(1 + i)^n}$$

n	$s_{\overline{n}|i}$	$a_{\overline{n}|i}$	n	$s_{\overline{n}|i}$	$a_{\overline{n}|i}$
1	1.000000	0.961538	51	159.773756	21.617485
2	2.040000	1.886095	52	167.164706	21.747582
3	3.121600	2.775091	53	174.851294	21.872675
4	4.246464	3.629895	54	182.845345	21.992956
5	5.416322	4.451822	55	191.159159	22.108612
6	6.632975	5.242137	56	199.805525	22.219819
7	7.898294	6.002055	57	208.797746	22.326749
8	9.214226	6.732745	58	218.149655	22.429567
9	10.582795	7.435331	59	227.875641	22.528429
10	12.006107	8.110896	60	237.990667	22.623490
11	13.486351	8.760477	61	248.510293	22.714894
12	15.025805	9.385074	62	259.450704	22.802783
13	16.626837	9.985648	63	270.828732	22.887291
14	18.291911	10.563123	64	282.661881	22.968549
15	20.023587	11.118387	65	294.968356	23.046682
16	21.824530	11.652295	66	307.767089	23.121809
17	23.697511	12.165669	67	321.077773	23.194048
18	25.645412	12.659297	68	334.920883	23.263507
19	27.671228	13.133939	69	349.317718	23.330295
20	29.778077	13.590326	70	364.290426	23.394515
21	31.969200	14.029160	71	379.862043	23.456264
22	34.247968	14.451115	72	396.056524	23.515639
23	36.617887	14.856841	73	412.898785	23.572730
24	39.082602	15.246963	74	430.414735	23.627625
25	41.645906	15.622080	75	448.631325	23.680408
26	44.311742	15.982769	76	467.576577	23.731162
27	47.084212	16.329585	77	487.279640	23.779963
28	49.967580	16.663063	78	507.770825	23.826888
29	52.966284	16.983714	79	529.081656	23.872007
30	56.084935	17.292033	80	551.244922	23.915392
31	59.328332	17.588493	81	574.294718	23.957107
32	62.701465	17.873551	82	598.266505	23.997219
33	66.209524	18.147645	83	623.197166	24.035787
34	69.857905	18.411197	84	649.125051	24.072872
35	73.652221	18.664613	85	676.090053	24.108531
36	77.598309	18.908282	86	704.133654	24.142818
37	81.702242	19.142579	87	733.299000	24.175787
38	85.970331	19.367864	88	763.630957	24.207487
39	90.409144	19.584485	89	795.176195	24.237969
40	95.025510	19.792774	90	827.983241	24.267278
41	99.826530	19.993052	91	862.102572	24.295459
42	104.819591	20.185627	92	897.586673	24.322557
43	110.012375	20.370795	93	934.490139	24.348612
44	115.412870	20.548841	94	972.869744	24.373666
45	121.029384	20.720040	95	1012.784531	24.397756
46	126.870560	20.884653	96	1054.295909	24.420919
47	132.945382	21.042936	97	1097.467747	24.443191
48	139.263197	21.195131	98	1142.366453	24.464607
49	145.833724	21.341472	99	1189.061112	24.485199
50	152.667073	21.482184	100	1237.623554	24.504999

$i = 5\%$ (interest rate per period) $n =$ number of periods

$$s_{\overline{n}|i} = \frac{(1 + i)^n - 1}{i} \qquad\qquad a_{\overline{n}|i} = \frac{(1 + i)^n - 1}{i(1 + i)^n}$$

n	$s_{\overline{n}|i}$	$a_{\overline{n}|i}$	n	$s_{\overline{n}|i}$	$a_{\overline{n}|i}$
1	1.000000	0.952381	51	220.815391	18.338977
2	2.050000	1.859410	52	232.856160	18.418073
3	3.152500	2.723248	53	245.498969	18.493403
4	4.310125	3.545950	54	258.773917	18.565146
5	5.525631	4.329477	55	272.712612	18.633472
6	6.801913	5.075692	56	287.348243	18.698545
7	8.142008	5.786373	57	302.715655	18.760519
8	9.549109	6.463213	58	318.851437	18.819542
9	11.026564	7.107822	59	335.794010	18.875754
10	12.577892	7.721735	60	353.583710	18.929290
11	14.206787	8.306414	61	372.262896	18.980276
12	15.917126	8.863252	62	391.876039	19.028834
13	17.712983	9.393573	63	412.469841	19.075080
14	19.598632	9.898641	64	434.093334	19.119124
15	21.578563	10.379658	65	456.798000	19.161070
16	23.657492	10.837770	66	480.637899	19.201019
17	25.840366	11.274066	67	505.669795	19.239066
18	28.132384	11.689587	68	531.953284	19.275301
19	30.539004	12.085321	69	559.550949	19.309810
20	33.065954	12.462210	70	588.528495	19.342677
21	35.719251	12.821153	71	618.954919	19.373978
22	38.505214	13.163003	72	650.902666	19.403788
23	41.430475	13.488574	73	684.447799	19.432179
24	44.501998	13.798642	74	719.670188	19.459218
25	47.727098	14.093945	75	756.653697	19.484970
26	51.113453	14.375185	76	795.486382	19.509495
27	54.669126	14.643034	77	836.260701	19.532853
28	58.402582	14.898127	78	879.073734	19.555098
29	62.322711	15.141074	79	924.027421	19.576283
30	66.438846	15.372451	80	971.228793	19.596460
31	70.760789	15.592810	81	1020.790232	19.615677
32	75.298828	15.802677	82	1072.829742	19.633978
33	80.063770	16.002549	83	1127.471228	19.651407
34	85.066958	16.192904	84	1184.844790	19.668007
35	90.320306	16.374194	85	1245.087029	19.683816
36	95.836321	16.546852	86	1308.341380	19.698873
37	101.628137	16.711287	87	1374.758448	19.713212
38	107.709544	16.867893	88	1444.496370	19.726869
39	114.095021	17.017041	89	1517.721189	19.739875
40	120.799772	17.159086	90	1594.607245	19.752262
41	127.839761	17.294368	91	1675.337609	19.764059
42	135.231749	17.423208	92	1760.104489	19.775294
43	142.993336	17.545912	93	1849.109716	19.785994
44	151.143003	17.662773	94	1942.565195	19.796185
45	159.700153	17.774070	95	2040.693453	19.805891
46	168.685160	17.880066	96	2143.728127	19.815134
47	178.119419	17.981016	97	2251.914536	19.823937
48	188.025389	18.077158	98	2365.510255	19.832321
49	198.426659	18.168722	99	2484.785771	19.840306
50	209.347992	18.255925	100	2610.025058	19.847910

Table II Annuities (continued)

$i = 6\%$ (interest rate per period) n = number of periods

$$s_{\overline{n}|i} = \frac{(1 + i)^n - 1}{i}$$

$$a_{\overline{n}|i} = \frac{(1 + i)^n - 1}{i(1 + i)^n}$$

n	$s_{\overline{n}|i}$	$a_{\overline{n}|i}$	n	$s_{\overline{n}|i}$	$a_{\overline{n}|i}$
1	1.000000	0.943396	51	308.756049	15.813076
2	2.060000	1.833393	52	328.281411	15.861393
3	3.183600	2.673012	53	348.978296	15.906974
4	4.374616	3.465106	54	370.916993	15.949976
5	5.637093	4.212364	55	394.172013	15.990543
6	6.975318	4.917324	56	418.822333	16.028814
7	8.393838	5.582381	57	444.951673	16.064919
8	9.897468	6.209794	58	472.648773	16.098980
9	11.491316	6.801692	59	502.007700	16.131113
10	13.180795	7.360087	60	533.128160	16.161428
11	14.971642	7.886875	61	566.115851	16.190026
12	16.869941	8.383844	62	601.082800	16.217006
13	18.882137	8.852683	63	638.147769	16.242458
14	21.015066	9.294984	64	677.436635	16.266470
15	23.275970	9.712249	65	719.082832	16.289123
16	25.672528	10.105895	66	763.227802	16.310493
17	28.212879	10.477260	67	810.021470	16.330654
18	30.905652	10.827603	68	859.622755	16.349673
19	33.759991	11.158116	69	912.200122	16.367617
20	36.785591	11.469921	70	967.932127	16.384544
21	39.992726	11.764077	71	1027.008055	16.400513
22	43.392289	12.041582	72	1089.628537	16.415578
23	46.995827	12.303379	73	1156.006250	16.429791
24	50.815576	12.550357	74	1226.366622	16.443199
25	54.864511	12.783356	75	1300.948621	16.455848
26	59.156381	13.003166	76	1380.005534	16.467781
27	63.705764	13.210534	77	1463.805867	16.479039
28	68.528110	13.406164	78	1552.634216	16.489659
29	73.639797	13.590721	79	1646.792271	16.499679
30	79.058184	13.764831	80	1746.599804	16.509131
31	84.801676	13.929086	81	1852.395794	16.518048
32	90.889776	14.084043	82	1964.539537	16.526460
33	97.343163	14.230230	83	2083.411913	16.534396
34	104.183752	14.368141	84	2209.416623	16.541883
35	111.434777	14.498246	85	2342.981621	16.548947
36	119.120864	14.620987	86	2484.560511	16.555610
37	127.268116	14.736780	87	2634.634147	16.561896
38	135.904202	14.846019	88	2793.712188	16.567827
39	145.058455	14.949075	89	2962.334920	16.573421
40	154.761961	15.046297	90	3141.075010	16.578699
41	165.047679	15.138016	91	3330.539515	16.583679
42	175.950540	15.224543	92	3531.371874	16.588376
43	187.507572	15.306173	93	3744.254194	16.592808
44	199.758026	15.383182	94	3969.909436	16.596988
45	212.743508	15.455832	95	4209.104005	16.600932
46	226.508118	15.524370	96	4462.650238	16.604653
47	241.098605	15.589028	97	4731.409255	16.608163
48	256.564521	15.650027	98	5016.293804	16.611475
49	272.958392	15.707572	99	5318.271438	16.614599
50	290.335895	15.761861	100	5638.367708	16.617546

$i = 8\%$ (interest rate per period) n = number of periods

$$s_{\overline{n}|i} = \frac{(1 + i)^n - 1}{i}$$ $$a_{\overline{n}|i} = \frac{(1 + i)^n - 1}{i(1 + i)^n}$$

n	$s_{\overline{n}|i}$	$a_{\overline{n}|i}$	n	$s_{\overline{n}|i}$	$a_{\overline{n}|i}$
1	1.000000	0.925926	51	620.671751	12.253227
2	2.080000	1.783265	52	671.325489	12.271506
3	3.246400	2.577097	53	726.031528	12.288432
4	4.506112	3.312127	54	785.114049	12.304103
5	5.866601	3.992710	55	848.923175	12.318614
6	7.335929	4.622880	56	917.837026	12.332050
7	8.922803	5.206370	57	992.263989	12.344491
8	10.636628	5.746639	58	1072.645104	12.356010
9	12.487558	6.246888	59	1159.456715	12.366676
10	14.486562	6.710081	60	1253.213249	12.376552
11	16.645487	7.138964	61	1354.470310	12.385696
12	18.977126	7.536078	62	1463.827931	12.394163
13	21.495296	7.903776	63	1581.934169	12.402003
14	24.214920	8.244237	64	1709.488897	12.409262
15	27.152114	8.559479	65	1847.248009	12.415983
16	30.324283	8.851369	66	1996.027847	12.422207
17	33.750225	9.121638	67	2156.710075	12.427969
18	37.450243	9.371887	68	2330.246878	12.433305
19	41.446263	9.603599	69	2517.666628	12.438245
20	45.761964	9.818147	70	2720.079956	12.442820
21	50.422921	10.016803	71	2938.686356	12.447055
22	55.456754	10.200744	72	3174.781254	12.450977
23	60.893295	10.371059	73	3429.763757	12.454608
24	66.764758	10.528758	74	3705.144851	12.457971
25	73.105939	10.674776	75	4002.556443	12.461084
26	79.954414	10.809798	76	4323.760948	12.463967
27	87.350767	10.935165	77	4670.661830	12.466636
28	95.338828	11.051078	78	5045.314764	12.469107
29	103.965934	11.158406	79	5449.939954	12.471396
30	113.283209	11.257783	80	5886.935134	12.473514
31	123.345866	11.349799	81	6358.889949	12.475476
32	134.213535	11.434999	82	6868.601137	12.477293
33	145.950617	11.513888	83	7419.089235	12.478975
34	158.626667	11.586934	84	8013.616357	12.480532
35	172.316800	11.654568	85	8655.705661	12.481974
36	187.102144	11.717193	86	9349.162105	12.483310
37	203.070315	11.775179	87	10098.095077	12.484546
38	220.315940	11.828869	88	10906.942661	12.485691
39	238.941216	11.878582	89	11780.498081	12.486751
40	259.056512	11.924613	90	12723.937900	12.487732
41	280.781033	11.967235	91	13742.852951	12.488641
42	304.243515	12.006699	92	14843.281143	12.489482
43	329.582997	12.043240	93	16031.743671	12.490261
44	356.949636	12.077074	94	17315.283134	12.490983
45	386.505607	12.108401	95	18701.505798	12.491651
46	418.426055	12.137409	96	20198.626205	12.492269
47	452.900140	12.164267	97	21815.516296	12.492842
48	490.132150	12.189137	98	23561.757575	12.493372
49	530.342722	12.212163	99	25447.698181	12.493863
50	573.770138	12.233485	100	27484.514007	12.494318

Table III   Values of Exponentials

x	e^x	e^{-x}	x	e^x	e^{-x}
0.01	1.010050	0.990050	0.51	1.665291	0.600496
0.02	1.020201	0.980199	0.52	1.682028	0.594521
0.03	1.030455	0.970446	0.53	1.698932	0.588605
0.04	1.040811	0.960789	0.54	1.716007	0.582748
0.05	1.051271	0.951229	0.55	1.733253	0.576950
0.06	1.061837	0.941765	0.56	1.750673	0.571209
0.07	1.072508	0.932394	0.57	1.768267	0.565525
0.08	1.083287	0.923116	0.58	1.786038	0.559898
0.09	1.094174	0.913931	0.59	1.803988	0.554327
0.10	1.105171	0.904837	0.60	1.822119	0.548812
0.11	1.116278	0.895834	0.61	1.840431	0.543351
0.12	1.127497	0.886920	0.62	1.858928	0.537944
0.13	1.138828	0.878095	0.63	1.877611	0.532592
0.14	1.150274	0.869358	0.64	1.896481	0.527292
0.15	1.161834	0.860708	0.65	1.915541	0.522046
0.16	1.173511	0.852144	0.66	1.934792	0.516851
0.17	1.185305	0.843665	0.67	1.954237	0.511709
0.18	1.197217	0.835270	0.68	1.973878	0.506617
0.19	1.209250	0.826959	0.69	1.993716	0.501576
0.20	1.221403	0.818731	0.70	2.013753	0.496585
0.21	1.233678	0.810584	0.71	2.033991	0.491644
0.22	1.246077	0.802519	0.72	2.054433	0.486752
0.23	1.258600	0.794534	0.73	2.075081	0.481909
0.24	1.271249	0.786628	0.74	2.095936	0.477114
0.25	1.284025	0.778801	0.75	2.117000	0.472367
0.26	1.296930	0.771052	0.76	2.138276	0.467666
0.27	1.309965	0.763379	0.77	2.159766	0.463013
0.28	1.323130	0.755784	0.78	2.181472	0.458406
0.29	1.336428	0.748264	0.79	2.203396	0.453845
0.30	1.349859	0.740818	0.80	2.225541	0.449329
0.31	1.363425	0.733447	0.81	2.247908	0.444858
0.32	1.377128	0.726149	0.82	2.270500	0.440432
0.33	1.390968	0.718924	0.83	2.293319	0.436049
0.34	1.404948	0.711770	0.84	2.316367	0.431711
0.35	1.419068	0.704688	0.85	2.339647	0.427415
0.36	1.433329	0.697676	0.86	2.363161	0.423162
0.37	1.447735	0.690734	0.87	2.386911	0.418952
0.38	1.462285	0.683861	0.88	2.410900	0.414783
0.39	1.476981	0.677057	0.89	2.435130	0.410656
0.40	1.491825	0.670320	0.90	2.459603	0.406570
0.41	1.506818	0.663650	0.91	2.484323	0.402524
0.42	1.521962	0.657047	0.92	2.509290	0.398519
0.43	1.537258	0.650509	0.93	2.534509	0.394554
0.44	1.552707	0.644036	0.94	2.559982	0.390628
0.45	1.568312	0.637628	0.95	2.585710	0.386741
0.46	1.584074	0.631284	0.96	2.611697	0.382893
0.47	1.599994	0.625002	0.97	2.637945	0.379083
0.48	1.616075	0.618783	0.98	2.664456	0.375311
0.49	1.632316	0.612626	0.99	2.691235	0.371577
0.50	1.648721	0.606531	1.00	2.718282	0.367879

x	e^x	e^{-x}	x	e^x	e^{-x}
1.10	3.004164	0.332871	5.60	270.426253	0.003698
1.20	3.320116	0.301194	5.70	298.867344	0.003346
1.30	3.669294	0.272532	5.80	330.299308	0.003028
1.40	4.055198	0.246597	5.90	365.037329	0.002739
1.50	4.481689	0.223130	6.00	403.428793	0.002479
1.60	4.953030	0.201897	6.10	445.857515	0.002243
1.70	5.473946	0.182684	6.20	492.748947	0.002029
1.80	6.049649	0.165299	6.30	544.572014	0.001836
1.90	6.685892	0.149569	6.40	601.844808	0.001662
2.00	7.389056	0.135335	6.50	665.141633	0.001503
2.10	8.166165	0.122456	6.60	735.094769	0.001360
2.20	9.025012	0.110803	6.70	812.405670	0.001231
2.30	9.974184	0.100259	6.80	897.847463	0.001114
2.40	11.023172	0.090718	6.90	992.274337	0.001008
2.50	12.182494	0.082085	7.00	1096.633158	0.000912
2.60	13.463743	0.074274	7.10	1211.967537	0.000825
2.70	14.879729	0.067206	7.20	1339.430509	0.000747
2.80	16.444650	0.060810	7.30	1480.300210	0.000676
2.90	18.174138	0.055023	7.40	1635.983806	0.000611
3.00	20.085537	0.049787	7.50	1808.042414	0.000553
3.10	22.197960	0.045049	7.60	1998.196657	0.000500
3.20	24.532526	0.040762	7.70	2208.347571	0.000453
3.30	27.112644	0.036883	7.80	2440.602443	0.000410
3.40	29.964117	0.033373	7.90	2697.283872	0.000371
3.50	33.115452	0.030197	8.00	2980.957987	0.000335
3.60	36.598248	0.027324	8.10	3294.469332	0.000304
3.70	40.447297	0.024724	8.20	3640.949613	0.000275
3.80	44.701193	0.022371	8.30	4023.873161	0.000249
3.90	49.402477	0.020242	8.40	4447.069292	0.000225
4.00	54.598150	0.018316	8.50	4914.768840	0.000203
4.10	60.340311	0.016573	8.60	5431.661663	0.000184
4.20	66.686382	0.014996	8.70	6002.916797	0.000167
4.30	73.699808	0.013569	8.80	6634.245272	0.000151
4.40	81.450915	0.012277	8.90	7331.977735	0.000136
4.50	90.017131	0.011109	9.00	8103.083928	0.000123
4.60	99.484354	0.010052	9.10	8955.296120	0.000112
4.70	109.947256	0.009095	9.20	9897.136610	0.000101
4.80	121.510441	0.008230	9.30	10938.021294	0.000091
4.90	134.289857	0.007447	9.40	12088.387647	0.000083
5.00	148.413301	0.006738	9.50	13359.739570	0.000075
5.10	164.021970	0.006097	9.60	14764.787198	0.000068
5.20	181.272380	0.005517	9.70	16317.619647	0.000061
5.30	200.336848	0.004992	9.80	18033.748367	0.000055
5.40	221.406543	0.004517	9.90	19930.381842	0.000050
5.50	244.692166	0.004087	10.00	22026.486801	0.000045

Answers to Selected Problems

Chapter 1. Fundamental Concepts of Modern Mathematics

Exercise Set 1.1, page 7

1. a. True   **c.** True   **e.** False   **g.** False   **i.** True

2. a. $\{x \mid x$ is a counting number less than or equal to 16$\}$
   c. $\{x \mid x$ is a counting number between 8 and 15, inclusive$\}$
   e. $\{x \mid x$ is a counting number greater than 10$\}$

3. a. 4   **c.** 7   **e.** 2

4. a. $R \cup T = \{5, 10, 15, 20\}$ **c.** $A \cup B = \{0, 10, 100, 1000\}$ **e.** $A \cup B = \{x, y, z, r, s, t\}$
   $R \cap T = \{15\}$ $A \cap B = \{10, 100\}$ $A \cap B = \{x, y\}$

5. a. 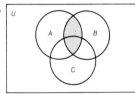   **c.** 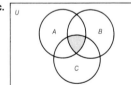   **e.**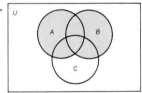

7. a. True   **c.** False   **e.** True   **g.** True   **i.** True

8. a. A student at Hard College who is not majoring in business
   c. A person who is not a student at Hard College (if U is the universe for the problem, then U' is an empty set)

9. a. $X \cup Y = \{a, b, c, d, e, f\}$ **c.** $X \cap Y = \{c, d\}$ **e.** $Y \cap X' = \{e, f\}$ **g.** $(X \cup Y)' = \{g\}$

10. a. $\varnothing, \{a\}, \{b\}, \{a, b\}$ **c.** $\varnothing, \{a\}$

11. a. In $A \subseteq B$, every element in A is also in B, and it is possible that A contains all elements of B. In $A \subset C$, every element in A must be in C, but A cannot contain all elements of C.
   c. Yes. If two sets are equal, the sets contain identical elements—every element in one set is an element in the other. Therefore, if $\{a, b\} = \{b, c\}$, then a must equal c.
   e. Yes. The null set is a subset of every set.

12. a. 1   **c.** 4   **e.** 16   **13.** 2^n

14. a. 350   **c.** 150   **e.** 850   **g.** 650   **15.** 3

17. a.

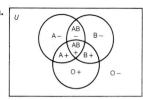

19. a. $\{A, B, C, D, E\}, \{A, B, C, D\}, \{A, B, C, E\}, \{A, B, D, E\}, \{A, C, D, E\}, \{B, C, D, E\}, \{B, C, D\}, \{B, C, E\},$
$\{A, B, C\}, \{A, B, D\}, \{A, B, E\}, \{A, C, D\}, \{A, C, E\}, \{B, C\}, \{A, B\}, \{A, C\}$

Exercise Set 1.2, page 14

1. a. H, R **c.** Q, R **e.** Q, R **g.** H, R

2. a. True   **c.** False   **e.** True   **g.** False

3. a. $x \geq 7$ **c.** $x \leq 5$ **e.** $1 \leq x < 3$

4. a. $4x^2 - 8z + x$ **c.** $-5x^2 + 8x - 4$ **e.** $6x - 6$

5. a. 11   **c.** 11   **e.** 7   **6. a.** -1 **c.** -1

7. a. $-1, 0, |-3|$ **c.** $-|2|, -1, |-2|$

8. a. $\frac{1}{5}$ **c.** $\frac{80}{3}$ **e.** Undefined   **g.** $\frac{1}{2}$ **i.** 0   **k.** -280 **m.** $2xy$ **o.** -1

9. a. $<$

10. a. $\frac{56}{9} = 6\frac{2}{9}$ **c.** $-\frac{941}{63} = -14\frac{59}{63}$ **e.** $-\frac{57}{2} = -28\frac{1}{2}$

g. -1.6848 **i.** $-\frac{65}{2} = -32\frac{1}{2}$ **k.** $-\frac{522}{275} = -1\frac{247}{275}$

11. a. 2.551   **c.** -1.36465 **12. a.** Yes   **c.** Yes

13. Year	Fraction	Allowable Depreciation
1	$(\frac{8}{36})5{,}000$	1,111.11
2	$(\frac{7}{36})5{,}000$	972.22
3	$(\frac{6}{36})5{,}000$	833.33
4	$(\frac{5}{36})5{,}000$	694.44
5	$(\frac{4}{36})5{,}000$	555.56
6	$(\frac{3}{36})5{,}000$	416.67
7	$(\frac{2}{36})5{,}000$	277.78
8	$(\frac{1}{36})5{,}000$	138.89
		5,000.00

15. $\frac{1}{2}$, 0.36, 0.015, 0   **17.** 18

Exercise Set 1.3, page 23

1. $x = 5$ **3.** $x = 3$ **5.** $x = -1$ **7.** $x = 1$

9. $x = 5$ **11.** $x = -4$ **13.** $x > 3$

15. $x < -21$ **17.** $x > \frac{28}{5}$

$5\frac{3}{5} = \frac{28}{5}$

19. $r = \dfrac{A - P}{Pt}$

21. $b = y - mx$

23. $r = 1 - \dfrac{a}{S} = \dfrac{S - a}{S}$

25. $x = 2$

27. $x = \frac{2}{3}$

29. $x = 9$

31. $x = 3$ or $x = 5$

33. $x = 1$ or $x = -2$

35. $-6 \le x < 1$

37. $-\frac{25}{2} < x \le -8$

39. Ed is 10 years old.

41. Joe has 25 books, and Tom has 50.

43. $P = \dfrac{A}{1 + rt}$

45. $y^2 = \dfrac{1 + 3x}{x^2 - 2z^3}$

47. $1.696 > x$

49. Smith's bill is $72, Jones' is $12.

51. $1,000 at 8%, $1,000 at 10%

53. At least 68¢ a pound

55. When $x = 40$

57. $t = \dfrac{y - 430}{1.5}$; year 1993

Exercise Set 1.4, page 32

1. a. First quadrant

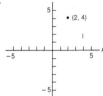

c. Third quadrant

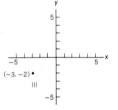

2. a.

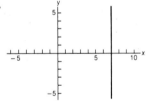

c.

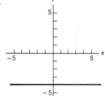

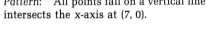

Pattern: All points fall on a vertical line that intersects the x-axis at (7, 0).

Pattern: All points fall on a horizontal line that intersects the y-axis at (0, −4).

e.

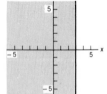

g.

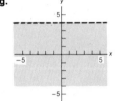

Pattern: All points fall in the half-plane to the left of the vertical line that intersects the x-axis at (3, 0) or on the line.

Pattern: All points fall in the half-plane under the horizontal line that intersects the y-axis at (0, 4).

3.

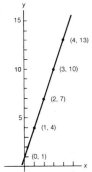

4. a.

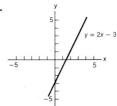

c.

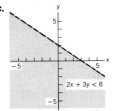

e.

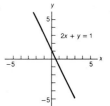

g.

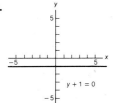

i.

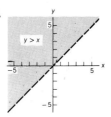

k.

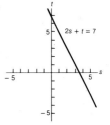

5.

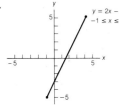

7.

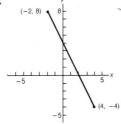

9.

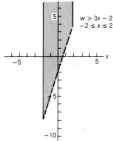

10. a.

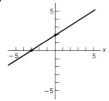

c.

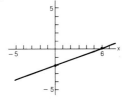

Intercepts at $(-3, 0)$ and $(0, 2)$

Intercepts at $(6, 0)$ and $(0, -2)$

11. *Pattern:* The value of m affects the slope of the line.

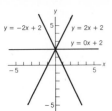

13. Equation: $y = 2x - 3$

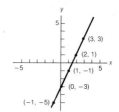

15. a.

Months	0	5	10	15	20	25	30	35	40
Average Dollar Value of a Machine	10,000	9,700	9,400	9,100	8,800	8,500	8,200	7,900	7,600

16. a. 12.5   **c.** Demand becomes 0.

17. a. 2.5; 7.5   **c.** When $x = 6$ **e.** When $x > 6$

18. a.

   c. 100; 100

19.

Height	63	66	69
Weight	120	130	140

Exercise Set 1.5, page 39

1. a. -5 **c.** 1   **e.** -1 **g.** The slope is not defined.   **i.** 0

2. a.

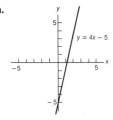

c.

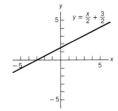

3. a. $m = 3$; $b = 2$ **c.** $m = 3$; $b = -1$ **e.** $m = \frac{1}{2}$; $b = -2$ **g.** $m = -\frac{4}{3}$; $b = \frac{7}{3}$

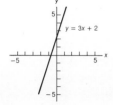

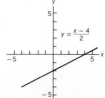

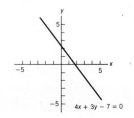

4. a. False   **c.** False

5. a. $x - 2y = -5$ **c.** $x + 3y = -7$

6. a. $4x - y = 3$ **c.** $x = 1$

7. a. $8x - 3y = 17$ **c.** $x - y = -8$ **e.** $5x - y = -4$

8. a. $y = -6$ **c.** $y = 0$ **9.** $a; b$

10. a. $\dfrac{x}{2} - \dfrac{y}{3} = 1$ **11.** $b = -8$

13. a. $x - 2y = -4$ **c.** $x + 3y = 11$ **14. a.** $2x + y = 7$ **c.** $3x - y = 3$

15. a. $V = 10{,}000 - 500t$ **c.** At the end of 20 years

17. a. $S = 150{,}000 - 10{,}000t$ **c.** \$90,000   **19.** $P = 110 + 30t$; 230; 290

Exercise Set 1.6, page 45

1. a. 0.055   **c.** 0.0031   **e.** 0.436   **2. a.** 120%   **c.** 40%   **e.** 27.5%

3. a. 25%   **c.** 32   **e.** 12.48   **g.** 300%   **5.** 6.67%

7. 60.8%   **9.** \$66.92   **11. a.** \$1,736   **c.** \$70

12. a. 19.3%   **c.** 16.7%   **13.** \$20.00

14. a. 57.25%   **c.** They are the same.   **15.** 31.6%

16. a. \$1,400; \$1,120; loss of \$80   **c.** \$905.80; \$1,086.96; profit of \$3.62

17. They are not making any money.

19. 110,000; 121,000

Review Exercise Set 1.7, page 47

1. a. $\{4, 6, 8, 9\}$ **c.** $\{1, 2, 3, 5, 6, 7, 9\}$ **e.** $\{1, 2, 5, 7\}$

2. a. $\{2\}$ **c.** $\{-2, -\tfrac{1}{2}, 0, 2\}$ **e.** $\{-2, -\tfrac{1}{2}, -\sqrt{2}\}$

3. a. $y = -\tfrac{3}{4}x - \tfrac{7}{4}$; $m = -\tfrac{3}{4}$ **c.** $y = \tfrac{4}{5}x - \tfrac{3}{5}$; $m = \tfrac{4}{5}$

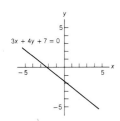   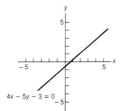

5. $2x + 3y = 19$

7. a.   **c.**   **e.**

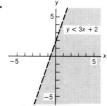   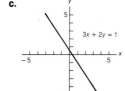   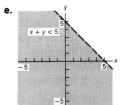

8. a. $x = -\dfrac{43}{2}$

9. a. $y \le \frac{24}{7}$

c. $x \ge -8$

11. 87¢; $3.33   **13.** 20.512%   **15.** 72.75%; 42.11%

17. 30 minutes; 25 miles   **19.** $3.80   **21.** $x = -0.1$

22. a. $x = 29.18$ **23** $4\frac{1}{2}$ months   **25.** 92 pounds   **27.** 69

29. $t = \dfrac{-b}{a - 2}$

31. a. Because a number not zero divided by zero does not exist.

Chapter 2. Systems of Linear Equations and Matrices

Exercise Set 2.1, page 58

1. a. $\{(2, 3)\}$

c. $\{(x, y) \mid 2x + y = 4\}$

e. $\{(1, 3)\}$

g. $\{\ \}$

i. $\{(1, 2)\}$

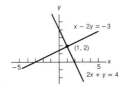

2. a. $\{(2, 3)\}$ **c.** $\{(x, y) \mid 2x + y = 4\}$ **e.** $\{(1, 3)\}$ **g.** No solution because the lines are parallel
i. $\{(1, 2)\}$

3. a. $\{(5, -7)\}$ **c.** $\{(12, -5)\}$ **e.** $\{(0, 2)\}$ **4. a.** $\{(2, 3)\}$ **c.** $\{(2, 7)\}$ **e.** $\{(5, 3)\}$

5. a. $\{(-\frac{40}{133}, \frac{116}{133})\}$ **c.** $\{(50, 3)\}$ **7.** 84, 72

9. a. $\{(1.341732, 0.076087)\}$ **c.** $\{(87, 103)\}$

11. 32 pounds of $3-per-pound candy and 48 pounds of $4-per-pound candy

13. The management should allow the service company to operate the club.

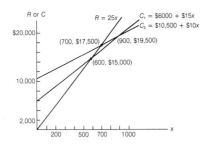

15. The change should be made if the number produced is greater than 1600.

17. The change should be made if the number produced is greater than 150 items per day because the second cost function allows greater profit after this number.

19. 640 men, 360 women

Exercise Set 2.2, page 65

1. $3x + y = 13$
$2x - y = 2$

3. $x = 4$
$y = 6$

5. $\begin{bmatrix} 2 & 3 & | & 5 \\ 4 & -1 & | & 3 \end{bmatrix}$

7. $\begin{bmatrix} 5 & 2 & | & 3 \\ 1 & 3 & | & -2 \end{bmatrix}$

9. $\begin{bmatrix} -2 & 2 & | & -6 \\ 1 & -2 & | & -5 \end{bmatrix}$

11. $\{(3, 4)\}$ **13.** $\{(1, 1)\}$ **15.** $\{(1, -1)\}$ **17.** $\{(11, 8)\}$

19. $\{(x, y) \mid 4x + 3y = 7\}$ **21.** No solutions   **23.** $\{(4.34, 0.89)\}$

25. 100 pounds   **27.** 7 runs of Best Paper, 13 runs of Good Paper

29. (100, 200)

Exercise Set 2.3, page 77

1. a. $[1 \quad 2 \quad 9]$ **c.** $\begin{bmatrix} 23 & 31 & 30 \\ -6 & -7 & 5 \end{bmatrix}$ **e.** $\begin{bmatrix} 1 & 7 & 6 \\ 2 & 8 & 10 \\ 3 & 7 & -1 \end{bmatrix}$

2. a. $\begin{bmatrix} 6 & 3 \\ 0 & 15 \end{bmatrix}$ **c.** $\begin{bmatrix} 35 & -5 & 9 \\ -2 & 28 & -21 \end{bmatrix}$ **3. a.** Impossible   **c.** [23]

4. a. $\begin{bmatrix} -1 & 2 \\ -3 & -4 \end{bmatrix}$ **c.** $\begin{bmatrix} 0 & 0 & 0 \\ 0 & 0 & 0 \end{bmatrix}$ **5.** $x = -3$

6. a. $x = -4, y = 8, z = 20$ **c.** $x = 0, y = 0, z = 0$

7. a. $\begin{bmatrix} 24 & 2 & 38 \\ 6 & -4 & 25 \end{bmatrix}$ **c.** $\begin{bmatrix} 3 & 19 & 13 \\ 1 & 5 & -3 \\ 2 & 12 & 10 \end{bmatrix}$ **e.** $\begin{bmatrix} 0 & 0 & 0 \\ 0 & 0 & 0 \\ 0 & 0 & 0 \end{bmatrix}$ **g.** $\begin{bmatrix} 11 & 1 & 17 \\ 16 & 2 & 25 \\ 21 & 3 & 33 \end{bmatrix}$ **i.** $\begin{bmatrix} 3 & 15 & 12 \\ 7 & 35 & 28 \\ 2 & 10 & 8 \end{bmatrix}$

8. a. $\begin{bmatrix} 24 & 2 \\ 6 & -4 \end{bmatrix}$ **c.** $\begin{bmatrix} 0 & 0 & 0 \\ 4 & 4 & 4 \\ 0 & 0 & 0 \end{bmatrix}$ **9.** $\begin{bmatrix} 2 \\ -3 \end{bmatrix}$

13. a. $\begin{bmatrix} -3 & 0 \\ -2 & 4 \end{bmatrix}$ **c.** $\begin{bmatrix} 3 & -6 \\ 10 & 0 \end{bmatrix}$ **e.** $\begin{bmatrix} 3 & -6 \\ 10 & 0 \end{bmatrix}$ **g.** $\begin{bmatrix} 3 & 0 \\ 0 & 3 \end{bmatrix}$ **i.** $\begin{bmatrix} 0 & 0 \\ 3 & 1 \end{bmatrix}$

14. a. $\qquad AB \neq BA$ **c.** $\begin{bmatrix} -3 & -2 \\ 2 & -4 \end{bmatrix} - \begin{bmatrix} 3 & 0 \\ 0 & 3 \end{bmatrix} \neq \begin{bmatrix} 0 & 0 \\ 3 & 1 \end{bmatrix} \begin{bmatrix} 2 & -4 \\ 1 & -1 \end{bmatrix}$

$\begin{bmatrix} -3 & 0 \\ -2 & 4 \end{bmatrix} \neq \begin{bmatrix} 3 & 2 \\ 3 & -2 \end{bmatrix}$ $\begin{bmatrix} -6 & -2 \\ 2 & -7 \end{bmatrix} \neq \begin{bmatrix} 0 & 0 \\ 7 & -13 \end{bmatrix}$

15. a. $[150 \quad 200 \quad 300 \quad 100]$ **c.** [$52,800]

17. Process A = 3.4, process B = 2.6, process C = 4.2, and process D = 8.8 milliliters of pollutants

19. $A^2 = \begin{bmatrix} 2 & 1 & 1 & 1 \\ 1 & 2 & 1 & 1 \\ 1 & 1 & 0 & 2 \\ 2 & 2 & 0 & 2 \end{bmatrix}$ $A^3 = \begin{bmatrix} 3 & 4 & 1 & 3 \\ 4 & 3 & 1 & 3 \\ 3 & 3 & 2 & 2 \\ 4 & 4 & 2 & 4 \end{bmatrix}$

Exercise Set 2.4, page 86

1. $x = 3, y = -1, z = 4$ **3.** $x = 3 - 2c, y = 1 - c, z = c$

5. No solution   **7.** $x = -2, y = 4, z = 6, w = 1$

9. No solution

11. $x = 1 - c$, $y = 3 + 2c$, $z = c$

13. $x = 10$, $y = 3$, $z = 15$

15. $x = 1$, $y = -1$, $z = 1$

17. $x = 1$, $y = 3$, $z = 0$

19. There is an infinite number of solutions: $x = 3c - 2$, $y = 4 - c$, $z = c$

21. $x = \dfrac{c}{3} + \dfrac{10}{3}$, $y = \dfrac{4c}{3} - \dfrac{2}{3}$, $z = c$

23. a. There is no common solution.
   c. There is an infinite number of solutions: $x = 3c_1 + 2c_2 - 3$, $y = c_2$, $z = c_1$

24. a. There is an infinite number of solutions: $x = 2c + 1$, $y = c - 2$, $z = -c + 3$, $t = c$
   c. $(1, -1, 0, 2)$
   e. There is an infinite number of solutions: $x = c + 2$, $y = 2c - 3$, $z = c + 1$, $t = c$

25. $3,000 with 9%, $5,400 with 10%, $4,000 with 11%

27. $11 blue-collar workers, $8 office workers

29. $A = 200$, $B = 100$, $C = 300$

31. 1150 lower-division, 1000 upper-division, and 750 graduate students

Exercise Set 2.5, page 94

1. a.

c.

e.

2. a. x, z-plane: $3x + 2z = 14$
   y, z-plane: $7y + 2z = 14$
   x, y-plane: $3x + 7y = 14$
   intercepts: $z = 7$, $y = 2$,
     $x = 4\frac{2}{3}$

   c. x, z-plane: $5x + 3z = 15$
   x, y-plane: $5x + 2y = 15$
   y, z-plane: $2y + 3z = 15$
   intercepts: $z = 5$, $y = 7.5$,
     $x = 3$

   e. x, z-plane: $2x - 4z = 12$
   x, y-plane: $2x - 3y = 12$
   y, z-plane: $-3y - 4z = 12$
   intercepts: $x = 6$, $z = -3$,
     $y = -4$

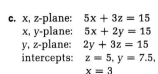

3. a. False **c.** True **e.** True **g.** True **i.** True

4. a.

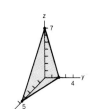

c.

e.

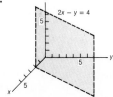

5.

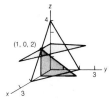

7. The system has no solution as two of the equations represent parallel planes.

9. The system has no solution as two of the equations form parallel planes.

10. a. $y = 2z$ **c.** $3x + y = 8$

11. \$15,000 at 10%, \$10,000 at 12%, and \$10,000 at 15%

13. Species A, 5166.67; species B, 1000; species C, 4166.67

Exercise Set 2.6, page 103

1. a. $\begin{bmatrix} 1 & 2 \\ 1 & 3 \end{bmatrix}\begin{bmatrix} 3 & -2 \\ -1 & 1 \end{bmatrix} = \begin{bmatrix} 1 & 0 \\ 0 & 1 \end{bmatrix}$ **c.** $\begin{bmatrix} 5 & 7 \\ 3 & 4 \end{bmatrix}\begin{bmatrix} -4 & 7 \\ 3 & -5 \end{bmatrix} = \begin{bmatrix} 1 & 0 \\ 0 & 1 \end{bmatrix}$

2. a. $\begin{bmatrix} \frac{1}{7} & \frac{1}{7} \\ -\frac{2}{21} & \frac{5}{21} \end{bmatrix}$ **c.** $\begin{bmatrix} 4 & -19 \\ -1 & 5 \end{bmatrix}$

3. a. $\{(4, -2)\}$ **c.** $\{(3, 2)\}$

4. a. $\begin{bmatrix} 0 & 0 & 1 \\ 0 & 1 & 0 \\ 1 & 0 & 0 \end{bmatrix}$ **c.** $\begin{bmatrix} 0 & 1 & 0 \\ \frac{1}{4} & 0 & 0 \\ \frac{1}{4} & 0 & 1 \end{bmatrix}$ **e.** $\begin{bmatrix} \frac{1}{18} & \frac{7}{18} & -\frac{1}{9} \\ -\frac{1}{6} & -\frac{1}{6} & \frac{1}{3} \\ \frac{7}{18} & -\frac{5}{18} & \frac{2}{9} \end{bmatrix}$

5. a. $\{(3, -2, 1)\}$ **c.** $\{(1, -1, 2)\}$

7. a. $\begin{bmatrix} \frac{7}{11} & -\frac{5}{11} \\ -\frac{2}{11} & \frac{3}{11} \end{bmatrix}$ **c.** $\begin{bmatrix} 1 & -1 \\ -5 & 6 \end{bmatrix}$ **8. a.** $\begin{bmatrix} -1 & -1 \\ 3 & 2 \end{bmatrix}$ **c.** $[A^{-1}]^{-1} = A$

9. a. $\begin{bmatrix} 2 & 1 & 1 & 0 \\ 6 & 3 & 0 & 1 \end{bmatrix}$ Multiply the first row by -3 and add it to the second row: $\begin{bmatrix} 2 & 1 & 1 & 0 \\ 0 & 0 & -3 & 1 \end{bmatrix}$

Since $\begin{bmatrix} 2 & 1 \\ 0 & 0 \end{bmatrix}$ cannot be reduced to $\begin{bmatrix} 1 & 0 \\ 0 & 1 \end{bmatrix}$, the matrix does not have an inverse.

c. The inverse does not exist.

10. a. The inverse does not exist.   **c.** $\begin{bmatrix} \frac{1}{3} & \frac{4}{3} & \frac{5}{3} & -\frac{7}{3} \\ -\frac{1}{6} & \frac{1}{3} & -\frac{5}{6} & \frac{2}{3} \\ -\frac{1}{2} & 0 & -\frac{1}{2} & 1 \\ \frac{1}{6} & -\frac{1}{3} & -\frac{1}{6} & \frac{1}{3} \end{bmatrix}$

11. $(AB) = \begin{bmatrix} 22 & 9 \\ 39 & 16 \end{bmatrix}$ $(AB)^{-1} = \begin{bmatrix} 16 & -9 \\ -39 & 22 \end{bmatrix}$

$A^{-1} = \begin{bmatrix} 2 & -1 \\ -5 & 3 \end{bmatrix}$ $B^{-1} = \begin{bmatrix} 3 & -2 \\ -7 & 5 \end{bmatrix}$ $B^{-1}A^{-1} = \begin{bmatrix} 16 & -9 \\ -39 & 22 \end{bmatrix}$

13. \$32,000 in type A and \$68,000 in type B bonds

15. $\begin{bmatrix} -2 & 3 \\ -\frac{1}{5} & \frac{1}{5} \end{bmatrix}\begin{bmatrix} 6,000 \\ 10,500 \end{bmatrix} = \begin{bmatrix} 29,500 \\ 900 \end{bmatrix}$ **17.** 40 days for team I, 35 days for team II

Exercise Set 2.7, page 109

1. $\begin{bmatrix} 20 \\ 28 \end{bmatrix}$

3. $\begin{bmatrix} 80 \\ 55 \end{bmatrix}$

5. $\begin{bmatrix} 32 \\ 29 \\ 18 \end{bmatrix}$

7. **a.** .1   **b.** 20   **c.** A

9. $\mathbf{X} - \mathbf{AX} = \begin{bmatrix} 3.0 \\ 0.2 \\ 0.2 \end{bmatrix}$

11. $\begin{bmatrix} 0.3 & 0.2 & 0.3 \\ 0.5 & 0.2 & 0.1 \\ 0.1 & 0.3 & 0.2 \end{bmatrix} \begin{bmatrix} 10 \\ 7 \\ 5 \end{bmatrix} = \begin{bmatrix} 5.9 \\ 6.9 \\ 4.1 \end{bmatrix}$ $\mathbf{X} - \mathbf{AX} = \begin{bmatrix} 4.1 \\ 0.1 \\ 0.9 \end{bmatrix}$

13. 71 units of services, and 43 units of manufacturing are needed.

Review Exercise Set 2.8, page 111

1. **a.** $(3, -4)$ **c.** $x = \frac{3}{11}c + \frac{7}{11}, y = c$

2. **a.** $(1, 2)$ **c.** $(2, 3)$

3. **a.** No solution   **c.** $x = 3c_1 + 2c_2 - 3, y = c_2, z = c_1$

4. **a.** $(1, 1, 1)$

5. **a.** $(1, 1, 1)$

6. **a.** $x = 2c + 1, y = c - 2, z = -c + 3, t = c$ **c.** $(1, -1, 0, 2)$

7. $6,000 at 9%, $3,700 at 10%, and $4,000 at 11%

9. $3,000 at 7%, $3,500 at 8%, and $2,500 at 9%

11. $A = 200, B = 125,$ and $C = 250$

13. 150 faculty, 100 staff, and 50 administration employees

Chapter 3. Introduction to Linear Programming

Exercise Set 3.1, page 118

1.

3.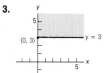

5.

7.

9.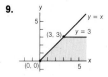

11.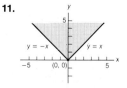

13.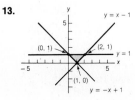

15.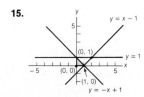

17.

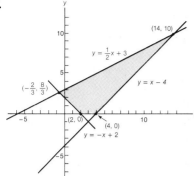

19.

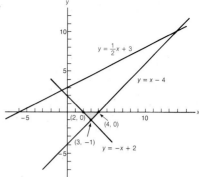

21.

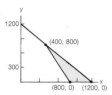

23.

25.

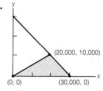

27.

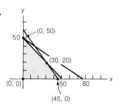

29.

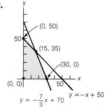

Exercise Set 3.2, page 127

1. a, b, c, d

3. b, c, f

4. a. Convex polyhedral

yes, yes, no

Corner point $(0, 0)$

e. Bounded polygonal convex

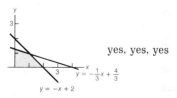

yes, yes, yes

Corner points are $(0, 0)$, $(0, \frac{4}{3})$, $(1, 1)$, $(2, 0)$

c. Bounded polygonal convex

yes, yes, yes

Corner points are $(0, 0)$, $(0, \frac{4}{3})$, $(4, 0)$

g. Bounded polygonal convex

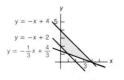

yes, yes, yes

Corner points are $(1, 1)$, $(4, 0)$, $(0, 2)$, $(0, 4)$

5. a. $P = 0$ is minimum at $(0, 0)$; no maximum   **c.** $P = 4$ is maximum at $(4, 0)$; $P = 0$ is minimum at $(0, 0)$
   e. $P = 3$ is maximum at $(1, 1)$; $P = 0$ is minimum at $(0, 0)$
   g. $P = 8$ is maximum at $(0, 4)$; $P = 3$ is minimum at $(1, 1)$

6. a. no maximum, no minimum   **c.** $P = 4$ is maximum at $(4, 0)$; $P = -\frac{8}{3}$ is minimum at $(0, \frac{4}{3})$
   e. $P = 2$ is maximum at $(2, 0)$; $P = -\frac{8}{3}$ is minimum at $(0, \frac{4}{3})$
   g. $P = 4$ is maximum at $(4, 0)$; $P = -8$ is minimum at $(0, 4)$

7. a. Maximum is 180, minimum is 0   **c.** Maximum is 245, minimum is 0
   e. Maximum is 245, minimum is 50

8. a. Maximum is 180, minimum is 0   **c.** Maximum is 195, minimum is 0
   e. Maximum is 175, minimum is 50

9. a. Maximum is 100, minimum is -175 **c.** Maximum is 100, minimum is -245
   e. Maximum is 66.67, minimum is -245

10. a. Maximum is 245, minimum is 50   **c.** Maximum is 290, minimum is 70

11. a. Maximum is 100, minimum is -245 **c.** Maximum is 200, minimum is -245

12. a. Maximum is 210, minimum is 40   **c.** Maximum is 400, minimum is 40

13. Four of item 1, two of item 2

15. \$37,500 in AA bonds, \$12,500 in B bonds

17. $P = \$250x + \$225y$; $P = \$12,000$ at $(30, 20)$
   George should plant 30 acres of wheat and 20 acres of corn for a maximum profit of \$12,000.

19. 35 instructors, 6 graduate assistants

Exercise Set 3.3, page 133

1. False

3. True

5. True

7. True

9. False

11. a. 3   **c.** $4x + y + s = 3$ **e.** x and y

13.
$$
\begin{array}{ccccc|c}
x & y & r & s & P & \\
0 & -\frac{7}{4} & 1 & -\frac{5}{4} & 0 & \frac{5}{2} \\
1 & \frac{3}{4} & 0 & \frac{1}{4} & 0 & \frac{3}{2} \\
\hline
0 & \frac{5}{2} & 0 & \frac{5}{2} & 1 & 15
\end{array}
\qquad
\begin{aligned}
-\tfrac{7}{4}y + r - \tfrac{5}{4}s &= \tfrac{5}{2} \\
x + \tfrac{3}{4}y + \tfrac{1}{4}s &= \tfrac{3}{2} \\
\tfrac{5}{2}y + \tfrac{5}{2}s + P &= 15
\end{aligned}
$$

15.
$$
\begin{array}{ccccc|c}
x & y & r & s & P & \\
1 & 0 & \frac{1}{2} & -\frac{1}{4} & 0 & 2 \\
0 & 1 & -\frac{1}{4} & \frac{3}{8} & 0 & 1 \\
\hline
0 & 0 & 4 & 1 & 1 & 40
\end{array}
\qquad
\begin{aligned}
x + \tfrac{1}{2}r - \tfrac{1}{4}s &= 2 \\
y - \tfrac{1}{4}r + \tfrac{3}{8}s &= 1 \\
4r + s + P &= 40
\end{aligned}
$$

17.
$$
\begin{array}{cccccc|c}
x & y & r & s & t & P & \\
\frac{5}{2} & 0 & 1 & 0 & -\frac{1}{2} & 0 & \frac{1}{2} \\
\frac{5}{4} & 0 & 0 & 1 & -\frac{3}{4} & 0 & \frac{1}{4} \\
\frac{1}{4} & 1 & 0 & 0 & \frac{1}{4} & 0 & \frac{5}{4} \\
\hline
-\frac{5}{2} & 0 & 0 & 0 & \frac{3}{2} & 1 & \frac{15}{2}
\end{array}
\qquad
\begin{aligned}
\tfrac{5}{2}x + r - \tfrac{1}{2}t &= \tfrac{1}{2} \\
\tfrac{5}{4}x + s - \tfrac{3}{4}t &= \tfrac{1}{4} \\
\tfrac{1}{4}x + y + \tfrac{1}{4}t &= \tfrac{5}{4} \\
-\tfrac{5}{2}x + \tfrac{3}{2}t + P &= \tfrac{15}{2}
\end{aligned}
$$

19.
$$
\begin{array}{cccccc|c}
x & y & r & s & t & P & \\
-10 & -4 & 1 & 0 & 0 & 0 & 1 \\
3 & 1 & 0 & 0 & 1 & 0 & 1 \\
-2 & -2 & 0 & 1 & 0 & 0 & 4 \\
\hline
11 & 3 & 0 & 0 & 0 & 1 & 11
\end{array}
\qquad
\begin{aligned}
-10x - 4y + r &= 1 \\
3x + y + t &= 1 \\
-2x - 2y + s &= 4 \\
11x + 3y + P &= 11
\end{aligned}
$$

21.

$$\begin{array}{c} \quad\quad x \quad\quad\; y \quad\quad r \quad\quad\; s \quad P \\ \left[\begin{array}{ccccc|c} 0.548780 & 1 & 0.406504 & 0 & 0 & 0.723577 \\ 1.767806 & 0 & -0.601626 & 1 & 0 & 1.469106 \\ 0.055852 & 0 & 1.048780 & 0 & 1 & 3.206829 \end{array}\right] \end{array}$$

Exercise Set 3.4, page ▮▮▮

1. a. False   **c.** True   **e.** False

3.

$$\begin{array}{c} \;\; x \quad\; y \quad r \;\; s \;\; P \\ \left[\begin{array}{ccccc|c} 2 & 1 & 1 & 0 & 0 & 7 \\ ③ & 1 & 0 & 1 & 0 & 8 \\ \hline -35 & -25 & 0 & 0 & 1 & 0 \end{array}\right] \end{array}$$

5.

$$\begin{array}{c} \;\; x \quad\; y \quad r \;\; s \;\; P \\ \left[\begin{array}{ccccc|c} 2 & 3 & 1 & 0 & 0 & 15 \\ ③ & 1 & 0 & 1 & 0 & 12 \\ \hline -25 & 35 & 0 & 0 & 1 & 0 \end{array}\right] \end{array}$$

7.

$$\begin{array}{c} \;\; x \quad\; y \quad r \;\; s \;\; P \\ \left[\begin{array}{ccccc|c} 2 & ① & 1 & 0 & 0 & 7 \\ 3 & 1 & 0 & 1 & 0 & 8 \\ \hline -25 & -35 & 0 & 0 & 1 & 0 \end{array}\right] \end{array}$$

9.

$$\begin{array}{c} \;\; x \quad\; y \quad r \;\; s \;\; t \;\; P \\ \left[\begin{array}{cccccc|c} 1 & 1 & 1 & 0 & 0 & 0 & 7 \\ 2 & 1 & 0 & 1 & 0 & 0 & 9 \\ ③ & 1 & 0 & 0 & 1 & 0 & 12 \\ \hline -35 & -25 & 0 & 0 & 0 & 1 & 0 \end{array}\right] \end{array}$$

11.

$$\begin{array}{c} \;\; x \quad\; y \quad r \;\; s \;\; t \;\; P \\ \left[\begin{array}{cccccc|c} 1 & 1 & 1 & 0 & 0 & 0 & 7 \\ 2 & 1 & 0 & 1 & 0 & 0 & 9 \\ ③ & 1 & 0 & 0 & 1 & 0 & 12 \\ \hline -35 & 25 & 0 & 0 & 0 & 1 & 0 \end{array}\right] \end{array}$$

13.

$$\begin{array}{c} \;\; x \quad\; y \quad r \;\; s \;\; t \;\; u \;\; P \\ \left[\begin{array}{ccccccc|c} 2 & ③ & 1 & 0 & 0 & 0 & 0 & 6 \\ 1 & 3 & 0 & 1 & 0 & 0 & 0 & 21 \\ 2 & 3 & 0 & 0 & 1 & 0 & 0 & 24 \\ 2 & 1 & 0 & 0 & 0 & 1 & 0 & 16 \\ \hline -25 & -35 & 0 & 0 & 0 & 0 & 1 & 0 \end{array}\right] \end{array}$$

15.

$$\begin{array}{c} \;\; x \quad\; y \quad r \;\; s \;\; t \;\; u \;\; P \\ \left[\begin{array}{ccccccc|c} 1 & 1 & 1 & 0 & 0 & 0 & 0 & 5 \\ ③ & 2 & 0 & 1 & 0 & 0 & 0 & 7 \\ 1 & 4 & 0 & 0 & 1 & 0 & 0 & 9 \\ 3 & 5 & 0 & 0 & 0 & 1 & 0 & 12 \\ \hline -30 & -18 & 0 & 0 & 0 & 0 & 1 & 0 \end{array}\right] \end{array}$$

Exercise Set 3.5, page 142

1. False   **3.** False   **5.** True

7. $P = 9$ at $(3, 0)$ or $(1, 3)$ or at any point on the line segment between these

9. $P = 17$ at $(1, 3)$ **11.** $P = 245$ at $(0, 7)$ **13.** $P = 175$ at $(0, 7)$

15. $P = 1920$ at $(120, 0, 200)$ **17.** $P = 49$ at $(12, 0, 5)$ **19.** $P = 132.83$ at $(0, 56.52)$

21. $P = 15$ at $(0, 6.25)$

23. Four of type II for a maximum profit of \$56

25. 192 of I, none of II

27. \$18,000 in good quality, \$9,000 in high risk

29. 1800 liters by the new process

31. Eddy should answer 12 short-answer questions and 8 true-false questions.

1. Minimize $\quad 15y_1 + 12y_2 = C$
$\quad$ subject to $\quad 2y_1 + 3y_2 \geq 25$
$\qquad\qquad\qquad 3y_1 + y_2 \geq 35$
$\qquad\qquad\qquad\qquad y_1 \geq 0$
$\qquad\qquad\qquad\qquad y_2 \geq 0$

3. Maximize $\quad P = 5x_1 + 21x_2$
$\quad$ subject to $\qquad\quad x_1 + 3x_2 \leq 4$
$\qquad\qquad\qquad\quad x_1 + x_2 \leq 7$
$\qquad\qquad\qquad\qquad\quad x_1 \geq 0$
$\qquad\qquad\qquad\qquad\quad x_2 \geq 0$

5.

	x_1	x_2	y_1	y_2	P	
	2	3	1	0	0	15
	3	1	0	1	0	12
	−25	−35	0	0	1	0

7.

	x_1	x_2	y_1	y_2	P	
	1	3	1	0	0	4
	1	1	0	1	0	7
	−5	−21	0	0	1	0

9. Maximize $\quad P = 7x_1 + 4x_2$
$\quad$ subject to $\quad 3x_1 + 2x_2 \leq 5$
$\qquad\qquad\qquad x_1 + 3x_2 \leq 8$
$\qquad\qquad\qquad\qquad x_1 \geq 0$
$\qquad\qquad\qquad\qquad x_2 \geq 0$

Dual: Minimize $\quad 5y_1 + 8y_2 = C$
$\quad$ subject to $\quad 3y_1 + y_2 \geq 7$
$\qquad\qquad\qquad 2y_1 + 3y_2 \geq 4$
$\qquad\qquad\qquad\qquad y_1 \geq 0$
$\qquad\qquad\qquad\qquad y_2 \geq 0$

11. Maximize $\quad P = 6x_1 + 8x_2$
$\quad$ subject to $\quad 2x_1 + 3x_2 \leq 4$
$\qquad\qquad\qquad x_1 + 2x_2 \leq 7$
$\qquad\qquad\qquad 3x_1 + x_2 \leq 6$
$\qquad\qquad\qquad\qquad x_1 \geq 0$
$\qquad\qquad\qquad\qquad x_2 \geq 0$

Dual: Minimize $\quad 4y_1 + 7y_2 + 6y_3 = C$
$\quad$ subject to $\quad 2y_1 + y_2 + 3y_3 \geq 6$
$\qquad\qquad\qquad 3y_1 + 2y_2 + y_3 \geq 8$
$\qquad\qquad\qquad\qquad y_1 \geq 0$
$\qquad\qquad\qquad\qquad y_2 \geq 0$

13. $C = 23$ at $(2, 3)$ $\qquad$ **15.** $C = 28$ at $(7, 0)$ $\qquad$ **17.** $C = 0$ at $(0, 0)$ $\qquad$ **19.** $C = 50$ at $(2, 0)$

21. $C = 11$ at $(1, 2, 0)$

23. 40 tons from A to II, 50 tons from B to I, and 35 tons from B to II, for a minimum cost of $970

25. 5 days for refinery I and 0 days for refinery II, at a cost of $750

27. Eight units of food II and no units of food I

29. Abdul should eat no units of food I and five units of food II

31. 0 grams of medicine I, 8 of medicine II, for a minimum of 16 milligrams of drug X

32. 8 hours of work, 3 hours of play, for a maximum of 3 hours of study time

Review Exercise Set 3.7, page 153

1.

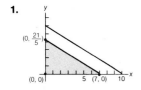

Bounded polygonal convex; corner points are
$(0, 0)$, $(0, \frac{21}{5})$, and $(7, 0)$

5.

	x	y	r	s	P	
	3	5	1	0	0	30
	3	5	0	1	0	21
	−3	−4	0	0	1	0

3. $P = 0$ is minimum at $(0, 0)$;
$\quad P = 21$ is maximum at $(7, 0)$

7. Minimize $\quad 30y_1 + 21y_2 = C$
$\quad$ subject to $\quad 3y_1 + 3y_2 \geq 3$
$\qquad\qquad\qquad 5y_1 + 5y_2 \geq 4$
$\qquad\qquad\qquad\qquad y_1 \geq 0$
$\qquad\qquad\qquad\qquad y_2 \geq 0$

9. $P = 21$ is maximum at $(7, 0)$; *Dual:* $C = 21$ is minimum at $(0, 1)$

11. 25 tons from A to I, 75 tons from A to II, 25 tons from B to I, for a minimum cost of $875

13. 2 days for refinery I, 4 days for refinery II, at a cost of $1,500

15. Three units of food I and one unit of food II, for a minimum of 130 calories

17. $C = 2.08$ at $(2.4, 6.8)$

Chapter 4. Mathematics of Finance

Exercise Set 4.1, page 160

1. a. $I = \$3,200$; $A = \$13.200$ **c.** $I = \$640$; $A = \$16,640$

2. a. $6,800   **c.** $15,360   **3. a.** 23.5%   **c.** 12.5%   **5.** $666.67

7. $3,000   **9.** $1,545   **11.** $52.67

13. $r = I/Pt$ **15.** $d = (A - P)/At$ **17.** 8.69%

19. $2,014.20   **21.** $550 six months from now   **23.** $4,460.82

Exercise Set 4.2, page 167

1.

	Simple Interest	Compound Interest
First year	$I = \$8$	$I = \$8$
Second year	$I = \$8$	$I = \$8.64$
Third year	$I = \$8$	$I = \$9.33$
Fourth year	$I = \$8$	$I = \$10.08$

3. 8.16%   **5.** 26.824%

6. a. $I = \$5,794.63$; $A = \$10,794.63$ **c.** $I = \$6,040.20$; $A = \$11,040.20$

7. a. $I = \$3,126.61$; $A = \$5,126.61$ **c.** $I = \$3,150.17$; $A = \$5,150.17$

9. $4,053.38   **10. a.** $3,194.71   **11. a.** $5,466.36

13. Approximately 9.3 years   **15.** About 7 years   **17.** 8.7 years

19. $8,074.76   **21.** $486.11   **23.** $1,421.58   **25.** $N = 182$

Exercise Set 4.3, page 174

1. a. $r = 3$; 9, 27, 81   **c.** $r = -\frac{1}{3}$; $-\frac{1}{3}, \frac{1}{9}, -\frac{1}{27}$ **2. a.** $\frac{255}{32}$ **c.** $\frac{21}{8}$

3. a. $\frac{63}{4}$ **c.** $\frac{4118}{81}$ **5. a.** $4,697.06   **6. a.** $7,243.28   **7.** $10,737,418.23

9. $5,992.05   **11.** $5,866.60   **13.** $2,644.60   **15.** $1,060.36

17. $3,092.79   **19.** $2,211.24   **21.** $7,840.30

Exercise Set 4.4, page 181

1. a. $45,761.96   **c.** $7,203.66   **2. a.** $9,818.15   **c.** $4,866.54

3. a. $A = \$15,992.73$; $P = \$6,152.77$ **5.** $284.91

7.

Period	Outstanding Principal	Interest Due	Payment	Principal Repaid Each Period
1	$2,000.00	$60.00	$284.91	$224.91
2	1,775.09	53.25	284.91	231.66
3	1,543.43	46.30	284.91	238.61
4	1,304.82	39.14	284.91	245.77
5	1,059.05	31.77	284.91	253.14
6	805.91	24.18	284.91	260.73
7	545.18	16.36	284.91	268.55
8	276.63	8.30	284.91	276.63

8. a. $20,875.32   **9. a.** $18,319.74   **11.** $101.24   **13.** $3,397,192.30

Exercise Set 4.5, page 185

1. $15,000   **3.** $150   **5.** $1,060.36   **7.** $1,358.36

9. $5,355.70   **11.** $337.26   **13.** $99.01

Exercise Set 4.6, page 187

1. $150   **3.** $180   **5.** 12.36%

7. $A = \$5,794.62$; $P = \$2,684.03$ **9.** $246,305.42   **11.** $55.24

13. $989.75

15.

Period	Outstanding Principal	Interest Due	Payment	Principal Repaid
1	$10,000.00	$400.00	$1,907.62	$1,507.62
2	8,492.38	339.70	1,907.62	1,567.92
3	6,924.46	276.98	1,907.62	1,630.64
4	5,293.82	211.75	1,907.62	1,695.87
5	3,597.95	143.92	1,907.62	1,763.70
6	1,834.25	73.37	1,907.62	1,834.25

17. $255,468,811,500   **19.** $12,576.99   **21.** $4,136.64

Chapter 5. Counting Techniques and Probability

Exercise Set 5.1, page 196

1. a. $\{A, B, C\}$ **c.** $\{1, 2, 3, 4, 5, 6\}$

2. a. $P(A) = P(B) = P(C) = \frac{1}{3}$
c. $P(1) = P(2) = P(3) = P(4) = P(5) = P(6) = \frac{1}{6}$

3. $\{1, 2, 3, 4, 5, 6\}$
$P(1) = P(2) = P(3) = P(4) = P(5) = P(6) = \frac{1}{6}$

5. a. $\{A, B, C\}$ $\qquad P(A) = P(C) = \frac{1}{4}, P(B) = \frac{1}{2}$

7. 0

8. a. Probability cannot be negative. **c.** .001 can be a probability.
e. Probability cannot exceed 1. **g.** Probability cannot exceed 1.

9. $\{(H, 1), (H, 2), (H, 3), (H, 4), (H, 5), (H, 6), (T, 1), (T, 2), (T, 3), (T, 4), (T, 5), (T, 6)\}$

10. a. $\{(A, R), (A, G), (B, R), (B, G), (C, R), (C, G)\}$
c. $\{(A, 10), (A, 11), (A, 12), (A, 13), (B, 10), (B, 11), (B, 12), (B, 13), (C, 10), (C, 11), (C, 12), (C, 13)\}$
e. $\{(10, R), (11, R), (12, R), (13, R), (10, G), (11, G), (12, G), (13, G)\}$

11. a. There could be 0 heads.
c. 4 is not a possible outcome of this experiment.
e. This is the empty set and contains none of the outcomes.
g. This is the sample space.

13. a. $\{R, B\}$ **c.** $\{RRR, RRB, RBR, BRR, RBB, BRB, BBR, BBB\}$

14. a. $\{(1, 1) (1, 2) (1, 3) (1, 4) (2, 1) (2, 2) (2, 3) (2, 4) (3, 1) (3, 2) (3, 3) (3, 4) (4, 1) (4, 2) (4, 3) (4, 4)\}$

15. a. $\{$red marble, blue marble, green marble$\}$

17. $\{ABC, ABD, ABE, ACD, ACE, ADE, BCD, BCE, BDE, CDE\}$

18. a. $\frac{2}{5}$ **c.** $\frac{7}{25}$ **e.** $\frac{1}{4}$ **g.** $\frac{1}{100}$

19. a. $\frac{4}{5}$ **c.** $\frac{1}{26}$

20. a. $\frac{7}{55}$ **c.** $\frac{27}{55}$ **e.** $\frac{7}{22}$ **21.** $\frac{37}{40}$ **22. a.** $\frac{9}{32}$ **c.** $\frac{7}{33}$ **e.** $\frac{1}{16}$

Exercise Set 5.2, page 204

1. a. $\frac{1}{4}$ **c.** $\frac{1}{52}$ **2. a.** $\frac{1}{2}$ **c.** $\frac{1}{3}$ **e.** 1 **3. a.** $\frac{1}{2}$ **c.** 0

5. a. Any 1 of the 35 students would be an equally likely outcome. **c.** $\frac{1}{35}$ **e.** 1

6. a. $\frac{2}{5}$ **c.** $\frac{3}{5}$ **e.** $\frac{11}{40}$ **7.** $\frac{1}{10}$ **8. a.** $\frac{1}{6}$ **c.** $\frac{1}{9}$

9. a. $\frac{1}{4}$ **c.** $\frac{3}{4}$ **10. a.** $\frac{2}{7}$ **c.** $\frac{1}{2}$ **e.** $\frac{11}{14}$

11. a. This statement assumes that a person has an equal chance of being born in any of the 50 states, when in actuality this is not true. Births are more likely to occur in those states containing more people.
c. This outcome could possibly indicate that the coin is biased in favor of heads since, according to the concept of a priori probability, 10 of the outcomes should be heads.

13. No; the events are not equally likely. **14. a.** $\{1, 3, 5\}$ **c.** $\{5\}$

15. a. $\frac{1}{12}$ **c.** $\frac{1}{6}$ **e.** 0

16. a. $\{(1, 1), (1, 2), (1, 3), (1, 4), (2, 1), (2, 2), (2, 3), (2, 4), (3, 1), (3, 2), (3, 3), (3, 4), (4, 1), (4, 2), (4, 3), (4, 4)\}$
c. $\frac{5}{8}$

17. A head followed by a head; a head followed by a tail; a tail followed by a head; and a tail followed by a tail.

18. a. $\frac{1}{4}$ **c.** $\frac{1}{50}$ **19. a.** $\frac{25}{27}$ **c.** $\frac{1}{36}$

20. a. (V, W, Z), (V, X, Z), (V, Y, Z), (W, X, Z), (W, Y, Z), (X, Y, Z) **c.** (W, X, Y), (W, X, Z), (W, Y, Z), (X, Y, Z)

21. a. $\frac{15}{34}$ **c.** $\frac{1}{34}$

Exercise Set 5.3, page 213

1. a. Six **2. a.** 24 **3.** 18

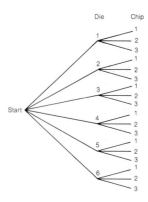

5. 2 **7.** 24 **8. a.** $\frac{1}{36}$ **c.** $\frac{1}{18}$

9. a. $\frac{1}{16}$ **c.** $\frac{5}{16}$ **10. a.** $\frac{1}{14}$ **c.** $\frac{1}{35}$ **11.** 72

13. a. 358,800 **c.** 456,976 **14. a.** $\frac{1}{169}$ **15.**

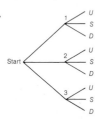

17. 60 **18. a.** $\frac{1}{4}$ **c.** $\frac{3}{4}$ **19. a.** $\frac{1}{8}$ **c.** $\frac{1}{2}$ **20. a.** $\frac{1}{16}$ **c.** $\frac{5}{16}$

21. a. $\frac{5}{32}$ **c.** $\frac{1}{2}$ **22. a.** 14 **c.** 6 **23.** Yes $(2 \cdot 3 \cdot 3 = 18)$

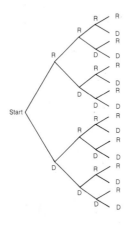
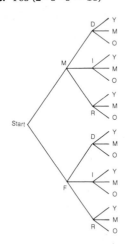

Exercise Set 5.4, page 222

1. a. Six: $\{W, X\}, \{W, Y\}, \{W, Z\}, \{X, Y\}, \{X, Z\}, \{Y, Z\}$ **c.** $\{W\}, \{X\}, \{Y\}, \{Z\}$

2. a. $\frac{5!}{2!}$ **c.** $\frac{44!}{22! \cdot 22!}$ **e.** $\frac{6!}{0!} = 6!$ **g.** $\frac{7!}{5! \cdot 2!}$ **i.** $\frac{100!}{89! \cdot 11!}$

3. a. 210 **c.** 15 **e.** $\dfrac{r(r-1)}{2}$ **4. a.** 60 **c.** 8 **e.** 42

5. 120 **7.** 5040 **9.** 2,598,960

11. a. r **c.** $r!$ **e.** $k(k-1)(k-2)$ **13. a.** 10,000

15. a. 1,050,739,900 **c.** .9 **16. a.** $\dfrac{13}{55}$ **17.** $\dfrac{7}{95}$

18. a. $1/(26)^3$ **19.** $\dfrac{63}{125}$ **21. a.** 1716 **c.** 725,010

23. $n!$

25. a.
$$n = 4$$
$$(4^2 - 4) \cdot (4 - 2)! = 4!$$
$$12 \cdot 2! = 4!$$
$$24 = 24$$
$$(n^2 - n) \cdot (n - 2)! = n(n-1)(n-2)! = n!$$

c.
$$n = 4$$
$$4! - 3! = 3^2 \cdot 2!$$
$$3!(4 - 1) = 3^2 \cdot 2!$$
$$6 \cdot 3 = 9 \cdot 2$$
$$18 = 18$$
$$n! - (n - 1)! = (n - 1)!(n - 1)$$
$$= (n - 1)(n - 2)!(n - 1)$$
$$= (n - 1)^2(n - 2)!$$

26. a. 1, 1, 1 **27. a.** 3, 7, 9 **28. a.** 1, 1, 1 **29. a.** 28

30. a. 28 **31.** $C(n, r) = C(n, n - r)$ **33.** 48,450

35. $\dfrac{3}{7}$ **36. a.** 45 **c.** 24 **37. a.** 1900 **c.** 648 **e.** 220

38. a. $\dfrac{1}{3}$ **39. a.** 1140 **c.** $\dfrac{8}{19}$ **40. a.** 120 **43. a.** $\dfrac{2}{7}$ **c.** $\dfrac{3}{7}$

Exercise Set 5.5, page 232

1. a. $\dfrac{1}{2}$ **c.** $\dfrac{1}{4}$ **2. a.** .4 **c.** .7

3. a. Getting zero or one head $\{TTTTTTT, TTTTTTH, TTTTTHT, TTTTHTT, TTTHTTT, TTHTTTT, THTTTTT, HTTTTTT\}$
   c. Getting at least two tails or no tails

5. a. $\dfrac{1}{2}$ **c.** $\dfrac{12}{13}$ **6. a.** $\dfrac{1}{2}$ **c.** $\dfrac{13}{24}$ **7. a.** $\dfrac{2}{13}$ **c.** $\dfrac{4}{13}$ **e.** $\dfrac{1}{4}$

8. a. $\dfrac{10}{13}$ **c.** $\dfrac{9}{13}$ **e.** 1

9. a. $E = \{(2, 4), (3, 3), (4, 2)\}$
   c. $\{E \text{ and } F\} = \{(3, 3)\}$
   e. $F = \{(1, 1), (1, 2), (1, 3), (1, 4), (2, 1), (2, 2), (2, 3), (2, 4), (4, 1) (4, 2), (4, 3), (4, 4)\}$

11. a. $A = \{(HHHH), (HHHT), (HHTH), (HHTT), (HTHH), (HTHT), (HTTH), (HTTT), (THHH), (THHT), (THTH). (THTT), (TTHH), (TTHT), (TTTH), (TTTT)\}$
   c. $B = \{(HHHT), (HHTH), (HHTT), (HTHH), (HTHT), (HTTH), (HTTT), (THHH), (THHT), (THTH), (THTT), (TTHH), (TTHT), (TTTH), (TTTT)\}$
   e. $A \text{ and } B = \{(HTTT), (THTT), (TTHT), (TTTH)\}$

13. a. $\dfrac{1}{2}$ **c.** $\dfrac{8}{9}$ **e.** $\dfrac{16}{225}$ **15. a.** 20% **c.** 7% **16. a.** $\dfrac{3}{4}$ **c.** $\dfrac{17}{20}$

17. a. $\dfrac{17}{20}$ **c.** $\dfrac{23}{25}$ **18. a.** $\dfrac{3}{10}$ **c.** $\dfrac{1}{10}$

Exercise Set 5.6, page 241

1. a. $S = \{$the card is black, the card is a heart, the card is a club$\}$ **c.** 0 **e.** 1

2. a. $\dfrac{2}{3}$ **3. a.** .42 **c.** .4

4. a. .35 **c.** .3 **e.** .8 **g.** $\dfrac{4}{7}$ **i.** $\dfrac{2}{3}$ **5. a.** $\dfrac{2}{3}$ **c.** $\dfrac{4}{5}$ **e.** $\dfrac{1}{5}$ **g.** $\dfrac{1}{3}$

6. a. $\dfrac{1}{3}$ **c.** $\dfrac{1}{4}$ **e.** $\dfrac{1}{3}$ **g.** $\dfrac{2}{3}$ **7. a.** $\dfrac{3}{4}$ **c.** $\dfrac{7}{20}$ **e.** $\dfrac{13}{16}$

9. a. $\frac{4}{13}$

10. a. $\frac{1}{4}$ **c.** $\frac{2}{5}$ **e.** $\frac{5}{7}$ **g.** $\frac{5}{13}$

11. Her probability of being selected will decrease.

13. a. $\frac{1}{56}$ **c.** $\frac{10}{11}$

Exercise Set 5.7, page 250

1. .63

3. $\frac{15}{56}$

5. $\frac{1}{4}$

6. a. $\frac{1}{169}$

7. a. $\frac{16}{49}$

9. a. $\frac{1}{5}$ **c.** $\frac{11}{20}$

11. $\frac{7}{8}$

12. a. $\frac{1}{4}$ **c.** $\frac{1}{2}$ **e.** 1

13. .665

14. a. $\frac{4}{77}$ **c.** $\frac{8}{77}$

15. a. $\frac{6}{121}$

17. $\frac{3}{10}$

19. $\frac{8}{663}$

21. a. .048   **c.** .552

23. .3275

25. a. .0005

27. $\frac{42}{95}$

29. a. $\frac{1}{15}$ **c.** $\frac{3}{20}$

31. .17

32. a. $\frac{1}{16}$ **c.** $\frac{1}{16}$

33. a. $\frac{1}{16}$ **c.** $\frac{1}{256}$

34. a. $\frac{1}{2}$ **c.** $\frac{1}{2}$ **e.** $\frac{1}{8}$ **g.** $\frac{5}{8}$ **i.** $\frac{5}{8}$

35. a. $\frac{1}{20}$ **c.** $\frac{3}{20}$

37. $\frac{5}{12}$

Exercise Set 5.8, page 259

1. a. .6   **c.** .4   **e.** .28   **g.** .63

2. a. $\frac{1}{9}$ **c.** $\frac{10}{27}$

3. a. $P(B_1|A) = \frac{1}{5}$; $P(B_2|A) = \frac{4}{15}$; $P(B_3|A) = \frac{8}{15}$ **c.** $P(B_1|A) = \frac{1}{9}$; $P(B_2|A) = \frac{8}{27}$; $P(B_3|A) = \frac{16}{27}$

4. a. $\frac{11}{20}$ **c.** $\frac{1}{10}$ **e.** $\frac{4}{7}$

5. a. $\frac{5}{11}$ **c.** 1

7. $\frac{48}{133}$

9. a. $\frac{24}{31}$

11. $\frac{90}{199}$; $\frac{40}{199}$

13. $\frac{36}{103}$

15. a. $\frac{9}{11}$

Review Exercise Set 5.9, page 262

1. a. $\frac{55}{100}$

2. a. {red, black, green}
   c. {(red, red), (red, black), (red, green), (black, red), (black black), (black, green), (green, red), (green, black), (green green)}

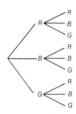

   e. {(red, red, red), (red, red, black), (red, red, green), (red, black, red), (red, black, black), (red, black, green), (red, green, red), (red, green, black), (red, green, green), (black, red, red), (black, red, black), (black, red, green), (black, black, red), (black, black, black), (black, black, green), (black, green, red), (black, green, black), (black, green, green), (green, red, red), (green, red, black), (green, red, green), (green, black, red), (green, black, black), (green, black, green), (green, green, red), (green, green, black), (green, green, green)}

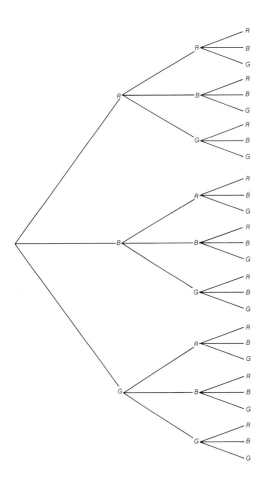

3. a. $\frac{10}{13}$ **c.** 1   **e.** $\frac{9}{13}$ **g.** 1   **i.** 1   **4. a.** $\frac{36}{169}$ **c.** $\frac{16}{169}$

5. a. $\frac{1}{3}$ **6. a.** .65   **7.** $\frac{1}{3}$ **9.** $\frac{1}{36}$

10. a. .7   **c.** .6   **11. a.** $\frac{1}{8}$ **c.** $\frac{1}{8}$ **12. a.** $\frac{11}{4165}$ **c.** $\frac{44}{4165}$

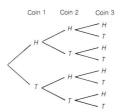

13. a. Two aces   **c.** Mutually exclusive   **e.** Mutually exclusive

15. $\frac{199}{400}$ **17.** $\frac{463}{800}$ **18. a.** $\frac{25}{102}$ **c.** $\frac{1}{221}$

19. a. 24   **c.** $\frac{1}{2}$ **20. a.** $\frac{1}{6.35(10)^{11}}$ **c.** 0   **21.** $\frac{26}{51}$

22. a. $\frac{29}{30}$ **c.** $\frac{7}{30}$ **23. a.** $\frac{3}{14}$ **c.** $\frac{15}{56}$ **24. a.** $\frac{1}{2}$

25. 4   **26. a.** $\frac{1}{40,425}$ **27.** 17%

28. a. $\frac{68}{271}$ **c.** $\frac{118}{271}$ **e.** $\frac{110}{271}$ **29.** $\frac{14}{27}$

Exercise Set 6.1, page 272

1.

Number of Rides	Tally	Frequency
1	|	1
2	||||	4
3	|||	3
4	|||	3
5	|	1
6	|	1
7	||	2
8	卌 |	6
9	||	2
10	|	1
		Total 24

2. a.

Interval (Age)	Tally	Frequency
4.5–14.5	|||	3
14.5–24.5	卌 卌 |||	13
24.5–34.5	|||	3
34.5–44.5	|||	3
44.5–54.5	||	2
54.5–64.5	卌	5
64.5–74.5	卌 ||	7
		Total 36

3. a. 14.5–19.5   **c.** 20   **e.** 16
19.5–24.5
24.5–29.5
29.5–34.5
34.5–39.5

5.

Interval (Grades)	Tally	Frequency
44–51	|||	3
52–59	卌	5
60–67	卌 卌	10
68–75	卌 卌 ||||	14
76–83	卌 卌 ||||	14
84–91	卌 卌 |	11
92–99	卌 ||||	9
		Total 66

6. a. $\frac{4}{15}$ **c.** $\frac{2}{3}$ **e.** 1

7. a.

x	1	2	3	4
P(x)	$\frac{1}{4}$	$\frac{1}{4}$	$\frac{1}{4}$	$\frac{1}{4}$

c.

x	1	2	3	4
P(x)	$\frac{1}{4}$	$\frac{1}{4}$	$\frac{1}{8}$	$\frac{3}{8}$

9.

x	P(x)
2	$\frac{1}{18}$
3	$\frac{2}{18}$
4	$\frac{3}{18}$
5	$\frac{3}{18}$
6	$\frac{3}{18}$
7	$\frac{3}{18}$
8	$\frac{2}{18}$
9	$\frac{1}{18}$

11.

Class	Frequency
42.5–50.5	2
50.5–58.5	5
58.5–66.5	9
66.5–74.5	13
74.5–82.5	13
82.5–90.5	10
90.5–98.5	8

13.

x	P(x)
46.5	$\frac{2}{60}$
54.5	$\frac{5}{60}$
62.5	$\frac{9}{60}$
70.5	$\frac{13}{60}$
78.5	$\frac{13}{60}$
86.5	$\frac{10}{60}$
94.5	$\frac{8}{60}$

15.

x	P(x)
0	.020
1	.080
2	.120
3	.250
4	.260
5	.190
6	.080

16.

Interval	x	P(x)
−.5–4.5	2	.06
4.5–9.5	7	.46
9.5–14.5	12	.30
14.5–19.5	17	.10
19.5–24.5	22	.04
24.5–29.5	27	.02
29.5–34.5	32	.02

a. .30   **c.** 1

17.

Class	Frequency
100–149	5
150–199	21
200–249	14
250–299	5
300–349	3
350–399	4
400–449	2
450–499	2
500–549	4
550–599	2

19.

Class Boundaries	Frequency
449.5–491.5	4
491.5–533.5	7
533.5–575.5	6
575.5–617.5	5
617.5–659.5	3

Exercise Set 6.2, page 282

1. a. 14%   **c.** 19%

2. a.

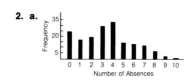

3. a. 24.5, 34.5, 44.5, 54.5, 64.5, 74.5, 84.5   **c.**

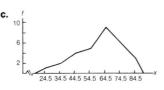

4. a.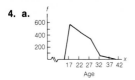
Age

5. a.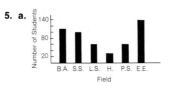
Field

c.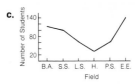
Field

6. a.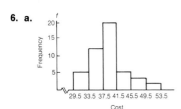
Cost

c.
Cost

7. a.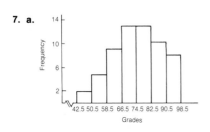
Grades

c.
Grades

9.

Class	Frequency
60–74	30
75–89	35
90–104	36
105–119	34
120–134	28

11.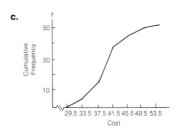

12. a. $2,200   **c.** $2,000

13.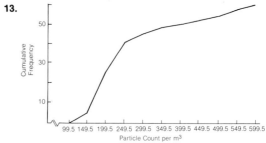
Particle Count per m³

14. a. 45% for Democratic candidates and 3% for Republican candidates; 16% for Democratic candidates and 30% for Republican candidates

   c. $5.94 million

Exercise Set 6.3, page 292

1. a. Mean = 6; median = 5; no mode   **3.** Mean = 27

   c. Mean = 34/9; median = 4; mode = 6

   e. Mean = 137/8; median = 19.5; mode = 23

4. a. 5, 6, 7, 8   **c.** 3, 4, 4, 5   **e.** 3, 6, 6, 9   **5.** 520

7. a. Median   **c.** Mode   **8. a.** Mean = 266.23 pounds; median = 254 pounds

9. a. Mean = 82.725   **c.** Mode = 80   **11. a.** 118.21

12. a. 223

13. 135. Hence, it is impossible if the tests are each worth 100 points.

15. a. 83.33

17. a. Mean salary   **c.** Median salary is more representative as the president's salary skews the mean.

19. a. No, he did not use the frequency.   **21. a.** 8.75 million gallons

23. Mean = 106.33; median = 101.5

Exercise Set 6.4, page 303

1. 3.82   **3.** 3.5 miles   **5. a.** 2.7¢   **7.** 5.31 minutes

9. 10.5 (that is, expect either 10 or 11)   **11. a.** $187.50   **c.** $2,933.33

13. a. $10   **c.** $12.63

14. a.

c. $4.46

| | Number in Stock | | | | | | | | | | |
	40	41	42	43	44	45	46	47	48	49	50
40	4.00	3.85	3.70	3.55	3.40	3.25	3.10	2.95	2.80	2.65	2.50
41	4.00	4.10	3.95	3.80	3.65	3.50	3.35	3.20	3.05	2.90	2.75
42	4.00	4.10	4.20	4.05	3.90	3.75	3.60	3.45	3.30	3.15	3.00
43	4.00	4.10	4.20	4.30	4.15	4.00	3.85	3.70	3.55	3.40	3.25
44	4.00	4.10	4.20	4.30	4.40	4.25	4.10	3.95	3.80	3.65	3.50
Demand 45	4.00	4.10	4.20	4.30	4.40	4.50	4.35	4.20	4.05	3.90	3.75
46	4.00	4.10	4.20	4.30	4.40	4.50	4.60	4.45	4.30	4.15	4.00
47	4.00	4.10	4.20	4.30	4.40	4.50	4.60	4.70	4.55	4.40	4.25
48	4.00	4.10	4.20	4.30	4.40	4.50	4.60	4.70	4.80	4.65	4.50
49	4.00	4.10	4.20	4.30	4.40	4.50	4.60	4.70	4.80	4.90	4.75
50	4.00	4.10	4.20	4.30	4.40	4.50	4.60	4.70	4.80	4.90	5.00

15. a.

| | Number of Cases in Stock | | | | |
	100	110	120	130	140
100	350	305	260	215	170
110	350	385	340	295	250
Demand 120	350	385	420	375	330
130	350	385	420	455	410
140	350	385	420	455	490

16. a.

Number of Crates	
4	E = $40
5	E = $48
6	E = $52
7	E = $48
8	E = $39

c.

	100	110	120	130	140
100	350	315	280	245	210
110	350	385	350	315	280
Demand 120	350	385	420	385	350
130	350	385	420	455	420
140	350	385	420	455	490

17. a.

Demands	Profit
10	$5,000
11	5,000
12	5,000
13	5,000
14	5,000

c.

Demands	Profit
10	$4,800
11	5,400
12	6,000
13	6,000
14	6,000

e.

Demands	Profit
10	$4,600
11	5,200
12	5,800
13	6,400
14	7,000

19. $207.51 **21.** $268

Exercise Set 6.5, page 311

1. a. Range $= 8$; $s_x^2 = 12$; $s_x = 2\sqrt{3}$ **c.** Range $= 12$; $s_x^2 = 20$; $s_x = 2\sqrt{5}$ **e.** Range $= 11$; $s_x^2 = 20$; $s_x = 2\sqrt{5}$

3. Standard deviation $= 5.40$ **5.** 14.15   **6. a.** 1   **c.** -2.9 **e.** 4

7. 12.58   **9.** 3.015   **10. a.** C

11. a. 23; 95.83%   **13.** 1975   **15.** 15.42

17. The potato peeling corps

Exercise Set 6.6, page 317

1. a. $\frac{16}{81}$ **c.** $\frac{8}{27}$ **e.** $\frac{1}{81}$ **3.** .054

5. a. .24   **c.** .000064   **7.** .205

9. $E(x) = 5$; $P = \frac{7}{128}$ **10. a.** .1115   **c.** .0017   **e.** .0001

11. Mean $= 5$; $P = .9087$; 1.55 standard deviations below the mean

12. a. .354   **c.** .47   **13.** $2.5(10)^{-12}$

15. .013, approximately 3   **17.** .738

Exercise Set 6.7, page 326

1. a. 0.4918   **c.** 0.4525   **2. a.** 0.7698   **c.** 0.9070

3. a. .0179   **c.** .5398   **e.** .0668   **g.** .9821   **i.** .0886   **k.** .5028

4. a. .3770

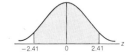

c. .9840

5. a. .9332   **c.** .8904   **6. a.** .8413   **c.** .3830   **e.** Approximately 1

7. a. .5000   **c.** .1587   **e.** .1587   **g.** .5403   **8. a.** .2611   **c.** .4838   **e.** .6826

9. a. 62.12%   **c.** 100%   **e.** 49.57%   **10. a.** .4772   **c.** .5000

11. a. 68.53%   **12. a.** 18.51%   **c.** 0.43%   **13.** 0.62%

15. a. .9525   **16. a.** 68.26%   **17.** 49.38%

19. .0228

Review Exercise Set 6.8, page 329

1. a. 18   **c.** 20   **e.** 8.11

3. Perhaps there are four employees with salaries of $10,000, $11,000, $12,000, and $13,000 and the president's salary is $104,000.

5. a.

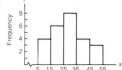

6. a. 75   **c.** 94   **e.** 15.27

7.

Interval	Frequency
30–34	1
35–39	0
40–44	0
45–49	0
50–54	1
55–59	0
60–64	5
65–69	0
70–74	3
75–79	4
80–84	3
85–89	2
90–94	4
95–99	1

a. 75.125   **c.** 60–64 modal class   **e.** 15.24

8. a.

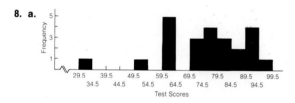

9.

11. 9

13. a.

D	200	225	250	275	300	325	350	375	400
P(D)	.045	.089	.240	.259	.227	.053	.040	.033	.013

c. $38.47

14. a. $\dfrac{1}{40,425}$ **c.** $\dfrac{304}{2695}$

15. A loss of $40.32

Chapter 7. Applications of Probability

Exercise Set 7.1, page 337

1. a. Yes   **c.** No   **e.** No   **g.** No   **i.** Yes

2. a. .3

3. a. .4   **c.** .4

5.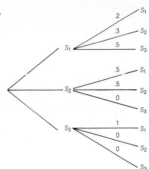

6. a. $\begin{bmatrix} \frac{9}{16} & \frac{7}{16} \\ \frac{7}{18} & \frac{11}{18} \end{bmatrix}$

7. a. $\frac{7}{16}$ **c.** $\frac{109}{216}$

8. a. 0 **c.** .16

9. $p_{11}(2) = .60$
$p_{12}(2) = .40$
$p_{21}(2) = .35$
$p_{22}(2) = .65$

$$A^2 = \begin{bmatrix} .60 & .40 \\ .35 & .65 \end{bmatrix}$$

11. 0

13. It is equally likely to be in either state 2 or state 4.

14. a. .2 **c.** .350

15. a.

	Use x	Don't use x
Use x	.90	.10
Don't use x	.40	.60

c. .15

16. a.

	In	Out
In	.80	.20
Out	.10	.90

c. .83

17. a. 0 **c.** $\frac{1}{2}$

18. a. $\begin{bmatrix} 0 & .90 & .10 \\ 1 & .20 & .80 \end{bmatrix}$

19. a. .10 **c.** .03665

20. a. .2 **c.** .19

Exercise Set 7.2, page 345

1. a. [1500 1500] **c.** [.46 .54] **e.** [.61 .39]

2. a. Not regular **c.** Not regular **e.** Regular **g.** Not regular **i.** Not regular
k. Regular **m.** Regular

3. e. $[\frac{3}{5} \quad \frac{2}{5}]$; $\begin{bmatrix} \frac{3}{5} & \frac{2}{5} \\ \frac{3}{5} & \frac{2}{5} \end{bmatrix}$ **k.** $[\frac{9}{13} \quad \frac{4}{13}]$; $\begin{bmatrix} \frac{9}{13} & \frac{4}{13} \\ \frac{9}{13} & \frac{4}{13} \end{bmatrix}$ **m.** $[\frac{1}{3} \quad \frac{4}{9} \quad \frac{2}{9}]$; $\begin{bmatrix} \frac{1}{3} & \frac{4}{9} & \frac{2}{9} \\ \frac{1}{3} & \frac{4}{9} & \frac{2}{9} \\ \frac{1}{3} & \frac{4}{9} & \frac{2}{9} \end{bmatrix}$

5. a. [120 0]; $\begin{bmatrix} 1 & 0 \\ 1 & 0 \end{bmatrix}$ **c.** $[\frac{3400}{19} \quad \frac{3000}{19} \quad \frac{5000}{19}]$; $\begin{bmatrix} \frac{17}{57} & \frac{5}{19} & \frac{25}{57} \\ \frac{17}{57} & \frac{5}{19} & \frac{25}{57} \\ \frac{17}{57} & \frac{5}{19} & \frac{25}{57} \end{bmatrix}$

6. a. $\begin{bmatrix} \frac{4}{7} & \frac{3}{7} \\ \frac{4}{7} & \frac{3}{7} \end{bmatrix}$ **c.** $\begin{bmatrix} \frac{17}{57} & \frac{5}{19} & \frac{25}{57} \\ \frac{17}{57} & \frac{5}{19} & \frac{25}{57} \\ \frac{17}{57} & \frac{5}{19} & \frac{25}{57} \end{bmatrix}$

7. $A^2 = \begin{bmatrix} .65 & .35 \\ .40 & .60 \end{bmatrix}$, $A^3 = \begin{bmatrix} .475 & .525 \\ .60 & .40 \end{bmatrix}$, $A^4 = \begin{bmatrix} .5625 & .4375 \\ .50 & .50 \end{bmatrix}$, $A^5 = \begin{bmatrix} .51875 & .48125 \\ .55 & .45 \end{bmatrix}$; guess: [.50   .50]

8. a. State 2   **c.** State 3

9. a. Star $\frac{9}{20}$, Times $\frac{11}{20}$ **c.** Star $\frac{3}{7}$, Times $\frac{4}{7}$

10. $\begin{bmatrix} .75 & .20 & .05 \\ .30 & .50 & .20 \\ .30 & .10 & .60 \end{bmatrix}$ **a.** $[\frac{33}{80} \quad \frac{18}{80} \quad \frac{29}{80}]$ **c.** $[\frac{6}{11} \quad \frac{17}{66} \quad \frac{13}{66}]$

11. a. $[\frac{57}{160} \quad \frac{42}{160} \quad \frac{61}{160}]$ **c.** $[\frac{6}{11} \quad \frac{17}{66} \quad \frac{13}{66}]$

13. $[\frac{1}{5} \quad \frac{3}{5} \quad \frac{1}{5}]$. The probabilities eventually become $\frac{1}{5}$ of the offspring recessive, $\frac{3}{5}$ hybrid, and $\frac{1}{5}$ dominant.

15. The long-term prediction will be 80,000 members for party I, 74,286 members for III, and 45,714 members for II.

Exercise Set 7.3, page 352

1. a. [0   1   0]; absorbing   **c.** [0   1   0]; absorbing   **e.** [1   0   0   0] and [0   1   0   0]; absorbing

g. [1   0   0   0]; absorbing   **i.** [0   0   1   0]; absorbing

2. a.
$$\begin{array}{c} \\ S_2 \\ S_1 \\ S_3 \end{array} \begin{array}{ccc} S_2 & S_1 & S_3 \\ \begin{bmatrix} 1 & 0 & 0 \\ .5 & .1 & .4 \\ .4 & .6 & 0 \end{bmatrix} \end{array}$$

c.
$$\begin{array}{c} \\ S_2 \\ S_1 \\ S_3 \end{array} \begin{array}{ccc} S_2 & S_1 & S_3 \\ \begin{bmatrix} 1 & 0 & 0 \\ .6 & 0 & .4 \\ \frac{1}{3} & \frac{1}{3} & \frac{1}{3} \end{bmatrix} \end{array}$$

e.
$$\begin{array}{c} \\ S_1 \\ S_2 \\ S_3 \\ S_4 \end{array} \begin{array}{cccc} S_1 & S_2 & S_3 & S_4 \\ \begin{bmatrix} 1 & 0 & 0 & 0 \\ 0 & 1 & 0 & 0 \\ \frac{2}{5} & 0 & \frac{3}{5} & 0 \\ 0 & \frac{1}{3} & \frac{1}{3} & \frac{1}{3} \end{bmatrix} \end{array}$$

g.
$$\begin{array}{c} \\ S_1 \\ S_2 \\ S_3 \\ S_4 \end{array} \begin{array}{cccc} S_1 & S_2 & S_3 & S_4 \\ \begin{bmatrix} 1 & 0 & 0 & 0 \\ .1 & .1 & .7 & .1 \\ 0 & 1 & 0 & 0 \\ .6 & .3 & .1 & 0 \end{bmatrix} \end{array}$$

i.
$$\begin{array}{c} \\ S_3 \\ S_1 \\ S_2 \\ S_4 \end{array} \begin{array}{cccc} S_3 & S_1 & S_2 & S_4 \\ \begin{bmatrix} 1 & 0 & 0 & 0 \\ .2 & .4 & .4 & 0 \\ 0 & .1 & .6 & .3 \\ 0 & .2 & .1 & .7 \end{bmatrix} \end{array}$$

3. See answer 2.

4. a. $\begin{bmatrix} \frac{50}{33} & \frac{20}{33} \\ \frac{10}{11} & \frac{15}{11} \end{bmatrix}$ **c.** $\begin{bmatrix} \frac{5}{4} & \frac{3}{4} \\ \frac{5}{8} & \frac{15}{8} \end{bmatrix}$ **e.** $\begin{bmatrix} \frac{5}{2} & 0 \\ \frac{5}{4} & \frac{3}{2} \end{bmatrix}$ **g.** $\begin{bmatrix} \frac{25}{4} & \frac{71}{16} & \frac{5}{8} \\ \frac{25}{4} & \frac{87}{16} & \frac{5}{8} \\ \frac{5}{2} & \frac{15}{8} & \frac{5}{4} \end{bmatrix}$ **i.** $\begin{bmatrix} 5 & \frac{20}{3} & \frac{20}{3} \\ 5 & 10 & 10 \\ 5 & \frac{70}{9} & \frac{100}{9} \end{bmatrix}$

5. a. Expected transitions $= \frac{70}{33}$ (S_1).
Expected transitions $= \frac{25}{11}$ (S_3).
c. Expected transitions $= 2$ (S_1).
Expected transitions $= \frac{5}{2}$ (S_3).
e. Expected transitions $= \frac{5}{2}$ (S_3).
Expected transitions $= \frac{11}{4}$ (S_4).
g. Expected transitions $= \frac{181}{16}$ (S_2).
Expected transitions $= \frac{197}{16}$ (S_3).
Expected transitions $= \frac{45}{8}$ (S_4).
i. Expected transitions $= \frac{55}{3}$ (S_1).
Expected transitions $= 25$ (S_2).
Expected transitions $= \frac{215}{9}$ (S_4).

6. a. $\frac{50}{33}$ is the expected number of times the system in state 1 will be in state 1. $\frac{20}{33}$ is the expected number of times the system in state 1 will be in state 3. $\frac{10}{11}$ is the expected number of times the system in state 3 will be in state 1. $\frac{15}{11}$ is the expected number of times the system in state 3 will be in state 3.
c. $\frac{5}{4}$ is the expected number of times the system in state 1 will be in state 1. $\frac{3}{4}$ is the expected number of times the system in state 1 will be in state 3. $\frac{5}{8}$ is the expected number of times the system in state 3 will be in state 1. $\frac{15}{8}$ is the expected number of times the system in state 3 will be in state 3.

e. $\frac{5}{2}$ is the expected number of times the system in state 3 will be in state 3. 0 is the expected number of times the system in state 3 will be in state 4. $\frac{5}{4}$ is the expected number of times the system in state 4 will be in state 3. $\frac{3}{2}$ is the expected number of times the system in state 4 will be in state 4.

g. $\frac{25}{4}$ is the expected number of times the system in state 2 will be in state 2. $\frac{71}{16}$ is the expected number of times the system in state 2 will be in state 3. $\frac{5}{8}$ is the expected number of times the system in state 2 will be in state 4. $\frac{25}{4}$ is the expected number of times the system in state 3 will be in state 2. $\frac{87}{16}$ is the expected number of times the system in state 3 will be in state 3. $\frac{5}{8}$ is the expected number of times the system in state 3 will be in state 4. $\frac{5}{2}$ is the expected number of times the system in state 4 will be in state 2. $\frac{15}{8}$ is the expected number of times the system in state 4 will be in state 3. $\frac{5}{4}$ is the expected number of times the system in state 4 will be in state 4.

i. 5 is the expected number of times the system in state 1 will be in state 1.
$\frac{20}{3}$ is the expected number of times the system in state 1 will be in state 2.
$\frac{20}{3}$ is the expected number of times the system in state 1 will be in state 4.
5 is the expected number of times the system in state 2 will be in state 1.
10 is the expected number of times the system in state 2 will be in state 2.
10 is the expected number of times the system in state 2 will be in state 4.
5 is the expected number of times the system in state 4 will be in state 1.
$\frac{70}{9}$ is the expected number of times the system in state 4 will be in state 2.
$\frac{100}{9}$ is the expected number of times the system in state 4 will be in state 4.

7. a. Yes **c.** 26 **e.** 33

9. a.

$$\begin{array}{c} & \begin{array}{cccc} R_1 & R_2 & R_3 & R_4 \end{array} \\ \begin{array}{c} R_1 \\ R_2 \\ R_3 \\ R_4 \end{array} & \left[\begin{array}{cccc} 0 & \frac{2}{3} & \frac{1}{3} & 0 \\ \frac{2}{3} & 0 & \frac{1}{3} & 0 \\ \frac{1}{3} & \frac{1}{3} & 0 & \frac{1}{3} \\ 0 & 0 & 0 & 1 \end{array} \right] \end{array}$$

c. 12 **e.** 9

Exercise Set 7.4, page 360

1. a. 0
c. 3 in second row, first column; or 3 in first column, third row; or 3 in second column, third row
e. 4 in third row, third column

2. .a. 0; [1 0] and $\begin{bmatrix} 1 \\ 0 \end{bmatrix}$

c. 3; [0 1 0] and $\begin{bmatrix} 1 \\ 0 \\ 0 \end{bmatrix}$; or [0 0 1] and $\begin{bmatrix} 1 \\ 0 \\ 0 \end{bmatrix}$; or [0 0 1] and $\begin{bmatrix} 0 \\ 1 \\ 0 \end{bmatrix}$

e. 4; [0 0 1] and $\begin{bmatrix} 0 \\ 0 \\ 1 \end{bmatrix}$

3. a. Value $= 0$; fair; strategies $=$ [1 0] and $\begin{bmatrix} 1 \\ 0 \end{bmatrix}$ **c.** Value $= 0$; fair; strategies $=$ [0 1] and $\begin{bmatrix} 0 \\ 1 \end{bmatrix}$

e. Value $= 0$; fair; strategies $=$ [1 0] and $\begin{bmatrix} 0 \\ 1 \end{bmatrix}$ **g.** Value $= 0$; fair; strategies $=$ [0 1] and $\begin{bmatrix} 1 \\ 0 \end{bmatrix}$

i. Value $= 0$; fair; strategies $=$ [1 0 0] and $\begin{bmatrix} 1 \\ 0 \\ 0 \end{bmatrix}$ **k.** Value $= -1$; not fair; strategies $=$ [1 0] and $\begin{bmatrix} 0 \\ 1 \\ 0 \end{bmatrix}$

4. a. $\frac{47}{9}$ **c.** $\frac{7}{4}$ **5.** x $= 0$, 1, or 2

6. There are five possible conditions for x in relation to y and z:

Case 1: x > y and z
In this case, there are three possible conditions for y and z: y > z, y < z, or y = z. If y > z, then y is the saddle point; if y < z, then z is the saddle point. If y = z, then they both are saddle points. In any case, the game is strictly determined.

Case 2: x < y and z
Again, either y < z, y > z, or y = z. In any of these situations, x is the saddle point, and, hence, the game is strictly determined.

Case 3: x = y
In this case, either y > z, y < z, or y = z. If y > z, then both y and x (in the a_{11} position) are saddle points. If y < z, then x (in both positions) is the saddle point. If y = z, then all four positions are saddle points. In any case the game is strictly determined.

Case 4: x = z
By the same argument as case 3, the game is strictly determined.

Case 5: x > y and x < z   or   x < y and x > z.
If x > y but x < z, then x is the saddle point. If x > z but x < y, then x is the saddle point. Hence, the game is strictly determined.

7. $\begin{bmatrix} 0 & 1 & 2 \\ -4 & -1 & 6 \\ ⓶ & ⓶ & 4 \end{bmatrix}$

9. The Hats

$$\begin{array}{cc} & \text{The Wigs} \\ & \begin{array}{cc} \text{III} & \text{IV} \end{array} \\ \begin{array}{c} \text{I} \\ \text{II} \end{array} & \begin{bmatrix} 300 & -100 \\ 400 & -150 \end{bmatrix} \end{array}$$

Value $= -100$; strategies $= \begin{bmatrix} 1 & 0 \end{bmatrix}$ and $\begin{bmatrix} 0 \\ 1 \end{bmatrix}$

Exercise Set 7.5, page 367

1. a. Value $= \frac{17}{11}$; strategies $= \begin{bmatrix} \frac{9}{11} & \frac{2}{11} \end{bmatrix}$ and $\begin{bmatrix} \frac{8}{11} \\ \frac{3}{11} \end{bmatrix}$ **c.** Strictly determined; value $= 3$; strategies $= \begin{bmatrix} 1 & 0 \end{bmatrix}$ and $\begin{bmatrix} 1 \\ 0 \end{bmatrix}$

e. Value $= \frac{68}{15}$; strategies $= \begin{bmatrix} \frac{2}{15} & \frac{13}{15} \end{bmatrix}$ and $\begin{bmatrix} \frac{11}{15} \\ \frac{4}{15} \end{bmatrix}$

2. a. Value $= \frac{44}{7}$; strategies $= \begin{bmatrix} \frac{1}{7} & \frac{6}{7} & 0 \end{bmatrix}$ and $\begin{bmatrix} 0 \\ \frac{6}{7} \\ \frac{1}{7} \end{bmatrix}$

c. Value $= -68/-14 = \frac{34}{7}$; strategies $= \begin{bmatrix} 0 & 0 & \frac{11}{14} & \frac{3}{14} \end{bmatrix}$ and $\begin{bmatrix} \frac{5}{7} \\ 0 \\ 0 \\ \frac{2}{7} \end{bmatrix}$

3. a. Value $= \frac{23}{10}$; strategies $= \begin{bmatrix} 0 & \frac{7}{10} & \frac{3}{10} \end{bmatrix}$ and $\begin{bmatrix} \frac{1}{10} \\ \frac{9}{10} \\ 0 \end{bmatrix}$ **c.** Value $= \frac{4}{6} = \frac{2}{3}$; strategies $= \begin{bmatrix} \frac{5}{6} & \frac{1}{6} & 0 \end{bmatrix}$ and $\begin{bmatrix} \frac{2}{3} \\ \frac{1}{3} \\ 0 \end{bmatrix}$

e. Value $= -1$; strategies $= \begin{bmatrix} 1 & 0 \end{bmatrix}$ and $\begin{bmatrix} 1 \\ 0 \\ 0 \\ 0 \end{bmatrix}$

4. a. Value = $\frac{83}{11}$; strategies = $[\frac{9}{11} \quad \frac{2}{11}]$ and $\begin{bmatrix} \frac{8}{11} \\ \frac{3}{11} \end{bmatrix}$ **c.** Value = 4; strategies = $[1 \quad 0]$ and $\begin{bmatrix} 1 \\ 0 \end{bmatrix}$

e. Value = $\frac{158}{15}$; strategies = $[\frac{2}{15} \quad \frac{13}{15}]$ and $\begin{bmatrix} \frac{11}{15} \\ \frac{4}{15} \end{bmatrix}$

5. a. Value = $\frac{51}{11}$; strategies = $[\frac{9}{11} \quad \frac{2}{11}]$ and $\begin{bmatrix} \frac{8}{11} \\ \frac{3}{11} \end{bmatrix}$ **c.** Value = 9; strategies = $[1 \quad 0]$ and $\begin{bmatrix} 1 \\ 0 \end{bmatrix}$

e. Value = $\frac{68}{5}$; strategies = $[\frac{2}{15} \quad \frac{13}{15}]$ and $\begin{bmatrix} \frac{11}{15} \\ \frac{4}{15} \end{bmatrix}$

7. Katie
$$\begin{array}{c} \text{Jeannie} \\ \begin{array}{cc} 1 & 2 \end{array} \\ \begin{array}{c} 1 \\ 2 \end{array} \begin{bmatrix} -2 & 3 \\ 3 & -4 \end{bmatrix} \end{array}$$
; value = $\frac{1}{12}$; strategies = $[\frac{7}{12} \quad \frac{5}{12}]$ and $\begin{bmatrix} \frac{7}{12} \\ \frac{5}{12} \end{bmatrix}$

9. Value = 2; strategies = $[1 \quad 0]$ and $\begin{bmatrix} 1 \\ 0 \end{bmatrix}$

11. Republicans promise
$$\begin{array}{c} \text{Democrats} \\ \text{promise} \\ \begin{array}{cc} A & B \end{array} \\ \begin{array}{c} \text{I} \\ \text{II} \end{array} \begin{bmatrix} 1800 & -1200 \\ 600 & 700 \end{bmatrix} \end{array}$$
; value = $\frac{19,800}{31}$; strategies = $[\frac{1}{31} \quad \frac{30}{31}]$ and $\begin{bmatrix} \frac{19}{31} \\ \frac{12}{31} \end{bmatrix}$

Exercise Set 7.6, page 372

1. a. Value = $\frac{5}{3}$; strategies = $[\frac{7}{12} \quad \frac{5}{12} \quad 0]$ and $\begin{bmatrix} \frac{1}{3} \\ \frac{2}{3} \end{bmatrix}$ **c.** Value = 1; strategies = $[\frac{1}{2} \quad \frac{1}{2}]$ and $\begin{bmatrix} \frac{1}{2} \\ \frac{1}{2} \\ 0 \end{bmatrix}$

e. Value = $2\frac{1}{2}$; strategies = $[\frac{1}{4} \quad \frac{3}{4}]$ and $\begin{bmatrix} \frac{1}{2} \\ 0 \\ \frac{1}{2} \end{bmatrix}$

g. Reduced matrix = $\begin{bmatrix} -2 & 5 & 0 \\ 2 & -3 & -2 \end{bmatrix}$; value = $-\frac{2}{3}$; strategies = $[\frac{2}{3} \quad \frac{1}{3}]$ and $\begin{bmatrix} \frac{1}{3} \\ 0 \\ \frac{2}{3} \\ 0 \end{bmatrix}$

2. a. Strategies = $[\frac{5}{9} \quad \frac{4}{9} \quad 0]$ and $\begin{bmatrix} 0 \\ \frac{7}{9} \\ \frac{2}{9} \end{bmatrix}$; value = $\frac{1}{9}$ **c.** Strategies = $[0 \quad \frac{1}{2} \quad \frac{1}{2} \quad 0]$ and $\begin{bmatrix} 0 \\ \frac{1}{2} \\ \frac{1}{2} \\ 0 \end{bmatrix}$; value = $\frac{1}{2}$

3. $\begin{bmatrix} \dfrac{m}{n+m-l} & \dfrac{m-l}{n+m-l} \end{bmatrix}$; $\begin{bmatrix} \dfrac{m}{n+m-l} \\ \dfrac{m-l}{n+m-l} \end{bmatrix}$

5. They are identical. **7.** Value = 2; strategies = $[0 \quad 0 \quad 1]$ and $\begin{bmatrix} 0 \\ 1 \end{bmatrix}$

9. Value = $\frac{13}{7}$; strategies = $[\frac{2}{7} \quad 0 \quad \frac{5}{7}]$ and $\begin{bmatrix} \frac{3}{7} \\ \frac{4}{7} \end{bmatrix}$

1. a. Value $= \frac{5}{3}$; strategies $= [\frac{7}{12} \quad \frac{5}{12} \quad 0]$ and $\begin{bmatrix} \frac{1}{3} \\ \frac{1}{3} \\ \frac{2}{3} \end{bmatrix}$ **c.** Value $= 1$; strategies $= [\frac{1}{2} \quad \frac{1}{2}]$ and $\begin{bmatrix} \frac{1}{2} \\ \frac{1}{2} \\ 0 \end{bmatrix}$

e. Value $= 2\frac{1}{2}$; strategies $= [\frac{1}{4} \quad \frac{3}{4}]$ and $\begin{bmatrix} \frac{1}{2} \\ 0 \\ \frac{1}{2} \end{bmatrix}$ **g.** Value $= -\frac{2}{3}$; strategies $= [\frac{2}{3} \quad \frac{1}{3}]$ and $\begin{bmatrix} \frac{1}{3} \\ 0 \\ \frac{2}{3} \\ 0 \end{bmatrix}$

2. a. Strategies $= [\frac{5}{9} \quad \frac{4}{9} \quad 0]$ and $\begin{bmatrix} 0 \\ \frac{7}{9} \\ \frac{2}{9} \end{bmatrix}$ **c.** Strategies $= [0 \quad \frac{1}{2} \quad \frac{1}{2} \quad 0]$ and $\begin{bmatrix} 0 \\ \frac{1}{2} \\ \frac{1}{2} \\ 0 \end{bmatrix}$

3. a. Value $= \frac{1}{3}$; strategies $= [\frac{2}{3} \quad \frac{1}{3} \quad 0]$ and $\begin{bmatrix} \frac{1}{3} \\ \frac{2}{3} \\ 0 \end{bmatrix}$ **c.** Value $= \frac{11}{7}$; strategies $= [\frac{2}{7} \quad 0 \quad \frac{5}{7}]$ and $\begin{bmatrix} \frac{5}{7} \\ \frac{2}{7} \\ 0 \end{bmatrix}$

5. Value $= \frac{7}{5}$; strategies $= [\frac{2}{5} \quad \frac{3}{5}]$ and $\begin{bmatrix} \frac{4}{5} \\ \frac{1}{5} \\ 0 \end{bmatrix}$ **7.** Value $= \frac{19}{40}$; strategies $= [\frac{5}{8} \quad 0 \quad \frac{3}{8}]$ and $\begin{bmatrix} \frac{3}{4} \\ \frac{1}{4} \end{bmatrix}$

1. $\frac{1}{3}$

2. a. Strategies $= [0 \quad 1]$ and $\begin{bmatrix} 1 \\ 0 \end{bmatrix}$; value $= 1$ **c.** Strategies $= [0 \quad 1]$ and $\begin{bmatrix} 0 \\ 1 \end{bmatrix}$; value $= -2$

e. Strategies $= [0 \quad 1 \quad 0]$ and $\begin{bmatrix} 0 \\ 1 \\ 0 \end{bmatrix}$; value $= 5$ **g.** Strategies $= [\frac{4}{5} \quad \frac{1}{5}]$ and $\begin{bmatrix} 0 \\ \frac{2}{5} \\ \frac{3}{5} \end{bmatrix}$: value $= -\frac{3}{5}$

i. Strategies $= [0 \quad 0 \quad 1]$ and $\begin{bmatrix} 0 \\ 1 \end{bmatrix}$; value $= 4$

3. a. $[\frac{19}{72} \quad \frac{25}{72} \quad \frac{28}{72}]$ **5.** The sum of elements in the last row exceeds 1.

7. a. $[\frac{5}{7} \quad \frac{2}{7}]$ **c.** $[0 \quad 0 \quad 1]$ **9. a.** It is regular. **c.** $\begin{bmatrix} \frac{8}{15} & \frac{2}{15} & \frac{5}{15} \\ \frac{8}{15} & \frac{2}{15} & \frac{5}{15} \\ \frac{8}{15} & \frac{2}{15} & \frac{5}{15} \end{bmatrix}$

11. 7 **13. a.** [.376 .301 .323] **15.** 3

Chapter 8. Functions and Graphs

1. a. $\sqrt{7}$ **c.** $\sqrt{5y}$ **e.** $\sqrt[3]{xy}$ **g.** $\sqrt[5]{x^3}$

2. a. $x^{4/3}$ **c.** $x^{1/2}y^{3/4}$ **3. a.** -3 **c.** 10 **e.** x^4y^2 **g.** $3x^2y$

4. a. $24x^2y^3z^5$ **c.** $\dfrac{5b}{a}$ **e.** $\dfrac{az^4}{3xy^2}$ **5. a.** 3 **c.** 4 **e.** 16 **g.** 5

6. a. x^7 **c.** $x^{1/2}$ **7. a.** $\dfrac{1}{x^5y^3z^3}$ **c.** 3 **e.** a^4y^5

8. a. $2x^2\sqrt{2x}$ **c.** $xy\sqrt[3]{2y}$ **9. a.** $\dfrac{\sqrt{2}}{2}$ **c.** $\dfrac{2\sqrt{2x}}{x}$ **e.** $\dfrac{2\sqrt[3]{3}}{3}$ **g.** $\dfrac{\sqrt{xy}}{y}$

10. a. $2xy^2\sqrt{2xy}$ **c.** $2a\sqrt{3a}$ **e.** $\dfrac{\sqrt[3]{4x}}{2}$

11. a. $\dfrac{3^{5/3}}{2^{1/3}5^{4/3}}$ **c.** $\dfrac{4x}{y^{7/2}}$ **e.** $\dfrac{2^{1/2}+1}{2}$ **g.** $a(2)^{1/2}$

12. a. \$8,000   **c.** \$5,120; \$1,677.72

13. \$500,000; \$250,000; \$125,000; \$4,487.10; \$2.577.16; \$850.15

15. 100, 60.6531; 36.7879; 13.5335; 4.9787; 1.8316; 0.6738

Exercise Set 8.2, page 394

1. a. Function   **c.** Function   **e.** Function   **g.** Function   **i.** Not a function

2. a. Doesn't define a function   **c.** Doesn't define a function   **e.** Defines a function
g. Doesn't define a function

3. $f(-2) = -4; f(1) = -1; f(0) - f(3) = -21$

5. a. Defines a function   **c.** Doesn't define a function   **e.** Doesn't define a function

7. $f(-2) \cdot f(2) = 0; f(z) = (z + 2)(z - 1); f(3w) = (3w + 2)(3w - 1); f(t + 3) = (t + 5)(t + 2)$

9. $x \le 3$ **11.** $x < 0; 0 < x < 2; x > 2$ **13.** $x \le -4$ or $x \ge 0$

14. a. 6.091   **c.** -2 **e.** $6t + 6 - \frac{3}{2t}$

15. a. Domain $= \{x \mid x \in \text{real numbers}\}$ **c.** Domain $= \{x \mid x \in \text{real numbers} \ge -1\}$
e. Domain $= \{x \mid x \in \text{real numbers} \ge 0\}$

17. a. $h[l(x)] = \dfrac{2x^2 - 7}{2x^2 - 8}$ **c.** The domain is all real x except for $x = \pm 2$.

19. a. No

21. a. $R(x) = (400 + 2x)(200 - x)$ **c.** \$79,950; 79,800; 79,200; 76,800; 60,000

22. a. $D = 12.5$ **c.** $D = 0$ **23. a.** 2.5; 7.5   **c.** $x = 6$ **e.** $x > 6$

24. a. D(x) and S(x)   **c.** Equilibrium supply and demand are each 100 at $x = 40$.

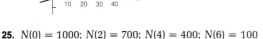

25. $N(0) = 1000; N(2) = 700; N(4) = 400; N(6) = 100$ **27.** $N(5) = 165; N(7) = 165; N(15) = 245$
1986 has the smallest class.

Exercise Set 8.3, page 401

1. $3x^2 - 10x + 9$ **3.** $-12x^2 + 9x - 25$ **5.** $6x^3 + 12x^2$ **7.** $x^2 - x - 6$

9. $3x^2 + 5x - 2$ **11.** $24x^2 + 44x - 28$ **13.** $3x^2(y - 4)$ **15.** $(x + 5)(x + 5)$

17. $(2x - 3)(2x + 3)$ **19.** $(x + 5)(x - 2)$ **21.** $(x + 3)(y - 1)$ **23.** $9xy - 5y^2$

25. $3x^3 - 7x^2 + 6x - 8$ **27.** $2x^4 + 2x$ **29.** $x(x - 4)(x + 2)$ **31.** $y^2(3 + x)(y - 1)$

33. $x(3 + y)(x - 1)$ **35.** $3y^2(x^2 - 4y)(x^2 + 4y)$ **37.** $4x^2 - 3x - 15$

39. $6x^4 - 3x^3 + 9x^2 - 13x - 22$ **41.** $2y(3x + 7y)(x - 2y)$ **43.** $(3x + y)(x^2 + y^2)$

45. $A = P(1 + rt)$ **47.** $V = 20,000\left(\dfrac{1}{10,000} - x^2\right)$

Exercise Set 8.4, page 410

1. a. $x = -\frac{1}{2}$ **c.** $x = -1$ **e.** $x = -\frac{3}{2}$ **g.** $x = \frac{7}{12}$ **i.** $x = \frac{5}{16}$ **k.** $x = -\frac{3}{2}$

2. a. Minimum $= (-\frac{1}{2}, -\frac{25}{4})$ **c.** Maximum $= (-1, 25)$ **e.** Minimum $= (-\frac{3}{2}, -\frac{75}{4})$
   g. Maximum $= (\frac{7}{12}, \frac{121}{24})$ **i.** Maximum $= (\frac{5}{16}, \frac{121}{32})$ **k.** Maximum $= (-\frac{3}{2}, \frac{29}{4})$

3. a. Upward **c.** Downward **e.** Upward **g.** Downward **i.** Downward **k.** Downward

4. a.

x	−2	−1	0	1	2
y	−4	−6	−6	−4	0

c.

x	−2	−1	0	1	2
y	24	25	24	21	16

e.

x	−2	−1	0	1	2
y	−18	−18	−12	0	18

g.

x	−2	−1	0	1	2
y	−35	−10	3	4	−7

i.

x	−2	−1	0	1	2
y	−39	−10	3	0	−19

k.

x	−2	−1	0	1	2
y	7	7	5	1	−5

5. a.

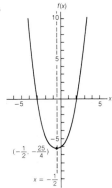

c.

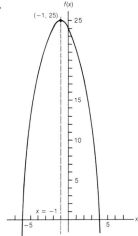

e.

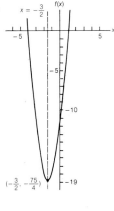

g.

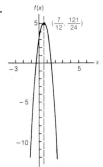

i.

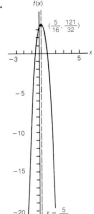

k.

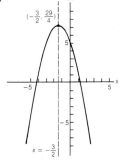

7. $x(3x - 7)$; $\{0, \frac{7}{3}\}$ **9.** $\{\pm 3\}$ **11.** $\{5, -3\}$ **13.** $\{-6, 4\}$

15. $\{-2, 7\}$ **17.** $\{3, -1\}$ **19.** $x = 2 \pm 2\sqrt{2}$ **21.** $x = -\frac{1}{3}$; $x = 2$

23. No real roots   **25.** No real roots   **27.** No real roots   **29.** $\{\frac{1}{3}, \frac{1}{2}\}$

31. $\{\frac{1}{3}, 5\}$ **33.** $\{-\frac{1}{2}, 1\}$ **35.** $x = \dfrac{7 \pm \sqrt{69}}{10}$ **37.** $\{\ \}$

38. a. No   **c.** No   **39. a.** No   **c.** No   **40. a.** No   **c.** No   **41.** $\{6.34, -0.73\}$

43. 7 days before payday, and 8 days after   **44. a.** $P(5) = 25$ **c.** \$153.13

45. $x = 3$; minimum cost $= \$17.00$

47. Equilibrium point $= (\frac{3}{2}, 6\frac{1}{4})$; demand $= 1500$ items

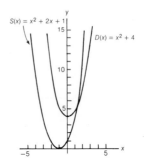

49.

Break-even point $= (49, 4899)$

51. $\{0, 100\}$

53.

1. a.

c.

e.

2. a. Vertical, $x = 0$; horizontal, $y = 0$ **c.** Vertical, $x = -4$; horizontal, $y = 0$
   e. Vertical, $x = 3$; horizontal, $y = 2$ **g.** Vertical, $x = \pm 2$; horizontal, $y = 1$
   i. Vertical, $x = 4$, $x = -1$; horizontal, $y = 1$

3. a.

c.

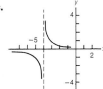

e.

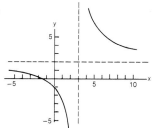

4. a. $x = 0, 1, -2$
  $x < -2,$ y is $-$
  $-2 < x < 0,$ y is $+$
  $0 < x < 1,$ y is $-$
  $x > 1,$ y is $+$

c. $x = 0, 4$
  $x < 0,$ y is $-$
  $0 < x < 4,$ y is $-$
  $x > 4,$ y is $+$

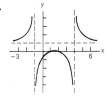

e. $x = 0, -1, \pm 2$
  $x < -2,$ y is $+$
  $-2 < x < -1,$ y is $-$
  $-1 < x < 0,$ y is $+$
  $0 < x < 2,$ y is $-$
  $x > 2,$ y is $+$

5. g.

i.

7. a. $x = 0, \frac{2}{3}, -1$
  $x < -1,$ y is $+$
  $-1 < x < 0,$ y is $-$
  $0 < x < \frac{2}{3},$ y is $-$
  $\frac{2}{3} < x,$ y is $+$

c. $x = -1, 1, 3$
  $x < -1,$ y is $-$
  $-1 < x < 1,$ y is $+$
  $1 < x < 3,$ y is $-$
  $3 < x,$ y is $+$

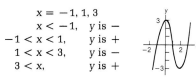

11.

13.

15. After the twentieth year.

Review Exercise Set 8.6, page 420

1. a. Function   **c.** Not a function

2. a. 7   **c.** 4   **e.** 3.92

3. a. $6xy^2z$ **c.** $15x^2 - 12$ **e.** $\dfrac{y}{x^4}$

4. a. $3(xy - 4z)(xy + 4z)$ **c.** $2y(x - 3y)(x + 2y)$

5. $\dfrac{x\sqrt{2x}}{2}$

7. a. $x = 4, -1$

8. a. $x = \frac{2}{3}, -1$

9. a. $x = \frac{1}{2}$ **c.** $x = \frac{5}{2}$ **e.** $x = 2$ **g.** $x = \frac{5}{4}$

10. a. $(\frac{1}{2}, -\frac{25}{4})$ **c.** $(\frac{5}{2}, -\frac{49}{4})$ **e.** $(2, 16)$ **g.** $(\frac{5}{4}, -\frac{41}{8})$

11. a. Upward   **c.** Upward   **e.** Downward   **g.** Upward

12. a.

x	−3	−2	−1	0	1	2	3
y	6	0	−4	−6	−6	−4	0

c.

x	−1	0	1	2	3	4	5	6
y	0	−6	−10	−12	−12	−10	−6	0

e.

x	−2	−1	0	1	2	3	4	5	6
y	0	7	12	15	16	15	12	7	0

g.

x	−1	0	1	2	3	4
y	5	−2	−5	−4	1	10

13. a.

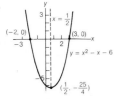

c.

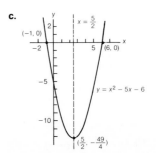

e.

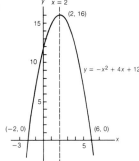

g.

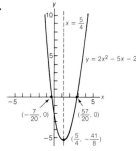

14. a.

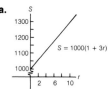

15. $y = \sqrt{x + 3}$ is a real function when $x \geq -3$

17. $\varepsilon = \$900 + \$0.03x$

19.

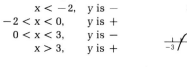

20. a. $4x(2x + 3y)(5x - y)$

21. $x = 0, 3, -2$ are zeros
   $x < -2,$ y is $-$
   $-2 < x < 0,$ y is $+$
   $0 < x < 3,$ y is $-$
   $x > 3,$ y is $+$

Chapter 9. Differential Calculus

Exercise Set 9.1, page 428

1. a. $f'(x) = 0$ **c.** $f'(x) = 0$ **e.** $f'(x) = 0$ **2. a.** $f'(x) = 4$ **c.** $f'(x) = -3$ **e.** $f'(x) = \frac{2}{3}$

3. a. $f'(x) = 8x$ **c.** $f'(x) = -6x$ **e.** $f'(x) = \frac{4}{3}x$

4. a. $f'(x) = 12x^2$ **c.** $f'(x) = -9x^2$ **e.** $f'(x) = 2x^2$

5. a. $f'(x) = 5$ **c.** $f'(x) = 6x - 5$ **e.** $f'(x) = 12x + 4$ **g.** $f'(x) = x - 2$ **i.** $f'(x) = 2x^2 + x - 5$

6. a. $m = 9$ **c.** $m = 6.3$ **7.** $f'(1) = 6$ **8. a.** $m = -15$ **c.** $m = -8.2$

9. $f'(2) = -8$ **10. a.** $m = 2$ **c.** $P'(200) = 0$

11.

$-100, 0, 100$

13. a. $t = 4$ seconds   **c.** $v = 128$ feet per second   **14. a.** $m = 78.6$

15. a. $m = 5$ **16. a.** $m = 8$

Exercise Set 9.2, page 436

1. 8   **3.** 0   **5.** -3

7. 6   **9.** -1 **11.** 3

13. 14   **15.** 42   **17.** 21

19. 0   **21.** 7   **23. a.** 2   **c.** Does not exist

25. -3 **27.** 1   **29.** $\frac{3}{4}$

31. Does not exist   **33.** 3   **35.** 1

37. -2 **39.** 3   **41.** 0

45. 12   **47.** 27   **49.** 3

51. 2   **52. a.** 1700   **c.** $\frac{1100}{3}$ **53. a.** 5

54. a. 40,000   **c.** $\frac{800,000}{11}$ **55. a.** $\frac{17}{60}$ **c.** $\frac{77}{240}$

Exercise Set 9.3, page 443

1. Continuous   **3.** Continuous   **5.** Continuous

7. Continuous at $x = -1$ and $x = 2$; not continuous at $x = 0$

9. Continuous at $x = 0$ and $x = 1$; not continuous at $x = -2$

11. Continuous at $x = -1$ and $x = 0$; not continuous at $x = 2$

13. Continuous

15. Continuous at $x = -3$ and $x = 0$; not continuous at $x = 3$

17. Continuous at $x = -1$; not continuous at $x = 0$ and $x = 1$

19. Continuous at $x = 0$; not continuous at $x = -2$ and $x = 2$

21. a. Not continuous at $x = 2$ since function is not defined at $x = 2$

22. a. Not continuous at $x = 2$ since $\lim_{x \to 2} f(x)$ does not exist

23. Continuous at $x = -1$ since $\lim_{x \to -1} g(x) = g(-1)$; not continuous at $x = 0$ since $g(0)$ does not exist

25. Not continuous at $x = -2$ since $g(-2)$ does not exist; continuous at $x = 2$ since $\lim_{x \to 2} h(x) = h(2)$

27. Continuous at $x = -\frac{2}{3}$ since $\lim_{x \to -2/3} p(x) = p(-\frac{2}{3})$; continuous at $x = -\frac{3}{2}$ since $\lim_{x \to -3/2} p(x) = p(-\frac{3}{2})$

29. Continuous at $x = 0$ since $\lim_{x \to 0} g(x) = g(0)$; continuous at $x = 1$ since $\lim_{x \to 0} g(x) = g(1)$

31. Continuous everywhere

33. Discontinuous at $x = 3$

35. Discontinuous at $x = 0$ and $x = 2$

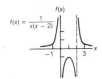

37. Discontinuous at $x = 1$ and discontinuous for $x \le -1$

39. Continuous everywhere

41. a. 50　　**c.** 240　　**e.** 550　　**g.** At $x = 25$, $x = 50$, and $x = 100$

42. a. At $x = 4$ and $x = 6$　　**c.** 5　　**e.** 5　　**g.** 15　　**43. a.** 99　　**c.** 2500　　**e.** Yes

45.

Continuous for $t > 0$

46. a. At $t = 2$, $t = 3$, and $t = 5$

47. a. .2　　**c.**

48. a. 80　　**c.** 160　　**e.** Continuous for $0 < x < 16$　　**49. a.** 30　　**c.**

50. a. 68　　**c.** 148　　**e.** Continuous for $0 < t < 8$

Exercise Set 9.4, page 452

1. $f'(x) = 3$, $f'(0) = f'(1) = f'(2) = 3$　　**3.** $f'(x) = f'(0) = f'(1) = f'(2) = 3$　　**5.** $f'(x) = f'(0) = f'(1) = f'(2) = 4$

7. $f'(x) = f'(0) = f'(1) = f'(2) = 5$　　**9.** $x = 2$　　**11.** $x = 1$

13. $f'(x) = 6x$, $f'(0) = 0$, $f'(1) = 6$, $f'(-1) = -6$　　**15.** $f'(x) = 7 + 2x$, $f'(0) = 7$, $f'(1) = 9$, $f'(-1) = 5$

17. $f'(x) = 4 - 6x$, $f'(0) = 4$, $f'(1) = -2$, $f'(-1) = 10$　　**19.** $f'(x) = 2x + 1$, $f'(0) = 1$, $f'(1) = 3$, $f'(-1) = -1$

23. a. $f'(x) = 2x$　　**c.** $y = 2x$, $y = 2x + 1$　　**25. a.** $C'(x) = 300 + 2x$　　**c.** $C'(3) = 306$

26. a. $D'(x) = -2x$　　**c.** $D'(6) = -12$　　**27. a.** $D'(x) = -2x$　　**c.** $D'(5) = -10$

29. a. $P'(x) = 10 - 10x$　　**c.** $P'(3) = -20$

Exercise Set 9.5, page 459

1. $f'(x) = f'(0) = f'(2) = f'(-3) = 0$　　**3.** $f'(x) = f'(0) = f'(2) = f'(-3) = 0$

5. $f'(x) = f'(0) = f'(2) = f'(-3) = 0$　　**7.** $f'(x) = f'(0) = f'(2) = f'(-3) = 1$

9. $f'(x) = f'(0) = f'(2) = f'(-3) = 2$　　**11.** $f'(x) = f'(0) = f'(2) = f'(-3) = -3$

13. $f'(x) = 4x$, $f'(0) = 0$, $f'(2) = 8$, $f'(-3) = -12$　　**15.** $f'(x) = 6x$, $f'(0) = 0$, $f'(2) = 12$, $f'(-3) = -18$

17. $f'(x) = 8x$, $f'(0) = 0$, $f'(2) = 16$, $f'(-3) = -24$　　**19.** $f'(x) = 4x - 4$, $f'(0) = -4$, $f'(2) = 4$, $f'(-3) = -16$

21. $f'(x) = 15x^2 - 6x$, $f'(0) = 0$, $f'(2) = 48$, $f'(-3) = 153$

23. $f'(x) = 24x^3 - 6x$, $f'(0) = 0$, $f'(2) = 174$, $f'(-3) = -630$

25. $f'(x) = -3x^{-2} + 4$, $f'(0)$ does not exist, $f'(2) = \frac{13}{4}$, $f'(-3) = \frac{11}{3}$

27. $f'(x) = -8x^{-3} - 8x$, $f'(0)$ does not exist, $f'(2) = -17$, $f'(-3) = \frac{656}{27}$

29. $f'(x) = 2x^{-1/2}$, $f'(0)$ does not exist, $f'(2) = \sqrt{2}$, $f'(-3)$ is not real

31. $y' = 0$, $y'' = 0$, $y''' = 0$

33. $y' = 3$, $y'' = 0$, $y''' = 0$

35. $y' = 70x - 27$, $y'' = 70$, $y''' = 0$

37. $y' = 6x^2 + 6x - 1$, $y'' = 12x + 6$, $y''' = 12$

39. $y' = 12x^5 + 9x^2 - 2$, $y'' = 60x^4 + 18x$, $y''' = 240x^3 + 18$

41. $y' = 2x^3 + x^2$, $y'' = 6x^2 + 2x$, $y''' = 12x + 2$

43. $y' = x^{-2/3}$, $y'' = -\frac{2}{3}x^{-5/3}$, $y''' = \frac{10}{9}x^{-7/3}$

45. $y' = 4x^{-1/3} + 2x^{-1/2}$, $y'' = -\frac{4}{3}x^{-4/3} - x^{-3/2}$, $y''' = \frac{16}{9}x^{-7/3} + \frac{3}{2}x^{-5/2}$

47. $y' = 6x + 2x^{-3/2}$, $y'' = 6 - 3x^{-5/2}$, $y''' = \frac{15}{2}x^{-7/2}$

49. $y' = \frac{7}{2}x^{-1/2} + 3x^{-2/3}$, $y'' = -\frac{7}{4}x^{-3/2} - 2x^{-5/3}$, $y''' = \frac{21}{8}x^{-5/2} + \frac{10}{3}x^{-7/3}$

51. a. $P' = x + 4$ **b.** $P' > 0$ when $x > -4$ **c.** $P' = 0$ when $x = -4$ **d.** $P' < 0$ when $x < -4$

52. a. $C'(x) = 400 + 2x$ **c.** $C'(2) = 404$

53. a. $D'(x) = -2x$ **c.** $D'(5) = -10$

54. a. $R'(x) = 20 - \dfrac{x}{250}$ **c.** 50,000

56. a. $P'(x) = -.4x^{-3}$ **c.** $-.05$

57. a. $f'(x) = 24x^{-1/2}$ **c.** $f'(4) = 12$

58. a. $f'(x) = 24x^{-2/3}$ **c.** $f'(8) = 6$

Exercise Set 9.6, page 464

1. $y = 6x + 15$; $y' = 6$

3. $y = 6x - 5$; $y' = 6$

5. $y = 9x + 10$; $y' = 9$

7. $y = 12x^2$; $y' = 24x$

9. $y = -12x^2$; $y' = -24x$

11. $y = -4x^2 + 3$; $y' = -8x$

13. $y = 12x^2$; $y' = 24x$

15. $y = 4(3x + 5)^2$; $y' = 24(3x + 5)$

17. $y = -3(2x - 3)^2 + 2$; $y' = -12(2x - 3)$

19. $y = 8x^4 - 6x^2$; $y' = 32x^3 - 12x$

21. $y' = 3(24x + 53)$

23. $y' = 12x^5 - 72x^3 + 108x$

25. $y' = 320x^3 + 1440x^2 + 2144x + 1056$

27. $y' = 48x^3 - 36x^2 - 74x + 20$

29. $y' = 81x^2 + 216x + 144$

31. $y' = 6(3x - 1)(3x^2 - 2x + 1)$

33. $y' = 20(x + 1)(x^2 + 2x - 1)$

35. $y' = \frac{1}{2}(x^2 + x - 1)^{-1/2}(2x + 1)$

37. $y' = 12(x^2 - 2x + 1)^3(2x - 2) = 24(x - 1)(x^2 - 2x + 1)^3 = 24(x - 1)^7$

39. $y' = \frac{4}{9}(x - 4)^{-1/3}$

41. $y = 3u^2$; $u = 2x + 5$; $y' = 12(2x + 5)$

43. $y = 2u^2 + u$; $u = 3x - 2$; $y' = 12(3x - 2) + 3$

45. $y = 4u^3 + 5$; $u = 3x + 2$; $y' = 36(3x + 2)^2$

47. $y = -5u^3 - 7$; $u = 2x + 1$; $y' = -30(2x + 1)^2$

49. $y = 3u^2 - 2u + 4$; $u = 2x - 3$; $y' = 12(2x - 3) - 4$

51. $f'(x) = 2(2x^2 + x + 1)(4x + 1)$; $f'(1) = 40$; $f'(3) = 572$

52. a. $C'(x) = 6(3x - 10)$ **c.** $C'(\frac{10}{3}) = 0$

53. a. $R'(x) = 124 + \dfrac{2}{3}\left(12 - \dfrac{x}{3}\right)$ **c.** $R'(9) = 130$

54. a. $P'(1) = -\frac{8}{625}$

55. a. $L'(1) = 48$

Exercise Set 9.7, page 468

1. $y = 3x^2 - 7x - 6$; $y' = 6x - 7$

3. $y = 8x^2 - 2x - 3$; $y' = 16x - 2$

5. $y = 10x^2 - 9x - 9$; $y' = 20x - 9$

7. $y = x^4 - 1$; $y' = 4x^3$

9. $y = x^3 - 1;\ y' = 3x^2$

11. $y' = \dfrac{-10}{(2x - 3)^2}$

13. $y' = \dfrac{-13}{(2x - 3)^2}$

15. $y' = 36x^2 + 14x - 6$

17. $y' = \dfrac{-10x}{(x^2 + 1)^2}$

19. $y' = \dfrac{-3x^2 + 4x - 9}{(x^2 - 3)^2}$

21. $y' = \dfrac{2x - 9}{2(x - 1)^{3/2}}$

23. $y' = 2(3x + 2)^{1/2} + \frac{3}{2}(2x - 3)(3x + 2)^{-1/2}$

25. $y' = 2x + 1 + \dfrac{5}{(x - 3)^2}$

27. $y' = -4x^{-3} - \dfrac{3}{(x - 2)^2}$

29. $y' = \frac{5}{2}(x - 2)^{-1/2} - \dfrac{4}{(x + 1)^2}$

31. $y' = 3(3x - 2)(x + 2)^2(5x - 2)$

33. $y' = 18(2x + 5)^2 + 2(3x - 5)^2 + 12x(3x - 5)$

35. $y' = \dfrac{2x(2x^2 - 1)(-2x^3 + 3x + 4)}{(x^3 + 1)^3}$

37. a. $\bar{C}(x) = 7x - 3 + 10x^{-1}$ **c.** $\bar{C}'(x) = 7 - 10x^{-2}$

39. a. $C'(t) = \dfrac{-16t^2 + 63}{(16t^2 + 10t + 63)^2}$ **c.** $C'(1) = \dfrac{47}{7921}$

40. a. $L'(t) = \dfrac{272}{(18t + 17)^2}$ **c.** $L'(8) = \dfrac{272}{25{,}921}$

Review Exercise Set 9.8, page 470

1. $y' = 14x - 3$

3. $y' = 6x - 3x^2 + 8x^3$

5. $y' = 15x^2 + 2x^{-2}$

7. $y' = 24x^3 + 5x^{-3}$

9. $y' = 12x - 1$

11. $y' = \dfrac{-19}{(3x - 2)^2}$

13. $y' = 36x^2 + 16x - 6$

15. $y' = \dfrac{23}{(2x + 3)^2}$

17. $y' = 18(2x + 5)^2$

19. $y' = 30(3x - 2)$

21. $y' = x^{-1/2} + 6x$

23. $y' = x^{-1/2} + 2x^{-3/2}$

25. $y' = -2x^{-3/2} + 4x^{-5/3}$

27. $y' = (2x - 3)(18x + 11)$

29. $y' = 2(4x + 1)(2x^2 + x - 1)^{-1/2}$

31. $y' = \dfrac{2(3x - 2)}{x^{1/2}}(15x - 2)$

33. $y' = \dfrac{-24x}{(2x - 3)^3}$

35. $y' = 108x^3 - 270x^2 + 150x - 2$

37. $y' = 6(2x + 5)(4x^2 + 7x + 5)$

39. $y' = \dfrac{9x^2 - 12x - 7}{(3x - 2)^2}$

41. $y = 72x - 66$

42. a. $C'(x) = 24(3x - 2)$ **c.** $\bar{C}'(x) = 36 - 16x^{-2}$

43. a. $D'(x) = 240{,}000x^{-3} + 6000x^{-2}$ **c.** $D'(2) = -28{,}500$

44. a. $C'(t) = \dfrac{-18t^2 + 61}{(18t^2 + 8t + 61)^2}$ **c.** $C'(2) = \dfrac{-11}{27{,}225}$

45. a. 64

Chapter 10. Additional Derivative Topics

Exercise Set 10.1, page 478

1. $y = 4x^2 - 3x;\ y' = 8x - 3$

3. $y = -\frac{1}{2}x - \frac{3}{2}x^2;\ y' = -\frac{1}{2} - 3x$

5. $y = \frac{2}{7} + \frac{3}{7}x - \frac{4}{7}x^2;\ y' = \frac{3}{7} - \frac{8}{7}x$

7. $y = -\frac{2}{5} + \frac{3}{5}x - \frac{x^2}{5};\ y' = \frac{3}{5} - \frac{2}{5}x$

9. $y = \frac{1}{2}x + \frac{1}{2}x^2 + \frac{3}{2}x^3$; $y' = \frac{1}{2} + x + \frac{9}{2}x^2$

11. $y = \frac{4}{3}x$; $y' = \frac{4}{3}$

13. $y = \frac{3}{2x} - \frac{5}{2x^2}$; $y' = -\frac{3}{2}x^{-2} + 5x^{-3}$

15. $y = \frac{4}{1 + 3x}$; $y' = \frac{-12}{(1 + 3x)^2}$

17. $y = \frac{-3x}{1 + 2x^2}$; $y' = \frac{9x^2 - 3}{(1 + 2x^2)^2}$

19. $y = \frac{2x}{1 - 3x^2}$; $y' = \frac{2 - 2x}{(1 - 3x^2)^2}$

21. $y' = \frac{3}{2y + 1}$

23. $y' = \frac{-8x}{6y - 1}$

25. $y' = \frac{4 - y}{x + 2y}$

27. $y' = \frac{-3y^2}{6xy - 2}$

29. $y' = \frac{3y - 2y^2 - 3x^2}{4xy - 3x}$

31. $y = -\frac{2}{3}x + \frac{5}{3}$

33. $y = -\frac{3}{7}x + \frac{13}{7}$

35. $y = 2$

39. $y' = \frac{-x}{\sqrt{-1 - 2x}} - 2$; $\left.\frac{dy}{dx}\right|_{(-1, 3)} = 3$

41. $y = \frac{5}{4}x - \frac{9}{4}$

$x^2 - y^2 = 9$

43. $y = -6x + 20$

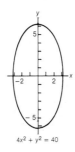
$4x^2 + y^2 = 40$

45. $y = -\frac{1}{2}x + 4$

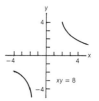
$xy = 8$

46. a. $s' = \frac{40 - s}{1 + x}$

47. $p' = \frac{-x^2}{p^2}$

49. $P' = \frac{-2P(1 + x)}{(1 + 2x + x^2)} = \frac{-2P}{1 + x}$

50. a. $L' = \frac{128}{L}$ **c.** $L'(9) = \frac{128}{9}$

Exercise Set 10.2, page 483

1. $\frac{dy}{dt} = -3$

3. $\frac{dy}{dt} = \frac{9}{2}$

5. $\frac{dy}{dt} = \frac{3}{\sqrt{2}} = \frac{3\sqrt{2}}{2}$

7. $\frac{dy}{dt} = \frac{9}{\sqrt{2}} = \frac{9\sqrt{2}}{2}$

9. $\frac{dy}{dt} = 12$

11. $\frac{dy}{dt} = -3$

13. $\frac{dy}{dt} = -\frac{9}{2}$

15. $\frac{dy}{dt} = \frac{-5}{3}$

17. $\frac{dy}{dt} = 7$

19. $y' = \frac{-51}{25}$

21. a. $\frac{\sqrt{2}}{2}$ centimeters per second

22. a. 40π square centimeters per second

23. a. 64 square centimeters per second

25. 72 square centimeters per second

26. a. $R' = 488$ **c.** $P' = 370$

27. $p' = -\frac{9}{5}$

28. a. $\dfrac{dv}{dt} = 300{,}000\pi$ cubic centimeters per minute   **c.** $\dfrac{dv}{dt} = \dfrac{25\sqrt{3}}{3}$ centimeters per minute

30. $R' = -\frac{5}{98}$

Exercise Set 10.3, page 489

1. No critical points   **3.** No critical points   **5.** $(0, 0)$ **7.** $(-1, -1)$

9. $\left(-\frac{3}{8}, -\frac{41}{16}\right)$ **11.** $(-2, -17)$ **13.** $\left(\frac{2}{5}, \frac{11}{5}\right)$

15. $c < x < e,\ f < x < g,\ g < x < i$ **17.** c **19.** f

21.

$y = 2x^2$

$(0, 0)$ is the critical point; $(0, 0)$ is the relative minimum; decreasing for $x < 0$; increasing for $x > 0$

23.

$y = -2x^2 + 3$

$(0, 3)$ is the critical point; $(0, 3)$ is the relative maximum; increasing for $x < 0$; decreasing for $x > 0$

25.

$y = 3x^2 + 3x + 2$

$\left(-\frac{1}{2}, \frac{5}{4}\right)$ is the critical point; $\left(-\frac{1}{2}, \frac{5}{4}\right)$ is the relative minimum; decreasing for $x < -\frac{1}{2}$; increasing for $x > -\frac{1}{2}$

27.

$y = x^3$

$(0, 0)$ is the critical point; increasing for $x < 0$; increasing for $x > 0$

29.

$y = x^3 + 3x$

No critical points; increasing for all x

31.

$y = x^3 + 6x^2$

$(-4, 32)$ and $(0, 0)$ are the critical points; $(-4, 32)$ is the relative maximum; $(0, 0)$ is the relative minimum; increasing for $x < -4$; decreasing for $-4 < x < 0$; increasing for $x > 0$

33. (0, 0) is the relative maximum; (2, −8) is the relative minimum; increasing for x < 0; decreasing for 0 < x < 2; increasing for x > 2

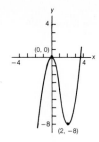

35. (3, 0) is the relative minimum; (1, 4) is the relative maximum; increasing for x < 1; decreasing for 1 < x < 3; increasing for x > 3

37. No relative maximum and no absolute maximum; no relative minimum and no absolute minimum; increasing for all x ≠ 1

39. (0, 0) is the relative minimum; (−1, 1) is a relative maximum and absolute maximum; (1, 1) is a relative maximum and absolute maximum; increasing for x < −1; decreasing for −1 < x < 0; increasing for 0 < x < 1; decreasing for x > 1

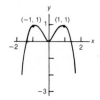

41. a. Increasing   **c.** $S = 20$

42. c. Decreasing

43. a. 80 feet   **c.** 144 feet   **e.** 96 feet per second

44. a. Decreasing   **b.** $t = 3$ **c.** 20,000

45. Increasing

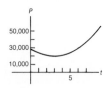

Exercise Set 10.4, page 497

1. Concave upward everywhere; no inflection points

3. Concave upward everywhere; no inflection points

5. Concave upward everywhere; no inflection points

7. Concave downward for $x < 0$; concave upward for $x > 0$; inflection point at $(0, 0)$

9. Concave downward for $x < 1$; concave upward for $x > 1$; inflection point at $(1, -2)$

10. Concave upward for $x < -\dfrac{\sqrt{3}}{3}$ or $x > \dfrac{\sqrt{3}}{3}$; concave downward for $\dfrac{-\sqrt{3}}{3} < x < \dfrac{\sqrt{3}}{3}$; inflection points at $\left(-\dfrac{\sqrt{3}}{3}, \dfrac{-5}{9}\right)$ and $\left(\dfrac{\sqrt{3}}{3}, \dfrac{-5}{9}\right)$

13. Concave upward for $x < -\frac{1}{2}$ or $x > 0$; concave downward for $-\frac{1}{2} < x < 0$; inflection points at $(0, 0)$ and $(-\frac{1}{2}, -\frac{1}{16})$

15. Concave downward for $x < 0$; concave upward for $x > 0$

17. Concave upward for $x < -1$; concave downward for $x > -1$

19. Concave upward for $x < -\frac{2}{3}\sqrt{3}$ or $x > \frac{2}{3}\sqrt{3}$; concave downward for $-\frac{2}{3}\sqrt{3} < x < \frac{2}{3}\sqrt{3}$; inflection points at $(-\frac{2}{3}\sqrt{3}, \frac{64}{9})$ and $(\frac{2}{3}\sqrt{3}, \frac{64}{9})$

21. Critical point at $(\frac{1}{8}, -\frac{1}{16})$; relative minimum at $(\frac{1}{8}, -\frac{1}{16})$; absolute minimum at $(\frac{1}{8}, -\frac{1}{16})$; no absolute maximum and no inflection points

23. No absolute extrema; no relative extrema; critical point at $(0, 0)$; inflection point at $(0, 0)$

25. Critical points at $(0, 0)$ and $(2, -4)$; relative maximum at $(0, 0)$; relative minimum at $(2, -4)$; no absolute extrema; inflection point at $(1, -2)$

27. Critical point at $(0, 0)$; relative minimum at $(0, 0)$; absolute minimum at $(0, 0)$; no absolute maxima; no inflection points

29. Critical points at $\left(-\dfrac{\sqrt{2}}{2}, -2\sqrt{2}\right)$ and $\left(\dfrac{\sqrt{2}}{2}, 2\sqrt{2}\right)$; relative maximum at $\left(-\dfrac{\sqrt{2}}{2}, -2\sqrt{2}\right)$; relative minimum at $\left(\dfrac{\sqrt{2}}{2}, 2\sqrt{2}\right)$; no absolute extrema; no inflection points

31. Critical points at $(1, 2)$ and $(3, -2)$; relative maximum at $(1, 2)$; relative minimum at $(3, -2)$; no absolute extrema; inflection point at $(2, 0)$

$y = x^3 - 6x^2 + 9x - 2$

33. Critical points at $(\frac{1}{3}, \frac{4}{27})$ and $(1, 0)$; relative maximum at $(\frac{1}{3}, \frac{4}{27})$; relative minimum at $(1, 0)$; no absolute extrema; inflection point at $(\frac{2}{3}, \frac{2}{27})$

$f(x) = x(x - 1)^2$

35. Critical point at (0, 0); no relative extrema; absolute minimum at (0, 0); no inflection points

37. No critical points; no relative extrema; no absolute extrema; no inflection points

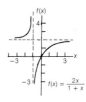

39. Critical points at (0, 9), ($\sqrt{3}$, 0), and ($-\sqrt{3}$, 0); relative maximum at (0, 9); relative minimum at ($\sqrt{3}$, 0) and ($-\sqrt{3}$, 0); absolute minimum at ($\sqrt{3}$, 0) and ($-\sqrt{3}$, 0); inflection points at (-1, 4) and (1, 4)

41. Relative minimum at $\left(-\dfrac{b}{2a}, \dfrac{-b^2 + 4ac}{4a} \right)$; absolute minimum at $\left(\dfrac{-b}{2a}, \dfrac{-b^2 + 4ac}{4a} \right)$

43. $y'' = 2a$, and since $2a \neq 0$ there cannot be an inflection point.

45. 120

47. a. At $t = 3$ **b.** $c(3) = \frac{1}{50}$

Exercise Set 10.5, page 502

1. $x = 1, C = 3$ **3.** $x = 4, C = 4$ **5.** $x = 5, C = 5$ **7.** $x = 150, P = 45{,}000$

9. $x = 100, P = 50{,}000$ **11.** $x = 2$ **13.** $x = 3$ **15.** $x = 6, P = 1776$

17. $x = 6, P = 7296$ **19.** $x = 6, P = 156$ **21.** 26 and 26   **23.** 1

25. The cutouts should be 10 centimeters. The maximum volume is 16,000 cubic centimeters.

29. 30 feet by 45 feet, with the dividing fence parallel to the 30-foot side

31. 1000 feet by 500 feet

32. a. $C'(x) = 10 + 0.03x^2$ **c.** $\bar{C}'(x) = -30x^{-2} + 0.02x$

33. 100; $10,000   **35.** In 6 weeks   **37.** $300 per month   **39.** $x = 7$

41. a. In 3 days   **42. a.** 3 inches   **43.** 8 hours

44. a. $N' = 6t - 3t^2$ **c.** At $t = 1$

Review Exercise Set 10.6, page 504

1. Critical point at (1, 2); relative minimum at (1, 2)   **3.** Critical point at (1, 1); relative minimum at (1, 1)

5. Critical points at $(0, 0)$ and $(-2, 4)$; relative maximum at $(-2, 4)$; relative minimum at $(0, 0)$; inflection point at $(-1, 2)$

$y = x^3 + 3x^2$

7. Critical points at $(-1, 4)$ and $(1, 0)$; relative maximum at $(-1, 4)$; relative minimum at $(1, 0)$; inflection point at $(0, 2)$

$y = x^3 - 3x + 2$

9. Critical point at $(1, -2)$; relative minimum at $(1, -2)$

$y = x^4 - 4x + 1$

11. Critical point at $\left(-2, -\frac{1}{4}\right)$; relative minimum at $\left(-2, -\frac{1}{4}\right)$; inflection point at $\left(-3, -\frac{2}{9}\right)$

$y = x^{-1} + x^{-2}$

13. Critical points at $(0, 0)$ and $(-3, 3)$; relative minimum at $(-3, 3)$; inflection point at $(0, 0)$

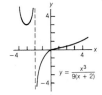
$y = \dfrac{x^3}{9(x + 2)}$

15. Critical points at $(2\sqrt{2}, 4)$ and $(-2\sqrt{2}, -4)$; relative maximum at $(2\sqrt{2}, 4)$; relative minimum at $(-2\sqrt{2}, -4)$; inflection point at $(0, 0)$

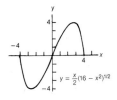
$y = \frac{x}{2}(16 - x^2)^{1/2}$

17. Critical points at $(0, 0)$ and $(3, -9)$; relative minimum at $(3, -9)$; inflection points at $(0, 0)$ and $(2, -\frac{16}{3})$

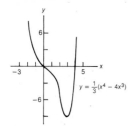

$$y = \tfrac{1}{3}(x^4 - 4x^3)$$

19. Critical points at $(\frac{2}{3}, \frac{64}{27})$ and $(2, 0)$; relative maximum at $(\frac{2}{3}, \frac{64}{27})$; relative minimum at $(2, 0)$; inflection point at $(\frac{4}{3}, \frac{32}{27})$

$$y = 2x(x - 2)^2$$

21. $a = 4$, $b = 2$; a minimum value

23. a. Increasing   **b.** $0 < 5 < 15$ **c.** $15

25. a. \$5,408.33   **c.** \$75

27. Width $= 4\sqrt{3}$ inches, height $= 4\sqrt{6}$ inches

29. Relative maximum at $(3, 81)$; relative minimum at $(4, 80)$

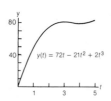

$$y(t) = 72t - 21t^2 + 2t^3$$

Chapter 11. Integral Calculus

Exercise Set 11.1, page 510

1. $5x + C$

3. C

5. $\sqrt{3}x + C$

7. $-x^2 + C$

9. $\dfrac{\sqrt{2}}{2}x^2 + C$

11. $\dfrac{x^3}{3} + C$

13. $2x^3 + C$

15. $\dfrac{x^4}{4} + C$

17. $\dfrac{3x^4}{4} + C$

19. $\frac{2}{3}x^{3/2} + C$

21. $\dfrac{x^{-2}}{-2} + C$

23. $\dfrac{3}{-2}x^{-2} + C$

25. $-x^{-1} + C$

27. $-x^{-1} - x^2 + C$

29. $\frac{3}{2}x^2 - 2x + C$

31. $\dfrac{x^3}{3} - \frac{7}{2}x^2 - 3x^{-1} + C$

33. $\frac{3}{5}x^{5/3} - \frac{3}{2}x^{2/3} + C$

35. $\frac{12}{11}x^{11/4} - \frac{20}{3}x^{3/4} + C$

37. $S = 4t^2 + 6t$; $S(2) = 28$

39. $y = x^3 + x^2 + x + 2$

Exercise Set 11.2, page 515

1. $\frac{3}{2}x^2 + \frac{4}{3}x^3 + C$

3. $4x + x^2 - \frac{x^3}{3} + C$

5. $2x - 2x^2 - x^3 + \frac{x^4}{4} + C$

7. $\frac{x^2}{2} + x + C$

9. $\frac{x^4}{2} + x^3 - x^2 + 4x + C$

11. $x^5 + x^4 - \frac{3}{2}x^2 + 2x + C$

13. $\frac{3}{5}x^5 - \frac{x^4}{2} + \frac{x^3}{3} + \frac{x^2}{2} - x + C$

15. $2x^3 - \frac{x^2}{2} - 15x + C$

17. $TO = \frac{7}{2}x^2 - \frac{1}{3}x^3$; maximum output $= \frac{343}{6}$ at $x = 7$

19. $TO = 5x^2 - \frac{x^3}{3}$; maximum output $= \frac{500}{3}$ at $x = 10$

21. $TS = \frac{5}{2}x^2 + 3x$; maximum value $= 25{,}300$

23. $TR = 800x - 0.2x^2$; revenue $= \$600{,}000$; maximum revenue $= \$800{,}000$

25. $TP = 500x - 2x^2$; maximum profit $= \$31{,}250$

28. $s(t) = 32t - 16t^2 + 128$; 144 feet above the ground; $t = 4$ when $s = 0$

29. $L(30) = 21.6$, or approximately 22; $L(40) = 35.2$, or approximately 35

Exercise Set 11.3, page 519

1. $\frac{1}{3}(x - 3)^3 + C$

3. $\frac{1}{6}(2x - 3)^3 + C$

5. $\frac{1}{9}(3x + 2)^3 + C$

7. $\frac{1}{9}(3x - 7)^3 + C$

9. $-(x - 2)^{-1} + C$

11. $-\frac{1}{8}(4x + 5)^{-2} + C$

13. $-\frac{1}{9}(3x + 2)^{-3} + C$

15. $\frac{1}{18}(3x + 5)^6 + C$

17. $-\frac{1}{8}(2x - 5)^{-4} + C$

19. $\frac{2}{3}(4 + x)^{3/2} + C$

21. $-\frac{2}{3}(5 - x)^{3/2} + C$

23. $\frac{1}{6}(3 + 4x)^{3/2} + C$

25. $-\frac{1}{3}(5 - 2x)^{3/2} + C$

27. $4(x + 3)^{3/2} + C$

29. $-\frac{4}{9}(4 - 3x)^{3/2} + C$

31. $\frac{3}{28}(3 + 7x)^{4/3} + C$

33. $\frac{3}{8}(2x + 3)^{4/3} + C$

35. $\frac{2}{5}(3 + 2x)^{5/4} + C$

37. $-\frac{3}{4}(4x - 3)^{-1} + C$

39. $\frac{3}{20}(4x - 5)^{5/3} + C$

41. $\frac{1}{7}(2x^2 - 7)^{7/4} + C$

43. $\frac{1}{3}(x^2 + 4)^{3/2} + C$

45. $\frac{2}{9}(1 + x^3)^{3/2} + C$

47. $\frac{1}{2}(5 + x^3)^{4/3} + C$

49. $\frac{1}{9}(5 + 3x^4)^{3/2} + C$

51. $TS = \frac{1}{3}(x^2 + 16)^{3/2}$; $TS(3) = \frac{125}{3}$

53. 320 feet

Exercise Set 11.4, page 524

1. 4

3. 7

5. 12

7. 30

9. 14

11. $\frac{63}{2}$

13. $\frac{81}{4}$

15. $\frac{69}{2}$

17. $\frac{8}{3}$

19. -4

21. $\frac{2}{3}$

23. 820

25. $\frac{12}{5}\sqrt[3]{4}$

27. $\frac{2}{3}\sqrt{2} - \frac{1}{3}$

29. $\frac{11}{9}\sqrt{11} - \frac{2}{9}\sqrt{2}$

31. $\frac{13}{3}\sqrt{13} - \frac{1}{3}$

Exercise Set 11.5, page 531

1. 10

3. 24

5. 34

7. $\frac{26}{3}$

9. 50

11. 10

13. 36

15. 46

17. $\frac{56}{3}$

19. 92

21. $\frac{64}{3}$

23. $\frac{202}{3}$

25. The function does not exist at $x = 0$.

27. The function does not exist at $x = 2$.

Exercise Set 11.6, page 538

1. 15

3. 12

5. $\frac{31}{2}$

7. 3

9. 16

11. 10

13. 36

15. $\frac{500}{3}$

17. 9600 hours

19. $TC = \frac{3}{2}x^2 + 8x + 10; \ TR = 23x; \ P(x) = -\frac{3}{2}x^2 + 15x - 10$

21. $TC = 2x^2 + 9x + 10; \ TR = 37x; \ P(x) = -2x^2 + 28x - 10$

23. $TC = 2x^2 + 7x + 10; \ TR = 19x; \ P(x) = -2x^2 + 12x - 10$

25. $CS = \frac{9}{2}; \ PS = \frac{9}{2}$

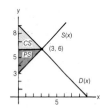

27. $CS = 8; \ PS = 2$

29. $CS = \frac{32}{3}; \ PS = \frac{16}{3}$

33. 60

Review Exercise Set 11.7, page 541

1. $\frac{10}{3}x^{3/2} + C$

3. $\frac{3}{2}x^2 - 5x + C$

5. $x^3 + \frac{5}{2}x^2 - 7x + C$

7. $-(x + 3)^{-1} + C$

9. $-\frac{1}{3}(x^3 + 3)^{-1} + C$

11. $\frac{1}{4}(x^2 - 5)^2 + C$

13. $\frac{2}{9}(3x - 7)^{3/2} + C$

15. $\frac{3}{4}x^4 + 2x^3 + C$

17. $\frac{81}{4}$

19. $\frac{45}{4}$

21. a. \$23,333.33   **b.** \$56,533.33

23. $TR = 900x - 0.3x^2; \ TR(1200) = \$648,000;$ maximum revenue $= \$675,000$ at $x = 1500$

25. 216

Chapter 12. The Calculus of Exponential and Logarithmic Functions

Exercise Set 12.1, page 549

1. $1, 2, \frac{1}{2}, 4, -\frac{1}{4}$

3. $1, \frac{1}{2}, 2, \frac{1}{4}, 4$

5. $-1, 0, -\frac{3}{2}, 2, -\frac{7}{4}$

7. $9, \frac{49}{9}, 41, \frac{409}{81}, 329$

9. a. 2; 2.255; 3.086; 7.524   **c.** 3; 1.025; 1.051; 1.105   **e.** 4; 4.010; 4.020; 4.040

10. a.

x	−3	−2	−1	0	1	2	3
y	8	4	2	1	$\frac{1}{2}$	$\frac{1}{4}$	$\frac{1}{8}$

c.

x	−3	−2	−1	0	1	2	3
y	$\frac{9}{8}$	$\frac{5}{4}$	$\frac{3}{2}$	2	3	5	9

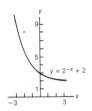

e.

x	−3	−2	−1	0	1	2	3
y	10	6	4	3	$\frac{5}{2}$	$\frac{9}{4}$	$\frac{17}{8}$

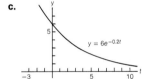

11. a.   **c.**

12. a.

x	−3	−2	−1	0	1	2	3
y	$-\frac{15}{8}$	$-\frac{7}{4}$	$-\frac{3}{2}$	−1	0	2	6

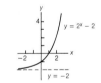

c.

x	−2	−1	0	1	2
y	$-\frac{99}{100}$	$-\frac{9}{10}$	0	9	99

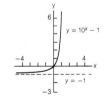

13. a. $y = 3(2)^x$ **c.** $y = 3\left(\frac{1}{2}\right)^x$

14. a.

x	−3	−2	−1	0	1	2	3
y	31	19	13	10	$8\frac{1}{2}$	$7\frac{3}{4}$	$7\frac{3}{8}$

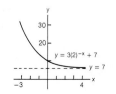

c.

x	-3	-2	-1	0	1	2	3
y	39	23	15	11	9	8	$7\frac{1}{2}$

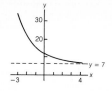

e.

x	-3	-2	-1	0	1	2	3
y	2921	329	41	9	$5\frac{4}{9}$	$5\frac{4}{81}$	$5\frac{4}{729}$

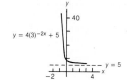

15. a.

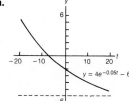

c.

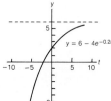

16. a.

c.

e.

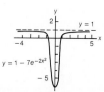

17. \$8,262.77 **19.** \$36,000 **21.** 18.77%

23.

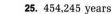

25. 454,245 years

27. a. $c = 0.110$ **c.** Approximately 267

28. a. 0 **c.** 29.29 **e.**

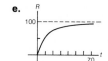

Exercise Set 12.2, page 556

1. a. $\log_3 81 = 4$ **c.** $\log_3 \frac{1}{9} = -2$ **e.** $\log_8 2 = \frac{1}{3}$

2. a. $7^2 = 49$ **c.** $3^{-2} = \frac{1}{9}$ **e.** $10^{-2} = \frac{1}{100}$

3. a. 4 **c.** 3 **e.** 1 **g.** -1 **4. a.** 4 **c.** 2 **5. a.** $x = 2$ **c.** $x = \frac{1}{1000}$

7. $\frac{2}{3} \log_b x - \frac{1}{3} \log_b y$ **9.** $\log_b \dfrac{x^2}{\sqrt{y}}$ **11.** $\log \dfrac{x-1}{\sqrt{x}}$

13. a. $\ln x - \ln y$ **c.** $2 \ln x + \ln y$

14. a.

15. a.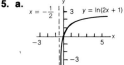

16. a. 0.9030   **c.** 2.1070   **17. a.** 0.9542   **c.** 1.2552   **18. a.** 2.1972   **c.** 2.0793

19.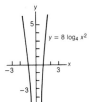

20.

21. a. 0   **c.** 1   **e.** 2   **22. a.** \$10,000   **c.** \$18.71

23. a. $\dfrac{500}{\ln 1000}$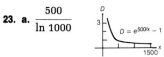

25.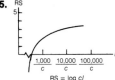

27.

Exercise Set 12.3, page 561

1. $y' = \dfrac{3}{x}$

3. $y' = \dfrac{2}{2x + 3}$

5. $y' = \dfrac{12}{3x + 2}$

7. $y' = \dfrac{4(3x + 1)}{3x^2 + 2x + 5}$

9. $y' = 6x + 2 + \dfrac{2}{2x + 5}$

11. $y' = (3x + 5)^2(2x - 3)^4(48x + 23)$

13. $y' = \dfrac{6(3x - 2)^3(x + 8)}{(2x + 3)^4}$

15. $y' = \dfrac{1}{2x} + \dfrac{6}{2x + 1}$

17. $y' = \dfrac{4(3x - 1)}{3x^2 - 2x + 5} \ln \left| 3x^2 - 2x + 5 \right|$

19. $y' = \dfrac{-x - 6}{(2x - 4)^3(3x + 2)^{2/3}}$

21. $\frac{1}{2}$

23. $(\text{pH})' = -\dfrac{1}{H^+}$. Since $(\text{pH})' < 0$ when $H^+ > 0$, the function is decreasing.

Exercise Set 12.4, page 564

1. $y' = 4e^{4x}$

3. $y' = 2e^{2x}$

5. $y' = 4 + 3e^{-3x}$

7. $y' = 4 - 3(5^{3x}) \ln 5$

9. $y' = 2e^x + 3e^{-x}$

11. $y' = 6xe^{4x} + 12x^2e^{4x}$

13. $y' = \dfrac{1}{x} + 6e^{2x}$

15. $y' = 3(7^{3x}) \ln 7 - e^x$

17. $y' = \dfrac{3(e^{2x} + 5)}{3x - 5} + 2e^{2x} \ln |3x - 5|$

19. $y' = 2xe^{2x} + e^{2x} + \dfrac{15}{3x + 2}$

21. $y' = 7(5^{7x}) \ln 5 + \dfrac{e^x}{x} + e^x \ln |x|$

23. a. $y' = -2xe^{-x^2}$ **c.** $y = 1$ **e.**

24. a. $-40,000e^{-0.1} = -36,193.48$ **b.** $-40,000e^{-0.3} = -29,632.72$ **c.** $-40,000e^{-1} = -14,715.16$

25. $R'(x) = -6xe^{-0.06x} + 100e^{-0.06x}; \ x = \frac{100}{6} = 16\frac{2}{3}$

Exercise Set 12.5, page 570

1. $6 \ln x + C$

3. $4e^x + C$

5. $6e^x + x^2 + C$

7. $2 \ln x + e^x + C$

9. $e^2 - e$

11. $3 \ln 4 - 3 \ln 2 = 3 \ln \frac{4}{2} = 3 \ln 2$

13. $2 \ln 3 + 15 - 2 \ln 1 - 5 = 2 \ln 3 + 10 - 2(0) = 2 \ln 3 + 10$

15. $\dfrac{x^2}{2} + \ln |x| + C$

17. $e^9 - e$

19. $3 + \ln 2$

21. $\frac{3}{2} \ln |2x + 5| + C$

23. $\ln 15 - \ln 7$

25. $N(t) = 500,000 - 500,000e^{-2.2t}$

27. $P(t) = P_0 e^{-rt}$

29. $y = 60(1 - e^{-kt})$

Review Exercise Set 12.6, page 571

1. $3, 5, \frac{7}{3}, 11, \frac{19}{3}$

3. $6, \frac{14}{3}, 10, \frac{38}{3}, 22$

5. $3, 3e^2, 3e^{-2}, 3e^4, 3e^{-4}$

7. $2 \ln 7, 2 \ln 10, 2 \ln 4, 2 \ln 13, 0$

9. $\log_3 \frac{1}{27} = -3$

11. $\log_2 \frac{1}{64} = -6$

13. $\dfrac{\ln 5}{\ln 3}$

15. $\dfrac{\ln 7}{3 \ln 4}$

17. $y' = 6e^x + 8e^{-2x} + 2e^{-x}$

19. $y' = 8x^3 e^{2x} + 12x^2 e^{2x}$

21. $y' = 6e^{2x} \ln (2x + 1) + \dfrac{6e^{2x}}{2x + 1}$

23. $y' = \dfrac{3x[(4x + 3) \ln (4x + 3) - 2(2x + 1) \ln (2x + 1)]}{(2x + 1)(4x + 3)[\ln (4x + 3)]^2}$

25. $y' = 3e^{3x} + 9xe^{3x} + 4x \ln (3x + 1) + \dfrac{6x^2}{3x + 1}$

27. $50; P(50) = 500 \ln 250 - 100$

29. a. $R' = 200e - 0.1x$ **b.** Maximum revenue of $200,000e^2$ at $x = 2000e$

31. $N'(t) = -1.6e^{0.02t}$ **a.** $N'(6) = -1.6e^{0.12}$

Chapter 13. Additional Integration Methods

Exercise Set 13.1, page 576

1. $6(x - 2)^{1/2} + C$

3. 8

5. $2(x^2 + 2)^{1/2} + C$

7. $\frac{5}{2} \ln |e^{2x} + 1| + C$

9. $2x - 10 \ln |x + 5| + C$

11. $2\sqrt{x} - 6 \ln |\sqrt{x} + 3| + C$

13. $4 - 8 \ln 7 + 8 \ln 5$

15. $\frac{4}{3}(x + 8)^{3/2} - 32(x + 8)^{1/2} + C$ **17.** $6(e^x + 4)^{1/2} + C$ **19.** $\frac{2}{3}(\ln x)^{3/2} + C$

21. $\frac{886}{5}$ **23.** $x - 12\sqrt{x} + 36 \ln \left|\sqrt{x} + 3\right| + C$

25. $-\frac{1}{2}e^{1/x^2} + C$ **27. a.** $\frac{1}{5}(208 - 36\sqrt{6})$

29. $\frac{1}{300}(400\sqrt{10} - 384\sqrt{6}) = 1.081°$

Exercise Set 13.2, page 581

1. $3xe^x - 3e^x + C$ **3.** $-2xe^{-x} - 2e^{-x} + C$

5. $xe^x - 2e^x + C$ **7.** $\frac{2}{3}xe^{3x} - \frac{5}{9}e^{3x} + C$ **9.** $-\frac{3}{2}xe^{-2x} - \frac{5}{4}e^{-2x} + C$

11. $\frac{5}{2}x^2 \ln x - \frac{5}{4}x^2 + C$ **13.** $\frac{1}{3}x^3 \ln x - \frac{1}{9}x^3 + C$ **15.** $\frac{1}{4}x^4 \ln x - \frac{1}{16}x^4 + C$

17. $2x(1 + x)^{3/2} - \frac{4}{5}(1 + x)^{5/2} + C$ **19.** $2(x - 5)(x + 2)^{1/2} + C$

21. $\frac{1}{3}x^2e^{3x} - \frac{2}{9}xe^{3x} + \frac{2}{27}e^{3x} + C$ **23.** $\frac{3}{2}(\ln x)^2 + C$ **25.** $\frac{1}{2}x^2e^{x^2} - \frac{1}{2}e^{x^2}$

27. 345.78 or 346   **29.** $\frac{100}{9} - \frac{340}{9}e^{-2.4} = 7.684$

Exercise Set 13.3, page 587

1. $\frac{1}{2}$ **3.** 2   **5.** $\sqrt{2}$ **7.** Does not exist

9. 1   **11.** $\frac{1}{2}$ **13.** Does not exist   **15.** $\frac{1}{2}$

17. $\frac{1}{10}$ **19.** $\frac{1}{3}$ **22. a.** 0   **c.** .94   **e.** 0

23. a. .25   **c.** .94   **e.** 1   **24. a.** .5   **c.** $1 - e^{-1/2}$ **e.** $1 - e^{-3/2}$

25. 1368 thousand barrels; 16,250 thousand barrels   **27.** $\frac{100}{9}$ milliliters

Exercise Set 13.4, page 592

1. $\frac{1}{10} \ln \left|\dfrac{x - 5}{x + 5}\right| + C$ **3.** $\frac{1}{12} \ln \left|\dfrac{6 + x}{6 - x}\right| + C$ **5.** $\ln \left|x + \sqrt{x^2 + 36}\right| + C$

7. $-\frac{1}{5} \ln \left|\dfrac{5 + \sqrt{x^2 + 25}}{x}\right| + C$ **9.** $-\dfrac{\sqrt{49 + x^2}}{49x} + C$ **11.** $\dfrac{\sqrt{x^2 - 49}}{49x} + C$

13. $\frac{1}{8}[x(2x^2 + 25)\sqrt{x^2 + 25} - 625 \ln \left|x + \sqrt{x^2 + 25}\right|] + C$

15. $\sqrt{x^2 + 25} - 5 \ln \dfrac{\left|5 + \sqrt{x^2 + 25}\right|}{x} + C$ **17.** $\frac{1}{2}(x\sqrt{x^2 + 49} - 49 \ln \left|x + \sqrt{x^2 + 49}\right|) + C$

19. $\frac{1}{5}(\ln \left|x - 2\right| - \ln \left|x + 3\right|) + C$ **21.** $\frac{1}{5} \ln \left|5x + \sqrt{25x^2 + 16}\right| + C$ **23.** $-\frac{8}{5} \ln \left|\dfrac{5 + \sqrt{25 - 4x^2}}{2x}\right| + C$

25. $\frac{1}{36}[3x(9x^2 + 8)\sqrt{9x^2 + 16} - 128 \ln \left|3x + \sqrt{9x^2 + 16}\right|] + C$

27. $-\dfrac{\sqrt{25x^2 + 16}}{3x} + \frac{5}{3} \ln \left|5x + \sqrt{25x^2 + 16}\right| + C$ **29.** $\frac{1}{13}(\ln \left|2x - 3\right| - \ln \left|3x + 2\right|) + C$

31. a. $2 + \frac{1}{3456}(57\sqrt{10} - \ln \left|3 + \sqrt{10}\right|) = 2.05$ **c.** 10.24

33. $R = 144 \ln \left|\dfrac{5 + \sqrt{41}}{4}\right| = 151.2$

Review Exercise Set 13.5, page 594

1. $4\sqrt{7} - 4\sqrt{3}$ **3.** $\frac{3}{10} \ln \left|5e^{2x} + 2\right| + C$ **5.** $\frac{3}{2}x - \frac{9}{4} \ln \left|2x + 3\right| + C$

7. $6\sqrt{x} - 24 \ln \left|\sqrt{x} + 4\right| + C$ **9.** $\frac{8}{27}(3x + 1)^{3/2} - \frac{8}{9}(3x + 1)^{1/2} + C$

11. $-\frac{3}{2}xe^{-2x} - \frac{3}{4}e^{-2x} + C$ **13.** $\frac{4}{3}x^3 \ln x - \frac{4}{9}x^3 + C$

15. $3\sqrt{2}$ **17.** $\frac{3}{2}$

19. $\frac{1}{144}(6x\sqrt{36x^2 - 25} + 25 \ln |6x + \sqrt{36x^2 - 25}|) + C$

21. $\frac{4}{19}(\ln |2x - 5| - \ln |3x + 2|) + C$

23. $\frac{20,000}{3} - \frac{27,200}{3}e^{-0.36}; \frac{20,000}{3}$ thousand barrels

25. $\dfrac{150,000}{7}$

27. $\frac{3}{10}$

Chapter 14. Multivariable Calculus

Exercise Set 14.1, page 600

1. $f(0, 1) = 1$ **3.** $f(-1, 0) = 3$ **5.** $f(2, 1) = 9$

7. $g(0, 0) = 7$ **9.** $g(2, 3) = 7$ **11.** $h(1, 2) = 6$

13.   **15.**

17. a. $4x$ **b.** $2y$ **19. a.** $2x$ **b.** $6y$

21. a. $6x$ **b.** $2 - 2y$

23.   **25.**

27.   **29.**

31. a. $P(3, 2) = 44$ **c.** $P(3, 4) = 78$

32. a. $P(x, y) = -x^2 + 3xy - 3y^2 + x - 7$ **c.** $C(2, 3) = 36$

33. a. $\frac{6755}{13}$ **34. a.** $I(14, 10) = 140$ **c.** $I(10, 10) = 100$

Exercise Set 14.2, page 605

1. $\dfrac{\partial z}{\partial x} = 2; \dfrac{\partial z}{\partial y} = 0; f_x(3, 2) = 2; f_y(3, 2) = 0$

3. $\dfrac{\partial z}{\partial x} = 3; \dfrac{\partial z}{\partial y} = -2; f_x(3, 2) = 3; f_y(3, 2) = -2$

5. $\dfrac{\partial z}{\partial x} = -6x - 2y; \dfrac{\partial z}{\partial y} = -2x + 3y^2; f_x(3, 2) = -22; f_y(3, 2) = 6$

7. $\dfrac{\partial z}{\partial x} = 3e^x; \dfrac{\partial z}{\partial y} = -2e^y; f_x(3, 2) = 3e^3; f_y(3, 2) = -2e^2$

9. $\dfrac{\partial z}{\partial x} = 2x + \dfrac{3}{x}; \dfrac{\partial z}{\partial y} = \dfrac{3}{y}; f_x(3, 2) = 7; f_y(3, 2) = \frac{3}{2}$

11. $\dfrac{\partial^2 z}{\partial x^2} = 0; \dfrac{\partial^2 z}{\partial y^2} = 0; f_{xy}(1, 3) = 0$

13. $\dfrac{\partial^2 z}{\partial x^2} = 20y^3; \dfrac{\partial^2 z}{\partial y^2} = 60x^2 y; f_{xy}(1, 3) = 540$

15. $\dfrac{\partial^2 z}{\partial x^2} = 10y; \dfrac{\partial^2 z}{\partial y^2} = -18xy; f_{xy}(1, 3) = -71$

17. $\dfrac{\partial^2 z}{\partial x^2} = 3e^x; \dfrac{\partial^2 z}{\partial y^2} = -2e^y; f_{xy}(1, 3) = 0$

19. $\dfrac{\partial^2 z}{\partial x^2} = 3y^2 e^{xy}; \dfrac{\partial^2 z}{\partial y^2} = 3x^2 e^{xy}; f_{xy}(1, 3) = 12e^3$

21. $\dfrac{\partial^2 z}{\partial x^2} = \dfrac{24xy^2}{(3x^2 + 2y^2)^2} + \dfrac{6x}{3x^2 + 2y^2}; \dfrac{\partial^2 z}{\partial y^2} = \dfrac{12x^3 - 8xy^2}{(3x^2 + 2y^2)^2}; f_{xy}(1, 3) = \frac{20}{49}$

23. $\dfrac{\partial^2 z}{\partial x^2} = e^x \ln (3x + 2y) + \dfrac{6e^x}{3x + 2y} - \dfrac{9e^x}{(3x + 2y)^2}; \dfrac{\partial^2 z}{\partial y^2} = \dfrac{-4e^x}{(3x + 2y)^2}; f_{xy}(1, 3) = \frac{4}{27}e$

25. $\dfrac{\partial^2 z}{\partial x^2} = -(2x + 3y)^{-3/2}; \dfrac{\partial^2 z}{\partial y^2} = -\frac{9}{4}(2x + 3y)^{-3/2}; f_{xy}(1, 3) = -\dfrac{3}{22\sqrt{11}}$

27. a. $P(1, 2) = 28$ **c.** $P_x(1, 2) = 6$

28. a. $P(x, y) = -x^2 + 2xy - 3y^2 + 3y - 5$ **c.** $C_x(2, 3) = 1$ **e.** $P_x(2, 3) = 2$

29. a. $I(65, 30) = 35.42$ **c.** $I_d(65, 30) = -0.54$; for each increase of 1 unit in depth, time decreases by 0.54.

30. a. $L(2000, 50) = 70$ **c.** $L_w(3000, 55) = 0.04235$

31. a. $I(13, 10) = 130$ **c.** $I_M(13, 10) = 10$

Exercise Set 14.3, page 611

1. (0, 0) is a critical point; $f(0, 0) = 0$ is a relative minimum

3. (0, 0) is a critical point; $f(0, 0) = 4$ is a relative maximum

5. (0, 0) is a critical point; $f(0, 0) = 10$ is a relative maximum

7. (0, 0) is a critical point; $f(x, y)$ has a saddle point at (0, 0)

9. (2, 0) is a critical point; $f(2, 0) = 9$ is a relative maximum

11. $(-2, 3)$ is a critical point; $f(x, y)$ has a saddle point at $(-2, 3)$

13. (0, 0) is a critical point; $f(x, y)$ has a saddle point at (0, 0)

15. $(2, -1)$ is a critical point; $f(2, -1) = -2$ is a relative minimum

17. (3, 2) is a critical point; $f(3, 2) = 13$ is a relative maximum

19. (0, 0) is a critical point; $f(x, y)$ has a saddle point at (0, 0).
(1, 1) is a critical point; $f(1, 1) = 1$ is a relative maximum.
(0, 3) is a critical point; $f(x, y)$ has a saddle point at (0, 3).
(3, 0) is a critical point; $f(x, y)$ has a saddle point at (3, 0).

21. (0, 3) is a critical point; $f(x, y)$ has a saddle point at (0, 3).
(0, −1) is a critical point; $f(0, -1) = 5$ is a relative maximum.
(4, 3) is a critical point; $f(4, 3) = -59$ is a relative minimum.
(4, −1) is a critical point; $f(x, y)$ has a saddle point at (4, −1).

23. $(L/3, L/3)$ is a critical point; $S(L/3, L/3) = L^2/3$ is a relative minimum. Each part is thus of length $L/3$.

25. $x = 2$, $y = 4$; $P(2, 4) = 15$

27. (2, 3) is a critical point; $C(2, 3) = 6$ is the minimum cost

Exercise Set 14.4, page 616

1. 75 at (5, 5) **3.** 18 at $(3, \frac{3}{2})$ **5.** 6 at $(\frac{2}{3}, 2)$ **7.** $\frac{68}{3}, \frac{34}{3}$

9. $\frac{250}{9}$ at $(\frac{10}{3}, \frac{5}{6})$ **11.** 47, 47 **13.** $\frac{850}{289}$ at $(\frac{35}{17}, \frac{15}{17})$ **15.** $\frac{146}{3}, \frac{146}{3}, \frac{146}{3}$

17. $-\lambda = \dfrac{80}{3\sqrt[3]{2}} = 21.16$; hence, an increase of \$1,000 would increase the maximum production about 21.

19. 75 feet by 75 feet **21.** Length = width = $10\sqrt{2}$ feet, depth = $5\sqrt{2}$ feet

Exercise Set 14.5, page 624

1. $\frac{3}{2}x^2 + 2xy + C(y)$ **3.** $2x^2y + 3xy^2 + C(y)$ **5.** $5x + \frac{1}{3}e^{3x} + xe^{2y} + C(y)$

7. $12 + 4y$ **9.** $6y + 12y^2$ **11.** $4 + \frac{2}{3}e^6 - \frac{2}{3}e^3 + 3e^{2y}$

13. $\frac{16}{3}$ **15.** 22 **17.** $e^3 - e^2 - e + 1$

19. 6 **21.** 5 **23.** 6

27. $9e + 9$ **29.** $\frac{1}{3}\ln 5$ **31.** \$49,733.33

Review Exercise Set 14.6, page 626

1. $\dfrac{\partial z}{\partial x} = 6x + 2y$; $\dfrac{\partial z}{\partial y} = 2x - 10y$; $f_x(1, 2) = 10$; $f_y(1, 2) = -18$

3. $\dfrac{\partial z}{\partial x} = 8xy + 2e^x$; $\dfrac{\partial z}{\partial y} = 4x^2$; $f_x(1, 2) = 16 + 2e$; $f_y(1, 2) = 4$

5. $\dfrac{\partial z}{\partial x} = 3y + \dfrac{2x}{x^2 + 2y^2}$; $\dfrac{\partial z}{\partial y} = 3x + \dfrac{4y}{x^2 + 2y^2}$; $f_x(1, 2) = \frac{56}{9}$; $f_y(1, 2) = \frac{13}{3}$

7. $\dfrac{665}{9}$ **9.** 50

11. $f(x, y) = -4$ is a relative minimum at (0, 2) **13.** $f(x, y) = -\frac{28}{3}$ is a relative minimum at $(\frac{10}{3}, -\frac{2}{3})$

15. 210 **17.** $6e^4 - 6e^2 + \frac{56}{3}$

19. $2\ln 5 - 2\ln 2$ **21.** $x = 2814$; $y = 1860$; $P(2814, 1860) = \$788,460$

23. $x = y = z = \sqrt[3]{V}$

Index